Cyclopedia
of
LITERARY
PLACES

Cyclopedia
of
LITERARY
PLACES

Volume Two
Glengarry Glen Ross—The Pit

Consulting Editor
R. Baird Shuman
University of Illinois at Urbana-Champaign

Editor
R. Kent Rasmussen

Introduction by
Brian Stableford
King Alfred's College

SALEM PRESS, INC.
Pasadena, California   Hackensack, New Jersey

Editor in Chief: Dawn P. Dawson

Editor: R. Kent Rasmussen	*Acquisitions Editor:* Mark Rehn
Manuscript Editors: Melanie Watkins	*Research Supervisor:* Jeffry Jensen
Christine Steele	*Production Editor:* Joyce I. Buchea
Assistant Editor: Andrea E. Miller	*Layout:* William Zimmerman

Library of Congress Cataloging-in-Publication Data

Cyclopedia of literary places / editor, R. Kent Rasmussen.
    p. cm.
Includes bibliographical references and index.
   ISBN 1-58765-094-0 (set : alk. paper) — ISBN 1-58765-095-9 (vol. 1 : alk. paper) — ISBN 1-58765-096-7 (vol. 2 : alk. paper) — ISBN 1-58765-097-5 (vol. 3 : alk. paper)
   1. Setting (Literature) 2. Literary landmarks. 3. Literature—Encyclopedias
I. Rasmussen, R. Kent.
  PN56.S48C97 2003
  809′.922—dc21

2002156159

First Printing

CONTENTS

CONTENTS

CONTENTS

CYCLOPEDIA OF LITERARY PLACES

COMPLETE LIST OF CONTENTS

Volume 1

Volume 2

Volume 3

KEY TO PRONUNCIATION

As an aid to users of *Cyclopedia of Literary Places*, guides to English pronunciations of foreign place-names are provided for particularly difficult words. These guides are rendered with easy-to-understand phonetic symbols enclosed in parentheses after boldfaced subheads and use the symbols listed in the table below. Stressed syllables are indicated by capital letters, as in "**Yoknapatawpha County** (YOK-nuh-puh-TAW-fuh)." It should be understood that some of the phonetic pronunciations are merely approximations, as both English and foreign pronunciations of many place-names vary.

Symbols	*Pronounced as in*	*Phonetic spellings*
Vowel sounds		
a	answer, laugh, sample, that	AN-sihr, laf, SAM-pul, that
ah	father, hospital	FAH-thur, HAHS-pih-tul
aw	awful, caught	AW-ful, kawt
ay	blaze, fade, waiter, weigh	blayz, fayd, WAYT-ur, way
eh	bed, head, said	behd, hehd, sehd
ee	believe, cedar, leader, liter	bee-LEEV, SEE-dur, LEED-ur, LEE-tur
ew	boot, lose	bewt, lews
i	buy, height, lie, surprise	bi, hit, li, sur-PRIZ
ih	bitter, pill	BIH-tur, pihl
o	cotton, hot	CO-tuhn, hot
oh	below, coat, note, wholesome	bee-LOH, coht, noht, HOHL-suhm
oo	good, look	good, look
ow	couch, how	kowch, how
oy	boy, coin	boy, koyn
uh	about, butter, enough, other	uh-BOWT, BUH-tur, ee-NUHF, UH-thur
Consonant sounds		
ch	beach, chimp	beech, chihmp
g	beg, disguise, get	behg, dihs-GIZ, geht
j	digit, edge, jet	DIH-jiht, ehj, jeht
k	cat, kitten, hex	kat, KIH-tehn, hehks
s	cellar, save, scent	SEL-ur, sayv, sehnt
sh	champagne, issue, shop	sham-PAYN, IH-shew, shop
ur	birth, disturb, earth, letter	burth, dihs-TURB, urth, LEH-tur
y	useful, young	YEWS-ful, yuhng
z	business, zest	BIHZ-ness, zest
zh	vision	VIH-zhuhn

Cyclopedia
of
LITERARY
PLACES

GLENGARRY GLEN ROSS

Author: David Mamet (1947-   )
Type of work: Drama
Type of plot: Psychological realism

Time of plot: 1982
First performed: 1983; first published, 1983

There are only two settings in this play. While the city is not specified, the atrocious profanity of the principal characters establishes them as modern, big-city Americans. The settings symbolize the barren lives of the salesmen, who are never free; they are forced to make appointments by day and meet with prospects by night, when they would otherwise be with their families.

Chinese restaurant. Act 1 takes place in what is understood to be a typical Chinese restaurant in any large American city. No description of the interior is provided except that it has booths. Unlike many Chinese restaurants, this establishment serves alcoholic beverages, as the reader learns when Roma buys a round of gimlets for himself and Lingk. The salesmen are always talking about big sums of money, but they give the impression that they subsist on dishes of rice or noodles and chopped up vegetables. The restaurant is not much more than a door or two away from their office.

Real estate office. This place looks like every other real estate office in a big city, except that it has been ransacked. A broken window has been boarded up, and there is broken glass all over the floor. Even the telephones have been stolen in a vain attempt to divert suspicion from the real purpose of the burglary, to steal the fabulous Glengarry Glen Ross leads. It is immediately obvious that there is little in such an office worth stealing because no merchandise or money is kept on the premises. There is an outer office for the salesmen and an inner office for the manager, where Baylen, the detective, questions the salesmen one by one.

*Glengarry Glen Ross. Real estate subdivision in far-off Florida, parcels of which are sold sight unseen by the high-pressure salesmen. The outlandishly romantic Scottish name, designed to help attract mailed-in "leads," suggests the ironic contrast to the likely reality—flat, barren, grossly overpriced land infested with mosquitos and alligators, totally unimproved except for a billboard promising a future retirement paradise.

— *Bill Delaney*

GO DOWN, MOSES

Author: William Faulkner (1897-1962)
Type of work: Novel
Type of plot: Psychological realism

Time of plot: 1859-1941
First published: 1942

Like most of William Faulkner's fiction, this episodic novel is set in Yoknapatawpha County, a fictional locale in northern Mississippi modeled after Lafayette County, where Faulkner lived. The land is central to the conflict in the novel; its history is the history of conquest and enslavement, miscegenation and incest.

McCaslin plantation. Located seventeen miles from Jefferson, this plantation was established by Carothers McCaslin near the end of the eighteenth century. The land's passage through the generations of McCaslins and Edmonds tells the story of the McCaslin family. The land is handed down through the white side of the family, but worked chiefly by the family's black side— the illegitimate descendants of the plantation's founder through miscegenation with his slave Eunice and his incest with Thomasina—his own daughter by Eunice. The story titled "Was" reveals that by 1859, Carothers McCaslin's twin sons, Uncle Buddy and Uncle Buck, have moved into a log cabin they have built and moved their slaves into the unfinished big house, turning the world upside down. Uncle Buck's son, Isaac, repudiates his inheritance, so the plantation that was his birthright passes through the female line of the family to his cousin Carothers McCaslin Edmonds ("Cass"), then to his son Zack and his grandson Roth.

No further miscegenation is recorded until 1940, when Roth fathers a son by an unnamed black woman who is, like Roth, a great-great-great grandchild of the family patriarch, Carothers McCaslin. Like much of the agrarian South, the McCaslin plantation is a dark and bloody ground, on which black and white coexist uneasily, each group suffering the consequences of McCaslin family history as the sins of the father are continually visited upon the sons. "Was" begins on the McCaslin plantation, while nearly all of "The Fire and the Hearth" takes place there.

*Tallahatchie River.** Mississippi river whose alluvial "big bottom" region (also called "the woods") contains Major de Spain's hunting camp. Here Sam Fathers teaches the young Ike McCaslin to shoot and here the yearly hunts for Old Ben take place. Later, Uncle Ike, Roth Edmonds and the others go hunting in what is left of the big bottom in 1940. For Ike, the center of consciousness as a boy in "The Old People" and "The Bear," and as an old man in "Delta Autumn," the big bottom represents the wanton destruction of the land, its game, and its people. In the woods, Ike learns a deep and abiding love for all three.

Jefferson. Seat of **Yoknapatawpha County**, located approximately seventy-five miles southeast of the real city of Memphis, Tennessee. Modeled after the real town of Oxford, Faulkner's home, Jefferson appears in many of Faulkner's works. Parts of "The Fire and the Hearth" and all of "Go Down, Moses," the final story in this episodic novel, are set in Jefferson, where Gavin Stephens maintains his office, and where he takes up a collection to return the body of Molly and Lucas Beauchamp's grandson, Samuel Worsham ("Butch") Beauchamp, home for burial after Butch is executed for murder in Illinois in 1940. Jefferson represents modern law, or rather, its inadequacy. The authorities in Jefferson cannot untangle the stories of Lucas Beauchamp and his son-in-law, George Wilkins, during their comic trial for bootlegging. Here, too, attorney Gavin Stephens does what he can to right the wrongs of the past. What he can do seems little enough: Unlike Moses, he cannot save Butch Beauchamp but can only retrieve his corpse.

Warwick. Plantation owned by Hubert Beauchamp and his spinster sister, Sophonsiba, approximately twenty miles from the McCaslin farm. Most of the comic action of "Was" takes place at Warwick, so called because Sophonsiba ("Sibbey") believes her brother is the rightful earl of Warwick, England. Sophonsiba stations a slave boy at the gate to blow a fox horn when guests arrive, and her pretentiousness regarding the plantation satirizes the aspirations of frontier society and the comical attempts of southern men to adhere to an aristocratic code, while providing an appropriate setting for the comical "foxhunt" that occurs as Uncle Buck hunts his escaped slave—and half brother—Tomey's Turl.

— *Craig A. Milliman*

GO TELL IT ON THE MOUNTAIN

Author: James Baldwin (1924-1987)
Type of work: Novel
Type of plot: Social realism

Time of plot: 1880-1935
First published: 1953

This novel makes extensive symbolic use of place, employing settings in New York City and especially Harlem in the real-time of the plot. The novel also works metaphorically and psychologically, through recollections of life in the American South, place-bound memories that unfold within the inner landscapes of characters' consciousness during their prayers and visions. The novel makes particularly strong use of particular structures, such as a movie theater and a storefront church.

*Harlem. Predominantly African American neighborhood in New York City's Upper Manhattan. Harlem is the scene of the real-time narrative of the novel, an urban community in which the lives of the central characters intertwine. Harlem is also symbolic of the historic northward migration of African Americans seeking escape from the Jim Crow South in the early twentieth century. As a physical marker of historical transition, Harlem symbolizes an ambiguous free space for the Grimes family, providing the sanctuary of a black-defined neighborhood in America, but also signifying restricted space on another level for the characters. For example, when John Grimes and his biological father, Richard, try to create a life outside the boundaries of Harlem, they must struggle with external racial barriers and internalized mental barriers to do so.

*American South. As a region, the South resonates with symbolic importance in the memories, prayers, and visions of the novel's characters. None of the real-time action of the novel occurs in the South; however, the South is symbolic of the psychological and historical origins of the Grimes family and other key characters. The South also works symbolically on other levels. It signifies the legacy of slavery in American history, with all of its physical, mental, spiritual and political implications for the characters, for African American history, and for the country as a whole. As embodied in the consciousness of the characters, the South also signifies the continued reality of American apartheid, which through the literary device of visionary prayer is projected "north" and played out in the present of the novel, and, by extension, it is projected into the 1950's context of the novel's original publication. As the place from which many of the key characters come, the South profoundly affects "where they are."

Pentecostal church. Harlem church in which John Grimes, his family, Elisha and the "Saints" gather for prayer services on the threshing floor as the symbolic (and ironic) center of African American history and consciousness. This temple is also the place where the characters confront American history and culture, through the intense visionary experience of their prayers. Interpreters of *Go Tell It on the Mountain* disagree regarding whether or not John Grimes has a religious conversion on the threshing floor, and whether whatever kind of conversion he does experience is toward, or away from, the tradition represented by Gabriel and the black church. However, among these differing interpretations, there is no dispute about the importance of the threshing floor as the altar, so to speak, where John "descends" into history and where he experiences his ultimate epiphany.

Movie theater. Midtown Manhattan theater that John visits on his birthday, the day of his profound rebirth. The movie theater becomes a secularized temple for John, a place where the film he sees symbolizes the world of art, open sexuality, and creativity. Drawn toward the "temptation" of art, John struggles throughout the novel to see his history and the history of his people, as a source for the liberating possibilities of artistic expression.

*Central Park. Large park in the middle of Manhattan that serves as a transitional space, working symbolically within the richly textured biblical imagery of the novel as a whole. Early in the novel, John crosses the park, the wilderness, to climb to the summit of a hill, and is gripped by a prophetic presentiment of freedom, power, and transcendence. His brief but sharply focused encounter with an elderly white man in the open space of the park symbolically affirms the possibility of a mutually acknowledged shared humanity. This encounter occurs in a space away from the city streets, where the characters are protected for a brief moment from the identity pressures and pre-set patterns of American society.

— *Sharon Carson*

GOD'S LITTLE ACRE

Author: Erskine Caldwell (1903-1987)
Type of work: Novel
Type of plot: Naturalism

Time of plot: Late 1920's
First published: 1933

Land on a small and impoverished Georgia farm motivates the characters of this novel. The farm has the potential to sustain TyTy Walden and his family in relative comfort; instead it becomes a landscape of huge craters and mounds of dirt because TyTy is obsessed with the notion that there is gold on his land, which he is perpetually excavating. As the land continually fails to give forth gold, the family is driven further away from realistic aspirations toward ultimate tragedy.

Walden farm. Sixty-acre farm in Georgia with more than twenty acres cratered with excavated holes from ten to thirty feet deep. The holes and craters make it impossible to cultivate the land around the farmhouse. The promise of gold, based on an old report that a nugget was found there, keeps the Waldens from planting crops that could allow them to live reasonably well. Instead they live from hand to mouth, waiting for a gold strike that never happens. Eventually, the land is tainted by the blood of one of the Waldens' sons, when Buck shoots and kills his brother Jim Leslie in a jealous rage.

God's little acre. Constantly shifting parcel of the Walden farm that TyTy dedicates to God. In a none-too-pious concession to his Christian beliefs, TyTy dedicates one acre of his land to God but regularly negates the gesture by reassigning the acre whenever it stands in the path of his gold-digging work. The acre represents TyTy's belief that there is within him "some aspect of God." As he shifts the parcel around, however, he devastates more and more of the land. TyTy moves the acre each time he, his sons, and the African American workers start a new hole. The final time that he moves the acre is after his son Buck shoots Jim Leslie. Wanting to ensure that Buck will be on God's land as he walks away from the killing, TyTy wishes that the acre will follow Buck everywhere he walks that evening.

*****Augusta.** Georgia city, close to the South Carolina border, where TyTy's son, the cotton broker Jim Leslie, has a fine home and an upper-class wife. It is a place where temptations as well as opportunities beckon. Financial gratifications are also to be gotten there: Jim Leslie gives his father money that will ease some of the constraints on the family. On the other hand, Jim Leslie develops an unwholesome interest in Buck's wife Griselda. The family leaves Augusta fairly quickly, once they are given money by Jim Leslie. That they go to Augusta only rarely and stay there only briefly is indicative of a reluctance to leave the familiarity of their farm to attempt a different, more promising approach to life.

Scottsville. Cotton mill town in Horse Creek Valley, in South Carolina near the Georgia border. TyTy's daughter Rosamond lives here in a company house with her union-activist husband Will Thompson. Will is killed at the mill trying to force the mill management to reopen after a lockout. Erskine Caldwell worked in a mill and was well aware of the hardscrabble lives endured by the workers. Horsecreek Valley is also mentioned in Caldwell's *Tobacco Road* (1932).

Rosamond and Will's home. Small company house in which the couple lives throbs with the sexual tension between Will and Rosamond's sister Darling Jill. As the unfettered emotions of the girl build to the predictable climax, they are matched by the increasing violence among the mill workers and the mill owners.

— *Jane L. Ball*

THE GOLD-BUG

Author: Edgar Allan Poe (1809-1849)
Type of work: Short fiction
Type of plot: Detective and mystery

Time of plot: Early nineteenth century
First published: 1843

The setting of the story is the remote South Carolina coast, an appropriate location for the hiding and later discovery of buried pirate treasure.

*Sullivan's Island.** Barrier island off the coast of South Carolina, near Charleston. During the early nineteenth century, the sea islands near Charleston were barren, isolated locations, accessible only by water and inhabited by relatively few people. Sullivan's Island, at the mouth of Charleston harbor, was notable mainly for Fort Moultrie, which guarded the entrance to the port. Edgar Allan Poe was quite familiar with Sullivan's Island, since he had been stationed at Fort Moultrie during his brief service in the U.S. Army and selected the island as the suitable location for a story about the discovery of treasure buried by pirate captain William Kidd.

Despite its proximity to Charleston, Sullivan's Island's distinguishing characteristic was its isolation. Aside from the garrison of the fort and a few summer residents, there were only a few year-round inhabitants of the place. Densely covered with myrtle trees, the narrow, sandy island becomes home to the once-wealthy William Legrand, who has left New Orleans because of some misfortunes. Legrand lives with his single slave, Jupiter, in a small hut located at the center of an almost impenetrable growth of myrtle trees. He is literally, as well as figuratively, cut off from the world he has left behind.

*Mainland.** Region between Sullivan's Island and Charleston. Although not separated from civilization by water, the land just beyond Sullivan's Island is equally wild and barren. When the narrator, Legrand, and Jupiter go there in search of the treasure, they pass into a desolate area without evidence of human life. In his emphasis on the strangeness of the area, Poe departs from the realities of southern geography, transforming the level, sandy landscape into one filled with inaccessible hills, huge crags, and deep ravines. Although unrealistic, these touches add to the atmosphere of the story, which requires an isolated, wild, and exotic location.

Tulip-tree. Tree on the mainland that allows Legrand to determine the exact location of the buried treasure. Jupiter climbs this extremely tall, old tree, where he finds a skull attached to an upper limb; lowering the "gold-bug" of the title through the empty eye socket of the skull reveals the burial site of Captain Kidd's treasure.

— *Michael Witkoski*

THE GOLDEN APPLES

Author: Eudora Welty (1909-2001)
Type of work: Short fiction

Time of plot: Early to mid-twentieth century
First published: 1949

Neither a novel nor a collection of unrelated short stories, these seven tales are structurally linked in that each draws from a shared set of characters living in or hailing from the little town of Morgana, Mississippi. As the stories reveal the lives of these characters over four decades, they create a mosaic of life as it is lived among those who stay in Morgana, those who leave it behind, and those who having left are drawn back to it. Morgana, more than anything else, is the unifying thread that ties the seven stories into something more than each is alone.

Morgana. Mississippi town about nineteen miles from Vicksburg, by way of a gravel road that crosses thirteen little bridges and the bridge over the Big Black River, Morgana is little more than a wide place in the road. From the MacLain house at one end of the road to the Starks' at the other, each story is set in Morgana or draws on the emotional ties that Morgana exerts on its sons and daughters. As one story after another unfolds, the reader pieces together the whole cloth that is the communal life of Morgana's inexorably linked inhabitants.

MacLain house. In its outlying position at the end of the road that runs through Morgana, the MacLain house was built for two outsiders, King MacLain of nearby MacLain Courthouse and his albino wife Snowdie Hudson, daughter of the storekeeper at Crossroads. From the beginning, the life of the house seems doomed: "Shower of Gold" tells of the unfaithful King, a rambler who

456 / *The Golden Ass*

leaves his wife and twin sons to struggle on alone, and the always hopeful Snowdie, who finally moves back to her own people when she can no longer keep the house up. In "June Recital," the children of the Morrison house next door watch in fascination as the MacLain house is set afire by the old spinster boarder who once gave piano lessons there. By the last story, "The Wanderers," the house too is gone, although the townspeople still refer to the lot as the old MacLain place.

Morgan's Woods. Old-growth southern forest of magnolia, oak, and cedar functions metaphorically as the dark place of danger in several of the collection's stories. Here Snowdie MacLain goes to meet the returning King in "Shower of Gold." Here the simple-minded Mattie Will Holifield has sexual encounters with both King and his twin sons in "Sir Rabbit." Here Eugene MacLain, exiled in far-off San Francisco, feels the call of home as he pictures his twin Ran still hunting the familiar hills and gullies of the Woods in "Music from Spain."

Moon Lake. In the story of the same name, Moon Lake refers both to the lake itself and the girls' camp on its shore. The camp was modeled on an actual camp Eudora Welty attended as a child, Camp McLaurin in Rankin County, Mississippi, near Welty's hometown of Jackson. The overhanging willows, the mud bottom and dark mud-stirred waters, the threat of cottonmouth moccasins in the water, the adjacent swamp all evoke a primordial quality in this intense story where life hangs in the balance.

Vicksburg. Mississippi city. When Ran MacLain wants to get even with his unfaithful wife Ginny Love Stark in "The Whole World Knows," it is Vicksburg where he goes to seduce the innocent country girl Maideen Sumrall. Nineteen miles and another world away, Vicksburg offers Prohibition liquor on a river barge, a midnight drive through the eerie Confederate and Union monuments of the Vickburg National Military Park, and an illicit night at the decrepit Sunset Oaks Cabins.

San Francisco. Fifteen hundred miles from Morgana lies the anonymity of San Francisco, where "Music from Spain" explores the world of Morgana's diaspora. From his apartment near Sacramento Street to California Street to Market Street and eventually all the way to Land's End on the ocean shore, Eugene Hudson MacLain wanders as a lost soul before he returns home to an early death in MacLain Courthouse. San Francisco is where husband and wife experience the death of a child and still remain strangers, where native son and foreigner spend an intensely personal (though unspeaking) day together and yet remain strangers, where a man from the close-knit southern community that is Morgana loses himself.

Rainey house. *The Golden Apples* ends where it begins, with the relationship between Snowdie MacLain and her cross-road neighbor Katie Rainey. From "Shower of Gold" where two young mothers first share sewing days and shy companionship, to "The Wanderers" where forty years later Snowdie lays out Katie's corpse, from the new-built but ill-fated MacLain house to the rundown old Rainey place forty years later, Welty's stories come full circle in theme, character, and setting. Katie's daughter Virgie, herself destined to become one of Morgana's dispersed, and the other mourners who gather to wake the newly dead Katie look across the road to the burned-out MacLain house and on past cotton fields to the Big Black River beyond, the moving road that flows from Morgana to bear away its sons and daughters.

— *Diane L. Chapman*

THE GOLDEN ASS

Author: Lucius Apuleius (c. 124-probably after 170 C.E.)
Type of work: Folklore
Type of plot: Picaresque

Time of plot: Early second century
First transcribed: *Metamorphoses*, second century (English translation, 1566)

This tale's plot unfolds in the Greek region of Thessaly, known for its connections with the supernatural. The protagonist, Lucius, is fascinated by magic, and while staying in the capital of Hypata, is anointed with cream that turns him into an ass. Much of the novel is taken up with his sad life as a quadruped, and the stories he hears as he serves robbers, a gardener, a miller, and other country folk. He finally escapes humiliating public intercourse with a condemned woman in decadent Corinth, and is cured by the aid of the divine Isis, of whose cult he becomes a devotee.

*Greece.** Apuleius locates his action in the Greek portion of the Roman Empire, at its height during the Antonine era of the mid-second century C.E. Roman distrust of supposed Greek decadence and sharp dealing made the Greeks easy targets of a critical pen. Roman superstition and fear of sorcery made them both wary and respectful of Greek conjuring. Indeed, Thessaly itself Apuleius calls a crucible of the art of magic. In general, the eastern Roman Empire was also the home of both the Olympian gods, who appear in Apuleius's stories, and the so-called mystery cults, which promised salvation through a life devoted to one of the eastern divinities, such as Cybele, Mithras, or, in Lucius's case, Isis.

*Hypata.** Capital of Thessaly; a resort for the wealthy where Lucius is taken in by the wealthy Milo and his witch-wife, Pamphile. Hypata vaguely piques Lucius's fascination with magic, and indeed, he feels as if everything in the town is somehow touched by magic. In Milo's house Lucius finds a willing sex partner in the servant Fotis, and his undoing as he dabbles in his hostess's arts. Milo's wealth draws robbers who seize both it and Lucius, who has been turned into an ass.

*Thessaly.** Region of east-central Greece on whose countryside Apuleius's critique of Roman society is focused. Rather than bucolic, Thessaly is filled with dangers of every sort, most of which stem from human greed, fear, ignorance, and general decadence. For example, the robbers' cave is a brutal setting for brutish deeds. The people who live in the rural areas are uncultured, dishonest, violent, and oppressive when they can get an upper hand. Lucius's sufferings at the hands of several of these people cause him to reflect on the "heavy storms" of fortune with which he is beset while on his journey to find the roses that will transform him back into human form. The very namelessness of most places at which he stops renders them beyond the pale of civilization.

*Corinth.** City of southern Greece that was colonized by Romans in the first century C.E. and became more Hellenic again in the early second century. Corinth's reputation for sexual immorality was unmatched in the Roman Empire. Apuleius uses this reputation by having Lucius—who is still in the form of an ass—couple with an eager free woman in private, then prepare and escape a second unnatural act in a public arena with a condemned woman. It is perhaps here more than at any other point that Lucius hits bottom and flees to what some might call a conversion experience, his fascinations with sex and magic both drained of life.

*Cenchreae** (SENG-kree-ee). Small Greek port town, about six miles from Corinth, where Lucius has his vision of the goddess Isis/Venus. He follows her instructions to his mortal salvation, and joins her cult. The town's Temple of Isis becomes Lucius's new home and refuge—a place of "intense affection," in which he undergoes the lessons and rituals that make him a devotee. Its stability not only replaces his own previous anomie as man and beast, but also contrasts sharply with the wandering devotees into whose service he was pressed.

*Rome.** Capital of the Roman Empire that is Lucius's final destination and the place where he will serve his new savior. Rome is a place as far from the superstitious and violent Greek countryside as can be imagined.

— *Joseph P. Byrne*

THE GOLDEN BOWL

Author: Henry James (1843-1916)
Type of work: Novel
Type of plot: Psychological realism

Time of plot: c. 1900
First published: 1904

Although this novel is set in and around London, its main characters are Americans and Italians. Having these characters act outside the contexts of their native cultures highlights what they bring from their own cultures, as well as the ways in which they consciously resist cultural expectations in England. More generally, the setting allows Henry James to compare European and American values and behaviors. James lived in England through much of his adult life; the experience of Americans living in Europe is a common theme in his novels.

*London.** Great Britain's capital is the home of most of the novel's main characters. Most of its scenes are set within the homes of Adam and Charlotte Verver, Prince Amerigo and Maggie, and, less frequently, their friends Bob and Fanny Assingham. James provides little description of these interior spaces, but instead focuses almost exclusively on the contents of the characters' thoughts. As is typical of James's later novels, the characters do not voice their most important thoughts and learn, not from hearing, but from seeing one another. Long passages detailing their thoughts contain much of the motivation for the plot development. The reader is typically reminded of where a passage is set after the passage has begun.

The setting in London is significant because it is the true home of neither the Ververs nor Prince Amerigo. The Ververs are free of Adam's business and financial and business concerns; the prince is free of family and aristocratic tradition.

Bloomsbury Street. London street that is the location of the shop in which Charlotte and the prince—and later Maggie—find the golden bowl of the novel's title. Here, Maggie learns that her husband spent time with Charlotte on their wedding day; from this information, she comes to understand that they had been much more intimate than she had realized.

Matcham. Home of friends in which the prince and Charlotte spend a weekend. Away from their spouses, they are free to be together. While they are gone, Maggie realizes that her husband is interested in Charlotte and begins working to keep them apart.

Fawns. Country home of Adam Verver, in southeastern England's Kent County, which Maggie arranges to visit with the prince, Adam, and Charlotte, at a time when she is trying to keep the prince away from Charlotte. The peaceful estate, which the characters think of as "out of the world," contrasts with the emotional turmoil of the two women competing for the man's affection. Maggie's victory over Charlotte is sealed when, during the stay at Fawns, Adam decides that he and Charlotte should return to American City to live.

American City. American home of Adam and Maggie Verver in which Adam uses his wealth to build a museum. He collects treasures to send to his museum, and it is in the spirit of collecting that he sees the acquisition of his son-in-law, an Italian prince, conspicuously named Amerigo. Although no scenes in the novel are actually set in American City, it is important symbolically in the novel. The city's very name stresses its differences from Europe. Through Adam's collecting, European culture is reduced to objects for display in the museum.

Although the Ververs, Charlotte, and many other characters in the novel are Americans, they clearly view their native country as an inferior place to live. Charlotte's final loss of the prince to Maggie at the end of the novel is accentuated by her move to American City, a decision made by her husband Adam.

*Rome.** Italy's capital city is the home of Prince Amerigo. Although he retains his royal title, his family has lost its wealth; through him, this city is depicted as a place where the aristocracy is in decline. Although no scenes in the novel are set in Rome, both Charlotte and Maggie fondly remember their romances with the prince there. The city thus reminds both women of happy and less complicated times.

— Joan Hope

GOLDEN BOY

Author: Clifford Odets (1906-1963)
Type of work: Drama
Type of plot: Social realism

Time of plot: 1930's
First performed: 1937; first published, 1937

Clifford Odets's play presents a conflict between the fist and the fiddle—Joe Bonaparte's boxing ambitions versus his musical aspirations. The play's sets represent this conflict: The Bonaparte home and the park bench are opposed by Tom Moody's office, the dressing room, and the gymnasium.

Bonaparte home. New York City home of young boxer Joe Bonaparte and his family. The furnishings of its combination dining-living room suggest a world of culture and the arts. Its plaster busts of composers Wolfgang Amadeus Mozart and Ludwig von Beethoven and piles of newspapers reflect the family's interest in music and the arts. Mr. Bonaparte has bought Joe an expensive violin; Joe is initially drawn to the violin, but eventually he chooses to leave it with his father when he chooses boxing over music. At the end of the play Joe's father hears about his son's accidental death and talks about bringing him home.

Park bench. Set used only by Joe and his mistress, Lorna. The bench is associated with their developing romantic interest in each other and with Joe's discussion about boxing versus music.

Moody's office. Office of Joe's boxing manager, Tom Moody. Its meager furnishings are appropriate because Tom is almost broke and needs a successful fighter to stay financially secure. It is the place where Joe gets his start in the ring, where plans are made for his future, where his relationship with Lorna begins to sour.

Gymnasium. Facility in which Joe trains. While he works out there, the mobster Eddie Fuseli argues with Moody about Fuseli's owning "part" of Joe, and Tom encourages Lorna to become friendly with Joe to protect Tom's interest in him. Here, the emphasis is not on sports; it is on the dark underside of the boxing business.

Dressing room. Dressing room at the arena in which Joe boxes with the Chocolate Drop King, where all the play's characters gather at the end of act 2. Mr. Bonaparte, whom Joe describes as his "conscience," watches as he reveals that he has broken his hand, rendering him unable to play the violin. For Joe, it is "the beginning of the world." However, it is also the end; in the next dressing-room scene Joe discovers that he has killed his opponent. In his desire to escape from his actions, he speeds away with Lorna in a car and dies in an accident that is foreshadowed by his preoccupation with speed and a remark that his violin case looks like a coffin.

— *Thomas L. Erskine*

THE GOLDEN NOTEBOOK

Author: Doris Lessing (1919-   )
Type of work: Novel
Type of plot: Social realism

Time of plot: 1940's-1950's
First published: 1962

The main action of this novel takes place in London, where Anna Wulf and Molly Jacobs, divorced women with children, are conscious of the constraints placed on them, as well as the freedoms made possible to them as unmarried British women in the mid-twentieth century.

Molly's house. London home of Molly Jacobs, in which most of the novel's action is set. Molly's house and Anna's apartment are interior spaces that function as containers for the heroines' emotional lives. Although the two friends refer to themselves as "free women," they recognize the confines that their culture and their own thinking about gender relationships place on their actions and emotions. They are as enclosed by cultural conventions as they are by the spaces they inhabit.

When Anna and Molly are living together in the house, Molly's house provides a space for their growing friendship. They pursue their careers and relationships with men as they please. After Molly's son blinds himself in a suicide attempt, he spends most of his time at home and moves into the main room, making it impossible for Molly even to make a private phone call. At the end of the novel, Molly plans to marry and move to her new husband's house; the change in residence signifies a new phase in her emotional life.

Anna's apartment. Anna rents an apartment for herself and her daughter after her long affair with Michael ends. She wants to get away from the place in which she has spent so much time with him but also wants a space for the notebooks she begins to keep. The author of a successful novel, *Frontiers of War*, Anna lives off the royalties while trying to decide what to write next. In her four notebooks, she records parts of her life. Experiencing her life as fragmented, she can find no single truth to record. At the end of the novel, she decides to stop writing, get a job, and move to another apartment. As with Molly, Anna's life begins a new phase, as evidenced by her decision to find a new place to live.

*Central Africa. Setting of Anna's novel *Frontiers of War* and the place where Anna lived for several years during World War II. Anna's novel tells the story of a British fighter pilot's tragic love affair with an African woman. In her black notebook, Anna records her own experience in Africa, which provides the raw material for her novel. The stories of Africa stress several themes of *The Golden Notebook*—the process of translating experience into art and the difficulty of realistically recording experience. This second theme is evidenced by Anna's constant questioning of whether her memory is accurate and wondering whether the story would be the same if told by one of the other participants.

In describing Central Africa, Doris Lessing draws on her own experience of living in Southern Rhodesia (now Zimbabwe) from the age of five until 1949, when she moved to London.

Mashopi Hotel. Hostelry in the African countryside where Anna and her friends spend weekends and holidays. Although the group goes there primarily to take breaks from their Communist Party activities, it is there that they experience most deeply the politics of the country, particularly the racial divide between the white settlers and black Africans. One white friend of Anna's has had a long-term affair with an African women, the wife of the hotel's cook, and has fathered one of her children. Despite his rejection of the color bar and his desire to help his lover, he cannot acknowledge this child without jeopardizing his job and harming his own wife, his children, and his elderly parents and in-laws who depend on him. Jackson, the cook, loses the job he has held for fifteen years because of a misunderstanding by the owner. He is forced to leave immediately with no opportunity to explain.

*Soviet Union. Although neither Anna nor Molly visits the Soviet Union, they both join and later leave the Communist Party. The contrast between their political ideals and reports of possible atrocities taking place in the Soviet Union accentuates the novel's theme of the difficulty of discerning a single truth.

— Joan Hope

GONE WITH THE WIND

Author: Margaret Mitchell (1900-1949)
Type of work: Novel
Type of plot: Historical

Time of plot: 1861-1873
First published: 1936

This epic novel of the South traces the lives of the O'Hara and Wilkes families through the Civil War and its aftermath. The South is personified first in Ellen O'Hara and later in her daughter Scarlett, with all their positive and negative qualities. Like Scarlett, the South is not broken by death, starvation, poverty, deprivation, or war; both do whatever is necessary to survive. Pride and belief in land, home, family, and ideals fuel the flames of battle of both Scarlett and her beloved South.

*The South. Southern region of the United States. Most of the characters of Margaret Mitchell's novel see the "South" as encompassing the states between the Lower Mississippi River on the west to the Atlantic Ocean on the east, from Tennessee on the north to the Gulf of Mexico and Florida to the south. However, the novel's central characters—with the exception of Rhett Butler—have a narrower view of the South, which they see as encompassing the region between their part of Georgia, east to Charleston, South Carolina, and Savannah, Georgia. To others, the limited area includes only the Clayton County and Atlanta area.

The novel depicts the South as a great lady who sheds tears of blood on the Civil War battlefields. Her strength endures just as the strength of the Southern women when fighting to hold on to a way of life that is fast sliding away with the loss of each Confederate soldier and the destruction of homes, plantations, and towns. During the Civil War, Union general William T. Sherman—who became famous for his devastating march through Georgia—said that the spirit of the Southern matriarch would have to be broken for the Union to win the war. As the novel progresses, the South slowly relinquishes her gentility and gracefulness to the realities of an unfamiliar, unwelcome, and harsher way of life.

Tara. Elegant plantation of Gerald O'Hara and his family, located in Clayton County, Georgia. Tara symbolizes the way of life and the entire world as perceived by plantation families. Her graceful hospitality, the well-greased joints of farming, entertaining, caring for the sick and elderly, reflect the strength and loving care of the matriarchal society. The functioning of this family within a Celtic society symbolizes the work supervised and completed to conquer the wilderness and create the lavish homes, in which white women rule supreme and their men sit back and bask in the glory of their smiles. Just as the characters feel security within the arms of the matriarch and her "mammy," Tara itself provides safety and security for all of those who live within its confines.

*Jonesboro. Seat of Clayton Country, immediately southwest of Atlanta. As the home of the central government of Clayton County, this town provides the controlling elements. In the prewar period, it embraces the formation of the Troop, maintains its status as transportation and communication center, and houses county governmental agencies and privately owned commer-

cial businesses. During the war, the railroad creates the impetus for the Union armies to attack and occupy the town. Many beautiful homes are destroyed by fire, looting, and occupation by both Confederate and Union troops. Their headquarters and hospital is the Warren House. Reconstruction creates an unknown world of scalawags, carpetbaggers, Union soldiers, and free blacks, and a general feeling of fear previously unknown to the residents of Clayton County.

*Atlanta. Capital and largest city of Georgia. Established as the cultural, social, commercial, and transportation crossroads, Atlanta symbolizes the genteel Southern matriarch in a comfortable urban setting without the ever-present supervision of a plantation. Before the war, new money and aristocratic hostesses rub elbows for the benefit of the Southern cause. During the war, these same women nurse the wounded in the Atlanta hospitals, care for the graves of both Confederate and Union soldiers in Oakland Cemetery, feed the hungry, and defend their homes before they are forced to evacuate to places they hope will be safer. Postwar Reconstruction brings military law under Union troops, roaming bands of free blacks, and carpetbaggers. The matriarchs who have returned to their homes must protect themselves with both bodyguards and weapons. The establishment of the Ku Klux Klan and nightriders creates fear as well as antagonistic courts and law enforcers. No one wins this war. In attempting to break the spirit of the Southern women, Reconstruction creates an even firmer resolve, not to restore the slave-labor society, but to maintain the family property despite heavily levied taxes and foreclosures.

Butler home. House that Rhett Butler builds for Scarlett when they are married after the war ends. The house is gaudy, pretentious, dark, and unfriendly; it symbolizes everything that Scarlett believes she has lost in the war. It may be characterized as a sporting house, built with money from a man for a kept woman who resents being kept. Just as rebuilding other areas of the South supposedly provides a better life for free blacks, more opportunities for "white trash," and a harder life for the genteel white Southerners, this new house supposedly secures all that Scarlett regards as having been lost at Tara. However, the component all Southerners most need does not appear. Contentment, security, and the loving arms of the matriarch are gone forever.

Aunt Pittypat's house. Home of Sara Jane Hamilton on Atlanta's Peachtree Street. A small house by prewar standards, it provides respite and security for Emily and Wade Hampton and freedom from the rigidity of widowhood for seventeen-year-old Scarlett before the war. During the war, the small but steadfast house feeds and cares for battle-worn soldiers and allows occupants to view the steady trail of soldiers early in the war. Later, the wounded and dead pass by the house on their way to the hospital and cemetery. Like many Southern women who survive the Union siege of Atlanta, this small secure house is gray, tired, worn, and ragged, but unbroken. After the war, it provides security for Aunt Pittypat, her coachman, Uncle Peter, Scarlett, Wade Hampton, and Ella Kennedy, Scarlett's daughter by Frank Kennedy, her second husband.

Twelve Oaks. Plantation home of the Wilkes family; patterned after the real Lovejoy Plantation near Jonesboro. It is even more graceful than Tara, but the Union army burns it as it sweeps across Georgia. Although battle worn, Twelve Oaks provides a kitchen garden of withered vegetables for the starving residents of Tara after the Yankees plunder and destroy all sources of income and food at the O'Hara plantation.

Fontaine plantation. This yellow-stucco house, home of three generations of strong Southern women, provides moral support and some food for Scarlett and her family.

Tarleton plantation. Largest horse-breeding farm in Georgia. All of its horses and men serve in the "War Against Yankee Aggression."

— *Anna Hollingsworth Hovater*

THE GOOD COMPANIONS

Author: J. B. Priestley (1894-1984)
Type of work: Novel
Type of plot: Social realism

Time of plot: 1920's
First published: 1929

J. B. Priestley's valentine to small-time theater companies centers on a touring Pierrot troupe, the Good Companions, as it plays England's Midlands and northern counties during a winter off-season. The troupe's world is illuminated by outsiders from Yorkshire, the Cotswolds, and East Anglia who join forces with them. Setting in the story is significant, with each of the newcomers' geographical and cultural backgrounds being established early, and each small city in which the troupe performs representative of a certain kind of English society. Nearly all the places in which the story is set are purely imaginary.

Bruddersford. Industrial town of north-central England modeled on Bradford, in which Priestley grew up. The novel opens with an almost cinematic longshot of the Pennine Range, "the knobbly backbone of England," moves in on the black, windy moors of the Yorkshire-Lancashire border, and then targets Bruddersford in one of the range's valleys, looking at the town's tramlines, enormous factories (many now idle), and slimy canals. Bruddersford's streets are stifling, and in spite of the city center's Free Library and Imperial Music Hall, life on Jesiah Oakroyd's Ogden Street is narrow and mean. Jesiah dreams about his beloved married daughter in Canada, and the loss of his job, coupled with a family quarrel, sends him off on the Great North Road.

Hitherton-on-the-Wole. Town in the hills of the Cotswolds in southwestern England, which are not like the Pennines in northern England. Here, the wind is gentle, the scale is smaller, and sunlight turns the stone houses a soft pink. Hitherton-on-the-Wole may be less picturesque than Broadway or Chipping Campden, but it is still a pretty Cotswold village, where thirty-seven-year-old Elizabeth Trant has long tended her elderly father at the hall. His death and her inheritance free her to change direction, and on impulse she buys a small car and embarks on adventure (though her initial plan is only to visit a few cathedral towns, such as Ely).

Washbury Manor School. Redbrick boarding school for boys in East Anglia. Here the land is flat and dreary, crisscrossed by drainage canals that make the fens habitable. Winds blowing down from the North Sea scour the desolate landscape. The school stands near a tiny hamlet, where Inigo Jollifant, a young schoolmaster, labors unhappily. A Cambridge graduate with an undiscovered gift for songwriting, he decides to leave the cheerless classrooms and cabbage-water-smelling precincts of the school to take to the road.

Rawsley Station. Small-town depot in which the novel's principal characters converge—the three outsiders and a theatrical company down on its luck owing to its manager's having absconded with its funds, leaving the players unpaid. The proprietor of the station's dismal tearoom behaves harshly, and Miss Trant impulsively takes on the company's debts and management. Inigo replaces the departed pianist, and Jesiah Oakroyd handles backstage chores.

Sandybay. Second-tier resort town on the east coast in which the troupe enjoys its first big success. Through the autumn the troupe plays a number of small inland cities in various "Winter Gardens, Alfresco Pavilions, Kursaals, Châlets, and Playhouses" from the Rawsley Assembly Rooms to Dotworth, "a one-eyed hole." Sandybay is a fishing village but big enough to support a pier with a "Pavilion, which looked like an overgrown and neglected greenhouse," equipped with a real stage, proper lights, curtain, and grand piano.

Winstead. Pleasant market town with a cobblestone square, sophisticated shops, fine churches, gabled houses, and a small playhouse, in which the Good Companions play to responsive audiences.

Haxby. "Hateful" town, dirty, economically depressed, smelly, full of empty failed shopfronts, an example of a community with poor morale and little hope.

Tewborough. Failed industrial town, "a money-making machine that had almost stopped working," one of the ugliest towns in the Midlands, a place of dust, cobwebs and decay. Among the bleakest stops in the troupe's travels.

Luddenstall. Provincial Yorkshire town that looks "like a Gas Works all spread out" but is nevertheless the home of appreciative theater-goers. Surrounded by dark, steep, snow-drifted moors and hills netted with tram lines in stony vertical streets, it is a warm and satisfactory place for the company to perform at Christmas time.

The Triangle. Nickname for three industrial towns—Gatford, Mundley, and Stort—devoted to automobile manufacturing. The growth of little redbrick suburbs has drawn the three communities into one "Tin Triangle" whose borders are indistinct. Here the company has its greatest success but also comes to its dissolution when a cinema owner whose business has been hurt by live theater pays hooligans to disturb a performance, leading to a riot and fire damage to the Gatford Hippodrome. Miss Trant remains near Gatford and marries a doctor she met years earlier. The other members of the troupe scatter to various real places.

— *Nan C. L. Scott*

THE GOOD EARTH

Author: Pearl S. Buck (1892-1973)
Type of work: Novel
Type of plot: Social realism

Time of plot: Early twentieth century
First published: 1931

Drawn from her experiences of living in China, Pearl Buck's novel traces the life of a peasant in a province hundreds of miles west of China's great cities who must pin his survival upon the yields of his land, which above all else, preoccupies and absorbs him. The novel uses three houses—a simple rural farmhouse, a mansion with many courtyards, and a refugee's mat hut—as the settings for the novel's action.

*Anhui. Large inland province in east central China divided by the great Yangzi (Yangtze) River. The far northern part of the province, in which the novel is set, is part of the broad northern China plain that is usually hot and dusty but subject to frequent flooding from the Yellow River.

Wang Lung's farmhouse. Rural farmhouse that is the scene of most of the novel. The house is located in Wang village, described as composed of only a half dozen households, within an hour or so walk of an unnamed walled administrative town in the inland province of Anhui. The changes the farmhouse undergoes closely mirror the fortunes of Wang Lung and his family. Wang Lung toils daily in the fields and has a deep attachment to the land—the "good earth" of the title. In famine he lets the house go into disrepair and sells the household goods but will not sell his land. A multitude of trials face the family and threaten the farmhouse, but both survive. In prosperity, Wang Lung buys additional land and improves his house.

The house first appears as a run-down three-room, earthen-floored structure made of mud-and-straw bricks with a thatched roof in which Wang Lung and his widowed father live. When a wife, O-lan, joins the household, the interior of the house improves through her skill and hard work. Additions to the house come as the frugal and hard-working family members raise themselves up. These improvements include sheds for animals and a room in which laborers reside. Eventually a tile-roofed, brick-floored addition is built for Wang Lung's secondary wife, Lotus. The house sits above the high-water marks of the frequent floods and so both the house and Wang Lung's family survive flooding.

Hwang family mansion (wang). Walled compound located in an unnamed walled administrative city in Anhui that has its own imposing gates. The unnamed city is probably Nansuzhou (now known as Suxian), in northern Anhui, where Buck lived from 1917 through 1919. Wang Lung's wife, O-lan, comes to him from the Hwang mansion where she grew up as a harshly treated orphan kitchen servant. In the course of the novel, Hwang family members dissipate the family fortune and eventually sell land to Wang Lung. The Hwang mansion falls into ruins, leaving only a servant or two living in its collapsing courtyards. In his greatest period of prosperity, after O-lan's death, Wang Lung purchases the property. Now a great extended Chinese family, the Wangs move into the refurbished mansion, where Wang Lung falls heir to some of the same excesses and faults of the Hwang family. He can never find peace in the mansion and prefers his modest farmhouse.

City in Jiangsu (Kiangsu) province. Unnamed city to which Wang Lung and his young family flee by train during a famine in Anhui. There they live in a "little village of sheds clinging to the wall." Country folk who are never comfortable with city life, they eke out a living through Wang Lung's work as a rickshaw puller. O-lan and the children beg on the streets. After Wang Lung comes into some money by chance, the family immediately return to their farmhouse and land. Although never named, this city is clearly modeled on Nanjing (Nanking).

— *David D. Buck*

THE GOOD SOLDIER

Author: Ford Madox Ford (Ford Madox Hueffer, 1873-1939)
Type of work: Novel
Type of plot: Psychological realism
Time of plot: Early twentieth century
First published: 1915

John Dowell, a wealthy member of an old Philadelphia family marries a New England beauty of a family with comparable distinction; the prestige of being part of upper-class America does not satisfy his wife, who insists on living in Europe, with the ambition of owning an elegant country house in Hampshire, England, from which her ancestors came. Sexual intrigue and ironic bad luck leave Dowell, in the end, owning just such a house in just such a place, but his wife is dead, and he is left trying to make sense of what has happened.

Branshaw Teleragh. Edward Ashburnham's English country estate. The physical manifestation of the glory of the English gentry, the upper class of England, has been, for centuries, the country house surrounded by acres of woods and working farm land. In the lush countryside of Hampshire, southeast of London, John Dowell lives in the dream house of his deceased wife, Florence. She never lived there, not because the couple were not wealthy enough, but because she had been living a life of lies, and adding to them, until eventually she thought that suicide was her only way out. For both of them the great country house represents the finest example of civilized living. However, the magnificent house becomes, as Dowell says, a prison. His wife is dead, and the man he most admired, Edward Ashburnham, the former owner, has committed suicide, finding himself in various ways constantly betraying the obligations of the ideal English gentleman that Dowell thought he was, and which he often was when his wife allowed him to practice his duty as a benevolent landlord.

*Nauheim (now-HIM). Health resort in western Germany, usually called Bad Nauhiem, that was popular with the wealthy for rest, recreation, and often as an elegant refuge for the ill and the aged to soothe and sometimes heal their illnesses, serious or trivial. The Ashburnhams and the Dowells meet here on a regular basis over several years to cosset the heart problems of Edward Ashburnham and Florence Dowell, although both parties, for different reasons, are only pretending to be ill. Only the "best" people can afford to spend time there, in expensive hotels, enjoying the international company, and the occasional naughty dalliance. Nauheim is not so much a symbol of upper-class extravagance as it is the real thing—a place where Dowell's wife and the English gentleman whom Dowell admires and would seek to emulate, carry on an affair that eventually results in one fatal heart attack, two suicides, one mental breakdown, and misery for the two most innocent characters.

*Europe. When not at Nauheim, the Dowells have a permanent home in Paris, and spend the winters in smart hotels on the south coast of France. The irony of all this fine living is the fact that their lives are spent in places other than the one they yearned for. Florence would not live in America, and it was a condition of their marriage that Dowell take her to live permanently in Europe. However, the European continent, where they first land, is the end of the line for Florence. Because she does not want her husband to touch her sexually, she fakes a heart attack on their honeymoon voyage to France, bribing a doctor to confirm this illness; the doctor eager to please, forbids any further sea voyages as likely to kill her. England is only a comparatively short ferry ride from France; however, there is no other way to reach the island country from France, so Dowell, a conscientious husband, refuses to take his seemingly fragile wife across the English Channel to her ideal home. She, somewhat comically, terrified of what he might do, does not dare to tell him the truth. She may roam the fleshpots of Europe, but she is forever punished for her wayward conduct by her own lie. She is an exile from the dream that could be so easily fulfilled if she could tell the truth.

*Philadelphia. Pennsylvania city that is one of the great urban centers of eastern United States, where John Dowell's family is one of the oldest, richest families. Neither the family's nor the city's stature is, however, sufficiently august to satisfy the ambitions of Dowell, who is an educated, cultured gentleman of substance, but in a typically American way is in awe of European culture. This innocence of the American abroad contributes to the marital disasters of the novel. Dowell yearns for the longer history, the deeper traditions and the acquisition of the country house in the "place" where such civilized living occurs, and as he sees them in the Ashburnham family history.

*Waterbury. One of the older small cities of Connecticut, a New England state rich in the history of the founding of the American nation. Waterbury is the home of Florence Hurlbird, who, even more intensely than her future husband, John Dowell, sees her home as a poor copy of the real gentility of England. The Ashburnham holding lies in the very part of England from which Florence's family emigrated, and she is determined to escape the prison, as she sees it, of Waterbury for the glory of an English country home.

— *Charles Pullen*

THE GOOD SOLDIER ŠVEJK

Author: Jaroslav Hašek (1883-1923)
Type of work: Novel
Type of plot: Satire
Time of plot: World War I

First published: Osudy dobreho vojáka Švejka ve světove války, 1921-1923 (English translation, 1930; unabridged translation, 1973)

Set in the Austro-Hungarian Empire during World War I, this novel abounds with references to place, yet includes little description. The novel relies heavily on dialogue and monologue, with most references to place occurring within the rambling monologues of the title character. Every anecdote that Švejk relates identifies a character as a resident of a specific neighborhood or village and names the street or establishment where events transpire; however, rather than provide specific information about characters and events, such details merely extend Švejk's digressions. Individually, the references to place hold little significance, but considered collectively, they help to establish character and theme and to reinforce the universality of the novel's antiwar message.

***Austro-Hungarian Empire.** Central European empire ruled by the Habsburg Dynasty from 1867 to 1918 whose territory included the region that became Czechoslovakia, where much of the novel takes place. Although the novel is based on Hašek's experiences as a Czech conscripted to serve in the Austrian army, Austria-Hungary represents any corrupt and oppressive regime, a fact readily apparent to Germany's Nazi regime, which banned this book in the 1930's.

Anabasis. Term for a military advance. Not surprisingly, in the chapter titled "Švejk's Budéjovice Anabasis" the Good Soldier retreats from Ceské Bodévice, a town in southern Bohemia from which troops are deployed to the Russian front. Unlike Hašek himself, who traveled without incident to Ceské Bodévice, then on to Kirilyhida in Hungary and finally to the front, Švejk misses his train and sets off on foot to rejoin his regiment, traveling in the opposite direction. In Cecil Parrott's English translation of this novel Švejk's "anabasis" is conveniently plotted on a map. However, what is important is not the towns and villages themselves, but the circular path of the journey, which replicates in physical terms the themes of circularity that form much of the novel's structure. Just as Švejk attempts to circumvent authority by launching into monologues that digress wildly before returning to the original point, so the anabasis allows him to delay being sent into combat. He inhabits a world in which oppressive authority is inescapable and in which history is doomed to repeat itself.

***Prague.** Capital city of Bohemia and later capital of Czechoslovakia and the Czech Republic, where the first volume of the novel is set. A life-long resident of Prague, Hašek displays his knowledge of the city on nearly every page, naming streets and landmarks and businesses, such as the Chalice.

After being arrested at the Chalice, Švejk spends time in Pankrák, which is the Prague prison, a psychiatric clinic, a hospital, and a garrison jail. Hašek alternates periods of confinement with periods of freedom during which the Good Soldier faces few restrictions—and in the case of his "anabasis" roams the countryside. This pattern not only reinforces the themes of circularity and repetition, but also contributes to characterization. No matter what the situation, Švejk responds in a cheerful, cooperative manner. Although he appears to be both a shrewd manipulator bent on avoiding combat and a person who cherishes his freedom, space—whether open or closed—seems to have little effect on him. A key to his survival in a world of inescapable authority is his ability to remain unfazed by the world around him; consequently, he often seems oblivious to his surroundings.

***Chalice.** Prague pub that was a favorite of Hašek and is now a popular tourist attraction. In the novel it serves as the starting point for Švejk's adventures when he is arrested by an undercover member of the Austrian police who eavesdrops on Švejk's conversation with the barkeeper. This is the first of a series of arrests and incarcerations throughout the novel.

*Konopisté (KON-o-pish-tyeh). Fourteenth century castle outside Prague converted to a hunting lodge for Austrian archduke Francis Ferdinand, whose assassination in 1914 triggered World War I. Hašek's references to Konopisté exemplify the indifference to description that many critics consider a failing of the novel. The archduke was an insatiable hunter who killed thousands of animals and filled his castle with hunting trophies.

Although his obsession with killing animals was well known at the time of his death, nothing in Hašek's novel suggests any connection between the horrors of war, the deployment of Czechs as cannon fodder, and the archduke's corpse-lined residence. Konopisté is simply the place where the archduke stayed when he was in Bohemia.

— *K. Edgington*

GOOD-BYE, MR. CHIPS

Author: James Hilton (1900-1954)
Type of work: Novel
Type of plot: Sentimental

Time of plot: 1870-1933
First published: 1934

In the enduring tradition of British public school novels, this short novel is uncommon, not only because its central character is a kindly, humane master and not a tortured schoolboy, but also because, in James Hilton's narrative, the public school, typically portrayed as rugged training grounds that make men out of boys or as penal institutions posing as utopias of higher education, becomes a symbolic world of infinite possibilities—a place that upholds the belief in the comic resolution of the tragic, indeed, a sympathetic representation of England as it perceived itself at the height and the waning of the Victorian era and the period ushering in and following World War I.

Brookfield School. English public school (comparable to an American "private" school, that is, one that is not government run) at which Mr. Chipping (nicknamed "Mr. Chips") spends his entire career teaching boys. Of unspecified location, the school functions as an idealized and realistic microcosm of England. The men who lead it and the boys who develop under their tutelage are allegorical inhabitants of this symbolic design. As a benevolent archetypal mentor, casting his personality over and through everything and everyone, Chipping is the paragon of all that is held dear to the English heart.

Brookfield is "an old foundation," its history dating to the reign of Queen Elizabeth I of the sixteenth century, when England first asserted itself as a major world power brimming with self-confidence. However, Brookfield's fortunes throughout the centuries have gone up and down. Unlike famous schools such as Harrow and Eton, Brookfield has never achieved first-rate status; it has attracted students from the middle class and masters who are solid but not brilliant scholars. Such a setting al-

lows for a realistic representation of England as a whole and also underscores the unpleasant British emphasis on class and social standing, which Chipping, in his quiet way seeks to make more democratic, though he reveres much that is traditional.

Under different headmasters, the school, like England, changes, abandoning the classics for the moderns and altering the organizational structure that Chipping struggles to preserve when made acting headmaster. Ultimately, Brookfield School, like England, is compelled to change not only because of the Great War, in which its own great losses mirror those of the nation as a whole, but also because of social issues such as woman's suffrage and class distinctions. Through Chipping's reactions and solutions and the pains Brookfield School must endure, readers recognize the paradox of English life in those times, indeed the paradox of any society in a period of upheaval: While change is as inevitable as growth, one must be careful of what may be lost in the gain and cherish that which the past has taught and bequeathed. In great part from the lessons Chipping learns from his brief marriage to a young nonacademic woman, who comes to Brookfield and introduces new ways and ideas, he steers Brookfield through the perils of change with grace and understanding and support.

Brookfield School symbolizes all that is believed good, decent, traditional, and sacred about English life during the period in which it is set. Beneath this paean to society, however, lies a deep irony, one of which Chipping is well aware: To preserve the ideals embodied in the symbol, sometimes the physical structure of the symbol must be altered, even transformed, and in overly ambitious or inefficient hands, such as Headmaster Ralston's, change can spell disorder. However, the faith of the British people in themselves as phoenixlike is embodied in Chipping and Brookfield as school and nation and man rise again and again from their own ashes to adapt to and fashion the times.

Mrs. Wickett's house. Boardinghouse in which Chipping lives. In his retirement, he can watch the school from his room and experience its life vicariously. The house is close enough to the school for him to invite boys to tea, thus allowing him to maintain his connections; he still knows all the boys and is a part of the whole while technically apart. His books, his papers, his photographs, all the trappings of his life make up his room, which serves as a symbolic cave of death and rebirth, as he retires to it and emerges again, reborn, to lead the school through difficult times during the war, only to return to die there, and live on, reborn, in the hearts of all who knew and loved him.

*Lake District. Region in northern England that is a popular tourist destination and the subject of much Romantic poetry, a symbol of poetic genius and inspiration. In this English shrine of Romanticism and celebration of nature and life, Chipping goes on vacation in 1896 and meets young Kathy, with whom he falls in love and marries. For all her youth, Kathy teaches Chipping more about humanity in their short time together than he could ever learn in the greatest books. Though she and her baby die when she is in childbirth, Kathy's presence is with Chipping throughout the novel and is an indispensable element of the spiritual setting of the novel.

— *Erskine Carter*

A GRAIN OF WHEAT

Author: Ngugi wa Thiong'o (James Ngugi, 1938-   )
Type of work: Novel
Type of plot: Social realism

Time of plot: Mid-twentieth century
First published: 1967

Ngugi's third novel, generally hailed as his masterpiece, portrays the nation of Kenya at the moment of its independence from British colonial rule. Through a series of flashbacks, the novel explores a complex web of motivations and characters—disillusioned colonialists, Mau Mau freedom fighters, and Kenyans who collaborated with colonial rule—gradually unveiling the real identity of a traitor to the Mau Mau cause. The colonial era, the novel implies, is defined by a series of betrayals and mixed motives, and the question for an independent Kenya is whether it can surmount that troubled and divisive past.

*Kenya. East African nation that became independent from the British Empire in 1963. While the novel embraces the whole nation of Kenya, from its "one horizon" touching the Indian Ocean to its "other," touching the shores of the great Lake Victoria, it focuses on central Kenya's Gikuyu (also known as Kikuyu) people, from whom British settlers took large tracts of the country's best land for their own use. Indeed, land was central to the colonial conflict—to both the settler farmers and the agricultural Gikuyu. As a result, place in this novel is the object of struggle but also symbolic of the various betrayals that occur in the course of that struggle.

Rung'ei (roong-AY). Fictional town in which most of the novel's action takes place that is modeled on Limuru, an important settlement twenty miles northwest of Kenya's capital, Nairobi. Rung'ei stands on the edge of the so-called White Highlands, where European settlement was most dense. The Mombasa-Uganda railway line runs through the town, on its way from the coast to the interior. The railroad itself is at once an item of fascination for the villagers and an unavoidable symbol of the colonial presence. During Kenya's independence day celebrations, a highly symbolic footrace—essentially a contest to win the heart of the new nation—takes place on Rung'ei's main sports field.

Thabai (thah-BI). Gikuyu village near Rung'ei that is home to most of novel's main characters. It is a fictional version of the author's own home village of Kamiriithu. Because of the village's proximity to Nairobi and the White Highlands, and consequently to the most intense conflict during the Mau Mau fight for independence during the 1950's, its residents are profoundly affected by the stresses that colonialism has placed on their way of life.

*****Nairobi** (ni-ROH-bee). Kenya's capital city and the seat of colonial power until independence. Entirely a colonial creation, Nairobi, as the young carpenter Gikonyo notes, "was never an African city." It was, however, the site of important early resistance to colonial rule, and in this regard the novel highlights the work of such historical Kenyan leaders as Harry Thuku and Jomo Kenyatta. At independence, Nairobi's street names are changed, but the actions of a newly installed Kenyan member of parliament suggest that Kenya's new leaders will continue to exploit the people in the same way that the colonial rulers have been doing.

*****Kinenie Forest** (kee-neh-NEE-eh). Also known as the Kikuyu Escarpment Forest, a small wooded area near Limuru in which Mau Mau fighters took refuge.

Githima Forestry Research Station (gee-THEE-mah). Fictional name for Muguga, a research station northwest of Nairobi established by the colonial administration. Like Rung'ei, its location at the edge of the Kinenie Forest makes it a crucial meeting point for the colonial enterprise and the Gikuyu resistance.

Rira Detention Camp (REE-rah). Government holding center for captured Mau Mau fighters in a remote and inhospitable area near the coast of northeastern Kenya. During the Mau Mau uprising, the colonial administration demolished Gikuyu villages and relocated and consolidated villagers and put suspected Mau Mau collaborators in detention camps. Rira, where the protagonist Mugo and others are detained, is modeled on a real-life detention camp at Hola.

Green Hill Farm. Prime agricultural land in the White Highlands that Thabai villagers hope to purchase and return to Gikuyu use at independence. It is a profound betrayal of the hopes of independent Kenya when the villagers' own member of parliament uses his position to grab the choice farm land for himself.

— *J. Roger Kurtz*

THE GRANDISSIMES: A Story of Creole Life

Author: George Washington Cable (1844-1925)
Type of work: Novel
Type of plot: Regional

Time of plot: 1804
First published: 1880

One of George Washington Cable's best novels, this book, like most of his work, is set in New Orleans and is an excellent example of local color fiction, concentrating as it does on those elements of a particular setting and society that distinguish them from other American locales and cultures.

*****New Orleans.** Louisiana's leading city, located on the Mississippi River near the Gulf of Mexico. New Orleans is essentially an island, surrounded by Lake Pontchartrain to the north; the Mississippi River, which curves in a semicircle around it; and numerous bayous and swamps. Because of its status as the most foreign of all American cities, New Orleans, especially the old French Quarter, in which most of the action of the novel occurs, seems itself a character in the novel. Founded by the French in 1718, the city became part of the United States after the sale of Louisiana in 1803. Following the purchase and the American occupation, the city remained very much a French and Spanish city, with language, culture, and food more associated with Europe than with the rest of the United States. Cable was a native of New Orleans and was fascinated by the Creoles, descendants of French and Spanish settlers; their history and unique lifestyle, so different from his own, intrigued him, even as certain aspects of their existence repulsed him.

The plot of *The Grandissimes* could not have occurred in any other American city, for only in New Orleans did the peculiar institution called *placage* exist as an established and accepted part of society. White Creole men frequently took mistresses of mixed blood, known as "quadroons" or "octoroons." They housed these young women in their own homes on the periphery of the French Quarter and proceeded to father and rear second families. The result was a mixed population unique to New Orleans and unlike any other in the country. This type of situation is dramatically exhibited in the story of the two branches of the Grandissime family. Although Creoles tended to be secretive about their lives and distrustful of outsiders, the practice of *placage* was common knowledge and seems to have intrigued even as it repelled the staunchly religious Cable.

***Louisiana.** When the United States acquired Louisiana from Napoleon, the territory consisted of more than one million square miles that stretched west from the Mississippi River to the Rockies and north from Mexico to the Canadian border. From this enormous area, several states were carved, including what is now the state of Louisiana.

***French Quarter.** New Orleans's old Frenchtown district, also known as the "Vieux Carre." After 1718, the district grew up around the original settlement on the banks of the Mississippi. By 1804, the Quarter had expanded up and down the river. White Americans found themselves unwelcome in the French Quarter—a conflict dramatized in the struggle between Joseph Frowenfeld, Cable's protagonist, and the hot-tempered young Creole men. The Americans soon moved outside the Quarter, many to an area upriver that became known as the Garden District.

At the point on the river where the Creoles landed, they set apart a square where the militia could drill. This was known as the Place d'Armes (place of arms). After the mid-twentieth century it became known as Jackson Square.

***Congo Square.** Quadrangle on the outskirts of the French Quarter. It was so named because, before the Civil War, many of the slave owners in the Quarter brought their slaves to the area on Sunday afternoons for their only recreation, which consisted of singing and dancing to the music that would later evolve into jazz. Cable wrote an essay, "Dance in Place Congo," in which he collected several of these songs.

— *W. Kenneth Holditch*

THE GRANDMOTHERS: A Family Portrait

Author: Glenway Wescott (1901-1987)
Type of work: Novel
Type of plot: Family

Time of plot: 1830-1925
First published: 1927

The old Northwest frontier is the primary setting for this novel, which uses a family's migration to the American West in pursuit of their dream as a metaphor for the role of pioneer families and immigrants in the development of the young American republic. The family's individual histories of courage and despair, triumph and failure illustrate the nation's conflicts and struggles to incorporate the wilderness areas and warring factions into a united and civilized homeland.

Hope's Corner. Frontier farm of Henry and Rose Hamilton Tower, located on Stony Creek, north of Milwaukee, which became Wisconsin's Washington County. Hope's Corner is the primary setting for the novel. Alwyn Tower, the first-person narrator of the novel, grows up in the farmhouse occupied by his grandparents and his parents. A huge boulder by the hitching post looks like the Ark of the Covenant in Grandmother Tower's Bible, and the kitchen doorstep is a discarded marble gravestone with the lettering turned toward the ground—symbols of the promise of a land of their own and the sacrifices required to realize that dream. During Alwyn's childhood, the wilderness is already gone; he can see only plowed land and farm machinery of all kinds creeping like mechanical spiders over the slopes.

Tower House. The house itself, the third built on Hope's Corner, is a work in progress, as new rooms and porches are added to accommodate the generations of Towers who call it "home." From this house, Tower descendants scatter throughout the West, and a few go to Europe. Some return home to live for a while or to be buried in the family cemetery, which for Alwyn, takes the place of a city child's park.

In the house's parlor, furnishings brought from New York by canal boat give evidence of the family's hopes of becoming landed gentry in the West. The upholstered couch, on which Alwyn's grandfather takes his daily nap, has the proportions of a lion's body, with carved claws for legs and one end raised in a mass of fringed pillows. Above a writing desk a single frame contains embossed portraits of literary masters such as Ralph Waldo Emerson, Henry Longfellow, James Russell Lowell, and John Greenleaf Whittier. A wall rack over the couch holds plates painted by the family daughter Nancy, who marries after the Civil War and moves to Iowa. After intermittent bouts with madness and recovery, she comes home to rest in the "silent land" of the family cemetery.

The kitchen is Grandmother Tower's domain. Filled with treasures of the past—a dented copper kettle used as a foot-bath, a sugar barrel, and hand-hewn chests, the kitchen is a place where Grandmother Tower shares family histories with Alwyn. As she exercises her talents for cooking, sewing, and story telling, she teaches Alwyn that America is a land to be guarded and used for the glory of God, "the owner." However, her stories also teach Alwyn of the "darkness of life" in the Land of Promise, as Grandmother Tower relates the personal tragedies that comprise the chapters of this novel.

Duff house. Home of Alwyn's maternal grandparents, Ursula and Ira Duff, in Aaronsville, Wisconsin, where Alwyn stays while he attends school. A typical middle-class house, it has a front lawn fenced by hedges, a vegetable garden, and a stable. The house reflects Grandmother Duff's stiffness and modesty, which becomes a "form of madness" as she grows older. The antagonistic relationship between Ursula and Ira makes the house uncomfortable for family and friends.

Fielding house. Chicago home of Alwyn's "third grandmother," the mother of Uncle Jim's wife, Caroline Fielding. The widow of a descendant of Cromwell Fielding, merchant tycoon of Chicago, Mrs. Fielding reigns in her house like royalty. She is a fearful person who rarely leaves home and forces her daughters to remain by her side. When Jim's wife dies, Mrs. Fielding insists that he compromise his own ambitions and live in her home. Alwyn is a frequent visitor there, as he loves his Uncle Jim.

*Paris. Capital of France in which Alwyn spends time while wandering through Europe during the 1920's. Apparently a member of America's self-exiled "lost generation"—artistic expatriates who spend their days pondering the American republic and trying to explain it—Alwyn decides to publish the stories of his grandmothers so that others might better understand the American character. The people who settled the American West, he concludes, could not bring civilization to the frontier because they were "perpetual pioneers," too caught up in the individual dramas of everyday life to build an orderly, sophisticated society. Yet they had given birth to a composite American character that was the "hero" of all his grandmothers' stories. In comparison with that character's dwelling place, Europe seemed merely the "scene of a classic play continually repeated."

— *Marguerite R. Plummer*

THE GRAPES OF WRATH

Author: John Steinbeck (1902-1968)   *Time of plot:* 1930's
Type of work: Novel   *First published:* 1939
Type of plot: Social realism

This novel reflects the importance of land during the Great Depression—when it was so quickly lost by farmers in the south-central states—at the same time it reveals John Steinbeck's focus on the crucial relationship between human beings and their environment.

*Dust Bowl. Central region of the United States that was devastated by great dust storms during the 1930's. The first part of *The Grapes of Wrath* is set in Oklahoma, at the center of the Dust Bowl. Tom Joad returns from four years in prison to find that his family has lost its farm, and many of his neighbors have been made homeless by the banks and land companies that have taken over their farms when the tenants could not keep up with their payments through several disastrous seasons. Lured by handbills distributed by West Coast growers, Tom and his family begin the long trek from the devastated Dust Bowl to the promising fields of California.

The epic structure of the novel becomes a triptych of Oklahoma/journey/California. In the intercalary chapters—those interchapters of the novel, such as five and fourteen, in which Steinbeck gives important sociohistorical background—he explains what happened to this land and why, and how the loss of their farms led thousands of "Okies" to leave for California.

*Route 66. Highway leading out of Arkansas, Oklahoma, and Texas toward California. This narrow strip of highway, bordered by hamburger stands and gasoline pumps, is the escape route for the Joads and other families hit hardest by the Depression. It is also the place where they come together and form extended families moving westward. In the evenings, in their makeshift camps, "a strange thing happened: the twenty families became one family." Route 66 is thus the setting for one of Steinbeck's major themes, which is how communities form and provide strength for all their members. As the Joad family loses members along the way, Ma Joad emerges as the leader and helps shape a larger, matriarchal family as others join them. "They ain't gonna wipe us out," she says. "Why, we're the people—we go on."

*California. Site of fruitful fields and bountiful crops. Steinbeck describes the Joads' first sight of the San Joaquin Valley's rich farming land in almost biblical language, as he does in other passages in the novel: "The vineyards, the orchards, the great flat valley, green and beautiful, the trees set in rows, and the farm houses." The contrast to Oklahoma's impoverished farms could not be stronger; however, Steinbeck makes it clear in intercalary chapters 19 and 21 that similar economic and agronomic policies are exploiting the land and its people in both locales, and that "when a majority of the people are hungry and cold they will take by force what they need." This second theme—that of revolutionary socialism—emerges in *The Grapes of Wrath*, not in the Dust Bowl, but in California, where so many migrants have been drawn to the harvests by the promise of work that they see their wages steadily reduced because of the surplus of workers. The Okies are thus transformed from tenant-farmers to migrant workers. The next step, Steinbeck says, is certain: "On the highways the people moved like ants and searched for work, for food. And the anger began to ferment."

Steinbeck shows no California cities in the novel, but reveals the contrast between the bountiful fields and the "Hoovervilles," the temporary camps in which migrant workers are forced to live without adequate water or sanitation in California's great Central Valley. "There is a crime here that goes beyond denunciation," Steinbeck writes. "In the souls of the people the grapes of wrath are filling and growing heavy, growing heavy for the vintage." Steinbeck's thematic metaphors, including his novel's title, grow directly out of the land he describes.

Weedpatch. Government-run camp for migrant workers located below Bakersfield in central California (based on the Arvin Sanitary Camp) where the Joads stay for several weeks. Weedpatch is the emotional high point of the novel, and a clear contrast to the Hoovervilles. When the Joads arrive, they are greeted by migrants like themselves who run the camp with efficiency and care. The community theme in the novel is thus reinforced in these chapters, culminating in the festive Saturday night dance. Given a chance, Steinbeck is showing, people will manage their own affairs well and work for better lives. The local land owners want the camp removed and try to cause a disturbance at the dance, however, for Weedpatch gives people hope for a better life and reveals that they only want the same opportunities as other Americans.

Pixley peach farm. Dirty migrant cabins and a depressing contrast to living conditions at Weedpatch. When the Joads are forced to leave Weedpatch in order to find work farther north, they arrive at a peach farm where the owners have reduced wages so low that workers go on strike. It is here that Jim Casy—the labor organizer who travels west with the Joads—is killed and Tom leaves the family to join the organizers fighting the terrible conditions for migrant workers in California.

Boxcar. Last home of the Joads in the novel. Drawn by the promise of cotton picking, the depleted Joad family ends up living in a boxcar with other displaced families. It is in a field near which Tom says good-bye to Ma with the promise that he'll always be near: "Wherever they's a fight so hungry people can eat, I'll be there. . . . An' when our folks eat the stuff they raise an' live in the houses they build—why, I'll be there."

Black barn. Last shelter for the Joads. Forced out of the boxcars by torrential rains, the family seeks shelter in a barn on higher ground, and the novel ends when Rose of Sharon, whose own baby is stillborn, suckles a dying old man and smiles "mysteriously" across the barn. In the biological metaphor that defines the novel, life is being nurtured even at this last site, and hope for the people survives.

— *David Peck*

GRAVITY'S RAINBOW

Author: Thomas Pynchon (1937-   )
Type of work: Novel
Type of plot: Historical realism

Time of plot: 1944-1945
First published: 1973

This novel is set primarily in Western Europe at the close of World War II, with its protagonist, Tyrone Slothrop, traveling in search of Germany's V-2 rocket. The novel also contains episodes in the United States. Places in the novel are sometimes real and sometimes allegorical—such as the resort town of Bad Karma.

*****London.** Capital of Great Britain in which the novel opens during the final days of the European theater of World War II. Although Germany is facing almost certain defeat, it continues to bombard London with V-2 rockets—weapons of great psychological power because the noise they make while approaching and striking their targets gives a menacing resonance to the military's use of the word "theater" to describe war zones.

*****The Zone.** Parts of Western Europe liberated from German occupation. As the war ends, Slothrop travels from London to the liberated zone, in which former national boundaries have not yet been fully reestablished. As the Allies negotiate over the spoils of their victory, Slothrop travels on a quest for information on the V-2 rocket. His sometimes frantic search is motivated by his paranormal intuition regarding his own personal connection to the rocket. He is in danger, he knows, because

he has aroused the curiosity of powerful intelligence agents who have discovered his ability to predict exactly where the rockets would strike in London. Slothrop reasons that he needs to uncover information about the rockets that will explain his intuitive powers, which he does not understand.

For Slothrop, the zone is a study hall in which he needs to lose his innocence. Everyone is looking for something: drugs, money, power, revenge, redemption, and most of all information. The places Slothrop visits in the Zone include the Casino Hermann Göring, a posh Riviera gambling casino named after a top Nazi that has not yet had its name changed to something more appropriate for the victors. He also visits cafés and apartments in Geneva, Zurich, and Berlin that are filled with spies and drug fiends; the underground German rocket factory at Nordhausen; Potsdam, a German town dedicated, before the "theater" of the war, to making movies; Peenemünde, where V-2 rockets were tested; and various bodies of water. The vessels Slothrop encounters or hears of include a U-boat hijacked by Argentine anarchists and a black marketeer's large speedboat on which a group of musicians, chorus girls, and a troupe of performing chimpanzees get into some cases of vodka and start a riot. Slothrop also travels on a balloon laden with spies and descends on a train underground into what remains of the V-2 assembly line.

The seeming anarchy of the zone does not entirely conceal its rigid, ruthless order. To Slothrop, the zone is a tightly controlled "rocket-state." At all times, even as he constantly changes identity and zigzags across Europe, he is aware that he is not merely being followed but is being anticipated. He can never be sure he has escaped his role as a pawn in some larger drama.

*Los Angeles.** Southern California capital of the movie industry and the center of secret weapons development. During the 1970's, a specially produced rocket that was the particular object of Slothrop's quest that was launched in Europe in 1945 comes down. The rocket apparently carries a nuclear payload and triggers World War III.

Gravity's rainbow. Allusion to the parabolic shape of the flight path of a rocket. A realm of mathematically described space is on locales that exist on levels at once as real as a wartime bombardment and as allegorical as geometry.

— *Eric Howard*

GREAT EXPECTATIONS

Author: Charles Dickens (1812-1870)
Type of work: Novel
Type of plot: Bildungsroman

Time of plot: Early nineteenth century
First published: 1860-1861

Like most of Charles Dickens's novels, this book is largely set in London. However its beginning and end are set in the Kentish marshes, some twenty to thirty miles east of London, an area Dickens knew in his youth, when his father was stationed at Chatham, a naval base. The link between the two settings is the River Thames, which runs through the novel like a leitmotif. To its west lie the fashionable suburbs of London; to its east, the decaying marshes and the rotting prison ships. Dickens's vision of English society sees both as inextricably joined, though that society's illusion is to separate them.

*River Thames** (tehmz). River in southern England that runs through London to the North Sea. Several places that figure in the novel stand along the river. Some eight miles to the west of London lies Richmond, on the river's south bank, a stylish town in Surrey. After her "finishing school," Estella comes to live here in Mrs. Brandley's house on Richmond Green, to be introduced into fashionable London society, to continue to break men's hearts. It is thus an extension of Satis House as a locus for Miss Havisham's revenge.

*Hammersmith.** Town on the northern bank of the Thames, west of London. There the Pockets have a small riverside house, in which Pip is tutored together with Bentley Drummle and Startopp.

*The Temple.** Central London district in which Pip and Herbert take rooms overlooking the river. Although this place symbolizes the pretentiousness of Pip's life of expectations, it also marks the point where he enables Magwitch to escape, thereby bringing his false expectations to an end.

*Chinks Basin.** District in London, downriver from the Temple, in the dock area below London Bridge, where Magwitch is secreted at the home of the father of Clara, Herbert's girlfriend, at Mill Pond Bank.

*Marshes.** Region along the lower reaches of the River Thames in which Pip grows up. The region is featured ambiguously as a place of childhood innocence and adult menace. Here Pip's life is threatened by Magwitch and then Orlick; however, it is also where the warmth of Joe Gargery's forge lies. Dickens seems to collapse notions of innocence, safety, and corruption at the same time he extends motifs of imprisonment and entrapment in the symbolic Hulks, dismasted naval ships used as floating prisons near the marshes. Ironically, the Thames reaches from the pretensions of Estella Havisham in the west to the sordid reality of her paternal origin in the east. The novel refocuses these two places by seeing the river's flow, not as time, but as inevitable moral process. Estella and Pip's frequent coach journeys from one end of this space to the other are like the shuttle of a web, broken only by the last thwarted journey downriver of Magwitch, where full revelation of the moral failures of the past is made.

Satis House. Decaying mansion home of Miss Havisham, standing along the edge of an unnamed town next to the marshes. Within its grounds once stood a brewery, which was the source of Miss Havisham's inherited wealth. While *satis* is the Latin word for "enough," within this novel the name represents the opposite: unfulfilled desire and expectation. Within the Satis House, Estella is raised to use her charms to entrap men. In the end, everyone in the house is entrapped, and Miss Havisham is burned to death purgatorially. Finally, the contents are auctioned off and the house sold as scrap, again symbolically signifying the end of all the unreal expectations of Pip and Estella.

*London. Great Britain's capital city, a different version of which Dickens presents in each of his novels. In *Great Expectations*, the reality of London is particularly symbolized by **Newgate Prison**, a notorious institution in which violent prisoners were kept along with those awaiting execution. Dickens made a close study of prison conditions, perhaps because of his own parents' imprisonment for debt. Here, the nearness of Jaggers's chambers in Little Britain to the prison symbolizes how near criminality is to the sinister order of the law as practiced by so-called respectable practitioners such as Jaggers.

Jaggers himself lives in Soho, a mile to the west of Newgate; his clerk, Wemmick, lives in Walworth. In the early nineteenth century this was a disorganized northern suburb of London. His small wooden house is built like a miniature castle, with a moat and drawbridge round it, symbolizing his attempts to cut himself off from the sordid legal activities he is engaged in. His aging father lives with him, and they celebrate Sunday, their day off, by raising the Union Jack on a flagstaff.

Another site of pretentiousness is Pip's own dining club, the **Finches of the Grove**, which meets at Covent Garden, an area of central London famous for its great flower and vegetable market, as well as London's main opera house. Thus, low-life and fashionable society share the same space, though pretending not to, just as Jaggers's office is situated near Smithfield, the London meat market.

*Barnard's Inn. Apartment block to which Pip is assigned when he first comes to London to live up to his expectations of a fortune, and which he shares with his friend Herbert Pocket. Confusingly, the term *inn* in London has a legal significance, often being the place where a group of lawyers may have or may have had their offices (or chambers). Barnard's Inn, though not presently being used by lawyers, does lie in the legal district round Holborn Hill. Pip's first impression of it is its dinginess, rottenness, and dilapidation, again symbolizing the quality of life he is destined to live there. Later on, he and Herbert move to the Temple, another inn.

— *David Barratt*

THE GREAT GATSBY

Author: F. Scott Fitzgerald (1896-1940)
Type of work: Novel
Type of plot: Social realism

Time of plot: 1922
First published: 1925

Both the theme and much of this novel's symbolism can be found in F. Scott Fitzgerald's use of setting and place. Fictional and real places are combined not only in order to illuminate character, provide realism, and focus on the specific time period (aptly termed by Fitzgerald the "Jazz Age") but also to imaginatively create physical contrasts that highlight the author's examination of the corruption and disintegration of the so-called American Dream.

Gatsby's mansion. Garish, multilevel home located on "West Egg." The narrator Nick Carraway describes it as colossal, as ostentatious as it is roomy. Situated on forty acres, the mansion is the site of numerous glitzy and riotous parties thrown by Gatsby, hoping to pique Daisy Buchanan's interest. The mansion, however, is much more than a lure for Gatsby's long lost love; it is a symbol of the man himself and his dream of materialism as a vehicle to success both literally and romantically. Gatsby's home parallels his persona—grand, mysterious, and richly adorned. It is the emblem of a successful businessman and the symbol of what he hopes to recover in Daisy and her love. The mansion is also a representation of a shortsighted American Dream: that material success, in and of itself, will bring one status and happiness. Unfortunately, the dream is based on hollow underpinnings, on the vacuous Daisy and the misguided concept that large amounts of money can be made and used without responsibility. Conversely, the mansion serves also as a symbol of Gatsby's vision, aspiration, idealism, and belief in the American Dream of the self-made man. Thus, it is simultaneously a symbolic representation of the "great" Gatsby and of the flawed one. Ultimately, Nick Carraway describes the mansion as "that huge incoherent failure of a house." The mansion exists as both a vision and failure of such a vision.

East Egg and **West Egg.** Fictionalized opposing peninsulas of Long Island Sound described as resembling a giant pair of eggs. They are contrasted in terms of fashionableness, color, and type of wealth. The East Egg mansions glitter along the water; they are more chic and are representative of older, Eastern, inherited wealth. The West Egg residences are more derivative and imitative, representative of the nouveau riche, affluent newcomers not yet accepted into the highest echelons of wealth. It is Gatsby's habitation in West Egg that denotes his aspiration to a social status that seems unattainable. The Buchanans, who reside on East Egg, represent the arrogance of an exclusive clique who attend Gatsby's parties and share in the fruits of his wealth but who essentially despise him. Tom Buchanan, who has inherited his fortune, does not value it in terms of the traditional American ethics of hard work, integrity, fairness, and success coupled with responsibility. The two Eggs also represent the larger framework of an East symbolic of European antiquity, old money, and corruption, and a West symbolic of independence, new money, and the pioneering spirit. Certainly Nick Carraway values Western ideals over Eastern, and at the conclusion of the novel he returns, in a westerly direction, to the traditional and conservative Midwest whence he came.

Valley of Ashes. Generally considered to be Flushing in New York City's borough of Queens, this place exists as a gray, dead, powdery area—even the homes seem to be composed of ashes—passed by motorcars on their way to New York. Here Myrtle and George Wilson live and operate a garage and gasoline station. The valley is a metaphoric representation of the wasteland the American Dream becomes when ethics and morals are disassociated from it. The valley is also the locus of those, such as George and Myrtle, who are victimized by the arrogant wealthy who base their lives on pleasure, avoidance of boredom, and dishonesty. If East and West Egg are two renditions of attainment of the American Dream, the Valley of Ashes is its demise. Literally it is the site where Daisy kills Myrtle, without compunction, and George decides to murder Gatsby. Finally, overlooking the valley are the giant blue eyes of Dr. T. J. Eckleburg, who stares down on the ashes from a billboard. A central symbol of guilt, judgment, and God, it invests the valley with a moral intensity that allies the novel with existential themes and statements about the moral bankruptcy of the modern world, a vast gray, ashen wasteland.

*New York City. Certain integral scenes take place in this city and often entail irresponsibility, adultery, violence, and drunkenness. New York is where Tom Buchanan takes his mistress, where Nick witnesses Tom brutalizing her, where Gatsby reveals his illicit love affair with Daisy, and where a lot of alcohol is consumed. Symbolically, the city represents careless consumption and irresponsible immorality. New York in the 1920's was a glittering den of writers, socialites, wealthy entrepreneurs, and other moneyed persons who were known for their extravagance and excesses.

— *Sherry Morton-Mollo*

GREEN GROW THE LILACS

Author: Lynn Riggs (1899-1954)
Type of work: Drama
Type of plot: Regional

Time of plot: 1900
First performed: 1931; first published, 1931

In his preface to this play, Lynn Riggs states his purpose as seeking to create a nostalgic glow emanating from the memories of his childhood. He also states his wish to explore the ways in which his characters relate themselves to the earth, as well as to one another. Few dramatic works are more grounded in place than Green Grow the Lilacs.

Williams farmhouse. Well-kept farmhouse in Indian Territory (later Oklahoma), occupied by young Laurey Williams and fifty-year-old Aunt Eller Murphy. The stage directions introducing the first scene of the six-scene play describe a radiant summer morning and a landscape dotted with men, cattle in a meadow, blades of young corn, and streams. Much of the play centers on the Williams farm.

*Indian Territory. Federal territory in which the play is set, before it merged with Oklahoma Territory to become the state of Oklahoma in 1912. Oscar Hammerstein II and Richard Rodgers, who adapted the play to create the musical *Oklahoma!* (1943), stated that Riggs's opening stage directions inspired the magical atmosphere of "Oh, What a Beautiful Morning," the song that opens *Oklahoma!* In a sense, *Green Grow the Lilacs* is itself a musical play, throughout which Riggs intersperses traditional folk songs and ballads. The first scene opens with Curly McClain, a brash young cowboy who is Laurey's suitor, approaching the Williams farmhouse singing "Chisholm Trail," immediately establishing the play's frontier setting. Later, Curly sings an old ballad containing the lyrics that give the play its title.

Riggs further reinforces the sense of place through dialogue. He attempts to render the characters' speech on the page just as he remembers that of his own Oklahoma boyhood. One stage direction describes their speech as lazy and drawling, but warns against use of a generalized southern or "hick" dialect. He wants his characters' dialect to be true to that of Indian Territory in 1900.

After the murderously jealous farmhand Jeeter dies while trying to burn Curly and Laurey alive, Curly is taken to the territorial capital, Claremore, for an inquiry. However, he escapes and returns to the Williams farmhouse. Much of the sixth scene of the play reflects the primitive state of law and order in Indian Territory in 1900.

Old Man Peck's house. Backyard of a place across Dog Creek, where a party is in progress in the play's fourth scene. Riggs devotes almost two pages of stage directions to dozens of period details. The revelers square dance outside and pull candy in the kitchen. Here also Curly and Jeeter become enemies in their pursuit of Laurey.

— *Patrick Adcock*

GREEN HENRY

Author: Gottfried Keller (1819-1890)
Type of work: Novel
Type of plot: Autobiographical

Time of plot: Mid-nineteenth century
First published: Der grüne Heinrich, 1854-1855;
    revised, 1879-1880 (English translation, 1960)

Settings in this novel alternate between the great cities Zurich and Munich and the rural region north of Zurich, with its villages and varied wild terrain. Like his protagonist Henry Lee, author Gottfried Keller was born in Zurich and studied art in Munich; his place depictions demonstrate the interplay between art and life, as well as progress from earlier times to the present reality. While the countryside, as the scene for love and courtship, immerses Henry in sensual and concrete nature, the cities serve as the backdrop for his artistic training and exposure to enlightened, cosmopolitan ideas.

*Zurich. Large city in northeastern Switzerland in which the Swiss painter (Heinrich) Lee lives. The Preaching Church, visible from Henry's room, is a symbol of his Protestant upbringing with its doctrinaire religious instruction. Freethinkers who gather at the secondhand shop across from Henry's home, stories of heterodox historical residents, and Swiss returning from long sojourns abroad provide critical perspectives.

A childhood experience playing a bit part on stage fascinates Henry by revealing the dichotomy between art and life, onstage glitter and backstage chaos. The one-room schoolhouse for the poor and the cadet training in middle school with prosperous middle class youths promote Henry's self-reliance and social integration. Henry's apprenticeship in an artist's workshop, as stuffy as the old monastery it is housed in, contrasts with his training in the elegant house of an artist just returned from Rome.

Lee home. House in which Lee lives in Zurich, the model for which is the tall, narrow house in the old quarter of Zurich where Keller himself grew up. While connecting Henry to the past, the house also lets him observe present activities of neighbors. The secret places in its dark corridors create a space for fantasy. Henry's room, overlooking the rooftops of Zurich, contained collections of homemade toys, minerals, and small animals when he was a boy. Decorating the attic room with etchings and picturesque objects, Henry as a teenager made it his art studio. Henry associates the house with mixed feelings toward his mother, including love, guilt, and shame of family poverty and debt.

*Canton Zurich. Northeastern province of Switzerland, whose mountains, fertile plateaus, rivers, forests, and meadows provide the backdrop for much of the action in the novel. The history and folk traditions of the Swiss are reflected in their consciousness as developed in artistic expression and by interaction with their unique landscape. The carnival celebration that ranges through towns and countryside, reenacting Friedrich Schiller's 1841 play about William Tell, illustrates this well. The play and wider folk festival show how art and life are connected, for Henry personally, as well as for the people generally.

Village. Henry's summer retreat and source of his direct experience with nature is modeled on Glattfelden (canton Zurich, on the Rhine), the ancestral home of Keller's parents. While the rural Swiss traditions of the parsonage, the farm, and the hunt are symbolically integrated in the uncle's house, the flowers, fruits, and animals of the village convey freedom, color and movement that gratify Henry's heart and inspire him as an artist. His cousin Judith's house, with its orchard garden hanging with ripe fruit to be picked and eaten, contrasts with the schoolmaster's house, with its profusion of flowers and contemplative view of the lake. Whereas the schoolmaster's house is associated with spiritualized love, Judith's house represents erotic awakening and temptation.

*Munich. Bavarian city in which Henry studies art. Described as the "abode of the Muses," Munich is filled with folk music and dance, but especially represents the art world, with its museums, exhibits, and art studios. In addition to exposing Henry to Germany's Roman Catholic heritage to supplement his Protestant training, Munich lets him experience German monarchy to contrast with Swiss republicanism. Interacting with all classes, Henry meets artists from the outer reaches of the old German empire. During Carnival time, the Bavarian royal palace becomes a workshop for artists and artisans, reflecting the royal patronage of King Ludwig I of Bavaria. The carnival's parades and festivities gratify the playful and artistic impulses as well as serving an important social function: creation of a German identity anchored in the past (Renaissance Nuremberg), but also open toward the future.

Count Dietrich's estate. Home of the nobleman who becomes Henry's patron. The estate's buildings and rooms point to aristocratic activities: hunting, gardening, agriculture, and patronage of the arts. With its library, work tables, and decorations, the count's room demonstrates his own liberal sentiments. His active promotion of art is shown when he pays Henry a handsome fee for his paintings and decorates his room with them. The Hall of the Knights, with its historic manuscripts, ancestor portraits, and old armor, stimulates the imagination as well as establishing continuity with a proud past.

— *Julie D. Prandi*

THE GREEN HOUSE

Author: Mario Vargas Llosa (1936-   )
Type of work: Novel
Type of plot: Social realism

Time of plot: Forty years that include World War II
First published: La casa verde, 1965 (English translation, 1968)

Mario Vargas Llosa's memories of his life in the Peruvian jungle town of Piura, together with the story of a brothel known locally as the "Green House," form the basis of this complex novel. A nonlinear narrative runs through many stories about the brothel, the family that owns it, one of its prostitutes, the military that runs the town, and a local dealer in stolen rubber.

*Piura. Provincial city in Peru where Vargas Llosa grew up, attended college, and wrote for a local newspaper. *The Green House* draws upon experiences he had there; its story line about the virgin Bonifacia, who is taken from the Amazon jungle to the Piura brothel is inspired by a trip he made with anthropologists on which he saw how Indian girls were drafted into prostitution.

Green House. Piura brothel around which the novel's stories are interwoven in a nonlinear narrative. The novel's title links the primal lusts of civilization in Piura, embodied by the whorehouse, with the primitive world of the lush, green jungle.

*Amazon basin. Rain forest region that extends from Brazil into eastern Peru. The novel opens on a tributary of the great Amazon River on which two nuns are being boated downstream by a rowdy crew of police and military men. The characters melt into a landscape of casual talk and flood of visual observation. No narrator sorts out which characters are important or what is going on. After thirteen pages without a single paragraph break, the novel suddenly cuts to a scene with different characters, who seem unrelated to what has gone before them. The entire book follows the pattern established in its opening pages. Past and present flow together. What happens first is never told first. Every beginning is instead the end of something begun earlier. In this way Vargas Llosa suggests that the jungle river, like the oddly constructed house painted green, is a metaphor for the world of Piura and for the Latin American experience in general. This experience involves struggles to separate what is real from what is fiction, what is indigenous from what is European culture, what is men's life from what is women's life, what is the modernity of urbanization and what is traditional culture as experienced through the magical landscapes of both city and jungle.

Vargas Llosa relies on a spiral, flowing narrative mode, characterized by a flood of text, unmarked by paragraph indentations, or quotation marks—much like that of the Maranon River with its "six violent miles of whirlpools, rocks, and torrents."

— *Elaine Laura Kleiner*

GREEN MANSIONS

Author: W. H. Hudson (1841-1922)
Type of work: Novel
Type of plot: Fantasy

Time of plot: Nineteenth century
First published: 1904

Few novels are as rich in geographical detail as this one, in which real and imaginary place names are frequently presented in expansive lists. These names provide a conceptual map of humankind's long journey from a mythical prehistory to an all-too-real modernity, via intermediate savagery. The significantly named Abel tracks South America's Orinoco River toward its source in a journey of discovery.

Ytaioa (ee-TI-oh-ah). Solitary hill situated in the savanna region west of Parahuari, whose lower slopes protect a densely forested oblong basin. In the heart of this forest—the "green mansions" of the novel's title—the wanderer Abel finds a kind of natural paradise which contrasts as sharply with the Native American village in the neighboring Parahuari hills as with the turbulent civilization he had earlier fled. It is a vivid place, roofed by the crowns of tall trees and lavishly furnished with ferns, mosses, creepers, and shrubs. The shade of the canopy creates a perpetual twilight, full of the music of birdsong.

Rima is the incarnate spirit of this forest, integrated into its lush ecology more fully and more intimately than would ever be possible for the corrupt Native Americans of Parahuari or for refugees from civilization like Abel and the old man who passes himself off as her grandfather. The rain forest is, in this metaphorical reckoning, the edenic garden which humankind's ancestors deserted when they fell into the bad habits exhibited by savage Native Americans and technologically sophisticated colonists alike. Unfortunately, it remains a wild place, subject to the harsher vagaries of nature, as Abel discovers when he is bitten by one of its serpents. It is, however, the consequences of that bite that allow him to forge a more intimate relationship with Rima.

Abel takes Rima up the slopes of Ytaioa in order to show her more distant peaks. She has her own names for some of them, but has no idea how big the South American continent really is. The geography lesson he gives her changes her notion of the world and of her situation within it; it is this new sense of place that drives her to leave her petty garden in a desperate attempt to find a greater "Eden," from which even she is an exile. This further Eden is supposed to be situated in the legendary mountains of Riolama for which Rima was named, but it is irredeemably lost—and while she and Abel absent themselves in the search for it, the fragment of Eden that they had is invaded and despoiled by the Native Americans. Rima is destroyed by fire, the first and foremost of all technological devices.

Parahuari (pehr-ah-WAHR-ee). Hilly region to the west of the part of the Orinoco River which flows from north to south between what became the Venezuelan province of Amazonas (known in the novel as "Guayana") and the Colombian province of Guainia (which was also part of Venezuela when the novel was written). Parahuari is the site of the Native American "village"—a single mud-walled and palm-thatched hut with subsidiary extensions—where Abel's journey comes to its first terminus, in a haze of drunken idleness.

Manapuri (mah-nah-PEW-ree). Native American settlement on the Orinoco between its confluences with the River Meta and the River Guaviare, consisting of a number of hovels with walls of mud or plastered wattle and roofs of thatched palm leaves. In the story, it represents one of the intermediate stages of civilization through which Abel "descends" as he journeys up the Orinoco into the dark heart of the continent.

*Georgetown. Capital and chief port of British Guiana (now Guyana), to the east of Venezuela. This is where the second phase of Abel's odyssey comes to an end, when his haunted flight from Rima's ashes finally brings him "home" to civilization. It is where the narrator listens sympathetically to his tragic story, in a house on Main Street symbolizing all the anaesthetic comforts of modern life.

— *Brian Stableford*

GREENE'S GROATS-WORTH OF WITTE BOUGHT WITH A MILLION OF REPENTANCE

Author: Robert Greene (1558-1592)
Type of work: Short fiction
Type of plot: Satire

Time of plot: Late sixteenth century
Locale: A city resembling London
First published: 1592

In this vitriolic pamphlet, Robert Greene warns his friends not to follow his dissolute example and depicts a great city as an entity so corrupt that he himself faces an early death from poverty, disease, and despair. His deathbed repentance warns others of the dangers that lurk beneath the glittering facade of the city and its theatrical world.

***London.** The great city in this novel is never mentioned by name, but topical references, not to mention the prefatory material by the printer and the editor, clearly establish London as the novel's principal setting. Indeed, the pamphlet is so steeped with the gritty reality of the sixteenth century London underworld that the dangers Greene points out seem as real to modern readers as those of any modern metropolis.

Autobiographical fables that begin the pamphlet set up the contrast between the bucolic delights of the poet's country home and his years at Cambridge with the grimy, deceitful, rough-and-tumble, and ultimately destructive environment of the city. "Roberto," the persona Greene gives himself at the beginning of this work, is easily swayed by the attractions of an irregular life in the underworld of London in the sixteenth century. He goes through a succession of seedy lodgings from which he flits one step ahead of the landladies who demand rent from him. He frequents taverns filled with thieves and con men. He is also a well-known patron of the brothels of the Bankside where, much to the despair of his long-suffering wife, he consorts with prostitutes, finally taking one as his mistress, only to contract a venereal disease from her. He loses whatever meager earnings he ekes out as a writer in the gambling dens. Finally, on his deathbed, he not only repents of his misspent life but warns his friends of how easily they may also become entrapped in the illusory pleasures offered by the city.

In Greene's mind the city becomes a diseased living organism that reaches out and pulls naïve and innocent young men into its clutches with the sole intention of destroying them.

Theaters. One of the self-proclaimed "university wits" who thought he should be able to take the theatrical world by storm, Greene is particularly virulent in his condemnation of the theatrical milieu. While his pique is undoubtedly brought on by the failure of the playing companies to reward his talent and the audiences to appreciate it, the world of the theaters is filled, in his mind, by atheists (Christopher Marlowe), pretenders to talent (Thomas Nashe and George Peele), but, most offensively, by one upstart crow (William Shakespeare) who manages to attain the popular and financial success Greene envies despite his lack of a university education. He takes none of the blame on himself, despite his professed repentance for his follies, but rails against a setting in which these evils exist solely to lead unsuspecting country gentlemen astray. Greene professes that an entire book cannot contain the wrongs that exist and the temptations that abound in the playhouses of sixteenth century London. There is no escape from their evil for Greene in this world but only in the world to come.

— *Mary Anne Hutchinson*

GROUP PORTRAIT WITH LADY

Author: Heinrich Böll (1917-1985)
Type of work: Novel
Type of plot: Social realism

Time of plot: 1922-1970
First published: Gruppenbild mit Dame, 1971 (English translation, 1973)

Heinrich Böll's novel is an endearing depiction of the beautiful protagonist Leni through her fictitious biographer, Au. The novel is set in western Germany along the Rhine River, covering a whole generation of lives that associated with Leni in many fascinating ways during the period of World War II. Social and economic changes in Germany during this time reflect a German culture and heritage that really challenge the human spirit.

*Rhineland.** Region surrounding the Rhine River in western Germany. The Rhineland experienced heavy militarization in 1936 and severe destruction by Allied bombing during World War II. The novel's time frame and settings are revealing in that they signify harsh living conditions and the political socioeconomic climate that affect Leni and those around her in a war-torn environment. Civilians must cut back on luxury and food items, and bombing raids are frequent during the war.

During the years of Adolf Hitler's Third Reich, nationalism and political ideals are instilled in the German people at all levels, to such an extent that Leni's school votes her the "most German" girl in the city, district, province, and perhaps even the whole country. Despite the honorary title, however, she is actually German only in her physical heritage and place of birth—nothing more.

Nursery. Business concern for which Leni works in the Rhineland. During the economic instability of wartime, Leni's boss creatively sets up a place to sell wreaths to funerals. He and his workers efficiently make the business into a lucrative enterprise because of the war. Since people are dying everyday, floral wreaths are in demand. The business becomes even more lucrative, thanks to Leni's ingenuity in recycling wreaths and ribbons to save production costs.

Leni also meets a Russian prisoner of war at the nursery, where to work is a special privilege. During air raids, she and the Russian make love in a graveyard—the only place where they can find privacy together. Leni is often happy during the air raids and hopes they will last a long time each time they occur so she can be with her Russian lover as long as possible.

*Rome.** Capital city of Italy, where the fictitious biographer Au goes to interview an informant on the relationship between Leni and a nun. In addition to uncovering fascinating information on the nun, Au is charmed by another nun, Sister Klementina, in one of several instances where he projects himself into the narrative.

Leni's apartment. Home of Leni in a apartment building owned by the Hoyser family in a Rhineland reminiscent of Cologne, where for the first time Au finds himself in the physical presence of his biographical subject. His biographical affection for Leni is still strong. All his perceptions of her prove to be true and correct. Even meeting her here, she is still bewitchingly enigmatic to him due to her reticence.

— *Hanh N. Nguyen*

GROWTH OF THE SOIL

Author: Knut Hamsun (Knut Pedersen, 1859-1952)
Type of work: Novel
Type of plot: Social realism

Time of plot: Late nineteenth century
First published: Markens grøde, 1917 (English translation, 1920)

As this novel's title suggests, transformation of a place is its subject. Gradually, with the assistance of his wife, a Norwegian peasant changes the barren wilderness into a valuable and beautiful estate. At the same time the land shapes the characters of the man and woman who love it and who will eventually lie buried within it. Knut Hamsun uses place to dramatize his belief in the old-fashioned values of work, integrity, and simplicity. "Growth of the soil," thinks his farmer Isak, is "something different, a thing to be procured at any cost; the only source, the origin of all."

Sellanraa. Farm of the Norwegian protagonist, Isak, and his wife, Inger. Hamsun was in many ways the opposite of Isak, a simple, honest, and hard-working subsistence farmer who leads the kind of life that Hamsun might have wished for himself. As an aspiring writer, however, he was not attached to the soil or even to his native Norway. He worked for many years as an itinerant farm laborer in North America, where he saw the Industrial Revolution tearing millions from the soil. He suffered loneliness, poverty, and spiritual alienation, as suggested by the titles of some of his other books, such as *Hunger* (1890), *Vagabonds* (1930), and *The Road Leads On* (1934). Through his description of the transformation of Sellanraa, his utopia, Hamsun eloquently expresses his thesis that country life is more wholesome than town life.

Breidablik. Farm of Brede Olsen, whose character is undermined by town life. Scatterbrained, impractical, and lazy, he is used to taking orders from others and is unable to think independently. He envies Isak but fails to realize how much sweat and perseverance are behind Sellanraa's development. Brede lacks the knowledge required to cultivate the soil, raise livestock, build dwellings and barns, repair tools, store fuel and fodder, and perform all the other tasks necessary for independent survival. As Isak passes Breidablik on his way to and from the village, he notices tangible signs of neglect and deterioration, which proceed from Brede's weak character. When Breidablik is auctioned off by Olsen's creditors, Hamsun's description of the dilapidated farm, its few scrawny animals, and farm implements ruined by neglect eloquently expresses his contempt for dreamers whose characters are undermined by modern civilization.

Maaneland. Axel Ström's farm. Maaneland is not as successful as Isak's Sellanraa, although Axel shares Isak's values. The major difference is that Axel does not have a faithful, industrious, and skillful wife like Isak's Inger. Axel's servant, and later wife, Barbro, has been corrupted by city living and causes Axel much anxiety and heartache.

Storborg. Combination farm and general store owned by Aronsen. Unfit to be a farmer, Aronsen sells out to Isak at a loss when the local mine closes down. Isak's son receives the place as a gift, but he is too corrupted by city living to make a go of it, either as store or farm. He invests in such unsaleable merchandise as bird whistles and rocking horses. Eventually Storborg passes into the hands of Andresen, another man who loves the land and is content with a simple lifestyle.

Mine. Local copper mine that changes hands many times and creates both wealth and poverty. The mine illustrates the vanity of capitalistic speculation and the plight of wage slaves everywhere. It attracts a horde of rootless working men, whose interests are limited to drinking, gambling, and womanizing. Their shiftless lives undermine their characters, and they themselves have a harmful influence on the simple folk who live in the wilderness.

Village. Unnamed hamlet that is important to Isak and his family only as a place to sell surplus goods, such as cheeses and eggs, for which they obtain staples they cannot produce themselves, such as coffee and sugar. The village illustrates the dependency and insecurity of all those who have lost the skill and inclination to wrest their own livings from the land, the source of all wealth.

Cities. Norway's big cities of Trondheim and Bergen are almost legendary places to people like Isak. Never used for scenes in the novel, they are only mentioned in conversations. City dwellers seem like a different race of people. They can manage to eat and drink and wear fine clothes without ever doing any productive labor. At most they live by talking, scheming, and manipulating pieces of paper. City people are cold, selfish, materialistic, and dehumanized in direct proportion to the size of their city's population.

— *Bill Delaney*

GUARD OF HONOR

Author: James Gould Cozzens (1903-1978)
Type of work: Novel
Type of plot: Psychological realism

Time of plot: Three days during World War II
First published: 1948

The narrative of this novel focuses narrowly on a hot, isolated U.S. Army Air Force base near a seedy Florida town. The shabbiness and physical discomfort of the setting provide a symbolic background for a study in moral ambiguity and ambivalence. Just as the town is suspended between its once-dreamed-of importance and the reality of its decay, the novel's characters encompass a spectrum of courage, cowardice, and meanness.

Ocanara Army Air Base. Sprawling makeshift military facility in Florida comprising landing strips and hastily built temporary structures—a military base similar to many that sprang up in the United States—especially in the South—during World War II. The makeshift nature of the base's buildings represents perfectly the character of the Army Air Force personnel stationed there. Most of the men and women at Ocanara are not military professionals; rather, they have been moved by patriotism or shame into joining the service. Although the majority of these ex-civilians perform tasks at the base that are similar to what they did in civilian life, most of them would rather be somewhere else—perhaps in combat, probably not. The base is claustrophobic: men and women work together, socialize, and sometimes sleep together. The setting clearly represents a microcosm, not only of the 1940's South, but of American culture of that era.

The moral perspectives of the novel's characters constitute a full range of choices and positions. Hence, just as there exist contrasting qualities among the physical characteristics of the air base and the nearby town, Ocanara, the characters' multiple points of view create a good deal of tension among base personnel. Questions of morality surface in the forms of discussions, arguments, and debate concerning not only military dereliction of duty but marital fidelity and sexual conduct—and, what is most important, racial prejudice.

Among people on the base, the line between personal and professional relations is vague. And tensions that exist or develop between officers and enlisted personnel, between career men and temporary soldiers, between men and women and, what becomes most critical, between African Americans (a significant minority on the base) and whites are exacerbated by the base's close working and living quarters and the oppressive heat.

Officers Club. Base facility for commissioned officers that is the scene of a clash between angry black airmen and military police in which racial tensions on the base come to the surface. The club is an effective embodiment of the ways in which reality intrudes on illusion, pretense, and dreams in *Guard of Honor*. In keeping with the racial segregation that pervaded the U.S. armed forces, entry into the club is restricted to white officers; however, the building itself is merely a dreary, cheap, concrete-block structure. Appropriately, it is painted white. The club is near lakes (which are really ponds) bearing names that allude to dream worlds and myths: Oberon and Thisbe. A swimming pool planned for the club was never built. The unfinished club is a kind of physical aborting.

Oleander Towers Hotel. Hostelry that represents not only the dashed hopes of the town of Ocanara but the confusion and instability—social and moral—of the air base personnel. Once expressive of Ocanara's hopes for tourism, the hotel is now quarters for male officers from the air base. Like the base's Officers' Club, the hotel is stunted, even distorted; a fire has destroyed some of the building's original structure. Its grounds are overgrown. A hodgepodge of architectural styles, the hotel is, in a word, shabby.

Lake Lalage. Florida lake near the base's airstrip that is representative of the geography of central Florida, which has numerous lakes. The lake also serves as an emblem of military incompetence; Army Air Force commanders were warned that Ocanara was no place for parachute jumping because of its many lakes. The largest of the base's lakes, Lalage is the scene of the novel's critical moment: the drowning of seven paratroopers during a demonstration jump in a celebration staged for General Ira Beal. Ironically, the tragedy also is the occasion of the heroism of several black army engineers who try to save the drowning paratroopers.

— *Gordon Walters*

THE GUIDE

Author: R. K. Narayan (1906-2001)

Type of work: Novel

Type of plot: Social realism

Time of plot: Mid-twentieth century

First published: 1958

Like most of R. K. Narayan's fiction, this novel is set in and around the imaginary south Indian city of Malgudi. Narayan grew up and lived all his life in Mysore, a city in south India that probably served as Malgudi's model.

*India. South Asian nation in which the novel is set during the 1950's, after it became independent. Because of India's vastness and its population's relative stability, the various parts of the country differ dramatically in climate and terrain, customs, languages, architecture, food, and manners. During the country's long colonial period, southern India was less influenced by the presence of the British Empire than other parts of India. Southern Indian cities and countryside thus tend to be "more Indian" and colorful than such metropolitan centers as Delhi, Bombay, and Calcutta.

During the 1950's, India's northern cities and the areas around them still retained vestiges of colonialism. However, there is nothing British about the novel's Malgudi; it is pure Indian. Its authenticity and its central role in Narayan's work has been aptly compared to William Faulkner's Yoknapatawpha County in Mississippi. Both serve as microcosms for the writers' explorations of the human condition, which prevents them from evolving into places marked by maudlin regionalism.

Malgudi (mahl-GEW-dee). Fictional city in southern India. During nearly seventy years of writing fiction, Narayan built this memorable city street by street, building by building, and neighborhood by neighborhood. Lying next to a river, Malgudi is a bustling place, full of schools, restaurants, temples, the humble stands of street vendors, a hodgepodge of businesses, cinemas with garish posters, hotels from the grand to the shabby, and open places where people gather to talk and gossip. Like all Indian cities, Malgudi brims with humanity, noises and turmoil, animals wandering the streets, beggars and loiterers, an abundance of vehicles ranging from carts to motorcars, and odors—some pleasant, some not so pleasant. Because of Malgudi's warm climate, many of its shops are open to the street, and much of the daily living takes place outdoors.

The concept of community assumes its fullest meaning in an Indian city like Malgudi, in which much of life is carried on publicly and collectively. This spirited place, so familiar to Narayan's readers, serves as the backdrop for the novel. Much of the action takes place at the railway station where the main character, Raju, in his better days offers guide services to Malgudi visitors. In remote Indian cities railway stations serve as nerve centers. They are chaotic places, often dilapidated and unkempt, yet teeming with vitality. When trains pull in, the arriving passengers face armies of guides, porters, hawkers, and others offering varied services. Raju moves through the city, which unfolds naturally in the course of the action. Descriptions of Malgudi are never excessive. The environs simply emerge and blend with the characters and their behavior.

Temple. After his imprisonment Raju undergoes a transformation from a travel guide to a spiritual guide. This duality, which takes Raju from the mundane to the spiritual, serves as the book's theme. Thus, in his new life the temple, not the railway station, becomes his office. India is dotted with temples, so many, in fact, that it should not be difficult to find a deserted one, as Raju does. In the novel's first paragraph Raju is described assitting beside an ancient shrine, whose original significance has probably been long forgotten. From this point onward, though, the ancient shrine takes on new meaning, which is typical of Narayan's focus on spiritual progression in his fiction. As the opening dialogue proceeds, the appearance of the temple and its setting slowly and subtly emerge, with one detail building on another.

— *Robert L. Ross*

GULLIVER'S TRAVELS

Author: Jonathan Swift (1667-1745)

Type of work: Novel

Type of plot: Satire

Time of plot: 1699-1713

First published: 1726

The narrator of Jonathan Swift's masterpiece, Lemuel Gulliver, a ship's surgeon, finds himself stranded on four strange and wondrous lands scattered around the globe. Each land corresponds to a facet of the eighteenth century European Enlightenment movement in general and English society and culture, in particular, which remain Swift's satirical targets throughout.

*Bristol. Port town in southwestern England, where the down-on-his-luck, good-natured Lemuel Gulliver begins his travels. A solid English citizen, Gulliver represents England's optimistic, rationalistic, and scientific philosophies, which Swift abhorred. A Church of England cleric, Swift maintained that England should look back to the ancient Greeks and Romans and to the Christian Church teachings for guidance and inspiration.

Lilliput (leel-lee-pewt). Island southwest of Sumatra that is the first strange land Gulliver visits after his first ship, the *Antelope*, is wrecked on its coast. Lilliput is Swift's satirical representation of the pettiness and small-mindedness inherent in church and state; its inhabitants are barely six inches tall, and features of its landscape are correspondingly tiny. Because of his immense size relative to the Lilliputians, Gulliver feels like a king and becomes an important court minister. In the manner of England's opposing political parties, two factions of Lilliputians—the Whigs and the Tories—govern the island's capital city of **Mildeno**. Despite Gulliver's enormous size, and his ability to see everything, his shortcomings and his inability to view human nature properly become clear. While attempting to explain England's politics to the ruler of both Lilliput (and later Blefescu) Gulliver voices Swift's hatred for humanity in general and England's Whig Party in particular.

Blefescu (bleh-feh-skew). Island empire that is Lilliput's northern neighbor and archenemy; its inhabitants, like Lilliput's, are six inches tall. While Lilliput represents eighteenth century England, Blefescu represents eighteenth century France, England's traditional enemy. By the eighteenth century, both England and France had been fighting wars on and off for centuries for both political and religious reasons. Reminiscent of the channel that separates England from France, a channel eight hundred yards wide separates Lilliput from Blefescu. Gulliver wades across this channel, captures Blefescu's entire fleet of warships, and delivers them to Lilliput. He comes to understand the cruelty of the Lilliputians only after they begin using him as a war machine against Blefescu.

Brobdingnag (brohb-deeng-nag). Long peninsula off California in the North Pacific that is the second strange land visited by Gulliver. In book 2 he continues his satire on Enlightenment ideals and English society in Brobdingnag, a land that accentuates human grossness because of the inhabitants' stupendous size. After a short return to England, Gulliver boards the ship *Adventure* bound for India, but it is blown off course and winds up on Brobdingnag, whose people are twelve times larger than ordinary human beings. Rats are the size of lions and eat grain that grows forty feet high. Gulliver becomes a sort of pet to the giant queen. Through their dialogues, Gulliver begins to see the foolhardiness of the English court and England in general which Brobdingnag represents.

Laputa (lah-pew-tah). Circular-shaped floating island about ten thousand acres in area that hovers over the terrestrial island of Balnibari; also called the **Flying Island** by Gulliver. His experience in this land makes obvious just how dangerous are his rationalistic, scientific, and progressive views. On another of his ocean voyages, pirates from a Chinese vessel attack his ship and place him on a rocky island, from which intellectuals who inhabit Laputa rescue him. In their free-floating domain, these scholars literally have their heads in the clouds and do not stand on solid ground.

Balnibari (bal-nee-BAR-ee). Island between Japan and California in the North Pacific over which Laputa floats. It is ruled by an absent-minded king who endorses impractical projects put forth by his Grand Academy.

Glubbdubdrib (glahb-DUHB-drehb). Also known as the **Island of Sorcerers**, a small island, about fifteen hundred miles southwest of Balnibari, that Gulliver reaches by boat. The island is ruled by magicians, who have the power to bring back the dead. There a magician introduces Gulliver to Alexander the Great and Julius Caesar.

Luggnagg (lahg-nag). Large island located about three miles southeast of Japan, with which its people conduct trade. This island's king shows Gulliver the immortal Struldbrugs, who represent the ultimate outcome of the Enlightenment's theory of the perfectibility of man. After a short trip to Japan—another real land then little known in Europe—Gulliver heads home to England.

Houyhnhnm-land (wheen-num-land). Island in the South Seas on which Gulliver is marooned by the crew of the ship that he captains. Swift's satire, established in the land of the little people and the giant people in books 1 and 2, is continued in the land of the Houyhnhnms in book 4, in which the author demonstrates the eventual results of the rationalistic philosophy that permeated English thought during the late seventeenth and eighteenth centuries.

While everything in Houyhnhnm-land is in correct human proportions, the setting is that of the familiar English countryside. Thus, its impact on the English reader was greater. After Gulliver leaves Portsmouth in 1710, destined for the South Seas, he is cast adrift during a mu-tiny and washes up on a land where intelligent horses—the Houyhnhnms—are the masters, and slow-witted silent humans—Yahoos—the beasts of burden.

The land of the Houyhnhnms is presented as a utopia with decency, benevolence, and civility ruling every horse's actions. Here, Gulliver finds no wars and no courts and passes his time in contemplation and light labor. However, love of family is also unknown because the Houyhnhnms regard it as unnecessary, though marriage is regarded as rational, necessary purely to maintain the population. The birth rate is maintained impeccably and scientifically so there is no poverty, but the Houyhnhnms' overwhelmingly rationalistic ethos results in life being dull and meaningless.

The land of the horses exemplifies the eighteenth century philosopher John Locke's philosophy that argues that the human mind is a blank slate controlled and developed entirely by impressions made by the environment. Ashamed of being thought a Yahoo, the rational-minded Gulliver lives in perfect contentment among the Houyhnhnms until his master, a horse, throws him out: Gulliver is, after all, in the horses' estimation, nothing but a filthy Yahoo, and his existence as a talking, thinking human among them is entirely irrational. By now a miserable and bitterly disillusioned misanthrope, Gulliver sails back to England, where he has no chance of ever finding a truly rational man. He lives out the rest of his life in misery, forced forever, he believes, to live among filthy Yahoos.

— *M. Casey Diana*

GUY MANNERING: Or, The Astrologer

Author: Sir Walter Scott (1771-1832)
Type of work: Novel
Type of plot: Historical

Time of plot: Eighteenth century
First published: 1815

This novel's eighteenth century Hieland setting, in the mountainous coastal southwestern border of Scotland, prefigures the struggle of its nineteenth century English readers to make sense of the changes taking place within their class structure: Merchants with ready capital are superseding those with family history and property in the quest for social stature. Family estates and farms become objects of either inheritance or purchase and are intermingled with rugged and often dangerous places of ancient and superstitious legend in an attempt to find some harmony between modern gentility and regional history.

Ellangowan (el-lan-GAO-an). Ancient Scottish home of the noble Bertram family, located in Dumfries, a region in the southwest of Scotland, near the fictional village of **Kippletringan**. The Auld Place, the ruins of the family castle, overlooks the Point of Warroch and commands an impressive view of the bay. The family now resides in the New Place, built by Lewis Bertram using stones from the original castle's ruins. Central to the book's plot is the question of whether society and the legal system will allow the estate to be auctioned off to the family's agent—a man of no family history or prowess who drove the Bertrams into debt in the first place—or whether the missing "laird," young Harry Bertram, will return to claim his inheritance.

Physically, the estate is at the intersection of three contrary and warring worlds, each with its own excesses and vices. It is bordered on one side by Warroch Bay, a favorite landing place for smugglers hoping to avoid Great Britain's high tariffs on goods such as tea and brandy imported from Holland. On another side is Woodbourne, the estate rented by Mannering as his temporary residence in the region. Although he provides a home for Lucy Bertram when she is ousted from Ellangowan, the house is the site of a standoff between revenue officers and smugglers that results in the death of Vanbeest Brown, one of Hatteraick's crew and an accomplice of the local gypsy clan.

Ellangowan estate is also close upon the Kaim of Derncleugh, a site of local folklore and superstition, supposed by the region's peasants to be haunted. Ultimately the disposition of the estate successfully combines ready money got by trade, through Captain Brown's own industry and his involvement with the Dutch trading company Vanbeest and Vanbruggen; landed gentry, in the person of Lord Henry Bertram; and ancient gypsy superstition, through the machinations and pronouncements of Meg Merrilies.

Kaim of Derncleugh (kaym av dayrn-CLEW). Ruins of a tower situated in the Wood of Warroch surrounding Ellangowan. Legend has it that on this site rebellious members of the MacDingawaie clan killed themselves rather than be captured alive. The locals consider the spot to be haunted and shun it, which is precisely why Meg Merrilies uses it as a hideout for her gypsy clan. Here she watches over Vanbeest Brown's death while hiding young Captain Brown, or, as she knows him, Lord Bertram of Ellangowan. Here also, Meg herself breathes her last, but not before proclaiming the ascendancy of Lord Bertram. Her deathbed pronouncement in this den of superstition transcends the legal proof that Colonel Mannering and Mr. Pleydell are so desperately seeking and allows Henry Bertram to claim the estate of Ellangowan uncontested.

Gauger's Loop. Cliff overlooking Warroch Bay near Ellangowan. The bay is a convenient port for smugglers due to its proximity to the Isle of Man. The cliff has local renown as the point from which Frank Kennedy meets his death at the hands of Captain Dirk Hatteraick, and it is the site from which the same notorious high seas trader kidnaps young Lord Bertram. It is therefore fitting that from a cave under the cliff the captain is captured at Bertram's hands.

Charlies-hope. Dandie Dinmont's farm in Cumberland. In what becomes a typical strategy for Scott, the farm is the site of several days of old-style hunting and hospitality that introduces the young foreigner Captain Brown to the rusticity and grace of the Scottish clansmen.

Singleside. Estate belonging to Lucy Bertram's only remaining relation. It is her last hope for fiscal independence, which would allow her to marry her suitor, Charles Hazelwood, but, in a fit of superstition brought about by an encounter with the gypsy sibyl Meg Merrilies, Mrs. Margaret Bertram leaves it in trust to her lawyer until the young Lord Bertram returns.

— *L. Michelle Baker*

GUY OF WARWICK

Author: Unknown
Type of work: Poetry
Type of plot: Romance

Time of plot: Tenth century
First transcribed: Gui de Warewic, c. 1240 (English translation, 1300)

This romance encompasses almost the full extent of medieval Europe's known world. Guy of Warwick's name associates him with the "Heart of England," and two of his three greatest triumphs are to save England: He slays a dragon in the north and a giant in the south. He is also an exemplar of Norman expansion in the Mediterranean and Middle East. Guy's participation in tournaments and adventures takes him across Europe to Constantinople and the Holy Land, and part of his son Reinbrun's story unfolds in Africa. The poem abounds with place names; each subsequent version modifies these to reflect local interests and increasing knowledge of geography.

Warwick. City in north-central England in which Ethelfleda, daughter of Alfred the Great, first built a fortress and Normans began the present castle, which includes Guy's Tower and still displays relics of the mythic hero. Nearby is **Guy's Cliffe**, where the penitent Guy died as a hermit, just before identifying himself to his alms-giving wife Felice. Other places still to be seen that bear Guy's name include a cave, a well, and a colossal statue in a late medieval chapel.

York. City in northern England built and developed by ancient Britons, Roman, Saxons, Danes, and Normans, where Guy meets King Athelstan before slaying the Irish dragon that is ravaging Northumberland.

Winchester. Capital of England's early Anglo-Saxon kings and the place where Christianity was introduced in 634. Winchester's Norman cathedral and nearby religious houses at Chilcombe and Hyde Meed recorded Guy's most famous victory over the Saracen giant Colbrond, a literary transformation of King Athelstan's triumph over the Danes at Brunanburh in 937.

Constantinople. Capital of the Eastern Roman Empire, an entry point for Crusaders, and the start of the great Norman trade route along the Danube and Rhine to Lorraine. Guy's first visit to Constantinople is to assist the Greek emperor Hernis against the Soldan's siege. The steward Morgadour's envious opposition to Guy reflects the uneasy relations between the Greeks and the Normans, just as the feud between Guy and Duke Otun of Pavia, leader of the Lombards and vassal of the emperor of Germany, shows Norman antagonism and superiority to the Holy Roman Empire.

Holy Land. Middle Eastern center of a long struggle for control of religious sites during the Middle Ages between Christians and Muslims. Guy goes to the Holy Land as a pilgrim and visits Jerusalem and Bethlehem. At the Norman capital of Antioch, he meets Earl Jonas, whom he champions by slaying the Saracen giant Amoraunt in an episode infused with religious symbolism and thrilling combat.

— *Velma Bourgeois Richmond*

H

THE HAIRY APE

Author: Eugene O'Neill (1888-1953)
Type of work: Drama
Type of plot: Expressionism

Time of plot: Early twentieth century
First performed: 1922; first published, 1922

This one-act, eight-scene play introduces its central character, a steamship stoker, while he is stoking coal on a ship at sea, then follows him to New York City's fashionable Fifth Avenue, a jail, a union hall, and finally at the monkey house of a zoo, as he becomes increasingly alienated and tries to find his proper place in the world.

Steamship. Ocean liner at sea on which the hairy, bare-chested Yank is stoking the boilers when the play opens. The stokehole into which he shovels coal is at the very bowels of the ship, where the low ceilings force workers to stoop, making them seem apelike. When Mildred Douglas, a wealthy passenger aboard the ship insists on visiting the stokehold, she is so frightened by what she sees that she faints. Yank's buddy Paddy tells him that the woman looks as if she has seen a hairy ape. The incident shatters Yank's self-identity and sense of belonging, and he vows to get even.

In another shipboard scene, well-to-do passengers lounge on deck chairs under the open sky, a setting in stark contrast to the dark underworld in which the stokers who keep the ship running live. Whereas the stokehold is enclosed, dark, and constricted, the passenger deck is open, light, and airy. O'Neill uses this contrast to emphasize the difference between the privileged and working class.

*Fifth Avenue. Fashionable avenue in New York City noted for its exclusive stores. Yank visits Fifth Avenue three weeks after his encounter with Mildred on the ship. Enraged by the thought that Mildred called him a "hairy ape" (which she did not), Yank—unwashed and dressed in greasy clothing—strides defiantly through a crowd of prosperous people who are pouring onto Fifth Avenue as their Sunday church services end. Eugene O'Neill presents Fifth Avenue as the churchgoers see it

but later in the scene, in a stage direction, he offers Yank's inner, expressionistic vision of what Fifth Avenue is: "The women are rouged, calcimined, dyed, overdressed to the nth degree." Enraged when the crowd seems oblivious to his presence, Yank behaves increasingly violently until he is arrested.

*Blackwells Island. Now known as Welfare Island, small island in New York's East River that had a penal institution at the time when the play was written. Yank is taken to the island's jail after he is beaten and arrested by police. Scene 6 opens in the jail, in which a row of cells are exposed. The police have arrived, beaten Yank, and arrested him. While in the jail, Yank learns about the Wobblies, a labor organization that he thinks he must join.

Cages of various types are a recurring motif throughout the play. O'Neill's stage directions in the first, third, and fourth scenes suggest that he sees the ocean liner's stokehold as a cage. In the jail scene, Yank truly is in a cage; he awakens there thinking he is in a zoo. In the play's final scene, he visits an actual zoo.

Union Hall. Meeting hall of the "Wobblies," the International Workers of the World (IWW), located near New York's waterfront. After being released from jail, Yank goes to the hall to join the union. Thinking the members will welcome him because of his willingness to dynamite steel plants and go to prison if necessary, he announces his intentions but is turned away as a dangerous dissenter. The union hall, which should be a haven for Yank, turns into another threatening locale, further alienating him.

Monkey house. Area at a public zoo (presumably the Bronx Zoo) in which the final scene is set. Failing to gain acceptance among human society, Yank goes to the zoo, where he tries to talk to a caged gorilla. He breaks the lock on the gorilla's cage and releases the huge animal. However, when he tries to shake the gorilla's hand in friendship, it turns on him, crushes him, throws his body into the cage, and wanders off. Yank is left to die in an ape's cage, reinforcing the motif O'Neill has been building throughout the play.

— *R. Baird Shuman*

THE HAMLET

Author: William Faulkner (1897-1962)
Type of work: Novel
Type of plot: Psychological realism

Time of plot: Late nineteenth century
First published: 1940

One of the fifteen novels and many short stories William Faulkner set in his fictional Yoknapatawpha County, Mississippi, this novel is probably his most accessible, and perhaps the best introduction to the private kingdom of his inspired imagination.

Yoknapatawpha County (YOK-nuh-puh-TAW-fuh). County in Mississippi that resembles the region in northern Mississippi where Faulkner spent most of his life. Faulkner regarded his fictitious county (of which he called himself "sole owner and proprietor") as a microcosm of the post-Civil War South. It is suffering through the disastrous legacy of slavery and, in a larger sense, is a microcosm of the entire world, with its lust, greed, exploitation, chicanery, violence, and endless struggle for existence.

Hamlet. Unnamed village of about three dozen dwellings; a general store; a cotton gin; a gristmill, which also serves as a blacksmith shop; a dilapidated one-room schoolhouse; a church; a livery barn; and a small hotel. Most businesses in this community and much of the surrounding farmland belong to Will Varner.

Frenchman's Bend. Plantation that before the Civil War was a single enormous farm worked by slaves. The plantation was destroyed by General Ulysses S. Grant's army on his way to capture Vicksburg. After the war the plantation was subdivided into small farms, many of which are worked by sharecroppers. As in many of Faulkner's novels, *The Hamlet* is haunted by a sense of the dramatic contrast between the past and present.

Old Frenchman's place. Great mansion that once stood like a feudal castle over the rich farmland, symbolizing the Old South. The name of the owner has been forgotten, and it is simply called the "Old Frenchman's place." The estate's land is now "parcelled out . . . into small shiftless mortgaged farms for the directors of Jefferson banks to squabble over before selling finally to Will Varner." Over the years the illiterate, indigent farmers of Frenchman's Bend have stripped the stately building of its fences, banisters, oak floors, and outer walls for use as firewood. At night furtive figures can be seen digging around the ruin looking for the money the Frenchman reputedly buried before fleeing from Grant's advancing army. Besides symbolizing the glory of the Old South, the Old Frenchman's place plays an important role in Faulkner's novel because it enables the hateful protagonist Flem Snopes to take the first major step in his rise from poverty to riches.

The people of Frenchmen's Bend are tough because tough conditions make tough people. Cotton is king, but the one-crop economy is largely responsible for the general poverty. If crops are good, the price of a bale is driven down by the iron law of supply and demand. If the price of cotton is high in any given year, it is because crops are poor due to drought, floods, insect infestation, or other problems. In addition, the ignorant farmers are cheated by the local cotton buyer, Will Varner, who also forces them to buy their groceries and other necessities from his store. His prices are high, but his customers have nowhere else to go. They buy on credit and remain in debt all their lives. Most farmers and their wives and children go barefoot because they cannot afford shoes. They ride horses and mules in this era before the automobile.

Women have even harder lives than men here. They are dependent on the men and lack rights. Most are treated little better than farm animals. They are expected to bear large broods of children, who provide free labor for their husbands. The children grow up in the same ignorance and poverty that has kept their parents bound to the soil and enslaved to their creditors.

Racism is the norm: "There was not one negro landowner in the entire section. Strange negroes would absolutely refuse to pass through it after dark." Lynchings and murders are commonplace. The male inhabitants are dangerous because most are embittered by toil and poverty. All possess guns and often enforce their own justice. They have been brutalized by hard, thankless, endless labor which profits other people and not themselves or their children.

All the inhabitants of Frenchman's Bend take an interest in one another because there are no radios, no telephones, and not enough literacy to support a newspaper. Everybody knows everybody else's business. Most conversation is gossip—but people express themselves in cautious circumlocutions and innuendo. The people's characters, opinions, and modes of expression in Yoknapatawpha County have been shaped by the cruel, decaying environment in which they are forced to struggle for existence.

— *Bill Delaney*

HAMLET, PRINCE OF DENMARK

Author: William Shakespeare (1564-1616)
Type of work: Drama
Type of plot: Tragedy

Time of plot: c. 1200
First performed: c. 1600-1601; first published, 1603

Elsinore Castle is an appropriate setting for this darkly interior tragedy in which each answer seems to lead to another question. Almost the entire play's action takes place within the castle, which makes a suitable backdrop for the spying and betrayal that constitute the play's main plot elements.

***Elsinore Castle.** Thirteenth century Danish castle that is the site of the main action of the play. Elsinore is a real city in modern Denmark, where it is known as Helsingor in Danish. The official modern name of the castle is Kronborg. However, William Shakespeare was not interested in creating the historical Elsinore (a place he almost certainly never visited) but in creating a castle suitable for a play with themes dealing with treachery and revenge, a play in which it seems almost impossible for the revenging hero to know exactly what is true and what is not.

Significantly, all but two scenes of the play are set within the castle or on its battlements, and all the characters seem to live in the castle, at least temporarily. These include King Claudius and his wife, Hamlet's mother, as well as the aged courtier Polonius and his daughter Ophelia. Prince Hamlet, like his counterpart, Laertes, was evidently away, living at his university town, until called home for his father's funeral. Horatio, Rosencrantz, and Guildenstern, Hamlet's school friends, seem to be long-term guests at the castle. Even the acting company that stages *The Mousetrap* is lodged there. The exception is the Norwegian Prince Fortinbras, who lives in his own country except when he is waging war on his neighbors.

From its opening, the play's action involves spying, an activity well suited to the labyrinthine layout of an ancient building in which one room opens into another and passageways twist unpredictably, leading from royal audience rooms to chapels to private rooms or "closets." In such a setting, audiences see Hamlet decide to adopt his disguise of an "antic disposition" in order to test the veracity of the ghost. In this setting Polonius asks a spy to observe his son's behavior in Paris, Claudius and Polonius spy on Hamlet's conversation with Ophelia, Claudius asks Rosencrantz and Guildenstern to spy on Hamlet, and Polonius is killed while spying on Hamlet and Gertrude. The fact that Claudius cannot find where Hamlet has hidden Polonius's body—near the stairs to the "lobby"—suggests that the castle's structure is as complicated as the play's.

The task of the spy is always the same, to learn the truth, a problem central to *Hamlet*'s theme wherein truth is evasive and every answer seems to lead to more questions. The ghost's truth-telling, Claudius's guilt, Gertrude's complicity, Hamlet's unstable state of mind, and his apparent delaying are all subjects for questions in the course of the play, and the answers they bring forth are as confusing as the setting in which they are asked.

Exterior locations. *Hamlet* is an unusually interior play. Aside from its scenes on battlements, only two scenes seem to take place outdoors. One of those takes place on the Danish coast as Hamlet watches Fortinbras's army march to make war on Poland. There Hamlet compares Fortinbras's energetic action to his own proclivity for delaying action. Significantly, the other of the exterior scenes is set in a graveyard. There Hamlet seems to arrive at an answer which frees him to act out his revenge. As he watches preparations for Ophelia's funeral, he concludes that even the greatest lives end in the grave, and soon after that he tells Horatio that he recognizes his own fatal destiny and is ready to sweep into his revenge.

Battlements. Defensive structures around Elsinore's walls that are the location of some of the play's most gripping early action, as when the ghost of the dead king appears first to the watchmen and later to Hamlet. It is appropriate that the king, who appears in his armor, should want to walk on the structure that symbolizes his military power, the position from which he once defended Elsinore, since he is about to ask his son to undertake another sort of castle defense in avenging his death.

*Wittenberg. Location of the Germany university which Hamlet has attended. Wittenberg is closely associated with Martin Luther, whose studies there precipitated the Protestant Reformation in 1517. The university was still strongly associated with Protestantism in 1603, although Shakespeare never indicates that Hamlet is involved in any religious study. Wittenberg stands in strong contrast to Paris, where Polonius's son Laertes has been studying and where Polonius suspects he may be overly involved in the city's temptations to loose living.

*Denmark. General setting of the play. Shakespeare adopted the Danish setting along with the action of the play (which has its roots in thirteenth century Danish folklore) from a source almost contemporary to him; many scholars believe he used a version of the story written around 1589 by the English playwright Thomas Kyd. Shakespeare made no attempt to recreate early medieval Denmark; instead he set the action in a sort of timeless past. However, he included action and references that evoke the early modern period of 1600, when Denmark was an important naval power that competed with England and when both Paris and Wittenberg were significant educational centers. Hamlet's references to the Danish court's reputation for drunkenness must have amused Shakespeare's audiences. Ironically, Shakespeare makes Claudius portray England as a state so eager to stay in the favor of powerful Denmark that its king will surely commit any political executions Claudius requests, including the execution of Hamlet.

— *Ann D. Garbett*

A HANDFUL OF DUST

Author: Evelyn Waugh (1903-1966)
Type of work: Novel
Type of plot: Social satire

Time of plot: Twentieth century
First published: 1934

Evelyn Waugh uses this novel's principal settings—an English estate, the city of London, and a Brazilian jungle—as vehicles of the values he wishes to expose as shallow, foolish, and cruel. In these places, where evil lurks beneath the surface of both civilized and uncivilized worlds, vice does not even pay lip service to virtue.

Hetton. Estate of the Last family, located between the villages of Hetton and Compton Last in the English countryside. Although the novel begins at a house in Sussex Gardens in London, where the man who will cuckold the central character lives, its most important place is Hetton. In this story of the disintegration of a marriage, Waugh uses Hetton, whose owner, Tony Last, is trying to rehabilitate and renovate it, to symbolize Last's anachronism, since he, like his beloved estate, fits neither in medieval nor in modern England. In the Middle Ages the estate had been an abbey, where monks prayed, practiced penance, and sought God, but with England's abandonment of Roman Catholicism Hetton's religious character withered, and in the nineteenth century, during a revival of Gothic architecture, the ancient buildings were demolished and replaced by a Victorian edifice with battlements and towers, stained-glass windows, a massive clock with booming chimes, and bedrooms named after characters from Arthurian myth. In the twentieth century Hetton had become uncomfortable and unfashionable, somewhat like its proprietor, a naif who values his inheritance and wants to pass it on to his son but whose ignorance of the evil forces in both modern and savage societies leads to his and his estate's horrendous fate.

From the perspective of Brenda, Tony Last's wife, Hetton is big, ugly, and expensive. Brenda wants to refurbish its rooms with chromium plating and sheepskin, following the suggestion of Mrs. Beaver, with whose son John she is having an affair. At Hetton, Brenda and Tony sleep in separate bedrooms, and Brenda's room is named Guinevere after a woman in Arthurian legend notorious for her infidelity. Brenda begins to spend more and more time away from Hetton, whereas Tony, who spent time in France and Italy when he was a young man, now finds that he is never happy away from Hetton.

*London. Brenda's London, which, in the 1930's, was suffering from the Great Depression, is populated with dismal flats, stores filled with trivialities, and private clubs that, despite their Georgian facades and paneled rooms, have neither the tradition nor the character of Hetton. Brenda's flat is in Belgravia, a fashionable residential district of southwest London centered on Belgrave Square. Tony has sacrificed some of the funds needed to improve Hetton in order to provide his wife with a place to stay while she pursues her studies in economics. In reality the flat becomes the location of her infidelities. Unlike Hetton, her flat has no individuality, and its vulgar furniture and slapdash bathroom convey the thoughtlessness of her sordid love of John Beaver.

Waugh depicts the sophisticated London of Brenda's affair as a world of sham. The antiquity of the clubs, restaurants, and residences frequented by Brenda is counterfeit, as are the people with whom she associates. Brenda's charmless flat is also where she learns of the death of her son in an accident at Hetton. This tragedy eventually reveals to Tony his wife's duplicities, since she asks for a divorce to marry John. Consequently Tony feels that Hetton no longer serves as his impregnable citadel in a heartless world. Nevertheless, when Brenda expects him to sell Hetton to provide an income for her and her lover, Tony refuses to part with his inherited home. Instead, he forsakes it and England, which have become poisoned for him because of the death of his son and his marriage.

*Amazon Basin. His illusions destroyed, Tony is forced to seek a new place of sanctuary and stability in a world grown unpredictable and chaotic. Hearing from an explorer of a lost city in the Brazilian jungle, Tony travels to South America. He envisions this lost city as an idealized Hetton—a multitowered castle on a green hill where evils can be locked out and happiness pursued. As he and his guide journey south from Georgetown, in British Guiana, they fail to find the lost city; instead, they become trapped in the green hell of the Amazon Basin. Waugh juxtaposes scenes of savagery in the jungle, as Tony wanders, sick with malaria and abandoned by his guide, with scenes in London, where Brenda, now abandoned by her lover, who has gone to the United States, and excluded from Hetton, now in the hands of Tony's relatives, is trapped in the "jungle" of an avaricious London. "Civilized" London is as savage as the primitive world of the South American cannibals.

Tony is rescued by James Todd, the illiterate son of a Barbadian missionary. Todd nurses Tony to health in his house, which has a mud floor, wattle walls, and palm-thatched roof. During the hallucinations brought on by his fever Tony envisions a transformed Hetton in the jungle, but with his recovery he has to recognize that the fabled city, founded by the Incas at the height of their wealth and power, is a legend. Instead, he is now a prisoner of a community of savages controlled by the cunning crazy man Todd, who expects Tony to read Charles Dickens's complete works to him over and over again. The Hetton Tony lived in and loved had been built in the Victorian period, and now he is forced to revisit those places through the imagination of Dickens, who was highly critical of the greed that corrupted London and from which Tony was trying to escape by creating an ideal world at Hetton.

When a rescue party from England fails to find Tony, who has been drugged by Todd, Tony finally realizes that he has been cut off from his Hetton in England and his lost city in Brazil. Meanwhile, in England, Hetton has been taken over by Richard Last, one of Tony's cousins, since Tony has been declared dead. The new owners have closed many of the rooms and have turned the estate into a silver-fox farm. Waugh, a Roman Catholic convert, believed in Saint Augustine's City of God, but in this novel he shows that neither the Hetton of Tony and his cousin nor the London of Brenda and her friends nor the lost city of Brazil represent the City of God. Instead, they represent the triumph of barbarism and the powers of darkness over a vanishing Christian civilization of grace and light.

— *Robert J. Paradowski*

THE HANDMAID'S TALE

Author: Margaret Atwood (1939-   )
Type of work: Novel
Type of plot: Psychological realism

Time of plot: The future
First published: 1985

This novel is set in the United States in an unspecified future, after the country has been transformed by a civil war and become a theocracy called "Gilead." Readers find themselves in a landscape both troubling in its familiarity and frightening in its strangeness, as they read about a country irrevocably changed by a right-wing, conservative Christian coup d'état. In Gilead, women have no money, no property, and no rights. Indeed, the oppression is so great that young, fertile women are forced to serve as "handmaids" to bear children for sterile Christian couples.

Gilead. Future name for the northeastern section of the United States. In Margaret Atwood's vision of the future, the government of the United States has been overthrown by a group of right-wing, conservative Christians bent on transforming what they see as a decadent society into a theocracy. Atwood draws on the culture of the United States in 1985 and extrapolates what might happen if trends present in that year were to continue into the future. For example, in Gilead, birth rates have plummeted as a result of widespread contamination of the air, water, and earth. Further, Christians, sickened by divorce, pornography, and abortion, outlaw all three. They also take away a woman's right to own property or have money of her own; everything is in her hus-

band's name. Women who have been divorced but who are proven to be fertile, such as the main character in the novel, are found guilty of the crime of adultery, and are given to the rulers of Gilead in order to provide children for childless couples.

Atwood deliberately places Gilead in New England; landmarks such as the library and the wall are clearly taken from Cambridge, where Harvard University is located. The irony in this location is twofold: In the first place, Massachusetts was first established as a theocracy by the pilgrim fathers, who applied a strict interpretation of the Bible to all aspects of life. Indeed, it was the Puritans of the seventeenth century who were responsible for the Salem witch trials and subsequent burnings.

As a side note, Atwood, a Canadian writer, dedicates the novel to her ancestor, Mary Webster, a woman convicted of witchcraft in Salem and sentenced to hang. When she was cut down from the scaffold in the morning, she was found to be still alive and was thus set free. Webster immigrated to Canada soon after. The second irony is that Harvard University is the premier site of learning in the United States. Gilead, by contrast, is a country ruled by keeping people ignorant. Written language is reserved for only the most powerful men; pictographs replace signs, and women are not permitted to read. Furthermore, Atwood's second dedication is to Perry Miller, her professor of American literature at Harvard University. In the closing sequence of the book, an academic recognized by critics as being a parody of Miller addresses a large academic assembly. The academic reveals himself to be both ignorant and patronizing in his analysis of the state of Gilead.

Colonies. Unspecified location where infertile women, or "unwomen," and divorced women are sent to clean up toxic waste. The major threat made against the handmaids is that they will be sent to the colonies if they do not comply with the demands of the commanders and Gileadian society. In addition, handmaids who have three assignments without producing an offspring are automatically sent to the colonies. Postmenopausal and divorced women who refuse to become handmaids are also sent to the colonies. Life is extremely cruel in this location, and most women survive only a short time.

*Canada. While none of the action of the book takes place in Canada, the country represents freedom to the persecuted of Gilead. Indeed, the narrator of the book and her husband are arrested as they try to flee to Canada with their daughter. The final section of the book suggests that the narrator once again tried to flee to Canada and hid for a time in a barn in Maine, a hideout on the underground "frailroad," modeled on the Underground Railroad instituted by abolitionists in the years before the American Civil War.

— *Diane Andrews Henningfeld*

HARD TIMES

Author: Charles Dickens (1812-1870)
Type of work: Novel
Type of plot: Social realism

Time of plot: 1840's
First published: 1854

The squalid industrial landscape of northern England is no mere backdrop to this novel; rather, the desolation of its setting and period is central to Charles Dickens's social criticism. While his apparent target is the factory system that creates such desolation, his true quarry is utilitarianism, a shallowly statistical philosophy which results in a coldheartedness reflected in the settings of the novel.

Coketown. Fictional factory town in northern England that offers nothing that is not "severely workful." Coketown is center of Dickens's social criticism. As "a triumph of fact," it is grim, unnatural, and mechanical, from the polluted purple river to the identical laborers who all "do the same work, and to whom every day was the same as yesterday and to-morrow." Forested with the smokestacks of its textile mills, it is a "sulky blotch upon the prospect," abandoned by the sun even in sunny midsummer. Its tenements, such as Stephen Blackpool's home, tainted by poverty and by the drunken wife to whom he is irrevocably tied, reflect the miserable sameness and grinding labor of the workers' lives, empty of leisure and of fancy, which the utilitarian mill owners and politicians see as mere idleness. While Coketown is often associated with the real industrial towns of Leeds, Preston, and Manchester in the north, Dickens saw his commentary as touching on English workers everywhere.

Factory. Textile mill in Coketown, owned by Josiah Bounderby. Bounderby's factory is typical, for Dickens, of the factory system. Lit up by night, the factories look from a distance like "Fairy palaces." Yet they are not the dream palaces of fairies; instead they are nightmarishly inhabited by the "melancholy mad elephants," the pistons of steam engines working up and down. In its bitter monotony, its dreary labor, and in the polluted air that kills child workers and adults alike, the factory is a harsh metaphor for the tyrannical facts that govern all the stunted lives of the novel.

Sleary's horse-riding. Traveling circus, featuring clowns, equestrian exhibitions, tumbling, and tightropes. Typically found in that "neutral ground" which is "neither town nor country," the circus brings the old paternalist values of sentiment and charity into the new, alienated economy in which, as in the factory, the master knows nothing of the enslaved. Sissy Jupe, who brings to the Gradgrind house that "wisdom of the Heart" learned in the circus but absent from utilitarianism, is the abandoned daughter of a clown in this circus. Tom Gradgrind hides here from a vengeful Bounderby and the law after his robbery is discovered. Despised as trivial idleness by Gradgrind and Bounderby, the circus stands for that scorned leisure that proves a necessary antidote to the inescapable facts of Coketown: factory life, rampant capitalism, and domestic misery.

Gradgrind's school. Privately funded elementary school, financed by Gradgrind, and taught by Mr. M'Choakumchild on the monitorial system, in which student "monitors" repeat lessons they have learned from the schoolmaster to a row of children. The method emphasizes repetition and the rote learning of facts; Dickens here satirizes both the new model of teacher training and the absurdity of such fact-based rote learning.

Stone Lodge. Home of the Gradgrind family. Like Bounderby's town house, "cheerless and comfortless, boastfully and doggedly rich," Stone Lodge reflects the character of its owner, Thomas Gradgrind. From the outside, it is perfectly symmetrical; from the inside, perfectly mechanical, its time measured off by the "deadly statistical clock" in Gradgrind's study. For young Tom, it is the "Jaundiced Jail" he longs to escape, for Louisa the "great wilderness," without graces, without sentiments, without heart. Both Stone Lodge and the Gradgrinds are ultimately redeemed by the admission of Sissy Jupe into this monument of fact.

Bounderby country house. "Snug little estate" outside Coketown, on which Bounderby's bank has foreclosed. Here Bounderby, "the Bully of humility," grows cabbages in the flower garden and allows the estate's former elegance to fall into disrepair. The country house highlights Bounderby's secret allegiance to aristocratic rank and status, even as his lies about his own origins pretend to humility. It is also the site of Mrs. Sparsit's imaginary staircase, down which she imagines Louisa approaching "a dark pit of shame and ruin" with every day and hour of knowing James Harthouse. The image of the staircase was emblematic, for the Victorians, of a woman's progress into sexual sin and social ruin.

— *Susan Johnston*

A HAZARD OF NEW FORTUNES

Author: William Dean Howells (1837-1920)
Type of work: Novel
Type of plot: Social realism
Time of plot: 1880's
First published: 1889

Many of the cosmopolitan features of New York in this novel prove intensely interesting to a transplanted Bostonian magazine editor, but the city is also a place of severe economic disparities and a culturally diverse and largely unassimilated population. In this setting, with the seeds of disorder sown, an outbreak of violence catches the protagonist by surprise when dissatisfied streetcar workers decide to strike.

*New York City.** City in which the protagonist, Basil March, and his family settle early in the novel. March, who in his dislocation as in other respects resembles his creator, has come here to assume editorship of a magazine at a time when New York is replacing Boston as the literary capital of the nation. The specific settings are varied, but collectively they form the backdrop of the "new fortunes." To March, New York, especially the borough of Manhattan, is the place of new professional opportunity.

To other characters, this largest of the American urban environments offers a variety of other opportunities and challenges. March's wife Isabel compares New York unfavorably to Boston, their former home. To her it is too large and full of uncultivated and uncivilized newcomers, both native and foreign. To the fiery German socialist Lindau, who once taught March German, and whom March hires to review foreign literature for the magazine, New York provides an opportunity to associate with his fellow poor. Lindau views them as victims of the robber barons of the era and strives to undermine the power of the latter. The publisher of the magazine, a transplanted midwesterner named Dryfoos, is a boorish man for whom the big city is just the place to augment his already considerable fortune. In short, New York is a magnet drawing together people of all sorts and in the process exacerbating their inevitable social conflicts.

Third Avenue Elevated. Section of Manhattan's earliest rail transit system, the Third Avenue Line, before the advent of subways in the twentieth century. March rides this train regularly, and it gives him the opportunity to observe the variety of New York life and realize that on Manhattan's East Side his own dominant Anglo-Saxon stock is actually a minority among a swarm of diverse immigrants. The author first presents March as enjoying the picturesque view but thinking little about the hopes, fears, and sufferings of the people he studies. Only gradually does he become aware of the potentially destructive forces at work in the teeming streets.

Union Square. Park bounded by Fourteenth and Seventeenth Streets and by Broadway and Park Avenues, in lower Manhattan. Here labor and radical groups tend to gather, and stump orators present their views to passersby. In this area the activities of striking streetcar workers lead to violence in which Conrad Dryfoos, the publisher's idealistic son, is killed and the equally idealistic but more excitable Lindau is clubbed by a policeman. This area serves as the focus of the conflict, previously little understood either by March or Dryfoos, that brings home one "hazard" that the possessors of the "new fortunes" face: the resentment of oppressed laborers who have been inflamed by Lindau and his radical kindred spirits.

Washington Square. Another public park in lower Manhattan, a retreat for fashionable folk but now also for New York's growing Italian population. The Marches often sit in the park and observe those who congregate there. These visits demonstrate the limited extent of their contact with less privileged New Yorkers.

Greenwich Village (GREH-nich). Residential section of Lower Manhattan. While wandering through the streets of the adjacent Greenwich Village, March again fails to see poverty's warning signals. Here, in Lindau's neighborhood, March talks to a young boy who has listened to the socialist's declamations but fails to understand the extent to which they have influenced even this boy.

Madison Avenue. Street that is not yet the center of New York commercial life but an avenue of elegant houses interspersed with prospering shops. When the Marches walk here, they are led to question the dullness of material civilization. March prefers shabby Greenwich Village as more vital and colorful but again cannot, prior to the climactic violence of the streetcar strike, grasp the implications of vast economic disparities in neighborhoods in close proximity to one another.

— *Robert P. Ellis*

HEADLONG HALL

Author: Thomas Love Peacock (1785-1866)
Type of work: Novel
Type of plot: Fiction of manners

Time of plot: Early nineteenth century
First published: 1816

Headlong Hall, like all aristocratic British houses of the early nineteenth century, is facing the prospect of dramatic changes brought by the Industrial Revolution. The hall and its grounds form a quiet battleground, but a battleground nonetheless. New technologies guided by an entrepreneurial spirit hold out both the promise and the threat of a complete transformation of life within and without the hall.

Headlong Hall. Welsh manor house in the vale of Llanberis in Caernarvonshire. Its four principal "scenes of action" are explicitly identified in chapter 2 as the cellar, the library, the picture gallery and the dining room. The last is the most important as a setting for the philosophical conversations that form the principal substance of Thomas Love Peacock's story. The hall's grounds are, however, far more important than the house itself as a backdrop to these discussions. These wild spaces have been targeted by the landscape gardener Marmaduke Milestone, who is eager to substitute lawns and flowerbeds—embellished by pagodas, Chinese bridges, and artificial fountains—for the surroundings that nature has provided.

Milestone's specific proposals are contrary to the tide of contemporary fashion; in 1816 many of the orderly lawns and flowerbeds of southeastern Britain were torn apart in favor of artificial wildernesses, complete with the ready-made ruins that were known by the appropriate name of "follies." The hall's grounds already contain an authentic ruined tower, which Milestone purposes to obliterate in the service of his relentless desire to change things, thus demonstrating the authority of human ingenuity and technological power. His ambitions, as fostered by Squire Headlong, form the context of the arguments between Mr. Escot, the "deteriorationist" philosopher who asserts that humankind has been corrupted by civilization and luxury, and Mr. Foster, the "perfectibilian" champion of progress. As these and other characters arrive at the hall for a weekend party they all have opinions regarding the "tremendous chasms" that surround them as their coach makes its way along the rough-hewn road.

Cemetery. Graveyard in the grounds of Headlong Hall that provides a second significant location. Located in the estate's churchyard, the cemetery symbolizes the continuity of past and present, although the sexton's fanciful claims about the identity of one of the skulls in the bone-house remind readers that history, also, is a cultural artifact.

Ballroom. Although not listed as one of the four principal scenes in the early pages of the novel, the most significant interior setting, apart from the dining room, is the hall's ballroom. This is the location in which the various romantic couplings that provide the story's closure are finally cemented, and it is another setting whose cultural significance is ingeniously debated by Mr. Escot, this time in discussion with Mr. Jenkison. Although the making of various marriages complements the lessons of the churchyard, stressing the continuity of the family and human nature, Headlong Hall is—as its name indicates—in danger of losing its balance as it hurries into an unknown future.

*****Vale of Llanberis** (hlan-BEHR-us). Ancient county of Caernarvonshire (now part of the county of Gwynedd) that forms the northwestern part of Wales, facing the Isle of Anglesey. The town of Llanberis is five miles inland, in a valley between two spurs of the foothills of Snowdonia. Most of the region's inhabitants still speak Welsh even now, and in the early nineteenth century there would have been clear-cut distinction between the region's intrusive English aristocrats and the indigenous Welsh population—although the Headlongs are careful to claim descent from an ancient Welsh family, the Cadwalladers.

The landscape of the region outside the Headlong estate includes the pass of Aberglaslynn, which the text describes as "sublimely romantic," and mountain peaks that symbolize the unchangeable. This scenery functions within the story as an opposite extreme to the supremely civilized interior of the hall; the hall's grounds extend between the two extremes as an intermediate territory whose fate is yet to be determined—although it is the desires of its human owners rather than the dictates of nature that will decide the issue. The fact that Mr. Milestone's illustration of the merits of gunpowder as a means of clearing land goes awkwardly awry, nearly causing the death of Mr. Cranium, is a clear indication of where Peacock's own sympathies lie.

— *Brian Stableford*

THE HEART IS A LONELY HUNTER

Author: Carson McCullers (1917-1967)
Type of work: Novel
Type of plot: Psychological realism

Time of plot: 1930's
First published: 1940

Although this novel explores psychological emotions such as loneliness and reveals a young girl growing into adulthood, its story depends to a great extent on its setting. The attitudes of the characters and the way various community members react to them are representative of those found primarily in the South during the 1930's.

Southern town. Unnamed town that provides the novel's principal setting. The town is based on Columbus, Georgia, where Carson McCullers spent her formative years. McCullers left the South when she was seventeen and continued to express her hatred of the region, especially its racism, throughout her life. For example, she refused to donate her manuscripts to a library in Columbus, Georgia, because it was segregated. She also stated sarcastically that she had to revisit the South occasionally to renew her sense of horror. *The Heart Is a Lonely Hunter* is the only novel McCullers wrote while residing in the South.

Mick Kelley's house. One of the biggest houses on the north side of town. Three stories tall, this large building is a boardinghouse in which some of the main characters reside. The house has a large front porch, where people gather to talk. The house needs repairs and painting and sags on one end. Its interior symbolizes the psychological and emotional states of the characters; the huge house often feels empty to the people who dwell in it, just as the people frequently feel lonely and isolated even though they are surrounded by others. Mr. Singer, the character in whom the other characters confide, rents a room from the Kelleys.

Mr. Singer's room. This room is small and has minimal furniture. There is a closet in the room, where Singer keeps wine and snacks for his guests. Jake Blount lives with Singer in this room when he first arrives in town.

Dr. Copeland, Jake Blount, Mick Kelley, and Biff Brannon frequent Singer's room to confide in him. Singer's room is symbolic of his role in the novel: His guests feel comfortable sitting in his small room and confiding their secrets to him.

New York Café. Restaurant near the Kelley's house where locals go to eat and socialize. The main characters of the novel frequent the café, which Biff Brannon owns. Providing a place for community members to visit with each other, the café is typical of restaurants in southern communities.

African American neighborhood. Section of the unnamed town in which the black community resides. In this section of town, very small houses, some as small as two rooms, house up to fourteen people. Dr. Copeland, the black physician, treats this community and serves as its leader. Descriptions of the residences of Copeland's patients are important because they illustrate that the town is segregated. McCullers depicts the poverty and disease that plague the blacks in the novel. African Americans are denied decent jobs and are treated cruelly and unjustly by some of the white characters in the novel. The novel addresses racism by showing the unjust treatment of blacks. If the southern town is a microcosm of southern towns in the 1930's, McCullers is showing racism in the South as a whole during the 1930's.

— *Laurie Champion*

HEART OF AZTLÁN

Author: Rudolfo A. Anaya (1937-   )
Type of work: Novel
Type of plot: Social realism

Time of plot: 1950's
First published: 1976

This novel begins in Guadalupe, New Mexico, but its primary setting is Albuquerque after the Korean War. Transcending time and place, the novel also refers to the mythical city of Aztlán, which symbolizes the hope and the need for Mexican Americans spiritually to reconnect to their heritage, their homeland, and their culture to survive in a new land. Through one Mexican American family, the novel depicts the communal struggles Mexican Americans face as they make the transition between their old lives sustained by the land and their new lives in a city that often treats them as if they were aliens.

*Guadalupe. Small agrarian New Mexico community in which the central character, Clemente Chávez, is spiritually connected to his land: "His soul and his heart were in the earth." His family have lived on this same land for generations, so it is literally the "roots of his soul." As he is leaving his homeland, Clemente represents a problem that all Mexican Americans face when they leave their land in search of better economic opportunities in the cities: Without the land the relationship man created with the earth would be lost, old customs and traditions would fall by the wayside, and the people would be like wandering gypsies without a homeland where they might anchor their spirit.

Clemente's family not only leaves the physical land behind, they leave their spiritual connection behind them, too, and this loss will create enormous conflict in their lives. To ameliorate their feelings of being uprooted, they make a symbolic attempt to take the land with them by filling a coffee can with rich dirt from their garden.

*Albuquerque. New Mexico's largest city, the setting in which the novel's main action occurs. After leaving their home in Guadalupe, the Chávezes make their home in the Barelas barrio in downtown Albuquerque. This city is literally and figuratively "in a new time and in a new place." In this communal environment, the family at first feels accepted through the experiences they share with their neighbors. However, from Clemente's first attempt to mix the lush soil from his original home with the "hard city soil," the novel conveys the hostilities and difficulties the family will face.

The novel is filled with symbols that convey the violence, alienation, racism, poverty, and subjugation the family must confront and overcome if they are to survive. Some symbols are used ironically. For instance, a water tank next to a railroad yard might normally symbolize life, nourishment; here, however, it is a "black tower of steel [that] loomed over everything." It projects the inherent evil of those who own the railroad, a socioeconomic institution that controls its workers through threats and coercion. Eventually, the tank becomes known as "devil's tower" because of the injustices that take place there. The evil extends to the houses that surround the railroad yard as they are "dark with soot." Even the elm trees, normally symbols of fertility and life, are "withered and bare." The men who survive working in dismal, life-threatening conditions are covered with the black soot, which eventually creeps into their souls and destroys them.

The Roman Catholic Church, which should be a safe haven that offers its parishioners solace and hope, refuses to get involved in the strike against the injustices leveled against the people in the barrio. The public schools instead of being the great equalizer are places in which prejudice and violence flourish and are often even nourished. Rudolfo A. Anaya does not suggest that the people of the barrio should forsake the city and return to their rural environment. He does believe that if the family and the people of the barrio are to survive, they must reestablish their connection with their cultural heritage and forge new identities.

Aztlán. Mythical ancestral homeland of the Mexican American people that represents a spiritual reconnection to their culture, past, and pride as a people. When the people of the barrio rediscover Aztlán, their spiritual foundation, the "infusion of spirit into flesh," they unite and overcome the injustices, violence, and alienation. Aztlán is a mysterious, spiritual place that could only exist in the Southwest, in particular, Albuquerque.

— *Sharon K. Wilson*

HEART OF DARKNESS

Author: Joseph Conrad (Jósef Teodor Konrad Nałęcz Korzeniowski, 1857-1924)
Type of work: Novella
Type of plot: Psychological realism
Time of plot: Late nineteenth century
First published: serial, 1899; book, 1902

Although it may be read on a more superficial level, this novella is densely symbolic. An important part of that symbolism is that tropical Africa, and specifically the Congo Free State and the Congo River, represent the depths of the human heart and the extent to which human cruelty and depravity can reach.

***London.** Capital and largest city of Great Britain. The story opens with five men on a cruising yawl on the River Thames on a hazy evening at sundown. One of the men present is named Marlow. He is the only one of the men who is still active as a sailor or naval officer. Marlow begins telling a long story by remarking that the Thames has a dark history. He is referring to ancient times when the Romans first colonized England. At that time, London was an uncivilized place for the relatively sophisticated Romans to be entering.

***Brussels.** Capital city of Belgium. Marlow tells a story concerning his voyage to the heart of the African continent. The company that has hired Marlow to fix a river steamer and become its captain is headquartered in Brussels. At the time of the story, the 1890's, Belgium was a colonial power in control of a large portion of central Africa. Marlow must visit the company offices to obtain his commission and get orders concerning his new job. The people who work at the company headquarters treat him as though they do not expect him to return. The entire story Marlow tells shows that he has strong contempt for the way the Belgians have managed the country. He compares the city to a sepulcher—white on the outside but full of rotting bones.

***Congo River.** Greatest waterway in Central Africa. Joseph Conrad never names these places by their proper names, but it is obvious from his descriptions of them and their place on the map of Africa that he is referring to Congo Free State and to the lengthy Congo River. Marlow also discusses the company's lower station and a central station, analogous to Stanley Falls, far up the Congo River in the center of Africa. The trip that the steamer, captained by Marlow, makes up the Congo River to relieve Kurtz is eventful and dangerous both because of African attacks and because of tropical diseases. The journey into the heart of the dark rain forest is symbolic of the journey into the dark depths of the human soul.

— *Toni J. Morris*

THE HEART OF MIDLOTHIAN

Author: Sir Walter Scott (1771-1832)
Type of work: Novel
Type of plot: Historical
Time of plot: Early eighteenth century
First published: 1818

Many of Walter Scott's novels deal with aspects of Scottish history. This novel is unique in being about the whole of Scotland and its relationship to England. For Scott, the 1707 union between Scotland and England was necessary, but the politics of that union placed a great strain on justice, truth, and the Scottish national character. Most of the important places in this novel reflect aspects of these tensions and how the novel's central character, Jeanie Deans, overcomes them.

*Scotland. Scott's novelistic portrait of Scotland as a country, *The Heart of Midlothian* deals with the east and the west of Scotland, with Highlands and Lowlands. The novel presents the people of Scotland from many regions and classes, and the Scottish landscape in all its variety is described with great force and vividness. Scott sees Scotland as a country of beauty, independence, religious passion, courage, and, sometimes, violence and disruption. The finest qualities of Scotland are embodied in Jeanie Deans, who is virtually a national symbol in the novel.

*England. Scotland's rich and powerful neighbor to the south. The novel is set early in the eighteenth century, shortly after Scotland and England have been united under one crown; however, it is still an uneasy union. Scott shows an England that is more civilized than Scotland but also more corrupt. The Scottish heroine Jeanie Deans's simple honesty forms a striking contrast to the social facades and political intrigues of England. Also, England's attitude toward Scotland tends to be impatient and dismissive. Its intrusion into Scottish matters of law produces at least in part the legal injustice and cruelty that are at the novel's center. Jeanie Deans's most memorable encounter with England comes at Richmond, where she sees the luxuriant beauty of southern England but expresses a preference for Scotland. There, she also encounters and finally wins over Queen Caroline of England.

*Midlothian. Old name for the region of Scotland around the Firth of Forth and Edinburgh.

*Tolbooth of Edinburgh (edh-en-behr-OH). Edinburgh prison in which Effie Deans is confined. Known as the "Heart of Midlothian," the prison in the novel represents a justice that has been corrupted by politics, bad laws, English prejudice and power, and legal technicalities. The dark walls and grated windows of the Tolbooth form a symbolic and actual menace that hangs over Effie Deans and Scotland in general. The indignant Porteous rioters in the novel storm the Tolbooth, but Scott shows that the only effective answer to the inhumanity represented by the Tolbooth is provided by the love and truth of Jeanie Deans.

*Edinburgh-London road. Long road that Jeanie Deans travels in search of a pardon for her condemned sister Effie. As Jeanie, barefoot and alone, makes her often difficult way along this road she rises in her grand simplicity to heroic stature, and Scott compares her journey to those in John Bunyan's *Pilgrim's Progress* (1678, 1684). The great distance she travels and the difficulties she overcomes on this road form the central episode of the novel and the novel's greatest symbol of Jeanie's superb courage and determination.

Deans house. Home of Jeanie Deans and her father at St. Leonard's Crags through much of the novel. Jeanie's competent, careful, thoughtful, and wise management of the house is the school in which she learns the fundamental wisdom and integrity that make her one of Scott's great characters. Her simple life in the house, concerned with thrift, cleaning, making good cheeses, and tending livestock, may seem unromantic, but it is in the house of St. Leonard's Crags that Jeanie's character is formed.

*Dumbartonshire. Beautiful and well-administered realm of the duke of Argyle. After the duke becomes Jeanie's patron, Jeanie, her husband, and her father all move to this idyllic region where the duke's wisdom and generosity create a world which is happy and harmonious. The duke of Argyle's Dumbartonshire provides a fitting reward for Jeanie's goodness and a dramatic contrast to the tragedies of Edinburgh, the corruptions of London, and the neglect of Dumbiedikes.

*Muschat's Cairn. Mysterious and frightening place near Edinburgh where Jeanie first meets the guilty George Staunton. Associated with ghosts, Gothic ruins, a horrible murder, and the madness of Madge Wildfire, Muschat's Cairn forms an eerie and appropriate setting for Jeanie's introduction to the Byronic and brooding Staunton.

*Haribee Brow. Bleak area near the northern English town of Carlisle where, in passing, Jeanie sees the horrific hanging of Meg Murdockson and the violent events that lead to Madge Wildfire's death. Scott's painting of this place and the violence associated with it form an unforgettable vision of cruelty which contrasts with the love which leads to Effie's salvation.

Dumbiedikes. Estate of the two squalid, incompetent, but occasionally generous Dumbies. Dumbiedikes reveals the Scottish provincial laird at his bumbling and unintelligent worst, but it is on this estate that the young and innocent Jeanie and Reuben Butler come to love each other.

— *Phillip B. Anderson*

THE HEART OF THE MATTER

Author: Graham Greene (1904-1991)

Type of work: Novel

Type of plot: Psychological realism

Time of plot: World War II

First published: 1948

Graham Greene's first-hand experience in West Africa during the war years gives the African setting of this novel a feeling of authenticity. The motivations and actions of his protagonist are couched in wartime conditions that correspond to psychological tensions and challenges he encounters as an agent of imperialism in a remote tropical colony.

West African colony. Unnamed British colony in West Africa, but probably modeled on Sierra Leone, in whose colonial service Graham Greene worked during the early 1940's. Major Scobie, his novel's protagonist, is a deputy commissioner in the colony's police service and works out of the colony's chief port city. The secretariat for which he works represents British imperial control. Juxtaposed with the British presence are the enticing young African women who sit at the windows of the high school, and black clerks who move "churchward" with their wives in brilliant dresses.

In this mixed setting, Scobie goes past the secretariat to meet the commissioner at the police station and learns that he has again been passed over for promotion, despite his fifteen years of service with exemplary integrity. Instead of accepting any of the usual options offered to an officer in his position, Scobie refuses to resign, retire, or transfer to another colony; he wants to stay because he "likes the place." He knows the colony so well that he has no need of maps because he carries the "whole coastline" in his mind's eye. However, his disappointment at being denied promotion combines with the lassitude of the tropical colony to change him in ways that ultimately lead to his destruction.

Scobie's house. House originally built for a Syrian trader near a swamp in which Scobie lives with his wife, Louise. The last time Scobie had been on leave, he was ousted from his government bungalow in the town's European quarter. Louise, already unhappy with her living conditions, is even more anguished by Scobie's being denied promotion. She feels humiliated and wants to go to South Africa to prepare a home there for his retirement. Unlike Scobie, Louise can never feel at home in West Africa. The novel's primary conflict arises from the widening distance between Scobie and his wife over where they should live.

Bamba. Backcountry town in which another government officer, Pemberton, commits suicide, prompting an order for Scobie to go inland to retrieve Pemberton's body. Scobie's trip to Bamba, with its river crossings, marks a turning point in his domestic and professional life and foreshadows his own suicide. At Bamba, the shady Syrian merchant Yusef—a suspected smuggler—offers Scobie a loan to pay for Louise's trip to South Africa. This incident begins a relationship between Scobie and Yusef that intensifies suspense through suspicion, spying, and blackmail.

Nissen huts. Shabby one-room quarters for government officers and their dependents near the coastline. Wilson and Harris live in one of these huts. Likewise, Helen Rolt, a freshly widowed woman rescued after her ship is torpedoed by Germans during her honeymoon, occupies one. Scobie believes that his relationship with Helen is "safe," but when they are alone in the hut, they begin an adulterous affair. This setting provides a center to the theme of betrayal at the novel's conclusion. Wilson not only lives in close proximity to Yusef's office, he uses bribery, enticing promises, and the blood bond between his servant and Yusef's servant to spy on Yusef. Scobie's desire to conceal his visits to Helen shake his trust in his servant, Ali. The pervasive atmosphere of mistrust in this setting leads to Ali's murder and Scobie's suicide.

— *Mabel Khawaja*

HEARTBREAK HOUSE: A Fantasia in the Russian Manner on English Themes

Author: George Bernard Shaw (1856-1950)
Type of work: Drama
Type of plot: Play of ideas

Time of plot: 1913
First published: 1919; first performed, 1920

Through its first two acts, the play is set in an unusual room in the English country mansion of Captain Shotover. This room is built and furnished to resemble the after quarters of an old-fashioned sailing ship and thereby symbolizes the English ship of state at the beginning of World War I.

Shotover's house. Sussex mansion of the eccentric and visionary Captain Shotover. Through the play's first two acts, its characters seem completely unaware of the war in which Great Britain is engaged or their leadership responsibilities. Instead, they obsess over social niceties and their shallow affairs of the heart. Shaw's satire of this aristocratic household culminates in the third act, in which Lady Utterword says that the only thing England needs to become quite comfortable, sensible, and healthy is for every country manor to have horses and proper stables.

Ellie Dunn dubs Shotover's mansion "Heartbreak House" because of the many disappointed romances that surface there. However, George Bernard Shaw also implies that the name is appropriate because it represents the failure of the English ruling classes to lead England energetically and effectively through the turbulent war years.

Shotover's garden. Garden outside Shotover's house that is the scene of the third act. The garden symbolizes the possibility that the characters might move out of the center of their paralysis and frivolity toward meaningful political action. In the garden, the characters cannot ignore the war because there are enemy airships flying overhead dropping bombs in the distance. However, their response to a bomb that nearly hits the house is only a bizarre disappointment that the attack is not more devastating and thus exciting enough to rouse them out of their lethargic boredom.

— *Terry Nienhuis*

THE HEAT OF THE DAY

Author: Elizabeth Bowen (1899-1973)
Type of work: Novel
Type of plot: Psychological realism

Time of plot: 1942-1944
First published: 1949

In common with many novels set in World War II, place assumes a paramount importance in this novel set in wartime London, as the German air force is bombing the city almost constantly. Against the backdrop of the war, Stella Rodney, the female protagonist, falls in love with an enemy spy, and a British counterspy blackmails her.

***London.** Great Britain's capital city that provides the novel's primary setting. London is the center of the last European Allied country to withstand German conquest, although it endures continuous German bombing attacks. These attacks cause enormous destruction to the city, leaving no area untouched—including the royal Buckingham Palace. Seeking cover in air raid shelters becomes a daily occurrence for Londoners, for whom being roused from sleep by air raid sirens is a nightly ritual. Smoke from each night's bombs drifts throughout the city, giving off an acrid smell. Melancholy nights filled with the ever-present danger of falling bombs evokes the darkened mood in London and becomes almost surreal.

***Ireland.** Island country west of Britain that Stella visits on family business. Ireland remains neutral throughout the war and is depicted in the novel as representing what is still good and innocent as the war rages elsewhere. When she visits Mount Morris, she finds it a pastoral retreat from the devastation of London. Meanwhile, the British are unable to understand why the Irish do not join the alliance against Germany; to prevent Ireland from supporting Germany, Britain blockades Ireland's main ports. Stella's son Roderick claims that Cousin Nettie's madness is a result of Ireland's decision not to fight against Germany.

Holme Dene. Foreboding Irish family home of Robert Kelway, the enemy spy, where Stella goes to meet Kelway's parents. Built around 1910, the house is three stories high and much too large for the four people living in it. It has French windows and three balconies. Begonias grow in flowerbeds under each window, and the grounds have a tennis court, a pergola, a sundial, a rock garden, a dovecote, a seesaw, and a birdbath. The interior of the house has dark furniture, and its heavy draperies allow little light to enter its dark interior. Holme Dene appears to be linked to a horrible and evil power. The surrounding woods seem to be bewitched.

Mount Morris. Rodney family estate in southern Ireland that Stella's son inherits from her cousin Francis.

After visiting Holme Dene, Stella goes to Mount Morris to attend to her son's interests because he is legally underage and is away in the army. In contrast to what she experiences at Holme Dene, she feels that Mount Morris seems to exist outside of time. Harrison, the British counterspy, describes Mount Morris as a white elephant whose last owner has badly neglected, leaving its heating, lighting, and plumbing systems in almost their original states. Moreover, he claims that the estate's farm uses equipment known in his grandfather's day.

When Cousin Francis was alive, he lived much of his life in his home's library, in which an ancient smell emanates from the books that line the walls, and oil paintings are arranged over the fireplace. To complete the feeling of antiquity, a Shakespearean calendar from 1927 hangs in the room. Despite this antiquated atmosphere, the young and innocent Roderick will put his Irish estate to proper use. It is an illusion of pastoral innocence that to Roderick represents a future of possibilities that other characters in the novel lack; it thus becomes the center of his imaginary life. Roderick understands the obligations of possession and heritage in a way that the inhabitants of Holme Dene do not.

— Ronald L. Raber

HEDDA GABLER

Author: Henrik Ibsen (1828-1906)
Type of work: Drama
Type of plot: Social realism

Time of plot: Late nineteenth century
First published: 1890 (English translation, 1891); first performed, 1891

Neoclassical in construction, this play compresses its plot into about thirty-six hours and observes the unity of place by confining everything to a single location. All four acts take place in the same large drawing room of the house that George Tesman has recently purchased for his bride, the former Hedda Gabler.

*Christiana. Now called Oslo, the capital of city of Norway, located on the country's southeastern coast, and the largest and most important city in Norway.

Tesman Villa. House coveted by Hedda Gabler, located in a fashionable section of Christiana, when it belonged to the prime minister's widow. She casually remarked to George Tesman that she would marry the man who bought it for her. Tesman and his aunts go into debt to purchase and furnish the property, and the feckless pedant finds himself husband to the beautiful, imperious daughter of an aristocratic general. George and Hedda honeymoon in Italy, and Henrik Ibsen begins his play the morning after their return to Norway, as the newlyweds wake up for the first time in their elegant new home.

The plot of *Hedda Gabler* unfolds as a succession of visitors—Auntie Juju, Mrs. Elvsted, Judge Brack, and

Eilert Loevborg—enter and exit the drawing room. Thea Elvsted and Eilert Loevborg both arrive from the rural north, where Thea is wife to a magistrate and Eilert serves as tutor to his children. The sophisticated salon that Hedda Gabler presides over in Christiana is a stark contrast to the provincial world that Thea, abandoning her husband, has fled.

A fateful interlude at a brothel, involving Tesman, Brack, and Loevborg, occurs offstage, before each returns to the drawing room. Hedda's father's pistols are seen onstage early in the proceedings, and they serve as accessories to the drama's deadly finale. A table in the room elicits an early indication of Hedda's superciliousness, when she disdains the kitschy hat that Auntie Juju leaves on it.

A portrait of the late General Gabler hangs in the room, and his august image serves throughout the proceedings as a kind of verdict on Tesman's social pretensions in presuming to marry his haughty daughter and obtain a professorship. The room also contains a piano that, as a demonstration of her regal extravagance, Hedda insists not on replacing but on supplementing with a grander model. An orphan reared by his two unmarried aunts, George is accustomed to more modest accommodations than what Judge Brack, who provided the loan that made the acquisition possible, calls Tesman's "palatial" home. George insists that his financial risks were necessary, that he could not have expected the exquisite Hedda Gabler to live like an ordinary housewife. The play's setting is a continuing reminder of Tesman's folly and of the mismatch between an academic drudge of limited means and a lady of privilege in an upwardly mobile era when birth counts for less than effort.

Of all the other characters in the play, Brack is the only one who belongs to the same social class as Hedda, an aristocracy that has become superannuated by the ascendancy of the middle class. Brack and Hedda meet as equals in the drawing room, but they are acutely aware that their world is vanishing, displaced by upstarts who are not at home in Hedda's fancy villa. The house thus serves as both a focal point for the play's action and a thematic metaphor. Like the cherry orchard in Anton Chekhov's play of that name, Tesman's villa is a locus of nostalgia, symbolizing the passing of a privileged way of life.

— *Steven G. Kellman*

THE HEIDI CHRONICLES

Author: Wendy Wasserstein (1950-   )
Type of work: Drama
Type of plot: Social morality

Time of plot: 1965-1989
First performed: 1988; first published, 1988

This play opens with Heidi Holland lecturing on art history at Columbia University in 1988. As she marvels on how far she has come, the play unfolds in a series of flashbacks on moments from earlier stages of her life that reveal how she and her peers experimented with the different roles open to women.

*Columbia University. Ivy League university in New York City in a lecture hall in which the prologue to this play is set. Now a successful art historian, Heidi Holland is surprised to find herself lecturing on woman painters in so august an academic setting. Her very presence in this lecture hall proves that she has come a long way from her turbulent life in the 1960's and 1970's to have a meaningful career and still be a woman who has everything.

Church basement. Place in Ann Arbor, Michigan, where Heidi and other women meet to discuss women's issues in 1970. The emergence of socially conscious groups such as hers reflects the rise of collective movements during the 1960's and 1970's. Heidi herself merely observes the group's discussion in the play.

*Chicago Art Institute. Place where Heidi and a friend try to persuade passersby to participate in a protest against the lack of representation of women in art in

1974. Heidi speaks on a bullhorn, purposely creating a spectacle to attract an audience. She appropriately chooses an art institute to protest because the setting is patriarchal in itself.

Television studio. New York City television station in which Heidi and some of her associates are interviewed for a program in 1982. Heidi and the other interviewees represent the baby-boom generation, who are well off, white-collar professionals living in cosmopolitan cities such as New York City. Their presence in the studio gives them a sense of success, as the studio offers them exposure as representatives of an elite who have it all. However, Heidi is reticent to speak during this interview because she senses that the limelight is not really what she wants. With bright lights pouring on her and a camera aimed at her, Heidi realizes that the limelight of any aspect of a person's life is ephemeral.

— *Hanh N. Nguyen*

HEIMSKRINGLA

Author: Snorri Sturluson (1179-1241)
Type of work: Folklore
Type of plot: Saga

Time of plot: Legendary times to twelfth century
First transcribed: c. 1230-1235 (English translation, 1844)

Though the kingdom of Norway is central to this collection of tales, the numerous settings of the sixteen sagas it contains are reflected in the collection's name, which means "circle of the world." The hundreds of characters that populate its texts—whether kings, raiders, explorers, traders, or crusaders—make their presence known from the fringes of western Iceland to the Baltic Sea and from Finland to the Holy Land. In general the measure of a character's greatness is substantially drawn from his achievements abroad and in maintaining control over a contentious homeland. Consequently, the individual narratives never linger long in one place.

Asgarth (AHS-gahrth). Legendary homeland of the wandering warrior and king Odin, which is thought to be located somewhere in southwest Asia. Asgarth is considered to be the ancestral place of origin for the Norwegian royal line. Snorri thus obliquely links the kings of Norway with the generally accepted medieval belief that western European kingdoms were founded by expatriate members of the ancient Trojan nobility.

*****Norway.** Scandinavian kingdom whose governance is the central concern of the tales. The sagas detail how Norway is united by Harald Fairhair, converted to Christianity by Olaf Tryggvesson and Holy King Olaf, and subjected to foreign rule by Canute of Denmark. Many of Norway's kings spend a great deal of time traveling through its mountainous regions in the north, with their fjords and islands in the west and fertile valleys in the south, ever seeking to maintain control by quelling discontented farmers and chieftains alike. In many ways the Norwegian kingdom itself is truly the main antagonist for all the central figures of the narratives.

*****Nitharos** (NIHTH-ah-rohs). Norwegian town founded by Olaf Tryggvesson that serves as a royal residence for numerous kings of Norway. After Tryggvesson's martyrdom, his body is laid to rest in Nitharos's Church of St. Clement, thereby elevating the city's spiritual and symbolic significance.

*****Sweden.** Kingdom adjacent to Norway that appears throughout the sagas as both a rival to Norway and a place of refuge. At times Norway comes under Swedish rule, and at other times, Norwegian nobility flee to Sweden to escape hostility at home. The most notable refugee is Holy King Olaf, who after exile to this neighboring kingdom, returns to Norway and is martyred at the Battle of Stiklarstathir.

*****Iceland.** Island country in the north Atlantic that is settled by displaced members of the Norwegian nobility after Harald Fairhair's consolidation of Norway under one rule. Iceland represents one frontier of Scandinavian influence due to its remoteness and isolation. The fact that it is ruled not by a king but by a judicial and legislative assembly made up of freemen makes it a point of contrast with every other kingdom in the text.

***Denmark.** Powerful Scandinavian kingdom to the south of Norway that stands as the single-greatest foreign threat to Norway. At some times Denmark holds power over its northern neighbor; at other times it comes under Norwegian control.

***England.** With its many wealthy religious and economic centers, England is a target for many Scandinavian raiding parties, a number of them headed by Norwegian kings during their youth. For King Harald Hardruler, England represents his overweening ambition, as his attempt to conquer it ends in his own death at the Battle of Stamford Bridge. Because England was Christianized long before Scandinavia, it becomes the avenue by which Norway begins its conversion. Both Hakon the Good and Olaf Tryggvesson are baptized there.

***Miklagarth** (MIK-la-gahrth). Better known as Byzantium (now Istanbul), the capital of the Byzantine Empire, to which many Scandinavian warriors go to serve in the emperor's Varangian guard. As their leader, Harald Hardruler launches numerous campaigns in North Africa and the Mediterranean, he earns great wealth and fame before returning to Norway to claim half the kingdom from King Magnus.

***Holmgarth** (HOLM-gahrth). City in Russia (modern day Novgorod) that serves as a place of refuge for the young Olaf Tryggvesson and later for Holy King Olaf and his son Magnus when they flee Norway for their safety. Harald Hardruler also serves the king there and marries his daughter Ellisif.

***Jerusalem.** City in the Holy Land to which Christian pilgrims go. A journey to this city signifies great piety on behalf of pilgrims and crusaders. Thorir Hound's journey there after the king's death seems to be sign of his contrition for his slaying of Holy King Olaf. After the First Crusade King Sigurth of Norway brings an army there and receives a splinter of the true cross from King Baldwin.

— Joseph R. Carroll

HENDERSON THE RAIN KING

Author: Saul Bellow (1915-   )
Type of work: Novel
Type of plot: Mock-heroic

Time of plot: Late 1950's
First published: 1959

Though Saul Bellow's novels most often employ identifiably real American settings, this novel places his antihero Eugene Henderson in several imaginary East African locales. In quest of a spiritual ordeal that will give his life meaning, Henderson at first tries, and fails, to confront Africa with American nerve. Bellow's vividly drawn Africa serves both as a backdrop for Henderson's flamboyant personality and as a reflection of his inner moods: Africa is dry and dusty when Henderson is depressed, shimmering, riotously alive, and vaguely menacing when he taps into his inner strength and wisdom.

Wariri village. Domain of King Dahfu of the imaginary East African Wariri people. More lush than neighboring areas, the Wariri land also boasts a few of the modern amenities that Henderson associates with "civilization": firearms, books, and Western furniture. Bellow often shows the village as a place of confinement; Henderson and his African guide are held captive when they first arrive, as they are again after Dahfu's death, and Dahfu himself seems a prisoner in his own palace, chained by the obligations of his throne.

An atmosphere of death and danger hangs about the village, emphasized by Bellow's repeated use of the color red. The Wariri people have a fearsome reputation, yet Henderson finds the inhabitants attractive and their traditional garb stylish. The opulence and pageantry of Wariri culture contrasts with the pervasiveness of death in the village, exemplified by the corpse with which Henderson wrestles his first night there and the fondness of the Wariri for ornaments made of human bone. This weaving together of death and life underscores one of

Bellow's favorite themes: In order to live fully, human beings must come to terms with their own mortality.

Dahfu's palace. Home of the Wariri monarch, a place where human and animal, intellectual and sensual converge. Dahfu keeps lions in one part of his palace and a harem in another. He and Henderson discuss philosophy, yet Dahfu must live (and die) by the most elemental facts. Henderson at first envies Dahfu his exotic luxuries, but soon learns that they, like his own wealth, are accompanied by heavy burdens. Both characters, too, are displaced people: just as Dahfu once renounced his medical studies in Syria to assume his place as the Wariri king, so must Henderson renounce his Western arrogance in order to emulate the equipoise he admires in Dahfu.

The palace can be taken both as a literal location—one in which Henderson's friendship with the king deepens and where, under Dahfu's guidance, he faces some of his starkest fears—and as an allegory of Henderson's inner self, with the harem symbolizing his many raging lusts and the lions, in contrast, his dormant potential for nobility and serenity. The subterranean location of the lions' den is significant: In order to earn the freedom of his soul, Henderson must first descend into an allegorical Hell. Interestingly, Henderson's and Dahfu's friendship comes to its climax on a tower, outdoors, in direct antithesis to the palace's enclosed underground lions' den.

Bush. Wild areas surrounding the Arnewi and Wariri villages. Bellow repeatedly uses fire imagery to hint at the evanescence of life in this harsh setting, and at the way the land makes permeable the boundaries between matter and energy. Henderson's greatest fears are death and chaos, and thus he must learn to accept decay and disorder before he can live with the ease and mastery he desires. Henderson finally confronts death unflinchingly as Dahfu dies trying to catch a lion that his people believe contains the soul of his father. It is fitting that Dahfu's death and Henderson's redemptive attempt to save him occur in the bush, beyond the reach of both Western and African culture, at the "changing point between matter and light."

Earlier in the novel, Dahfu explains that people's surroundings influence their mentality and physical appearance. While Henderson at first finds this philosophy bizarre and depressing, he later, while in the bush, realizes that Dahfu is correct, connecting the African king's ideas with Albert Einstein's equation of matter and energy. Henderson, then, is changed by his time in Africa, especially the time he spends around the unselfish, noble Dahfu and his lions. Near the end of the novel, for example, Henderson begins to display a generosity that is, for once, unmotivated by expectation of reward. His adoption of Dahfu's lion cub ensures that he will take a part of Africa back to his home in the United States and thereby bring a healing element of the bush and its wildness into his domesticated, suburban American life even as he preserves the memory of his lost friend.

Arnewi village. First stop on Henderson's journey in East Africa. In ironic allusion to the Old Testament's Book of Exodus and the wasteland motif from the Grail mythos, Bellow depicts the village afflicted both by drought and a plague of frogs infesting its water supply. Henderson's attempt to become a hero by killing the frogs ends in disaster that leaves the parched village worse off than before, mirroring Henderson's arid, unsatisfied soul.

*Newfoundland. Eastern Canadian province in which Henderson's plane makes a refueling stop on the last leg of his return trip to the United States. The contrast between the African bush and Newfoundland's "gray Arctic silence" could not be more pronounced and serves to underscore the changes Henderson has undergone. Energized by the cold and by his sense of carrying on Dahfu's lineage, Henderson runs and leaps like the lions that for the Wariri symbolize the sovereignty of the soul.

*Connecticut. Henderson's New England home at the beginning of the novel. There he raises pigs, to the consternation of his neighbors. His house's disorder and his unkempt appearance indicate his alienation from the world and from himself. Feeling unhappy and confined at home, Henderson indulges in displays of temper; during one of these tantrums an elderly female neighbor dies of a heart attack, and his guilt over her death, as well as his dismay at seeing that her house is as cluttered as his, shocks Henderson out of his inertia and prompts him to travel to Africa. He realizes that he, too, will die one day, and that he must make some kind of peace with the world.

*France. Country in which Henderson lived for a time as a child; it is also the country where he lives with his first wife and begins the affair that will become his second marriage. As he tours France in adulthood, Henderson's memories of his cultured, accomplished parents fuel his feelings of inadequacy and discontent, and he quarrels with his lover, Lily. At the height of his misery he visits an aquarium and is both mesmerized and horrified by the sight of an octopus, the seeming embodiment of the randomness and death that terrify him.

— *Hayes Hampton*

HENRY IV

Author: Luigi Pirandello (1867-1936)
Type of work: Drama
Type of plot: Psychological realism

Time of plot: 1922
First performed: 1922; first published, 1922 as *Enrico IV* (English translation, 1922)

Although this play's actions all occur in one house, an unnamed Italian villa, the play's comparatively simple stage settings are important thematically, for they in themselves suggest the thin line between "reality" and "illusion" or, perhaps, between "sanity" and "madness" in this story about a modern man who imagines himself to be the eleventh century ruler of the Holy Roman Empire, Henry IV.

Henry's throne room. Villa salon designed to look like the throne room of the historical Henry IV in Goslar, Germany. However, as the young "counsellors" of "Henry IV," the mad hero of the play, reveal, this room is not always in Goslar but sometimes in numerous other places. Nevertheless, for Henry IV, it has been a real throne room, even though he has not in actuality left the villa for all the years of his madness. However, in the third act, it is, for everyone, merely a room in the villa, where Henry suggests in the story of the Irish priest that we all play parts and so in a manner are as mad as he was or perhaps is. At the end, it is the room in which Henry must always be "mad," in order not to be punished for his truly insane stabbing of Belcredi.

Second room in villa. This room, although its furniture is described as simple and old, seems rather timeless. Still, there is an irony in that there are windows that look out upon a garden, a real world, and yet a door opens into the so-called throne room. But it is here that Henry tells his counsellors, who are merely his hired actors, that he is no longer mad, so that for the moment everyone seems to be living in the present and is, perhaps, sane.

— *L. L. Lee*

HENRY IV, PART I

Author: William Shakespeare (1564-1616)
Type of work: Drama
Type of plot: Historical

Time of plot: 1403
First performed: 1592; first published, 1598

Historical and fictional settings are used to build contexts for William Shakespeare's retelling of English history that focuses on honor and Prince Hal's character reformation. Shakespeare shrewdly concentrates on three principal settings that expose Prince Hal stranded between his father's court, Falstaff's court, and Hotspur's feudal countryside. In the first three acts, Hal moves from tavern to court, learning responsibility and earning his father's affection and respect before conquering Hotspur's world.

Royal palace. King Henry IV's principal seat of rule, where he plans political strategy and shows concern about his seemingly dissolute son, Prince Hal, who swears to redeem himself at Hotspur's expense. The text distinguishes this palace from Windsor Castle, where the king, Northumberland, Worcester, and Hotspur meet before the rupture between Henry and the Percys. Productions of the play usually generalize the setting, and in most productions, the palace exudes a mood of solemnity with its somber soldiers, counselors, and courtiers.

Boar's Head Tavern. Public house in London's Eastcheap district that is the scene of Falstaff's dishonest retelling of the Gad's Hill escapade and of the interview-game he plays with Hal. The tavern is also the place where Mistress Quickly (hostess of the tavern) and Bardolph appear as examples of Shakespearean bawdiness. The location is usually depicted onstage as a place with battered walls, barrels of sack, and a shingle to indicate its name. Taken as a place of common people, seedy characters, and reprobate behavior, the tavern represents the sort of social and moral disgrace into which Hal has fallen and out from which he must rise and redeem himself.

*****Warkworth Castle.** Stronghold in Northumberland—the principal seat of the Percy family—where Hotspur exasperates his wife with his intense preoccupation with military honor. It is here that Hotspur scoffs at a popinjay lord's affectation, just as his own courtly life is scoffed at by Falstaff and Hal in Eastcheap. Beneath the superficial charm of Lady Percy's hospitality and Welsh song, lies Hotspur's reckless restlessness, his extravagant sense of military honor.

*****Shrewsbury.** Climactic battlefield on which Hotspur is slain, and Hal distinguishes himself in hand-to-hand combat, that was earlier a stronghold of both Saxons and Normans.

— *Keith Garebian*

HENRY IV, PART II

Author: William Shakespeare (1564-1616)
Type of work: Drama
Type of plot: Historical

Time of plot: 1405-1413
First performed: 1597; first published, 1600

As in Henry IV, Part I, *scenes in this play tend to be either locations for comic action featuring buffoons or rascals or locations for serious action involving the king and the nobility. Most of the action occurring on London streets and in a tavern is comical, whereas scenes at the royal palace at Westminster represent the activity of high policy and the royal family's struggle against its enemies.*

*****London streets.** This location is usually the realm of the comic chaos of lower-class life that constitutes much of the background of the play. The tavern-haunting Falstaff and his villainous companions embody the vigor, confusion, and immorality of London street life.

*****Westminster Palace.** Royal palace, adjacent to Westminster Abbey in London, where King Henry agonizes over the outcome of the rebellion of Northumberland and his accomplices. As his health wanes, his son Prince Henry arrives, and he advises the prince to keep his nobles busy by pursuing "foreign quarrels."

King Henry had once been told that he would die in Jerusalem. After learning that a chamber in his palace is named "Jerusalem," he orders that he be taken there to die, and his son becomes King Henry V.

Justice Shallow's house. Gloucestershire location of Falstaff's ludicrous efforts to recruit soldiers for the royal army.

*****Warkworth Castle.** Northumberland headquarters of the earl of Northumberland, head of the Percy family and a leader of the rebellion against Henry IV.

*****Gaultree Forest.** Yorkshire location of the deception and capture of the rebel leaders Mowbray, Hastings, and the archbishop of York by Henry IV's other son, Prince John. The distance between Yorkshire and London makes it possible for the king and Prince Henry to dissociate themselves from this rather dishonorable action.

— *Robert W. Haynes*

HENRY V

Author: William Shakespeare (1564-1616)
Type of work: Drama
Type of plot: Historical

Time of plot: Early fifteenth century
First performed: c. 1598-1599; first published, 1600

William Shakespeare's classic retelling of the epic English victory over the French at Agincourt, demonstrates how a small stage can be transformed into the English court, the French court, a siege of a walled town, and a battlefield through the magic of words and imagination. The use of the past glory of Agincourt allows Shakespeare to connect the heroic past with the present of Elizabeth I.

***London.** Capital of England and the site of Henry's royal court, London serves as the setting for the opening scenes of the play. By the fifteenth century, the time in which Shakespeare sets his play, London is the economic, political, and religious seat of power in England. Such concentration of power is underscored by the opening scene in which the Archbishop of Canterbury and the Bishop of Ely plot to counter a bill before Parliament that would take away half of the Church's lands. The clerics propose to fund an English military campaign against the French, if Henry will overlook their taxes. Consequently, the churchmen devise an argument that Henry has clear title to the French throne, territory that the English held in earlier times. Thus, Shakespeare locates in London the imperial power, the political machinations, and the religious finances to support the conquest Henry wishes to undertake.

London also serves as the location of the opening scenes of the second act, when Shakespeare transports playgoers to a common street outside a boardinghouse. There, Bardolph, Nym, and Pistol, former companions of the King in wilder days, decide to follow Henry to France as common soldiers. Again, Shakespeare uses the setting of London to juxtapose the bawdy and common folk with the high royalty of the King. Henry's actions have consequences from the top to the bottom of society.

***Southampton.** Seaport on England's southern coast from which Henry's army embarks for France. Southampton is a place of transition: by crossing the water, Henry will leave the land of his own sovereignty to put himself and his men in harm's way in order to conquer France. Tellingly, it is in Southampton where Bedford and Exeter uncover a treasonous plot against the King. The traitors, according to Henry, have conspired and

"sworn unto the practices of France/ to kill us here in Hampton." Finding traitors on British soil, just at the moment of departure indicated by the setting at Southampton, forewarns the King of the dangers ahead.

***Harfleur** (hah-FLUR). Walled city in France under siege by Henry and his army. The third act opens with Henry's famous "Once more unto the breach, dear friends, once more;/ Or close the wall up with our English dead." In this scene, Shakespeare does as the opening chorus says he will; through words and imagination, he is able to transform a small stage into the site of a great siege. The siege at Harfleur allows audiences to experience all levels of the attack, from Henry's exhortations to his men, to Bardolph, Nym, and Pistol's cowardice, to the Welshman Fluellen's close attention to the rules of war. It also provides Henry's first victory on French soil.

***Rouen** (rew-AN). City in Normandy that is the site of the royal court of France during the time in which the play is set. Shakespeare shifts his scene immediately from the fray and bloodshed of Harfleur to the Rouen bedroom of Princess Katharine of France, where she is teasing her old serving woman for English lessons. Their light-hearted exchange—entirely in French—contrasts markedly with the discussion that follows among the French king, the Dauphin, and the lord constable about the English king Henry's sweep through France.

***Agincourt** (AH-zheen-kohr). Village in northern France that is the site of perhaps the greatest military victory ever enjoyed by the English. Without question, playgoers of Shakespeare's day would have known the history and significance of Agincourt. The setting, then, is at the core of this historical drama whose purpose is one of nationalism, patriotism, and imperialism. Using the words supplied by Shakespeare and their own imaginations, playgoers could once again relive the glory of being English. Indeed, the celebration of "Englishness" is one of the hallmarks of the Elizabethan Age. Shakespeare's choice of Agincourt as the crucial setting for his play reflects his desire to connect the late sixteenth century reign of Queen Elizabeth I with the heroic deeds of early sixteenth century King Henry V.

— Diane Andrews Henningfeld

HENRY VI, PART I

Author: William Shakespeare (1564-1616)
Type of work: Drama
Type of plot: Historical

Time of plot: 1422-1444
First performed: c. 1592; first published, 1598

Through effectively juxtaposing French and English settings, this history play depicts the decline of English power in France in the early fifteenth century and the beginning of England's internecine Wars of the Roses. The patriotic values of the early scenes are undercut by growing factions within the English government.

*Orleans. City on the Loire River in north-central France. Historically the English laid siege to Orleans in 1428 but were repelled by the heroic Joan of Arc, marking the turning point in the Hundred Years' Wars. In presenting Orleans onstage, William Shakespeare sacrifices historical accuracy to Elizabethan prejudice by having Lord John Talbot retake the city from Joan (known in the play as Joan de Pucelle). At Orleans, English valor wins over French duplicity, reminding the audience of past English glory and giving them a stirring battle scene that made this play popular with Elizabethan-era audiences.

*Temple Garden. Garden adjoining the Inns of Court in London. Gardens traditionally symbolize peace and harmony, serving as models for orderly governments. However, in this invented scene Shakespeare subverts that tradition by making the Temple Garden the starting point for the Wars of the Roses. In the heat of a quarrel, Richard Plantagenet (later the duke of York) plucks a white rose from a bush; his enemy, the duke of Somerset, then plucks a red rose. Their partisans do likewise to make the roses serve as emblems of their animosity. These personal signs, the white rose of York and the red rose of Lancaster, become the fighting symbols that define the Wars of the Roses.

*Bordeaux (Bor-DOH). Capital city of Gascony in France. In contrast to the English triumph at Orleans, Bordeaux is the scene of England's defeat and disgrace. Talbot, his forces surrounded by a French army, sends for reinforcements. However, the feuding English commanders, Somerset and York, ignore his pleas in order to spite each other. Talbot and his son die at Bordeaux, and with them dies English dominion in France. Shakespeare suggests that discord among the English leaders, "the vulture of sedition," is more to blame for Talbot's death and England's defeat than the French are.

— Anthony J. Bernardo, Jr.

HENRY VI, PART II

Author: William Shakespeare (1564-1616)
Type of work: Drama
Type of plot: Historical

Time of plot: 1444-1455
First performed: c. 1590-1591; first published, 1594

This history play presents the theme of social dissolution through English settings that exemplify political treachery, witchcraft, misrule, and civil war. The play's two main actions, the intrigues against the duke of Gloucester and the open violence of Jack Cade's Rebellion and the Wars of the Roses, allow William Shakespeare to depict England's loss of order.

Magic circle. Center of an occult ritual performed in the duke of Gloucester's house in London. Two priests and a witch draw the circle in which demons appear so that the duchess of Gloucester can advance her husband's career through magical prophecies. As stage entertainment, this séance can thrill an audience with its necromancy, artificial thunder and lightning, demons rising from a trap door, and prophetic riddles. However, Shakespeare also invests the scene with irony and menace. This diabolical action occurs in the house of the honest and patriotic duke of Gloucester without his knowledge, suggesting that the corruption spreading through England touches even decent people. Moreover, the séance is part of a plot by the duke's enemies, who will use the duchess's magical practices against her husband.

*St. Albans. English town north of London. St. Albans is a setting at both the beginning and the end of this play and highlights the play's main actions: the duke of Gloucester's fall and the coming of civil war. First, while King Henry vacations in the town, the political conspiracy against the upright Gloucester bears fruit when he is publicly disgraced by his wife's crime of witchcraft. Second, the Wars of the Roses begin in St. Albans with the first Battle of St. Albans. This fight occurs within the town rather than on an outlying battlefield, emphasizing the breakdown of law and order. The town's sufferings foreshadow those of England itself.

*Jack Cade's camp. Headquarters of a popular revolt against King Henry, which ended in London. Shakespeare transforms the historical Cade's Revolt into a violent, anarchic affair, suggesting the fragility of England under Henry VI. Cade promises his followers a carnival England of social equality, commonly held property, and free-flowing wine and beer. However, his camp is a bloody tyranny in which men are killed for being literate or for failing to call Cade by his assumed title. The violence in Cade's camp parodies and foreshadows the duke of York's impending coup.

— *Anthony J. Bernardo, Jr.*

HENRY VI, PART III

Author: William Shakespeare (1564-1616)
Type of work: Drama
Type of plot: Historical

Time of plot: 1455-1471
First performed: c. 1590-1591; first published, 1595

The English settings of this play—battlefields, royal courts, and prisons—present a nation torn asunder by the Wars of the Roses, in which the rival houses of York and Lancaster struggled for control of the country. William Shakespeare presents twenty years of civil war in one play through the severing of social and familial bonds.

*Towton. Small Yorkshire town near which a great battle is fought. For Shakespeare's audience, the Battle of Towton represented the Wars of the Roses at their worst. On stage political discord appears as familial discord when fathers and sons, fighting on opposite sides, kill each other. Elizabethans believed that civil war dis-membered the body politic, and on the battlefield physical bodies are dismembered as when Lord Clifford's head is cut off and put on the gates of York to replace the duke of York's head. The battlefield also juxtaposes King Henry's political weakness with his moral stature. Henry, dismissed by his own supporters and forgotten in this battle for his crown, sits on a molehill, a symbol of his departed authority. However, while the king sits stripped of his royal dignity, he serves as a chorus, testifying to the human costs of the battle around him.

*Tower of London. Famous castle and prison alongside the River Thames in London. Richard of Gloucester murders King Henry in the Tower, foreshadowing Richard's more famous Tower murders in Shakespeare's earlier play *Richard III* (1592-1593). In the tower, Henry VI, once the king of England and France, lives and dies as a helpless prisoner, an almost fitting end for a man who could not rule his powerful nobles. Paradoxically, however, it is inside this prison that the ineffectual Henry grows into a prophet, foreseeing in young Henry of Richmond a great future king and in Richard a tyrant.

*Royal palace. Edward IV's court in London. In a play dominated by battle scenes the royal palace serves as a theatrical respite. Edward, while at court and apparently secure on his throne, pursues the widow Elizabeth Grey as he had once pursued the crown. Romantic intrigues replace military strategy, and battles yield to bawdy jokes and double entendres. But any security here is temporary; the discord produced by civil war continues. Edward's wooing of and subsequent marriage to Elizabeth will only renew the Wars of the Roses. More ominously, it is at the court that Richard of Gloucester gives his famous soliloquy, announcing his ambition to become king.

— *Anthony J. Bernardo, Jr.*

HENRY VIII

Authors: William Shakespeare (1564-1616) with
  John Fletcher (1579-1625)
Type of work: Drama

Type of plot: Historical
Time of plot: 1520-1533
First performed: 1613; first published, 1623

Setting in this historical drama is important for the scale of pageantry. Episodic, incrementally repetitive in its depiction of a string of falls, the play has big set-pieces in a royal council, a ballroom, the Blackfriars trial, a coronation, a cardinal's valediction, the king's deathbed chamber, and a christening, which use historical locales in London, Westminster, and Kimbolton. By staying closely to the actual sites of Tudor history, William Shakespeare ensures verisimilitude.

*Westminster Palace. Royal palace in London in which most of the play is set. The vast palace affords the play's producers rich opportunities for sumptuous spectacle. Life at the royal court often consisted of revels, masques, and displays of splendor. There is plenty of pageantry in *Henry VIII*, but there is also harsh and cold realism. As Shakespeare shows, King Henry's court was a place of intrigue and counter-intrigue, of fulsome emotion and eloquence. His play exploits the size and layout of Henry's palace for the various conflicts that are played out.

The play uses various rooms for different dramatic purposes. An antechamber, for example, is the setting for the duke of Buckingham's outrage at Cardinal Wolsey and his aim—which is forestalled—to report to the king about the cardinal's treachery. The palace itself is the place in which news of the birth of the daughter of Anne Bullen (Anne Boleyn) is first heard, and it serves as the locale for the play's climax, in which the infant Elizabeth is baptized and eulogized by Thomas Cranmer, the archbishop of Canterbury, in the final scene. The council chamber is the place where Henry's first wife, Katherine of Aragon, makes suit to the king on behalf of the people who are upset by the court's extravagance. An anteroom and yard are used for brief scenes in act 5 dealing with the bishop of Winchester's unsuccessful attempt to destroy Cranmer.

— *Keith Garebian*

HERCULES AND HIS TWELVE LABORS

Author: Unknown
Type of work: Folklore
Type of plot: Adventure

Time of plot: Antiquity
First published: Unknown

The story of the labors of Hercules is part of an oral tradition recorded in variant versions over the centuries. While details vary, the story's basic setting is largely within the lands known to the ancient Greeks around the Mediterranean Sea. Most of the places Hercules visits while performing his twelve labors are real, but the writers who recorded the tales were prone to adding details that could not have been present during the remote time in which Hercules' story is set.

*Tiryns (TIR-inz). Ancient city in southern Greece that is home to Hercules' cousin King Eurystheus. Driven mad by Juno, Hercules kills his own wife and children and is required by the Delphic oracle to atone for his crime by becoming the vassal of Eurystheus, who sets twelve difficult labors for Hercules to perform. Juno and Eurystheus hope that Hercules will perish while performing one of them.

*Nemea (NEE-mee-ah). City of northern Argolis, northwest of Mycenae, that is the site of Hercules' first labor: to kill the lion that threatens to eat the people of Nemea. The lion's cave is on Mount Tretus, two miles from Nemea.

*Lerna. Coastal town, five miles south of Argos, where Hercules performs his second labor: killing the multiheaded hydra, a creature living in a swamp whose body odor kills all who breathe the fetid area. The hydra's lair is beneath a plane tree at the seven-fold source of the Amymone.

*Erymanthus (ir-a-MAN-thahs). Mountain range in southern Greece, in the northwest Peloponnesus, where Hercules performs another labor: killing the Erymanthian boar. Along his way to Erymanthus, he stops at Pholoë, where he has a dispute with the centaurs when he drinks wine they claim as their own. To escape, he kills most of the half-horse men.

*Arcadia (ar-KAY-dee-ah). Region west of Argolis through which the River Ladon runs. On the river's banks near Mount Artemisium, Hercules captures the Ceryneian Hind, a deer that he spends a full year chasing down, after following it all the way to Istria in the land of the Hyperboreans, on the coast of the Black Sea.

Stymphalian Marsh (stim-fal-ee-an). Wetland in the northeast corner of Arcadia, overlooked by a spur of Mount Cyllene, that is home to the loud man-eating birds that Hercules must remove. The marsh is neither solid enough to walk on nor liquid enough to float a boat on and can increase in size as the channels draining it are blocked. One version of the story has Hercules draining the marsh, probably by freeing these natural channels. Hercules startles the birds with a bell, shoots many of them with arrows, and causes the rest to fly away.

*Elis (EE-lis). Region west of Arcadia whose city of the same name lies near the River Peneius. Hercules' task is to clean the stables in which King Augeas keeps three thousand oxen; the stables have not been cleaned for thirty years. Hercules accomplishes the task by diverting the rivers Alpheus and Peneus through the stables and washing them clean in one day.

*Crete (kreet). Island in the eastern Mediterranean, south of Greece, where Hercules captures a bull that has been causing havoc around the fertile valley of the river Tethris. He takes the bull back to Eurystheus by making it swim across the sea, carrying him on its back.

*Thrace (thrays). Country to the north of the Aegean Sea and east of Macedonia where King Diomedes keeps four savage, flesh-eating mares. Hercules' eighth labor is to steal the horses. He drives them down to the coast, leaving them on a knoll, probably opposite the island of Thasos. To confuse his pursuers, he cuts a channel from the sea to flood the plain and create a lake.

Amazonia. Region on the southern coast of the Black Sea, renowned for its female warriors, who dwell on the plain of the River Thermodon, which rises in the mountains to the south. Hercules' task is to get Queen Hippolyta's girdle. The queen is willing to give it to him, but Juno interferes by telling the other Amazons that Hercules intends to kidnap their queen. In the battle that ensues, Hercules kills Hippolyta and takes the girdle from her dead body.

Erytheia (ayr-eh-THEE-ah). Island near the Atlantic entrance to the Mediterranean on which the monster Geryoneus keeps a herd of oxen that Hercules steals for Eurystheus. The precise location of the island is uncertain, but the story tells of Hercules having to cross Europe to reach Tartessus to accomplish his tenth labor. He drives the oxen overland to Mycenae, visiting Spain, Gaul, and Italy along the way.

Garden of the Hesperides (heh-SPEHR-a-dees). Garden on the slopes of North Africa's Mount Atlas where the chariot horses of the sun end the day. Here grows the tree bearing golden apples that Hercules is charged to collect as his eleventh labor. Solid walls surround the garden, and a dragon coils around the base of the tree. Hercules' greatest challenge, however, is simply locating the tree, which he roams far and wide to find. During his long search for the tree, he kills a giant, a host of pygmies, and burns alive some of his captors in Egypt. In India, he sets Prometheus free. At last, when he discovers Atlas holding up the heavens, he assumes the Titan's burden, releasing Atlas to go after the apples. After Atlas returns with the apples, he reluctantly takes up his burden again, while Hercules delivers the apples to Eurystheus.

Tartarus. Underworld home of Hades, at the bottom of which flows the River Styx, which Hercules crosses in Charon's boat to capture Cerberus for his twelfth labor. The three-headed dog Cerberus is chained to the gates of Acheron, where he guards the entrance.

— *Pauline Morgan*

HEREWARD THE WAKE: Last of the English

Author: Charles Kingsley (1819-1875)
Type of work: Novel
Type of plot: Historical

Time of plot: Eleventh century
First published: 1866

This novel's prelude argues that England's lowland fens are an unusual but apt place to nurture a hero. Although Hereward has adventures in other lands, he returns to Danelaw England after the Norman Conquest to oppose the brutalities of the invaders with a berserk spirit that Charles Kingsley believed necessary to rebuild Victorian England. Kingsley's last historical novel interlaces medieval lore with modern judgments to argue the need for earlier northern virtues and a continuity through the Princess of Wales, daughter of the king of Denmark, who brought Viking blood to strengthen the royal line.

*Cambridgeshire. Marshy fenland region around Cambridge, where most of the novel's action takes place. Kingsley's opening pages are a paean to the great beauty of this landscape, a site of historic importance because there the Saxons continued to fight the Norman forces of William I for seven years after the Norman Conquest in 1066. This expansive marshy area, now diked and cultivated, was forested in medieval times. On the low rolling uplands above the open flat lands that housed towns of the Danelaw and Christian monasteries at Crowland, Ramsey, and on the Isle of Ely, there Hereward builds his "Camp of Refuge."

The novel was published on the eight hundredth anniversary of the Battle of Hastings, and its subtitle identifies Hereward as the "Last of the English" because the race subsequently included a French strain, associated with the softening effects of civilization. In contrast, Kingsley regarded the preconquest invasions as a happy marriage, and he uses the imagery of gender to characterize them: the Anglo-Saxon woman impregnated by the Norse Viking, the "great male race." Kingsley believed that such revitalization was urgent for a Victorian England weakened by effete indulgences. Hereward's battle cry "A Wake!" proclaims his salient quality of alertness, and Kingsley called upon his nation to "awake" and rise from their decline.

Kingsley gives to England's early Anglo-Danish nobility, who lived in a hard but "cheerful" landscape, a mythic status as gallant—though not always efficient—warriors. Their proud personal independence and the free institutions that inform British liberty derive from the northern races of Denmark and Norway who came as invaders but achieved a stable society. This argument is crucial in the Victorian invention of the Vikings, whose history is defined by the need for more agricultural lands, skill as shipbuilders and the love of the sea, and a passion for personal freedom. Much of the novel's matter comes from Icelandic sagas, and Hereward's heroes are Harold Hardraade, Ragnor Lodborg, and Frithiof. Going into exile, he sails close to Orkney and encounters a "witch-whale"; as on many occasions Hereward's singing of Viking songs gives confidence to his followers.

Kingsley makes a sharp distinction between Hereward's northeastern homeland and the southern home of the men of Wessex and the Godwinssons who claim to be all of England. These counties, even before the Norman Conquest, were the most civilized and most French. The breadth of separation is evoked by several pages that describe Hereward's journey to meet King William at Winchester to seek peace after he concludes that further resistance is pointless.

*Greenwood. Region stretching from the fens to the Scottish border, for two hundred years the refuge of outlaws, including the famous Robin Hood. Hereward spends time in the greenwood before he acknowledges King William's superiority. Both a real landscape and a mythic place, the greenwood transforms lives of despair and poverty into something that is not only tolerable but pleasant. As with the fenland, this less cultivated place is superior to the overly civilized and developed parts of England. In the forest, lawless men soon form an ordered society, defined by hard knocks, strict rules, fair play, and equal justice for high and low—the English ideal, advocated especially in the public schools and fostered by popular historical novels like *Hereward the Wake*, of which there are several juvenile versions.

*Crowland Minster. Most significant of several religious houses in the novel, used by Hereward as a place of refuge. After richly describing its buildings and their functions, Kingsley subsequently notes its destruction and later rebuilding, a sign of Norman development. The local monks start a little school in a nearby town that eventually becomes Cambridge University.

— *Velma Bourgeois Richmond*

HERLAND

Author: Charlotte Perkins Gilman (1860-1935)
Type of work: Novel
Type of plot: Social realism

Time of plot: Early twentieth century
First published: serial, 1915; book, 1979

The major setting of this utopian novel is the lost land of Herland, with its all-female population, which is the primary vehicle through which Charlotte Perkins Gilman critiques Western civilization and envisions improvements.

Herland. Imaginary subtropical country ringed by heavily forested mountains as high as the Himalayas that is about the size of Holland. Its location is kept secret by the few outsiders who have visited it. Herland's Aryan inhabitants, now limited to three million women, once were in contact with the best Old World civilizations. Two thousand years before the events of Gilman's novel, the country extended beyond its mountain perimeter, reaching the coast of the "Great Sea." Because of wars with external enemies, the ancient Herlanders con-

tracted their settlements to within the protective mountains, defended the mountain pass, and built fortresses. When the men were fighting in the mountains, a volcanic eruption killed all of them and isolated Herland from the rest of the world. At the time of the novel, the country stands like a "basalt column," accessible only by airplane, with thick forests at the base of the mountains.

Bordered by a belt of forest, the interior of Herland ranges from mountain valleys with winter snow to a large valley in southeastern Herland with a climate similar to that of California. The valley contains broad plains and well-tended forests, almost all of whose trees are either hardwood or food-bearing varieties. The three male adventurers compare the entire land to a garden, a park, and a truck farm. They comment that the forests are better tended than Germany's, with no dead limbs and even with trained vines. Interspersed throughout the well-cultivated land are small glades with shaded stone furniture placed near fountains with birdbaths.

The dust-free roads crisscrossing Herland are constructed of a durable manufactured material. Sloped, graded, curved, and guttered as well as the best European highways, they lead to towns containing both white and pink houses, situated "among the green groves and gardens like a broken rosary of pink coral." The white buildings are for public use, whereas the pink ones, especially those near the town center, resemble palaces or college buildings in parklike settings. All of Herland's towns and cities are clean, orderly, and lovely, without the urban blight common in American and European population centers. The entire country of Herland underscores the virtues of its all-female inhabitants.

Herland castle. Massive fortress more than one thousand years old in which the three Americans are detailed after they enter Herland. In contrast to the town's pink and white buildings, the castle is built of gray stone with thick walls and is isolated in the hills. Its high, smooth walls, built of huge stones interlocked like puzzle pieces, are reminiscent of Peru's massive pre-Columbian architecture. Perched on a lofty rock, the castle's high walls line the edge of a sheer cliff, with a river at its base. Its location in northern Herland gives it a clear view of the open plains in the southeast of the country.

The castle has no bars, though initially the three men are not allowed to leave. In contrast to the European princesses imprisoned in castles in traditional medieval tales of Europe, these men are interned only until they learn the language and customs of Herland. Instead of trying to possess the men, the women of Herland want to liberate them and learn from them.

Herland's forests. Important because the women whom the three adventurers court and eventually marry all work in Herland's well-fertilized forests, as do the three men after they wed. The forests seem almost magical to the intruders; they are also practical, since their many food-producing trees require little upkeep and yield more produce in a smaller area of land than do traditional farming methods. Herland's women have enriched their soil and nurtured their trees until they have created an Eden-like country, a standard against which the three male American intruders and their civilization are judged and found lacking.

— *Shelley A. Thrasher*

A HERO OF OUR TIME

Author: Mikhail Lermontov (1814-1841)
Type of work: Novel
Type of plot: Psychological realism

Time of plot: 1830-1838
First published: Geroy nashego vremeni, serial, 1839; book, 1840 (English translation, 1854)

This novel is set in the Caucasus Mountains during the Caucasian War. Although none of its five sections takes place on the battlefield, they dramatize the bitter relations between the Russian occupiers and their subjects as well as the boredom suffered by the Russians. Drawing on his own extensive experiences in the region and using the real names of towns and other geographical features, Mikhail Lermontov wrote what is regarded as one of the first important novels in the Russian language.

*Caucasus** (KAW-kuh-zuhs). Region and range of mountains lying between the Black Sea and the Caspian Sea in the extreme southeast of Europe. The Caucasus Mountains are generally accepted as a dividing line between Europe and Asia, and the range includes Europe's highest peak, Mount Elbrus. At the time the novel takes place, Russia was fighting the region's indigenous peoples in a war of expansion destined to last until 1864. To

Russians, the Caucasus represented a frontier whose cities were outposts of what they regarded as civilized life.

Lermontov himself visited the Caucasus as a child, and served twice in the region as a military officer, having been banished there in 1837 and again in 1840. Besides being a novelist and poet, he was a gifted painter and describes the region's majestic yet forbidding terrain with quick, impressionistic strokes.

*Military Georgian road. Often precipitous road running from Georgia to Russia through the Caucasus Mountains. Besides linking the Caucasus to its occupiers, the road connects the novel's five sections. In "Bela," the first episode, two of the novel's characters meet on the road during the autumn, and since the station they have reached lacks rooms for travelers, they spend several hours in a smoky native hut as a snowstorm passes. Over tea, one of the travelers, Maksim Maksimich, begins a story about a striking officer named Pechorin, the hero of the novel's ironic title. Although the two resume their travels during the night, worsening weather forces them to seek shelter in a second hut.

In "Maksim Maksimich" the two travelers meet again, farther down the road, in a decrepit inn at Vladikavkaz, a town on the Terek River. Although the mountains loom over the landscape "like a crenelated wall," the town itself is uninspiring, consisting of a "multitude of squat little houses" built along the riverbank. Here the two unexpectedly encounter Pechorin, who offhandedly urges his old friend Maksimich to do what he wishes with the personal papers Maksimich has been saving for him. These papers turn out to be Pechorin's journal, sections of which form the novel's remaining sections.

Fort. Setting of the story Maksim Maksimich recounts in "Bela," lying beyond the Terek River in Chechnya. Although the fort itself is secure, Maksimich describes the surrounding countryside as highly dangerous for Russian soldiers not on their guard: "Either a lariat would be around your neck or there would be a bullet in the back of your head."

In the same area lies the **Cossack settlement** that is the setting for "The Fatalist." The Cossacks were a warrior people who fought for Russia in that country's wars of expansion, and in this case their settlement is also the station for a battalion of Russian troops. In the evening the Russians have little to do but gamble, an activity whose philosophical implications are explored in the story and throughout the novel.

*Taman (tah-MAHN). Small Russian port on the Black Sea that is the setting for the episode of the same name. Pechorin calls it "the worst little town of all the seacoast towns in Russia." Forced to stay in a shanty with broken windows on the edge of the sea, he quickly notices that the customary religious icon is missing from its walls—"a bad sign!" Taman is one of the many places in the novel that Lermontov himself had visited.

*Pyatigorsk (pyih-tyih-GORSK) and *Kislovodsk (kyih-slah-VOTSK). Fashionable Russian spas nestled in the Caucasus Mountains that are the settings for the "Princess Mary" episode. Noted for their mineral springs, the spas provide a vivid contrast to the more austere settings of the other episodes. Pechorin calls Pyatigorsk a "varicolored, neat, brand-new little town." Although the spas are far behind the lines of battle, many army officers on leave frequent them.

It was also in Pyatigorsk that Lermontov himself was killed in a duel at the age of twenty-six, an event eerily presaged in this episode.

— *Grove Koger*

HERZOG

Author: Saul Bellow (1915-　　)
Type of work: Novel
Type of plot: Psychological realism

Time of plot: 1960's
First published: 1964

In this novel of humanistic affirmation, the emotional and intellectual vicissitudes of Moses Herzog are closely associated with the romantic juxtaposition of city and country as Herzog travels back and forth among Chicago, New York, and the Berkshires in Massachusetts.

*Chicago. Gritty midwestern city in which the Canadian-born Saul Bellow grew up. Chicago figures prominently in his writings; indeed, Bellow's great strength is his portrayal of the density and fabric of modern urban life in America. The city is associated with the Jewish American social and cultural experience to which Bellow is drawn. Such major urban centers as Chicago, with its grinding poverty, street crime, youth gangs, and widespread racism—all the ills of modern society—are also focal points of cultural and intellectual life and thus are treated somewhat ambivalently in Bellow's fiction.

American intellectuals come to love and despise the modern urban civilization upon which their existences are ultimately based. Cities are places to which intellectuals are invariably drawn but from which they must also inevitably escape. Ever since the rise of modern urban centers, there has been a labeling of cities as sources of social alienation in which people no longer know their neighbors, a contrast to the idealized romantic notion of rural communities.

Chicago is, in part, representative of the domain of actuality or "real life" in the modern world with which the vain and emotionally confused professor of literature, Moses E. Herzog, is continually confronted and with which he must come to terms. As an intellectual and idealist who has written on the social and political aspects of European Romanticism, he prefers to view what is often a rather harsh and brutal reality in terms of abstracted notions and philosophical ideas. In the cities he meets the urban people—like the crude and mocking lawyer Sandor Himmelstein or the pompous professor Valentine Gersbach, the supposed friend who steals away Herzog's wife, Madeleine Pontritter—who take it upon themselves to be his "teachers" and to introduce him to a nihilistic vision of reality that he instinctively abhors.

Herzog's reaction to this spiritual malaise and philosophical nihilism, especially the loss of humanistic moral values in favor of mute and indifferent facts, is an expression of Bellow's own response to the alienation of human beings and the negativity of the fashionable existentialism taught in American universities during the 1950's and 1960's. In a time of great pessimism—in a post-Holocaust and Cold War Western world—Bellow's work stands as an existential affirmation of humanity.

*New York City. Second great American urban center in *Herzog*. The urban centers of America are the places where one finds the modern self-obsessed neurotic individual who seems unable to maintain healthy emotional relationships with others. Like the neurotic New York character types found in the cinematic texts of filmmaker Woody Allen, Bellow's cities harbor rather dysfunctional people who seem to dwell in a delusional state. The long-suffering and egocentric Moses E. Herzog (whose initials spell "me"), divorced three times, is one such plagued and pitiful person. Bellow intends for him to be, in this regard, an ironic representative of the modern city dweller, a poor self-involved soul who nonetheless possesses a great sense of human compassion and moral commitment. The character's name "Herzog" implies (from the German) that he is both a prince (*Herzog*) of a man and a man with great heart (*Herz*). Bellow's Herzog character suggests the author's firm conviction that despite the distortions of the personality that occur from the stresses of modern urban life and the excesses of human self-consciousness, there is a deeper and more "natural" self that remains healthy and that fundamentally affirms human existence. Herzog's decision at the novel's conclusion not to murder Madeleine and Gersbach indicate Bellow's belief that the natural and healthy instincts of the self—despite the negative influences of modern society and urban life—can assert themselves and can prevail. That Herzog makes his decision as he draws a deep breath would seem to suggest that his choice is a natural one (as opposed to a rationally moral one) and is an affirmation of intrinsic human nature.

*Berkshires. Mountainous region in western Massachusetts that is the location of **Ludleyville**, where Herzog owns a large and dilapidated summer country home. A romantic at heart, the urban intellectual Herzog is drawn to what he perceives to be nature and its supposed "healing" effects. When he first purchases his Berkshire home, he envisages it as becoming a kind of idyllic and princely country estate where he can devote himself to his academic work. However, its poor condition seems constantly to mock his grand vision of himself, and the isolated location becomes a major point of marital contention between him and Madeleine, who yearns for the intellectual and cultural stimulation of the city. The run-down condition of the vacation home where Moses Herzog is found at the novel's beginning serves as a symbolic commentary on the state of his life, a catalog of both his academic and personal failures. The fact that even in the country Herzog cannot succeed seems to suggest Bellow's belief that location, be it city or country, is ultimately not the source of a character's failures; the foibles and frailties of the human heart are the source. An escape to some idealized vision of a romantic idyll in the countryside is only a delusion. Herzog's retreat to the ramshackle home in Ludleyville suggests, however, his final acceptance of all that he is and has become, both the good and the bad.

— *Thomas F. Barry*

A HIGH WIND IN JAMAICA

Author: Richard Hughes (1900-1976)
Type of work: Novel
Type of plot: Psychological realism

Time of plot: Early nineteenth century
First published: 1929

This debut novel about pirates in the Caribbean—set long after the great age of Caribbean piracy—spins a fanciful narrative about seven children and their year-long adventure aboard a pirate ship. Real Caribbean locations function as backdrops for an ironic universe revealed through the eyes of the children and various narrative voices.

Pirate schooner. Unnamed vessel commanded by Captain Jonsen on which the five young Bas-Thornton children and two Fernandez children are inadvertently taken prisoner when the ship carrying them from Jamaica to England is captured. The seven children quickly adapt to life aboard the slovenly pirate ship, and it becomes for them a place of adventure and friendly companions, much like their home in Jamaica. They climb the ship's ratlines fearlessly and pass their days talking with the friendly crew and playing with the ship's animals. After carrying the children aboard his ship for a year, Captain Jonsen disguises his vessel as the merchant ship *Lizzie Green* and hails a passenger steamship, which takes the children to England.

The pirate captain's cabin serves as a refuge and a crime scene. With the others aboard the *Thelma* for the circus, young Emily, still recuperating from her injury, remains behind to guard the tied-up *Thelma* captain. When he struggles free to get the knife, Emily grabs it first and stabs him fatally. The pirates only take two prizes while the children are aboard: the *Clorinda*, a London-bound British merchant ship, and the *Thelma*, a Dutch steamer.

*Jamaica. West Indies island ruled by Great Britain. Formerly a tropical paradise, Jamaica is suffering from economic and social confusion following the emancipation of slaves there and throughout the British Empire in the mid-1830's. Once-thriving sugar plantations are now nearly in ruin.

Ferndale. Jamaican sugar plantation on which the Bas-Thornton family is living when the novel opens. Conditions have already deteriorated so badly that the family must live in the overseer's leaking house after the collapse of the family mansion. Although they share this house with farm animals and vermin, their lives seem circuslike, rather than ugly or macabre. The family's five children roam wild.

On her tenth birthday, young Emily Bas-Thornton accidentally discovers Liberty Hill, a squalid refuge originally built by runaway slaves. Within a week, two natural disasters strike the island. An earthquake occurs while the children are visiting the Fernandez estate, Exeter. After they return home, a hurricane razes the remaining plantation buildings. After the rebuilding of the plantation begins, the family sends the children back to England to be educated.

Clorinda. Ship on which the Bas-Thornton and Fernandez children are sent from Jamaica to England. With their families unable to afford passage on a steamer, the children are put aboard the *Clorinda*, a modest merchant barque captained by James Marpole. They freely roam the ship, make friends with the crew, and witness the death of the ship's mascot, a monkey, that plummets from the cross-trees to the deck. Before the ship is out of the West Indies, it is captured by Captain Jonsen's pirate crew, who board it dressed as women and strip it of all its valuables.

*Santa Lucia.** Port in Cuba where the pirates auction off the *Clorinda*'s cargo. Presided over by a mustached, fat-lady (the wife of the chief magistrate), the sale resembles a sideshow. Three of the children with their pirate guide observe a banquet honoring the pirate captain and mate; then they attend a nativity play in a warehouse, where John Bas-Thornton falls to his death, paralleling the fate of the monkey that died aboard the *Clorinda*.

Thelma. Small Dutch steamship carrying a cargo of wild animals destined for a circus that Jonsen's pirates capture. To placate the children, the pirates stage a circus for them on the *Thelma*'s deck; however, the animals are too weak and seasick to perform.

— *Stephen V. Myslinski*

HIPPOLYTUS

Author: Euripides (c. 485-406 B.C.E.)
Type of work: Drama
Type of plot: Tragedy

Time of plot: Antiquity
First performed: *Hippolytos*, 428 B.C.E. (English translation, 1781)

This play, revolving around the forbidden love of Queen Phaedra for her stepson Hippolytus, is set in the royal palace of Troezen and its environs. Much of the tragedy's symbolic significance is located in the nearby woods and meadows and particularly the seashore. Through the characters of Theseus and Phaedra, Athens and Crete also figure prominently.

*Troezen.** Greek city, on the eastern coast of the Peloponnesian Peninsula, that is home of the Athenian king Theseus and his new wife Phaedra. The play's action is set largely in and around their royal palace. In ancient times, aristocratic Greek women tended to be kept indoors, and in the play the interior of the palace is associated with Phaedra's incestuous desire for her stepson Hippolytus, which she tries to conceal. After her secret is revealed, Phaedra hangs herself in her bedroom. The palace is a location of containment and repression whose walls cannot, however, ultimately shut out the forces of desire unleashed by Aphrodite, the goddess of love.

Nature. In the mythical landscape of the play, natural locations are the realm of Artemis, the goddess of hunting and virginity, to whom Hippolytus is abnormally devoted, and of Aphrodite, who uses Phaedra to destroy Hippolytus. Bodies of water, trees, and meadows are suffused with sexual symbolism. For example, the bull that causes Hippolytus's death comes from the sea, which symbolizes, in turn, the elemental power of desire. In contrast to Phaedra, Hippolytus is thus associated with the outdoors, particularly with the forests, where he hunts, and the seashore, where he exercises his horses.

*Crete** (kreet). Greek island in the eastern Mediterranean that is the original home of Phaedra. In mythology, Crete is known for its people's sexual aberrations and excesses. By alluding to Phaedra's relatives, such as Ariadne, Pasiphae, and the Minotaur, and her Cretan origins, Euripides emphasizes her exotic origins and her otherness within Athenian society.

*Athens.** City that Theseus is visiting while most of the play unfolds; he returns to Troezen to find his wife dead. Like all tragedies written by Athenian poets, *Hippolytus* is really discussing issues of importance to citizens of the Athenian democracy. Troezen is, on many levels, a substitute for Athens.

— *David Larmour*

THE HISTORY OF HENRY ESMOND, ESQUIRE:
A Colonel in the Service of Her Majesty Q. Anne

Author: William Makepeace Thackeray (1811-1863)
Type of work: Novel
Type of plot: Bildungsroman

Time of plot: Late seventeenth and early eighteenth centuries
First published: 1852

This novel's title character thinks that he is merely a poor cousin of his family's main line, but he is actually the rightful heir to an English peerage and the family's great estate.

Castlewood (England). Great house in southern England's Hampshire County where Henry Esmond is raised by his cousins in the Castlewood family. There Henry is first succored by Rachel's solicitude, and there he falls in love with Beatrix. The house stands for all that is valuable in Henry's heritage. Henry is the rightful heir to Castlewood, but he stands in an oblique relationship to the Castlewood family inheritance. Castlewood has an art gallery containing portraits by Van Dyck and Dobson. It is in this room where an unhappy Henry is first taken into the bosom of the family.

The Esmond family came into possession of Castlewood in the sixteenth century, when a page named Esmond married the lady of the house. This line gave rise to the viscounts of Castlewood. Neglected by the second viscount, Castlewood Manor was damaged during the civil wars of the seventeenth century, when its clock tower was attacked. Thomas, the third viscount, embarked on an ambitious program of refurbishment, whose residue is still evident in Henry's day.

*Chelsea (CHEL-see). London neighborhood, near Kensington and north of the Thames, where the dowager Viscountess Castlewood maintains her residence. It is the third leg of the Castlewood-Cambridge-Chelsea triangle on which Esmond's family relationships are based.

*Cambridge. University town northeast of London where Esmond is educated. Cambridge is less important primarily as a symbol of how Esmond is distanced from his idyllic boyhood memories of Castlewood and Lady Rachel.

*Newgate Prison. London prison in which Esmond is falsely imprisoned and separated from all he loves. This period is the low point of Esmond's fortunes, although the prisoners are well fed and allowed a good number of visitors. Newgate is less a hellish place of torture than a site of confinement, in which Esmond hones his sense of his inner density and fortifies his moral convictions.

*Kensington (KEN-zing-ton). London neighborhood in which the Castlewoods maintain their in-town residence. Kensington is also the locale of the guard-table at which Henry meets Joseph Addison and other literary luminaries. The guard-table is associated with stimulating companionship and good cheer. William Makepeace Thackeray also uses the table as a vehicle through which to have leading historical figures of the day make brief appearances. The Old Pretender is brought to Kensington in secret and reveals his loutish ways. The Kensington scenes of the novel portray the dynamic coffee-house culture of the time and represent the public sphere as opposed to the aristocratic country-house culture of Castlewood Manor itself.

Castlewood (Virginia). The second Castlewood manor is an estate on the right bank of the Potomac River, in Virginia's West Moreland County, north of the Rappahannock. There Henry and Rachel spend the idyllic "Indian summer" of their lives. Their descendants flourish there growing tobacco.

— *Nicholas Birns*

THE HISTORY OF PENDENNIS: His Fortunes and Misfortunes, His Friends, and His Greatest Enemy

Author: William Makepeace Thackeray (1811-1863)
Type of work: Novel
Type of plot: Bildungsroman

Time of plot: Mid-nineteenth century
First published: serial, 1848-1850; book, 1849-1850

In tracing the development of Arthur Pendennis (Pen) as a writer and human being, this novel plays upon the age-old distinction between town (London) and country; however, the values accorded these areas are fluid and dependent on the mind of the beholder.

Fairoaks. Pen's family home, based upon Larkbeare, a real house near the town of Ottery St. Mary, in southern England's Devon County, where William Makepeace Thackeray's mother and stepfather lived. To its female inhabitants, Pen's mother and her ward, Laura Bell, Fairoaks is quite sufficient. When an urban observer notes its shortcomings, Laura almost boasts that it supports, not pheasants, but nine hens, a rooster, a pig, and an old dog. Near the end of the novel, Laura holds Fairoaks out as a haven to be returned to, although she admits temptation can enter even there.

Clavering Park. Village near Ottery St. Mary in which Pen appears to seduce a lower-class girl, setting off gossip that flashes throughout the village to reach the ears of his mother. Based on the real village of Escot Park, Clavering Park is typical rural village, parochial and insular. The narrator points out that the village is prettier from a distance; its Anglican church has lost members to the New Church, while a ribbon factory has opened on the banks of its river.

Clavering. Ancestral home to the Clavering family that at first appears as a romantic prospect to the young Pen, as he plays in its grounds. After the scion of the family reopens the house, its ludicrous allegorical depictions of Clavering ancestors are scathingly described, and the chief memory of Sir Frank about its hallowed halls is that his father caned him there. The house's old trappings and new furnishings are discussed in a purely financial light; their worth is solely monetary to its inhabitants, and their acquisition based on their fashionability.

Chatteris. Larger country town in which Pen first falls in love with an older actress appearing at its often less-than-full theater. Based on Exeter, Chatteris appears to be a representative rural town of the period before the appearance of the railroad.

Oxbridge University. Fictional university whose St. Boniface College Pen attends. The name "Oxbridge" is a conflation of the names of England's two greatest universities, Oxford and Cambridge, and St. Boniface is modeled on Cambridge's Trinity College, which Thackeray attended. The imaginary university has all the romantic apparatus of the real ones—dreaming spires, ivy-covered buildings, and gleaming green quads—but for Pen, it proves to be not a haven for learning but another place where he proves his capacity for irresponsibility.

***Tunbridge Wells.** Location of Lady Clavering's villa, to which she flees after Sir Frank's Derby day disaster. Among its recently built "antiquities," Pen and Blanche Amory seem to fall in love; however, the narrator's facetious reference to them as "Phillis and Corydon" (classical pastoral lovers) hints that in such an environment their romance will be short-lived.

***London.** Chief city of England which, to the inhabitants of Clavering Park, is "Babylon." In a sense, the city never loses an aura of temptation. Pen remarks on how the city changes people. In his case, he *is* changed, for a time, into a self-proclaimed "Sadducee," a person for whom life is a "transaction." Despite these moral dangers, the scope and variety of life in London appeal as much to Thackeray as they did to writers such as Charles Dickens and Samuel Johnson (who is referred to several times in the novel as having frequented a particular location). Pen, like Thackeray, welcomes the chance London gives him to observe the seamier side of life: boxers, pickpockets, burglars, cracksmen.

Lamb Court. London neighborhood near the city's legal center where Pen and George Warrington have rooms. As the narrator points out, the roses in the Middle Temple Gardens that once gave their colors to the war between York and Lancaster could not grow in polluted mid-nineteenth century London.

— *William Laskowski*

THE HIVE

Author: Camilo José Cela (1916-   )
Type of work: Novel
Type of plot: Social realism

Time of plot: December, 1943
First published: La colmena, 1951 (English translation, 1953)

The "hive" of this novel's title is Madrid—dark, crowded, chaotic, and impoverished. The narrative covers three days in the lives of numerous characters during the dictatorship and economic depression after the Spanish Civil War. The novel's realistic vignettes portray a decadent Madrid in which people cling, sometimes desperately, to their pretensions and hopes. Because of the novel's unflattering portrait of the city, for many years the Spanish government banned the book's publication.

***Madrid.** Spain's capital city, in which a person's fate is determined by economic status and simple chance. In one passage, Camilo José Cela writes of a Madrid street as assuming, at nightfall, a "half-hungry, half-mysterious air, while a little wind, prowling like a wolf, whistles between the houses." He then describes with the precision of an anthropologist who stays out late the rich seeking diversion, the homeless, those who wander from bar to bar.

In another scene, a poor man finds himself sitting next to a policeman in a bar and offers the policeman an opinion about the city's law enforcement policies. "'It doesn't seem fair to me to arrest the black-market women in the underground. People have got to eat. . . . I think if a few poor women sell cigarettes it's wrong for you of the police to be after them.'" The policeman answers that he does as he is told. The policeman's life story, revealed in a few stark paragraphs before this reply, helps make his short statement resonate throughout the book. For many in the novel, the best odds for survival lie in doing as one is told.

Café La Delicia (ka-FAY lah day-LEE-see-uh). Madrid café which, despite its name, offers less delight than tedium. Most of its patrons are impoverished, having barely enough to pay for the cups of coffee they buy so they will be allowed to spend their hours there. The café is owned and operated by the tyrannical Doña Rosa, who owns apartment buildings as well. A ruthless landlord who does not hesitate to express reactionary opinions, she is treated with obsequiousness by her employees and customers.

Doña Rosa represents the type of person who succeeds in Madrid's brutal social structure. She treats others with varying degrees of rudeness according to their economic standing. Nearly all of these others, including would-be writers, gypsies, and women grasping at the last straws of gentility, are neither as fortunate nor as able as she is with money. Doña Rosa screams at her waiters, orders them to run down and rough up a non-paying customer, and enjoys causing pain. Some of those who suffer her outbursts resent them, but frequently her staff and customers, in keeping with their oppressed and defeated state, rationalize their situation and even identify with her.

Apartment building. Madrid building in which an old woman, Doña Margot, is murdered. Its residents hold a meeting at which they discuss the crime and what they should do. For some, it is an opportunity to demonstrate their ability to speak and appear wise and capable. In truth, the residents are helpless. The police scarcely seem interested in the murder, and there is nothing the residents can do to remedy the social rupture of the crime. However, they waste no time in finding a scapegoat in the person of the victim's son, a homosexual man who is not present to defend himself against their insinuations.

The apartment building also represents a hive within the hive. Many of the novel's events either take place in, or are discussed in, the building's many rooms. In its various apartments, characters plan and tell lies to one another about what they hope to accomplish outside the building's walls. Readers can, to some extent, piece together how the various conversations relate to one another and how they accord with what actually occurs. In general, however, there is little honey to show for the considerable buzzing.

— *Eric Howard*

HIZAKURIGE

Author: Jippensha Ikku (1765-1831)
Type of work: Novel
Type of plot: Farce

Time of plot: Early nineteenth century
First published: Tōkaidōchū hizakurige, 1802-1822
  (English translation, 1929)

This popular Japanese novel is the story of two good-humored scoundrels, Yaji and Kita, who undertake a footloose journey of adventure and misadventure along the great Tokaido Highway leading from Edo to Kyoto. To the Japanese, the book's earthy humor typifies the true "Edokko"—the brash and devil-may-care Tokyoite of the nineteenth century. This novel portrays all the varied colors in Japan's Tokugawa Era but does not offer elaborate descriptions of the places that the travelers visit.

***Tokaido Highway** (toh-ki-doh). Also known as the Eastern Sea Road, a road running along Japan's Pacific coastline, on which Yaji and Kita travel. Organized and administered by the central government in the seventh century, the road was usually easier to travel on than others, except that its rivers were often more difficult to cross. The road was the most important communication route during the Edo period. In the modern era, the Tokaido saw heavy development as a transportation corridor, industrial belt, and the most heavily populated area of Japan.

***Edo** (ay-doh). Japan's capital city; later renamed Tokyo. Edo was a small fishing village with a run-down castle nearby when in 1590 it was given to Tokugawa Ieyasu to be the center of his domain. He developed a grand castle and town that by 1750 had a population of as many as one million people. It became the central political city and an important economic center. By the end of the Edo period in 1868, the city had grown so dominant that the new government retained the city as their capital, renaming it Tokyo, for "Eastern Capital," in deference to the former capital at Kyoto.

***Ise shrine** (ee-say). Shinto shrine dedicated to the ancestors of the Japanese imperial family that is considered to be the most sacred place in Japan. Located in the city of Ise, on the south-central coast of Hōnshu, the shrine is visited by thousands of pilgrims each year and is the destination of Yaji and Kita. They make a small offering of rice at the family temple but usually show little regard for religious customs or decorum.

***Hakone Range** (ha-koh-nay). Mountain range that Yaji and Kita cross during the journey. The climb of twenty miles across the mountains was one of the famous parts of the journey between Tokyo and Kyoto. A well-known Japanese poem states that it is not possible to cross the Hakone range even on horseback, but Yaji and Kita joke about loin cloths with a silly ballad singer before they begin their crossing.

***Kanazawa** (kah-nah-zah-wah). Seaside city where Yaji and Kita notice that all the teahouses have two stories with balustrades and overhanging galleries allowing for views of the sea. The girls who work at the teahouse beg for the two heroes to enter and try their food. The men enter, order fish and wine, joke with the serving girls, and then ask directions from a boy who happens by, but he refuses to talk with Yaji or Kita until they buy him a rice cake.

*Osaka (oh-sah-kah). Large city about 320 miles southwest of Edo where Yaji and Kita's journey ends. While passing through this city, Yaji and Kita tell stories and sing songs. The ancient name for Osaka is "Naniwa," used by the heroes in their singing and storytelling.

— *Jonathan L. Thorndike*

H.M.S. PINAFORE: Or, The Lass That Loved a Sailor

Author: W. S. Gilbert (1836-1911)
Type of work: Drama
Type of plot: Operetta

Time of plot: Late nineteenth century
First performed: 1878; first published, 1878

This play is set entirely on the quarterdeck of the imaginary British warship Pinafore *resting at anchor in a naval port. The ship becomes a microcosm of the nation in which the operetta satirizes contemporary British ideas about social class.*

Pinafore. Warship of the Royal Navy that is tied up at Portsmouth in southern England. The operetta is set on the ship's open quarterdeck and poop deck. Stage directions indicate that the curtain rises to show sailors polishing the ship's brasswork, splicing ropes, and engaging in similar busy work. Prominent in the stage set are the rigging and the bulwarks of a man-of-war of the Napoleonic era. Before designing his stage set, W. S. Gilbert, who was always interested in things nautical, visited Lord Nelson's flagship *Victory* in Portsmouth harbor, making sketches of the ship to familiarize himself with every physical detail. This realism, like the perfect seriousness that Gilbert required of his actors, gives piquancy to the whimsy of the play's topsy-turvy satire, which is exemplified most strikingly in the ship's distinctly non-bellicose name, taken from a word for a dress for a young girl.

Earlier in the nineteenth century, Britain's Royal Navy had been exceptionally class conscious. The details of the ship, typical of the era of the Napoleonic Wars, make the *Pinafore* distinctly obsolete in the rapidly evolving naval milieu of the later nineteenth century

and suggests that its Captain Corcoran's ideas about strict naval discipline and rigid class structure are equally outmoded. Warships were normally male domains, their quarterdecks reserved for officers; however, to the *Pinafore*'s quarterdeck Gilbert brings not only the entire crew but a female peddler, who is at the low end of the social scale, and the First Lord of the Admiralty and his large coterie of female relatives, who are at the other end. Thus the ship becomes a microcosm in which Gilbert can explore the absurdities of both the rigid British caste system and the extremism of social levelers who wanted to do away with all class distinction.

*Portsmouth. Major British naval base on the English Channel. Pictures of *H.M.S. Pinafore*'s original stage set show a backdrop depicting the buildings of Portsmouth. The great mutiny of the British fleet at nearby Spithead in 1797 was put down from Portsmouth—a circumstance that for knowledgeable audiences adds to the irony of Sir Joseph's naval reforms in the play.

— *David W. Cole*

HOMEWARD: Songs by the Way

Author: Æ (George William Russell, 1867-1935)   *First published:* 1894
Type of work: Poetry

This collection of sixty-seven short metaphysical poems explores the alienation of human beings from their celestial home in soft, evocative opposition of the natural world and one's true "home."

Celestial home. George William Russell depicts man as a king who has descended to earth from the celestial realm he never describes. In the opening poem, "Recognition" and later in "Tragedy," Russell anchors the idea: "Recognition's" plowman, though a "slave" on earth, "finds himself a king" deep inside. The "gods" his "brothers" reside in this realm. The reading man in "Tragedy" is scorned by the evening stars: "King . . . thou art slave and we are free." He is an "exile" turning "homeward" to the stars "sick and slow." In "Comfort": "In the great ancestral spheres waits the throne for you."

Nature. Russell views nature neoplatonically, as a window through which readers darkly see the higher reality. The wind, clouds, and ever-passing time remind readers of the instability of life. Its beauty (well served by Russell) is a dim reflection of the higher realm's beauty. Fittingly, the natural world provides metaphors: his arid heart is like the "arid desert sky" ("Dawn of Darkness"); the hills are altars on which "sacrifices burn." While in this life, the wanderer is closest to his real home while in nature.

Cities. Sparse references to the urban world in these poems are invariably negative, expressed in terms such as "iron city," the city's "din," and the "fierce-pulsed city." The poet's life typically is portrayed in villages, in cottages, and on hillsides, to which "the city" provides a dark counterpoint.

*India. Despite Russell's Irish roots, the only land he specifies by name is India, and that in but three poems. He taps the mystical side of the land and people.

— *Joseph P. Byrne*

THE HOMEWOOD TRILOGY

Author: John Edgar Wideman (1941-   )   *Time of plot:* Mid-nineteenth century to the 1980's
Type of work: Novel   *First published:* 1985: *Damballah*, 1981; *Hiding*
Type of plot: Psychological realism   *Place*, 1981; *Sent for You Yesterday*, 1983

Place is essential in this trilogy, as all three parts of this work are set in an African American neighborhood that defines the lives of characters in the present at the same time that it gives them important parts of their past. Homewood is thus the repository of values and history which supports many of the characters and their families in the novel.

*Homewood. Long-established black neighborhood in Pittsburgh, Pennsylvania. The three volumes brought together to form *The Homewood Trilogy* are set in, or circle around, this black section of Pittsburgh. As John Edgar Wideman writes in his preface to the volume, the trilogy offers an investigation from many angles, "not so much of a physical location, Homewood . . . but of a cul-ture, a way of seeing and being seen. *Homewood* is an idea, a reflection of how its inhabitants act and think."

The three volumes of *The Homewood Trilogy*—two novels and a collection of a dozen stories—depict the life and history of one black neighborhood, a district that has all the strengths and dangers of any inner city. It is a neighborhood of houses and yards, of gathering places (the barber shop, for example, or bars like the Brass Rail and the Velvet Slipper), and of other institutions like the Elks Club, the Homewood African Methodist Episcopal Zion Church, and the A&P supermarket on Homewood Avenue. It is the home of John French and his wife Freeda in the 1920's, of their daughter Lizabeth and her husband Edgar Lawson twenty years later, and their grandsons John and Tommy Lawson forty years later. Cassina Way is the street on which these generations live, and where John French dies after a heart attack (wedged between bathtub and toilet). It is a neighborhood in which crime is common, drugs are taking over by the 1980's, and characters may be killed.

Homewood is also an area with a history, even if that history is slipping away by the end of the twentieth century. The neighborhood dates all the way back to the middle of the nineteenth century (as related in the story "The Beginning of Homewood" in *Damballah*) and the escaped slave Sybela Owens fleeing north. Homewood provides myths and meanings that can be sustaining to its residents, especially the narrator (and Wideman persona), John Lawson, born here in 1941 and returning to Homewood after some years away, and just now beginning to understand its richness and meaning. This community—its history, music, and language—provides a cultural safety net for its residents in a hostile world. "Homewood wasn't bricks and boards," as Lucy Tate says of its residents in *Sent for You Yesterday*. "Homewood was them singing and loving and getting where they needed to get. They made these streets. That's why Homewood was real once."

The three volumes of the novel encapsulate this history and heritage, and describe the friendship, family, and community that are the antidotes to the isolation and alienation of so much of twentieth century urban life. The stories told by and about Lucy Tate, Mother Bess, Sybela Owens, John French, and the others are part of a living African American past that Wideman (like Toni Morrison, in novels such as *Beloved*, 1987) wants his readers to acknowledge and celebrate.

Bruston Hill. Neighborhood within and above Homewood. It is to Bruston Hill where Tommy (John Lawson's brother) goes in *Hiding Place* when he is wanted for murder. He hides out in the shack of Mother Bess, the family's matriarch and Sybela's granddaughter, and a hermit whose family history comes out in this section of *The Homewood Trilogy*.

— *David Peck*

THE HONORARY CONSUL

Author: Graham Greene (1904-1991)
Type of work: Novel
Type of plot: Psychological realism

Time of plot: Early to mid-1970's
First published: 1973

This story of a bungled kidnapping has a complex international flavor, with Paraguayan rebels mistakenly seizing a British honorary consul while trying to kidnap the American ambassador to Argentina. The novel provides a rich cross-cultural scope to the plot through its ethnically diverse characters, while weaving the protagonist's quest to find his father.

*Paraná River. River that forms part of the border between Paraguay and Argentina. The river also serves as a device that connects Dr. Eduardo Plarr's childhood memories and his current involvement in the kidnapping of a British honorary consul by Paraguayan rebels. Plarr was born near the river, of an English father and an Argentine mother. After studying to become a physician in Buenos Aires, Plarr has returned to the river town of Corrientes in the region of his birth. Thus, the Paraná becomes a symbol of cross-cultural movement while reinforcing the political enclosures that undermine family ties.

*Buenos Aires. Argentina's capital city which Plarr visits every three months to see his mother. After the British consul, Charley Fortnum, is kidnapped by Paraguayans who mistake him for the American ambassador,

Plarr visits the British embassy in a futile quest to get the British government to put pressure on the Paraguayan government to meet the rebels' demands so that Fortnum will be freed.

Kidnapper's hut. Situated between the Plarr's port city and the bend of the river, this mud hut consists of two sparse rooms. Charley Fortnum and his guards occupy one room, and the other room is used by the rest of the rebels. Plarr visits Fortnum there to treat a wound he receives while trying to escape. As both Fortnum and Plarr are cooped in this hut, Fortnum discovers that Plarr is the father of the child his wife is carrying and begins to understand "the tangle" of his unborn child's ancestry.

Cemetery. Site of the funeral of Plarr, who is shot by the Argentine police when he tries to help resolve the kidnapping crisis. Fortnum is rescued, however, and attends the funeral accompanied by his wife, who is pregnant with Plarr's baby. The scene is rich in dramatic irony. In his mind, Fortnum compares the funeral to the "diplomatic cocktails" that bring together select dignitaries, including Colonel Perez and the renowned author Jorge Julio Saavedra, who delivers the eulogy for Plarr. Fortnum and the readers know that Saavedra falsely accuses the rebels of killing Plarr to claim him as a local hero because of his Paraguayan ties.

— *Mabel Khawaja*

HOPSCOTCH

Author: Julio Cortázar (1914-1984)
Type of work: Novel
Type of plot: Parable

Time of plot: 1950's
First published: Rayuela, 1963 (English translation, 1966)

While this unusually structured novel's action is divided between Paris and Buenos Aires, its settings are not so much physical places as states of mind. Both cities serve as metaphysical game boards for protagonist Horacio Oliveira, who is trying to find a way of living that embraces life's absurdity and breaks free from the linear constraints of bourgeois thinking. The unusual locales toward the novel's end, including a circus and a madhouse, reflect Oliveira's increasingly disturbed mind, the effect of which is in turn made available to readers in the author's invitation to read the chapters in different orders.

*****Paris.** France's capital city is Oliveira's residence during the 1950's. Julio Cortázar's depiction of Paris focuses on the indolent, mostly nocturnal lives of a group of expatriate intellectuals and artists who call themselves the Serpent Club. They meet at the apartment of La Maga, Horacio's lover, to drink, listen to jazz, and discuss philosophy and the arts. Within this cramped set of rooms, Horacio confronts the incongruity between his friends' esoteric musings and harsh physical reality in the sudden death of Rocamodour, La Maga's neglected infant son. Despite the group's emotional intensity, Horacio regards his relationships with its members as transitory and contingent, as exemplified by his games of chance encounter with La Maga in the Parisian streets.

For Horacio, "Paris is one big metaphor," which he tries to decipher as a means of attaining a new kind of

clarity, the "heaven" associated with the novel's recurrent game of hopscotch motif. Despite his efforts to focus single-mindedly on his existential project, the city sometimes throws random encounters in his path that force him to acknowledge his bond to humanity; for example, both the old man run down in the street and the pathetic pianist Berthe Trépat draw him out of his solipsism temporarily.

*****Buenos Aires.** Argentina's capital is Horacio's native city, to which he returns after deciding that Paris cannot provide the answers he seeks. In Buenos Aires, Horacio continues his quest for an authentic life, which is aided and complicated by his renewed relationship with his childhood friend, known as Traveler. Although Horacio reacts to his homeland with a mixture of love and European condescension, Talita, Traveler's wife, discerns that "for Oliveira being in Buenos Aires was exactly the same as if he had been in Bucharest." More and more, Horacio withdraws into a cerebral solitude, devising complex word games and outlandish schemes, such as the bridge of boards that he and Traveler construct between their apartment windows, which face each other across a street. Talita is literally suspended between the two men, and her presence in Horacio's life acts both as a source of tension with Traveler and a reminder of Horacio's failure to love and comfort La Maga, whose apparition he begins to see frequently.

Circus. In contrast to his situation in Paris, Horacio is forced to devote more of his time to working, first in the circus as an odd-job man. While the circus provides an appropriately absurd venue for Horacio's considerations of life, it also gives him an inkling of transcendence; he gazes up to the hole in the top of the main tent

and sees it as "an image of consummation." This symbol is put in opposition to the madhouse bought by the circus owner.

Madhouse. Subterranean and infernal morgue in which Horacio, Traveler, and Talita all go to work. In this last consistent setting in the novel, Horacio feels perfectly comfortable, finding in the inmates representatives of humanity who are free from the prison of reason. At the same time, however, Horacio's own sanity gradually collapses, to a point at which his paranoid fear compels him to erect an elaborate and ridiculous system of defense in his room against the violent invasion that he believes Traveler plans to make. After this crescendo of madness, the text disintegrates into a number of "expendable chapters," jumping from location to location and idea to idea.

— *Lynn Wells*

HORACE

Author: Pierre Corneille (1606-1684)
Type of work: Drama
Type of plot: Tragedy

Time of plot: Antiquity
First performed: 1640; first published, 1641 (English translation, 1656)

Pierre Corneille's play is set in the house of the Roman Horace family as an avoidable civil war breaks out between two allies: Rome and Alba. In this domestic setting, the violence of the civil war is illustrated by the irrational and fanatical behavior of certain dysfunctional family members.

Horace house. Roman home of the play's title character, Horace, and his father, Old Horace. Corneille's tragedy nicely illustrates the disastrous effects of characters who strive to impose their will upon others. Both Horace and his father believe in male domination of women. Within their house, women's opinions and feelings are ignored and they expect their wives, daughters, and daughters-in-law blindly to obey them. Their home has become an elegant prison in which the female inmates fear violent outbursts by domineering males. Domestic violence is a constant threat to them, especially during a crisis, such as the civil war in which this play is set.

As this tragedy begins, Sabine, who was born in Alba, expresses to her Roman friend Julie her displeasure that

vain Roman and Alban leaders have undertaken an absurd war. Her sister-in-law Camille visits her and tells her of her desire to marry Curiace, who is Sabine's brother. Far from being a pleasant discussion between two sisters-in-law, who care for each other, their conversation reveals their deep understanding of the fanaticism and violent tempers of the younger and older Horaces. The two women understand all too well that the two Horace men have created a tense atmosphere at home because they do not tolerate disagreements from the women in their families. The closed space in which these women live magnifies their justifiable fears. They know that the younger and older Horaces will treat them violently, but they do not know what will provoke these irrational men. The younger Horace kills his sister

Camille because she dares to state the truth: that the war Rome has undertaken against a weaker ally is unjust. The murder takes place in his own home. This tragedy has a profound effect on theatergoers who come to rec-ognize the disturbing links between the cruelty of civil war with the very real dangers of domestic violence and male efforts to dominate the women in their homes.

— *Edmund J. Campion*

THE HORSE'S MOUTH

Author: Joyce Cary (1888-1957)
Type of work: Novel
Type of plot: Picaresque

Time of plot: Late 1930's
First published: 1944

This vivid portrait of a British artist is set in London, a city that the artist Gulley Jimson knows as well as his own skin. It is his hometown, the source of his inspiration, the site of his struggles and trials as a man and an artist, and the location of his vision for a "new Jerusalem," where the dream of a more humane world might be rendered in paintings. In this novel, Joyce Cary offers a reconstruction in language of the artist's evolving view of the city.

***London.** Capital city of the British Empire, whose neighborhoods, landmarks, public houses, and climate provide a constant source of energy for a maverick artist. His friends, admirers, rivals, and passersby represent the rich variety of life in Great Britain just before the war that significantly transformed the city. Other parts of the city are brought into the narrative as Jimson pursues his quest for a place to paint. The wealthy patron Hickson lives in "Portland Place, top end, near the park," one of the more affluent sections of the city. The Beeders, who are collectors, live in a modern development called Capel Mansions, a relatively tasteful, slightly ostentatious group of town houses that Jimson describes as "fine large new buildings in the playbrick design." The sculptor's model Lolie is described as good stock by her husband, who identifies her as being from Bethnal Green. Sara Monday, Jimson's lifelong, truest love, lives with her common-law husband in Chattfield Buildings, grim, squalid, deteriorating tenements probably built as inexpensive lodgings for the poor. These locations, as well as public houses in Chelsea, Hammersmith, and Belgravia—bohemian quarters near the city's center—contribute to the ambience of the metropolis and deftly suggest its complexity. A bus tour that Jimson and his admirer Nosy Barbon take provides additional details to deepen the picture.

***River Thames** (tehmz). England's greatest river and London's connection to the sea. Jimson refers to the river as "the old serpent, symbol of nature and love," suggesting its timeless allure, as well as its primal power and its capacity for engendering the strongest emotional response. The river's serpentine course through London is suggestive of Jimson's peregrinations through the city, and its Greenbank section, near the city's center, is the location of Jimson's home. Familiar London landmarks, such as the fabled Tower of London and the London Bridge, are just upriver from Greenbank. What Jimson calls his old studio is actually a deserted boathouse down by the water.

Greenbank. Maps of London list the section that Cary calls "Greenbank" as two words, and while he is clearly using the geographical facts of that site, his adjustment of the name is designed to permit a degree of imaginative alteration. His intention is to draw on fundamental features that his British readers would recognize to highlight his rendition of the neighborhood. Not far from many world-famous tourist spots, Jimson's Greenbank is a working-class realm, gritty and blunt, where the homeless shelter Elsinore is placed. Cary gives it an Ellam Street address, another invention as there is no Ellam Street in London, and also places his friend Plantie's cobbler shop there in a basement off Greenbank.

— *Leon Lewis*

THE HOUND OF THE BASKERVILLES

Author: Sir Arthur Conan Doyle (1859-1930)
Type of work: Novel
Type of plot: Detective and mystery

Time of plot: Late nineteenth century
First published: serial, 1901-1902; book, 1902

Like most Sherlock Holmes stories, the case in this story begins in Victorian London, at the lodgings shared by Holmes and his chronicler, Dr. John Watson. From there, the action quickly moves to Baskerville Hall and the surrounding moors, which provide one of the most atmospheric settings in any Sherlock Holmes story.

*Baker Street. London street at whose imaginary 221B address Holmes and Watson share lodgings. There, visitors are admitted by Mrs. Hudson, the landlady who lives on the ground floor and takes them upstairs to Holmes and Watson's sitting room. The novel opens with the house being watched during the visit of Dr. Mortimer, a concerned neighbor of Sir Henry Baskerville.

Baskerville Hall. Ancestral Devonshire home of the Baskerville family, located on the edge of Dartmoor, a wild, rugged area in the south of England. Baskerville Hall is fourteen miles from Princetown, which is best known for is proximity to the high-security prison of Dartmoor, from which the convicted murderer Selden escapes. The hall is approached through ornate wrought iron gates at the end of a tree-lined drive that opens out onto an area of turf. The central and original part of the house has two towers that indicate the house's age, as they are crenellated and have loopholes. The inside of the house also indicates an age going back to Tudor times; it has a large, high-ceilinged central hall raftered with age-blackened oak. The room also has a large fireplace and oak paneling and is illuminated by high windows set with stained glass depicting family coats of arms. A gallery running around the hall is reached by a double stair. The narrow, dimly lit dining room that opens from the hall has a raised dais at one end, where members of the family dine; in earlier times, their dependents would have dined on the lower level. At one end of this room is a minstrels gallery. The walls here are adorned with family portraits, including one that provides Holmes with the clue to the identity of the villain.

Baskerville Hall has been recently expanded and has wings on each side of the original house constructed from granite blocks, with high chimneys and high, angled roofs. The bedrooms in one wing are reached from the gallery off the central hall. The room in which Watson stays overlooks the front lawn and has views of the moor beyond. The other wing is not occupied, except when Barrymore uses an empty room to send secret signals to Selden.

The grounds of Baskerville Hall contain a long yew alley, in which Sir Charles Baskerville is found dead. The thick yew hedges are twelve feet tall and eight feet apart. There is a central gravel path with grass on either side running from the house to a dilapidated summerhouse at the far end. About half way down the alley a four-foot-high, white-painted wicket gate gives access to the moor. It is kept padlocked.

*Dartmoor. Wild, sparsely inhabited part of southern England Devonshire region that is dotted with steep rocky peaks and valleys. Sheep and ponies roam freely, and the hillsides are covered with heather, bracken, and gorse. In autumn—the season in which the novel is set—the moors are bleak, and the weather can quickly change, covering the moors with thick fog. The novel describes the hillsides as covered with stones circles, the remains of numerous Neolithic hut circles. The novel's stone circles are both more numerous and larger than the real Neolithic circles found in that region of England.

Grimpen. Hamlet on the edge of Dartmoor, four miles from Baskerville Hall that contains only two large buildings—a public inn and Dr. Mortimer's house, which stands on the hillside above the rest. Also close by is Lafter Hall, the home of Mr. Franklin, whose rooftop telescope is instrumental in tracking the comings and goings of people on the moors.

Merripit House. Home of Stapleton and his sister. Located near Grimpen, it is reached along a narrow grass track from the road between Grimpen and Basker-ville Hall. It was once a farm and is surrounded by an orchard of old, stunted trees. Outwardly, it appears to be as bleak as its surroundings, but inside it is elegantly furnished. Not far away is **Grimpen Mire**, a treacherous part of the moor, which looks green, but whose bright patches mask bog holes which can swallow a man. Mr. Stapleton discovers a path running through the moor that leads to Grimpen Mine, where the hound is hidden.

— *Pauline Morgan*

THE HOUSE BY THE CHURCHYARD

Author: Joseph Sheridan Le Fanu (1814-1873)
Type of work: Novel
Type of plot: Horror

Time of plot: Mid-eighteenth century
First published: 1863

Set in a small Irish town on the outskirts of Dublin, this novel evokes a nostalgic sense of the past through its panoramic depiction of ordinary people who seem to embody the sensibilities of small-town life a century earlier. Joseph Sheridan Le Fanu deliberately romanticizes the story's homely setting to offset revelations of dark deeds in the lives of several characters.

*Chapelizod. Small town on the banks of Ireland's River Liffey, described as "the gayest and prettiest of the outpost villages in which old Dublin took a complacent pride." Chapelizod serves as the setting for several of Le Fanu's early ghost stories, and like other Irish country towns in his fiction, its mundane character helps throw into sharp relief the extraordinary experiences of individual townsfolk.

At first, the town seems the picture of country charm and simplicity. The narrator, reviewing his fond childhood memories of the place, imagines it even quainter a century before with many comforting features: a mix of orchards and formally planted poplar trees along the river banks, "merry" streets lined by houses with colorful doors, cozy inns and public houses in which the locals congregate, and a church that serves the entire populace. Banquets, parties, and fairs provide regular diversions. Although Chapelizod is home to a variety of people, its social life is centered around a local regiment of the Royal Irish Artillery, which at the time of the story is not engaged in battle and seems less a military presence than a social class seamlessly woven into the fabric of town life. The foibles and eccentricities of the soldiers do not differ from those of the rustics native to the town, and Chapelizod seems to nurture their more amusing personality quirks.

Despite the appearance of harmony it projects, Chapelizod is not without problems. The story proper begins on a somber note, with an approaching storm conveying "a weight in the atmosphere, and a sort of undefined menace brooding over the little town, as if unseen crime or danger—some mystery of iniquity—was stealing into the heart of it." The storm sets the mood for the midnight burial at the church with which the story opens. This event introduces the melancholy Arthur Mervyn and eventually proves the catalyst for uncovering duplicitous behavior of several of the town's more prominent figures, notably Captain Devereaux and Charles Nutter, each of whom will eventually be exposed for marital indiscretions, and Paul Dangerfield, who will be revealed a murderer living under an assumed identity. Because the community is so familiar and tightly knit, nearly every person in town is disturbed by the revelation of these crimes.

Though the appeal of Chapelizod is not illusory, the idealized version evoked by the narrator is. The passage of a century has reduced the old village to a handful of artifacts and ruins that allow the imagination to conjure a more romantic image than is seen in Chapelizod's current industrialized incarnation. But the truth of life in the town is somewhat less rosy than nostalgia admits. At best, it shows that "the palmy days" of Chapelizod are "more pleasant to read about, and dream of, than they were to live in." At worst, they confirm that "the golden age lingers in no corner of the earth, but is really quite gone and over everywhere."

Tiled House. Gloomy mansion on a lonely bend of the road leading away from Chapelizod. Among all the residences described in the novel, it provides the sharpest contrast to the pleasant facade of life in Chapelizod. In its anecdotal history, the house is haunted by both the spirit of a man with a cut throat and a spectral hand. Similarly, its temporary tenant, Arthur Mervyn, is haunted by the ghosts of the dead—in this case the memory of his father, who died in shame after being betrayed, and whom Mervyn has sworn to avenge upon his return to Chapelizod. The mystery surrounding the house is symbolic of the mystery surrounding Mervyn, who dresses in black and fraternizes with the townspeople under an alias.

— *Stefan Dziemianowicz*

THE HOUSE BY THE MEDLAR TREE

Author: Giovanni Verga (1840-1922)
Type of work: Novel
Type of plot: Impressionistic realism

Time of plot: Mid-nineteenth century
First published: I Malavoglia, 1881 (partial English translation, 1890, 1953; complete translation, 1964)

While this family saga avoids lengthy descriptions of the Sicilian village in which it is set, it projects the right images, strategic details, and resonant words to throw readers directly into the village's atmosphere.

*Trezza.** Village on the east coast of Sicily. Verga's family saga could only take place in a village as claustrophobic and as removed from the opportunities offered by the broader world as Trezza. There, superstition motivates action more strongly than the nominal Roman Catholic religion. Villagers all know one another and know each other's family histories. They wrest their livings from land and sea, and the novel presents details of their daily work realistically. The very repetitiveness of the descriptions conveys the monotony of existence in the village.

Villagers thrive in good times and almost perish in evil ones. Members of families work together to pay their debts and provide dowries for their daughters. Marriage is sometimes for love but more often because of family needs. Some strive to rise above their class and discover how impossible this is. When one member of the Malavoglia family commits an act of violence and runs afoul of the law, the entire family is stigmatized. Even the innocent are defeated because of the bad reputation of one family member. Neighbors gossip and foretell misfortune. Honor must be upheld at any human cost.

Uncle Crucifix, the local usurer, is a known cheat with whom villagers must nevertheless conduct business. Padron 'Ntoni, the Malavoglia patriarch, slaves to repay a loan. His life is guided by the wisdom of ancient Sicilian proverbs. A younger Malavoglia serves a prison term. A daughter sacrifices herself by leaving home when she brings disgrace upon her family. The tragedy of the Malavoglia family is that of limited possibilities, and the village is one of the reasons their possibilities are limited.

A real Sicilian village, approximately ten miles north of Catania, modern Trezza is overrun by tourists who savor its quaint charm. In Verga's time, the village was more remote, a hinterland of Western civilization, though still in Sicily, an island associated with pastoral poetry since antiquity.

*Sicily.** Island off the southern tip of the Italian peninsula, which, while an integral part of modern Italy, has a distinctive history and culture of its own. The island is a real presence throughout *The House by the Medlar Tree*. Verga knew well its loneliness, isolation, and sometimes hostile face, and he never forgot the courage and dignity of its people. The sense of humans at the mercy of fate—

or naturalistic determinism—is especially strong in his Sicilian stories. In this novel and in his other writings, he developed a standard Italian diction that echoes in every sentence the rhythms of the Sicilian dialect, a tongue which itself has a substantial poetic literature. This is sparse, dignified writing, resembling classical tragedy in some ways. Verga founded a school of southern Italian writing that is not unlike "southern schools" in the United States and elsewhere.

Deeply influenced by the writings of Émile Zola and Zola's belief in the effects of environment and heredity, Verga was nevertheless an inverted romantic. He admired the Sicilian code of honor and the eloquence and courtliness of the island's people. He respected the hard work and strength of character that enabled Sicilians to endure poverty and whatever the fates that brooded over the land sent.

Medlar tree. Tree growing beside the Malavoglia house in Trezza that symbolizes the family, whose roots go deep into the Sicilian soil and who—like the tree—are dependent upon the erratic elements of nature for their survival. (A member of the rose family, the medlar produces a fruit resembling crab apples that is used in making preserves.)

— *Allene Phy-Olsen*

THE HOUSE IN PARIS

Author: Elizabeth Bowen (1899-1973)
Type of work: Novel
Type of plot: Psychological realism

Time of plot: Post-World War I
First published: 1935

This novel's movement from present to past and back again to present creates a sense of place that provides a significant backdrop for its characters, actions, and theme. The primary setting is a house in Paris.

***Fisher house.** Parisian home of Naomi Fisher and her mother; the house of the novel's title and the place in which the main action of the first and third parts of the novel unfolds. It is here that eleven-year-old Henrietta Mountjoy meets Leopold Moody. The house, in its narrow and confining way with its "thin frame," "tight blinds" and air of sternness, suggests the secrets concerning Leopold's parentage and the adults' passions against which the two children struggle for a sense of their own understanding and identities. The presence of the dying Madame Fisher in her upstairs room emphasizes the need for the children to be quiet—a need reflecting the effect of the past's secrecy on the present.

The unfamiliarity of the house to both Henrietta and Leopold provides a visual context for the situation in which the children find themselves. Both are feeling their way through unfamiliar territory. Henrietta, whose mother has died and whose father has sent her to spend time with her grandmother in Mentone, is visiting the Paris house during a stopover before another chaperon accompanies her on the next leg of her journey. Leopold, who has traveled from Spezia, is anxiously awaiting a meeting with Karen Michaelis, the natural mother whom he has never seen. Although the children are unaware of it, Miss Fisher and her dying mother are deeply connected to Leopold's past, as is the house itself.

The events that occur in this house have great meaning, particularly to Leopold. In earlier days Madame Fisher provided rooms in this house for English and American girls undergoing a finishing-school experience in France. It was here that Karen, as a young girl, was first infatuated with Max Ebhart, who later became engaged to Miss Fisher.

***Rushbrook.** Irish town that is home to Karen's Aunt Violet and Uncle Bill. Their house and the adults in it suggest the possible entrapment of life that both children have yet to unravel. For Karen this house, too, seems like a stopover between her life with her parents and her coming marriage to Ray.

Mony's Restaurant. Dark, chilly restaurant in Boulogne, France, where Max and Karen eat. The fact that Max has "known" the restaurant before, presumably with other women, makes it even darker for Karen. Their meeting and conversation there parallel some of the confusion of Henrietta and Leopold about their own history, sexuality, and personal identity. Max and Karen share very little before they meet at the restaurant, but there they plan their second meeting where Leopold will be conceived and where they will create their own shared history in him.

— *Linda L. Keesey*

HOUSE MADE OF DAWN

Author: N. Scott Momaday (1934-   )
Type of work: Novel
Type of plot: Psychological realism

Time of plot: 1945-1952
First published: 1968

A harsh yet beautiful landscape of bare valleys, sandstone mesas, and red rock canyons provides the hub around which scenes and individuals revolve in N. Scott Momaday's first novel. This landscape, at and around the Jemez Pueblo in north-central New Mexico, is both setting and character.

***Wolatowa.** Main village in the Jemez Pueblo, a sovereign Native American nation in the Jemez Mountains, west of Santa Fe in New Mexico. Momaday, who moved with his Kiowa parents to Jemez at age twelve, has stated that life events "take place," by which he means that "place," or landscape, is indivisible from self. Momaday felt indivisible from Jemez Pueblo, and the central theme of his novel is that Abel, his Native American protagonist, is spiritually ill because he is emotionally separated from some aspects of the land after returning from military service during World War II. The land has its own terms, and to heal himself Abel must be possessed by the land under those terms. Throughout the book, physically harsh landscapes are shown to best nurture the Native American spirit. For Abel, only such a place, Wolatowa, can heal his personal agonies.

The central plaza at Wolatowa, called the Middle, is where ancient human dwellings have become indivisible from the earth. Here, Abel first encounters the albino, a man who comes to embody a snake-like evil for Abel. Later, outside Paco's, a bar about four miles south of the pueblo, Abel kills the albino as he would kill a snake.

***Seytokwa.** Location of an early Jemez settlement. The Winter Race, run by Pueblo men for bountiful harvests and good hunting, starts here, when the first sliver of the sun appears over Black Mesa (today's Mesa Chamisa). The race winds along the wagon road for several miles to end in Wolatowa's Middle. The novel's prologue, a flash-forward, shows Abel running in the Winter Race, through snow that covers the dunes, through cold rain that turns the juniper and mesquite trees black with wetness. At the book's end—after Abel's grandfather dies—Abel is shown again as the "Dawn Runner," his spiritual sickness healed in communion with the land.

***Valle Grande** (VAH-yay grahn-DAY). Large volcanic crater on the western slope of the mountains above Wolatowa described as "the right eye of the earth." The crater's valley is grassy, with a river running through it and clouds drifting above in the pure sky. On the crater's rim, Abel's separation from the land becomes apparent. He admires two great eagles as they "dance" with a rattlesnake, taking turns dropping it and diving to catch it again. Abel seems at one with the "eagle spirit" that can possess the land, but is uncomfortable with the "snake spirit" that is possessed *by* the land. The latter is the same spirit that Abel symbolically slays when he kills the albino.

***Benevides house** (beh-neh-VEE-dehs). Large white house of stucco and stone in the canyon north of Jemez Pueblo. The novel places this house at the settlement of

Los Ojos, which is not the modern town of that name. The Los Ojos of the novel is called Jemez Springs today. Staying at this house is the beautiful Angela St. John, a married white woman who comes to the springs alone to take the mineral baths. The canyon landscape comes alive to Angela. At night she even sees the Benevides house as part of the landscape, as a "black organic mass" as old as the canyon itself. Later, Angela has an affair at this house with Abel, who becomes, for her, an animal extension of the land.

*Los Angeles.** California city in which Abel settles after spending six years in prison for murder. Although the middle portion of the book takes place here, Abel's spiritual separation from his Jemez homeland is intensified by the huge city's alienness. Abel relives the pattern that took place earlier at Wolatowa, but, being further removed from the healing land, has no more success than before at curing his inner sickness. However, while he is in Los Angeles, he learns of two more "holy" landscapes from other displaced Native Americans. One is Rainy Mountain, a knoll arising from the Oklahoma plain, a place of blizzards and tornados where, one senses, creation began. (Momaday later wrote a book about Rainy Mountain.) The second holy place is Wide Ruins, Arizona, an austere landscape of brush and red rock gullies.

— *Charles A. Gramlich*

THE HOUSE OF BLUE LEAVES

Author: John Guare (1938-   )
Type of work: Drama
Type of plot: Absurdist

Time of plot: October 4, 1965
First performed: 1971; first published, 1971

The setting of this place is essential to its meaning. Artie Shaughnessy and his sickly wife, Bananas, live in a poorly furnished, cramped, and cold apartment in Queens, New York. The play uses this setting to show the humiliation the Shaughnessys must endure in their lives.

*Queens.** Borough of New York City across the East River from Manhattan in whose Sunnyside neighborhood the Shaughnessys live. John Guare describes Queens in great detail in a foreword to the play. He imagines it as the least elegant and least proud in heritage and prestige of the five boroughs that make up New York City—a place from which to move away to the more comfortable, wealthier, and lovelier suburbs of Westchester County, New York, or Connecticut. The zookeeper and would-be songwriter Artie Shaughnessy has grandiose dreams about making his fame and riches in the music industry; to enhance both the poverty of his daily life and the ludicrous desperation driving Artie, Guare contrasts these two images in his use of Artie's shabby Queens apartment, which lacks proper heating or any decorative, pleasing features. Artie has achieved almost nothing of note in life, as his surroundings testify.

House of Blue Leaves. Artie's name for a sanatorium that he tells Bananas he has found for her. The sanatorium, he tells her, has a lovely tree with blue leaves, leaves that have blown away in the form of a flock of bluebirds to canopy another tree, leaving the first one bare.

*California.** Home to the glamorous and lucrative film industry and a place where people can achieve their dreams, according to the characters in this drama. Guare uses the comic chaos of the Shaughnessy household to call attention to the American obsession with facile success and with a value system in which the pope and movie stars are indistinguishable media gods, television is a shrine, and assassins are glorified in headlines.

— *Patricia E. Sweeney*

A HOUSE OF GENTLEFOLK

Author: Ivan Turgenev (1818-1883)
Type of work: Novel
Type of plot: Psychological realism

Time of plot: Nineteenth century
First published: Dvoryanskoye gnezdo, 1859 (English
translation, 1869)

This novel depicts an idealization of pre-emancipation rural Russia in which the aristocracy (the title's "gentle-folk") are cultured and Westernized, wise and worthy people who handle their serfs firmly, yet fairly. Those who seek to liberalize the system are portrayed as foolishly spoiling their menials and creating trouble for themselves and society at large. This is a striking contrast to Turgenev's earlier A Hunter's Notebook *(1847-1852), which was notable for his realistic portrayal of brutality toward serfs, a portrayal that aroused the wrath of conservative elements but lent support to reformists' calls for change in the institution of serfdom, ultimately leading to Czar Alexander II abolishing it entirely. However, this discrepancy of portrayal is not necessarily a contradiction, if one considers* A House of Gentlefolk *to be a portrayal of Ivan Turgenev's ideal of society as it ought to be.*

O-. Russian town in which the principal events of the novel take place. Turgenev never gives a full name for the town, suggesting that it may be a real place, and that he is protecting the privacy of its inhabitants. However, it may be an entirely imaginary town, a composite of his observations of many such towns throughout central Russia, in which case he may merely be using the device of an incomplete name to create verisimilitude. O- is the capital of a *gubernia*, a prerevolutionary province, and as such is a fair-sized municipality, large enough to have outlying areas called suburbs in which many of the more fashionable families have homes. Although O- is located well away from Russia's capital, St. Petersburg, and the imperial court, members of its upper class pride themselves in their culture and their familiarity with Western customs.

*Moscow. Traditional Russian capital. Although it is not the political capital of Russia at the time in which Turgenev's novel is set, it is in many ways more immediate and important to the characters of this novel than the actual political capital of St. Petersburg in the far northwest of Russia. The characters live close enough to Moscow to visit it on a regular basis, and the city is a much greater presence in their consciousness than the distant northern capital and its imperial court. Turgenev also takes the narrative to Moscow in a way he never does St. Petersburg, and there the younger Lavretsky sees a girl who will completely change the course of his life.

*St. Petersburg. Capital of Imperial Russia. Created in 1712 by the order of Czar Peter the Great to be his "window on the West," it is a very un-Russian city with its grid of streets and stone buildings. Here the Russian nobility speak French and follow the manners of Paris and Berlin. However, the city is usually glimpsed from afar in this novel, as a place to which a character may go or has returned from. Even Fyodor Ivanovich's lengthy stay there with his wife, Varvara Pavlovna, is glossed over in narrative summary, rather than being shown in actual scenes. However, in many ways this period is critical to the plot, since it is among St. Petersburg's high society that Varvara Pavlovna becomes engrossed and is led to prefer frittering away her life in Paris, abandoning her husband, thereby setting the stage for the final tragic misunderstanding that blights Fyodor Ivanovich's hopes for happiness, with either her or Liza.

Lavriky (LAH-vree-kee). Estate not far from the town of O- that is the principal patrimony of the Lavretskys. It is a sizable estate but is portrayed as having been largely ruined by Ivan Petrovich's liberal management. When Petrovich is stricken with a sudden mysterious illness that progressively debilitates him and ultimately kills him, his more traditional sister, Glafira Petrovna, takes over the task of managing the estate. Turgenev portrays this change as restoring proper order to the estate.

— Leigh Husband Kimmel

THE HOUSE OF MIRTH

Author: Edith Wharton (1862-1937)
Type of work: Novel
Type of plot: Naturalism

Time of plot: Early twentieth century
First published: 1905

Places in this novel, especially the houses of the rich and those who aspire to be rich, are symbols of social class and status. In the course of the novel, Lily Bart moves downward from residence to residence, looking for her own comfortable place in this world, finding it finally only in death.

***Grand Central Station.** Major railroad terminus in New York City. The first scene in the novel is set in the afternoon rush at Grand Central, but there is much more significance to this railroad station. Trains play a large part in Lily Bart's life: They are the means of transportation to and from the country houses where she spends her weekends and where she is supposedly seeking a husband. The train is also an apt metaphor for Lily's life: a journey with a number of stops along the way, but generally headed downhill socially and economically.

Benedick. Apartment house near Grand Central Station. When Lily meets Lawrence Selden at the station, he invites her to tea at his apartment at the top floor of a building fronted by a "marble porch and pseudo-Georgian façade." Benedick means "bachelor," and it is a perfect name for Selden and his lodgings for he is confirmed in his single state. Lily meets Sim Rosedale, the owner of the Benedick, on her way out and lies to explain where she was. This is the first in a series of untruths which help propel her journey downward.

Bellomont. Country home of the Trenors, located on the Hudson River several miles north of the city. Most of the upper-class characters in *The House of Mirth* maintain apartments in the fashionable sections of New York City but also have country homes a few miles outside the city. Lily exists on the edge of this society: She lives at the home of her wealthy aunt and is dependent on the hospitality of friends for her social life. Lily's beauty and charm are apparently the compensation for her lack of money. She ought to be trying to catch a husband; however, she cannot bring herself to do it. At Bellomont, for example, she allows the wealthy Percy Gryce to elude her. Rather than attend church with him, she slips away to spend time with Selden, who is unable to make a commitment to her. At a later visit to Bellomont, Lily participates in a *tableau vivant*, a "living picture," in which she holds a pose many of the men find seductive.

Mrs. Peniston's house. Lily Bart's aunt's house on Fifth Avenue. Since her parents' deaths, Lily has lived with Aunt Julia. When Mrs. Peniston hears rumors about Lily and Gus Trenor, she tells Lily that she has been disgraced and refuses to help her with her financial troubles.

***Monte Carlo.** Capital of the principality of Monaco on the Riviera known for its casinos and luxurious hotels. Lily is saved from her aunt's fury by an invitation to accompany the Dorsets on their cruise to the Mediterranean. Bertha Dorset has invited her to come in order to hide her own affair with Ned Silverton. Lily meets Selden here, who warns her to abandon the yacht before she is further compromised, but it is already too late. In Monte Carlo, the American upper class appears even more decadent and immoral than at home in New York.

The pace of Lily's descent quickens in the last third of the novel. Mrs. Peniston dies, and Lily is disinherited. She is forced to become a social secretary for Mrs. Hatch, who lives in a fashionable New York City hotel. When she loses that position, she briefly gets a job at Madame Regina's, a fashionable haberdasher. She is "a star fallen" and even stays in the rooms of Gertie Farish, a friend as impoverished as herself. She makes a final visit to Selden's apartment in the Benedick, and visits the small, clean rooms of Nettie Struther, a working-class woman Lily has earlier helped, and then returns to her own poor room, where she dies from an overdose of sleeping pills. Edith Wharton shows that Lily has been the victim of a rigid social class system that allows women few opportunities in their lives and little freedom. Lily finds, not a "house of mirth," but the house of death.

— *David Peck*

THE HOUSE OF THE SEVEN GABLES: A Romance

Author: Nathaniel Hawthorne (1804-1864)

Type of work: Novel

Type of plot: Gothic

Time of plot: 1850

First published: 1851

An old mansion located in a small nineteenth century New England town provides the ideal setting for Nathaniel Hawthorne to demonstrate that the pride, greed, and revenge of one generation can taint another and to show how the power of love can heal past wrongs.

House of the Seven Gables. Colonial house built in the English style of half-timber and half-plaster on Pyncheon Street in an unnamed town in Massachusetts. The house had been built by Colonel Pyncheon, who had wrested the desirable site from Matthew Maule, a poor man executed as a wizard. Colonel Pyncheon was responsible for Maule's execution and took the doomed man's land. At the moment of his execution, Maule declared that God would give the Pyncheons blood to drink. Despite this grim prophecy, the colonel had his house, and its builder was Thomas Maule, son of the condemned wizard.

Just as the personality of a character evolves over the course of a story, the personality and appearance of the house change as the narrative unfolds. In the late 1600's, when Colonel Pyncheon first erects the building, it is the most opulent structure in the town. Located on the outskirts, it reflects the colonel's wealth, social position, and love of fine things. However, because he swindled Maule out of the land on which the house stands, it is also a symbol of the colonel's cold, greedy, and dishonest nature.

In the years that follow, Gervayse, the colonel's grandson, and Gervayse's beautiful daughter, Alice, occupy the house, and it again reflects the character of its occupants. The narrator points out that, although the dwelling is beginning to show its age, it is still a solid, pleasant mansion, whose interior has been redecorated to reflect Gervayse's sophisticated European tastes. The presence of the lovely and exotic-looking Alice gives the place a graceful air.

By 1850, when the spinster Hepzibah Pyncheon lives in the house, nature and age have taken their toll on the building. Moss covers its roof and windows, and flowering shrubs known as Alice's posies grow between two of the house's gables. The interior of the house is dark and dusty, much like the old woman who inhabits it. Once a public symbol of the Pyncheons' wealth and power, the mansion now represents decay and physical and psychological isolation, in addition to the family's material decline. Through most of the novel, Hepzibah never leaves the house. Her pride in her family's illustrious heritage prevents her from socializing with her middle-class neighbors. When her brother Clifford, who was falsely imprisoned, returns home, he reinforces her reclusive tendencies. The only contact Hepzibah has with the outside world is through the shop she is forced to open because of her extreme poverty.

Meanwhile, throughout the novel, the house stands as a metaphor for the human heart. Animated by memories of generations of Pyncheons, it embodies all human emotion and experience, including joy, sorrow, greed, hatred, and pride. As it ages, the house seems to mellow. Finally, after it is redeemed from its troubling history by the love of Phoebe Pyncheon, a distant cousin who comes to live with Hepzibah, and Holgrave Maule, it becomes no more than an empty shell after the last Pyncheons leave its dark rooms for a brighter mansion in the country.

Various attempts have been made to connect an actual physical place with the novel's wooden house. The best-known example of this is a brown, gabled mansion still standing in Salem, Massachusetts. Once owned by Hawthorne's cousins, the Ingersoll family, it is now a popular tourist attraction billed as the "House of the Seven Gables." Other Salem locales have also been proposed as Hawthorne's model for the house, including the Curwen mansion and a dwelling belonging to Philip English, another Hawthorne relative. Hawthorne may have drawn his portrait of the fictional house from all three structures. However, in his preface to the novel, he cautions against assigning a real place to the imaginary events of the novel. Hawthorne's disclaimer frees him artistically to use the house as both a character and as a symbol.

Town. The unnamed town in which the House of the Seven Gables stands is described as orderly and home-loving. The town's history parallels that of Salem, Massachusetts, especially in regard to the witchcraft trials of 1692. Because Hawthorne does not name the town, he has the freedom to use it as a symbol for the wider world, the human society from which Hepzibah and Clifford are separated by the walls of the house.

Train. Railroad train on which Hepzibah and Clifford take an impromptu ride into the countryside to escape the oppressiveness of the house, which is now Jaffrey Pyncheon's temporary tomb after he dies. This is the first time they leave the house. Filled with people, the train helps them to reconnect with humankind. "Here we are in the world, Hepzibah!—in the midst of life!—in the throng of our fellow beings! Let you and I be happy!" Clifford exclaims. However, his exuberance is short-lived, for he loses his nerve at the last stop and asks Hepzibah to take him back to the familiar, though repressive, environment of their home.

— *Pegge Bochynski*

THE HOUSE OF THE SPIRITS

Author: Isabel Allende (1942-   )
Type of work: Novel
Type of plot: Magical Realism

Time of plot: 1920's-1970's
First published: La casa de los espíritus, 1982
   (English translation, 1985)

Set in an unnamed South American country, this novel chronicles the lives of the Trueba family over several generations. The story ends shortly after a military coup overthrows the country's first socialist president. Although the setting resembles Isabel Allende's native Chile (whose toppled socialist president, Salvador Allende, was her uncle), the country of her novel is a place not only of realistically described political strife, but also a place where magical events occur commonly.

Tres Marías. Hacienda of the Trueba family, which the family patriarch, Esteban Trueba, rebuilds from ruin several times. After growing up poor and working several years in a diamond mine to earn money, Esteban puts his money and energy into rebuilding the ruined country estate, making it one of the most successful in the country and enhancing his wealth considerably. He rebuilds it again after the house is destroyed by an earthquake and yet again after the land is turned over to the peasants for two years during the socialist administration and then returned to him following the military coup.

Esteban's work on his hacienda confirms for him his political views. As the local *patrón*, Esteban opposes rights and freedoms for his tenants. Tenants caught passing out political tracts or discussing rights for the tenants are punished and banished from the hacienda. While Esteban takes pride in providing his tenants with the only brick houses on any hacienda in the area, he also feels justified in raping the women at will and taking no responsibility for the many children who result. Esteban's wealth and political conviction eventually lead him to become a senator.

Ironically, it is at Tres Marías that Esteban's daughter Blanca falls in love with one of the tenants, her childhood friend Pedro Tercero García. Pedro Tercero becomes a popular singer and political figure who helps the socialist president win his election and who fights against the military coup. Alba, Blanca and Pedro Tercero's daughter, likewise falls in love with a left-wing activist. Esteban's love for Alba encourages him to soften his political views after the military coup.

Big house on the corner. Home that Esteban Trueba builds in the capital city in preparation for his marriage to Clara. He erects the house in the city's finest neighborhood, sparing no expense on either construction or furnishings. This house becomes a meeting place for Clara's spiritualist and clairvoyant friends and thus becomes the "house of the spirits" of the novel's title. The many spirits who visit Clara there suggest adding rooms or knocking down walls to look for treasure. While the front of the house remains unchanged, the back becomes a labyrinth of small rooms because of Clara's constant remodeling. These rooms prove extremely useful during the nation's coup. Esteban hides guns for the military in one of them; Alba and Blanca hide political dissidents wanted by the military police.

Capital city. Unnamed capital of the country. As with the novel's descriptions of the hacienda Tres Marías, its descriptions of the city accentuate its political themes. The earlier generations in the novel—Esteban Trueba, Clara, Esteban's mother and sister, and Clara's parents—remain in the aristocratic sections of the city.

Later in the novel, younger generations visit the lower-class sections of the city.

Esteban and Clara's son Nicolás seeks out his girlfriend Amanda in the capital after not seeing her for several weeks. He finds her in her boardinghouse, pregnant and miserable. Nicolás is shocked by her poverty. Looking around he realizes that until that moment he has known almost nothing about her. In fact, he has never visited the home of a poor person before and never considered what it would be like to live without money. Nicolás's twin brother, Jaime, becomes a doctor devoted to helping the poor. He exhausts himself trying to cure the sick without adequate money, food, or medicine, spending most of his time in the poorest sections of the city. The powerful contrasts between the city's wealthy neighborhoods and its slums show why many of the younger Truebas support political reform.

— *Joan Hope*

THE HOUSE ON MANGO STREET

Author: Sandra Cisneros (1954-   )
Type of work: Novel
Type of plot: Bildungsroman

Time of plot: Mid-1960's
First published: 1984

The setting for this novel is the neighborhood around Mango Street in the Hispanic quarter of Chicago. In a series of vignettes, Esperanza Cordero, the narrator, shows the lives of people who live in the run-down tenements and shabby houses.

*****Mango Street.** Street in the Hispanic neighborhood of Chicago, where author Sandra Cisneros was born. The young narrator of her novel, Esperanza, lives with her family in a small, redbrick house at 4006 Mango Street. Its bricks are crumbling in places, and its front door is swollen and hard to move. The house has no front yard, only four skinny elm trees the city has planted by the curb, trees that manage to grow in the cement. The house's small backyard looks even smaller because it is enclosed by buildings on either side. Esperanza is ashamed of her house and longs to move away from Mango Street to a larger house in a better neighborhood.

The neighborhood is a busy place filled with children and adults engaged in a number of activities. Children play volleyball in the alley, and boys riding homemade bicycles shout at girls walking by. Kids bend trees, bounce between parked cars, and hang upside-down from their knees. A boy pushes Esperanza into an open water hydrant, and other boys sit on bikes in front of a house pitching pennies. Neighbors come out to see the crash of a big yellow Cadillac, listen for the sirens, and watch as cops handcuff the driver. In front of the tavern, a bum sits on a stoop. People wait to take the subway train to downtown. Strangers to the neighborhood fear that it is dangerous; however, the neighborhood is a place in which Esperanza feels safe.

Precious Blood Church. Center of social life for Esperanza's family and neighbors. On the day of a cousin's baptism, the family members dance in the church basement, which has been rented out for the occasion. People wear their finest clothes and enjoy the party, the dancing, and eating tamales as children run all over the place.

Monkey Garden. Secret place in a neighborhood yard where a family that owned a monkey once lived. After the family left, Esperanza and her friends make a clubhouse of the yard, using the back of an old blue pickup. Filled with sunflowers, spiders, worms, beetles, ants, ladybugs, and a hibiscus tree, the Monkey Garden is a place where the children's mothers cannot find them.

*****Mexico.** Original home to many people in the neighborhood whose culture continues to influence their lives. Esperanza's father flies to Mexico for the funeral of his mother after she dies. When Mamacita's husband brings her to Chicago to be with him, she becomes homesick for Mexico and does not come out of the apartment because she does not speak English.

White house. Esperanza's dream home. One day Esperanza wants to escape her dreary surroundings and move to a home of her own, not a flat or apartment, not a man's house, or a daddy's house, but her own house—one with a porch and pretty purple petunias. She yearns for a house as quiet as snow, a white house surrounded by trees with a big yard and no fence. Her dream house would have running water, a basement, and at least three washrooms. It would have no nosy neighbors watching, no motorcycles and cars, no sheets and towels and laundry, only trees and plenty of blue sky. Esperanza wants a house on a hill like the one with a garden where her father works. She thinks that people who live on hills sleep so close to the stars they forget the people who live on earth. As she describes the house she wants to own, she points to the dismal surroundings of her present life. Esperanza's dream house becomes synonymous with individual economic and social independence, which one can obtain through education and the cultivation of one's native talents.

— *Judith Barton Williamson*

THE HOUSE ON THE HILL

Author: Cesare Pavese (1908-1950)
Type of work: Novel
Type of plot: Psychological realism

Time of plot: 1943-1945
First published: La casa in collina, 1949 (English translation, 1956)

Set in northwestern Italy during World War II, this novel follows a bachelor schoolteacher who is searching constantly for shelter from the increasingly dangerous air raids on Turin. As Italy's political turmoil deepens, he is forced into increasingly precarious strategies to avoid arrest. As his personal situation becomes more perilous, he comes to understand that his need for refuge expresses not only an attachment to a beloved landscape but also a kind of evasion, a personal habit of detachment from society that implicates him in Italy's political fate.

*****Turin.** Principal city of northwestern Italy's Piedmont region that provides the narrator, Corrado, with his occupation and his status as an intellectual; however, both the city and Corrado are threatened by wartime instability. Corrado's work as a schoolteacher, as well as the school where he teaches, are given only a shadowy identity. Despite the increasingly difficult situation in Turin, Corrado's description of the city is remote. The city is the only place where Corrado admits the possibility of love; however, two early affairs in Turin have left

him with unhappy memories, and much of the early part of the novel concerns his attempt to redeem the rashness and futility of an early relationship with Cate, a former lover from Turin's suburbs whom he meets again by chance after eight years.

House on the hill. Place outside Turin where Corrado seeks safety from air raids on the city. The relative safety of the distant suburban hills moves many people to spend their nights outside the city in temporary quarters. Corrado takes lodgings in a hilltop owned by Elvira, a middle-aged woman who tends his needs with an anxiety that betrays her interest in marrying him. Although the hill on which Elvira's house stands is only one hill location among many, it is the one that best allows Cesare Pavese to illuminate his character's ambivalence about the Italian political landscape, by showing Elvira's reactions not only to the events of the day but also to her boarder's views about them.

Le Fontane. Rustic inn located below and at some distance from Elvira's large house to which people of a lower station in life go to avoid the dangers of Turin. There, Corrado encounters his former lover Cate and her young son, Dino. In Dino, who he imagines may be his own son, Corrado finds both a companion and a reflection of himself as a boy. Accompanied by Corrado's dog, Belbo, Corrado and Dino roam the woods, where Corrado passes on a knowledge and love of the natural world that is both scientific and deeply personal. In the scenes of Corrado and Dino abroad in the woods and fields, Pavese achieves a lyricism that con-

trasts effectively with the anxious tone of much of the novel.

The inhabitants of Le Fontane are peasants and workers who do not enjoy the detachment of well-off people like Elvira. Among them are partisan fighters whose presence ultimately condemns the entire group to arrest and perhaps execution. Le Fontane is the most uncertain of refuges and the first to collapse.

*Belbo. Corrado's name for his home village, where he seeks refuge at the end of the novel. He travels there, southeast from Turin, in a tensely wrought account of risky, clandestine travel. In this region Corrado still finds his true life of the forest, as he dreamed of it as a boy. However, he knows that the war will soon find its way to Belbo, and that then, even the "melancholy" and "solitary" will agree to make war.

Pavese himself was born in San Stefano Belbo, one of several small towns that take their names from the Belbo River flowing northeastward from the hills.

— Clyde S. McConnell

HOW GREEN WAS MY VALLEY

Author: Richard Llewellyn (Richard Dafydd Vivian
  Llewellyn Lloyd, 1906-1983)
Type of work: Novel

Type of plot: Regional
Time of plot: c. 1890-1910
First published: 1939

The novel charts the environmental degradation of a remote coal-mining village in Wales and the troubles of a mining family over several decades, as seen through the eyes of Huw Morgan, the narrator, who wistfully recalls how green it was before the refuse of the mines destroyed its beauty.

Valley. Unnamed valley in an unspecified region of Wales that is semi-rural, without most modern social institutions. There are no formal schools, only one church, and no police stations. The inhabitants look askance on most signs of modern social life, preferring to solve their own problems and making do with what they have. The valley seems to exist in a world of its own, as the narrative provides few allusions to the outside world.

From his early childhood, the narrator, Huw Morgan, is critical of the valley's coal mines and the harm they bring. For instance, both the miners and owners want to

keep bringing up coal from the ground; a stop in production means children go hungry. However, the owners do not properly dispose of the slag that also comes up. Instead, the slag is dumped on open ground in the valley. No one except Huw seems to care about the resulting slag heaps. As Huw gets older, the slag heap becomes a monstrous eyesore, long, and black, without life or sign, stretching along the floor of the valley on both sides of the river, crushing the grass, reeds, and flowers. Eventually, the narrator anthropomorphizes the slag heap, hating it as the enemy of his family and village, as it expands and threatens to crush everything in the valley. The mine's impact on the environment and on the human spirit are one and the same.

Mountain. Lush and majestic mountain that separates the valley from the town that provides an easy escape from the growing ugliness of industrial life for Huw. He describes it as a place of intense though terrible beauty, with spring flowers and the song of nightingales, but also deep winter snows and river water so cold it takes his breath away. When he is injured as a youth, he goes to the mountain to recover his strength. As an older boy, he finds it a place to wander with his father and learn life lessons. As a teenager, he uses it as a place for secret trysts with his sweetheart. However, even the mountain is no escape from the valley's slag heap.

Town. Unnamed town near the valley. With various stores, a national school, and several nearby estates, the town is big enough to attract traveling companies of actors. It is significant in the novel only insofar as it demonstrates a difference between urban life and life in the valley. Townspeople in the novel are prone to mob violence. This is indicated near the beginning when Huw is beaten at school by a group of bullies and later when a riot takes place near a theater.

National School. Secondary school in the town that is run by English educators and has a self-hating Welsh teacher who tyrannizes his fellow Welsh students. The school is another significant setting that demonstrates the difference between urban industrial life and the life of the valley. The school provides a potential escape for Huw from the valley, but only at the cost of his selfhood. On his first day at the school, he is chided for speaking Welsh and ordered to only speak English—both at the school and at home. As he continues in school, Huw comes into conflict with his teacher Mr. Jonas, who has only contempt for his Welsh neighbors. Finally, the headmaster at the school pushes Huw toward greater scholarship, holding out the offer of entrance to Oxford or Cambridge as an inducement. Being a man of the valley, however, and unwilling to leave his family to face the troubles alone, Huw stays in the valley, also working in the mines until his father is killed in a mine collapse.

— *Michael R. Meyers*

HOWARDS END

Author: E. M. Forster (1879-1970)
Type of work: Novel
Type of plot: Domestic realism

Time of plot: Early twentieth century
First published: 1910

A symbol of "little England" as opposed to the commercial and imperial interests of Great Britain, Howards End is the place with which all other places in this novel—the sprawling city of London, the rolling hills of Shropshire, the upper class country manor—are contrasted.

Howards End. Modest farmhouse near Hilton owned by Mrs. Wilcox, an hour by train north of London, England. E. M. Forster based the house on his boyhood home, called Rooksnest, in Hertfordshire. Both Rooksnest and Howards End are just outside the suburban ring of 1910 London. Although it takes Aunt Juley an hour to get to Hilton by train, following the Great North Road, this is still a journey too far for Paul Wilcox to commute to the city daily for work. As he says, it is somewhere between country and town.

The house is heavily symbolic. To Ruth Wilcox, "it had been a spirit, for which she sought a spiritual heir." On her deathbed Mrs. Wilcox tries to leave Howards End to Margaret Schlegel. Both Howards End and Mrs. Wilcox are tied to the past of working farmers with owners and laborers living side by side, not of manor houses, domestic servants, and vast estates. The house and grounds stand for England itself and embody the native mythology of the countryside. Modern England is seen to be encroaching on this land: The Wilcox children and their father are ill-suited to it, and they all end the novel inside while Helen and her son are out in the fields. Meanwhile, the "red rust" of the city is moving nearer.

London. Capital of Great Britain and city in which the Schlegel family has a house. The Schlegel's Wickham Place address is a middle-class row house in the fashionable southwest section of the city. The house is to be torn down and replaced by a block of flats when the Schlegel's ninety-nine-year lease has expired. It is into a flat across the street that Mrs. Wilcox moves when she becomes ill. Forster's attitude toward London is ambiguous. London stands opposed to the country, to nature, in the novel. Forster sees London as modern, as the place of "telegrams and anger," while the country holds the true values of English society.

London has created and nurtured the class of people that the Schlegels represent, that is, intelligent, cultured liberals. At the same time, another class of people is not as nurtured as the Schlegels. These are the Leonard Basts of England, former country dwellers whose occupations have been made obsolete by the industrial revolution and who are drawn to the city by menial, low paying jobs. Located in a newly built block of flats ("constructed with extreme cheapness") on the south side of the River Thames, Leonard's flat is also on the edge of the abyss of poverty.

Swanage. Town in Dorset, along the southern coast of England. The Schlegels' Aunt Juley lives in a house at The Bays. Forster's paean to the English countryside begins with a view of the nearby Purbeck hills and encompasses rivers, valleys, villages, and churches, and "beyond that onto Salisbury Plain itself," the site of Stonehenge. The view also encompasses suburbia and "the gates of London."

Oniton Grange. Country estate in Shropshire near the border of England and Wales. Oniton is the symbol of the transitional state of the English class system in the early twentieth century. It is a grand country manor acquired from an aristocratic family by the rich industrialist Henry Wilcox, who has made his money from the Imperial and West Africa Rubber Company. Forster treats a similar situation in *Maurice* (1971), in which the Durhams' estate is crumbling due to declining income and rising costs. As at Howards End, Wilcox is hardly aware of the history and cultural significance of his estate. Rather he sees Oniton as an investment and a status symbol, much as he sees his London house on Ducie Street.

— *James J. Berg*

THE HUMAN COMEDY

Author: William Saroyan (1908-1981)
Type of work: Novel
Type of plot: Sentimental

Time of plot: Twentieth century
First published: 1943

William Saroyan blends three distinct motifs into this sentimental novel: his gifts as a misplaced Middle Eastern storyteller, his love of classical Greek literature, and his grasp of middle American life during World War II. Against the particular setting of small-town America, Saroyan develops the universal themes of the search for identity, maturity, integrity, and family. Places in this novel serve as vital components in a modern day mystery play about loss and recovery, the strange mix of tragedy and comedy that constitutes life.

Ithaca. California town in which the novel is set. The fictional Ithaca has two models. The first is from classical Greek literature—the Ionian island kingdom of Ulysses in Homer's *Odyssey* (c. 800 B.C.E.). In that epic, Ithaca is a home that is painfully attained by the hero of the Trojan War after a long and difficult journey. Both "Homer" and "Ulysses" are names of characters in Saroyan's story.

Saroyan's second model for Ithaca is his own boyhood hometown in central California. Growing up in the "Little Armenia" section of Fresno, Saroyan knew at first hand small-town America, with its bakery (selling day-old pies), its grocery store (run by a clerk who fetched goods for customers), the train depot (where young boys waved to engineers as great trains sped by), the butcher shop, the newspaper office, the bus station, the telegraph office, the library, and so on. Ithaca's high school is modeled on Saroyan's own Emerson High School, with his own painful memories of studying ancient history and of athletic competitions on the race track with the hurdles (again the imagery of ancient Greece intrudes).

In Saroyan's mind the two Ithacas merge to become one, not only an archetypal Norman Rockwell small town, but one recognizably real and representative of real American towns during the 1940's.

Macauley house. Ithaca home of the Macauley family, headed by the widowed Katey Macauley. The modest house stands on a tree-lined street; it has a large, inviting front porch, complete with swing, and friends and neighbors pause, while walking, to chat up those outside the house. Singing is a part of the family's daily life, as are the long heart-to-heart chats in the kitchen, which was often the center of life in working-class American homes during the period in which this novel is set. The household follows regular hours: the hour when children eat breakfast and dash off to school, the hour when the mail arrives, the afternoon break between school and work, the return, late at night, for a cup of coffee before retiring for the day. It is very much a 1940's routine, set in a pre-media era, when entertainment was largely self-generated and interpersonal, and interaction was the norm. The Macauley house is more than merely a place in Ithaca; it represents America to soldiers uprooted and sent overseas by the war.

Telegraph office. Part of Saroyan's genius was to set the dramatic against the prosaic. While Ithaca symbolizes tranquillity, and the Macauley home represents security, the local telegraph office is the door to the wider, more dangerous world beyond rural California. Through it comes the daily news that often transforms the town, as when reports of its sons killed in the war arrive. It is thus not surprising that the telegraph clerk, Mr. Grogan, drinks and takes heart medicine and eventually has a fatal heart attack. His death is symbolic of the frequent bad news that enters tiny Ithaca.

— *C. George Fry*

THE HUMAN FACTOR

Author: Graham Greene (1904-1991)
Type of work: Novel
Type of plot: Spy

Time of plot: Late Cold War era
First published: 1978

Settings in this novel span four continents, linking the covert operations of the Cold War era to the conflicting interests and collaborative ventures of Western bloc nations. The mystery of the plot emerges from the protagonist's involvement in espionage and counterespionage activities that connect to the theme of family ties. The novel also illustrates the barriers between a polarized world in which superpower rivalries endorse racial barriers and ethnic divisions in the postcolonial era.

*London. Great Britain's capital city is the central location of the British Secret Service. The novel's protagonist, Maurice Castle, works as a trusted intelligence officer in a London firm but is actually selling secrets to the Soviet Union. He returns to England from Africa and lives in the country, commuting to London by train. His movements between the city and his country home highlight the contrast between his dual allegiances: In London he is a secret agent; in the country he uses an old childhood hideout to drop secret information to the Soviets. The ironic framework of Greene's novel unfolds several relationships, including Castle's interracial marriage, that challenge cultural perceptions through plausible and possible relationships of strong commitments.

London itself is not free of racial prejudice. Castle mistakenly believes that no one in London would mind the "African blood" of his wife. However, a passerby addresses her with the derogatory term "Topsy"—echoing a nickname for a black slave girl in Harriet Beecher Stowe's novel *Uncle Tom's Cabin* (1851-1852). Greene ridicules London's class-conscious society through Sir Hargreaves's marriage to an American woman who brought him wealth, status, and a promotion in the London office at a time when he was an inexperienced man in the firm.

*South Africa. Homeland of Castle's wife, Sarah. Castle's flashbacks to his years in South Africa reveal a setting during the period when apartheid was supreme. At the same time, political rivalries among Western countries led to partnerships with South Africa's government that promoted economic imperialism that helped to perpetuate the apartheid system. The United States, Great Britain, and South Africa are collaborating in covert activities in support of Uncle Remus Operation as a joint endeavor, sharing of secret information on diverse issues, such as guerrillas, blockades, Cuban or Russian penetration, or economic interests.

While living in South Africa, Castle had to break the country's rigid racial-separation laws in order to be with Sarah. This experience opened his eyes to the evils of apartheid and made him sympathetic to the plight of black South Africans. In fact, he became a Soviet informant because of his sympathy for Africans.

*Moscow. Capital of the Soviet Union. When Castle fears that he will be discovered as a double-agent, the KGB arranges his escape from England to provide him sanctuary in Moscow. There, he discovers that he must learn a great deal about Russian culture and language. At the same time, he learns that the Russians have merely used the information Castle has sent them to make Western nations believe there is a double-agent in Moscow who does not actually exist. This disclosure comes to Castle only after he is virtually a prisoner in Moscow. Meanwhile, England turns into a prison for Castle's family because his wife does not have her son on her passport. There is an irony of fate in the separation of this family that had come together across continents; in the end, Sarah and her son are forced to remain in England, while Castle leads a life of an exile in Russia.

— *Mabel Khawaja*

HUMBOLDT'S GIFT

Author: Saul Bellow (1915-   )
Type of work: Novel
Type of plot: Psychological realism

Time of plot: 1970's
First published: 1975

This novel is set in and around large cities, beginning in Chicago and ending in the New York City area. Most of it occurs in the more affluent sections of those cities that are associated with Charlie Citrine during his wealthy years; but parts of it, especially those Charlie visits in memory, involve poverty-stricken areas.

*Chicago. Midwestern city where Charlie grew up and still lives. Chicago is also the home of his mistress, Renata, and his ex-wife, who calls Chicago a deadly, ugly, vulgar, and dangerous place. In American culture, Chicago is indelibly associated with gangsters, and Charlie has adventures involving a gangster, Rinaldo Cantabile, who has Charlie's beautiful Mercedes bashed repeatedly with a baseball bat and who takes Charlie up to a girder high on an unfinished skyscraper, where he throws down money Charlie lost to him in a poker game. To escape from Chicago and all the problems it represents to Charlie, he plans to fly directly to Europe with Renata but decides to stop at New York first to find out about a legacy he has been left by his late friend, Von Humboldt Fleisher.

*New York City. Largest city in the United States, a place of great poverty and great wealth. When Charlie visits New York, he stays in the plush Plaza Hotel and enjoys all the luxuries money can buy. He and Renata visit an old-age home on Coney Island, where Humboldt's uncle Waldemar lives. There Charlie gets the legacy Humboldt has left him, in a sealed package.

The last time Charlie sees Humboldt alive occurs while he is on a business trip to New York City. There, in the company of the state's two current U.S. senators, Jacob Javits and Robert Kennedy, he flies over the city in a Coast Guard helicopter and attends a political luncheon at the expensive restaurant, Tavern on the Green in Central Park. While on this business trip to New York, he sees the impoverished Humboldt on the street eating a pretzel for lunch. Charlie takes advantage of the anonymity the city offers to hide behind a parked car and watch Humboldt but does not approach his old friend. Two months later, Humboldt dies in the elevator of a flophouse near Times Square while taking out his trash. Afterward, Humboldt is buried in a crowded cemetery in the fictitious New Jersey city of Deathsville.

Valhalla Cemetery. Graveyard in the New York City area, where the novel ends in early spring, when Charlie, Waldemar, and one of Waldemar's friends have Humboldt reinterred. This cemetery, with its blooming flowers, represents a new beginning for Charlie.

*Madrid. Capital of Spain where Charlie is supposed to meet Renata. He wants to meet her there, rather than in Milan, Italy, where they first planned to meet, so he can begin writing a chapter for a cultural travel guide about Europe that will begin in Madrid. Through this travel guide, he hopes to make enough money to free himself from his creditors, the Internal Revenue Service, and especially his ex-wife. However, he eventually finds that no publisher is interested in his book.

*Paris. Capital of France in which Charlie finds himself with the gangster Cantabile among the crowds on the Champs Élysées, one of the most fashionable streets in the city, waiting to see the film Cantabile mentions in Madrid. In Paris, Charlie also uses the package from Humboldt to prove that he and Humboldt did write the movie's scenario and begins to engage in a series of deals that will enable him to rebury Humboldt as well as solve all of his economic problems and many of his personal problems.

— *Richard Tuerk*

THE HUNCHBACK OF NOTRE DAME

Author: Victor Hugo (1802-1885)
Type of work: Novel
Type of plot: Historical

Time of plot: 1482
First published: Notre-Dame de Paris, 1831 (English translation, 1833)

The full French title of Victor Hugo's novel, Notre Dame de Paris, *reflects the importance Hugo gave to the setting that dominates the experiences of all the characters including the hunchback Quasimodo. Although all the action in the novel takes place in a small area in the center of Paris, contrasts between the cathedral, the Palace of Justice, and the streets reflect the various forces acting upon the characters. To an extent, all the locations also reflect the power of fate, which Hugo specifies as determining the action.*

*Notre Dame Cathedral. Roman Catholic cathedral on Paris's Ile de la Cite. The iconic presence of the cathedral dominates the novel, especially through the lives of Claude Frollo, the archdeacon of Notre Dame, and Quasimodo, the cathedral's deaf bell-ringer. The forces that control the ultimate tragedy of the story arise from the hopeless love of these two men for Esmeralda, the gypsy woman who is herself besotted with the unfaithful soldier, Phoebus de Châteaupers. Frollo's love for Esmeralda would not drive him to such madness, were he not restrained by his clerical vow of celibacy. The Church separates him from women while his vocation continues his torment. When Frollo plots to have Esmeralda hanged if she will not love him, Quasimodo rescues her by hiding her in the cathedral, where she can claim sanctuary. So long as she remains there, she is safe, even during the violence of the beggars' attack on the cathedral.

The public square in front of Notre Dame unites the cathedral with the people. As the main characters are drawn together there, it reflects through this coincidence the role of fate. After Frollo has Esmeralda sentenced to death, she must make penance in front of the cathedral before being executed. It is from the square that

Quasimodo carries her away to the sanctuary of the church, but not before she sees Phoebus on a nearby balcony. This sight proves that Phoebus is not dead—although Esmeralda has been charged with killing him—and renews Esmeralda's hope that Phoebus will return to her. Phoebus sees Esmeralda just at the moment he is swearing to another woman that she, Esmeralda, means nothing to him. The square weaves together the multiple relationships that control the characters.

*Place de la Grève** (plahz deh lah grehv). Public square on which Quasimodo is applauded as Prince of Fools and where he must serve time in the pillory for his role in Frollo's attack on Esmeralda. The Place de la Grève also contains the gallows where Esmeralda is destined to be hanged. Hugo would have been especially aware that this square was later named Place de la Concorde to erase the memories of the guillotine it had held during the French Revolution.

*Palace of Justice.** Great hall in which the novel opens, when a crowd gathers to choose a Prince of Fools at the same time a morality play is being presented. The palace is later the scene of the trials of both Quasimodo and Esmeralda. Quasimodo is interrogated even though he is deaf and unable to understand what is being asked. Esmeralda is tortured until she confesses. Both are condemned in proceedings that show both the power and the fallibility of the law. The role of the Palace of Justice is ambiguous in the novel, just as the concept of justice in the novel seems quite variable.

Court of Miracles. Courtyard close to other places of action that serves as a refuge for the beggars who display artificially contrived wounds or disabilities in order to beg money in the streets. The "miracles" refer to what happens when they return to their own territory and suddenly can walk normally. This courtyard represents the people of the street, Esmeralda's people, who as gypsies or other marginal characters make a living as best they can. When Esmeralda is in danger, these people rally to her defense, just as Esmeralda comes to the defense of Gringoire by offering to marry him so he will be accepted by her people. The solidarity of this group sets itself against the forces of authority when the beggars attack the cathedral.

— *Dorothy M. Betz*

HUNGER

Author: Knut Hamsun (Knut Pedersen, 1859-1952)
Type of work: Novel
Type of plot: Impressionistic realism

Time of plot: Late nineteenth century
First published: Sult, 1890 (English translation, 1899)

This novel details the madness that comes over a young writer during his encounter with Norway's large capital city, to which many people come hoping to fulfill their dreams. However, their dreams are soon dashed by the very nature of how a large industrial city functions. In this "modern" age, the writer as artist finds it almost impossible to make his way in the urban environment without compromising his nature, his very being.

*Kristiania (Christiana).** Norway's capital city (now Oslo) is the destination for many young writers who wish to capitalize on their supposed talent and become rich and famous. The young narrator of *Hunger* is one of those who struggles to make ends meet in the big and unfeeling city. He rarely has enough to eat, and his consequent hunger leads to erratic behavior. The room he lives in does not protect him from the elements. When he cannot find work, he is forced to sell his belongings at a pawnshop, borrow money from friends, or beg on the street. A pawnbroker is amused when the young writer attempts to sell the buttons from his coat.

The city is made up of many different types of people, including beggars, beautiful girls, policemen, pawnbrokers, editors, and managers. Struggling to get his writing projects sold, the narrator is worn down by the city's indifference to him and his needs. He seems doomed to failure in this urban environment and must try to earn a living doing other work that he is not trained to do. The industrial city does not need artists. The narrator is not suited for city life. His own worst enemy, he is incapable of playing by the rules, of putting his life in order.

Hamsun based a good deal of the novel on his own desperate experiences living in Kristiania during the early 1880's, as well as the time he spent in Chicago, Illinois, during the mid-1880's. The isolation that Hamsun so poignantly writes about in the novel is largely a retelling of what he went through in large cities himself.

Attic room. Room that the narrator rents in a house in Kristiania. Its walls are plastered with old newspapers from which the narrator reads advertisements. The room is empty except for a bed and a red rocking chair. The room has no stove and no lock on its door. The narrator thinks of the room as a poorly constructed "coffin." From his attic window, he can look out onto a clothesline, an open field, and debris. Street noises tempt him to leave his room. Because the narrator is always strug-

gling to come up with enough money to pay his rent, his landlady finally rents the room to a sailor. The young writer is allowed to sleep on the sofa downstairs, but this is only temporary. Toward the end of the novel, he is forced out of the house and must decide what he can do to change his situation.

Copégoro. Ship flying a Russian flag that catches the narrator's eye at Kristiania's wharf. There, he persuades the captain to take him on as an extra member of the crew. The ship is heading for England. Once the ship sets sail, the narrator looks back at Kristiania and notices that the "windows of the homes shone with such brightness." Not only is he escaping from the city that has left a mark on him, he is also admitting that he has failed to make his way on the streets of Kristiania.

— *Jeffry Jensen*

HYDE PARK

Author: James Shirley (1596-1666)
Type of work: Drama
Type of plot: Comedy of manners

Time of plot: Early seventeenth century
First performed: 1632; first published, 1637

This sprightly comedy contrasts the conventional everyday manners of members of the London gentry with their more liberated behavior on a festive occasion in the open and pastoral venue of Hyde Park, which provides a bucolic escape from urban London—a playground for enjoyment of nature, sports, and courtship.

Hyde Park. Large public park in central London. As the central backdrop for acts 3 and 4 of James Shirley's play, the park combines an atmosphere of natural beauty with the presence of sports—especially horse racing—that provides a diversion for most of the cast in act 4. The park also offers private paths where the lovers can carry on their courtships and quarrels. An additional touch of rural atmosphere is provided by a milkmaid who carries a pail of fresh milk. Clearly the park's atmosphere of freedom and release from inhibition is central to the play's effect.

An old tradition suggests that Shirley's comedy was written in order to commemorate the opening of the park to the public in 1632.

Mrs. Bonavent's house. Large London mansion belonging to the supposedly widowed Mrs. Bonavent. This

structure is the home and arena for two major women characters and the scene of Carol's initial pert assertions about the follies of men and the joys of living a single life. Though dominated by Mrs. Bonavent and Carol, the house is the setting both for ensemble scenes, such as the final festive celebration of Mrs. Bonavent's wedding, and for relatively intimate courtship scenes, including Carol's final battle of wits with Fairfield, where the two reach a truce in their struggle for dominance in the relationship and agree to wed. In contrast to her behavior in the neutral area of the park, where she is unable to manage events as she intends, Carol exerts more control over her relationship with Fairfield on her home ground, Mrs. Bonavent's house.

— *Edgar L. Chapman*

HYPATIA: Or, New Foes with an Old Face

Author: Charles Kingsley (1819-1875)

Type of work: Novel

Type of plot: Historical

Time of plot: Fifth century

First published: 1853

This historical novel centers on Egypt's Alexandria, one of the great cities of the late Roman Empire. The novel's subtitle, "New Foes with an Old Face," suggests that this apparently obscure period of ancient history is being used to make a comment on and give a warning to Charles Kingsley's own society. The flux and fanaticism of fifth century Alexandria bear directly on the confused values and antagonisms of Victorian England.

*Alexandria. Egyptian port city founded by the Greeks some three hundred years before the Christian era and named after the great leader and conqueror Alexander. The Greek foundation still survives in Kingsley's fifth century city in its language, basic town-plan, museum, and lecture halls, where a form of Greek philosophy known as neoplatonism, was expounded, particularly by Hypatia, a young goddesslike and charismatic philosopher. Alexandria also has Roman buildings, notably the Caesarium, now being used by Christians as their main church, and the port, which is crucial to Rome, for through it pass grain supplies and much of Africa's exported wealth. A Roman military garrison occupies the city, which is governed by a prefect appointed by Rome. The Roman games, or circus, are still used by the prefect to keep the mob on his side.

Two other cultures also compete for influence. Traditionally, Alexandria also had an influential Jewish population, academic and financial by nature. Kingsley shows the devious nature of this influence, and the destabilizing effect when its financial basis is largely destroyed by the mob. The "mob" is, in effect, a Christian one, comprising some two thirds of the city's population. They are led by Christian monks and church officers under the authority of Archbishop Cyril, the metropolitan of Egypt and third-most powerful figure in fifth century Christendom. The mob also destroys Hypatia and the last remnants of the high culture of neoplatonic philosophy.

A final culture in this restless and violent city is that of the pagan Goths, nomads from northern Europe who still worship their Germanic gods. As nomads, however, their influence in Alexandria is peripheral, unlike elsewhere in the Mediterranean.

Museum. Place where Hypatia lectures. More a library than a museum in the modern sense, this building includes picture galleries and a series of lecture halls, much like what is termed a university. The museum is the local center of Greek culture, especially its late Platonic forms, which still vie intellectually with newer Christian theologies. It also has a garden. In Museum Street is located the modest house of Hypatia and her father.

Archbishop's house. Home of the metropolitan of the Orthodox Church; located near the Serapeium and the center of the real power in the city. From here, Kingsley shows, comes good and evil: good in the way that only the church is seen to be dealing with the poverty and disorder in the city; evil, in the way fanatic hatred of "the heathen" is fanned into riots, civil disturbances, and murder. The novel's cool debates over the merits of Christianity versus Platonism take place in other locations and in contrast to these irreconcilable opposites.

Cyrene (si-REE-nee). North Africa town in what is now Libya that is the seat of Bishop Synesius, who, by contrast to Cyril, is shown to be a cultured and balanced churchman. Cyrene is also the power base of Heraclian, its governor, the count of Africa, whence he launches an ill-fated revolt against Rome. The resulting military weakness allows devastation by the Moorish inhabitants of the hinterland.

— *David Barratt*

THE HYPOCHONDRIAC

Author: Molière (Jean-Baptiste Poquelin, 1622-1673)
Type of work: Drama
Type of plot: Comedy

Time of plot: Seventeenth century
First performed: 1673; first published, 1674 as *Le Malade imaginaire* (English translation, 1732)

Molière, who despised and distrusted physicians, wished to satirize the medical quacks of his day who used incomprehensible jargon full of Latin or pseudo-Latin terminology. He realized he could not show numerous physicians prescribing worthless nostrums to an assortment of patients at a variety of locations. Observation of the Aristotelian unities, and especially unity of place, led to the creation of one of Molière's most famous characters, le Malade imaginaire. *This stroke of genius enabled the iconoclastic French playwright to confine his comedy to a single place, the sick chamber of a wealthy bourgeois hypochondriac.*

Argan's bedchamber (ahr-GAH[N]Z). Bedroom of the hypochondriac of the play's title. This play is an excellent example of how place can have critical importance in the creative process. The dramatic conventions of Molière's time required adherence to the Aristotelian unity of place. His creative solution to the problem of confining the action to a single location was to invent a character gullible and rich enough to employ a doctor and an apothecary on a full-time basis to treat his nonexistent maladies. Once Molière imagined this neurotic character, it was obvious that the complex plot could easily revolve around a single place, the imaginary invalid's bedchamber. The doctor and apothecary are attracted there by the lucrative fees. Dr. Diafoirus brings his son there in hopes of marrying him to the rich Argan's daughter. The intrusions of the unsympathetic and outspoken maidservant into Argan's bedchamber are logical because Argan demands constant attendance. The intrusions of his mendacious and avaricious wife are also logical because she wants to turn her husband against her two stepdaughters as well as to see how much closer he may have come to dying.

In addition to being rich, neurotic, and gullible, the hypochondriac had to be made parsimonious, as demonstrated in the opening scene where he is going over his apothecary's bills and deciding how much he can chisel on each item. Argan's imaginary ailments led to the creation of the most important plot element, his desire to obtain free medical advice for life by forcing his daughter to marry a doctor's son against her wishes. Moliere's invention of Argan was a case of necessity being the mother of invention.

— *Bill Delaney*

I, CLAUDIUS

Author: Robert Graves (1895-1985)
Type of work: Novel
Type of plot: Historical

Time of plot: 10 B.C.E.-41 C.E.
First published: 1934

This novel is presented as the lost autobiography of the fourth Roman emperor after the demise of the Roman Republic, Claudius, whose narrative concentrates on historical figures rather than on places. Claudius's descriptions of places in the years leading up to his accession as emperor are therefore sketchy, and the novel uses modern English names for places, rather than the latin names used by the Romans during Claudius's time.

*Rome. Ancient walled city of central Italy built around seven hills. The emperor Augustus's palace is on the Palatine Hill. During the Palatine festival in honor of Augustus, wooden stands for seating sixty thousand people are erected in the southern courtyard. After his death, his widow, Livia, has a magnificent gold statue of Augustus placed in the palace's hall. During the reign of Augustus's successor, Tiberius, Tiberius builds a two-story palace for himself on the northwest part of the hill that is three times larger than Augustus's palace. Most of the other houses on this hill belong to senators. The house where Claudius's father and his uncle Tiberius were brought up and in which Claudius lives through most of his childhood is near the hill. Nearby is the temple of Apollo built by Augustus and the Apollo Library, in which Claudius spends much of his time researching his histories of Etruria and Carthage.

The Palatine Hill looks down on the market place. Under the steepest part of the hill is the Temple of Castor and Pollux. Originally built of wood, it is rebuilt in marble by Tiberius, and its interior is richly painted and gilded. Later, Caligula transforms the temple into a vestibule for his own temple, cutting a passage between the statues of the gods. The Temple of Saturn is west of the Palatine Hill, where Tiberius builds an arch celebrating Germanicus's victories in Germany.

North of the Palatine Hill, on the Capitoline Hill, is the capitol, the Temple to Jove. Caligula orders the building of a shrine next to it with a gold statue of himself, three times larger than life, to celebrate his own godhood. Also on this hill is the Tarpeian Cliff from which traitors are hurled; great use is made of the cliff during Tiberius's reign.

To the northwest lies Mars Field, where the funeral pyres of leading citizens are lit. Augustus's mausoleum, in which the ashes of most of Claudius's relatives are interred, is at the north end. The amphitheater in which gladiatorial contests are fought is not the famous Roman Colosseum, which was not to be built for another seventy years, when Vespasian becomes emperor.

Claudius owns a villa with a farm attached to it near Capua, where he spends as much time as possible.

*German frontier. Northern extent of the Roman Empire that has the empire's only unsecured border. The frontier runs along the Rhine River; Claudius's brother Germanicus spends much of his time there commanding Roman legions. The territory across the Rhine is forested. Roman Germany is divided into two provinces. The upper province, whose capital is Mainz, extends into Switzerland. The lower province, whose capital is Cologne, reaches north to the Scheldt and Sambre. Germanicus builds a fleet of ships and sails them down the Rhine, through a canal, and by sea, to reach the mouth of the Ems. The Weser River runs parallel to the Ems, fifty miles to the north, a short march for the army, where the Germans are massing. The battleground is a narrowing plain on the far side of the Weser, between the river and a range of wooded hills. A birch and oak forest bounds the plain at its narrow end.

*Bay of Naples. Area off the Campanian coast of southern Italy. Naples is in the northern corner and Pompeii to the south. The Isle of Capri is about three miles off the southernmost headland. The climate is mild in winter and cool in summer. There is only one landing place, as it is surrounded by steep cliffs. Tiberius has twelve villas here, and it is the place where he spends most of his leisure time after leaving Rome. A number of rocky islands lie north of the bay where various members of the imperial family are exiled. Augustus's daughter, Julia, and later, her daughter Agrippina, are sent to Pandataria, Nero to Ponza, and Postumus to Planasia.

— *Pauline Morgan*

THE ICEMAN COMETH

Author: Eugene O'Neill (1888-1953)
Type of work: Drama
Type of plot: Tragedy

Time of plot: 1912
First performed: 1946; first published, 1946

Harry Hope's saloon, specifically sections of its bar and backroom, provides the bleak New York City setting of this play. This contained environment emphasizes the characters' isolation from the outside world as well as their inability to face reality, visually reinforcing the major theme of the play.

Harry Hope's saloon. Squalid barroom in lower New York City. Although a fictional creation, it is modeled on three actual spots familiar to Eugene O'Neill: Jimmy the Priest's, a flophouse where O'Neill landed after a stint at sea; the Hell Hole, a Greenwich Village establishment; and the taproom of the Garden Hotel near the old Madison Square Garden.

O'Neill's stage directions describe a "dirty black curtain" that separates the backroom from the bar. The backroom, the location of the primary action of the play, is so crammed with tables that it is difficult for anyone to pass through. There is a toilet built out into the room and a nickel-a-slot phonograph. The windows, which look out on a backyard, are filthy, and the walls and ceiling are "splotched, peeled, stained and dusty." Larry Slade, the "old Foolosopher," calls it the "No Chance Saloon" and "The Bottom of the Sea Rathskeller."

Walled from the street outside, Harry Hope's saloon provides a place of escape for its occupants, who are social outcasts, derelicts, and failures, existing with their five-cent whiskey, free lunch, and pipe dreams of tomorrow. It is a setting in which one can forget, repress, deny. Symbolically, Harry Hope's is like a womb: It is warm, cozy, dark, and filled with fluid.

At the end of the first act, the comfortable booziness of the backroom is disturbed by the entrance of Hickey, the salesman, arriving ostensibly to help celebrate Harry's birthday, as is his annual custom. However, he differs somewhat from usual: first, because he refuses to drink, and second, because he is determined to persuade the residents to act upon their dreams.

In the second act the backroom has been prepared for a party. It is midnight, signifying the beginning of a new day. The bar is closed off, the floor has been swept, tables have been pushed together to make one long table, and a space has been cleared for dancing. There is a birthday cake, red ribbons on the light fixtures, and presents and bottles of whiskey on the table. The setting has been transformed into something that grotesquely approximates the celebrations of the outside world. Similarly, Hickey seeks to transform his friends into participants in society by convincing them to confront their dreams.

The effort to alter the setting and its inhabitants continues through act 3 and into the next morning. Now more of the bar is seen, including its swinging doors to the street. Significantly, the doors will introduce the characters to the reality beyond Harry Hope's, and, one by one, seduced by Hickey's arguments relating to their peace of mind, they make abortive attempts to bring their illusions of tomorrow into reality.

In the last act the setting reverts to the original scene but with an "atmosphere of oppressive stagnation." Even the booze has no life to it. The patrons were unsuccessful in facing reality, and only when Hickey blurts out that he hated his wife and must be insane can they reinstate their pipe dreams and therefore their stasis. They, as all humankind, need their illusions to survive.

Jimmy the Priest's was a Raines Law hotel of the early twentieth century. It could allow service of liquor after hours and on Sundays if a meal was served with the liquor. Generally this meant a moldy sandwich festered in the middle of each table. The building was a narrow, five-story structure, with the proprietor occupying the second floor, while the upper floors were rented to the regulars. When O'Neill lived there for a while in 1912, he met many of the characters who appear in this play; and it was here that he probably attempted suicide and was saved by his friend, James Byth, the model for Jimmy Tomorrow.

— *Joyce E. Henry*

THE IDIOT

Author: Fyodor Dostoevski (1821-1881)
Type of work: Novel
Type of plot: Psychological realism

Time of plot: Mid-nineteenth century
First published: Idiot, 1868-1869 (English translation, 1887)

Set primarily in St. Petersburg, Russia, this novel draws heavily upon the special characteristics of that city in the Russian history and culture of its time.

*St. Petersburg. Russia's capital city and cultural and political center of Russia, where Prince Myshkin arrives, and where much of the novel's action takes place. The character of the city is very un-Russian. Traditional Russian cities grew up in concentric rings around their central fortresses—a pattern still visible in modern Moscow, with its three ring roads (boulevard, garden, and outer rings), linked by radial avenues to the city center, the Kremlin. By contrast, St. Petersburg is laid out in a Western-style grid pattern that was established by Peter the Great's decree. Moreover, while traditional Russian cities were built of wood and suffered frequent fires, St. Petersburg is a city of stone. However, it was threatened by frequent floods, particularly when strong winds from the Baltic Sea caused the Neva River to back up.

Because St. Petersburg is near the Arctic Circle, it has an extreme seasonal variation of its day-night cycle. During the winter, the sun scarcely peeks above the horizon, giving only a few hours of daylight each day. By contrast, at the summer solstice the sun barely sets, and even at midnight the sky remains bright, creating the fabled "white nights" for which St. Petersburg is famous. It is significant that Fyodor Dostoevski has Prince Myshkin's second and third arrivals in St. Petersburg (when he returns from his visit to Moscow and the traditional Russian heartland, and his disastrous return to find Nastasia Filipovna murdered) take place during the white nights. Dostoevski plays upon the idea that this period of nighttime light is a period in which the normal laws of nature are tenuous at best and can even be suspended.

Dostoevski follows an established Russian literary tradition that regards St. Petersburg as a city in which extraordinary and unnatural events take place. For example, Alexander Pushkin's "The Bronze Horseman" has the equestrian statue of Peter the Great come to life, and in Nikolai Gogol's "The Nose," the protagonist's nose absconds, assumes human form, and reaches a rank higher than that of its former owner. Since Dostoevski is writing realistic fiction, he does not include such fantastical elements, but the madness that leads Parfen Semyonovich Rogozhin to murder Nastasia Filipovna would be understood by Russian readers familiar with the white nights.

*Pavlovsk (pahv-LOFSK). St. Petersburg suburb visited by Prince Myshkin. This suburb, in which the czars had a palace as a vacation retreat, was also the terminus of the first Russian railroad. Myshkin and several of the other major characters retreat there in chapters in the middle of the novel.

Dr. Schneider's institute. Facility in Switzerland where Prince Myshkin is treated for epilepsy, and to which he returns after his disastrous breakdown. The institute and the village in which it is located are seen only in Myshkin's recollections, which reveal his otherworldly saintliness through his ability to forgive and love the fallen woman, Marie.

— *Leigh Husband Kimmel*

IDYLLS OF THE KING

Author: Alfred, Lord Tennyson (1809-1892)
Type of work: Poetry
Type of plot: Arthurian romance

Time of plot: Fifth century
First published: 1859-1885

Most writers of Arthurian romance are intentionally ambiguous about the setting of the legend. Alfred, Lord Tennyson, is no exception. While it may be difficult to link the places in Tennyson's poem to specific locations in England, it is clear that Tennyson uses location for specific thematic purposes. With great care he contrasts Camelot with other locales to draw parallels between the values of Arthur's kingdom and those held by others, who struggle to topple the Round Table and its King.

Camelot. Castle where King Arthur has his seat of government. As in most accounts of the Arthurian legend, Camelot is the place where Arthur and his knights meet at the Round Table, where they are ostensibly equals in upholding the chivalric virtues that lead to the practice of justice and mercy in the kingdom. In Tennyson's version, the knights are also committed to upholding a strict moral code. Tennyson's Camelot is a physical symbol of the perfect society, in which the will of the individual is subordinate to the grand plan of a benevolent and wise ruler. That association is made manifest in the second tale, "Gareth and Lynette." When the young knight first makes his way to Arthur's court, he sees the spires of the city emerging from the clouds and hears strange music. Meeting Merlin, the wizard who is the king's confidant and mentor, Gareth learns that, if he hears music, it is because "they are building still." As Merlin explains, "the City is built to music,/ Therefore never built at all,/ And therefore built for ever." Metaphorically, the city is like a symphony: It is built or sustained in existence only so long as each individual participant continues to play his or her role. The suggestion that there is a hierarchy of roles and a subordination of the individual will to the common good is a major theme of *Idylls of the King*. Tennyson's description of the construction of the city of Camelot is a metaphor for the way a perfect society should be constructed.

Forests and plains. Areas outside Camelot and the other dwelling places of the knights throughout the kingdom. Using a time-honored comparison, Tennyson contrasts the city and castle with the countryside. In Camelot, men and women exhibit both knightly and Christian virtues; in the natural world, however, men and women often resort to practices that demonstrate their kinship with the beasts. Far from being idyllic, the woods and fields of Arthur's kingdom are often places where danger lurks, principally because these regions are inhabited by outcasts from Camelot or people who choose to live by values contrary to the ones the king espouses.

Wastelands. Location where many of King Arthur's knights search for the Holy Grail. Like other writers of Arthurian legend, Tennyson creates vivid descriptions of the filth, squalor, and aridity of a land clearly in need of tending. In traditional versions of the legend, the discovery of the Grail was to lead to restoration of the land's fertility. For the knights in *Idylls of the King* the search for the Grail proves fruitless, and the land remains barren. The ill-fated quest provides Arthur an opportunity to explain to his subjects that it is not in seeking remote conquests that the kingdom is served, but rather in staying close to home and handling the domestic, social, and political tasks that are part of everyday living.

Red Knight's castle. Home of the knight Pelleas, who becomes disillusioned with Arthur's court after discovering that the woman he loves is unfaithful. Though mentioned in only one scene, the castle's importance to the theme of the poem is significant. After Pelleas leaves Camelot, he sets up an alternative order of knights, who behave openly as brigands, lechers, and moral degenerates. When Arthur sends a force to wipe out this rogue order, Pelleas tells the invaders from Camelot that his castle houses knights who, though immoral, are actually better than those in Arthur's city. They are not hypocrites like those at Camelot who publicly espouse high virtue but in fact act basely.

Battlefields. Locations of Arthur's initial struggles to unite the petty kingdoms of the country and of his last fight to preserve his kingdom against his nephew Mordred. In Tennyson's poem, battlefields are not only places of destruction, they are locales shrouded in mist and fog, places where friend and enemy are indistinguishable. Tennyson contrasts the mayhem of the battlefield with the civility of the court to demonstrate the precarious nature of the civilization Arthur establishes at Camelot.

— *Laurence W. Mazzeno*

IF NOT NOW, WHEN?

Author: Primo Levi (1919-1987)
Type of work: Novel
Type of plot: Adventure

Time of plot: 1943-1945
First published: Se non ora, quando?, 1982 (English translation, 1985)

Based on Primo Levi's activities as a partisan in northwestern Italy, this novel is about displacement—the continuously shifting search for place, and the vision of a promised land for Jews in Palestine as a shifting group of mostly Jewish resistance fighters makes its way from western Russia to Milan. At every turn, men and women torn by war from their homes and haunts seek a definable space that can permit physical survival and the maintenance of a social order.

*Pripet Marshes. Camp in western Russia built by one man around a downed aircraft that establishes the theme of personally created space. This is then expanded in the "Republic of the Marshes," a refuge built in relative safety on the hummocks of the Pripet Marshes of Belorussia. As a makeshift social group of resistance fighters coalesces but moves on, other forms of shelter are briefly occupied, such as a set of chambers dug out from the shaft of a well.

*Poland. Eastern European country caught between warring Germany and Russia. Although place is always being reidentified, as territory is yielded by the Germans or retaken by the Russians, the war is more than territorial. For many, not only place but also community has been eradicated: the destruction of Jewish towns, followed by the mass murder of Jews in the death camps. Even Poland itself risks disappearance. Earlier divided between Soviet Russia and Nazi Germany into zones of intended future influence, it is now being fought over. As the tide of war turns against the Germans, the partisans, with Mendel at the focus of the reader's attention, move westward behind enemy lines both to escape shelling and to continue their guerrilla war of harassment in the chaos of the once victorious army now falling back. Specific towns, rivers, and districts are mentioned early in the novel but the partisans' local knowledge is soon exhausted and they move westward into a nameless landscape and collapsing social order.

*Germany. Belligerent country through whose eastern region the partisans make their way to Austria, and from there to Italy. The partisans can rest at no one site for any lengthy period. In "the land of hunger" place is redefined daily by need, such as an abandoned field is marked off for an air-drop of relief supplies. The Soviets promote partisan activity behind German lines in the now emptying, so-called "Great Land" in order to lay better claim to future occupancy. Some of the illusion of emptiness is willed, since the Germans hope to destroy the evidence of the death camps before the day of judicial reckoning that many of them know must come. The partisans are more than the "displaced persons" of the postwar era, swept up and aside by events, because their sense of lost place is in part offset by growing group cohesion. Couples form—Mendel and Sissl, Leonid and Line, Mendel and Line; units realign themselves under leaders of varying ability and vision—Dov, Gedaleh.

*Milan. Italian city relatively untouched by the horrors of war that the partisans eventually reach. There they even meet Palestinian Jews who help refugees. By now, the civilized urban space and functioning human society of Milan seem oddities to the survivors. So complete is their divorce from the superficial attributes of settled urban culture that they feel an "undefined malaise, which was homesickness for the forest and the open road."

*Palestine. Middle Eastern territory mandated to British rule that after the events of this novel will form the basis of the independent Jewish-ruled state of Israel. The novel ends with the partisans being promised passage to Palestine on a ship; however, there are still hurdles to cross. British permission would be needed for a ship to come into port and for would-be settlers to disembark. Readers know what the partisans of the novel cannot: the contention over place, the birth and early life of the new Jewish nation will be no less marked by suffering than their flight across eastern Europe. From marsh to desert, place can be no more secure than before. Whatever their sense of reintegration into collective Jewish identity, their finest experience of community may lie in the past, in the makeshift camps along the path of flight and war. At the book's end, a child is born to two of the partisans—a promise of future life—but on that same day the United States drops the first atomic bomb on Japan, in history's relentless reconfiguring of place.

— *William Sayers*

THE ILIAD

Author: Homer (c. ninth century B.C.E.)
Type of work: Poetry
Type of plot: Epic

Time of plot: Antiquity
First transcribed: c. 800 B.C.E. (English translation, 1611)

The fact that this epic uses the name of the ancient city of Ilios, or Troy, for its title reflects the importance of place in this epic. The Greeks besieging Troy are not fighting merely to reclaim King Menelaus's wife, Helen, or to punish Paris, the Trojan prince who took her. They want to destroy the city and kill or enslave all its inhabitants. The aim of the Trojans is to kill enough Greeks so that those remaining will flee to their ships and set sail. However, both sides know that ultimately their fate will be decided not on the battlefield but on Mount Olympus, the home of the gods.

*Troy (Ilios). Ancient city on the plain of Troas, or Troad, on the eastern shore of the Aegean Sea in what is now Turkey. Homer knew the area so well it is assumed that he had visited it. However, the Troy about which he wrote was a city that existed perhaps four centuries before his own time.

Legend has it that Apollo and Poseidon constructed Troy, and the Greek divinities had much to do with destroying it, first providing the occasion for the war, then prolonging it by squabbling among themselves, and finally deciding the city's fate. However, historians believe that the cause of the war may have been the Greeks' wish to stop the Trojans from collecting tolls from land travelers and from ships moving in or out of the Dardanelles (Hellespont).

*Pergamos** (PUR-gah-muhs). Troy's walled citadel, or acropolis. The temple of Athena at its summit is the Trojans' place of worship. King Priam's palace, which is described in book 6, is also there. It serves not only as the residence of the royal family but also as the city's center of government. Whenever Hector goes out to battle or returns home, as he does in book 6, he uses the Scaean Gate on the west side of the Pergamos. His wife Andromache often watches him from the wall above. The city cannot be destroyed as long as the Pergamos remains in the hands of the Trojans; when it falls, the city will be destroyed.

Ship station. Area west of the city of Troy where the Greeks beach their ships. In book 15, Hector leads the Trojans through the Greek defenses and sets fire to one of the ships, leading the Greeks to fear that they will be defeated.

Greek camp. Area between the ships and the battlefield where the Greeks gather to rest, feast, argue, and discuss strategy. In book 7, Nestor persuades the Greeks to fortify their camp by building a wall with watchtowers and strong gates and by digging a moat just beyond it.

*Mount Ida.** Mountain southeast of Troy where the great god Zeus often stations himself so that he can watch the conflict below, periodically hurling thunderbolts to signal his disapproval. Zeus is often found near his altar on the peak Gargaron. In book 14, Zeus's wife Hera visits Mount Ida to charm and distract him so he will not be aware of the Greeks' victories below.

*Mount Olympus.** Mountain that is the highest point in Greece, located near the western shore of the Aegean Sea that is in legend the home of the gods. Homer's epic shows the gods meeting there, observing events below, and often quarrelling bitterly. Sometimes they leave their Mount Olympus homes, disguise themselves as mortals, and take part in battles. When they are wounded—as Aphrodite and Ares are in book 5, they return to Olympus to be made whole.

Hades (hay-deez). Legendary underworld, ruled by Hades, in which the spirits of the dead dwell forever and the guilty are punished. In book 23, the ghost of Patrocles appears to his friend Achilles, asking that his body be placed on a funeral pyre so that he can complete his journey into Hades, instead of wandering with the other unburied spirits outside the gates.

— *Rosemary M. Canfield Reisman*

IMMENSEE

Author: Theodor Storm (1817-1888)
Type of work: Novella
Type of plot: Pastoral

Time of plot: Mid-nineteenth century
First published: 1850; final version, 1851 (English translation, 1863)

This story is a study in profound regret, in which the eponymous lake is a symbol of the life that Reinhard has never dared embrace. He walks restlessly around it, and once plunges into it in quest of a symbolic flower—only to withdraw, defeated—but in the end he abandons it, just as he had abandoned his beloved once before, in favor of a sterile life of learning.

Immensee (Imm-uhn-ZEE). Site of the estate from which Reinhard Werner's former schoolfriend Erich sends Elisabeth the canary that replaces the linnet he gave her before going away to university. Erich was given the estate by his father. When Reinhard first visits the Immensee as Erich's guest, some years after Elisabeth's marriage to Erich, the estate is blue and calm, surrounded by green sunlit woods. The red roof of Erich's house rises out of foliage speckled with white blossom. It is accompanied by vineyards, hop gardens, and a vegetable garden—a perfect image of domestic self-sufficiency, as further exemplified by a stork (a symbol of good luck in German folklore) that flies up from the chimney before settling in the garden. The bees swarming there are a metaphorical reflection of Erich's own industry; he has added a distillery to the farm buildings erected by his father to supplement the dwelling built in his grandfather's time, emphasizing the progress as well as the continuity of family life.

Switzerland has a region called Immensee, but Theodor Storm uses the name in this novel because of its symbolic significance. The word means "lake of bees" in German.

Lake. Body of water on the estate. A path along the lakeshore, where the troubled Reinhard walks, leads through a birchwood to a small promontory where there is a bench that Elisabeth's mother has named the "sunset seat." While returning along the path one day in the rain, Reinhard thinks he sees Elisabeth among the trees, but she vanishes before he can catch up with her. The family's favorite room overlooks the garden; there Reinhard and Elisabeth rediscover their feelings when they sing folk songs together. Afterward, while walking along the lakeside, Reinhard sees a white water lily on the lake and impulsively wades in after it; he soon finds himself in deep water, and the lily seems to recede as he tries to approach it. On the following day, after Reinhard and Elisabeth have been walking on the opposite shore, Reinhard detects signs of repressed suffering in the reflexive gestures of Elisabeth's hand as it trails in the water—but Reinhard goes back across the lake alone, obsessively revisiting the places where he and Elisabeth had paused together, incapable of positive action.

Reinhard's home. Old Reinhard lives in a single upstairs room in a high-gabled house; one wall is occupied by book and display cases, another is hung with pictures. He sits in an armchair with red velvet cushions, with books beside him on a green baize-topped table. His long reverie ends with a vision of dark waters ceaselessly stirred by black waves, while a single white water lily floats forlornly.

Meadow. Field where Reinhard and Elisabeth build a turf house when they are children. Reinhard sets out to make a wooden bench for the house on an unexpected holiday, while Elisabeth gathers mallow seeds to make a necklace.

Woods. Setting of a picnic before Reinhard's departure for university. The road to it leads through a gloomy pine grove to a brighter beech wood, where the young folk search for edible berries. After Reinhard rescues Elisabeth from brambles they follow a brook and get lost; the sound of church bells enables them to get their bearings, but they find no berries.

Rathskeller. Basement barroom in Reinhard's university town, where Reinhard and his fellow students spend Christmas Eve drinking, while a gypsy fiddler and zither player reluctantly play and sing for them. When Reinhard returns to his lodgings after dark, he finds a package of Christmas cakes ornamented by Elisabeth with his initials, but he gives them away and sets himself to work.

Elisabeth's home. Although Reinhard calls on Elisabeth regularly on his first return from university, she spurns the gift of his poems chronicling their childhood, after fastening chickweed on the gilded cage where Erich's canary has replaced his linnet.

— *Brian Stableford*

THE IMPORTANCE OF BEING EARNEST: A Trivial Comedy for Serious People

Author: Oscar Wilde (1854-1900)
Type of work: Drama
Type of plot: Comedy of manners

Time of plot: Late nineteenth century
First performed: 1895; first published, 1899

This comedy of manners is situated in two settings, Algernon Moncrieff's flat on Half-Moon Street in London, and Jack Worthing's country home, the Manor House in Woolton, Hertfordshire. The resulting city-country dichotomy allows the play's two chief male characters freedom to escape their relations and female suitors.

Moncrieff's flat. Elegant London flat of the bachelor Algernon Moncrieff in which the first act of the play is set. The flat is complete with butler and other accoutrements of a life of leisure. This milieu provides the backdrop for Algernon's insouciance, wit, and idle life. The drawback to his lovely home is its proximity to the home of his aunt, Lady Bracknell, a dragon lady and master of the non sequitur. Her incursions into Algernon's life often force him to flee to the country to care for his invalid friend, Bunbury, whom he has invented for this purpose.

Manor House. Hertfordshire home of Algernon's friend Jack Worthing, who also has a London home. This house provides the setting for the second and third acts of the play. Worthing is the guardian of Miss Cecily Cardew, who is instructed in the German language by her governess, Miss Prism, and in religion by the Reverend Canon Chasuble; they all reside in this rural retreat. Worthing escapes to London by receiving phone calls from an imaginary brother whom he must rescue from scrapes.

While Algernon escapes London to care for his imaginary sick friend Bunbury in the country, Worthing escapes from the country by looking out for his imaginary brother in the city. The two worlds of the play collide and make for comic results when Algernon comes to the Manor House posing as Worthing's brother Ernest. The arrival of Lady Bracknell leads to exposure of the imaginary friendships and identities and makes possible true love among the young people.

— *Isabel Bonnyman Stanley*

IN COLD BLOOD

Author: Truman Capote (Truman Streckfus Persons, 1924-1984)
Type of work: Novel

Type of plot: Detective and mystery
Time of plot: 1959
First published: 1966

Set in Kansas, which is cast as a kind of Eden violated, Truman Capote's best-selling novel recounts the actual 1959 murder of an innocent farm family—Herbert Clutter, his wife, and teenage son and daughter—and the pursuit, trial, and punishment of their killers, Richard Hickock and Perry Smith.

*Garden City. Seat of Kansas's Finney County on the high wheat plains of Western Kansas. Here upright Herbert Clutter headed the building committee for the newly completed First Methodist Church. Capote reminds his reader that they are in "the 'Bible Belt,' that gospel-haunted strip of American territory in which a man must, if only for business reasons, take his religion with the straightest of faces." This idyllic setting has caused many readers to believe Capote's book is evoking the Christian story of the Fall in the Garden (City) of Eden, with Hickock and Smith as the snakes, that is, as infiltrating evil.

*Holcomb. Village of 270 people near Garden City, outside of which the Clutters reside on River Valley Farm, a spread of eight hundred acres owned outright by Herbert Clutter, with three thousand more acres farmed on a rental basis. Clutter calls the river valley "Eden on earth."

Open Road. *In Cold Blood* is structured in four sections, and the central two—"Persons Unknown" and "Answer"—detail Hickock and Smith's flight following the Clutter murders and the Federal Bureau of Investigation's pursuit of the men across the United States and into Mexico. During his six years of research, Capote retraced every step of the killers' seven-thousand-mile flight, beginning in Kansas City, where Hickock bounces bank checks, and moving through Oklahoma, Texas, Mexico, California's Mojave Desert, Nevada, Wyoming, Nebraska, Iowa, back to Kansas City (where Hickock writes more bad checks), Missouri, Arkansas, Louisiana, Alabama, Florida, and through Alabama, Louisiana, Texas, New Mexico, and Nevada, where they are arrested in Las Vegas on December 30 and returned to the Garden City jail. Capote's treatment of Hickock and Smith's hapless and circuitous flight seems to imply the end of America's open road as a symbol of escape and new beginning.

*Leavenworth Penitentiary.** Kansas prison in whose "Death Row" Smith and Hickock are held following their conviction for the Clutter murders. Death Row is "a dark two-storied building shaped like a coffin" from which Smith and Hickock can view the execution chamber, called "the corner." In titling the novel's final section "The Corner," Capote alludes to this literal place name, yet he also implies that Smith and Hickock are "cornered," trapped by a criminal justice system that refuses to accept the psychological testimony of the two men, a system of capital punishment that murders Smith and Hickock "in cold blood."

*Kansas.** Capote states in the opening lines of his volume that "the village of Holcomb stands on the high wheat plains of western Kansas, a lonesome area that other Kansans call 'out there.'" He goes on to say that "the countryside, with its hard blue skies and desert-clear air, has an atmosphere that is rather more Far Western than Middle West." This opening and many other details have spurred some readers to interpret this novel as a reverse Western, that is, a tale of Indian revenge, for Perry Smith is half Cherokee. However one reads the novel, one is left with the author's final haunting image of "the big sky, [and] the whisper of wind voices in the wind-bent wheat."

— *Barbara Lounsberry*

IN DUBIOUS BATTLE

Author: John Steinbeck (1902-1968)
Type of work: Novel
Type of plot: Social realism

Time of plot: 1930's
First published: 1936

The setting for this rehearsal for John Steinbeck's The Grapes of Wrath *(1939) is the Salinas Valley (Torgas Valley in the novel), a twentieth century Eden of apple orchards where the original battle between the forces of good and evil is being fought out again. Setting tends to be objective and neutral in* In Dubious Battle *but also carries a clear allegorical significance.*

City. Unnamed California city at the start of the novel that is probably San Francisco. The signs of the economic Depression are everywhere here. Steinbeck wastes little time describing this setting, but it is in this city that Jim Nolan begins his education, by joining the Communist Party. He has been "dead" in this modern and alienating urban environment for some time, but under the tutelage of Mac, a Party organizer, he makes his commitment to the causes of social justice and begins to come alive.

Torgas Valley. Rich farmland full of apple orchards some 150 miles southeast of the city (and closely resembling California's real Salinas Valley). Mac tells Jim that "Torgas is a little valley, and it's mostly apple orchards. Most of it's owned by a few men. . . . when the apples are ripe the crop tramps come in and pick them." Later, Steinbeck describes one orchard where the pickers are working: "The orchard was alive. The branches of·the trees shook under the ladders. The overripes dropped with dull plops to the ground underneath the trees. Somewhere, hidden in a tree-top, a whistling virtuoso trilled." Figuratively, this is an evocation of the innocence of the Garden of Eden before the Fall. The title of the novel is actually taken from John Milton's *Paradise Lost* (1667), which describes the forces of the fallen angels in league with Satan and, in the line Steinbeck uses as his epigraph, "In dubious battle on the plains of Heaven." The Torgas Valley is being linked with Milton's allegory of the figures of good and evil battling in a Christian Heaven, as well as with the mythology of the Garden of Eden.

Anderson place. Ranch owned by the one grower in the valley sympathetic to the workers. When the strike pushes the fruit pickers off other farms, they set up their camp on land owned by Mr. Anderson for the duration of the strike, which will include pitched battles with scabs and confrontations with local vigilantes. Later, the vigilantes burn down Anderson's barn and his crop, killing his hunting dogs in the process. In the final confrontation, Jim Nolan is shot by the vigilantes and becomes a Christ figure. On the last page of the novel, Mac is using Jim's murder to rally the disheartened strikers: "This guy didn't want nothing for himself."

Torgas. Small town that is the center of life in the valley. Many of the confrontations in the novel between strikers and those leagued against them (owners, police, and scabs) occur in this town, including a funeral march for another murdered organizer, but the town is only sketchily described. The central symbolic struggle in the novel is really between those who own property and those who can only work it, a theme Steinbeck would develop on the broader canvas of *The Grapes of Wrath* three years later.

— *David Peck*

IN THE HEART OF THE SEAS: A Story of a Journey to the Land of Israel

Author: Shmuel Yosef Agnon (Shmuel Yosef Czaczkes, 1888-1970)
Type of work: Novel
Type of plot: Folklore

Time of plot: Early twentieth century
First published: Bi-levav yamim: Sipur agadah, 1935 (English translation, 1947)

Place functions as a strong motivating force for this novel's Jewish characters, to whom the Land of Israel is both real and holy—a place where God's presence is powerfully felt. Their desire to migrate from Eastern Europe to Israel overwhelms their bonds to their hometown, which is described in realistic terms. To reach Israel, a place that serves as terminus for their religious aspirations, they embark on an adventurous voyage across land and sea. To the author, who actually undertook such a voyage, Israel is a spiritual place that provides the only real home to the Jewish people.

*****Jerusalem.** Holy Land city that is the holiest place on earth to the Hasidic travelers of the novel, as well as the final destination of their arduous journey. Jerusalem is both a real and a divine place to them. The novel describes the travelers' religious beliefs about the mythical powers of the city in the same tone of voice in which it describes the city's physical and architectural details, implicitly inviting readers to share these beliefs.

The history of Jerusalem and its religious importance have a strong emotional impact on the protagonists. Arriving at Jerusalem on the eve of the Sabbath, the travelers kiss its walls and tear their clothes in memory of the destruction of the last Jerusalem Temple by the Romans in the second century. The travelers are invited to stay at the House of Study of the Hasidic Jews in the city; on the Sabbath they wash themselves in a bath house before finally praying at the Wailing Wall, which is all that remains of the original Jerusalem Temple. Later, they rent a house with a view of the wall, and, with few exceptions, decide to settle in Jerusalem to remain in a place where they can feel God's presence in an especially powerful way.

*****Israel.** At the time in which the novel is set, the Ottoman Empire of the Turks ruled over what the Jewish voyagers of the novel call the Land of Israel—the Middle Eastern land that became a British Mandate Territory after World War I. Both the novel's characters and its author implicitly use the biblical boundaries of the Land of Israel when thinking of the place, which corresponds only roughly to what became the modern State of Israel in 1948. Landing on Israel's shores at Jaffa (now Tel Aviv), they are welcomed in the Courtyard of the Jews, the traditional reception center for Jewish visitors. As they continue inland, by donkey, on the road to Jerusalem, the desolate condition of the country, which is described in sad detail, reminds them of the loss of their homeland since Roman days. This sense of loss upon viewing the place is juxtaposed with their hope that God may restore this holy place to them.

*****Buczacz** (BEW-chahch; also spelled Buchach). Polish city, which is now in the Ukraine, that is hometown to both the Jewish voyagers of the novel and its author, who includes himself among them. At the time they begin their journey, Buczacz was part of the Austro-Hungarian

Empire, which ceased to exist in 1918. Buczacz lies to the east of the Carpathian Mountains, on a hill overlooking the Stypa River, and is part of the old district of Galicia. The town and its large Jewish population are described in lively, vivid, and lovingly recalled detail.

Before writing the novel, Shmuel Yosef Agnon revisited Buczacz and was saddened by its spiritual and economic decay under Polish rule. His descriptions thus carry a nostalgic tone remembering a better past. During World War II, German troops occupying the town murdered nine thousand of its ten thousand Jewish inhabitants. Only four hundred Jews returned to the city described in such loving terms in the novel.

*Yaslovitz (yah-SLOH-vihtz; now Jazlovicz, Ukraine). First major town to the south of Buczacz. Yaslovitz serves as an example for hostility among neighbors. Until the arrival of the voyagers, the members of Yaslovitz's Jewish community loathe Buczacz's Jews for having abducted their rabbi to minister to them.

*Eastern Europe. On their way to the Holy Land, the travelers pass through a variety of Eastern European cities before taking ship in Istanbul, Turkey. Their travels give Agnon opportunities to describe the different character of each town and comment on the conditions of the towns' Jewish inhabitants. However, these places are only way stations on the journey to Israel.

*Mediterranean Sea. The final obstacle between the travelers and the Holy Land is the eastern Mediterranean. Their sea voyage tests their faith and resolve when a storm threatens their lives and sends them back to port in Istanbul, from where they departed. While at sea, the travelers experience repeated sightings of Hananiah, a holy member of their group, who is seen sitting on the waters of the sea. Although Hananiah misses the ship's departure in Istanbul, he reaches Israel before all the others.

— *R. C. Lutz*

IN THE WILDERNESS

Author: Sigrid Undset (1882-1949)
Type of work: Novel
Type of plot: Historical
Time of plot: Early fourteenth century

First published: Olav Audunssøn i Hestviken and *Olav Audunssøn og hans børn*, 1925-1927 (*The Master of Hestviken*, 1928-1930; volume 3, *In the Wilderness*, 1929)

This second volume of Sigrid Undset's Master of Hestviken tetralogy is set in Norway at a time when Christianity was replacing the old Viking ways. In this stark setting, Olav Audunssøn gradually achieves a sense of personal redemption. The novel begins at gloomy Hestviken, where Olav agonizes over his wife's death. Two contrasting households—Rundmyr and Torhild Björnsdatter's farm—represent negative and positive forces acting upon Olav and his family.

Hestviken. Olav Audunssøn's ancestral home—a cold, isolated place on a rugged Norwegian landscape of rocky promontories and pounding fjord waves. Olav secretly carries bowls of ale out to an old Viking burial mound on his property to honor an adventurous ancestor. This practice demonstrates his longing for release from the constraints of his confining life.

Eirik, Olav's heir apparent to the estate, covets Hestviken's land and buildings and reacts with anger and jealousy to any perceived threats to his right to inherit them. However, Eirik fails to perform his share of

farm work, and household workers make fun of his lies and boasting.

Rundmyr. Farm near Hestviken that is overseen by Olav and occupied by the mentally deficient Arnketil and the corrupt Liv. A "den of iniquity," this site of slovenliness, thievery, and profligacy contributes to the corruption of Eirik. Olav can reform neither the farm nor Eirik's character.

Torhild Björnsdatter's farm. Home of Olav's former mistress at Auken. Contrasting completely with Rundmyr, this household is a place of virtue and accomplishment. Olav twice crosses the fjord to visit it, and each time is favorably impressed by Torhild's hard work and resourcefulness in managing the property. When Swedes invade Norway, the women of Hestviken flee to Torhild's farm for safety. Like Torhild herself, the farm stands for strength and resiliency.

*London. Capital city of England, which Olav visits. The novel provides a detailed account of London in the fourteenth century: the sights, sounds, and smells of its streets, its harbor, its markets, and its diverse population. Olav finds the city invigorating, a place in which to renew his downcast spirit. At a Dominican church in London Olav becomes infatuated with a young woman who resembles his late wife, Ingunn. After Olav leaves London, he wanders into a church attended by poor people and realizes that riches matter little when it comes to one's relationship to God. His pilgrimage to a shrine north of London leads him to understand that he has wrongly taken advantage of friends.

*Oslo. Norwegian city that bears the brunt of the Swedish invasion in 1308. The novel shows a masterful grasp of the locations and tactics of skirmishes and battles that eventually lead the invaders to withdraw. Though badly wounded in the face, Olav comes away from the battle exultant because he has fought valiantly for his homeland.

— *Nancy Conn Terjesen*

INDEPENDENT PEOPLE

Author: Halldór Laxness (Halldór Kiljan Guðjónsson, 1902-1998)
Type of work: Novel
Type of plot: Social

Time of plot: Twentieth century
First published: Sjálfstætt fólk, 1934-1935 (English translation, 1946)

This novel is set on a poor sheep farm nestled in a mountain dale of northern Iceland, beginning at the turn of the twentieth century. The farm's isolation reflects the spiritual and cultural isolation of its occupants, and their self-sufficiency. Its simplicity, exiguous conditions, and quasi-mystical closeness to nature also contrast with the ambitions, privileges, and artificialities of a wealthy farm nearby, a seaside town, and the distant national capital, Reykjavik. These contrasts expose changes in Icelandic culture that moved it away from its much-beloved heritage, as portrayed in its medieval sagas of warrior-farmers living a fiercely independent life on their freeholds.

Summerhouses. Small farm, formerly wintering pens for sheep, in a mountain valley of north-central Iceland. The story's protagonist, Gudbjartur Jonsson, fulfills his dream of becoming an independent man by buying Summerhouses, a marginal tract of heath, and raising his own flock. To the south rise desolate mountains with glaciers, and ranges extend to the east and west, making the farmstead an island of fertile land within the surrounding desert highlands. Furthermore, it lies under a legendary curse, haunted by the Irish sorcerer Kolumkilli and the witch Gunnvor. In a major theme, these spirits symbolize the harsh, alien hostility of the environment to human occupation; everyone before Bjartur has been driven from Summerhouses. To avoid the humiliation of eating the bread of others or accepting charity of any kind, Bjartur must have stony resolution as unforgiving as the natural environment. In the best of years the heath barely supports enough sheep to feed a family; during bad years Bjartur loses two wives and several children to starvation and disease. Bjartur represents all poor people who dream of standing on their own land and controlling their own fortunes, and his fate—he eventually loses Summerhouses after decades of struggle—reveals the brittleness of that dream.

*Iceland. North Atlantic island nation, whose countryside contains natural features that are both beautiful and terrifying—desert, heath, hot springs, freezing rivers, volcanic vents—all of it snowbound much of the year. On the northern part of Iceland, Bjartur and his family respond to the conditions variously. Bjartur himself finds nature a foe to tame with his strength and steadfastness. The summer pastures and native creatures imbue his youngest son, Nonni, with peace and contentment and inspire him to become a singer. The beauty of spring, especially its fragile wildflowers, reflects the innocent eroticism of Bjartur's daughter, Asta Sollilja.

To most others in the area, however, the north is either a place of social exile, a backwater retaining relics of medieval pastoral culture, as it is to the regional minister, the Reverend Godmundur, or it is a base from which to acquire larger wealth and status in greater Iceland, as it is for Bailiff Jon of Utirauthsmyri.

Rauthsmyri (roths-meer-ee). Small community, whose name means "Red Moors," centered on a wealthy farm, **Utirauthsmyri**, just north of Summerhouses. Bailiff Jon is the resident rural squire, whose large farm and household employ many locals (Bjartur was one for eighteen years) and dominate local politics and culture. Summerhouses originally was part of Utirauthsmyri, and it returns to the bailiff after Bjartur defaults on unwise loans made at the bailiff's urging. The prosperity of the bailiff's holdings and his shifty machinations to regain Summerhouses at a bargain contrast with Bjartur's wretched poverty and single-mindedness. Moreover, to Bjartur, Summerhouses is all the world he wants; the bailiff, on the other hand, uses his wealth and position to establish a farmers' cooperative that supplants local merchants in supplying loans and goods to members and finding markets for their sheep. His son, Ingolfur

Jonsson (Bjartur's foster brother), builds on these efforts to become a member of parliament, governor of the Bank of Iceland, and, even as Bjartur is reduced to a tenant farmer, prime minister.

Fjord (fee-yohrd). Icelandic seacoast town dependent on fishing and on merchants who cater to farmers. Perhaps modeled on Akureyri, now a major Icelandic city at the end of a long fjord, Fjord and its nearest neighbor Vik ("bay," possibly modeled on Husavik) indicate coastal topography, as well as identify settlements, and so contrast with the inland landscape of Summerhouses and Rauthsmyri. The townspeople set themselves apart from country folk, whose rustic clothes they laugh at because those in town pay attention to fashion, live in better houses, and consume more luxuries. For his part, Bjartur considers towns to be full of corruption, especially among greedy merchants who cheat farmers, and the refuge of lost souls who gave up the independent farm life to be wager earners.

*****Reykjavik** (RAY-kyeh-veek). Iceland's capital city, a seaport in the southwest. Whatever corruption exists in small towns is compounded many times in Reykjavik in Bjartur's eyes. The distant capital is the home of banks and the national government, both full of time-servers and middlemen who depend upon rural revenues and taxes and who make decisions that affect the independence of small landholders.

— *Roger Smith*

INDIAN SUMMER

Author: William Dean Howells (1837-1920)
Type of work: Novel
Type of plot: Domestic realism

Time of plot: Shortly after the American Civil War
First published: 1886

This novel unfolds in Florence, an Italian city with a dazzling cultural heritage but one with many presumed dangers for impressionable American visitors in the post-Civil War period. In contrast to more typical literary treatments of this theme, the novel makes the foreign city not a hotbed of intrigue and corrupting influences but the quiescent setting of the mischief created by a footloose American visitor who, in a futile endeavor to re-create his youth, becomes a bad influence on other Americans in Florence.

*****Florence.** Northern Italian city noted as a center of great artistic and architectural works that the young American architect Theodore Colville visited during his

youth. After becoming a journalist in a midwestern town, Colville, has sold his newspaper and returned to Florence twenty years later. At forty-one, he is unlikely to resume his early vocation, but he fails to recapture any of the vitality of his earlier experience in Florence. He proposed, unsuccessfully, to a young woman during his first visit to Florence; now he is still a bachelor and tries to win a woman less than half his age.

Florence is the home of Lina Bowen, a former friend and confidant of the woman he sought earlier, but now a widow with a young daughter. Florence has also attracted a young American woman for whom Mrs. Bowen is acting as a chaperone. W. D. Howells uses this novel as a variant on the theme of American "innocents abroad" that interested Howells's literary friends Mark Twain and Henry James in their distinctive ways. Whereas James typically focused on young American women at risk at the hands of worldly wise Europeans, Howells makes Colville—not a young woman—his central character. Colville persists in an inexcusable attempt to recover the romance of his earlier visit to Italy at the expense of Mrs. Bowen. Although he finally proposes marriage to Miss Graham, it is a selfish act that in effect is a kind of seduction. He agrees to wait, however, until her mother can come to Florence, a trip across the broad Atlantic that takes enough time to allow reason to prevail.

Des Vaches. Colville's Indiana hometown that is present only in his recollection. However, it is a powerful presence, particularly early in the novel. Howells drolly gives the town a name that means "cows." Colville, who has now lived there for many years, ludicrously finds himself preferring its Main Street Bridge to Florence's famous Ponte Vecchio. A long elapse of time and a life among the plain midwestern comforts of Des Vaches have rendered him incapable of recapturing the sensations and emotions that the sights and sounds of Florence once inspired in him.

Palazzo Pinti. Mrs. Bowen's Florentine home, which Colville finds "rather a grand affair." However, the Palazzo Pinti is a place of civility that reflects the maturity Mrs. Bowen has attained and Colville has not. She invites Colville to come on her afternoon for receiving guests, and soon he becomes a habitual guest. Because Mrs. Bowen loves him and must watch as he uses his opportunities at Palazzo Pinti to pursue the bewitching young Imogene, her home becomes for her a place of intense suffering, all the more because she is responsible for the young woman's welfare.

Pergola Theater. Florence theater that hosts a *veglione*, or masked ball, that Colville, Mrs. Bowen, her daughter Effie, and Imogene attend. To the very proper Lina Bowen, this theater is primarily the site of a dubious type of entertainment, and she attends the affair only reluctantly. The evening proves to be a most distressing one for her. Paradoxically, the behavior of the other maskers, including the native Florentines, proves to be polite and decorous, but Colville's behavior does not. In his attempt to charm Imogene, he leaves Lina and Effie alone for so long that they return home without him and Imogene. This gathering place of dubious reputation is thus the setting, but not the cause of her distress, which Colville himself generates with his ill-considered behavior.

— Robert P. Ellis

INDIANA

Author: George Sand (Amandine-Aurore-Lucile Dupin, Baronne Dudevant, 1804-1876)
Type of work: Novel

Type of plot: Sentimental
Time of plot: Early nineteenth century
First published: 1832 (English translation, 1833)

This first novel by George Sand, which takes its title from its central character, a girl named Indiana, contains many places and events that were inspired by Sand's life experiences. Place in this novel is used to emphasize the differences between the urban and the rural. Strongly influenced by Jean-Jacques Rousseau, Sand shows rural areas to be places where nature brings relative peace and innocence, while urban areas suffer from the corruption brought on by society.

*Réunion. Island in the Indian Ocean, four hundred miles east of Madagascar, Réunion is an overseas department of France. This is the island where Indiana, Noun, and Ralph were born. Although both Indiana and Ralph were unhappy as children, neither appreciated nor kindly treated by their families, they have happy memories of times they spent together in nature. It is because of these happy memories that Indiana and Ralph decide to return to Réunion to commit suicide. Sand's descriptions of this island are based on the memories and notes of her friend, Jules Néraud, who had visited the island. Despite this accurate information, Sand makes some errors in distance and in describing some areas.

*Bernica. Gorge on Réunion that is particularly beautiful and which was Ralph's favorite place in his youth. Ralph and Indiana return to the island intending to commit suicide by throwing themselves into a huge waterfall that flows into this gorge. However, when Ralph tells Indiana the secret story of his love for her, the two decide to stay alive and live together amid nature, isolated from society at Bernica.

Lagny. Château of the Delmares in the Brie area of France, east of Paris. While the château is imaginary, its location is accurate in a real area near the town of Melun. The house resembles Plessis-Picard, a country home owned by Sand's friends, where she met her husband. The main characters, Madame Delmare, Colonel Delmare, and Sir Ralph Brown, are at Lagny when Raymon de Ramière bursts into their life. His entry disturbs the peace of the family and the relationships between the three characters. He is a corrupt aristocrat and a product of Parisian society and brings no end of trouble to their bourgeois household. His country home, Cercy, where his sweet old mother lives, is near the Delmares' home.

Bellerive, Sir Ralph's family home, is located between Lagny and Crécy. This is a symbol of the way Ralph is constantly coming between Indiana and Raymon. Raymon came to Lagny for the first time to meet Noun, Indiana's maid and childhood friend, whom he has gotten pregnant before the beginning of the narrative. When Noun is deserted by Raymon after he attempts to seduce Indiana, she drowns herself in a stream near Lagny.

*Paris. Capital of France, in which Indiana begins to court Raymon, though he first meets her in the country. He dances with her at a Parisian salon, where she is chaperoned by her aunt, Madame de Carvajal. Both Raymon and Madame de Carvajal are products of Parisian society and, thus, are corrupted by it. Even though he had sworn to love her always and to do anything for her, Raymon abandons Indiana on two occasions when she has fled from her brutal husband. When she was abandoned the first time, she was already in Paris with her husband. The second time, Indiana had crossed the seas from Réunion, only to be spurned again by Raymon, who had married another woman. Madame de Carvajal refuses Indiana her support as soon as Indiana has "dishonored" herself by going to Raymon's house at five o'clock in the morning. Twice Indiana wanders along the banks of the Seine River contemplating suicide and is saved by Ralph. On the first occasion he is accompanied by Ophelia, his dog, who is later murdered in the water by sailors taking Indiana back to France. Indiana has some moments of happiness in Paris when she believes Raymon loves her; however, when she imagines Paris with anticipation, the narrator is quick to note that Paris was the site of her most unhappy moments.

— *Lucy M. Schwartz*

THE INFORMER

Author: Liam O'Flaherty (1896-1984)
Type of work: Novel
Type of plot: Psychological realism

Time of plot: 1920's
First published: 1925

This novel is Liam O'Flaherty's best-known work and offers a compelling view of the Dublin slums in the years following the Irish civil war. The city's streets and dilapidated buildings act as expressionistic mirrors of the protagonist's tortured conscience.

*Dublin. Capital of Ireland, in which the entire novel is set. Dublin's slums offer a squalid backdrop to the criminal activities of the novel's characters.

Dunboy lodging house. Dismal excuse for a flophouse where fugitive Frankie McPhillip meets his old comrade Gypo Nolan. Frankie, a member of a paramilitary organization, is wanted for the murder of a union organizer. The lodging house looms as an ugly monstrosity popular among Dublin's criminal underground. The accommodations are spartan, and the residents emerge as a haggard collection of the unwashed and forlorn. Over a paltry meal, Nolan impulsively decides to inform on his friend and collect the ransom money.

McPhillip home. Frankie's family residence. To protect himself from the suspicion of having informed on his friend and to offer condolences, Nolan wanders over to the McPhillip home, and the walk becomes an expressionistic odyssey. A street which was once familiar becomes threatening, as if inhabited by monsters. Thus begins a pattern repeated throughout the novel: Landscape and setting alternate between predatory threat and calming retreat.

The house itself is a refreshing haven from the storm on the lanes and in Nolan's head. It is the most respectable house on the street, with a parlor window, fresh curtains, spotless stairway, and polished brass railings. Photographs and ornaments decorate the rooms, the kitchen is spacious, and everything is immaculate except Nolan, who stands in motley high relief. In fact, except for the novel's final setting, another associated with the McPhillips, this house represents the best that Nolan's world can offer.

Fish and chips shop. Seedy restaurant on the slum streets where Nolan stops for nourishment. Overwhelmed by the sorrow of the McPhillip family, Nolan retreats to the neighborhood he knows best, and in an expansive mood, he buys meals for an assembled crowd. The group represents more of Dublin's losers, yet Nolan regards them as his loyal subjects as he plays king for the moment. Ironically, though, his generosity brings unwanted attention and the assurance that he is Frankie's informant and therefore responsible for his friend's death.

Aunt Betty's bordello. High-class brothel. Aunt Betty's stands as another contrasting portrait in a night of antitheses. Nolan usually visits Biddy Burke's place, where the prostitutes are slovenly drunks and the stout is watered down. Aunt Betty's, however, caters to a more fashionable crowd: a group of university students, an artist, and a doctor. Where Biddy's is an unkempt hovel, Aunt Betty's has a broad hearth, clean walls covered with titillating photographs, and delftware on a dresser. Once again Nolan is conspicuous in his working-class attire but wins the favor of the madam and the prostitutes when he impulsively throws his ransom money around.

Bogey Hole. Abandoned basement wine cellar used as a makeshift prison. Nolan is spirited off to this cavern for interrogation, which both literally and figuratively represents the nadir of his experience. Located in the bowels of a once-grand manor, the Bogey Hole sits under a crumbling structure in which water continuously drips, rubbish is strewn around, and rats scurry about.

*Tipperary. Village in south-central Ireland that is the location of Nolan's youth. Periodically the narrative is punctuated by Nolan's memory of his youth and the fact that he is ill suited for city life. After escaping from the Bogey Hole, he travels once more across north Dublin in the hope of crossing the Liffey River and heading south to the mountains. In another of the novel's dramatic antitheses, the mountains represent freedom, expansiveness, and a return to simplicity.

Church. Chapel in which Frankie's mother retreats to pray for her son. His body riddled with bullets, Nolan instinctively gropes his way toward church and begs Mrs. McPhillips's forgiveness before dying before the altar. Damp, threatening streets that hem Nolan in give way to the warm quiet of a sacred place in which his large body can finally rest. Ultimately those labyrinthine avenues act as metaphors for a conscience that has lost its moral compass, eventually restored in the melodramatic final scene.

— *David W. Madden*

THE INHERITORS

Author: William Golding (1911-1993)
Type of work: Novel
Type of plot: Allegory

Time of plot: Paleolithic period
First published: 1955

A primal prehistoric landscape whose simple elements—cave, river, island, and clearing—provide an uncluttered stage upon which is played out, in miniature, the great drama of modern human beings inheriting the earth from the Neanderthals.

River crossing. The first appearance of a family of Neanderthals occurs during their spring migration when they reach a river crossing and discover that an old fallen tree that long provided a bridge across the river is now gone. Their belief that the tree has somehow decided to go away, provides the first glimpse of the Neanderthal world view. Their ability to move another fallen tree into position to fashion a bridge shows their limited ability to manipulate nature and to learn. At the same time, the fact that old Mal falls into the river and catches a chill that later kills him also demonstrates the dangers of the world in which the Neanderthals live. Later, the moment when Lok returns to the crossing and finds the new bridge is gone provides one of the first inklings of the malign influence of the new race of humans.

Cave. Rudimentary shelter provided by an overhang on a cliff that is a summer home for the Neanderthals. Their sense of coming home when they arrive at the cave is palpable, and each member of the family group has a regular place within the cave. It is here that Mal dies, despite being cared for by the whole group, and he is buried by the fire. This scene demonstrates not only the gentleness of the Neanderthals, but also their sense of ritual and belonging, which they themselves cannot fully articulate.

The moment the newcomers raid the Neanderthal cave, killing two members of the family, not only marks the intrusion of violence into the family but also symbolizes the destruction of the Neanderthals' world. Once their carefully nurtured fire has been extinguished, they have no home left.

Island. Island in the river that the Neanderthals cannot reach because they are afraid of crossing water. However, the new race of humans are more sophisticated tool users and fashion boats from hollowed-out tree trunks that they use to make the island their first camp. The island therefore becomes a symbol of the technological superiority of the new people, as well as the threat they pose to the Neanderthals.

When two of the Neanderthals manage to get onto the island, they see many of the things that will help the new people conquer the world: They wear clothing, build rudimentary huts, practice organized rituals and dances, and use alcohol. Above all, they exhibit the beginnings of social organization, with the emergence of figures who might be formal leaders or shamans. None of these things is known to the Neanderthals, and in the long scene in which the two primitive groups are contrasted Golding shows not only the beginnings of modern human society, but also a moment in which innocence is lost—a recurrent theme in his fiction.

— *Paul Kincaid*

THE INSPECTOR GENERAL

Author: Nikolai Gogol (1809-1852)
Type of work: Drama
Type of plot: Satire

Time of plot: Early nineteenth century
First performed: Revizor, 1836 (English translation, 1890)

Set in a small town in rural Russia, Gogol's five-act play takes place in two rooms: one in the house of the town's chief of police, Anton Antonovich, and one in the town's inn. These limited settings facilitate the comic tension created as characters barge in and out bearing further news of the growing catastrophe engendered by the supposed arrival of the inspector general.

*Provincial Russia. At the heart of Gogol's satire is the inefficiency and corruption in Russia's rural provinces, due in large part to the central government's inability to maintain control from a distance. Setting the play in an unnamed rural village allows Gogol to illustrate this point by providing an intimate portrait of these two opposing forces, the central bureaucracy and its minor rural officials.

Antonovich's house. With the exception of act 2, the play is set entirely in one room of Anton Antonovich's house. Gogol's notes direct the play's actors to "pay particular attention to the last scene. The last speech should produce upon all a sudden electric shock." The frantic meetings held in this room, culminate in act 5 with the explosive news that the real inspector has arrived.

Inn. The second act is set in a small room in the town's inn, where Hlestakov and his servant Osip quarrel with the proprietor, trying to get him to extend them further credit. The small, untidy room provides a catalyst for the sustained confusion of identities at the center of the plot. Hlestakov's impoverished circumstances should indicate that he is little more than a petty con man. In his paranoia, however, Antonovich sees only a cleverly conceived disguise. The more ridiculous Hlestakov's behavior, set against the squalor of the room, the more convinced Antonovich becomes that he is the inspector.

— *Philip Bader*

THE INTRUDER

Author: Maurice Maeterlinck (1862-1949)
Type of work: Drama
Type of plot: Tragedy

Time of plot: Early twentieth century
First published: L'Intruse, 1890 (English translation, 1891); first performed, 1891

This one-act play says nothing about where it is set or what nationality its characters are. There is a sense of the Old World about its setting, but it is general enough to allow it to be universal; it could be anywhere. What it does is attempt to capture and sustain mood and atmosphere.

Country house. The play's only location is an ordinary setting in extraordinary circumstances: a dimly lit room in an old country. The room has doors at the left and right and a small concealed door in a corner. Stained glass windows on the back wall are predominantly green, giving an eerie cast to interior objects lighted by the light from the outside. A glass door beside them opens to a terrace. In another corner is a clock, and a lighted lamp provides illumination. There is also a table with chairs around it.

The play opens in the late morning, when a family assembles to wait for news of the mother's illness; the atmosphere is one of terror and foreboding. Doors open by themselves, and then refuse to close. The lamp casts flickering shadows. Sounds are heard for which no explanation can be found. With very little plot or characterization, Maeterlinck creates an atmosphere of mystery that gradually escalates into full-blown terror.

— *H. Alan Pickrell*

INTRUDER IN THE DUST

Author: William Faulkner (1897-1962)

Type of work: Novel

Type of plot: Detective and mystery

Time of plot: Early 1930's

First published: 1948

As in most of his books, William Faulkner's emphasis in this novel is on the complexities of a southern community. Here, a sixteen-year-old white boy struggling to prevent the lynching of a young black man gains often painful insights into both his own prejudice and the racial codes of his community. Although the novel's broad geographical setting is realistic, the places specifically mentioned are fictional representations of areas that Faulkner knew well.

Yoknapatawpha County (YOK-nuh-puh-TAW-fuh). Fictional county in northern Mississippi, modeled on the region in which William Faulkner lived most of his life—a region that constitutes the fictional world of most of his novels and stories. A representation of the South from its earliest settling to modern times, Yoknapatawpha serves as a repository of southern history, legends, and communal memories. Against this backdrop, Chick Mallison confronts his long-held attitudes, becoming, himself, an intruder in the dust.

Jefferson. Fictional seat of Yoknapatawpha County, based on Faulkner's hometown of Oxford, Mississippi. Jefferson is the home of Chick, who is horrified to see the throngs of people converging there to witness the impending lynching of Lucas Beauchamp that is expected to be carried out by the Gowries. The town assumes a holiday atmosphere; music blares; people, including families with children, arrive, eat, joke with one another, and gather outside the jail. Chick's lawyer uncle, Gavin Stevens, digresses endlessly about the South, while presuming Lucas's guilt and awaiting the inevitable.

Beat Four. Hilly region of Yoknapatawpha County that is inhabited by the Gowries and other poor white families. Living in unpainted one-room cabins, these independent, uncompromising, and clannish people pursue illegal whiskey making, bootlegging, and crimes of passion. Violent and vindictive, they want no black inhabitants near them, preferring instead their own community, religion, and code of values.

Chick stealthily enters the forbidding area of Beat Four with his black servant and friend, Aleck Sander, and feisty Miss Habersham. Together they sneak into the Gowrie cemetery at Caledonia Chapel to dig up Vinson Gowrie's body in order to determine what kind of bullet killed him. Beyond providing evidence that eventually clears Lucas of Vinson's murder, the trek to Beat Four inspires in Chick a realization of the essential humanity of the Gowries. The development of the novel hinges upon Chick's widening sympathies with other human beings, accomplished to a large extent through his association with the Gowries and his foray into the Gowrie cemetery.

Lucas's farm. Site where, several years before the main narrative of the novel begins, Chick fell into a creek while hunting with Aleck Sander, and was rescued by Lucas. Taken to Lucas's house to recuperate from his harrowing ordeal, Chick was so tainted by his belief in his own racial superiority that he failed to understand he was a guest in Lucas's house and attempted to force payment on him. Lucas resisted and continued to foil Chick's efforts to pay him back. The debt that was never repaid becomes the basis for Lucas's request for Gavin Stevens to represent him and for Chick to exhume Vinson's body.

The fact that Lucas owns his own land—ten acres that he inherited from his grandfather—is one of the reasons why he refuses to act as white people expect him to act, as a black man. Proud, strong, and individualistic, Lucas behaves in a free and nonsubservient manner similar to that of white persons. Angry white people consequently believe that Vinson's murder has something to do with Lucas's arrogant behavior and resolve to teach Lucas a lesson.

— *Mary Hurd*

INVISIBLE MAN

Author: Ralph Ellison (1914-1994)
Type of work: Novel
Type of plot: Social realism

Time of plot: Late 1930's and early 1940's
First published: 1952

The theme of this novel is the invisibility of African Americans in American society—the hiding of black character and individuality behind masks presented to fool whites, and the veil separating black and white society. Key settings reinforce theme by hiding the true character of the invisible man in particular and black America in general.

*Harlem. African American neighborhood of New York City's Upper Manhattan in which much of the action takes place. The unnamed narrator lives there after the explosion of the paint factory. A surrealistic vision of the real city, the Harlem setting allows him to mix with a wide variety of people, from wealthy white women, who believe him to be a powerful, savage lover, to poor black prostitutes, who mistake him for a pimp named Rinehart. In Harlem readers see that the "invisible man" is not only invisible to whites but to fellow African Americans, as well. None of the characters, white or black, can see past racial and cultural stereotypes into the real invisible man.

Jack-the-Bear's "hole." Apartment of the narrator in a white neighborhood near Harlem. Deep in the bowels of a "whites only" building, the apartment is a section of a basement that was walled off and forgotten in the nineteenth century, just as black America was walled off and forgotten after the passage of the Fourteenth Amendment in 1868. There the narrator steals electricity, thereby remaining invisible to the power company, and wires every inch of his walls and ceiling with more than one thousand light bulbs to bathe himself in brilliant light as he seeks knowledge about himself and his race.

State college. Unnamed black college in Alabama to which the narrator wins a scholarship. Modeled on Alabama's Tuskegee Institute, the college embodies the educational ideals of Booker T. Washington, who advocated gradual progress for blacks and continued separation of the races. The college's central fountain is broken and dry, suggesting the exhaustion of Washington's outmoded, conciliatory policies. The college is a model community in which "model" black citizens present to white benefactors a whitewashed version of black America—a veil behind which real black life is kept hidden.

The Quarters. Poverty-stricken black community near the state college. There one of the college's white founders, Mr. Norton, encounters black poverty in the flesh for the first time: People live in shacks as squalid as those from antebellum days, suggesting how little progress African Americans have been permitted to make. In contrast to the ivy-covered buildings and manicured lawns of the "show" college, the Quarters features the weathered shacks and shabby farms that typified much of southern black life in the age of widespread sharecropping and Jim Crow laws. Dr. Bledsoe, the president of the college, keeps his white benefactors from seeing the Quarters. Thus, the truth of black life remains hidden behind the veil that is the college.

Golden Day. Bar and brothel near the college, that is a microcosm of an insane society built on racism and hypocrisy. The Golden Day is filled with the "veterans," patients from a nearby asylum, a group that includes World War I veterans and a variety of educated black professionals. They are considered insane because the veterans expected to return from the war to a Golden Day of full integration, and the professionals—doctors, chemists, and others—also expected to take their rightful places in society. The Golden Day and the asylum are, like the Quarters, kept carefully hidden behind the whitewashed veil that is the college, and they, too, represent hidden truths about black American life and the effects of racism.

Liberty Paint Factory. New York factory in which the narrator gets his first job. There, too, he remains invisible as pro-union workers revile him as a scab and his supervisor, old Lucius Brockway, reviles him first as a spy, then as a union organizer. The enormous factory produces the whitest of white paints by adding a few drops of black pigment to each bucket, suggesting the hidden black foundations (stolen slave labor) underlying much of America's industry and culture.

Factory hospital. Medical facility in which doctors treat the narrator for injuries he receives in the paint factory explosion. They do not see him as a human being, but as a research subject, so he remains invisible even in the hospital.

— *Craig A. Milliman*

THE INVISIBLE MAN: A Grotesque Romance

Author: H. G. Wells (1866-1946)
Type of work: Novel
Type of plot: Science fiction

Time of plot: Late nineteenth century
First published: 1897

This novel is set in a combination of fictitious and real places in England. The contrast between the large urban area of London and the small villages in Sussex plays a key role in the hopes and plans of Griffin, the Invisible Man.

Iping. Fictitious town in southern England's Sussex County, where Griffin, a scientist who has made himself invisible, seeks refuge from the crowds and dirt of London. He hopes that the village will provide him with a place where he can continue his research without being disturbed by the people who live there, all of whom he considers of inferior intelligence. He also hopes that the village, with its relatively clean air and streets, will enable him to commit robberies whenever he needs money and remain undetected. Later, when he runs amok in the village, H. G. Wells satirizes, actually even mocks, the inhabitants of British villages who can have no idea what they are up against in the person of the Invisible Man. Griffin makes chaos of the town's celebration of Whit-Monday, the day after Whitsunday or Pentecost, when the small town has a kind of carnival in celebration of the holiday.

*****London.** Great Britain's capital city, where Griffin first becomes invisible. He soon learns, however, that London is no place for an invisible man. The streets are full of dirt that quickly makes his feet visible. The air is full of dirt that settles on his body and makes his form visible if he stays outside for any length of time. Moreover, London's weather is too cold for him to go naked in the streets, and he must remain naked to be completely invisible. The streets are full of people, carts, and other vehicles that present constant danger to him since they cannot see him and he cannot watch in all directions all the time. Even a large emporium or retail store where he tries to take refuge is too crowded to serve as a safe haven. Eventually, he robs a theatrical costume place on Drury Lane, a street in the theater district, taking money and a disguise that will, he hopes, enable him to survive long enough to get out of London and into the rural village of Iping.

Port Stowe and **Port Burdock.** Fictitious towns on the southern coast of England, across the English Channel from France, to which Griffin goes in the hope of finding a ship on which he can began a journey to reach Spain or Algiers, where he can survive without clothes in a warmer climate. Instead of boarding a ship, Griffin remains in the area in the home of a former scientific colleague, Dr. Kemp. When Kemp proves uncooperative, Griffin then decides to launch a reign of terror in the area and become its absolute ruler. However, he ends up dying in a village street.

— *Richard Tuerk*

IOLANTHE: Or, The Peer and the Peri

Author: W. S. Gilbert (1836-1911)
Type of work: Drama
Type of plot: Operetta

Time of plot: Nineteenth century
First performed: 1882; first published, 1882

The two settings of this comedy present a deliberate contrast, juxtaposing a fluid and unpredictable fairyland with the seat of urban Victorian government, suggesting the need for greater imagination, flexibility, and thought in the "real world" of the law.

Arcadian landscape. W. W. Gilbert called the setting of the play's first act "Arcadian," and his stage directions indicate a river and a rustic bridge. However, the scene in which the action of *Iolanthe* begins might be described more truly as **Fairyland**, a place in which an Arcadian shepherdess can be a ward of Chancery, wooed by a shepherd who is the son of a union between a mortal and a fairy and who is a fairy down to his waist but has the lower half of a mortal. To a picturesque vista of grassy lawns and goldfish ponds, Conservative peers come marching to pay their court to Phyllis, and in this realm of infinite possibilities the stout Wagnerian queen of the fairies has been able to nestle in a nutshell, dive into a dewdrop, and curl up inside a tiny flower.

*Westminster Palace. London home of the British Parliament, where the moonlit face of the clock below Big Ben anchors the play's second act in the reality of Victorian London. A sentry marches back and forth in precise fashion, meditating on the structure of party politics. The fairies have come to London in support of Strephon, the half-mortal shepherd, and the power they bring from their own magical world upsets the boundaries and expectations of Westminster and the House of Lords. Ultimately, the fairy queen reunites Strephon's mother with her long-lost husband, the lord chancellor, proposes marriage to the sentry, and pairs off her troops with members of Parliament, who immediately sprout wings, and "away [they] go to Fairyland," where "they will be surely happier."

— *Nan C. L. Scott*

IPHIGENIA IN AULIS

Author: Euripides (c. 485-406 B.C.E.)
Type of work: Drama
Type of plot: Tragedy

Time of plot: Beginning of the Trojan War
First performed: Iphigeneia ē en Aulidi, 405 B.C.E.
(English translation, 1782)

Set in ancient Greece, this play presents a dilemma based on personal honor and glory gained at the expense of a great moral wrong.

Aulis (AW-lis). Greek seaport, on the west coast of Euboea; a centrally located spot where Greek forces assemble to prepare for their invasion of Ilium. The play opens in front of the tent of Agamemnon, commander of the Greek armies. While the scene never changes, it is important that the audience know that just out of sight thousands of warriors and sailors are waiting impatiently for the wind to pick up so the fleet can set sail for Troy.

While stage directions indicate the setting, there is no certain knowledge as to how that setting was created on the ancient Greek stage. The more commonly accepted theory is that vertical prisms (*periaktoi*) were mounted on pivots between columns and rotated to show painted scenes. However, it is the pressure applied to the central character by the unseen thousands of men that creates the action of the play. Greek playwrights shaped much of their settings by their words and dialogue rather than actual physical objects, and the same is true of this play, even though there is the spectacle of characters entering in a chariot.

— *H. Alan Pickrell*

ISRAEL POTTER: His Fifty Years of Exile

Author: Herman Melville (1819-1891)
Type of work: Novel
Type of plot: Historical

Time of plot: 1774-1826
First published: 1855

This novel employs biblical typology to characterize the title character and the patriots who fought the American Revolution as giants, the patriarchs of a new "chosen people." Like the ancient Israelites, the title character endures captivity and enslavement as a brick maker in enemy country; like Joseph, he finds employment and protection under the enemy king; like Jesus, he is entombed and rises after three days. He also suffers forty years of exile and wandering before he can enter the promised land, the new nation of the United States. Consequently, there are dozens of different locations in the story, each one used to characterize Israel Potter and to strengthen the parallels between the American revolutionaries and the ancient Israelites.

*Berkshire. Range in western Massachusetts that is the birthplace of the fictional Israel Potter. Herman Melville describes this region as a nearly empty land of rocks and difficult soil—a physical image that suggests the desert regions inhabited by the ancient Hebrews, as well as the hardiness of the American pioneers. Many abandoned farmhouses are enormous, and the land is crisscrossed with walls built of enormous stones. Israel Potter comes from a land of Titans.

*Bunker Hill. Prominent hill in Charleston, Massachusetts, that was the site of the first major battle of the American Revolution in 1775. Historically, it is important because the poorly trained and poorly armed colonial volunteers were inflicting serious damage on an army of British regulars before a shortage of ammunition and superior British numbers resulted in a costly British victory. Israel Potter suffers severe wounds in the front line at Bunker Hill, which firmly establishes his credentials as an American hero.

*Kew Gardens. Royal gardens at Kew, a suburb of London, where Israel becomes a gardener after escaping from a British naval prison hulk at Spithead. There, he has an improbable and nearly incomprehensible conversation with King George III. Although he is an escaped rebel prisoner, Israel cannot, as an American patriot, bring himself to kneel to the king. Like the ancient Israelites—particularly Meshach, Shadrach, and Abednego, thrown into the furnace by Nebuchednezzar—Israel Potter cannot worship a "false god." Like Joseph, he enjoys the favor of the king.

Franklin's office. Parisian embassy office of Benjamin Franklin, who served as American ambassador to France during the American Revolution. The room reveals the powerful and eclectic intellect of America's greatest Enlightenment thinker; it is full of books on a wide variety of subjects and in many different languages. It also has models and drawings of new inventions, barometers, charts, and maps. The windows are open for cooling, and the room is full of flies, but Franklin's powers of concentration allow him to ignore the insects and continue with his work. Perhaps the most interesting detail is his map of the New World with the word "Desert" spanning much of the American West. Franklin has crossed the word out, Melville says, "in summary repeal" of it, as if he believes he can reclaim the deserts. This tiny detail suggests Franklin's—and the Enlightenment's—firm belief in the power of reason and science to change the world.

Potter's cell. Hiding place on the estate of Squire Woodcock, a nobleman sympathetic to the American cause, in Brentford, England. There Israel, now a spy carrying messages between the squire and Franklin, hides. The cell was originally built the size and shape of a coffin by the holy order of Knights Templars, who used it to punish impenitent members of their order. Like Jesus, Israel leaves the tomb after three days.

*Whitehaven. British coastal town that was the boyhood home of future American naval hero John Paul Jones. Israel ships with Jones during the captain's daring raids on England, including an attack on Whitehaven. The ground under the town is honeycombed with coal mines, and abandoned mines occasionally collapse, destroying the homes and warehouses above. Melville's description suggests the town's relation to Jones, who had, in a sense, been discarded by his country: Despite his extraordinary worth as a sea captain, he was barred from the British merchant service after the accidental death of a seaman under his command, and now, like the disused mines, he destroys part of the town with a surprise attack. In a larger sense, Whitehaven and Jones represent the American revolutionaries reared on English values, exploited, and provoked into rebellion.

*Latin Quarter. Bohemian section of Paris and the home of the Sorbonne, the famous college of the University of Paris. The Latin Quarter was so named because many of the students who lived there studied Latin. In the novel, Franklin maintains a home there and also installs Israel in a hotel room. As Israel represents the simple purity of America, his room in the Latin Quarter represents the decadence of Europe: it is equipped with brandy, sugar, cologne, expensive fragrant soap, and a chambermaid who moonlights as a prostitute. The vigilant, pragmatic Franklin rescues Israel from these ruinous temptations.

*England. As America is the Promised Land in the novel, England and her seas—which Israel sails with the famous John Paul Jones—represents Israel Potter's Egypt, his wilderness, and later his Babylon. Similar to the ancient Israelites in Egypt, Israel Potter suffers virtual enslavement as a brick maker. Later, a wildly comic accident of war brings him again to England, but not as a slave. Like the Israelites during the Babylonian Captivity of the first century B.C.E. Israel mingles freely with the English and even marries an English woman. Also like the Israelites, when he finally returns to the Promised Land, he finds himself forgotten and displaced.

Brickyard. Near the end of the novel, a destitute Israel finds work making bricks a few miles from London. Another biblical allusion, the brickyard strengthens the correspondence between Israel and the ancient Israelites, who were compelled to work as brick-makers in Egypt.

— *Craig A. Milliman*

THE ITALIAN: Or, The Confessional of the Black Penitents

Author: Ann Radcliffe (1764-1823)
Type of work: Novel
Type of plot: Gothic

Time of plot: 1758
First published: 1797

The primary settings of this novel, Naples and elsewhere in southern Italy, are characteristic of the gothic genre, in large part because Ann Radcliffe was so influential in shaping this genre. Setting is fundamental to the larger themes of the work: the sublimity of nature, especially the Italian landscape, and the corruption of powerful nobles and clergy.

Abbey of San Stefano. Religious complex used as a prison to incarcerate the central female character at the behest of an evil noblewoman. This structure serves two important purposes within the novel and supplements the themes of the work. First, the abbey is depicted as a place of coercive power and spiritual and physical darkness. It explains the criminality of the villain, an evil monk, as the environment within which his criminality was encouraged to grow. This representation is furthered later in the novel when the villain himself is incarcerated within the dungeons of the Inquisition. Virtually every religious person encountered in this novel is either a criminal or lacks the moral fiber to oppose criminality. This representation of religious criminality is to be expected in the eighteenth century English gothic novel since anti-Catholicism was deeply ingrained in English culture.

For instance, the novel opens with a scene in which English travelers in Naples are touring a darkened Catholic church. There they see an assassin who has been given sanctuary inside the building. This opening scene prepares the reader for the other religious institutions encountered in the novel and demonstrates that her novel is hardly a sociological study but rather an English fantasy of Italian vice and Catholic corruption.

The dark Abbey of San Stefano serves another purpose, that of illustrating the sublimity of the natural landscape. The incarcerated heroine is sometimes permitted to wander through the abbey, and frequently looks out on the landscape, expatiating on its beauties. She looks out on the mountainside and is spiritually reenergized. In turn, the sublimity of the landscape enables this character to endure the hardships she suffers.

*Southern Italy. In this novel, a region of striking natural beauties: towering mountains and sheer cliffs, glowing moonlit nights, glimmering lakes, and sheltering forests. For much of the novel, the central characters flee through this landscape, sometimes meeting rural inhabitants, sometimes dodging religious pilgrims, but always aware of the landscape through which they pass. In part, this landscape serves to illustrate the beauty of the natural world and to explain the inherent virtue of the rural people. For instance, the young hero and heroine come across an aged shepherd who provides them with the best food and drink he has and who shelters them from pursuers. As the novel suggests, this character's kindness results in part from such beautiful surroundings. In fact, throughout most of Radcliffe's novels, and this one in particular, danger is almost never to be feared in such surroundings. Danger only comes to the characters in this novel when they take shelter in towns and cities.

*Naples. Major city in southern Italy, sketchily described in the novel as a town of villas, churches, and beachside huts. Radcliffe's Naples is populated almost entirely by three sorts of people: a closed circle of rich and overbearing noblemen and -women, oppressive clergy, and happy albeit poor fishermen. Naples is barely described otherwise. The villas frequently have surrounding walls and central gardens and are tastefully decorated, the churches are decorated with statuary and vividly colored murals, and the huts of the fishermen are appropriately shabby. This representation of Naples illustrates Radcliffe's contention of the inequities of Italian society, which is dominated by nobles and clergy and is oppressive to the less fortunate. In Naples, a poor woman falls in love with a young nobleman, and the setting furthers the difficulties of this relationship. The young people are isolated within this environment and are well aware that those with power are all too eager to split their relationship apart.

— *Michael R. Meyers*

THE ITCHING PARROT

Author: José Joaquín Fernández de Lizardi (1776-1827)

Type of work: Novel

Type of plot: Picaresque

Time of plot: 1770's to 1820's

First published: El periquillo sarniento, 1816 (English translation, 1942)

This, perhaps the earliest Latin American novel, traces the adventures of Pedro Sarmiento, an upper-middle-class ne'er-do-well nicknamed the Itching Parrot, who goes from one tight spot to another. Set mostly in and around Mexico City in the years leading up to Mexico's independence from Spain, the novel satirizes the corruption of the university, the Roman Catholic Church, and the colonial government. In a call for social reform, the novel paints a vivid portrait of the seedy confidence men and card sharps who survive by any means necessary in the oppressive socioeconomic conditions of colonial New Spain.

College of San Ildefonso (eel-DAY-fohn-soh). College in Mexico City at which Pedro Sarmiento (also called "Poll") does not learn to behave but picks up the rude habits of his classmates, even though he eventually is awarded a bachelor's degree. In his satire of the university system, José Joaquín Fernández de Lizardi demonstrates that a college degree is neither difficult to obtain nor, ultimately, useful.

Januario's hacienda. Country estate owned by the father of Pedro's classmate Januario, whom he visits after he obtains his degree. Unable to ride a horse or fight a bull, he makes a fool of himself in front of Januario's family and is sent back to the city.

Monastery of San Diego. Franciscan monastery that Pedro enters to avoid having to learn a trade. However, he soon finds that he cannot stand the monks' life of religious devotion and sacrifice and is glad when his father's death gives him an excuse to leave the monastery. He then returns to a life of gambling and debauchery.

Prisons. Penal institutions in which Pedro is imprisoned for petty crimes and misdemeanors several times. Lizardi provides an unflinching description of the colonial prisons' hellish conditions. While incarcerated, the prisoners continue to gamble and steal. Lizardi exposes the corruption of the penal system through the character of Don Antonio, an innocent man who has been unjustly convicted.

*Tula. Village outside Mexico City to which Pedro flees after failing in brief and disastrous apprenticeships, first for a pharmacist and then for a physician, whose uniform and diploma he steals. He then pretends to be a physician and sees several patients die. When a plague hits Tula, he gives up and moves on to his next adventure.

Church of San Miguel. Church in which Pedro serves briefly as sacristan—the person in charge of watching over the church's most sacred objects—after finding nowhere else to turn. Blinded by greed, he finds nothing sacred and is caught trying to steal jewelry off a corpse.

*Tixtla. District in whose government Pedro becomes a government subdelegate, or representative. There he abuses his authority to such an extent that he is arrested and sent back to Mexico City in a vignette that satirizes the unscrupulous Spanish authorities who indulge their own desires to the detriment of others.

*Manila. Spanish colonial capital of the Philippines, to which Pedro is sent after being sentenced to eight years of service in the army. Far from the corrupting forces of his native city, Pedro finally becomes an honest man here. He earns the trust of the colonel and becomes his clerk. He is also able to stockpile a small fortune before he finishes his sentence and makes his way back to Mexico City.

Island. Remote Pacific island on which Pedro takes refuge after his ship sinks in a storm and he loses his entire fortune while returning to Mexico. On the island he is befriended by a wealthy man who takes him in. Because his island host does not know Western ways, Pedro tries to convince him of his noble status. The institutions of the West, and the abuses of power in New Spain, surprise and confound the islander.

San Augustín de las Cuevas (auh-guhs-TEEN deh las KWAY-vahs). Beautiful country house to which Pedro retires and leads a respectable life after marrying the daughter of Don Antonio. There he raises a family, surrounded by a well-cultivated orchard in a setting that contrasts starkly with the grime of Mexico City. With this ending, Lizardi suggests that reform is possible, and rewards wait for those who live an honest life.

— *Corinne Andersen*

IVANHOE: A Romance

Author: Sir Walter Scott (1771-1832)
Type of work: Novel
Type of plot: Romance

Time of plot: 1194
First published: 1819

The historic and heavily forested areas of north-central England are the foundation for this story about the rivalry between twelfth century England's Saxons and Normans.

*Don River.** Tributary of the Humber River, which drains much of north-central England into the North Sea, described by Scott as soft and gentle. The town of Doncaster is on the upper Don River. The territory south of the Humber and east of the Don is a beautiful valley that includes on the bank of the Don south of Doncaster the Saxon castle of Conisbrough, which Scott uses as the backdrop for much of his story.

*Pennine Hills.** Mountain range that forms the backbone of England and marks the western boundary for the events in *Ivanhoe*. Warncliffe Park, mentioned by Scott, is the area around Warncliffe Crags, which is part of the Pennine Hill Range. The crags are above Stockbridge and northwest of Sheffield.

*Ashby-de-la-Zouche.** Town in Leicestershire between Birmingham and Nottingham, where Ivanhoe enters the tournament upon his return from the Crusades. The area is used to create many of the action scenes of Scott's novel.

Rotherwood. Fictitious castle home of Ivanhoe's father, Cedric. It is probably based on the town of Rotherham, which is mentioned in chapter 20, in South Yorkshire near Sheffield. Because of this connection, Rotherwood figures often in the story.

*Sherwood Forest.** Dense forest in northern England's Nottinghamshire which is the scene of action involving Locksley—who becomes Robin Hood—and the location of **Torquilstone**, the imaginary castle of Front-de-Boeuf. The castle setting may have been the town of Harthill about nine miles southeast of Rotherham. The area contains the ruins of Middleham Castle, which may have been the model for Torquilstone. It is also the location of the Hermit's cell where King Edward spends the night on his hunting trip.

*Templestowe.** Castlelike structure known as a preceptory—a religious and educational house used in medieval times by the Knights Templer, who figure prominently in *Ivanhoe*. It is to Templestowe that Bois-Guibert flees from Torquilstone with his captive, Rebecca, and to which Isaac goes to negotiate his daughter's release. Templestowe is about a day's journey from Torquilstone.

— *Glenn L. Swygart*

J. B.: A Play in Verse

Author: Archibald MacLeish (1892-1982)
Type of work: Drama
Type of plot: Symbolism

Time of plot: 1940's to 1950's
First performed: 1958; first published, 1958

A brief but intense restaging of the biblical story of Job ("J. B."), this play is set in the shadows of an apparently abandoned circus site, where two circus vendors converse and alternately play the parts of God and Satan as the setting evolves into a play-within-a-play. Though the stage remains deliberately barren of props and staging, scattered around it are clothes that resemble vestments from the churches.

Heaven. Place where God and Satan dispute about the character of people on earth. The simple setting of this play symbolizes the ancient and timeless nature of this drama. Heaven is presented as a flat set of planks set six or seven feet off the floor of the main stage. As the vendors, Mr. Zuss, who sells balloons, and Garrick Nickles, who sells popcorn, search the upper stage, they discover two masks. The mask for God resembles the face of Michelangelo's *Night* sculpture with its closed eyes, and the mask for Satan has eyes "wrinkled with laughter," but a mouth "drawn down in agonized disgust." These masks recall the ancient Greek tradition of presenting plays by using masks through which actors spoke while conveying their characters through fixed expressions. Mr. Zuss also has a name resembling that of the Greek god Zeus. When he and Nickles don their masks, they take on the masks' characters and speak timeless insights, much like the Old Testament's Book of Job, which is thought by many scholars to be the oldest book in the Bible.

*Earth.** Place where the life and tragedies of the banker J. B. and his wife Sarah are worked out. This setting is also simple—with a table and chairs that make the events seem universal. As these parents lose their children to war, accidents, and crime, and as J. B. loses his wealth and health, they wrestle with the problem of evil in the world, until even Sarah abandons J. B. Once J. B. has lost everything, he is visited by Bildad, Zophar, and Eliphaz, the biblical characters who question his integrity. Eventually, the voice of God thunders and silences all questions, including J. B.'s. Then the love between Sarah and J. B. is restored and they begin to build anew on the ash heaps of past disasters. In the end, on Earth no one finds an answer to the problem of evil. Earth is filled with injustice and inexplicable disasters. Only in moving forward with love for the life God gives does life become bearable for J. B. and his wife.

— *Daven M. Kari*

JACK SHEPPARD

Author: William Harrison Ainsworth (1805-1882)
Type of work: Novel
Type of plot: Picaresque

Time of plot: 1702-1724
First published: 1839

Jack Sheppard and his nemesis Jonathan Wild became notorious by virtue of the reports of their lives and crimes contained in the Newgate Calendar, *a periodical account of the most celebrated inmates of London's Newgate Prison. William Harrison Ainsworth's fancifully embellished account of Sheppard's career and legendary escapes from custody takes in many of the great landmarks of early eighteenth century London, with particular reference to the haunts of its criminal underworld.*

*Newgate Prison. Famous London prison featured in the novel; named after the city's fifth gate, which was added in the twelfth century. The prison in this novel was the latest (but not the last) in a long series, replacing one destroyed in the great London fire of 1666. The famous court of the Old Bailey was established nearby for convenience. Chapter 9 of the novel's third part includes an elaborate description of the prison's architecture, in order to give due credit to Jack's two escapes, first from the Condemned Hold and then from the Stone Hold—allegedly its most terrible dungeon—where he is visited by painters anxious to obtain portraits of the notorious felon. (This, the most celebrated of Sheppard's escapes, is lavishly illustrated by George Cruikshank's steel engravings.) When Jack is sent back to Newgate for a third time, he is weighed down with inescapable fetters in the Middle Stone Ward. The other significant setting within the prison is the Press Room, where Blueskin is tortured. Jonathan Wild lives opposite the prison's main gate, next door to the Cooper's Arms.

*Moorfields. Site of London's Old Bethlehem Hospital, erected in 1675, allegedly modeled on the French king Louis XIV's Tuileries Palace, and popularly known as Bedlam. Mrs. Sheppard is confined here, a short distance to the north of Newgate. The "New Prison" in Clerkenwell, from which Jack escapes after the Dollis Hill robbery, is farther to the north.

*Southwark. District south of the River Thames connected to the City of London by Old London Bridge. When King Charles II obliterated "Alsatia," the thieves' kitchen which had taken advantage of the ancient sanctuary of Whitefriars, its inhabitants took up residence in Southwark, in the so-called Old Mint. Ainsworth's story begins here, in Mrs. Sheppard's dismal lodgings in Wheeler's Rents. The Cross Shovels, an inn used as a base by "Baptist" Kettleby, the so-called Master of the Mint, is also featured. Old London Bridge was the city's only bridge in 1703: an extraordinary edifice covered with houses and shops, with arched gateways at either end whose spikes were adorned with traitors' heads. The pier of each arch was protected by a spur called a starling, one of which enables Owen Wood to save Thames Darrell from the storm and Rowland Trenchard's murderous intentions.

*Wapping. Port district east of the City of London where the ship on which Thames Darrell is abducted is anchored. By the time Thames returns to England, Southwark's Old Mint has been purged of its underworld on the instructions of George I and a "New Mint" has been established in Wapping between Artichoke Lane and Nightingale Lane, Baptist Kettleby having replaced the Cross Shovels with the Seven Cities of Refuge.

*London. Other principal settings in the novel are distributed along an arc extended westward and northward from the City of London. Owen Wood's home and workshop are located immediately to the west in Wych Street, Drury Lane; William Kneebone's drapery, which subsequently moves into Wood's premises, is initially situated in the Strand, opposite St. Clement's Church. Westminster Hall, from which Jack begins his last journey, and the scaffold at Tyburn where it terminates, are arranged along a route curving away to the northwest, as is Southampton Fields, where Lady Trafford's Elizabethan Mansion is located. Although it is now part of Greater London, Willesden was then a country village even farther to the northwest; this is where Jack is caught stealing for the first time and makes the first of his many escapes from the constable's cage. Jack and his mother are eventually buried in Willesden Churchyard. Dollis Hill, to which Owen Wood's family retires, is nearby.

Ashton Hall. Stately home near Manchester, in the north of England, from which Mrs. Sheppard was allegedly stolen by gypsies, and to which Rowland Trenchard retires after his denunciation by Wild.

— *Brian Stableford*

JACQUES THE FATALIST AND HIS MASTER

Author: Denis Diderot (1713-1784)
Type of work: Novel
Type of plot: Picaresque

Time of plot: Mid-eighteenth century
First published: Jacques le fataliste et son maître,
   1796 (English translation, 1797)

Specific places have no real role in Denis Diderot's novel. Not only Jacques and his master but everyone and everything are constantly in motion. The reader is convinced that the multiplicity of places is infinite. As a materialist, Diderot believed that the world was in constant flux and completely lacking in permanence. Picaresque novels usually take their characters to specific places for specific reasons; in this novel, Jacques and his Master go wherever chance takes them or Diderot mischievously directs them. The inability of the characters and of the reader to find a stationary place in the novel throws the reader into confusion. Interested in exactly what a novel is or should be, Diderot was intrigued by the relationship between author and reader and virtually challenges the readers to determine where they are.

   *France. Interrupted tales bounce the main characters and readers from place to place throughout France. Settings include towns, inns, farms, roadways, houses, and even lofts and doorsteps. The constantly shifting scenes are so disorienting that even the narrator is not always sure where the characters are.

   Like his contemporary French writer Voltaire, Diderot often viewed sexual relationships between men and women as good sources of humor and satire. The novel includes several places which by their nature create humorous situations based on these relationships. The tale of the baker's wife and her lover, for example, is one in which place is essential to the action. When the local authorities come to arrest the baker, the wife's lover, not the baker, is with her. Later the lover leaves and is arrested in spite of his protests because "whoever sleeps with the baker's wife is the baker."

— *Shawncey Webb*

JANE EYRE: An Autobiography

Author: Charlotte Brontë (1816-1855)
Type of work: Novel
Type of plot: Domestic realism

Time of plot: 1800
First published: 1847

Although the title character's growth from child to young woman to governess to wife is the focus of this novel, the five houses in which she lives at various places in northern England play vital roles as the plot unfolds. These five houses—Gateshead Hall, Lowood School, Thornfield Hall, Moor House, and Ferndean Manor—are physical manifestations of Jane's initiation into adult society.

   Gateshead Hall. Upper-middle class home of the Reed family. Gateshead Hall, identified only as located in "—shire," England, is the home in which Jane spends the first ten years of her life with her aunt, Mrs. Reed, and her three cousins. It is here that Jane learns to take care of herself—training that prepares her for the hardships that are to follow during her years at an orphan asylum.

   Two places in particular within Gateshead Hall play prominent roles in Jane's life there. The **window seat** in which the reader first encounters Jane as she reads a book on the history of British birds is surrounded by thick red curtains and shelters her from both the cold, raw weather on the outside of the window and the cold, loveless environment of the Reed household on the other side of the curtain. Shortly after Jane leaves the womb-like safety of the window seat, she is banished to the red room, her late uncle's old bedroom, after being unjustly accused of fighting with her cousin John. It is from the unhappy atmosphere of Gateshead Hall that Jane acquires the strength of character to help her with the difficulties she must face in the future.

Lowton. Fictional town near which the Lowood Orphan Asylum is located, some fifty miles from Gateshead Hall. This school is believed to be based in part on the Cowan Bridge School that Charlotte Brontë and her sisters attended as girls.

Lowood Orphan Asylum. After the incident of the red room, Mrs. Reed contacts Mr. Brocklehurst, treasurer of the Lowood Orphan Asylum, to arrange for Jane to live at the school permanently. Jane's first year at Lowood, especially, is difficult because Mr. Brocklehurst forces the teachers and students to survive on inadequate nourishment and in harsh living conditions. By the spring of her first year at Lowood, typhoid fever ravages the school, resulting in an investigation of Brocklehurst's methods and leading to vastly improved conditions for the inhabitants of Lowood.

Jane spends the next eight years at Lowood—six years as a student and two years as a teacher. Though her remaining years at Lowood are less difficult than the first, Jane still yearns for more from life. During her years at Lowood, Jane learns from her close friend, Helen Burns, and the superintendent of Lowood, Miss Temple, what it means to live life as a true Christian.

Millcote. Fictional English village that is the location of Thornfield Hall, the home of Edward Fairfax Rochester. The village affords Jane the first glimpse of her new home after she leaves Lowood School and is also the scene of her near-marriage to Rochester.

Thornfield Hall. Home of Rochester, his ward Adela, and the housekeeper Mrs. Fairfax. It is there that Jane begins to enjoy life for the first time. However, as the house's name implies, the house is also a field of thorns, in which Jane learns the joys and pain of true love as well. Thornfield is a large upper-class estate with many rooms and an equal number of secrets. One secret that is kept from Jane and visitors to the estate is that on the upper floor of the mansion, Rochester is hiding Bertha, his legal wife, who has gone mad. After Jane's arrival, the house transforms from a place nearly abandoned by its master to the scene of family tranquillity, parties, and Jane and Rochester's growing love for each other. Later, however, it becomes a place of pain and regret that Jane must leave in secret in order to escape the prospect of love without the sanctity of marriage.

Whitcross. Fictional crossroads on the moors of northern England to which Jane flees from Rochester and the memories of their lost love. Left with no food, money, or clothes, Jane must beg for scraps of food and spends several nights sleeping outside.

Moor House. Home of St. John, Diana, and Mary Rivers. Left with no other options, Jane finds herself outside Moor House, hoping to find food, lodging, and possible employment. The cottage is warm and inviting, and the Rivers family takes in an ailing Jane and nurses her back to health. Finding Jane to be well bred and educated, St. John immediately employs Jane to run a school for village girls. In her small home and school Jane finds the contentment of employment to be both fulfilling and enjoyable. However, Jane soon discovers that she is both an heiress to a considerable fortune and the cousin of the Rivers family. She is also faced with a marriage proposal from St. John. Realizing that she loves only Rochester, she leaves Moor House to go to him. Upon arriving in Millcote, Jane learns that Thornfield Hall has burned down, Rochester's wife has died, and Rochester has moved to his other home, Ferndean Manor.

Ferndean Manor. One of Rochester's homes, located two miles from Millcote. After Jane learns of the change in Rochester's circumstances, she rushes to Ferndean Manor and finds that he is both blind and maimed as a result of the fire that destroyed Thornfield Hall and killed Bertha. Jane and Rochester decide on a quiet wedding with only the two of them present. It is at Ferndean Manor that Jane is rewarded for her years of suffering and longing for love and where the Rochesters finally begin a long and happy marriage.

— *Kimberley H. Kidd*

JASON AND THE GOLDEN FLEECE

Author: Unknown
Type of work: Folklore
Type of plot: Adventure

Time of plot: Antiquity
First published: Unknown

This mythical story of Jason's quest for the Golden Fleece depicts a journey from the Mediterranean to the Black Sea, from the known world to the unknown, from the realm of the living to that of the dead. In its developed form, the story incorporates the geography of most of the Mediterranean world, including the Danube basin, Italy, and North Africa. Probably derived from traders' reports, the myth becomes a means of defining Greece and Greekness against other cultures.

*Iolcus (i-ohl-kuhz). Greek city at the foot of Mount Pelion in Thessaly where Jason is a prince. From Iolcus, Jason and the crew of his ship, the **Argo**, set forth in their quest for the Golden Fleece. While Jason's uncle Pelias keeps Jason's father, Æson, the rightful king, imprisoned in the royal palace at Iolcus and rules illegally, Jason is secretly brought up on Mount Pelion, home to the centaur Chiron. When Jason returns to Iolcus as a man, Pelias sends him on his quest to find the fleece. Iolcus is a location of divine-human conflict: Hera hates Pelias and uses Jason to bring back Medea to destroy him. Iolcus was on the trade route to the Black Sea, and its commercial activity is an important underlying element of the myth.

*Lemnos. Greek island in the northeastern part of the Aegean Sea where Jason and his crew make their first stop after setting out from Iolcus. Inhabited only by women, Lemnos is the first of many locations where the Argonauts encounter representations of otherness—non-Greek, non-male, or non-human forms. Lemnos is a site of danger for the Argonauts, who risk being entrapped by sexual desire and diverted from their quest. This danger is reflected in the landscape, as the boy Hylas is pulled into a cooling spring by water nymphs and drowned.

Clashing Rocks. Known as the Symplegades in Greek, these massive rocks are shrouded in an impenetrable mist and by smashing together destroy anything that attempts to pass between them. They bar access to the Black Sea from the Aegean and are a mythical outgrowth of the narrow straits of the Bosporos, or perhaps the Hellespont. The rocks are a symbolic barrier between the world of the living and the realm of the dead, for the voyage of the *Argo* to Colchis is, on one level, the equivalent of the hero's journey to the underworld and his overcoming of death.

*Aea (EE-ah). Capital of the land of Colchis, a region at the eastern end of the Black Sea that included part of the Caucasus. Aea was ruled by King Æetes, who was a son of Helios the sun god and whose name means "earthman." Aea is an archetypal end-of-the-world location—a place where traditional boundaries and rules do not apply. There, the Golden Fleece hangs on an oak tree in a grove, guarded by an unsleeping dragon. Medea, whom the gods have made fall in love with Jason, helps Jason secure the fleece by using her knowledge of magic herbs and potions. She abandons her father and country to escape with the Argonauts and is the embodiment of Aea's close links with the earth and its old matriarchal powers.

*Libya. Ancient Greek name for much of the coastal area of North Africa, a region much larger than the modern country of the same name. One of the most fanciful locations in the story, Libya is marked by strange geography, harsh conditions, and close encounters with danger. The homeward journey of the *Argo* does not retrace the route taken to get to Colchis, but follows a path that mixes real and fictional geography. Traveling up the Danube River, to the Adriatic Sea, then up the Po River and through southern France to the coast of Italy, Jason and the Argonauts finally reach Libya, where a storm drives them into the Syrtis, a "dead sea" filled with seaweed. This episode includes a visit to an inland lake, Tritonis, a journey across the desert to the **Garden of the Hesperides** (mysteriously transposed from the far-western seas), and a return to the Mediterranean guided through treacherous waters by the god Triton.

Corinth. Greek city in the north of the Peloponnese. After a journey of four months, Jason returns to Iolcus and restores his father to the throne. Shortly thereafter, he and Medea are driven out of the city and travel to Corinth. There, Jason returns to his Greek self, abandoning Medea for the daughter of the local king; however, Medea takes her revenge by killing their two sons. She flies away to Athens, and Jason is killed by a beam that falls on his head from the rotting *Argo* on the seashore. Jason's pathetic death makes him a less than typically heroic character, and it happens by the sea, the element on which he had his greatest successes. Corinth represents the heart of Greece; although Jason attempts to fit into this location, he cannot do so, perhaps because he is now too tainted by otherness and the exotic.

— *David Larmour*

JEALOUSY

Author: Alain Robbe-Grillet (1922-   )
Type of work: Novel
Type of plot: Antistory

Time of plot: Probably the early 1950's
First published: La Jalousie, 1957 (English translation, 1959)

This plotless novel deals with the ways in which sexual heat, deceit, and violence disrupt a milieu of order and calm. The novel is appropriately set in an unspecified place with an oppressively hot and humid tropical climate where the narrator appears to be the owner of a banana plantation. The nature of the narrator's property and business sets order and disorder against each other.

House. Home of the novel's anonymous narrator and his wife, who is identified only as "A . . . " Located at the center of a series of squares or—boxes, the house is surrounded by other squares or partial boxes—a veranda, a garden, a courtyard, and the banana plantation, which encloses the house on all four sides of its square. The narrator-husband always remains in or close to his home. Readers see nothing that lies beyond his field of vision and are consequently at the mercy of the narrator's judgments.

A road leads from the house to a highway, which in turn, leads to the home of Franck, who is apparently A . . . 's lover. This road, which cuts through the boundaries around the narrator's home, constitutes then a means of escape for A . . . and Franck, who make at least one trip to a port city, several hours away by car.

The story's three major characters spend much of their time on a veranda that surrounds the house on three sides. The narrator notes that the chairs of Franck and A . . . are always very close together, which facilitates conversation—and conspiracy. On the other hand, the narrator-husband's chair is at the other end of a semicircle—separated from those of the others by a cocktail table and the empty chair reserved for Franck's always-absent wife, Christiane.

The narrator's garden, courtyard, and plantation represent his desire to carve out a civilized domain in a hostile environment—a triumph of humankind over savage nature. The garden and the courtyard separate the house from the groves of banana trees, from which shrill animal cries emanate.

Office. Principal vantage point of the narrator, from which he observes A . . . , Franck, and activities on his estate. He watches what goes on around him through jalousie blinds—whose name gives the novel's title a double meaning. Physically therefore, the narrator's view of things is never complete—just as his knowledge of what is in fact going on between Franck and his wife is fragmented.

A . . . 's bedroom. Directly across a corridor from her husband/narrator's office, the room in which A . . . primps before a vanity mirror, dresses, apparently writes letters to Franck, and stares out a window, in the direction from which Franck is most likely to approach the house. This room is referred to only as A . . . 's bedroom, *not* the bedroom of husband and wife. The narrator apparently sleeps in a small bedroom separated from A . . . 's room by a bathroom. The jealous narrator/ husband can see what A . . . does in her bedroom when the doors to his office and the bedroom are ajar; however, her room has corners in which A . . . cannot be seen from outside.

At the end of the novel, when the narrator's stress is critical, he sees spots and streaks of red (blood?) on the windowsill of A . . . 's bedroom and nearby. The incident leaves readers with the impression that the narrator has murdered his wife and/or Franck.

Living room. Main room of the home of the narrator and A . . . One wall of the room has a red stain left by a centipede that Franck has crushed during one of his visits to the house. Later, in the narrator's anguished view, the stain on the wall curiously resembles the red stain on the windowsill of A . . . 's bedroom.

— *Gordon Walters*

JENNIE GERHARDT

Author: Theodore Dreiser (1871-1945)
Type of work: Novel
Type of plot: Naturalism

Time of plot: 1880's-1890's
First published: 1911

This novel is set primarily in three cities—Columbus and Cleveland, Ohio, and Chicago, Illinois. Other places, both real and fictional, also play important but more tangential roles. The major function of place in the novel is to provide a backdrop for the author's investigation of the social implications of industrialization in late nineteenth century America—especially the widening gulf between the rich and the poor.

***Columbus.** Medium-sized industrial city in southern Ohio in which the novel opens. Jennie, the daughter of a German immigrant laborer, and her mother seek employment in the city's "principal hotel." While working there, she meets and is subsequently seduced by, a U.S. senator, whose illegitimate child she bears.

***Cleveland.** Northern Ohio city to which most of Jennie's family moves after she gives birth to a child and her father moves to Youngstown in search of employment. The members of the family see Cleveland as a place of superior opportunity—a good place "to seek a new start." While working as a domestic in Cleveland, Jennie meets Lester Kane, a member of a wealthy and influential Cincinnati family.

***Chicago.** Illinois city to which Lester takes Jennie as his mistress. They initially live in a North Side apartment near Lake Michigan; later they live in an old eleven-room house in South Hyde Park. Lester oversees the Chicago portion of his family's growing carriage empire. During the years they spend together in Chicago, Jennie grows more comfortable with wealth, and her relationship with Lester deepens. At the same time, the fact that they remain unmarried becomes a scandal in their Chicago social circle and causes a conflict within the Kane family. After Lester leaves Jennie to marry a wealthy widow, Jennie lives in "a simple cottage in a very respectable but not showy neighborhood near Jackson Park," and the Kanes occupy "a handsome mansion on the Lake Shore Drive"— clearly symbolic of the social distance that separates them.

***London.** Capital and leading city of Great Britain, which Jennie and Lester visit during a trip abroad that they make while trying to sort out their problems during the midst of a financial and social crisis. Another major stop on their journey is Cairo, Egypt. In the midst of the splendor and exotic character of these foreign settings, Lester meets and is again attracted to Mrs. Gerard, a wealthy widow whom he knew in Cincinnati, and decides to leave Jennie. Meanwhile, the same settings make Jennie realize that she can never truly be a part of Lester's world.

A poignant symbol of the gulf that separates Lester and Jennie can be seen in the grinding poverty of parts of Europe that impelled Jennie's father to emigrate to America to seek a better life. The harsh economic conditions in Europe are juxtaposed against the romantic elegance of these foreign locales for wealthy American travelers.

"Yalewood." Proposed real estate development in the southwest side of Chicago in which Lester invests, hoping to acquire enough wealth to allow him to distance himself from his family and remain with Jennie. When a large meat packing company plans to locate itself in the same area, Lester loses his investment.

Sandwood. Small Wisconsin town in which Lester helps Jennie find a house for her and her daughter after he leaves her. A pleasant place, the house has flowerbeds and trees and a lake view; it serves as a place of quiet retirement for her until the death of her daughter draws her back to live in Chicago.

— *Scott Wright*

THE JEW OF MALTA

Author: Christopher Marlowe (1564-1593)
Type of work: Drama
Type of plot: Tragedy

Time of plot: Fifteenth century
First performed: c. 1589; first published, 1633

All the action occurs on Malta, a Mediterranean island and commercial center epitomizing Renaissance attitudes toward venture capital: rich argosies sail to and from her port. Two lofty turrets and a fortified city wall make Malta formidable, but failures to pay Turkish tribute leave citizens fearful of reprisals. Its walls bombarded, eventually the city is sacked as Christians, Jews, and Turks struggle for dominance.

*Malta. Small Mediterranean island group south of Sicily on which the entire play is set. Because of its strategic location in the Mediterranean, Malta was occupied by a succession of foreign powers, including the Ottoman Turks, who are besieging the island at the time in which the play is set, when the island has a Christian government ruled by the Knights of St. John.

Barabas's house. Home of the wealthy merchant of the play's title, Barabas, who alienates Malta's governor by refusing to convert to Christianity or to give the government half of his property. The governor seizes his property to punish him, and transforms his home into a Roman Catholic convent, in which Barabas's daughter Abigail is entered as a novice. Much of the play's plot

revolves around Barabas's efforts to retrieve sacks of gold he has hidden under his house's floor and to exact his revenge.

The convent's upper and lower levels make for an effective scene on the stage with two voices in the dark. Barabas is on the lower level eulogizing his gold; Abigail is above eulogizing her father. Like the island itself, this protective enclosure is vulnerable; Barabas poisons everyone within his house, including his own daughter.

Barabas also has a second house, which he uses as a secret center for plotting against the city, its officers, and the nuns who occupy his first house.

— *Gina Macdonald*

JOHN BROWN'S BODY

Author: Stephen Vincent Benét (1898-1943)
Type of work: Poetry
Type of plot: Epic

Time of plot: 1859-1865
First published: 1928

This epic poem captures the rebirth of a unified nation from the disparate regions that existed before the Civil War. Setting is a critical component of the poem, as it is the combination of landscape and character that co-alesces to shape the American nation. Because the war affected men and women from Maine to Florida and from the Eastern seaboard to the Pacific shore, Stephen Vincent Benét shapes the poem as a series of vignettes, alternating between historical and fictional characters and among locations. Frequently a specific place in the poem is made to stand for an entire region and its people.

Ellyat farm. New England farm of the Ellyat family. Because Benét organizes his poem as alternating pictures of the Civil War as seen from the perspectives of Americans on both sides, he creates a number of fictional characters whose stories reflect those of the larger groups affected by the struggle. Jack Ellyat, the protagonist, comes from a small farm in New England. With great care, Benét sketches both the farm and the surrounding forests and meadows to give readers a sense of the region this character represents. Relying on the reader to bring to the poem certain preconceived notions of regionalism, the poet is able to use a kind of shorthand to suggest values associated with men such as Ellyat.

Wingate Hall. Plantation home of Clay Wingate and his family, which the poem contrasts with the simple farmstead on which Ellyat is raised. Benét's portrait of the southern plantation perpetuates many of the stereotypes about the South. Plantation lifestyle, founded on the system of slavery that Northerners considered an abomination, helps produce in Benét's young protagonist a sense of honor sometimes devoid of discretion, a predilection for paternalism in dealing with those beneath him in social standing, and an attitude of chauvinism masked as chivalry in his treatment of women. Wingate Hall could have been located in any one of the Southern states, making it an appropriate symbol for the lifestyle that was to disappear at the end of the war.

Vilas home. Home of the Vilas family in the wilderness of the Tennessee woods that becomes a refuge for Jack Ellyat after he escapes from the Confederates who capture him at the Battle of Shiloh. The frontier people in *John Brown's Body* are represented in the poem by a number of fictional characters from Kentucky and Tennessee, including the Vilas family. Benét uses the episodes at the Vilas home to discuss the effect of the war on those who still believe that America offers the chance to escape from civilization. The woods around the Vilas home are crisscrossed by soldiers of both armies, and it becomes clear to the Vilas clan that America as a frontier nation must inevitably give way to the encroaching modern industrial age.

*Battlefields.** Benét uses real battlefields, such as those at Bull Run, Shiloh, and Gettysburg, to emphasize the themes of heroism and self-development in his fictional protagonists. Both Ellyat and Wingate fight at these three major battles and, as a result, learn something of the horrors of war. Additionally, they come to understand something of themselves and the values for which they are fighting.

*Washington, D.C.**, and *Richmond, Virginia.** From time to time throughout the poem, Benét shifts the focus to the Northern and Southern capitals. Because this is a historical work, Benét is faithful to the historical record. His major reason for setting some of the action in these cities, however, is that the principal historical figures who determined the strategy for conducting the war were located here. Character studies of both Abraham Lincoln and Jefferson Davis are important to Benét's portrait of the country in crisis. Nevertheless, the cities also have metaphorical value. The mood of politicians and the populace in these two cities shifts with the vicissitudes of battle, and the poet makes it clear that the attitudes of citizens in Richmond and Washington reflect in great part those of the larger populations in the North and South.

— *Laurence W. Mazzeno*

JOHN HALIFAX, GENTLEMAN

Author: Dinah Maria Mulock (Mrs. George Craik, 1826-1887)

Type of work: Novel

Type of plot: Domestic realism

Time of plot: 1795-1834

First published: 1856

Domesticity is a central theme in this novel, in which homes are pivots of emotional and moral balance. Those who make successful homes are contrasted with those who cannot. Within this pivotal theme of home comes the geographical concept of house, since homes are formed within houses. The development of the protagonist John Halifax as gentleman is signified by his transition from one house to another.

Norton Bury. Small town in the county of Gloucestershire in the west of England; it lies on the flood plain of the River Avon. The River Severn and its estuary can be seen from the nearby Cotswolds Hills. There, Phineas Fletcher, the novel's narrator, is brought up, his Quaker father owning a tanner's yard and, later, a mill. The main historical features of the town are the abbey, now in ruins, and its gardens. The nearest large town, Coltham, a center of fashion, lies ten miles away.

Longfield. Second home of John and Ursula Halifax, who earlier live in a modest house in Norton Bury. Located some six miles from Norton Bury, Longfield is a small farmhouse that is periodically enlarged. It is the house to which John and his friend Phineas attach the greatest emotional warmth. John and Ursula's dream is to retire there—a dream cut short by their relatively early deaths. It is "a nest of love and joy," a place of blessing, where "liberty, fraternity and equality" are practiced. In fact, it is seen as Arcadia, the ideal pastoral setting in which to bring up a young family.

Enderley. Town in the Cotswold Hills, most of which is owned by the earl of Luxmore, where John Halifax leases a stream-driven mill that he tries to develop into a profitable cloth-weaving business. Lord Luxmore's refusal to upgrade the mill or workers' tied cottages leaves John to raise the capital for improvements himself. Luxmore's denial of adequate water to keep the mill running prompts John to install steam-driven machinery, which ensures his mill's success. John thus becomes an early industrialist, an ideal one in that he concerns himself with the well-being of his workers.

Beechwood Hall. "Great house" at Enderley that John Halifax buys to become a public figure and mix with people of influence in the county. John also sees that it is a fit setting for his sons to find a similar place of altruistic influence. The domestic desire here is expressed in terms of service and faith. As the center of the growing family, it is also a place of strife among the grown-up children. The loss of John and Ursula's blind daughter at Longfield is paralleled by their son Guy's self-imposed exile from Beechwood. The novel makes it clear that Eden is not achievable in any pastoral quest.

Mythe House. Home of Richard Brithwood, the local squire, and his wife, Lady Caroline, in Norton Bury, the first of the novel's "false" houses. Its great iron gates symbolize the barriers of class and privilege that Brithwood seeks to erect against the democratic likes of John Halifax. However, for Brithwood the outcome is divorce, debauchery, and the loss of his political influence. His failure to establish a family in his house is the sign of the moral bankruptcy of inherited power.

Luxmore Hall. Home of Lord Luxmore at Enderley; the second of the novel's "false" houses. Historically, the house served as a shelter for Roman Catholics when they, like the Quakers, were persecuted outsiders. However, it has lost its vocation as a place and is burdened by massive debts accrued by Luxmore before he dies, and the renunciation of title and place by his son, Lord Ravenel. The latter's marriage to John's surviving daughter signifies the final triumph of democracy and the possibility of a new home based on merit and hard work rather than privilege.

— *David Barratt*

JONATHAN WILD

Author: Henry Fielding (1707-1754)
Type of work: Novel
Type of plot: Social satire

Time of plot: Late seventeenth century
First published: The History of the Life of the Late Mr. Jonathan Wild the Great, 1743

In this novel, Henry Fielding uses settings from the seamiest area of London for an ironic purpose: to point out similarities amid strikingly obvious differences. The novel's theme is that however different the mansions of the rich and powerful appear to be from the homes of thugs, cheats, thieves, and murderers considered criminals, the rich and powerful themselves behave no differently.

Snap's house. London residence of Mr. Snap the younger, a bailiff. He uses part of his home as a sponging-house, where debtors are imprisoned until they are either bailed out or transported to jail. Since the debtors mix freely with the Snaps and their guests, the house becomes young Jonathan Wild's college of crime, with a resident tutor, the card sharp and confidence man, Count la Ruse, who has to stay with Snap until he can satisfy his creditors. The house is also significant because it is there that Wild meets Snap's daughter Laetitia, who convinces him that she is chaste, when in fact it is only Wild whom she will not admit to her bed. This bit of bad luck at Snap's house indicates that like every other "great" man, Wild has his weaknesses. In the end, it is his arrogance that brings him down.

On another level, Fielding intends Snap's house to represent the palace or castle where the king might be holding court. At both places, men talk of honor and women of chastity, but nothing really matters except not getting found out. At both places, everyone and everything is for sale; for example, during the eighteenth century, it was well known that one could buy one's way out of a sponging-house like Snap's, and it was just as well known that under the Whig prime minister, Sir Robert Walpole, whom Fielding equates with Wild, one could buy one's way into any post or out of almost any difficulty.

Newgate Prison. Largest prison in London until 1902, when it was torn down; an annex of the Old Bailey, the largest common law court in England. Newgate was crowded, dirty, and disease-ridden. In it, male prisoners were mixed with women, the young with mature criminals, and debtors with felons. As Mr. Heartfree discovers, anyone entering Newgate would first have to pay off the authorities and then would be stripped of everything he still possessed by the brutal gangs who ran free in the prison. On the other hand, someone as unscrupulous as Wild could eliminate his rivals and become a virtual monarch.

As a journalist and as a law student, Fielding knew Newgate well, and his sympathy for the unfortunate people who landed there, often through no fault of their own, is evident in his description of Heartfree's experiences. However, Fielding also utilizes Newgate for broad thematic purposes. Specifically, Newgate is a place where an evil man, Wild, corrupts those who fear him, just as Walpole corrupts his inferiors in the government. More broadly, Newgate is a microcosm of human society, which is dominated by a reverence for power, however attained, and by scorn for principle, which to the evil is mere weakness. Thus Newgate the prison stands as a symbol for the world itself, a prison in which human beings are confined both by their mortality and by the sins in their hearts.

Tyburn. Public execution place, once located where Oxford Street now meets Edgware and Bayswater Roads. Wild is taken to Tyburn in a cart, accompanied by a chaplain. At the "tree," or scaffold, the noose is placed over his neck while members of the crowd variously cheer for him and pelt him with stones and clods of dirt, sending the chaplain fleeing to the safety of a hackney-coach. Then the horses are driven on, leaving Wild to hang. Though Wild richly deserves his fate, the bloodthirstiness displayed by the onlookers and the chaplain's cowardice suggest that they are not much better than he. Literally, Tyburn is an extension of Newgate.

— *Rosemary M. Canfield Reisman*

JORROCKS' JAUNTS AND JOLLITIES

Author: Robert Smith Surtees (1803-1864) *Time of plot:* 1830's
Type of work: Novel *First published:* 1838
Type of plot: Wit and humor

With this novel, his first literary success, Robert Smith Surtees established himself as the foremost author in the genre of sporting novels, which enjoyed immense popularity in Victorian England, especially among sportsmen and the gentry. In the character of his London grocer, John Jorrocks (who also appears in other novels) Surtees created one of the great eccentrics in the gallery of English comic characters, an exuberant and passionate cockney devotee of the national sport of fox-hunting.

*London. Jorrocks's home and place of work are both in London. His grocer's business is located on the real St. Botolph's Street in the eastern part of the city, while his "elegant residence," as Surtees describes it, is on Coram Street, north of Russell Square. Friends and acquaintances with whom he goes hunting are encountered on the Strand and at such meeting places as the Piazza coffee room in Covent Garden.

Jorrocks's hunting excursions take him to the other side of London, south of the Thames, through what were in Surtees' time villages on the outskirts of London. Many of these places, such as Elephant and Castle, Kennington Common, Brixton Hill, and Streatham Common, are now part of metropolitan London. There are references to places further afield, which are now London suburbs: Blackheath, Eltham, Bromley, Beckenham, and Lewisham. Surtees' south London is peculiarly evocative in light of the fact that this is now a densely populated area, some of it the embodiment of urban decay.

*East Surrey. Region immediately southwest of London in which Jorrocks hunts with what is described as the Surrey Hunt. This hunt works the eastern part of the county and neighboring western Kent. The terrain is undulating and at times hilly, much of it consisting of the North Downs. The Surrey Hunt is quite unlike the hunts that Surtees himself knew in the north of England, which were patronized and supported by the landed gentry. The Surrey Hunt was a subscription-hunt, a new form of recreation in the early nineteenth century that appealed to prosperous members of the middle class. Unlike the county packs farther afield, the hounds in such packs were maintained by subscriptions that also paid for pro-

fessional masters of foxhounds—such as Jorrocks himself becomes in Surtees' *Handley Cross* (1843)—as well as for the hunt servants. The meets were held on Saturdays, when city merchants and those engaged in trade (still despised occupations in the eyes of gentleman-hunters) closed their businesses and rode out into the surrounding countryside—as Jorrocks does—to enjoy their sport.

*Croydon. Town outside London at which the London huntsmen meet. From there, they ride to Keston, where the Surrey Hunt foxhounds await them, after which the hunt sets off toward Tatsfield and Chipstead, or sometimes turns west over the Kentish border as far as Westerham. On one occasion, Jorrocks, against his better judgment as a fox-hunter, goes out with the Surrey stag-hounds, and this takes him as far as Tunbridge Wells.

*Newmarket. Village in Cambridgeshire at which Jorrocks attends a horse race with a friend. As an enthusiastic fox-hunter, Jorrocks scorns horse racing, but on one occasion he is persuaded to spend what becomes a wretched day at Newmarket, a principal venue of the racing fraternity since the seventeenth century.

*Margate. Fashionable resort town on the coast of Kent, southeast of London, that Jorrocks goes to when prevailed upon by a friend to pay a visit. He reaches Margate by steamer from London Bridge and finds it a vulgar, rackety place. His stay is definitely spoilt when he goes for a swim and his trousers are swept out to sea by the tide.

*Paris. Capital of France that Jorrocks visits after traveling by coach from London to Dover via Gravesend, Chatham, and Rochester, where the horses are changed. This journey provides Jorrocks with a fine occasion for observing coaching life on the eve of its disappearance. The sea crossing to Boulogne is followed by a coach journey to Paris in the company of the unscrupulous Countess Benvolio. Once in Paris, there is much scope for comic action and for misunderstandings between English and French.

— *Gavin R. G. Hambly*

JOSEPH ANDREWS

Author: Henry Fielding (1707-1754)
Type of work: Novel
Type of plot: Social realism
Time of plot: Early eighteenth century

First published: The History of the Adventures of Joseph Andrews, and of His Friend Mr. Abraham Adams, 1742

Places in this early English comic novel illustrate Henry Fielding's technique of conveying themes through contrasts, such as places that are examples of selfishness and pretense that contrast with those symbolizing selflessness and charity. The settings also illustrate Fielding's definition of a comic novel as a "comic Epic-Poem in Prose." Because its main characters are mock knights on a quest, places in the novel can be seen as contrasting parodies of epic castles and battlefields.

*London. Largest city both in England and in Europe, where the novel opens. London serves as a metaphor for vice and sham. The innocent Joseph later writes to his sister that "London is a bad Place." London's Hyde Park, former preserve of royalty, is a symbolic place associated with vanity, where people parade to be seen. Hyde Park is also the place where the vain widow Lady Booby walks with her handsome footman, Joseph.

Booby Hall. Country house of Sir Thomas and Lady Booby that is the setting for Lady Booby's and Mrs. Slipslop's attempted seductions of the innocent Joseph. Each woman masks a lascivious passion for Joseph with feigned modesty. High-born widow and low-born housekeeper, they are Fielding's opening examples showing that hypocrisy and self-interest infect all social classes.

*Somerset road. Route that Joseph follows to return to his Somerset home in the sequence that makes up the bulk of the narrative. Joseph's journey becomes a parody of Homer's ninth century B.C.E. epic *Odyssey*. Like Homer's Odysseus, Joseph must overcome obstacles and various symbolic monsters—people such as the robbers who beat him soundly and leave him lying naked and half dead in a ditch on his first night out from London. After a passing coach stops to help when its passengers hear his cries, he is taken to a nearby inn, where he recuperates. There he meets the generous Parson Adams, who pays his bill and accompanies him the rest of what becomes a long and complicated journey.

Inns. Places in which Joseph stays during his journey to Somerset. His first stop, after he is robbed, is at the Red Lion Inn in Surrey—the first of seven inns and alehouses in the novel. The **Red Lion Inn**—whose very name celebrates the noble animal symbol of England—is a model of hospitality and charity. His next stop, however, at the **Dragon Inn**, is a sharp contrast; its proprietors are the mean and stingy Mr. Tow-wouse and his dragon-like wife. Another of Joseph's stops is at the **George Alehouse**, whose name represents a contrast with that of the Dragon Inn, as St. George is England's patron saint, who is most famous for performing a religious and patriotic duty by killing the dragon, a symbol of evil.

Trulliber's parsonage. Of the six clergymen contrasted in the novel, the gluttonous, bad-tempered Parson Trulliber is the most uncharitable, refusing Parson Adams a loan to pay his bill at an inn. Trulliber's parsonage contrasts with that of Adams, a symbol of his familial and spiritual fatherhood by charity.

Wilson cottage. Somerset home of the kindly and generous Mr. Wilson, who turns out to be Joseph's father. Wilson and his wife are perfect hosts and turn out to be perfect parents. Their home thus proves to be a perfect contrast to the great Booby Hall.

— *H. George Hahn*

A JOURNAL OF THE PLAGUE YEAR

Author: Daniel Defoe (1660-1731)
Type of work: Novel
Time of plot: 1664-1665
First published: A Journal of the Plague Year: Being

Observations or Memorials of the Most Remarkable
Occurrences, as Well Publick as Private, Which
Happened in London, During the Last Great
Visitation in 1655, 1722

Greater London, the surrounding countryside of nearby counties, the River Thames, and relatively distant Oxford are all concretely, and even statistically, mapped out in this novel. This effect of realism as well as the urgency of concrete horrors in Daniel Defoe's world depends heavily on real places and real statistics of population and other urban details such as governmental jurisdictions.

***London.** Capital of England. In the voice of his thorough and even brilliantly factual narrator, who is a middle-class businessman and maker of saddles, Defoe educates the reader about numerous urban details governing the eighty to one hundred square miles of London at the time of the story. The population then was nearly 500,000 people, of whom about 20 percent died from the plague in 1665. Perhaps the most lurid detail, which lends itself nicely to statistics and charts in the text, is the weekly toll of deaths recorded as the Bills of Mortality by parish vestries in each of the approximately 130 Church of England parishes in greater London. The walled city, which constitutes what was left of the old London of the Middle Ages, has the most parishes in number, but the parishes outside the walls cover more territory and, by the time of the plague, are densely populated. Furthermore, the reader learns about county government in greater London, which included magistrates in Westminster at the West End of London and outside the walls as well as what are called the liberties, or districts, within a county such as Middlesex, which have their own independent magistrates. It is a vast honeycomb of jurisdictions, government officials, and record keeping. Overall the government is fairly effective in disposing of the dead and, especially, in boarding up buildings and in posting official watchmen or guards so that the sick may not spread disease. Nevertheless, the statistics map the remarkable progress of the disease from the West End, over the northern parishes of greater London, finally reaching awful proportions in the East End and in the parishes south of the river. Defoe's reader gets the sense that the narrator survives the plague not only because he is pious but also because his stoic and deterministic realism enables him to know greater London so well and to record what he knows with a matter-of-fact love of detail.

***Nearby counties.** Unlike the narrator, who resolves to remain in London in order both to protect his business and to collect data, many people flee to live in small, isolated groups. They are forced to subsist in caves and deserted farmhouses in the woods and fields. The narrator hears reports from some who are eventually forced to come back to London for financial reasons. He also reports on some thirty small towns no farther out from London than twenty miles where the number of plague deaths is high.

***Oxford.** University city to the northwest from London. Farther out from London than the nearby counties, this comfortable town that houses the ancient university is where members of the court of Charles II retreat to escape disease. They constitute a considerable body of people who usually live in London's West End, in Westminster. Moving to Oxford saves them.

***River Thames** (tehmz). England's greatest river and London's link to the sea. Merchant ships from Europe, especially from the Dutch low countries, which were fierce enemies of England at this time, are suspected of delivering plague. In fact, all vessels, friend and foe, are halted and wait downriver from London Bridge as far as Gravesend for many months. In addition, citizens of London flee to boats covered with awnings and furnished with straw in the middle of the river both downstream and upriver from London Bridge. The narrator depicts this broad water highway as both culprit and safe haven.

— Donald M. Hassler

JOURNEY TO THE END OF THE NIGHT

Author: Louis-Ferdinand Céline (Louis-Ferdinand Destouches, 1894-1961)

Type of work: Novel

Type of plot: Naturalism

Time of plot: World War I and after

First published: Voyage au bout de la nuit, 1932 (English translation, 1934)

To the misanthropic narrator of this novel, war-racked Flanders defines the essence of the human condition, which is violent, stupid, and disgusting. For the narrator, human debasement and immorality are reflected in the many places that his travels take him, from battlefields in Flanders, to the disease-laden jungles of Africa, to the vapid opulence of America, and to the slums of France. Each place reflects the nature of the people who inhabit it; in each place, human beings demonstrate to the narrator that greed, folly, and stupidity bordering on lunacy, have created a pit of human misery.

***Flanders.** World War I battlefield overlapping France and Belgium where the narrator, Ferdinand Bardamu, discovers the absurdity of war and its meaningless slaughter. The war symbolizes the disease that has infected Europeans, perhaps all humans, and its victims are not only the wounded and killed but the mentally injured—who include Bardamu. The battlefield literalizes the irrational spirit that has taken over the world.

***Paris.** Capital of France. To Ferdinand, this beautiful and historic city is seen from a hospital for mental patients. In his new abode, sexual promiscuity and superficial affairs run rampant. Although he escapes the slaughter of the battlefield by being sent to this hospital, it, too, is a place where stupidity and self-interest reign and is an apt symbol of the unstable mentality that has devastated Europe.

Ferdinand's search for understanding, truth, and fulfillment eventually brings him back to Paris for a second time, and finally to a mental hospital in a Paris suburb. As he advances geographically, spiritually, and materially, he descends further into nihilism and despair. Paris represents the nadir of his fortunes and his emotional development. In extreme poverty himself, he treats the sick in a neighborhood that is an extension of their moral and emotional illness.

In the City of Light, dark streets, buildings perpetually in shadows, and night scenes are all part of a place that reeks of death, disease, and decay. The mental institution where Ferdinand finds lasting employment, companionship, and purpose represents the ironic outcome of his quest for beauty, reason, and a meaningful life:

The sanest place in an insane world is an asylum for the insane.

Ship. Unnamed ship on which Ferdinand sails from Europe to Africa. This sultry, cramped microcosm introduces Ferdinand to another group of people who are idle, vain, self-indulgent, and bigoted. This European crowd further convinces him that, although he has changed places, human nature is the same—egotistical, narrow-minded, self-indulgent, and fundamentally and persistently mendacious and dishonest. Aboard the ship, as in Europe, self-interest and greed drive human beings, who ostracize and punish those who are perceived as threats to their complacency and selfishness. The ship serves as a bridge between the slaughter and insanity in Europe and the rapacity in Africa, giving Ferdinand a foretaste of the human character in a colonial setting.

***French West Africa.** Ferdinand's experiences in France's West African colonies provide further evidence of the corruption that rots the human character and turns every place into a festering sore. Africa symbolizes the cruelty and greed of the colonial population. Ironically, the Africans who are brutalized and enslaved by the Europeans are among the dark forces that undermine the white intruders and sap their spirit. The other forces are represented by the African jungle, whose insufferable heat, diseases, and discomforts assault the Europeans who plunder the continent. All together, Africa's pestilential creatures and miserable conditions constitute a fitting symbol of the disease of colonialism: As the Europeans suck the life blood out of Africa, the continent itself destroys their spirit and defeats their enterprises.

America. Ferdinand's first impressions of New York are of tall buildings and beautiful women. The essence of its appeal is typified by the Hollywood movies he discovers, dream-inducing fantasies that take his mind off the miserable world outside. The movie houses satisfy his need for beauty, order, and meaning and represent a refuge from the glaring light of a purposeless existence outside. The city lures people with its opulent promise then traps them in benumbing routine and superficial abundance. Its nature is typified by the movie house, which takes the individual from a squalid banality but encloses him or her in make-believe. Another aspect of modern America is symbolized by the Detroit factory where Ferdinand finds temporary employment: repetitive labor on an assembly line relieved only by empty intervals between work shifts.

— *Bernard E. Morris*

THE JOURNEY TO THE WEST

Author: Wu Ch'eng-en (c. 1500-c. 1582)
Type of work: Novel
Type of plot: Fantasy
Time of plot: Seventh century

First published: Hsi-yu chi, 1592 (abridged English translation, *Monkey*, 1943; English translation, 1977-1983)

Few places in this mythical, picaresque adventure story—which is also a quest of the soul for sundry spiritual matters, enlightenment, and immortality—are identifiable as geographic locations. The work starts in China whence the main characters take a journey to India and enter a kind of amalgamated Asian religious heaven and find the true scriptures of Buddha.

Monkey's cave. Home of Monkey at an unidentified location in China. Born from an egg transformed from a rock, Monkey reigns over the race of monkeys. Situated in mountains with trees and lakes, Monkey's habitat is more or less an everywhere place for this everyman character of myth. The monkeys come to think of their cave and the surrounding area as paradise, and they wantonly occupy their time by wandering through the Mountain of Flowers and Fruit.

Jambudvipa. City in which Monkey spends ten years studying and learning the ways of men. After leaving his cave and his fellow monkeys when he realizes his own mortality, he crosses the ocean to the east and goes to Jambudvipa. He then crosses what is called the Western Ocean to arrive at **Cave of the Slanting Moon and Three Stars**, where a Taoist patriarch (who has monklike qualities) first informs him that he can become immortal. While in his stay, he learns how to transform himself into innumerable physical objects, foremost of which is the pine tree.

Heaven. After an act of mischief in one of his transformations, Monkey is sent to Heaven itself where the Jade Emperor can both watch and train him. Here, in the Treasure Hall of Divine Mists in the Cloud Palace of the Golden Arches, Monkey continues his adventures with numerous other mythical characters, most of whom are from the Buddhist tradition. Heaven, here, is given to readers as a physical place, but one in which supernatural settings and characters larger than life can both thrive and clash. After one particular misadventure, Monkey is placed under a five-peaked mountain to serve penance and further perfect his spiritual existence; this mountain, so it turns out, had originally been Buddha's fingers.

Chiang-chou. Province of China. In something of a flashback of the work, the story returns to this region to relate the story of Hsuan Tsang (also called Tripitaka) and his murdered father, the governor. In this setting are villages, farms, and large towns, as well as a temple—all reveal the sinful nature of China at the time this conspiracy is related. Hsuan Tsang, after learning the details of his father's murder, makes a journey to the West, where he, too, comes to the Cloud Palace of the Golden Arches and meets the Jade Emperor. The trip occurs after Emperor T'ai Tsung of T'ang experiences a kind of Buddhist hell in a place called the World of Darkness.

Chinese countryside. In this epic trip, Tripitaka (accompanied by Monkey, Pigsy, and Sandy) experiences more-than-typical occurrences on their spiritual pilgrimage on some very physical roads. Bandits accost them, for example, but, similarly, the journey comprises places from the supernatural: a dragon appears to give battle, and Monkey rides it. They come to the Cloud Ladder Cave near the River of Flowing Sands, on the banks of which are monsters to provide even more adventures. They also pass through two kingdoms: Crow-cock and Cart-slow.

Flaming Mountain. Hellish place where flames consume everything over hundreds of square miles in which a significant part of the story is set. Because the mountain's flames are inextinguishable, the only way to get beyond them—and thus to Buddhist heaven to find enlightenment and achieve immortality—is to fly over them by means of using an iron fan. Of all the geographic impossibilities in the work, this one is far more formidable than any of the others. Tripitaka and Monkey are eventually able to put out the flames permanently, and thus they transform the landscape into a set of mountains, which are yet impassable.

Blessed Region of Buddha. Surprisingly few details are given about Buddha's actual habitat. It is a place in the spiritual world that has physical dimensions. Buddha lives in a most holy monastery where there is a Great Altar and the Great Hero Treasure Hall. It is a place of treasure chests and great feasts; the scrolls are kept in chests with precious jewels on the outside. Entrusted with these great religious scrolls, Monkey and the others are sent back to the Western Paradise; that is, they are sent back to China, where the people can now (because they have the scrolls) receive spiritual guidance and thereby remove themselves from their sinful ways of life.

— *Carl Singleton*

THE JOY LUCK CLUB

Author: Amy Tan (1952-   )
Type of work: Novel
Type of plot: Social realism

Time of plot: Twentieth century
First published: 1989

Set in California and China, this novel uses different locations and stories about the past to underline the generational conflicts among Chinese-born mothers and their American-born daughters. China emerges as the place of the past, where the identities of the mothers were shaped amid much suffering. California is the place of the present, where the daughters have to come to terms with their bicultural identity. Closure is achieved once one daughter meets her half-sisters in China, reunifying her family.

*San Francisco. Northern California city that is home to most of the novel's characters. Three of the four families of the Joy Luck Club settled in Chinatown on their arrival in America, seeking the comforts of a place with an established Chinese community, one filled with the fragrances of familiar foods, such as fried sesame balls; familiar landmarks, such as herb shops and fish markets; and people like them. Indicative of their mothers' drive to assimilate, Waverly Jong is even named after her parents' home on Waverly Place.

As these immigrant families became successful, they moved into upper-middle-class neighborhoods, such as Ashbury Heights. However, for Ying-Ying St. Clair, the move from Oakland, across the Bay, to San Francisco's North Beach neighborhood remains unsettling. Her attempt to use *feng shui* to create a harmonious spiritual balance fails when the child she conceives in the new home miscarries.

San Francisco mirrors the emotional conflicts of the characters. It is a place where a Bank of America building and a McDonald's restaurant rise up next to the shops and apartment buildings of Chinatown, threatening to tower over them, just as the mothers worry about the impact of American culture on their daughters' Chinese heritage.

*Kweilin (KWAY-lin; Guilin in Pinyin). City in China to which Suyuan Woo was evacuated after the Japanese invasion in 1937. She had no eyes for the beauty of the city; to her its fabled mountains merely looked like fish heads, behind which lurked an advancing enemy. Its caves provided shelter from air raids pounding the beleaguered town. The city teemed with refugees from all corners of China, and misery abounded. To preserve hope, Suyuan formed her first Joy Luck Club there.

*Kweilin-Chungking road. While fleeing Kweilin for Chungking as the Japanese were invading, Suyuan had to abandon her twin baby daughters along the road, which was choked with refugees. The despair of the refugees was echoed by the overcrowded road, the sides of which were littered with discarded possessions. Most refugees trekked through this bleak apocalyptic landscape on foot, while a fortunate few escaped in trucks.

The road holds the mystery of Suyuan's babies, which is the novel's framing device. When her American-born daughter, Jing-mei, first learns what her mother had done, she seems callous to her. However, after Jing-mei reaches China and learns the full story of her half-sisters' abandonment, she can forgive her mother.

*Wushi (wew-shee; Wuxi). Chinese city one hundred miles northeast of Shanghai at the shores of large and beautiful Tai Lake that was the site of Ying-Ying St. Clair's privileged youth. While living in San Francisco, she nostalgically remembers the splendor of the Moon Festival on the lake. Yet the lake also represents danger, for she nearly drowned there. Later, she fell in love with her husband on the lake.

*Shanghai. Great Chinese port city to which Ying-Ying went after learning of her husband's infidelity in Wushi. Taking advantage of the city's opportunities, Ying-Ying worked in a clothing store, where she met and married Clifford St. Clair. Like the friends she later finds in San Francisco, she leaves behind a China that holds bitter memories.

*Tientsin (TEEN-tseen; Tianjin). Bustling Chinese port city south of Beijing. One of China's "treaty ports," where foreigners had their own enclaves exempt from Chinese law. An-mei Hsu was amazed by the city's colorful life when she arrived there with her mother from their hometown of Ningpo, near Shanghai. Yet the city's sparkle and the splendors of their palatial, Western-style home quickly wore off when An-mei learned that her mother was forced to be a concubine.

*Taiyuan (TAY-ywan). Capital of China's Shanxi province that contains major parts of the Great Wall. Surrounded by rough mountains, the Fen River runs through it. Lindo Jong grew up there in a low-lying peasant house, which was inundated by a flood, while the house of her future husband was built on richer, higher ground and remained intact. After getting out of her arranged marriage, Lindo left Taiyuan for Beijing and later America.

Jordan house. San Francisco home of Rose Hsu and her husband, Ted Jordan. After her husband announces that he wants a divorce, Rose refuses to let him have the house; her refusal signifies her newly discovered sense of self-worth.

— *R. C. Lutz*

JUDE THE OBSCURE

Author: Thomas Hardy (1840-1928)
Type of work: Novel
Type of plot: Philosophical realism

Time of plot: Nineteenth century
First published: 1895

Set in late Victorian England, this novel explores the clash of modern thinking and nineteenth century religion. Thomas Hardy's fictionalized Wessex towns symbolize the conflicts found in the democratic, feminist, and labor movements. The villages of Marygreen, Melchester, Shaston, and Aldbrickham represent the prescriptive social conventions idealizing marriage and romanticizing religion.

*Wessex. Fictional region of England in which Thomas Hardy set most of his major novels. It is situated east of the Cornish coast, between the River Thames and the English Channel. There, Hardy freely constructs a partly real and partly fictional locale to accommodate a series of "local" novels, including *Far from the Madding Crowd* (1874). The countryside in many ways resembles that of southwestern England—rolling hills, babbling brooks, quaint villages, and rustic rural folk.

Marygreen. Jude's hometown village in Wessex, where he is reared by his aunt. Marygreen's landscape is idyllic and contrasts with the coarseness of its working-class population, as represented by Arabella's family. Jude is initiated into adulthood in Marygreen; he learns a work ethic and experiences the temptation of fleshly desires. Here he marries Arabella and gives up his dreams of pursuing an education. This town is set in opposition to the university town of Christminster, which Jude views as an enlightened place of learning. This village is based on Great Fawley, Berkshire, where some of Hardy's ancestors are buried and where his grandmother lived. Jude's surname is taken from this place.

Christminster. University city. Christminster represents a typical university institution of the nineteenth century. It professes Christian values of humility and generosity yet excludes applicants based on class and gender. Jude moves to Christminster after his failed marriage to Arabella. However, Christminster will not accept him because he is a stonemason and therefore part of the working class. Even though Jude is intelligent and has studied independently, his application is rejected. Thus the city represents the belittling attitude of the Victorian upper classes toward the lower classes. Here, too, Jude meets his cousin, Sue Bridehead. Sue's intellectuality is also dismissed at Christminster because she is a woman. At the end of the novel Jude returns to Christminster to die a broken man still enamored of the city's beautiful spires and colleges. This town is modeled on Oxford with its many colleges and exclusive intellectual atmosphere. Hardy identifies particular places in Christminster as real places in Oxford: The meeting place of Jude and Sue is the cross in the pavement on Broad Street (the cross marks the place where Protestant bishops were burned to death during the reign of Queen Mary); Cardinal College is modeled on Christ Church College; St. Silas is inspired by St. Barnabus.

Melchester. Village to which Jude follows Sue after his failed attempt at Christminster. Here Sue and Jude finally recognize their love for each another and its dangers. When Sue is expelled from the teachers' college after an innocent, all-night escapade with Jude, she redeems herself in the eyes of Melchester society by marrying Phillotson. Thus Melchester represents Victorian society's rigid social standards for women, which inhibit Sue from acting independently. Melchester is a city found in several of Hardy's Wessex novels and represents Salisbury, Wiltshire, with its well-known Salisbury Cathedral and Anglican religious foundation.

Shaston. Village modeled after Shaftesbury in Dorset that Hardy uses as the backdrop for Jude and Sue's troubled reunion. When Phillotson and Sue settle in this city in southern Wessex, where they teach together, she realizes that she has betrayed herself and can no longer stay with Phillotson. Sue and Jude reunite, and breaking all conventions for marriage standards, Phillotson reluctantly gives his blessing for their future. Because Shaston is a peculiar mixture of permanence in Gothic churches and unpredictability in itinerant workers, it becomes an appropriate symbol for Jude and Sue's relationship. Always struggling against society's expectations for marriage, they are unable to preserve their unique relationship.

Aldbrickham. This city symbolizes Jude and Sue's final downfall. Jude and Sue move to Aldbrickham to escape criticism and pose as a married couple, while Jude works repairing and creating ornamental Gothic architectural works. They further their deception by creating a family-like situation with Little Father Time (presumably Jude and Arabella's son) and their two children. When the vestry discovers that they are not married, they are ostracized from the community. Again they move to an out-of-the-way area, where Jude's health fails. In a run-down house, symbolic of their demise, the son kills his younger siblings and himself in what he thinks is an act of mercy. The horror of this act is symbolized in the derelict conditions to which Sue and Jude have been reduced. Fashioned after Reading, Berkshire, Aldbrickham represents a typical Victorian village with its rigid prescriptions for social behavior.

— *Kathryn N. Benzel*

JULIUS CAESAR

Author: William Shakespeare (1564-1616)
Type of work: Drama
Type of plot: Tragedy

Time of plot: 44 B.C.E.
First performed: c. 1599-1600; first published, 1601

Although most of this play is set in ancient Rome—a setting that gives the play weight and credibility—it is at heart an English play with Elizabethan, rather than classical, language and thought. Since historically accurate costuming was not a theatrical concern during William Shakespeare's time, actors in the play wore Elizabethan, not Roman, clothing. This alone made the play seem more immediate and universal than a play about a long-dead figure from the past might otherwise have seemed.

***Rome.** Capital of the ancient Roman Empire in which the bulk of the play is set. The various settings within the city used in the play are represented sparsely on stage; most of the Roman scenes are set in outdoor places, particularly public streets. The Elizabethan theater was a nonrealistic theater that operated within a context of narrow stage conventions. Only a small bit of scenery might be used to suggest place; for example, a single bush or shrub might suggest a forest, while a throne might suggest a palace. It was mainly spoken dialogue that identified, described, and specified settings for the audience.

That Shakespeare intended Rome, and by extension the Roman Empire, as an example for Elizabethan England there can be no doubt. Most of the literature of his age, including drama, modeled itself on Roman examples. Even the theaters, their stages, and theatrical presentations were modeled partly on the Roman stages and such ancient dramatic conventions as were known. The Roman Republic was an ideal to most of the educated elite; however, the concept and institutions of such a government seemed beyond them. Roman history and the Latin language were part of the formal English education of that time, and English rhetoricians were fond of likening Elizabethan England to Rome. A goodly portion of Shakespeare's audiences would have known something about the history of Julius Caesar and would have admired him. Like Elizabeth I, Caesar was charismatic and popular with the people. Caesar's assassination echoed several conspiracies that Queen Elizabeth fought against during her reign.

***Forum.** Great public square in Rome at which Caesar is assassinated by the conspirators. Afterward, Marc Antony delivers a powerful eulogy to Caesar on the steps of the Forum that turns the public mob against the conspirators.

***Sardis.** Ancient city in Asia Minor, near what is now Izmir, Turkey, where Brutus and Cassius maintain their military camp, in the civil war following Caesar's assassination. There, Brutus and Cassius quarrel constantly over trivial matters. Sardis is thus the site at which visible chaos into which the conspiracy falls becomes clear as the conspirators deal with mutual lack of trust, poor planning, and defeat from all sides.

***Philippi.** Greek town near the Aegean Sea near which Marc Antony and Octavian (Augustus) defeat Brutus and Cassius in the concluding scenes of the play. Afterward, the downward spiral of Rome halts only when Caesar's rightful heir ascends to power. Ancient Rome becomes a model for Elizabethan England in which natural order prevails. The play is a lesson for Shakespeare's audience where the setting of Rome equals their England.

— *H. Alan Pickrell*

JULY'S PEOPLE

Author: Nadine Gordimer (1923-   )
Type of work: Novel
Type of plot: Psychological realism

Time of plot: Soon after 1980
First published: 1981

The South African bush country is central to this story of a family fleeing from war-torn Johannesburg during a fictional revolution and whose servant, July, leads them to his village and provides them with shelter. In this setting the members of the family rapidly discover how drastically unprepared they are for life amid the raw forces of nature.

***South Africa.** Nadine Gordimer's homeland, a country in Southern Africa in which legal segregation, or apartheid, sanctioned racial inequality for decades. Although in reality apartheid was abolished when constitutional reforms led to democratic elections in 1994, Gordimer's novel describes a time when a long-feared civil war between blacks and whites has erupted. Major airports have closed due to antiaircraft fire, and ports have been bombed or blockaded. Black revolutionaries have received arms and military assistance from Russia and Cuba. Volunteers from neighboring countries have also joined the revolutionaries, adding to their strength. The Smales family, although sympathetic to reforms to improve the lives of blacks, have nevertheless lived the privileged life of whites and fear that the revolutionaries will find, torture, and kill them.

Hut. Dwelling in which the Smaleses take refuge. The importance of the hut as a setting is apparent as Maureen Smales, wife and mother, awakens slowly in the opening segment of the novel. It is the Smaleses' first morning in the hut, and their servant July has brought them tea, a common and expected South African custom.

July's efforts to care for the Smaleses in the manner to which they have become accustomed contrasts starkly with the reality of the dwelling. The hut loaned to the Smaleses is round and constructed of thick mud walls with a thatched roof. Its doorway is hung with a sack, and its floor is made of stamped mud and dung. Insects infest the interior, attracting chickens that enter and exit at will, adding fresh excrement to the already unhealthy conditions.

The hut is furnished with an iron bed and car seats removed from the "bakkie," the recreational vehicle in which the Smaleses arrived. A paraffin lamp provides light, and the cooking facilities consist of a wood fire in front of the hut. During the first rain, the many insects in the roof are awakened and further disturb the human in-

habitants. Gordimer uses these and other details to dramatize the Smaleses' struggle to adjust to the rudimentary shelter.

July's village. Small African settlement consisting of a few huts. The village also includes a goat kraal, chicken coops, and a pigpen of "thorny aloes, battered hub-caps, . . . plates of crumbling tin, mud bricks." Water for drinking and washing comes from a nearby river. Although Maureen insists that the children drink purified water and use toilet paper, the children soon adopt village ways, drinking river water and wiping themselves with a stick. The husband and father, Bam, attempts to fit into the village by using his gun to hunt for and provide food, but Maureen has little to contribute. July dismisses her efforts, telling her that wood gathering, for example, is only for the village women. Attempting to help nevertheless, she is rejected by these same women, especially July's mother, who scoffs at Maureen's inability to differentiate between edible and poisonous plants. July, however, is at home in the village environment and this increases his independence. Gradually his role of servant to the Smaleses decreases, and without informing them of his intentions, he learns to drive the bakkie.

Bush. Also known as veld (or veldt) or savanna, high grassland plateaus dotted with shrubs and trees. The menacing bush stretches out in all directions from the village. Its immensity confines the family to the relative safety of the village. The shifting appearance of the bush, especially subject to changes of light and weather, renders it unfathomable. The bush hides everything, but sounds travel easily here. Voices of people passing, cattle trampling the undergrowth, and various other unidentifiable noises carry a frightening message. The feared revolutionaries may emerge from the bush with little or no warning. Each time July drives away in the bakkie the marooned and isolated Smaleses await his return.

— *Margaret A. Dodson*

THE JUNGLE

Author: Upton Sinclair (1878-1968)
Type of work: Novel
Type of plot: Social realism

Time of plot: Early twentieth century
First published: 1906

Aside from flashbacks to Lithuania in early chapters, most of this novel's action takes place in the meat-packing areas of Chicago, Illinois, whose immigrant workers are overworked and economically exploited to a point that causes the human spirit to deteriorate.

*Chicago.** Midwestern American city to which many immigrants, mostly eastern European, flocked in the late nineteenth and early twentieth centuries to find work in the meat-packing industry. A major railroad terminus, Chicago had a brisk economy, but its wealth was unevenly distributed. The captains of industry exploited the workers, who worked under appalling conditions for paltry wages, swelling the owners' bank accounts.

*Lithuania.** Small eastern European country on the Baltic Sea from which Jurgis Rudkus, the novel's protagonist, emigrates hoping to find a better life in the United States. Early chapters of the novel contain flashbacks to Jurgis's life in Lithuania that reflect the environment from which he has come.

Packingtown. Industrial area in Chicago where meat-packing houses are concentrated. Workers in Packingtown typically live nearby in run-down dwellings. Noxious smells from the meat-processing factories fill the air, and Packingtown's sewers often overflow, sending streams of polluted water into the streets. In one such overflow, Jurgis's young son drowns.

In 1904, Sinclair gained firsthand experience with such conditions after being sent by a socialist newspaper to investigate Chicago's stockyards and packinghouses. He spent seven weeks living among workers in the packinghouses, after which he wrote *The Jungle*. While trying to touch the hearts of Americans, he also touched their stomachs by accurately reporting the deplorable sanitary conditions in meat-processing plants. After President Theodore Roosevelt read *The Jungle*, he pressured Congress to pass the Pure Food and Drug Act of 1906.

After his arrival in Chicago, Jurgis tours Durham's plant and marvels at the efficiency of the operation and at its assembly-line, not realizing the dehumanizing effects that such efficiency can create. Later, he takes a job in Brown's meat-packing plant, an assembly-line killing field much like Durham's. He is assigned to the killing beds, the most dehumanizing place in the packinghouse to work—the place where stunned animals are brought by conveyor belts to be killed and gutted. The killing beds symbolize what the packinghouses do to humans who work in them: They destroy them, killing their spirits, exploiting them, and discarding them when they cease to work up to speed.

Jurgis's house. House that Jurgis buys for his family. He buys the house thinking it is new, but it is actually only freshly painted after it has been lived in by five other families. To buy the house Jurgis takes out a heavy mortgage but does not understand that his loan requires payment of interest. Like the house's five previous owners, Jurgis loses the house when he cannot make his payments. Like America generally, the glittering house is a sham that sinks Jurgis's family deeper into ruin.

Saloons. Chicago's neighborhood saloons provide their customers with both warmth and free lunches that come with their drinks. Many of the hard-working immigrants in Packingtown are also hard-drinking. In winter, when piercing winds howl through Chicago's streets, workers flood into neighborhood saloons, which represent safe and comforting sanctuaries into which alienated, disenchanted workers can retreat.

Bridewell. Jail in which Jurgis serves a term after being convicted of assault on his foreman, Phil Connor, after learning that Connor is involved with his wife. Later, Jurgis is again sentenced to Bridewell, this time for assault on a bartender who has cheated him. In Bridewell, Jurgis meets Jack Duane, a safecracker who befriends him, paving the way for Jurgis to join the union and involve himself in politics.

Great Plains. After losing his wife, his son, and his home, Jurgis hops a freight train for the tranquility of the plains to assuage his sorrows and reflect on the futility of his life. There he spends a summer moving from place to place, taking whatever jobs he can find. The wholesome rural atmosphere restores him, but after he returns to Chicago, his life reverts to its previous hell.

Union hall. Meeting place in which Jurgis finds new direction in his life. During the first union meeting he attends there, he falls asleep when the speaker talks about matters unrelated to his own problems and he is ejected from the hall. The next night, however, when the speaker begins addressing problems of Chicago's working poor, his speech energizes Jurgis.

Hind's Hotel. Chicago hotel in which Jurgis works as a porter. There he comes into contact with socialists and political activists who take rooms there. This job marks another significant turning point in his life.

— *R. Baird Shuman*

THE JUNGLE BOOKS

Author: Rudyard Kipling (1865-1936)
Type of work: Short fiction
Type of plot: Fables

Time of plot: Nineteenth century
First published: The Jungle Book, 1894; *The Second Jungle Book*, 1895

The Jungle Books contain several tales set in Arctic regions and one in the Himalayas, but most of their tales are set in the jungles of north-central India during the nineteenth century, when India was under the British Raj. Settings in the tales typically depict jungle life among the animals and villagers who attempt to live with the animal kingdom.

*****India.** Because the locations given for Mowgli's world are vague, except for the reference to India's Waingunga River, the forest in which Mowgli lives is chiefly symbolic of a world in which the laws of the jungle prevail, much as legal systems prevail in civilization. Mowgli's jungle is made up of several settings, the first being the wolf cave in which he is sheltered as an infant and young boy by Father and Mother Wolf.

Several times Mowgli encounters human villages, usually as they relate to a woman named Messua who believes that Mowgli is her son who was taken from her years before. Through one season, Mowgli lives in the village and learns of the ways of humankind; however, he is run off when he unites the animals to trample Shere Khan the tiger. The villagers suspect that Mowgli is a demon possessed because he knows how to talk with the animals who helped raise him.

Later, Mowgli returns to this same village to rescue Messua and her husband, who are being prepared for ex-

ecution because their son Mowgli lives as a brother to the animals. This time Mowgli enlists the help of his jungle friends to help his human parents escape and, especially with the help of the chief elephant Hathi and his three sons, destroys the village without killing the people. For many years, Mowgli is convinced that villages are more dangerous places to live than the jungle, where he understands the laws of the beasts. Later, when Mowgli is seventeen, he finds Messua in another village and goes to live with her as he comes to accept his place among people.

Council Rock. Place in the jungle where the wolves and others of the jungle meet to make important decisions. At this location the infant man cub, named Mowgli, or "Frog," is spared from the wrath of Shere Khan the tiger by the help of Baloo the bear and Bagheera the black panther. Later, at this location, Mowgli defends the wolf pack's aging leader, Akela, by spreading fire, or the Red Flower, to frighten away the younger wolves of the Seeonee Pack, who seek Akela's and Mowgli's deaths.

Years later, when Mowgli is grown, he finally kills his sworn enemy, Shere Khan, and hangs his hide on the Council Rock. So the Council Rock is a symbol of leadership and power, where Mowgli finally wins a good name for himself.

Cold Lairs. Lost city that Mowgli visits several times, once when the monkey people take him captive there, and again when he explores the treasures stored in this forgotten place. A place of ruined houses and temples, Cold Lairs is a reminder of death. A white cobra guards the treasure, and when Mowgli takes a jeweled and thorn-pointed ankus into the jungle, he finds six men willing to kill one another for it before he returns it to Cold Lairs. The role of greed among men causes Mowgli to reject the gold coins and other treasures of this lost city. By the law of the jungle, Mowgli learns to live free of greed.

Other places. Other stories in this collection are set in a variety of places, such as St. Paul Island in the Bering Sea, Devon Island above Lancaster Sound in the Northwest Territories of Canada, and near a village in the Himalayan Mountains beyond Mutteeanee Pass. In each of these settings, whether Kipling is discussing white seals fighting for survival or men seeking the meaning of their lives, their isolation helps the reader focus on the essentials of life. Just as *The Jungle Books* as a whole focus on the law of the jungle, so the stories in other settings also focus on the principles of dignity, honesty, and valor in challenging circumstances.

— *Daven M. Kari*

JUNO AND THE PAYCOCK

Author: Sean O'Casey (John Casey, 1880-1964)
Type of work: Drama
Type of plot: Satire

Time of plot: 1922
First performed: 1924; first published, 1925

The setting in this play is tightly restricted to the decrepit Dublin tenement in which the Boyle family lives during the 1920's, when life was undergoing tumultuous change.

Boyle apartment. Tenement in Dublin, Ireland, in which are crammed the four members of the Boyle family. The atmosphere is one of claustrophobia—all actions occur in the front room of this two-room flat—while beyond its confines Ireland is struggling to gain independence from England and, in a larger sense, its colonial past.

Stage directions indicate a place that is sparse and dilapidated, though a few possessions are significant—a laborer's shovel, which sees no work given the captain's assiduous avoidance of employment. A clock rests face down on the mantel, and time seems to stand still for the Boyles; their concerns have less to do with the unfolding future than with a repetition of predictable patterns from the past. Historical changes are overtaking them and will belie their predictable lifestyle. Another symbolic ornament is a picture of the Virgin Mary, under which a votive candle remains perpetually lit until it burns out in act 3, signaling the end of son Johnny's life.

Beginning with act 2, the furnishings change dramatically when it appears that the captain has been blessed with a generous inheritance. Gone are the meager furnishings, replaced by "glaringly upholstered" chairs, cheap pictures, and artificial flowers. By act 3 all this has been repossessed, and the family's fortunes fall precipitously.

In many ways this apartment is a mirror of Sean O'Casey's own humble origins in the tenements of Dublin's poorest neighborhoods and a symbol of the lack of opportunity in Ireland.

— *David W. Madden*

JURGEN: A Comedy of Justice

Author: James Branch Cabell (1879-1958)

Type of work: Novel

Type of plot: Fantasy

Time of plot: Middle Ages

First published: 1919

The protagonist Jurgen in this novel roams from one fantastic kingdom to another during a year in which his physical youth is restored, though he keeps his old and experienced mind. Each realm represents a different way of relating to life or a different aspect of human hopes or beliefs. Jurgen tries out each realm with no real intention to stay, though in most, he finds a wife. Eventually, he forgoes all the strange realms for what is to him the dull day-to-day of Poictesme, where he is a middle-aged pawnbroker with a shrewish wife.

Poictesme (PWA-tem). Imaginary medieval French realm whose name is derived from the cities of Poictiers (modern Poitiers) and Angoulesme (modern Angoulême), although it lies in the south, along the Mediterranean Sea's Gulf of Lions. Poictesme corresponds geographically with France's modern district of Gard, overlapping Herault and Bouches-Du-Rhone. Poictesme is a central location in many of the novels in James Branch Cabell's eighteen-volume *The Biography of the Life of Manuel*, of which *Jurgen* is a part. It is a pleasant country of fields, mountains, and forests (some haunted), and walled cities with castles, including Storisende ("story's end"), the capital.

Cabell based Poictesme partially on country resorts in Virginia where he passed time as a young man among the elegant gentry of the South.

Garden Between Dawn and Sunrise. Place inhabited by the illusions of youth and idealistic love, including Dorothy La Désirée, sister of the ruler of Poictesme, as she was when Jurgen first loved her. The garden reflects Cabell's ambivalence toward the vision of the eternal feminine glimpsed by naïve, adoring love: It is a necessary ideal, humankind's window to transcendence, as well as a great deal of fool nonsense.

Amneran Heath. Unwholesome and magical place, with an entrance to a troll's cave. At the end of the book, Jurgen finds Koshchei—the creator of the world—at the back of the cave, working in a small office; however, he gets no satisfactory explanations of life or of himself from the dim and overbusy creator.

Cameliard (kah-MEEL-yard). Capital of **Glathion**, the realm modeled on Arthurian romances, that is home to Queen Guenevere and the chivalric ideal that everything one possesses is on loan to devote to the service of god, king, and woman. It is an ideal that Jurgen cannot grasp. With chivalry comes courtly love, which is essentially illicit or adulterous and, to Jurgen, hypocritical. His affair with Guenevere is winked at so long as it does not become public knowledge and ruin her marriage to King Arthur.

Cocaigne (koh-KAYN). Island realm of eternal evening ruled over by Dame Anaïtis (whose name is an anagram of "Insatia"), the Lady of the Lake. A place of pagan hedonism whose law is do whatever seems good to you. However, Jurgen tires of endless indulgence in the "curious pleasures" he finds "disappointing and messy." Cocaigne's name comes from the medieval French for the "land of Cockaigne," an imaginary land of pleasure, eternal youth, and endless sweets—presumably just as cloying.

Leuke. Island ruled by Queen Helen of Troy, who is now married to Achilles. Its capital, **Pseudopolis** (Greek for "unreal city"), is the home of the classical tradition at its most noble and ethereal. Helen, like Dorothy, is the transcendent loveliness always sought, but lost when it is won. When Jurgen has a chance to reveal Helen's full beauty by drawing her coverlet away while she sleeps, he refrains, leaving the ideal unattained.

Philistia. Land at war with Pseudopolis; a satire of contemporary American culture. Philistia's law is do whatever seems to be expected of you. Its gods are Sephra, Ageus, and Vel-Tyno, anagrams of "phrases" (representing catch phrases), "usage" (conformity), and "novelty" (faddishness).

Hell. Hell exists to assuage the pride of sinners, specifically Jurgen's father, Coth, who think he deserves the direst of punishments. In Hell, whatever Coth believes becomes real. Cabell uses the episode to show

how human beings insist on their beliefs, which then shape the world around them: People are the cause of their own suffering. In Hell, which is fighting a war with Heaven, the religion is patriotism, and the government is an enlightened democracy—Cabell's satire of America's government by the masses and of the jingoistic extremism of Americans during World War I, which ended while he was writing this book.

Heaven. Contiguous to Hell, Heaven (and its God) was created by Koshchei to satisfy Jurgen's grandmother, Steinvor, who insisted on an afterlife fitting her religious beliefs, and to honor her capacity for selfless love. Jurgen finds he loves and fears God, but cannot believe in Him. Even sitting on God's throne, he still does not know what he wants. Our beliefs and expectations shape what we find, perhaps all that we can perceive, even of good; unable to believe, Jurgen cannot be satisfied.

— *William Mingin*

KENILWORTH: A Romance

Author: Sir Walter Scott (1771-1832)
Type of work: Novel
Type of plot: Romance

Time of plot: 1575
First published: 1821

Places in Kenilworth, *as in virtually all Walter Scott novels, are central to his historically based fiction. Scott earned the sobriquet "Wizard of the North" because of his ability to revive Great Britain's past and make it present to readers, and his use of settings is an integral part of that feat. In this novel, he brings to life the panorama of sixteenth century English society during the reign of Queen Elizabeth, using precise and detailed depictions of the settings.*

*Kenilworth Castle. Castle near the central England village of Kenilworth in Warwickshire. First built in the twelfth century, this castle was given by Queen Elizabeth to Robert Dudley, earl of Leicester, and was the scene of his festivities for her in the summer of 1575. Against this background, Scott's novel presents an intimate portrait of Elizabeth's personality and her relationships with Sir Walter Raleigh, the earl of Sussex, and other historical figures.

Although Scott takes liberties with historical details about Dudley's guest list, he is accurate about his architectural and topographical details. He uses the actual castle's floor plan in his description of the seven acres at Kenilworth and bases his descriptions of its interior on an inventory list from Dudley's time of the castle's tableware, furniture, and hangings. The castle's pageantry becomes one of the vehicles in the book for Scott to present a complete and vibrant picture of Elizabethan society that includes traveling entertainers, court figures, country bumpkins, servants, and others.

When he was asked to write a book on Elizabeth—after his 1820 novel about Scotland's Queen Mary Stuart, *The Abbot*—Scott rejected the title of "Armada" suggested by his publisher because such a novel would have required a focus on Elizabeth's political prowess in the English defeat of the attempted Spanish invasion in

1588. As in his other novels, Scott prefers not to show history in the making during a pivotal historical event, but to present historical figures in the normal course of everyday life. He chooses, for this novel, a setting in which the story allows him to be free to focus on the grandeur of Elizabeth's court and to convey the atmosphere of that age.

*Cumnor-Place. Also called Cumnor Hall, the home of Dudley and his wife, Amy Robsart, in the village of Cumnor, in south-central England's Oxfordshire. Formerly a monastery, this country home has a small area that has been refurbished in contemporary Elizabethan style for the earl and his secret bride. As the setting in which Amy is first introduced and the scene of her murder at the very end, Cumnor-Place is the stage for the beginning and the end of Scott's narrative circle concerning his plot about Amy's fate. The gloomy darkness of this place in general reflects Leicester's desire to hide the marriage (for political reasons) and foreshadows the treachery of Amy's murder.

Scott considered calling the novel "Cumnor Hall" because its central plot focuses on the plight of Amy Robsart and because that name is also the title of a tragic ballad about the mystery surrounding Amy's death. Although Cumnor Hall is a main setting in the book, it is not a place well suited to presenting the whole social strata of England, so Scott eventually chose the more appropriate title "Kenilworth."

Black Bear Inn. Public house in Cumnor that functions to launch the story by introducing Michael Lambourne and Edmund Tressilian. Their simultaneous arrivals at Cumnor initiate the action concerning Amy's future. Each time the Black Bear Inn reappears, the town gossip at this location becomes Scott's narrative vehicle to convey information not only about a host of other characters but about the history, culture and customs of the time.

*Greenwich Castle (GREH-nich). Queen Elizabeth's favorite royal residence in southeast London on the River Thames. In choosing to have Elizabeth appear first in this place where she holds her council meetings, Scott emphasizes her royal function as queen. Scott's depiction of Elizabeth as a woman, which is his focus later in the scenes at Kenilworth, is subordinated here to his presentation of her as the royal monarch.

Lidcote Hall. Home of Sir Hugh Robsart, Amy's father, near Lidcote in Devonshire, in southwest England. Briefly depicted, it has a simple and honorable atmosphere that contrasts with the court atmosphere of jealousy and intrigue elsewhere in the story.

— *Marsha Daigle-Williamson*

KIDNAPPED: Being Memoirs of the Adventures of David Balfour in the Year 1751

Author: Robert Louis Stevenson (1850-1894)
Type of work: Novel
Type of plot: Adventure

Time of plot: 1751
First published: 1886

The character of the young protagonist in this novel is shaped by the Scottish Lowlands, and his understanding of what it is to be a man and a Scotsman is developed in the Scottish Highlands. David Balfour's family's history and his own destiny center on the place called the House of Shaws. David first learns about the dark side of men and society on board a ship, and his awareness of physical limitations and the need for physical courage is formed on a desolate islet, the rocks of Glencoe, and the Braes of Balquidder. Most of Robert Louis Stevenson's novels show a strong sense of place, but perhaps nowhere is that sense more highly developed than in this novel.

*Scottish Highlands. Mountainous region of northern Scotland that is the scene of many adventures of young David Balfour, who finds the Highlands a wild, frightening, demanding, and alien environment. However, with the help of Highlander Alan Breck Stewart, he learns to survive there and to understand himself in doing so. There, he learns what it means to be Scottish. His own upbringing in the Scottish Lowlands has made him ambitious, thrifty, careful, and a little selfish. In the Highlands, he encounters heroism, romance, honor, tragedy, and loyalty. The Highlands thus represent aspects of Scotland and of David himself which, after David's adventures with Alan Breck Stewart, he cannot ignore or forget.

House of Shaws. Balfour family estate that is David's birthright but which at the beginning of the novel is in the possession of David's wicked uncle, Ebenezer Balfour. The House of Shaws is a dark, forbidding, dangerous, and mysterious place. Its decayed and incomplete state reflects the grim family history and blighted lives of the Balfours. Its darkness and dangers mirror the evils of Ebenezer Balfour. David's retaking possession of Shaws at the end of the novel signals his achievement of maturity and the beginning of a much brighter future for both the Shaws and the Balfour family.

Covenant. Ship captained by Elias Hoseason on which David Balfour is carried away after being kidnapped on his uncle's orders. The ship's name evokes Scottish religious tradition, but for David the *Covenant* is merely a small and dangerous place in which he learns quickly about the concentrated wickedness, violence, treachery, and brutality of men and the ruthlessness of wind and sea. In the miniature world of the *Covenant* he also finds occasional kindness and the heroic fighting abilities of the Jacobite adventurer Alan Breck Stewart.

***Scottish Lowlands.** Region of Scotland below the Highland line that is the home of David Balfour. Stevenson treats Scotland's Lowlands as prosperous, commercial, materialistic, affluent, and governed by law and order. The Lowlands represent one side of Scottish character and the romantic Highlands another. David's prudence, ambition, common sense, and faith in law mark him as a Lowlander, just as the daring Alan Breck Stewart is the perfect Highlander in his bravery, honor, loyalty, and quick temper. Contrasts and conflicts between the Lowlands and the Highlands are among the novel's most important themes.

***Appin.** Region of the Scottish Highlands that is home to Alan Breck Stewart and his clan and is the scene of the murder of Colin Campbell. Stevenson's account of Appin provides views of clan life, the violence associated with clan feuds, the oppression and degradation of the Highlands after the Jacobite uprising of 1745, and the fearful but determined survival of clan loyalties and values under English oppression.

***Earraid** (ihr-AYD). Rocky islet onto which David is cast after the loss of the *Covenant*. Earraid is a small, barren, uninhabited, and inhospitable island among Scotland's Hebrides where David learns about life without even the most basic comforts. During his four-day stay on this islet, David is wet, cold, hungry, and sick, and this bleak place provides him an education in the basic realities of physical existence and physical pain. When he finally discovers that Earraid is a tidal islet from which he can escape during any low tide, the island also educates him in humility.

***Cluny's Cage.** Egg-shaped hanging house made of wattles and moss where, on the side of the mountain Ben Alder, the outlawed Highland chieftain Cluny Macpherson finds refuge. Cluny's Cage is not only a memorably strange dwelling but a symbol of Highland determination and ingenuity. In this hanging home, Macpherson remains in his dear Highlands, tricks the English army, and conducts his clan's business. At the same time, his prisonlike suspended cage reflects the extremes to which Highlanders must go to survive.

***Balquidder** (bal-KWI-tur). Highland region in which David recuperates for a month from exhaustion and where he and Alan Breck Stewart meet Robin Oig, son of the notorious Rob Roy. Stevenson describes this region of the Highlands as a wild country inhabited by outcasts and men without chieftains or major clan connections. This outlaw region essentially serves as a symbol for the decay and disintegration of Highland life. However, Stevenson shows the survival of Highlander honor and love of music even in this place of disorder.

***Glencoe.** One of the wildest areas in the Scottish Highlands where, amid waterfalls and rocks, David and Alan hide from pursuing English soldiers. The horrific sublimity of Glencoe adds to the terror of their situation, and Stevenson is careful to point out that Glencoe was the scene of a famous massacre in 1692. The day in which David and Alan spend hiding and broiling on a sun-baked rock in Glencoe, surrounded by English soldiers, is among the most memorable episodes in *Kidnapped*.

— *Phillip B. Anderson*

KIM

Author: Rudyard Kipling (1865-1936)
Type of work: Novel
Type of plot: Adventure

Time of plot: Late nineteenth century
First published: 1901

Most of the principal characters in this novel are identified with a region that they personify, except for Kim, who is a synthesis of them all. Kim represents a fusion of British and indigenous Indian culture—what Rudyard Kipling hoped the Indian subcontinent might become. In addition to presenting this ideal, this novel is also Kipling's nostalgic recollection of the land in which he spent his happy childhood and early manhood. He even further idealized it to please his father, who thought that an early version of the novel was unpatriotic because it depicted British secrets being sold in the bazaars.

*Lahore (le-HOHR). Now a city in northeastern Pakistan, Lahore was part of British India at the time in which this novel is set. Its museum or "Wonder House" (which represents the city's richness and cultural diversity) has a curator modeled on Rudyard Kipling's father, who was curator there from 1875 to 1894. It is appropriate that *Kim* opens in Lahore, because Kipling's earliest memories came from there. His appreciation of the city's ethnic and religious heterogeneity owes something to the Masonic Lodge, which he joined there as a young man; it was an organization teaching the brotherhood of all races and faiths. *Kim*'s presentation of India is best when it conforms to this Masonic spirit. However, from the novel's first sentence, Kipling overlays this tolerance with the presupposition that the British have won the right to rule Lahore, and, indeed, all of India.

*Afghanistan. Independent country west of India that was thought to threaten British India, particularly if Afghanistan were to ally itself with Russia or France. Personifying the best of Afghanistan, Mahbub Ali, repeatedly called the "Afghan," exudes courage and ferocious virility as well as guile, yet Kim wins his affection. To celebrate that boy's becoming a man, Mahbub Ali dresses Kim in the robes of a prince of his Afghan tribe. This incident symbolizes Kipling's hope that the British Empire will eventually expand into Afghanistan.

Such-Zen (sewtch-ZEHN). Fictional Tibetan Buddhist monastery, where an unnamed lama becomes Kim's teacher. Since Kipling renders a few other Tibetan place names correctly, the name "Such-Zen" is probably not merely a corrupted spelling of the real Tibetan monastery Tso-chen, but Kipling's deliberate allusion to two basic Buddhist concepts: *tathata* for absolute reality, which is usually translated as "suchness"; and meditation, the root meaning of the Japanese word *zen*. Kipling may have encountered that term during a trip to Japan that inspired his poem "Buddha at Kamakura," which he used as epigraphs for chapters in *Kim*. The lama's being a Tibetan Buddhist serves as a pretext for Kipling to write of India's having given the world Buddhism, a religion that fascinated Kipling during his adolescence. Kipling's fictional lama is under Kipling's protection just as Kipling presumably wished to see Tibet under British imperial protection.

*Simla (SIM-lah; now spelled Shimla). Cosmopolitan city in the cool foothills of the Himalayas that was the summer capital of British India. There, Kim studies under Lurgan Sahib, a character modeled on that city's most famous illusionist and seller of jewels, A. M. Jacob. To a lesser extent, Colonel Creighton (modeled on Colonel Thomas Montgomerie) is associated with Simla, though he first appears in another center of British military power, Umballa (now called Ambala).

*Lucknow (LUK-now). City in north-central India, southeast of Delhi, to which Kim goes to attend St. Xavier's School, which Kipling modeled on Lucknow's real La Martinière Academy. Like its real-life model, St. Xavier's is a place in which students manage to keep contact with India while they learn British civilization, in contrast to the purely British schools that Kipling attended at the cost of considerable culture shock.

*Sahuranpore (se-HAR-ren-pohr; now spelled Saharanpur). Hill town in northern India's Uttar Pradesh State, near Tibet. The Sahiba who lives there represents the high status of women in those hills, as, to a greater extent, does the relatively nearby Woman of Shamleigh, with her two or more husbands.

*Bengal (ben-GAWL). Province of northeast British India (since divided between India and Pakistan) whose intellectuals were particularly prone to anti-British protests of which Kipling disapproved. Consequently, the Bengali character Babu Hurree Chunder Mookerjee is portrayed as pretentious and comic. His probable model was Colonel Montgomerie's Bengali agent Babu Sarat Chandra Das. Like Kipling's character, this Babu undertook clandestine operations involving Tibet, as part of Britain's attempted expansion of its political and economic influence into the Himalayas.

— *James Whitlark*

KINFLICKS

Author: Lisa Alther (1944-   )

Type of work: Novel

Type of plot: Bildungsroman

Time of plot: 1960's, early 1970's

First published: 1975

This novel opens as young Ginny Babcock is flying from Vermont to her hometown in Tennessee, where her mother is dying and the family home is being auctioned off. As she reenters the landscape of her youth, memories, like the home movies she calls "kinflicks," flash before her eyes. The chapters alternate between the present, dealing with her mother, hospitals, the medical profession, and making sense of her life, and the hilarious recollections of her misspent youth in the South and her picaresque flight north through the sexual politics, intellectual fads, social experiments, and civil rights and antiwar conflicts of that era.

Hullsport. Fictional town in east Tennessee, modeled on the real Kingsport, Tennessee, Lisa Alther's hometown. Alther's protagonist, Ginny Babcock, grows up in Hullsport, where the local chemical plant owned by her father, Major Babcock spews smoke as it manufactures munitions to support the Korean War effort and ships top secret materials to Oak Ridge, Tennessee, for the manufacture of nuclear weapons.

When Ginny was growing up in Hullsport, debutante balls, bouffant hairdos, southern drawls, and flag waving were as much a part of town life as kudzu vines, Harley Davidson motorcycles, moonshine liquor, and cockfights. There country music blared from radios while Ginny and her football-playing boyfriend, Joe Bob Sparks, made out after a Southern Baptist revival meeting; however, after she lost her virginity to a boy from the wrong social class, she was shipped off to a college up north.

In the novel's present time, when Ginny returns to Hullsport and attends her mother, she sees the town as it now is—with new developments, new roads, and a new McDonalds. However, the town's river is still polluted, the flag-waving routine for the band is still the same, the medical profession is just as impersonal as ever, her former friends have grown older and heavier, and she herself still does not fit in. She and the townspeople have little in common except their shared past; moreover, their memories of that past are very different.

Worthley College. New England college in which Ginny is accepted because she fills the Appalachian slot in the college's quota system. (Alther models the fictional college on Wellesley College, near Boston, where she earned a bachelor's degree.) At Worthley, Ginny is exposed through her teacher, Miss Head, to the intellectual pursuits of philosophy, literature, cellular biology, classical music, and foods totally unlike the hamburger and pizza of her former life. Here she has her first lesbian encounter, with Eddie Holzer from Roxbury, Massachusetts, who introduces her to protest movements, rock music, psychedelic mushrooms, and the politics of war, and persuades her eventually to drop out of college.

*****Boston.** New England's largest city, where Ginny discovers opera, symphonies, art museums, and the culture of the elite under the tutelage of Miss Head. Here she learns that Harvard and Princeton boys are no different from the boys in Tennessee. She sides at first with the life of the intellect, urged on by Miss Head, but later, swayed by Eddie and the writings of Friedrich Nietzsche, she realizes that she will choose a life involving people, not merely ideas. She rejects capitalism and part of her trust fund and moves into slum housing in Cambridge with Eddie, with whom she attends demonstrations with a group they call the "Family," singing in bars, and exploring each other sexually, until their apartment is condemned and they move to a commune in Vermont.

Stark's Bog. Vermont town loosely based on the area around Hinesburg, Vermont, where Alther has lived for thirty years. This rural setting is where much of the rest of the flashbacks in the novel take place. Here with three other women, Ginny and Eddie become part of the back-to-the-land movement, "soybean people," milking cows, chopping wood, and organizing the Free Farm, as they call their place. They experiment with organic gardening, conduct fertility rites, and gradually mingle with the local townspeople by joining the volunteer fire department, going to square dances, setting up Planned Parenthood meetings, and celebrating sisterhood.

Eventually, Ginny moves out of the commune, marries a local man, Ira Bliss, and becomes a Tupperware housewife with a baby daughter. However, her new lifestyle ends abruptly when she is discovered doing tantric yoga exercises with Will Hawk, a tattooed Vietnam deserter and Appalachian Trail hiker. When Ira discovers them in a compromising position, he forces Ginny to leave at gunpoint.

Sow's Gap. Virginia town, loosely based on Big Stone Gap, where Ginny's grandparents began their married life and where her father left coal mining to move to Hullsport. Sow's Gap is a place of feuding, coal mines, slag heaps, corn liquor, and hairpin curves.

*****Montreal.** Canadian city to which Will Hawk flees when he deserts from the army and to which Ginny and Will flee when they are expelled by Ira. With its cold winters and language battles, Montreal gives Ginny and Will a sense of culture shock.

— *Newton Smith*

KING JOHN

Author: William Shakespeare (1564-1616)
Type of work: Drama
Type of plot: Historical
Time of plot: Early thirteenth century
First performed: c. 1596-1597; first published, 1623

This play divides its action between England and France, but the literal settings are not essential to William Shakespeare's theme of Commodity or to the fact that it is not John but Faulconbridge the Bastard who is the real king. In the nineteenth century, the play particularly suited the vogue for elaborate historically accurate sets. However, modern productions tend to ignore realistic settings in favor of expressionistic or symbolic ones.

*****England.** The play's English settings include King John's castle, a battlefield, and an orchard near Swinstead Abbey. All these places are merely backdrops for the debates, declamations, disputes, and lamentations of the characters. The main focus is on the opposition between John and the Bastard, and it is this conflict rather than any setting or place which is crucial to the play's shape. In fact, the play's momentum would be retarded by more than passing reference to particular settings. It is character or episode rather than setting which makes a dramatic impression here, for this play is most vivid in such scenes as the King's bellowing at the French ambassador as Elinor, his mother, is amused; the Bastard's speech on Commodity; the blinding of young Arthur by Hubert; and John's death by poisoning.

*****France.** The play's French settings—which include the king's pavilion, the Dauphin's camp at St. Edmundsbury, and the French camp—are significant only to mark the politics of international diplomacy. Once again, the play reveals that detailed settings would merely impede the momentum, for the political arguments occur at high speed. Some productions dispense almost totally with scenic elements, showing clearly that the only value of place in this play is that which comes from the fact that it is English history turned into a work for the stage.

— *Keith Garebian*

KING LEAR

Author: William Shakespeare (1564-1616)
Type of work: Drama
Type of plot: Tragedy
Time of plot: First century B.C.E.
First performed: c. 1605-1606; first published, 1608

Although William Shakespeare's stage directions are not specific, the many locations suggested in the text of his play contribute to the feeling of unrest and tension in Lear's ancient British kingdom. Against a background of castles, heath, and military camps, the action moves inexorably, as Lear progresses toward understanding and death.

Heath. Large tract of uncultivated land covered with small plants and shrubs (the type of landscape also known as a "moor" in Britain), on which the play's memorable scenes are set. Barren and desolate, far removed from civilized society, the heath represents elemental Nature, a place for fools and madmen—and tragic kings. In the pelting rain and stripped of the garments of majesty, Lear vents his grief and anger by railing against his daughters' ingratitude, the injustice rampant in society, and the forces of Nature surrounding him.

Lear's palace. Royal residence of King Lear in whose stateroom the play opens. The palace provides a visual contrast with the scenes on the heath, and the setting for the first scene displays Lear at his most powerful. Supported by this environment and invested with the external objects of majesty, Lear can function

arbitrarily in the division of his kingdom.

Gloucester's castle (GLAHS-ter). Residence of the duke of Gloucester, which is the site of two of the most painful scenes in the play—the moments when Lear is rejected by Goneril and Regan, and when Gloucester is blinded. Significantly, the setting is located halfway between the palace of absolute power and the heath of total nothingness.

Fields near Dover. Region in southeastern England, on the edge of the British kingdom, where Gloucester attempts suicide and Lear deteriorates into madness. It is the landing place for Cordelia and the forces that will restore order and justice. These fields are a place of the natural world, where men must deal with themselves as merely "poor, bare, forked animals."

— *Joyce E. Henry*

KING SOLOMON'S MINES

Author: H. Rider Haggard (1856-1925)
Type of work: Novel
Type of plot: Adventure

Time of plot: Late nineteenth century
First published: 1885

Fictional hunter Allan Quatermain's narrative recounts an almost fantastical journey into a region of Southern Africa's interior that was poorly known to Europeans at the time H. Rider Haggard published this novel. The narrative gives Africa's diverse landscapes an adversarial character that hinders Quatermain's quest and accentuates the contrast between European and African civilizations. Africa seems vast, savage, and unforgiving as Haggard's heroic characters refuse to give up their concepts of British civility that advocates of imperialism would later use as a rationale for imposing European rule over most of Africa.

*Durban. Port city in the British-ruled colony of Natal on South Africa's eastern coast that is Quatermain's base. Durban represents a mean between the exaggerated civilization and inflation of Cape Town and the unexplored, untamed open country of Southern Africa's interior. Inland expeditions outfit at Durban and depart from and return there; it is a frontier town in which the best and worst of European and African residents can be

found. Durban is a busy place in which the unexpected can always be expected to happen. The setting allows a preview of what can be expected in the interior and prepares readers for a fabulous adventure.

Dunkeld. Ship on which Quatermain meets Sir Henry Curtis and Captain John Good while sailing from Cape Town to Durban. Their voyage symbolizes the impact of progress and technology on Africa. Not many years earlier, rounding the Cape of Good Hope was dangerous, and shipwrecks were common. However, European progress and technology have tamed the seas to the point that such voyages have become the common and safe means of transportation between Southern Africa's two main ports. Eventually, the African continent, like the seas surrounding it, will be tamed by European progress.

*Southern Africa. Region below the Zambezi River—which now separates Zimbabwe from Zambia—that is the broad canvas for *King Solomon's Mines.* The trek on which Quatermain leads Curtis and Good takes them through dense forests, torrid deserts, and high mountains that exemplify the harshest, most unforgiving, and most extreme opposites in Southern Africa's wide range of climates and topography. These extreme variations lend a mood of unrest to the novel: a sense of foreboding and danger, which is exactly what the author intends.

Haggard inclined toward the sensational in his writings, and since the British reading audience of his era wanted to be thrilled by near-death adventures set in exotic locales, Haggard obliged them with fantastic tales set mostly in Southern Africa. Drawing on bits of authentic local lore, as well as legends and myths he heard about during the several years he lived in Southern Africa, he gave all his African novels an air of mystery and romance. By setting characters exemplifying refined British standards of culture and morality against Africans exemplifying largely imaginary savagery, his books made the continent seem far more dangerous and mysterious than it ever actually was.

Suliman Mountains. Imaginary great mountain range separating Kukuanaland from the Transvaal that takes its name from the biblical King Solomon. In the subzero temperatures near the top of the range, the travelers find the frozen body of a Portuguese man who died three centuries earlier, and an African member of their party freezes to death in his sleep. The extreme contrast between the low temperatures atop these mountains and the high temperatures on the lower plains adds to the novel's mystique. Although no real mountains in the region in which *King Solomon's Mines* is set resemble Haggard's fictional range, snow-capped equatorial mountains—such as Kilimanjaro—do exist in East Africa, to the north.

*Matabele country (mah-tah-BAY-lay). Also known as Matabeleland, the site of the historical Ndebele kingdom, in what is now southwestern Zimbabwe, through which Quatermain's party travels to reach Kukuanaland. Haggard never visited this region but while working in South Africa's Transvaal region, he heard many reports of the alleged fierceness of the Ndebele people to the north and modeled his fictional Kukuana people on them.

An important narrative thread of *King Solomon's Mines* was inspired by an actual incident in Ndebele history. In 1872 a man claiming to be the rightful Ndebele king, Nkulumane, made an abortive attempt to enter Matabeleland to claim his throne. That pretender's mission was materially aided by a British colonial official in Durban named Theophilus Shepstone, under whom Haggard later served in the Transvaal. Haggard's mysterious African character Umbopa in *King Solomon's Mines* accompanies Quatermain's party into Kukuanaland, where he reveals himself to be the rightful king, Ignosi. In contrast to the Ndebele pretender, Umbopa succeeds—thanks in large part to the intervention of the British characters.

Kukuanaland (koo-koo-AH-nah-land). Imaginary African kingdom, located north of Matabele country, where the quest of Quatermain's party ends. During the nineteenth century, legends of "lost" civilizations in the African interior abounded among Europeans, and some of these focused on the Zimbabwe region—the actual site of a former stone-building African culture. Although Haggard's Kukuanaland and its capital, **Loo,** are totally fictional, his use of a great stone road leading to a lost city in the wilderness seemed to conform to rumors about a lost ancient civilization in the Zimbabwe region and added greatly to his novel's sense of the mysterious and exotic.

Cave of death. Cavern in which Quatermain and his companions find a great mineral treasure in the novel's climactic chapters. Three gigantic stone idols guard the entrance to the ancient mine and add even more foreboding and danger to an atmosphere already heavily laden with ominous overtones. The cavern, like Africa generally, offers its riches to those bold enough to claim them, but it never gives them up willingly.

— *H. Alan Pickrell*

KISS OF THE SPIDER WOMAN

Author: Manuel Puig (1932-1990)
Type of work: Novel
Type of plot: Social realism

Time of plot: 1975
First published: El beso de la mujer araña, 1976
(English translation, 1979)

In this novel, set in a small, isolated Argentine prison cell, prisoners Valentin and Molina overcome their boredom with the help of Molina's imaginative retelling of films he has seen. These films, in contrast with the prison cell, are exciting and offer hope for the future if the prisoners are ever released.

*Argentina.** South American country in which the prison cell holding Valentin and Molina is located. Argentina is a poor country swarming with crime and revolutionaries (like Valentin) who are trying to make the country a better place for all. Near the end of the novel, Molina and Valentin feel safer in the prison than in the outside world.

Tropical island. Valentin dreams of this unnamed island at the end of the novel. The island is an amalgam of the various film scenes that Molina has described. A woman appears to him in this dream, weaving webs out of her own body. This woman represents Molina and his storytelling abilities. His attraction toward this figure is emblematic of Molina and Valentin's romantic feelings toward each other.

*France.** Two films that Molina recalls take place in France. The first film, the apparently fictional *Her Real Glory,* is set in Paris in 1942. In the romantic setting of Paris, the two lovers of the film parallel Molina and Valentin. They too are opposites fighting against a common enemy—the Argentine prison system. Even though it is wartime, the scenes Molina describes are romanticized. The cabaret where Leni works, the German officer's apartment, the final scene of the film in the German Pantheon—all are larger than life. The other film, about a race car driver, is more brutal, and Molina tells it because it reflects Valentin's feelings for antigovernment forces.

*New York City.** The city that Molina describes in this film is taken from the original version of the horror film *Cat People,* which was made in 1942. While Molina does not describe the cityscape at all, the details he offers about other aspects of the city make it come alive for Valentin and the reader. New York City is worlds away from the small prison cell Molina and Valentin occupy both physically and culturally; Irene, a character in the film, is free to go to the zoo, the doctor, or anywhere else she pleases; Molina and Valentin are not. If Argentina is a damp prison with little hope, then New York City is the exact opposite: various, sensual, and alive.

Caribbean island. Another film that Molina recollects, this time about zombies, takes place on a Caribbean island. The atmosphere of the island reflects the setting of the prison in its isolation.

*Mexico.** Another film that Molina recounts is set on the coast of Mexico. Even though the film is described in romantic terms, the heroine feels like a prisoner, reflecting the fact that a person can feel like a prisoner wherever he or she is. The heroine, who wears a costume, reflects Molina; like the woman hiding behind the mask, Molina, being homosexual, appears to the world as a male while he feels like a woman.

— *Kelly Rothenberg*

THE KNIGHT OF THE BURNING PESTLE

Author: Francis Beaumont (c. 1584-1616)
Type of work: Drama
Type of plot: Comedy

Time of plot: Early seventeenth century
First performed: 1607; first published, 1613

This play is set on the stage of a London theater during a performance of a play-within-a-play called The London Merchant. *A unique arrangement of simultaneous setting takes place as the characters of Nell and George observe the actors perform the play and as the "real" audience observes Nell and George.*

Stage. Only three lines into the Prologue of *The London Merchant*, a grocer, his wife, and his apprentice climb out of the audience onto the stage, interrupting the performance and transforming the stage from a simple setting for a specific play to what was known in the middle-ages as the "platea"—literally "the place." The stage becomes everyplace and anyplace as the apprentice Rafe extemporaneously takes on the leading role (playing his master) in the play, which George retitles *The Knight of the Burning Pestle.*

The stage becomes a liminal space where the play and the play-within-the-play are staged simultaneously. Inspired by tales of knights-errant rescuing damsels in distress, Rafe sets out on a great adventure, traveling to Moldavia. Throughout his travels mention is made that the location changes from scene to scene but as the players are forced to improvise to accommodate Rafe's character the stage becomes increasingly a site of the here and now as all attention is drawn to the reactions of George and Nell. All the while the "real" audience of Beaumont's play is aware that George and Nell are actors performing roles and understand that while the play invites the audience to see the stage as a real location in time and space, this too is an illusion; the relationship turns back on itself as the audience understands that all they observe is artifice.

— *Rhona Justice-Malloy*

THE KNIGHTS

Author: Aristophanes (c. 450-c. 385 B.C.E.)
Type of work: Drama
Type of plot: Satire

Time of plot: Fifth century B.C.E.
First performed: *Hippēs*, 424 B.C.E. (English translation, 1812)

Aristophanes' scathing attack on the Athenian demagogue Cleon, which he set in contemporary Athens in this play, is proof of the freedom of speech that Athenian playwrights enjoyed in his time. Athens and its allies were then fighting against Sparta in the early stages of the Peloponnesian War. Cleon had risen to public notice by claiming full credit for the Athenian victory at Sphacteria, which credit should have been shared with Demosthenes.

*Athens. Ancient Greek city-state, in which the action of the play is set in an open, public place—probably the agora, which was the heart of the political community. Though pseudonyms thinly veil the characters, the allegory of a gullible, shallow, and misled citizenry of Athens (personified as "Demos") finally rejecting the aid and counsel of the scoundrel slave Cleon (also called "Paphlagonian") directly reflected the politics of post-Periklean wartime Athens. The politicians Nicias, Cleon, and Demosthenes appear as slaves of Demos despite their powerful positions. Given the nature of the Athenian democracy, the leaders were essentially the slaves of public opinion, which Aristophanes pillo-ries for being swayed by Cleon's deceit and blandishments. The boorish, uneducated, and equally unscrupulous sausage-seller Agoracritus, rather than the men of education and character—Nicias and Demosthenes—successfully counters the rascally slave: Only a rogue and stupid fellow can successfully lead the Athenians.

*Areopagus. Athens's senate house. Paphlagonian is bested by the sausage-seller in the trial before this determinative body of the Athenian state, which is held off-stage. Only following this vindication is Demos directly confronted by the sausage-seller and the slaves.

— *Joseph P. Byrne*

KRAPP'S LAST TAPE

Author: Samuel Beckett (1906-1989)
Type of work: Drama
Type of plot: Absurdist

Time of plot: 1950's
First performed: 1958; first published, 1958

This play creates a haunting portrait of an aging writer who confronts an aspect of his past that he cannot over-come. Set entirely in the writer Krapp's sparsely furnished and dimly lit den, it conveys a sense of complete isolation. A tape recorder with a microphone on a small writing desk at center stage becomes almost a second character, as Krapp listens to a tape he recorded thirty years earlier, on his thirty-ninth birthday.

Krapp's den. The writer's den suggests the spiritual darkness and utter loneliness in which Krapp lives. The play opens with a series of seemingly unconnected and eccentric actions, as Krapp eats bananas, fingers an old envelope, and retires to a room offstage for a drink. As he listens to one of his tapes, in which a much younger version of himself describes his usual birthday routine, the audience discovers that Krapp is now repeating this ritual on his sixty-ninth birthday.

As the younger Krapp explains on the tape, he is searching for the "grain" of his life, which he defines as "those things worth having when all the dust . . . when all *my* dust has settled." Now, thirty years later, the aging and alcoholic Krapp does the same. However, he can only return to a prior tape, on which he recorded what his ledger describes as a "Farewell to love." The voice on the tape goes on to state with youthful conviction that he would not want the years back, when he was capable of happiness. "Not with the fire in me now." As the elder Krapp sits in the same room thirty years later, with the fire all but extinguished, he has only the darkness surrounding him. The room embodies the dismal reality of that future which compelled him to bid farewell to love.

— *Philip Bader*

THE KREUTZER SONATA

Author: Leo Tolstoy (1828-1910)
Type of work: Novel
Type of plot: Social realism

Time of plot: Late nineteenth century
First published: Kreytserova sonata, 1889 (English translation, 1890)

High society of nineteenth century Russia provides the social and geographical setting for Leo Tolstoy's novel. It shows the problem through one, typical, marriage, while employing one of Tolstoy's favorite metaphors, a train.

*Russia. Tolstoy's native land is the setting for all his fiction, which typically focuses on family problems. In his view, the human mind is the place where everything starts: love and hate, marriage and murder, and the family is a micro-unit of society, showing health or sickness of the whole body. This novel is Tolstoy's "peep show"— attempt to analyze causes of failed marriages. The conflict between human physical needs (sex) and spiritual (moral) needs, created by the strict Christian upbringing in patriarchal Russia is further complicated by the inequality and bigotry in raising male and female children, therefore not preparing them for a successful marriage and family life together. The natural differences in male and female needs and roles are further complicated by the clash between new, modern ideas (of women's liberation, among others) and the old societal mores, resulting in unhappy individuals and couples, psychological problems, neuroses, domestic violence, and murder.

Train. Tolstoy uses a train speeding across Russia metaphorically and symbolically to reflect his view of the Russian high society headed toward a fast moral and social disintegration brought by civilization from the West. Construction of the huge trans-Siberian railroad, a costly project, greatly diminished arable land and impoverished many landowners and peasants. For these reasons, Tolstoy treats trains as symbols of "unnatural" and destructive forces.

As Tolstoy's protagonist, Pozdnyshev, travels on the train, he expresses Tolstoy's ideas in great length and detail. Through the choice of passengers and their participation in the conversation, Tolstoy displays opinions of different segments of society: educated versus uneducated, modern versus traditional, male versus female. Tolstoy believes that peasants and women are closer to nature and land, by their role, therefore crucial for the health and well-being of the society. During the train ride, Pozdnyshev tells his life story: his "libertine" youth and premature sexual corruption, marriage based on the romantic love (lust), quickly turning into emptiness and boredom, ultimately escalating into obsessive hate and jealousy.

Polluted with debauchery and plagued by shame and guilt, Pozdnyshev's mind develops a mental aberration fabricating ugly and hateful illusions leading to murder without a rational justification. The furious speed and urgency of the train powerfully (though subliminally) creates the atmosphere of a sexual, obsessive frenzy. The compartmental confinement, like a sick cell of a brain, obsessively focuses on the final, destructive end—murder.

Pozdnyshev's mental state is similar to Anna Karenina's. Tolstoy's earlier novel *Anna Karenina* (1875-1877) uses train symbols six times to foreshadow violence and tragedy. Although Tolstoy's favorite metaphor powerfully serves his artistic purpose, the composition of *The Kreutzer Sonata* (unlike *Anna Karenina*) is simplified and impoverished by the plot being told during the ride instead of shown in direct, life-simulating action. Tolstoy's rich and character-revealing dialogues here are replaced by a didactic and less engaging monologue expressing the ideas that Tolstoy strongly represented.

— *Mira N. Mataric*

KRISTIN LAVRANSDATTER

Author: Sigrid Undset (1882-1949)
Type of work: Novel
Type of plot: Religious
Time of plot: Early fourteenth century

First published: 1920-1922 (English translation, 1923-1927): *Kransen*, 1920 (*The Bridal Wreath*, 1923); *Husfrue*, 1921 (*The Mistress of Husaby*, 1925); *Korset*, 1922 (*The Cross*, 1927)

In this novel the Christianity of medieval Norway infuses the manors, churches, and convents that are the settings of the love between Kristin Lavransdatter and Erlend Nikulaussön and its consequences. For Sigrid Undset, the lives and locales of her characters belong not only in a panoramic natural world but also to a mysterious and wonderful spiritual world.

Jörundgaard (jor-ewnt-GAYRD). Manor and farm inherited by Kristin Lavransdatter's mother. The farm is located in Sel, a central Norwegian region northwest of Lillehammer, where Undset herself spent much of her life and where she died. Although Kristin was born at her father's manor at Skog near Oslo, she spends her early life and a significant part of her adult life at Jörundgaard. Jörundgaard and its master, Kristin's father Lavrans Björgulfsön, who is deeply rooted in his lands, family, and the Roman Catholic religion, represent the patriarchal religious life against which Kristin rebels and to which she eventually returns.

Surrounding Jörundgaard are hills, dales, forests, and streams that Kristin enjoys exploring. Catholicism is so intimately connected with Jörundgaard that visiting a church is like traveling into the mountains. The church is also where Kristin's arranged marriage to a neighbor's son is to take place because Lavrans wants to join his and his neighbor's estates. Troubled in heart, Kristin asks her father to let her go to a nunnery, where their shared hope is that she will regain her peace of mind.

*Oslo. Large port city on the southeastern coast of Norway where Kristin meets the love of her life, Erlend Nikolaussön at a fair. Instead of isolating Kristin from her troubles, the nearby convent of Nonneseter compounds them. The piety of convent life is no match for the passion promised by this knight of the north. Oslo becomes the scene of their sins and deceptions, though Kristin is eventually able to overcome the objections of her family to marry Erlend at Jörundgaard.

Husaby (hew-sah-BEE). Erlend's estate, comprising thirty farms and homesteads, located about twenty miles southwest of Nidaros. Perched on a hillside between two valleys, its many buildings are situated above a lake. Though larger than Lavrans's estate, Husaby has rocky soil and is not as fertile as the flatlands around Jörundgaard. For Kristin, Husaby's deteriorated state contrasts unfavorably with the order and productivity of her father's farm. However, through her dedication and hard work, she helps to cure Husaby's ills and turns it into a prosperous inheritance for her seven sons. Plagued by guilt over her sins with Erlend, she also tries to restore her soul to health.

*Nidaros (NEED-ah-rohs). Now known as Trondheim, the historic capital of Norway on the country's central coast. Located within the archbishopric of Nidaros,

Nidaros contains a cathedral known as the Wonder of the North and the shrine of Norway's patron saint, Olav. As a child, Kristin sees pilgrims passing through Jörundgaard on their way to Nidaros. Later, like them, she is awestruck by the cathedral and experiences true contrition at the shrine of St. Olav.

Later, with the death of her father and husband, Kristin no longer feels part of the young generations at Jörundgaard and decides to enter a convent at Nidaros. During her journey to Nidaros over the Dovre Mountains, she reviews her life and sees it in the light of God's grace. She enters the convent at Rein, where she hopes to become a nun. When the Black Death arrives in Nidaros, the city and the convent become scenes of great suffering, but for Kristin these disease-ridden places become the means of her redemption. With a self-abnegation that was lacking in her early life, she cares for the sick and dying, and when the plague makes her, too, its victim, she realizes that her moves from place to place were not meaningless fragments or a disorganized story but the unified parts of God's plan for her salvation.

Haugen (HOW-gen). Small farm in the Dovre Mountains to which Erlend retires after losing his Husaby estate because of his involvement in a political plot. Uncomfortable with his subsequent role as the lord of Jörundgaard, Erlend abandons his family and goes to his Haugen farm. Though Kristin visits him and pleads for him to return, he insists on remaining on his "little croft" where he can be free. However, he does return to Jörundgaard to defend his wife's honor.

— *Robert J. Paradowski*

L

LADY CHATTERLEY'S LOVER

Author: D. H. Lawrence (1885-1930)
Type of work: Novel
Type of plot: Psychological realism

Time of plot: 1910-1920
First published: 1928

Combining unabashed eroticism and deft social commentary, D. H. Lawrence's novel explores the enigmatic and often adversarial relationship between the physical and intellectual selves. The bulk of the novel's action takes place in Tevershall, a dreary turn-of-the-century mining town in central England which Lawrence uses to symbolize the decay of the human spirit brought about by the rapid industrialization of the Victorian era. The continental European cities of Dresden and Venice—both centers of sophistication and culture—also host some of the novel's significant actions, serving in vibrant counterpoint to the lifelessness and emotional bankruptcy of England's industrialized interior.

***Dresden.** German city known for centuries as one of Europe's most beautiful and culturally refined cities. It serves as the place in which the novel's protagonist Constance Chatterley gets her first taste of the delights of social interaction and sexual awareness. Constance's father sends her there to summer at age fifteen, and it is in Dresden that Constance acquires a taste for art and politics, as well as the view that her burgeoning sexuality is an essential facet of her identity. In Dresden's shaded parks and secluded alcoves she has a number of brief but passionate sexual encounters and returns to England a mature young woman in full command of her sensuality.

Tevershall. Fictional village in the center of England's coal-producing region where most of the novel is set. Like many of the early twentieth century English coal towns on which it is modeled, Tevershall stands in ironic contrast to the traditionally idyllic, pastoral depiction of the English countryside offered in most nineteenth century Romantic literature. Lawrence describes the village as "trailed in utter hopeless ugliness . . .

and willful, blank dreariness." After Constance marries landed aristocrat Sir Clifford Chatterley, whose emotional and sexual indifference to her fuels the novel's central conflict, Tevershall serves as a fitting backdrop for the emotional impoverishment she suffers while living there. She regards the "soulless ugliness" of Tevershall as "unbelievable and not to be thought about" although she is never completely able to remove it from her mind.

Wragby Hall. Sprawling but undistinguished manor house in England's Midlands district into which Constance moves after marrying Chatterley. Lawrence describes the dwelling as "a long low old house in brown stone, begun about the middle of the eighteenth century, and added on to, till it was a warren of a place without much distinction." Wragby's warrenlike drabness reflects the desolation Constance feels while living there, trapped in a loveless marriage to an aloof, passionless aristocrat. Although Wragby stands in a stately wood overlooking the Tevershall colliery, the house has ironically fallen into the same state of neglect and obsolescence as the coal pits below it.

Gamekeeper's cottage. Spartan one-person dwelling nestled on the far side of the Wragby estate in a stand of thick woods in which the estate's caretaker ("gamekeeper"), Oliver Mellors, lives. The cottage is the site of numerous sexual encounters between Constance and Oliver, an itinerant former soldier. (Largely because of the sexually explicit scenes set in the cottage, the novel was banned from publication in the United States in its unexpurgated form until 1959.) Lawrence describes the cottage and its environs in beautifully lyrical terms—a stark contrast to the unflattering portrait he paints of Wragby Hall. Images of sunlight, birth, and hopefulness pervade his depiction of the cottage, reflecting how Constance views the passionate sexual reawakening she experiences under its roof with the reclusive but sensitive Mellors.

*Venice. Italian city to which Constance escapes toward the end of the novel after she discovers that Mellors has made her pregnant. As a ruse to convince her husband that she has been impregnated by an exotic stranger, and not by one of his own hirelings, Constance arranges a vacation in Venice with her sister citing health problems brought on by Wragby's dampness.

Venice is famed for its endless canals and romantic hideaways, but in adulthood Constance does not find the refuge in them she might have in her adolescence. Surrounded by the city's breathtaking architecture and art, but estranged from both her husband and her lover, she finds the city merely "pleasant in a way," its diversions *almost* enjoyment" but nowhere near the sublime ecstasy she previously experienced with Mellors in the bucolic gamekeeper's cottage.

— *Gregory D. Horn*

THE LADY FROM THE SEA

Author: Henrik Ibsen (1828-1906)
Type of work: Drama
Type of plot: Psychological realism

Time of plot: Nineteenth century
First published: Fruen fra havet, 1888 (English translation, 1890); first performed, 1889

The fjords of Norway, Henrik Ibsen's homeland, are an essential component of this play, as is the wider sea to which they lead. The major character, Ellida, feels stifled by her life in a settled bourgeois village hemmed in by the fjords and is only happy when she is bathing in the sea.

Wangel's house. Home of the prominent Dr. Wangel. Stage directions introduce the house, which is situated in a sleepy Norwegian town that has been kept from the wilder sea by protective fjords. Almost all the action of the play takes place not in the house proper but in the various corners of the garden, from which one can see a road with trees on either side along the water's edge. Between the trees can be seen the fjord and the high mountain peaks in the distance. The fact that the open sea can never be directly seen strongly affects Wangel's wife Ellida, who cannot adjust to the domestic world represented by her husband's garden.

*Fjords (fee-yohrds). Long, narrow inlets of the sea along Norway's coast that can be seen from Dr. Wangel's house. The stage directions constantly reinforce the fact that while the open sea itself cannot be seen, its proximity is indicated by the fjords. Ellida is only well and happy when she is bathing in the fjords' waters, although she complains that they are brackish and tepid. Instead, she yearns for the greater sea, the reality of which is indicated by a shadowy figure known as Friman, who materializes in Wangel's garden to tempt her to a new and dangerous life at sea, beyond the secure Norwegian villages and fjords.

— *Margaret Boe Birns*

LADY WINDERMERE'S FAN

Author: Oscar Wilde (1854-1900)
Type of work: Drama
Type of plot: Comedy of manners

Time of plot: Nineteenth century
First performed: 1892; first published, 1893

This, Oscar Wilde's third play, reveals the hypocrisies of Great Britain's upper classes in witty, and much quoted, dialogue. Misunderstandings between a husband and wife over the husband's relationship with another woman and the question of whether the wife should run off with a lover, are acted out in the precisely decorous London homes of the rich and powerful.

Windermere house. Home of Lord and Lady Windermere in the real and fashionable Carlton House Terrace adjacent to St. James's Park in central London that serves as the setting for three of the play's four acts. The play opens and closes in the morning room, one of the grand rooms used for entertaining by the Windermeres, who are important members of British society. As with all the aristocracy of the time, they have servants; only one butler, one maid, and a nonspeaking footman appear in the play, but at least another six or eight servants might be expected. The morning room should be large and immaculately decorated, containing more furniture than the few items specified for plot purposes. Among the pieces of furniture specified in the play's stage directions are a bureau, in which Lady Windermere finds a bank book of her husband's that contains apparently incriminating evidence; a table used by Lady Windermere to arrange flowers; a sofa used for seating; and a small table on which tea is served. French windows open onto a terrace, to which an impressionable daughter is sent to view the sunset so that she will not hear gossip about Mrs. Erlynne.

The house's drawing room is equally grand, adjacent to the ballroom, where during the play's second act a ball is held and a band is playing. A door leads onto the terrace. Because of crowds of guests, no furniture is specified, though some chairs and sofas around the walls might be expected. Wilde mentions only flowers and potted palms, which are typical of late Victorian era decor.

Lord Darlington's rooms. Home of the bachelor Lord Darlington, who has long loved Lady Windermere and tried to persuade her to leave her husband. In keeping with his station, Darlington's apartment should be a suite of rooms forming all or part of a floor of a large terraced house. Act 3 of the play is set in his sitting and entertaining room. Wilde's stage directions mention a sofa—where the fan of the title is accidently left—and three tables set with writing materials, alcohol, and cigars—all items typical for a man of his status.

— *Chris Morgan*

THE LADY'S NOT FOR BURNING

Author: Christopher Fry (1907-   )
Type of work: Drama
Type of plot: Comedy

Time of plot: c. 1400
First performed: 1948; first published, 1949

Almost as detailed in its social character as a place in a Shakespearean play, the setting in this play has palpable suggestions of English pastoralism and small-town attitudes toward life. The period and locale of this romantic comedy about a bitterly disillusioned ex-soldier and a woman falsely accused of witchcraft serve as context for their yearnings and frustrations and help demonstrate why the characters run afoul of their world.

Cool Clary. Fifteenth century English market village in which the entire play is set. The play's richly poetic and often abstract language is rife with details about the tenor and texture of daily social life. Cool Clary is a town whose business is administered by a council and in which every adult has a clear-cut duty—from Mayor Tyson and the chaplain to Justice Tappercoom, the rag-and-bone merchant Skipps, and Richard, the clerk. It is a structured town with strong communal feeling in which everyone seems to know everybody else's business, but it is also a place easily disturbed from its bland workaday life by nonconformists such as Thomas Mendip and Jennet Jourdemayne.

Fry's language and imagery amplify the English pastoralism. Cool Clary has fields, gardens, birds, rosebuds, and wheelbarrows in ample supply. But even as the hot sun shines on blackbirds, daffodils, and ponds, there is a rigid orthodoxy at the heart of the town's life, for Cool Clary is medievally Christian. Its families may form quiet circles of prayer, but there is rank insecurity and fear about the possibility of sin, and Christian superstition leads to fear—as is demonstrated by the community's generally hysterical and comically confused reaction to the appearance of Mendip the discharged soldier and Jennet Jourdemayne, an alleged witch.

— *Keith Garebian*

LANCELOT: Or, The Knight of the Cart

Author: Chrétien de Troyes (c. 1150-c. 1190)
Type of work: Poetry
Type of plot: Romance

Time of plot: Sixth century
First transcribed: Lancelot: Ou, Le Chevalier à la charrette, c. 1168 (English translation, 1913)

Perhaps the most widely read portion of this French version of the Arthurian stories, produced by Chrétien de Troyes, this work is a quest story in which the title character and King Arthur's chief knight must prove himself after failing to satisfy the demands of the code of chivalry.

*France. The opening passages of this romance are set in France, allowing the writer to give credit to Marie of Champagne, who was his patroness and his encouragement in this effort. It also serves to lay the foundation for the introduction of the concept of courtly love into the Arthurian legends.

Camelot. The romance's action opens at Arthur's court in Camelot near **Caerleon**, placing the knights in the proper setting before they go on their quest to accompany and rescue the queen. The major portion of the romance takes place on the road and in the wilderness, demonstrating that the knights' path would most often lead into the world of the unknown. Perhaps the most prominent symbol associated with the setting is that of the bridge.

Bridges. In order to realize his quest, the knight must cross the right bridge; often he is confronted by bridges that might take him in the wrong direction or even to his death. The completion of the quest demonstrates that the knight has taken the correct path and met the dictates of the code of chivalry, which are his guiding principles.

— *Tom Frazier*

THE LAST CHRONICLE OF BARSET

Author: Anthony Trollope (1815-1882)
Type of work: Novel
Type of plot: Domestic realism

Time of plot: Mid-nineteenth century
First published: 1867

This novel is the last of six by Anthony Trollope set in the fictitious English county of Barsetshire, exploring an ecclesiastical community based upon Anglican church life in and around Salisbury in the mid-nineteenth century.

Barchester. Episcopal seat of the Church of England's diocese of Barset, the site of the bishop's palace as well as all the ecclesiastical politics, which involves the Reverend Josiah Crawley's trials after being accused of stealing a bank draft. Bishop Proudie and his wife are the chief powers of the town. In fact, Mrs. Proudie leads the bishop by the nose and is actively working against the honest but obtuse Crawley. Barchester is also the site of the dean and chapter, who also wield influence in matters spiritual and temporal.

Hogglestock. Small bleak parish of which the Reverend Josiah Crawley is the perpetual curate. While no one in his right mind could aspire to live in this god-forsaken hamlet, Crawley serves his poor parishioners well. Nevertheless, Mrs. Proudie conspires to oust him for malfeasance and insert her obsequious dependant, the Reverend Caleb Thumble, in his place.

Silverbridge. Town on the railway line in Barset where Crawley is taken to face legal charges after he is accused of stealing a bank check. His daughter Grace, the romantic heroine of a subplot of the novel, teaches at the Misses Prettyman's School in Silverbridge but resigns her post in shame because of her father's accusation.

***London.** Great Britain's capital city is the site of the office of the barrister Thomas Toogood, a member of a respected law firm and cousin to the Reverend Crawley's wife. Toogood defends Crawley and solves the mystery of the missing check. His urban offices provide a contrast to the rural milieu of Barset.

Allington. Small Barset village that is the home of Squire Dale and his daughter Lily, who persuade Grace Crawley to live with them after she resigns her teaching post in Silverbridge. Archdeacon Grantly's son, Major Henry Grantly, courts Grace at Allington and eventually persuades her to marry him after her father's name has been cleared.

Bishop's palace. Site of many ecclesiastic and domestic struggles between Bishop Proudie and his lady wife, Mrs. Proudie. Other ecclesiastical disputes take place there as well. Mrs. Proudie's dominion at the palace is virtually complete until she is told to be silent by Crawley—which spurs Bishop Proudie finally to rouse himself and begin to assert his prerogatives. Mrs. Proudie repairs to her room in the palace and expires suddenly of a fit of pique at her waning influence over her husband. Thus dies one of Trollope's greatest comic inventions, the odious Mrs. Proudie.

Dragon of Wantly. Pub owned by Mrs. Eleanor Harding Bold Arabin, wife of the Reverend Francis Arabin. The Dragon of Wantly is the site of the theft of the check the Reverend Crawley is accused of stealing. A dishonest employee of the pub steals the check and puts in motion the central mystery, which drives the plot of *The Last Chronicle of Barset*.

— *Isabel Bonnyman Stanley*

THE LAST DAYS OF POMPEII

Author: Edward Bulwer-Lytton (1803-1873)
Type of work: Novel
Type of plot: Historical

Time of plot: 79 C.E.
First published: 1834

This novel was inspired by the architecture, lifestyles, and customs revealed by nineteenth century excavations of the Roman city of Pompeii, which was buried under volcanic ash when nearby Mount Vesuvius erupted nearly eighteen centuries earlier. Through detailed descriptions of reconstructed houses, temples, baths, and streets, the novel reconstructs Pompeii's culture and frames its plot in the cityscape up to the moment of its sudden destruction.

Pompeii. Ancient southern Italian city populated by Greeks and Italians until it was occupied by Rome during the wars that united Italy under Roman rule. In the first century B.C.E., the Roman general Sulla established a colony for his veterans on land near Pompeii that he and his army had taken from his enemies during the last days of the Roman Republic. The long-term effect of the Roman conquest of the Italian peninsula was the progressive decline of local cultures as Roman customs and culture became dominant. Although remnants of Greek and other cultures are seen in the characters of this novel, the romanization of Pompeii and the peninsula was virtually complete by the first century C.E., the period in which the novel is set.

Before Pompeii's destruction in the volcanic eruption of 79 C.E., the city was a jewel of the Roman world, featuring luxurious houses and seaside villas that were the fashionable dwellings and summer resorts of wealthy Romans. The houses, baths, streets, and temples described by Edward Bulwer-Lytton and peopled by his characters are those that had been excavated and restored when he wrote the book. For example, Glaucus's house, the House of the Tragic Poet, is a small gem of a house that is built in the typical Roman style but adorned by artworks that reveal his Greek heritage.

The Greek temple pictured with the Triangular Forum may have been the temple in which Glaucus, a wealthy Athenian, worshiped the gods of his ancestors. Glaucus meets his friends Lepidus and Sallust in the street near the Temple of Fortune, considered one of the most graceful examples of Roman architecture. The street's raised footpath allows passersby to view the interior artwork and frescoes through the open doors of the painted houses along the street. It is in the portico of the Temple of Fortune that Glaucus and his beloved Ione take refuge from the raining ash after Vesuvius begins to erupt.

Vesuvius. Volcano on the east shore of Italy's Bay of Naples whose eruption in 79 C.E. provides the novel's climax. Even before its eruption, the volcano's dark presence is suggested throughout the novel by a strange dark cloud that hovers over it and becomes more ominous with each mention. The growing cloud appears to be a prophetic omen of both the disaster to come and the dark deeds being plotted against the wealthy Greek Glaucus, his Neapolitan lover Ione, her brother Apaecides, and the blind flower girl of Thessalian origins. The primary evildoer is the Egyptian priest Arbaces, who performs evil rites and manipulations against them in the Temple of Isis. Adding to the evil foreboding is the wicked witch in her cavern on the deadly mountain, who curses Glaucus for attacking the snake that is her familiar creature.

Bulwer-Lytton's settings for his plot provide a cross section of the restored city and its romanized culture. Glaucus entertains his friends at an intimate dinner party at his house. A fashionable house party allows the guests of a wealthy Roman to meet and judge the gladiators and place their wagers before the scheduled games. Readers glimpse the private dressing room of a Pompeian beauty who wants the attention of Glaucus.

In the gates, marketplace, baths and forum of Pompeii, Bulwer-Lytton moves his plot along through encounters that presage doom for the lovers and doom for the city. The blind flower girl serves to personify the eternal darkness of the city soon to be buried by the mountain's rain of volcanic ash. Thus, in street scenes and descriptions of revelers in the amphitheater, forum, and marketplace, alongside mourners at Apaecides' funeral, the novelist weaves a tapestry of the doomed city's cultural life and religious practices.

— *Marguerite R. Plummer*

THE LAST OF THE MOHICANS: A Narrative of 1757

Author: James Fenimore Cooper (1789-1851)
Type of work: Novel
Type of plot: Adventure

Time of plot: 1757
First published: 1826

This novel is set in the upper regions of the Hudson River in mid-central New York State at a time when the region was still a British colony and many Native American peoples lived in the region. The dominant tribe when the Europeans arrived, and consequently the first to be dispossessed of their land and to disappear from history, was the Mohicans.

*Fort William Henry. Defensive fortification built by the British in the fall of 1756, in the midst of the French and Indian Wars. The fort was a strategic part of the British attempt to penetrate French territory. The fort was at the southern end of Lake George just west of the Hudson River and was on the important Hudson River-Lake Champlain waterway. The fort survived the first French and Native American attack against it in March, 1757. James Fenimore Cooper uses the war to create a realistic setting for his narrative. The setting for this adventure is during the summer months following, and it is focused on one battle of a long war. Throughout the book the author contrasts the wilderness atmosphere with the more civilized areas along the Atlantic coast. Cooper himself was raised in a village on the edge of the wilderness near Cooperstown, New York.

Fort William Henry no longer exists, but the area today is strikingly similar to its appearance in the time of Cooper's story. A small village stands where the fort had stood. There is a watering place near the spring from which the fictional Hawkeye drank, and present-day roads follow the paths blazed by Hawkeye and his friends. The wilderness described by Cooper is still mostly wilderness today, but only a few Native Americans still reside in the area.

*Fort Oswego. British fortification at the western end of Lake Ontario that was originally a trading post built by the British and Dutch in 1722. Fortified by the British in 1727, it was one of five small forts in the area. By 1757 it was used to supplement Fort William Henry, and was used by Cooper to enhance the story.

*Lake George. Called Horican by the Native Americans as reported by Cooper, the word is roughly translated "The Tail of the Lake" in reference to its connection to Lake Champlain. The British named it for King George II. It was part of an internal highway connecting the Hudson River to the St. Lawrence River, and was near a warpath used by Native Americans. A narrow lake, one to three miles wide and thirty-two miles long, Lake George was claimed by the French when Samuel de Champlain explored the area in 1609. When the British built Fort William Henry on the southern edge, the area became a strategic part of the French-British conflicts and the center of the fictional activities of Hawkeye.

*Lake Champlain. Much larger than Lake George, Lake Champlain is up to 14 miles wide and 107 miles long. In 1755 the French built Fort Ticonderoga between the two lakes to help secure the area. In 1759, after the events of this adventure, the fort was captured by the British. Lake Champlain and the fort were always on the periphery of Cooper's story.

— *Glenn L. Swygart*

THE LAST OF THE WINE

Author: Mary Renault (Mary Challans, 1905-1983)
Type of work: Novel
Type of plot: Historical

Time of plot: 430-402 B.C.E.
First published: 1956

This modern novel is primarily set in ancient Athens at a time when Greece was made up of a number of city-states, each with its own government and often at war with one another. During the struggles to preserve Athens's democracy outlined in the novel, the principal characters also visit other city-states. All of the major settings used in the novel were real places in the fifth century B.C.E.

*Athens. Ancient Greek city-state that is the capital of Attica at the time in which the novel is set. Standing on the southwestern coast of the Attican Peninsula, Athens is a walled city, in the center of which is a flat-topped hill known as the High City, or Acropolis, on which most of the city's temples are built. The most famous of these temples now is the Parthenon; it figures into the novel but is known only as the Temple of Athena.

Steps lead up to the High City, from where can be seen the harbor at Piraeus. Dominating the High City is the statue of Athena of the Vanguard with her triple-crested crown and huge spear. The statue of Athena in her temple is gilded, and sunlight seeping through the thin ivory tiles of the roof made her features gleam. The Anakeion is the precinct of a temple to Castor and Pollux at the foot of the High City and is the mustering place for the army, whose cavalry horses are assembled here.

Another high rocky outcrop within Athens's walls is the Pnyx, to the west of the High City. On its top is the Assembly where citizens meet to discuss the governance of the city. Orators address the people from the public rostrum there. There is a theater lying against the south flank of the High City where plays are performed.

Outside Athens's Dipylon Gate is the Academy, whose gardens are frequented by philosophers such as Sokrates. A sacred olive and the statue of the hero Akademos is found here. The palaestras, or gymnasia, are places youths are trained in athletic skills, including dance. The Sacred Way, near which is Lysis's house, runs to Eleusis and is the road along which the dead are carried to the cemeteries.

The Agora is the main public market place, along whose western side runs the colonnaded Stoa of Zeus, where Sokrates and his students often retire to talk. Outside the city walls are the farms that supply the markets. Further away the land is mountainous and cut with steep gorges.

Alexias's house. Athens family home of the protagonist, the young Athenian Alexias. The house stands in the Inner Kerameikos, near the Dipylon Gate, on the northern wall of the city. The house has a colonnaded courtyard, a fig tree, and a vine. There are stables behind it. The house's gabled roof has a border of acanthus tiles, and a herm, or small guardian statue, stands at the gate. The family also owns a farm in the foothills beyond Acharnai. The slope above the valley is terraced for vines, but the principal crop is olives. Barley is also grown in the olive fields and there is a well on the hillside.

Lysis's house. Home of Alexias's lover and mentor, Lysis. Located near Athens's Sacred Way, the large house has many marble and bronze fixtures but is now becoming shabby. Its dining room has an inlay of the goddess Athena fighting a Mede. The house also has a pleasure garden beyond which are the fields of flower sellers. The harness room has old yokes for chariots, leftovers from the days when Lysis's father raced.

*Piraeus (pi-REE-us). The port serving Athens. The road between Piraeus and Athens is protected by long walls that enable citizens to move freely between the two cities. These walls are lined with huts all the way to the harbor. Rich foreigners build houses here, and the air smells of spices hemp and pitch until trade ceases because of a Spartan siege. At Piraeus's slave market, Phaedo is taken to be sold. On the hill above Piraeus is Munychia fort, where young men are sent for garrison duty during peace time.

*Corinth. City overlooking the isthmus between the two major parts of Greece. Its port is Isthmia, where the Isthmian Games are held under truce. The Corinthian citadel is on a round-topped mountain, on the summit of which is the Temple of Aphrodite. The games are held in the precincts of the Temple of Poseidon, which is surrounded by gymnasiums and palaestras, a stadium, and a hippodrome. The dressing places and baths in Corinth are finer than their counterparts in Athens, with marble everywhere and bronze waterspouts. Corinthian shopkeepers set up stalls around the temple precinct.

Corinth's Acrocorinth is higher than the Acropolis of Athens. The sacred way winds up between shrines and holy springs. The crown is carpeted with heath and mountain flowers. The image of Aphrodite is armed with a shield and spear. Her temple is small and delicate with a terrace from which the slopes fall gently. From this height, the shipping channel is visible and Alexias and Lysis can see Spartan ships being hauled on rollers across the isthmus from the western to the eastern sea. It is just possible to see the High City of Athens from this point.

*Samos. Island in the east Aegean Sea, close to Ionia (modern Turkey), built on a spur jutting into the sea. On its western strand is the Temple of Hera. Its eastern hillsides are terraced for growing barley. Samos is used as a base for the Athenian war fleet, and the Athenian camp is built on the shore where the ships are beached, between the town and the temple. Originally tented, it becomes more permanent with huts of wattle and daub, thatched with reed. An ancient city, Samos is expanding during the period in which the novel is set. Painters, sculptors, and masons are busy along the streets, as new marble buildings are built on the city's hillsides.

*Phyle. Stone fortification on the border between Attica and the Theban city-state that overlooks the pass between the territories. The postern, from which the rubbish is thrown, overlooks the gorge known as the Cleft of the Chariot. Between Phyle and Athens is the Acharnian Plain which is crossed by a road. It is used as a gathering place for the army that retakes Athens from the Spartans.

— *Pauline Morgan*

THE LAST PURITAN: A Memoir in the Form of a Novel

Author: George Santayana (1863-1952)
Type of work: Novel
Type of plot: Social realism

Time of plot: Early twentieth century
First published: 1935

In George Santayana's only novel, alienation from place is a consistent theme set against a kaleidoscope of mostly New England locations. The novel is as much psychological as it is geographical, a study of "inner space" in juxtaposition to a variety of "external places."

*New England. Northeastern region of the United States whose first English settlers built on Protestant Puritanism. A product of two worlds, Puritanism famished in the Old World and flourished in New England. Oliver Alden, Santayana's protagonist in this novel, like Santayana himself, is torn between two societies— America, "the greatest of opportunities" and "the worst of influences," and Europe, which is "always dying gently, cheerfully." It is the contrast of productive diligence and delightful decadence. The soul of the author, like that of his lead character, remains divided between two worlds.

*Boston. Capital of Massachusetts and largest city in New England. Boston has been called the "Athens of America"; however, Santayana's Boston in this novel is more like Sparta—a "dark and constricted place." The Aldens' home, located near the State House in Boston, is "forlorn" and "uninhabitable," more a "pretense" than a residence. Proper folk, like the Aldens, frequent King's Chapel, where they learn "morality mingled with reason." As old-line Blue Book Anglo-Saxon, the Aldens avoid the immigrant Irish and Italians, who are "romanizing" their Puritan "Eden."

Santayana's Boston, like that of the Aldens, is "out of step" with the rest of America. The "puritanism" of the Aldens is at odds with the "idealism" of the new century, and their "pessimism" conflicts with the "optimism" of the Progressive Era. Their obsession with the "ancient" contrasts with the compulsion for the "recent" in a New America, with a "New Freedom," "a new woman," and "a New Idea." Their noblesse oblige democracy clashes with the egalitarianism of President Woodrow Wilson's New Democracy.

Great Falls. Fictional Connecticut town that Santayana depicts as a "prison" in which "puritan character" is formed. The psychiatrist Dr. Bumstead's house, like the adjacent mental asylum, is a place of illusions—of class, character, and conduct. The house is refurbished only because of a lucrative marriage (to an Alden of Salem and Boston) and the pretentious house, with its decorative white columns, is restored to its original Revolutionary era style and is filled with Empire (pronounced "ompeer") furniture. Bumstead's house, like the nearby mental hospital, is a place from which to escape. Great Falls is an oppressive community, one sage observes, "no wonder so many people go mad in these old puritan families."

At the town's high school, with its "common boys" and "mediocre teachers," the "proper Bostonian" Oliver Alden teaches the "lower classes." It is a place for the elite to master mixing with "commoners." Its classical curriculum, complete with competitive sports, provides a crucial rite of passage for the Puritan soul.

Old Junk and ***Black Swan.*** Sailing ships that provide respite for the Alden men from the "oppression" of Puritan New England. A "floating heritage," the *Swan* is "a Noah's Ark in the Deluge" of respectability, for it is a place of enlightenment and salvation. Aboard it, one can tell forbidden truths and reveal the "other self." Away from land, one can swim naked, associate freely with the lower classes, and abandon all middle-class pretense.

***Salem.** Massachusetts town, which was the home of some of the Alden ancestors, that is both legacy and license. It is also the site of a Benedictine monastery founded by a cousin who became a Roman Catholic in his rebellion against Puritanism.

***Harvard University.** One of New England's oldest and most prestigious institutions of higher learning, located in Cambridge, Massachusetts, adjacent to Boston. Sometimes called the "Puritan Mecca," Harvard is the apex of any Alden's moral odyssey. Father Peter Alden might learn Arabic in the Empty Quarter or master psychology in Paris, but his real "imprimatur" is a medical degree from Harvard. Like Santayana—who both studied and taught at Harvard—Oliver Alden "serves his time" as an athlete, average scholar, and member of the right secret societies in this institution, which has more to do with socialization than education. To people like the Aldens books are ornaments, like mirrors, and Harvard should be a "paradise of plain living and high thinking." Although Oliver lives in Ralph Waldo Emerson's former room in Divinity Hall, the experience does not lighten his sense of obligation. The Romanticism of the famous Concord sage cannot free Alden's bound Puritan conscience any more than did his exposure to Johann Wolfgang von Goethe through his German governess.

— *C. George Fry*

THE LAST TEMPTATION OF CHRIST

Author: Nikos Kazantzakis (1883-1957)
Type of work: Novel
Type of plot: Psychological realism

Time of plot: First century C.E.
First published: Ho teleutaios peirasmos, 1955
   (English translation, 1960)

Many settings in this novel are familiar names from the New Testament. The primary theme of the novel is simply the humanity of Jesus, whom the novel portrays as a model of man in struggle—not a god with divine powers and knowledge, but a man like others, with the same desires and fears. The novel fills its landscapes and homes with people who have human desires, human motives, and human imperfections, and with the sensual joys of life.

***Magdala.** Home of Mary Magdalene, the prostitute whom Jesus saves from stoning, located about ten miles northeast of Nazareth. Nikos Kazantzakis describes her home in suggestive detail. In the courtyard grow three trees, a pomegranate laden with fruit and two cypresses, one a male with a phallic trunk and the other a female, its branches spread wide. Seen through Jesus' eyes, as he wrestles with temptation, the trees suggest Jesus' all-too-human desire for love, sex, and progeny. Four merchants, each awaiting his turn with Mary Magdalene inside the house, suggest sin and corruption. Inside, Jesus finds Mary naked after her day's "work"—a powerful temptation. However, he also finds a night's peace as he sleeps there alone by the fire. At dawn he rises, and finds Mary, who is feigning sleep in her own bed, an even greater temptation, as he imagines not sex but marriage, a new life in a distant village, where Mary's past is not known. For Kazantzakis's Jesus, home and hearth, the joys of an ordinary life, are the greatest of earthly temptations. In Jesus' delirium on the cross, he returns to Mary Magdalene.

Lazarus's house. Home of Lazarus, located in Bethany, a village between Jerusalem and the northern tip of the Dead Sea. Lazarus shares his home with his beautiful unmarried sisters, Mary and Martha. There, Jesus rests and refreshes himself after his most famous temptation, his forty-day struggle with Satan in the desert. Lazarus's home is of greater danger to Jesus than all the riches and power offered by Satan. The house smells of sweet spices and is filled with the comforts of home and hearth. In his imagination, Jesus shares a long and happy life in this house with Mary and Martha, which ends when Satan reveals that all is a dream, the "last temptation." Jesus instantly rejects Satan and returns to the agony of the cross and his duty to God.

*****Nazareth.** Village in the hills of Galilee about seventy miles from Jerusalem that is both Jesus' birthplace and his hometown. Kazantzakis postulates that the story of Jesus' birth in Bethlehem, the city of kings, was invented by the apostle Matthew in order to support his claim that Jesus was the son of God. Indeed, historical records show that the census that traditional Christians believe drew Joseph and Mary to Bethlehem during her

pregnancy never took place. Kazantzakis seeks the man behind the Gospels, and the villages and countryside that made the man.

*****Temple of Jerusalem.** Center of Judaism in Roman-occupied Judea. Traditionally believed to be built on the foundations of the Temple of Solomon and actually destroyed by the Romans in 70 C.E., the temple was still under construction during Jesus' lifetime. The Gospels give but sparse descriptions of the temple; however, Kazantzakis depicts it as a beehive of activity, reeking from the slaughter of the animal sacrifice that was an essential ritual of Judaism in the time of Jesus. The temple also signifies temptation because of the richness of its furnishings and construction, which suggests the corruption of the religious establishment in Jerusalem.

*****Gethsemane** (geth-SEH-mah-nee). Olive grove on the lower slopes of the Mount of Olives near Jerusalem that is the scene of Jesus' arrest by the Levites, who make up the temple guards. Kazantzakis's version of this "garden" smells of pistachios, and its soil smells of resin and honey, and Jesus marvels at such "perfume." Like the homes of Mary Magdalene and Lazarus, Gethsemane contains the joys of the earth.

— *Craig A. Milliman*

THE LAST TYCOON

Author: F. Scott Fitzgerald (1896-1940)
Type of work: Novel
Type of plot: Social realism

Time of plot: 1930's
First published: 1941

Set in Hollywood during the golden age of the movie studio system of the 1930's, this novel both satirizes and eulogizes that system through the story of a film producer. One of F. Scott Fitzgerald's working titles for this book was The Love of the Last Tycoon: A Western, *for in many ways the novel is a story of the American West, of a stylized world that existed at the very end of the frontier. The producer's life is very much a working life, and this story is very much a novel about work, about an industry that defines the producer's life, just as it defines Southern California in the popular imagination.*

*****Hollywood.** Section of the city of Los Angeles that is traditionally regarded as the center of the American film industry. "Hollywood" is not so much a place as it is an idea, and Fitzgerald's novel is an attempt to under-

stand that idea and give it flesh and form. While the novel provides details of things that characterize Southern California—for example, the primacy of automobiles and the lassitude Stahr notices in those who have lived too long in the climate—there are also social observations peculiar to the film industry. In a subculture obsessed with celebrity and success, nothing is so chilling as the specter of failure, and the ghostly figures of has-beens stalk these pages: Manny Schwartz, a former studio boss who commits suicide; a cameraman mysteriously blacklisted after someone starts a rumor that he is going blind; a faded actress, and Johnny Swanson, a has-been cowboy star. The rarefied few who are successful live in a small, closed world, huddled together against threatening forces from outside.

Stahr's studio. The film studio is Stahr's true home, much more so than the house he is having built in Santa Monica or the lonely Bel Air home in which he currently is living. The studio is the place he knows better than any other, where he works and often where he sleeps, as well as the place where he meets Kathleen. Chapter 3 sketches out his typical working day at the studio; it consists of little of the "glamour" typically depicted in old Hollywood films about Hollywood. Instead, it depicts Stahr attending to his business: discussing filmmaking with a discouraged writer, acting as therapist to an impotent actor, holding a story conference with writers and directors, hosting a visiting Danish prince, defending his desire to make "quality pictures" to the studio's cautious money men, helping the blacklisted cameraman, and using all his resources to discover the identity of the attractive young woman whom he glimpsed the night before. The studio is a place of business, a company engaged in the manufacture of dreams, and Stahr, for all that he is a dreamer, is also a businessman. At one point he compares himself to a chief clerk who knows where everything is. However, the truest picture of Stahr's place in his world may be the scene following an earthquake in chapter 2, when Stahr walks through the studio and is hailed by

workers on the set who regard him as a hero, "the last of the princes."

*Hermitage. Former home of Andrew Jackson, the seventh president of the United States, a Greek Revival mansion near Nashville, Tennessee, where Manny Schwartz kills himself at dawn. The pilgrimage that Cecelia, Wylie White, and Schwartz make to the Hermitage begins as a joke, a spur-of-the-moment side trip when their cross-country flight is grounded by a storm. However, Fitzgerald uses the visit to contrast an older frontier America with the dream-America Stahr and the film industry are creating in Hollywood. Cecelia notices the green of the woodland trees and the real cows (her first glimpse of farm animals was a herd of sheep on a movie lot). Andrew Jackson, a self-made man like Stahr, is evoked as a heroic figure from America's past (like the actor costumed as Abraham Lincoln in the studio commissary), admired if not quite understood by those engaged in creating the present.

*Santa Monica. Seaside community in Southern California where Stahr is having a new home built. He takes Kathleen to the unfinished, roofless house, which has a quality similar to that of a movie set. Stahr even speaks of having grass brought in as a prop. The house's incomplete state, with some rooms finished, others not yet built, reflects Stahr himself. He has devoted himself only to work for such a long time that the domestic side of his character, symbolized by the house, is underdeveloped. It is here that he forges a tentative relationship with Kathleen, whom he takes to the beach for the running of the grunion. The image of the small silver fish coming in with the tides, "as they had come before Sir Francis Drake" (who visited California in 1579), evokes an unspoiled world already lost to the fickle and impermanent structures of human civilization.

— *Kathryn Kulpa*

THE LATE GEORGE APLEY: A Novel in the Form of a Memoir

Author: John Phillips Marquand (1893-1960)
Type of work: Novel
Type of plot: Naturalism

Time of plot: Late nineteenth and early twentieth centuries
First published: 1937

Boston, or at least the Boston of the long-established families with inherited wealth who dominate its upper-class society in the nineteenth and early twentieth centuries, is the foundation on which nearly every thought, word, and action of this novel's title character, George Apley, rests. At the end of his long life, he characterizes Boston as probably the "best place in this neurotic world" and the only place in which he cares to live. Not only is he enamored of Boston, he is molded by it.

*Boston. Massachusetts city in which the Apley family has lived since the seventeenth century. The novel's title character, George Apley, is born in his grandfather's house on Beacon Hill in 1866 and dies in his own Beacon Street house in 1933. Except for a few trips to Europe and occasional sojourns to New York City, he rarely leaves New England during his nearly seventy years. His life is characterized by an adherence to a worldview espoused by his peers, the rarified few with Puritan forebears and inherited wealth, sometimes referred to as Boston Brahmins. These self-styled patricians inhabit a world of strictly structured social etiquette, private schools, men's clubs with severely restricted membership, and a dogmatic devotion to tradition. This small minority of the city's population believe themselves to be the social arbiters of the country. Despite their commitment to financial generosity to pet charities, they shield themselves from those outside their narrowly confined world, especially their immigrant neighbors. George Apley and his neighbors and friends are, because of their mind-set, as parochial and restricted by their outlook as anyone in a small village or town.

*Beacon Hill. Residential enclave in Boston that is synonymous with wealth and privilege. This neighborhood, which is characterized by an abundance of Charles Bulfinch-designed federal style residences, is the primary home of George Apley and most of his friends and colleagues. Although it is close to the Boston Common, the Public Gardens, and the immigrant neighborhoods just over the crest of the hill, it stands socially aloof from the rest of Boston during the period in which this novel is set.

*Harvard University. Founded in Cambridge, Massachusetts in 1636, Harvard is one of the oldest institutions of higher education in the United States. It serves, in the novel as a microcosm of Boston elitism and is the only college Apley and his peers consider worthy of attending. Students in his day are quickly funneled into its strict social hierarchy, epitomized in its club system. Membership in the right club is more important to these Bostonians than even academic achievement.

Pequod Island. Fictional Maine island owned by Apley that could be any one of several small islands located off Maine's coast. For Apley, who buys and furnishes this private island as a vacation retreat, it is a means of escape that is acceptable to his Boston peers. Life on the island is relatively rustic and simple—despite the presence of servants like the local young women hired each season to serve as waitresses in the dining hall. Routines on the island are, nevertheless, nearly as structured as those in the city. From the rising bell at 6:30 A.M. to the formal evening reports of the day's activities, summer islanders are ruled by their Bostonian loyalty to structure.

*New York City. Great metropolitan center about 175 miles southwest of Boston that functions, in its role as a modern cosmopolitan city, as a foil to the manners and mores of Boston. In a letter to his wife, Apley claims that Bostonians in New York seem like strangers in a foreign city. When he and his Boston neighbors visit New York, they always stay in the same hotel, thus assuring themselves of congenial and like-minded company who can shield them from the excesses and familiarity of non-New Englanders.

— *Jane Marie Smith*

LAVENGRO: The Scholar—The Gypsy—The Priest

Author: George Henry Borrow (1803-1881)
Type of work: Novel
Type of plot: Autobiographical

Time of plot: 1805-1825
First published: 1851

George Henry Borrow's idealized account of his youth describes his wanderings around the British Isles and becoming acquainted with Gypsies. The preface to the first edition describes this novel as "a dream, partly of study, partly of adventure." Though roughly chronological, the book's one hundred chapters tend to impose the knowledge and opinions of middle age on the adventures of Borrow's youth and thus to create dreamlike memories rather than precise travelogue.

*Great Britain. Borrow's native country. Born in Norfolk, he grew up the son of a professional soldier from Cornwall and has his first-person narrator, Lavengro, travel constantly throughout England. Lavengro is educated at one army encampment after another. Near the squalid training camp at Norman Cross in Lincolnshire, he first encounters Gypsies, who recognize his unusual qualities and give him his Gypsy name, "Lavengro"—from a Gypsy term for "word-master." The novel's subtitle alludes to his three identities: a student of languages, an honorary Gypsy, and an evangelical Protestant.

Wherever military life takes his family, Lavengro learns the local language and customs. In Scotland, he studies under a master of Norse extraction, while his father's regiment is stationed at Edinburgh Castle. In Ireland, where he visits the Castle of Cashel, he trades a deck of playing cards for language lessons and begins a lifelong fascination with racing horses. In Wales, he is entranced by the ancient culture and astounds adults by learning to speak Welsh as quickly as he learned to ride horseback. By the time he returns to England, he is proficient in all the languages of the British Isles.

*Norfolk. Region in eastern England, along the North Sea, where Lavengro's family settles after the Napoleonic Wars, There, in East Anglia, Lavengro receives a modest amount of formal schooling. On rambles through the countryside, he meets Gypsy horse traders whose values he prefers to those of his Anglo-Saxon neighbors. One Gypsy youth, Jasper, becomes his lifelong friend. He briefly contemplates a career in the law, then opts for a literary life and looks for work as a translator of literature.

*London. Capital of Great Britain where, after arriving by coach, Lavengro stays in the hostels of Cheapside and wanders among bookshops. He meets a publisher who commissions him to write about the urban poor. He writes the stories of debtors and criminals in the notorious **Newgate Prison**. He also writes about the shopkeepers and peddlers on London Bridge. On long walks outside the metropolis, he discovers such remnants of "Old England" as the fair at Greenwich, south of London on the River Thames.

*Stonehenge. Neolithic stone circle dominating the Sarum Plain north of Salisbury that Lavengro travels to on foot. There, he talks to a shepherd about such matters as the meaning of life, where Stonehenge's great stones came from, where the stars are from, and where the local people originated.

*Chester. English town near the Welsh border where Lavengro interviews both officials and peasants. Half of his adventure is always mental. As he arrives at new destinations, he reflects on local legends and literature and especially on the words that people use.

Mumper's Dingle. "Beggar's valley" on the Welsh border where Lavengro builds a makeshift forge and supports himself briefly by shoeing horses. There he meets more traveling Gypsies, including a beautiful young woman who shares his passion for languages, and a widely traveled postman who tells of his travels overseas. There, Lavengro's episodic story ends. Borrow continued the story in *Romany Rye* (1857).

— *Thomas Willard*

THE LAY OF IGOR'S CAMPAIGN

Author: Unknown
Type of work: Poetry
Type of plot: Romance

Time of plot: Late twelfth century
First transcribed: Slovo o polku Igoreve, c. 1187
    (English translation, 1919)

This poem is one of the defining traditional stories of Russia, telling the story of the disastrous overconfidence of an early prince of Novgorod-Seversk, one of the cities of Kievan Rus, in a battle against nomads. The unknown bard or bards who composed the ballad clearly were familiar with the region in which the events took place, as can be seen in their descriptions of the creatures dwelling within it.

*Novgorod-Seversk (NOV-go-rod seh-VEHRSK). Home of Igor Svyatoslavich. Not to be confused with the northern city of Novgorod, this is a smaller city on the Desna River, in what would later become Ukraine.

*Don River. Location of Igor's first battle against the Polovetsians. This large river of Russia's southern steppe is a major waterway and would serve as a natural boundary difficult for a rapidly retreating army to cross.

*Donets River (DO-nehts). The lesser Don, a tributary of the Don River. In the rushes along its banks, Igor escapes from his Polovetsian captors with the aid of Ovlur the Polovetsian. The poet personifies the river, having it speak to Igor as he approaches and then loyally protect him in his escape. The bard also portrays the various animals and birds of the region as aiding Igor in his escape, except for the snakes, which prove faithless but can only slither.

*Kiev (kyehv). Principal city of the Russian nation prior to the Mongol invasion. In the hills overlooking the Dnieper River, Svyatoslav the prince of Kiev has his palace. There he has the prophetic dream of his son Igor's defeat at the hands of the Polovetsians.

— *Leigh Husband Kimmel*

LEAVES OF GRASS

Author: Walt Whitman (1819-1892)   *First published:* 1855
Type of work: Poetry

This volume, which represents Walt Whitman's life's work, joins him with the American nation that he saw as his ultimate subject, his truest inspiration, and the source of his heart's spirit. The linkage between Whitman's poetic consciousness and the land is the most fundamental element of his epic portrait of the cosmos, which he saw through a sensibility finely attuned to respond with awe and wonder to its myriad features. As an explanation of his ambition, he stated (in "Starting From Paumanok"), "I will trail the whole geography of the globe," and as evidence of his accomplishments, he maintained that " proof of a poet shall be sternly deferr'd till his country absorbs him as affectionately as he has absorb'd it."

*Paumanok. Village on Long Island east of New York City where Whitman was born. His early poem "Starting from Paumanok" describes the village as "fish-shaped," indicating its (and his) nautical origins, an idea that he developed in detail in "Out of the Cradle Endlessly Rocking," in which he envisions himself a "little boy again,/ Throwing myself on the sand, confronting the waves." Whitman recalls Paumanok's fragrance as "lilac-scent," its coastline as marked by "Fifthmonth grass" and "briers," and its seashore inhabited by "two feather'd guests from Alabama," signaling its fertility and hospitality. Later in the poem, now speaking from an adult's perspective, Whitman cites "Paumanok's gray beach" as the site of his initial and continuing poetic inspiration.

*Brooklyn. City, which is now part of New York City, to which Whitman's family moved when his father began work as a carpenter in 1823. Whitman lived in Brooklyn intermittently through the next three decades. He became editor of a leading local newspaper, *The Brooklyn Eagle*, in 1846, and formed a habit of walking in the city observing every aspect of urban life. His poem "Crossing Brooklyn Ferry" describes people traveling between Brooklyn and Manhattan, using the "heights of Brooklyn to the south and east" and the traffic in the passage between the Hudson and East Rivers as symbols of city life and energy. He describes the "fires from the foundry chimneys/ burning high and glaringly into the night" as an image of industrial might, and the terrain of Brooklyn—"Brooklyn of ample hills was mine"—as homeground.

*Manhattan. For Whitman, "million-footed Manhattan" was the central city of the new American nation. In admiration he asked, "Ah, what can ever be more stately and admirable to me than mast-hemm'd Manhattan?" Multiple vignettes of life in the street ("the blab of the pave") come together to form an indelible portrait, which images such as "blacksmiths with grimed and hairy chests environ the anvil."

*United States. In his preface to the first edition of *Leaves of Grass*, Whitman says that the "United States themselves are essentially the greatest poem." He saw himself as literally an organic element of the new land. "I bequeath myself to the dirt to grow from the grass I love." In boldly accepting Ralph Waldo Emerson's call for an American poet, Whitman frequently proclaimed himself a genuine voice of the nation. "In the name of these States"—a characteristic formulation—expresses his position, and through his poems, there are apostrophes to and evocations of individual states and regions. "We dwell awhile in every city and town," he asserts in "On Journeys Through the States," writing many passages like Section 14 from "Starting From Paumanok":

> Land of the pastoral plains, the grass-fields of the world!
>   land of those sweet-air'd interminable plateaus!
> Land of the herd, the garden, the healthy house of
>   adobie!
> Lands where the north-west Columbia winds, and where
>   the south-west Columbia winds!
> Land of the eastern Chesapeake! Land of the Delaware!

Whitman returns throughout his poetry to his evolving conception of the United States by using place-names such as "Okonee, Koosa, Ottawa, Monongahela, Sauk, Natchez, Chattahoochee, Kaqueta, Oronoco,/ Wabash, Miami, Saginaw, Chippewa, Oshkosh, Walla-Walla." He also uses physical features, sensual imagery, folkloric depictions as poetic persona, and some historic incidents.

— *Leon Lewis*

THE LEFT HAND OF DARKNESS

Author: Ursula K. Le Guin (1929-   )
Type of work: Novel
Type of plot: Science fiction

Time of plot: Hainish Cycle 93, Ekumenical year 1490-1497
First published: 1969

This novel's primary setting is the imaginary planet of Gethen, sometimes called Winter by the diplomats sent to it by the intergalactic political unit called the Ekumen. Inside that primary setting are a number of secondary ones, only two of which, Karhide and Orgoreyn, are of importance to the story.

Gethen/Winter. Planet similar to earth in size and having an atmosphere capable of supporting a humanoid but not human population. It exists in an unspecified galaxy and in a distant future. It is called Gethen by the people of Hain, an advanced and distant planet from which the protagonist comes, and is sometimes called Winter for reasons that quickly become obvious. The central figure is Genly Ai, a diplomat who represents an intergalactic political organization called the Ekumen; it is Ai's task to live on Winter for as long as it takes to slowly and gently convince the Gethenians that they want, of their own free will, to join the Ekumen. This organization, a noncoercive political confederation of loosely linked planets, is often alluded to in the novel but is never directly encountered. It is Ursula K. Le Guin's ideal political organization, and its purpose is to represent a potential alternative to the modern organization of competing nation-states.

Modern nationalism/patriotism is the subject against which the novel cleverly and entertainingly argues.

Genly Ai's mission is impeded by the two conditions that are the most significant features of the planet. First, Gethen is in the midst of an ice age: This means that every feature of the planet, from its flora and fauna to its various cultural rituals and religions to its machines and technology, is shaped by the fact that Gethen is at all times extremely cold. The second factor that shapes the planet and the most interesting feature of the novel is that the people of Gethen are completely hermaphroditic. These preoccupations clearly mark the novel as a product of the 1960's American fascination with "alternative lifestyles."

Karhide. Nation on the planet Gethen. While for the sake of symmetry Le Guin mentions several places on Gethen, none is ever seen or visited except the two central nations. The first and most significant is Karhide, which, with its dedication to a sort of quasi capitalism and to individual liberty of various kinds, seems to be intended as a simplified representation of early, even primitive, democracy. For all the talk about total equality between people, the novel clearly prefers this to the form of government represented by its chief rival, Orgoreyn.

Orgoreyn. The second of the two main places on Gethen/Winter. With its highly organized and regimented social system, it is presented as a simplified image of communism. Much less time is spent there, however, than in Karhide, and it is clear that Le Guin's purpose in creating it is to have a balance between competing social systems which will allow her to make comments about the governments of Gethen that apply equally well to modern political situations on earth.

— *Ronald Foust*

THE LEGEND OF SLEEPY HOLLOW

Author: Washington Irving (1783-1859)
Type of work: Short fiction
Type of plot: Tall tale

Time of plot: Eighteenth century
First published: 1820

This story manipulates details of ordinary farmyard and rustic settings to create an ominous atmosphere to convey its tall tale. Exaggeration and description enhance the mood of the various scenes throughout the tale.

Sleepy Hollow. Small Dutch community in New York, near Tarry Town (now commonly known as Tarrytown) and the Hudson River. Sleepy Hollow has two main characteristics. The first is a sense of "listless repose" that settles over the land and the inhabitants. This drowsiness fosters the other characteristic, the enhanced imaginations and superstitions of its inhabitants. For example, its inhabitants speculate that an Indian chief's powwows or a German doctor's enchantments might be the causes of the strangeness in the area.

Residents of Sleepy Hollow enjoy sitting by their fireplaces and telling one another tales of ghosts. Washington Irving attributes the hauntings and tales to the fact that this is a long-established Dutch community whose families remain there generation after generation. Chief among the ghost stories are those about the Headless Horseman, the main specter in the tale, who is often seen around the old church, where he was supposedly buried without his head.

Throughout most of the tale, natural surroundings convey mood. During the daylight hours, Sleepy Hollow is bright and cheerful. On the fall day that schoolteacher Ichabod Crane heads for the Van Tassel farm, the trees are bright orange, purple, and scarlet. Ducks fly overhead. Quail and squirrels can be heard. However, when Ichabod returns home at night, the scene changes. He passes by a tulip-tree whose limbs are "gnarled and fantastic" and a "group of oaks and chestnuts, matted thick with wild grape vines," that throws a "cavernous gloom" over the road. The ominous change in scenery alerts readers to the fact that Ichabod is about to encounter the Headless Horseman.

Van Tassel farm. Sleepy Hollow farm that is home to Ichabod Crane's love interest, Katrina Van Tassel. What is most remarkable about the farm is that it is portrayed as an agrarian paradise. Situated along the banks of the Hudson River, the farm is in "one of those green, sheltered, fertile nooks, in which the Dutch farmers are so fond of nestling." It has a spreading elm tree, bubbling spring, and babbling brook. As big as a church, its barn is filled with activity and treasures from the farm. Birds twitter among its eaves, large pigs and sucklings grunt in their pens, and a "stately squadron" of geese occupy the farm's pond. "Regiments of turkeys" and guinea fowl wander through the barnyard. The farm has rich fields of rye, buckwheat, wheat, and Indian corn, and the orchards are "burdened with ruddy fruit."

The inside of the Van Tassel farmhouse also speaks of its family's wealth. Farming and husbandry implements are hung from the rafters, while a spinning wheel and a butter churn stand in the piazza. On entering the hall, Crane is struck by "rows of resplendent pewter" on a long dresser. A huge bag of wool waiting to be spun rests in one corner, while in another stands "linsey-woolsey just from the loom." Dried apples and peaches and Indian corn are placed on strings and hung as decorations. The best parlor holds mahogany furniture, silver, china, and an ostrich egg hanging from the center of the room.

Descriptions of the Van Tassel farm are slightly exaggerated, using military terms such as "regiments" and "troops," that fit the nature of the tall tale. The farm represents the idea of America as a land of plenty. The Van Tassel family is rich because of the fertility of the Hudson Valley soil. Crane is attracted to the farm because of its prosperity; his interest in Katrina is fueled by her father's wealth. He daydreams of marrying Katrina and selling the farm to pay for his trip to "Kentucky, Tennessee, or the Lord knows where." This is a sharp contrast to the contented settlements of the Dutch community. It is thus no surprise when Ichabod is eventually driven out of Sleepy Hollow.

— *P. Andrew Miller*

THE LEOPARD

Author: Giuseppe Tomasi di Lampedusa (1896-1957)
Type of work: Novel
Type of plot: Historical

Time of plot: 1860-1910
First published: Il gattopardo, 1958 (English translation, 1960)

Set in Sicily in the late nineteenth century, this novel explores the effects of the island's isolation from the political changes sweeping over Italy on an old member of the Sicilian royal family. It opens in 1860, a crucial year in the island's history—when its old Bourbon monarchy collapsed and the House of Savoy's Victor Emmanuel became king of a united Italy.

San Lorenzo. Sicilian village in the Piani dei Colli district, between Monte Pellegrino and Monte Castellaccio, north of Palermo where the Villa Salina, home of Don Fabrizio Corbera, prince of Salina, stands. This fictitious residence is based on the actual Villa Lampedusa home of the author—a property that his great-grandfather Guilio Tomasi acquired in the 1840's. Tomasi also inspired the character Don Fabrizio.

At his observatory from which he studies the stars, Don Fabrizio skeptically contemplates the dawn of the glorious new days that may bring his comfortable aristocratic order to an end. However, whatever changes come, he knows they will occur within a familiar context: One set of rulers will replace another, and the effect on most people will be minimal. His villa, enclosed within its own walls, is a distant, separate world, but one that is nonetheless part of a common landscape that has been punished by a crude, drugging sun that keeps all things in "servile immobility," annulling every will. The dichotomy between psychological distance and social imperative is fundamental to the book's themes of decadence and impending decline.

Donnafugata. Village in which the Corbera family country is estate located, three days' journey by coach from the Villa Salina. The estate's main residence is a "restless baroque" palace with so many rooms that the prince boasts he has not set foot in all of them. This fictitious little town is patterned after the real Santa Margherita di Bèlice, which lies in the northwestern corner of Agrigento province, called in the book by its original name of Girgenti.

An absentee landowner and city dweller by choice, Don Fabrizio likes to stay here three months each year. He has a proud sense of feudal ownership that goes beyond the fact that ownership of this and other agrarian properties, thousands of hectares in all, that are the main source of his family's wealth. Donnafugata holds for him the prized memories of an "everlasting childhood" and produces a sense of "serene confidence," which he finds important in the current trying and unpredictable times. However, the safeness of his haven proves deceptive. Don Lorenzo eventually confronts problems that will bring about changes in himself, generated in part by a decline in his own prestige. He realizes that, despite the outward steadfastness of his physical surrounding, the old truths and old social verities are being eroded and that he is no longer able to sweep away difficulties with a wave of his hand.

Convent of the Holy Spirit. Religious retreat that Prince Fabrizio and his family visit in order to pray at the tomb of Blessed Corbera, a revered ancestor and founder of the establishment. They follow a centuries-old family tradition, but Don Fabrizio particularly enjoys the visit because of the deference he is paid. He and the king of Naples are the only men allowed to enter the convent itself. In fact, everything about the place pleases him, from the humble simplicity of its parlor, to a little wooden wheel used for passing messages, to the macaroons nuns bake for visitors.

*Palermo. Sicily's capital city is not one of happy memories for Don Fabrizio. There, at great ball at the Palazzo Pontelone in 1862, he senses his extreme isolation from the society that once nurtured him and broods on his own mortality. He is pessimistic about the future, feels out of place, and philosophizes that when he dies, so will the whole world. When his death finally does come nineteen years later, it does not occur among magnificent surroundings. He is at the less-than-luxurious Hotel Trinacria to which he has been taken because he is too ill to return to his villa and because his virtually deserted Palermo town house does not contain any beds. In alien, strange surroundings he looks back on his life and realizes that he has only truly lived for two, perhaps three, of his seventy-three years.

*Sicily. Italian island, off the southern tip of the Italian peninsula, that is closer to Africa than it is to northern Italy. Its location has a profound psychological effect on its inhabitants. This Sicily which aridly, comfortlessly, and irrationally undulates to the horizon "with no lines the mind could grasp," produces in Sicilians a longing for sleep and an attraction for things past only because they are dead. Don Fabrizio clearly believes that such a morose attitude is not mere rationalization, but reasons for his own spirit of resignation.

— *Wm. Laird Kleine-Ahlbrandt*

LIBER AMORIS: Or, The New Pygmalion

Author: William Hazlitt (1778-1830)
Type of work: Novel
Type of plot: Autobiographical

Time of plot: 1823
First published: 1823

The primary settings of this autobiographical novel are London and various parts of Scotland. In his London boardinghouse, William Hazlitt seems a prisoner of his all-consuming love for Sarah Walker, who works as a maid. In Scotland, where he goes to divorce his wife, his feelings expand and fluctuate between adoration of his beloved and abhorrence of her fickle treatment of him.

London. Great Britain's capital and greatest city. The London boardinghouse owned by Sarah Walker's father is the only city site identified in Hazlitt's tormented account of his romantic obsession. Hazlitt falls in love with Sarah the instant she walks into his room to serve him breakfast. The rest of the world seems to vanish as he concentrates on her graceful movements. Before long, she allows him to fondle her, and they exchange many kisses. This familiarity always takes place in Hazlitt's room, and he has almost no knowledge of Sarah outside the confines of their morning meetings. They create, in other words, their own little world. Gradually Hazlitt conceives the idea of divorcing his wife and marrying Sarah. Almost at the same time he catches a glimpse of her outside his room with another lodger. Hazlitt suspects that Sarah has also given this other man her attentions. Distraught, he nevertheless maintains plans to divorce his wife, and he departs for Scotland, where he can obtain a divorce quickly and without the legal complications he would encounter in England.

Hazlitt plans to return from Scotland and attempt to renew Sarah's affections. Indeed he seems drawn by an irresistible force as he describes the River Thames heaving her "name pantingly forth." However, Sarah has rejected him, and the intense obsession that Hazlitt experienced earlier in the boardinghouse returns as he takes up residence there once more, keenly observing her every move and finally following her outside the boardinghouse, where he witnesses her meeting with the rival male lodger and realizes he was never the exclusive recipient of her attentions.

Scotland. Hazlitt writes to a friend, explaining that he is forty miles outside of Edinburgh, serving out a term of what he calls "probation," for he is awaiting the outcome of divorce proceedings. He often walks by the road to London and is obviously thinking about Sarah and the boardinghouse. Indeed, he writes to a friend about his interpretations of Sarah's behavior and his ultimate hope that he can win her undivided love. However, he acknowledges that he is in a "state of suspense."

Hazlitt relates every experience in Scotland to the "raging fire" in his heart. Thus a steamboat trip turns into a hellish vision of the "prison-house" of his feelings, which are relieved only by his image of Sarah's smile, which is heavenly. Away from her he plunges into a "dungeon of despair." He walks by the sea, and the "eternal ocean" evokes his expression of "lasting despair" in his memory of Sarah's face. He hopes that a visit to the Scottish countryside will relieve his intense emotions and that he will be able to work on his writing. Edinburgh seems "stony-hearted" and the air "too thin," the place too far from his "heart's true home."

Even exquisite sites such as Roslyn Castle lead back to Sarah and Hazlitt's suspicion that she is now in the lap of the rival lodger. Indeed every landmark and place, however briefly mentioned, becomes another location to dwell on Sarah's infidelity. She haunts Hazlitt's journey, and he takes to calling her a witch. It is a romantic setting, but he fears his passion has made him into a fool.

Scotland lingers in Hazlitt's memory after his return to lodge at the boardinghouse. In Scotland, the "flint had been my pillow," he remarks, but now his proximity to Sarah only emphasizes their estrangement. After a long interview with her, Hazlitt reluctantly realizes that she will not have him. The only place left for her is the very book he writes in order to express and to rid himself of his obsession.

— *Carl Rollyson*

LIE DOWN IN DARKNESS

Author: William Styron (1925-   )
Type of work: Novel
Type of plot: Psychological realism

Time of plot: Mid-twentieth century
First published: 1951

The central action of this novel unfolds in the fictional Virginia Tidewater town of Port Warwick, which represents the industrial South shortly after World War II. The novel's plot follows the coffin of Peyton Loftis into Port Warwick, then to the cemetery where she is buried. Throughout the novel there are movements back in time, and these shifts follow the Loftis family members to Charlottesville, Virginia, and New York City.

Port Warwick. Industrial town in Virginia. The events of the central plot occur on one hot August day, in 1945, in the town of Port Warwick, based closely on William Styron's hometown of Newport News, Virginia. In the opening scenes of the novel, a train carrying Peyton Loftis's body arrives in Port Warwick, a town where heat and dust oppress the inhabitants. As the funeral procession drives toward the cemetery, the characters feel the omnipresent heat, smell the marsh and rotting fish, and hear the sounds of the shipyard. Peyton's father, Milton, his mistress, and the funeral home director drive Peyton's coffin past workers' houses, supermarket signs, freight yards, gas tanks rising from the marsh, garbage heaps, a deserted brewery, a decrepit garage, a hotdog stand, and a waterlogged tent belonging to an itinerant fortune-teller. In other words, the town, its industry, and its heat reflect Milton's pain and suffering; he has just lost his daughter, the one person he has loved above all others.

On the trip to the cemetery, as Milton remembers the past and Peyton, the narration shifts to other settings. In his memories and later in Peyton's memories, Port Warwick is occasionally a beautiful place. The Loftis house is located on the Chesapeake Bay, surrounded by gardens, cedars, and a beach. Peyton's mother loves the garden, and Peyton's disabled sister Maudie enjoys the outdoors and the rain. Images of water, of baptisms in the James River, and of rain in the cemetery contrast with the omnipresent heat. Peyton's fondest memories are of walks with her father along the Chesapeake Bay toward Hampton, the only "pure moments" in her troubled life. The novel ends by breaking the heat of Port Warwick with a thunderstorm and with the river baptisms. This contrast of heat and water symbolizes both an ending and a beginning, but in this transformation, there is no promise of a better life; there is only the suggestion that opportunities existed and that these opportunities were squandered.

*Charlottesville.** City in central Virginia that was the birthplace of Thomas Jefferson and the home of the University of Virginia. Milton graduates from the University of Virginia, and Peyton dates a young man who attends the university. In addition, Maudie is treated at the University of Virginia medical center, so the memories of the characters return them to Charlottesville, where Milton drinks to excess, attends a football game, and carries a Confederate flag. On the same weekend, Peyton drinks excessively at a fraternity party, and Maudie receives treatment at the university's shoddy medical center. After the football game, Milton becomes so drunk that he finds himself lost in an African American neighborhood, where he falls into an open sewage ditch. In these scenes, the Virginia of Jefferson stands in sharp contrast with the Virginia of the twentieth century. This contrast emphasizes how far these characters have fallen.

*New York City.** Great northern city in which Peyton spends her last days. In an attempt to escape her dysfunctional family, Peyton marries New York artist Harry Miller and moves to the city, but in New York, the heat and the family problems continue. Peyton and Harry separate, and Peyton moves in with Anthony, a milkman, and lives in a roach-infested apartment. In August, New York is as hot and uninhabitable as Virginia. The irony is that Peyton does not escape her problems by moving; the same heat continues, and this heat symbolizes her suffering. By shifting the setting to New York, Styron is showing that the dysfunctional family is not uniquely southern. The "lost generations" of modern times are a product of an industrialized society, and the hot oppressive places of this novel ultimately symbolize the inhospitable and dysfunctional environments of modern industrial society.

— *Roark Mulligan*

THE LIFE AND OPINIONS OF TRISTRAM SHANDY, GENT.

Author: Laurence Sterne (1713-1768)
Type of work: Novel
Type of plot: Satire

Time of plot: 1718-1766
First published: 1759-1767

Each character in this meandering narrative of Tristram Shandy's life is associated with a specific place. For example, Shandy Hall has become synonymous with the wacky schemes and half-baked ideas of its owner, Walter Shandy. Uncle Toby's miniature battlefield is as convoluted and sterile as its owner, and Widow Wadman's prim parlor reflects the good woman's proper but very purposeful assault on Uncle Toby's bachelorhood. Nothing seems to turn out right in this world of accident, misunderstandings, and foiled schemes. Central to all the misfortunes plaguing the narrator's life is the implication that Shandy Hall and its environs are the principal players in the unhinging of Walter's well-laid plans and the undoing of Tristram's fortunes.

Shandy Hall. Tristram's chief misfortune is to be born in Shandy Hall, a world ruled by his father, Walter Shandy, who is determined to give Tristram, his only child, the best possible chances of success in life, only to be defeated at every turn. A botched conception, birth, and christening are the genesis of Tristram's lifelong misfortunes, but they also mirror and mock the activities of those who attempt to control destiny with arcane lore, esoteric learning, and harebrained schemes.

Walter Shandy's hodgepodge of philosophical and psychological ideas, formal logic, and theories of child-rearing form a comic opera in which his best plans are overturned, throwing Shandy Hall into constant turmoil. Within this microcosm, classical rhetoric, medieval literature, and biblical references mingle with allusions to astrology, alchemy, bridge-building, and fortifications. Citations in Latin, Greek, French, and Italian mingle with a technical vocabulary borrowed from science, medicine, and the legal profession. A dissertation on whiskers mingles with a long tale about a man's nose. All of these disparate elements create a rich muddle that symbolizes not only Walter Shandy's fecund mind but also the larger world of human affairs, which is marked by endless misunderstanding and ubiquitous charlatanism.

The events that take place within Shandy Hall represent, by implication, Tristram's version of human history, a tragicomedy in which good-hearted simpletons and well-intentioned schemers continually collide with common sense, and high-toned discourse is constantly undercut by coarse humor, coarse talk, and bawdy innuendo. What drives Shandy Hall, and what continually defeats Walter Shandy's schemes, is the same force, or Fate, that directs human affairs.

Uncle Toby's battlefield. Probably no other place in this novel so well represents the way language can lead to mishap and misunderstanding as Uncle Toby's miniature fortification. It symbolizes the problematic interplay of language and learning and of human character and its relation to events. In this miniature world, mock warfare mirrors the assault by the Widow Wadman against Uncle Toby's resolute bachelorhood, and her failure to engage him in a frank discourse symbolizes the power of innocence to blind and the power of language to obscure and mislead. Uncle Toby's battlefield, with its overtones of a child's game and harmless pastime, reflects his childish nature and benign spirit—he could not hurt a fly, we are told—as well as the essential childishness of adult warfare.

Widow Wadman's parlor. Climactic place in which the romantic Widow Wadman lays her siege. Her parlor is the arena in which one of the book's principal themes—the unreliability of language as a medium of communication—is most central and where one of the book's other themes, that impotence imbues the individual with a kind of potency, is played out before the reader's eyes in a comic climax of cross-purpose and miscommunication. The parlor also represents the polite world of decorum and propriety as this world is undercut by the physical behavior of servants below stairs. In the parlor, too, Sterne's double meanings and double entendres proliferate more quickly than the characters themselves can manage.

Tristram the narrator glories in the ambiguous properties of his chief weapon, language, which gives him the power to control the events of his narrative and, at the same time, to demonstrate the equivocal nature of language and the unequivocal power of those who know how to use it well. The widow's parlor is the place where she parlays with Uncle Toby and discovers that there is more to communication than simple talk.

— *Bernard E. Morris*

THE LIFE OF MARIANNE

Author: Marivaux (Pierre Carlet de Chamblain
  Marivaux, 1688-1763)
Type of work: Novel
Type of plot: Psychological realism

Time of plot: Late seventeenth century
First published: La Vie de Marianne, 1731-1741
  (English translation, 1736-1742)

Paris is the only setting possible for this novel of manners. In eighteenth century France, Paris and society were synonymous. Readers of the period wanted to know about Paris, and they wanted novels that were anchored in their own contemporary reality.

***Paris.** France's capital city is the setting for the major part of the novel. Marivaux's novel examines the life available to a woman in the eighteenth century, when Paris was the center of society. All rules of social conduct and moral values were developed there and imitated elsewhere. Paris is definitely the place for Marianne's life to unfold. The story deals in a conventional manner with aristocratic society, which was the proper subject of novels at the time. Marianne gravitates toward this society. Although her origins are cloaked in mystery, she has a strong sense that her unknown parents were members of the upper class. By chance and good fortune, Marianne finds herself included in this society. Thus, Marivaux's novel conforms to the dictates of other novels of the period. As an observer and recorder of human experience, Marivaux was, however, intrigued by those who were not members of the aristocracy and took great pleasure in creating characters from other social milieus.

By setting his novel in Paris, Marivaux also affords himself the opportunity of including characters from other classes. His aristocrats and Marianne herself interact with the shopkeepers, coach drivers, and various other people of the city in such a way that Marivaux creates a wonderful panorama of characters not found in other novels of the period. At the shop where Marianne is employed for a short time, the reader meets the merchant Madame Dutour, a character almost as interesting as Marianne, and the shop girl Mademoiselle Toinon.

House outside Rennes (ren). The manuscript of Marianne's story is found here in a cabinet contained in a wall of this house, which has already had five or six owners, by a man who has just bought the house. At the time Marivaux was writing, it was unacceptable for a woman, particularly a woman of the upper class, to write and publish. Marianne's narrative is in the first person. Marivaux needed to create a fiction around the manuscript to protect Marianne's reputation and to make her believable as a woman of quality. He does so by having the manuscript, which was intended only to be read by a friend of Marianne, be discovered in this obscure and secretive location.

Church. Parisian church in which Monsieur De Valville first sees Marianne and is awed by her beauty. He falls in love with her immediately. Marianne takes particular note of him as well. During the period, churches were places to worship, but they were also convenient places to be seen, especially for women. Being noticed at the church opens the way for Marianne to enter into the upper-class world to which she aspires. This particular scene has caused a considerable amount of controversy over the character of Marianne. She always speaks of her naïveté and innocence, but many critics view her conduct at the church as evidence that she is not what she pretends to be.

Convent. Roman Catholic religious community for women to which Marianne repairs each time her life becomes difficult. The convent plays a conventional role in the novel. Abandoned by Valville, whom she hoped to marry, Marianne enters the convent. She intends to take the veil and renounce all secular life. At the time the book was published, novels abounded with rejected heroines who withdrew to convents to suffer and mourn lost love. Entering the convent symbolized the death of the woman. Marivaux uses this conventional literary device; however, he brings Marianne back to life by having her receive a visit from a nobleman of about fifty who offers her a marriage based solely on reason.

— *Shawncey Webb*

LIGEIA

Author: Edgar Allan Poe (1809-1849)
Type of work: Short fiction
Type of plot: Gothic

Time of plot: Early nineteenth century
First published: 1838

The primary setting of this short story is a Gothic bridal chamber, a room in the high turret of an ornately deco-rated abbey isolated in the English countryside. There, the narrator is haunted after the death of his second wife and reappearance of his first.

Bridal chamber. Room in an isolated abbey in the wild English countryside. Following the death of his be-loved first wife Ligeia, the narrator restores an ancient English abbey whose gloomy grandeur and remote set-ting match his own mental and spiritual desolation. In-spired by his opium addiction, he furnishes the abbey in a fantastic style of elaborate furniture, tapestries, wall hangings, and decorations in an attempt to overcome his sorrow. This mixture reaches its zenith in the narrator's bedroom, high in a turret, where the huge bed has a can-opy, and there is a gigantic sarcophagus of black granite from ancient Egypt. The jumbled mixture of exotic fur-niture and artifacts, and in particular its emphasis on the bizarre and the magical, are reflections of the narrator's own internal state and a hint of the supernatural events to come.

It is to this bedroom, which the narrator calls his bridal chamber, that he brings his new wife, the Lady Rowena Trevanion, of Tremaine. Theirs is a loveless marriage and the narrator feels little sorrow when the Lady Rowena sinks into an illness, declines, and dies. After she is pre-pared for burial and is lying in the bridal chamber, the narrator sits in an opium-induced stupor watching over Rowena. The room seems to take on a life of its own, with almost imperceptible shadows gliding across the floor and the figures in the tapestries assuming sinister yet not-quite-perceivable patterns. During the night, Rowena re-vives and the startled narrator rushes to her side only to watch her fade again into death. This process repeats it-self in the eerie atmosphere of the room until finally the dead Rowena reveals herself as the reincarnated Ligeia.

— *Michael Witkoski*

LIGHT IN AUGUST

Author: William Faulkner (1897-1962)
Type of work: Novel
Type of plot: Psychological realism

Time of plot: 1930
First published: 1932

This novel tells the story of several main characters, and so includes a number of past settings, along with the present one. The combined stories of the characters reveal the impact of place and history on their lives and the tragic collision of individual histories, needs, and obsessions with a community's strengths and shortcomings. The places from which the characters come also play important parts in the novel.

Yoknapatawpha County (YOK-nuh-puh-TAW-fuh). Imaginary Mississippi county in which William Faulk-ner set all his fiction from his third novel on. A map of the county that he drew for his novel *Absalom, Absa-lom!* (1936) provides details about where the events in

his novels occur. These details make it clear that Yokna-patawpha corresponds to Mississippi's real Lafayette County, in which Faulkner lived. *Light in August* is also set in Yoknapatawpha, with Lena Grove leading the ac-tion into Jefferson at the beginning and out at the end.

Jefferson. Seat of Yoknapatawpha. Almost all the action of the novel set in the present takes place in and around Jefferson. Byron Bunch and Joe Christmas work at the sawmill, Reverend Hightower lives on a quiet street, Byron Bunch and Lena live in the boardinghouse, and Joanna Burden lives on the outskirts of town. Lena literally walks into Jefferson in the beginning of the novel and walks out again at the end, providing the frame for the rest of the events. As she enters the town, a fire burns in the distance—at Joanna Burden's house, where Joanna has been murdered. The rest of the novel provides the background explaining what has led up to this moment.

Reverend Hightower observes the town through his window and receives news of the outside world through his visitor, Byron Bunch. Hightower's carefully maintained isolation crumbles as the outside events intrude on his home, both through Byron's stories and through Joe Christmas's murder there late in the novel. Joanna Burden's isolation, not self-imposed as Hightower's but forced on her by her neighbors, also crumbles, as Joe Christmas enters first her servants' quarters, then her home. The scene of gruesome death, her property also gives hope when Lena gives birth in her servants' cabin.

The people of Jefferson, named and unnamed, also play a role. Whether hounding Hightower out of his church, turning on Joe Christmas when they learn he is partly African American, or helping Lena when they really cannot afford it, these people show the compassion, pettiness, sensitivity, and bigotry of Jefferson.

Other locations. Faulkner constructs much of his narrative out of the stories of how its characters have come to Jefferson and thereby portrays a variety of places. For example, he describes the Alabama farmhouse that Lena left and the road that took her to Jefferson in a vain search for her unborn child's father. A long section of the novel occurs in the orphanage where Joe Christmas's grandfather placed him, the McEachern house in which he lived after his adoption, and the many roads and towns he wandered. Hightower recalls the house where he grew up hearing the stories of his grandfather's exploits in the Civil War, his seminary, and the Memphis hotel room in which his wife committed suicide. One of Joanna Burden's sections recalls the Burdens' long trek from New England, around the country, and finally to Jefferson, where Joanna's relatives are shot by Colonel Sartoris for allowing African Americans to vote during Reconstruction, leaving her alone and isolated.

In order to explain the circumstances of the brief present time of the novel, Faulkner gives the factors that shaped each character's motivations, responses, and actions. For example, the reasons behind Christmas's murder of Joanna goes back to his experiences in the orphanage, in the McEacherns' home, and during his travels.

— *Caroline Carvill*

LITTLE DORRIT

Author: Charles Dickens (1812-1870)
Type of work: Novel
Type of plot: Social realism

Time of plot: 1820's
First published: 1855-1857

Places in this novel are a mixture of the real and the imaginary. While Marshalsea debtors' prison was a real institution that existed during Charles Dickens's childhood, the "Circumlocution Office" is a fictional representation of what Dickens saw as governmental incompetence and indifference to the plight of those so unfortunate as to find themselves in debtors' prisons' neglected neighborhoods, such as the fictional Bleeding Heart Yard.

*Marshalsea. Debtors' prison in the London suburb of Southwark; a real place, but no longer a prison at the time Charles Dickens wrote *Little Dorrit*. Dickens's father had been incarcerated there in 1824 when Dickens was twelve, and Dickens routinely visited his father there each morning. In the novel, Dickens heightens the effect of the imprisonment of William Dorrit by having the Dorrits' daughter Amy—the "Little Dorrit" of the title—actually born there.

Aside from effectively preventing its inmates from satisfying their creditors, the prison also saps the will and spirit of its inmates. In what was presumably intended by government authorities as a merciful provision, the debtors' prisons in England allowed members of the debtors' families to live inside with them. Marshalsea is a place that plunges William Dorrit into despair. To Little Dorrit, the prison is the only home she knows during her childhood, and she and her brother and sister can come and go freely. As one pathetic consolation, William clings to a dubious prestige as "Father of the Marshalsea."

Marshalsea also symbolizes England itself, with its inmate citizens imprisoned by a legal system that ultimately denies justice by delaying it until victims such as William Dorrit—who is actually heir to a substantial fortune—are too broken by the system to shake off their prison mentality. After Dorrit is finally physically freed from the prison, he remains its psychological inmate.

Circumlocution Office. Imaginary government department described as the "most important . . . under Government." A place of bureaucracy and cynical disregard of the rights of citizens, it is the most comprehensive of Dickens's frequent depictions in his novels of governmental ineptness and oppressiveness. Its interminable tangle of red tape is the reason why Dorrit and other inmates unfairly languish in prison. The word "circumlocution" means "talking around," and this is what officials, members of the influential Barnacle and Stiltstalking families, do in the Circumlocution Office, while years pass without resolution of the issues on which the fates of the oppressed depend.

Clennam Counting House. London accounting firm near the River Thames. Early in the novel Arthur Clennam, the man whom Little Dorrit loves, comes "home" to the tottering structure in which previous generations of Clennams have carried on a family business. It is an old and decrepit building, which, but for "some half dozen gigantic crutches" that keep it propped up, would fall into the river. In an upstairs room that is virtually a prison in itself lives Arthur's reclusive and semi-invalided mother, a grasping woman who, for selfish reasons of her own, harbors a secret that if disclosed would free William Dorrit from Marshalsea. This is a place in which both moral and physical decay are tangible.

Bleeding Heart Yard. Poor London neighborhood inhabited by people afflicted in various ways by the Circumlocution Office and by greedy entrepreneurs, such as the Clennams and a rack-renting landlord named Casby. However, the inhabitants of the Yard are chiefly people of character who help those in need. Although they "bleed," these are people with "heart."

*London. Great Britain's capital city is the predominant larger setting in the novel. As the governmental, financial, and population center of England, London embodies the forces that must be redirected to permit the establishment of justice and decent living conditions for its citizenry.

*Swiss Alps. Favorite vacation ground for international travelers, to which the Dorrits go in the second half of the novel after they finally come into their fortune. There, the Dorrits find that while they can enjoy the pure air of freedom, they cannot escape their prison mentality.

*Venice. Northern Italian port city that is another European tourist mecca. Functioning similarly to the Alps, the flowing streets of this Italian city, delightful to its many visitors, bring no relief to the Dorrit family.

— *Robert P. Ellis*

THE LITTLE FOXES

Author: Lillian Hellman (1905-1984)
Type of work: Drama
Type of plot: Social realism

Time of plot: 1900
First performed: 1939; first published, 1939

The setting of this play is described simply as the Hubbards' living room in a small southern town. Its furnishings, though not of a particular style, are nevertheless of the finest quality. While the specific location is unclear, the fact that it is set in the South—and probably the Deep South—is central to the play.

*Deep South. Southern-most of the southern states. The South itself is an offstage and onstage presence that is at the very heart of the play. From the earliest moments in the play the South is described almost as a character, with feminine and masculine traits. Regina Hubbard embodies the graces of womanhood in the Old South as she flirts with the northern industrialist William Marshall. Ben Hubbard epitomizes those who, at the turn of the twentieth century, despoiled the South for private gain. The defining characteristics of the South shift from the pre-Civil War agricultural aristocracy that had once ruled, to the new wealth of industry and commerce. The mores and ethos of southern men and women are described as though they characterize the South itself. The audience begins to feel the presence of the South in a tangible way: It is a character in transition. From the ashes of a sentimental past the South will be transformed by a new industrialism bringing northern-style prosperity while exploiting poor white southerners and unlanded black southerners. The Hubbards will, in the end, destroy their beloved South in their drive for power, influence, and status through wealth. They will import the cotton mill along with all the social and economic misery it will cause.

— *Rhona Justice-Malloy*

LITTLE WOMEN

Author: Louisa May Alcott (1832-1888)
Type of work: Novel
Type of plot: Domestic realism

Time of plot: Mid-nineteenth century
First published: 1868-1869

Much of this novel takes place near a northern city during the Civil War. The suburb and city are never explicitly identified, but Louisa May Alcott spent her youth in Concord, a suburb of Boston. The novel depicts domestic scenes and a family's trials and successes.

March home. Home of the four March sisters, Meg, Jo, Beth, and Amy, in an unspecified northern city. The house is probably based on the Orchard House in Concord, where Alcott herself spent much of her youth. Alcott reveals few physical details about the March house; it seems to be threadbare but comfortable. The Marches live frugally because the girls' father has suffered financial reverses trying to help a friend. They often gather around the fireplace during the winter months, and Jo has scorched one of her best gowns by standing too close to the heat. The Marches' comfortable home contrasts with the dwelling of German immigrants to whom Mrs. March and the girls take food on Christmas Day. The Hummels' home has broken window panes, no heat, and no food; however, the Marches try to set things right before leaving.

Gardiner and **Moffat houses.** The comfortable but plain home of the Marches also contrasts with the more luxurious homes of the social-climbing Gardiners and Moffats. At a party at the Gardiner residence, Jo meets Theodore Laurence (Laurie), who is hiding in a curtained recess and realizes that he lives next door. Later, the novel follows Meg's activities at a party at the Moffats. It is here at "Vanity Fair" that Meg becomes troubled and angered when she overhears Mrs. Moffat suggesting that Mrs. March is scheming for one of her girls to marry Laurie.

Laurence mansion. Home of the prosperous Laurence family. It, too, provides a contrast to the Marches' home. Located immediately next door to the Marches' home, it is the home of the wealthy and kindly Grandfather Laurence and his grandson Laurie, who is about the same age as the March girls. At the beginning of the novel, the girls seem never to have visited the Laurence house; however, after Jo meets Laurie, they frequently visit the home. The mansion contains a conservatory filled with rare and beautiful plants, which to the March girls is almost a paradise. The mansion also contains a piano, which is particularly attractive to Beth, and a library which is attractive to Jo. One senses that this house reflects a concern with human values rather than mere wealth.

Great Aunt March's house. Another home depicted in detail is that of Jo's father's aunt. Jo visits her great aunt daily to take care of the cranky elderly woman. The house possesses a library that belonged to Great Aunt March's deceased husband, and Jo reads interesting books while the old lady sleeps and her parrot squawks out insults. At the end of *Little Women*, readers discover that Jo has inherited the house from Great Aunt March and plans to use it to open a school for boys.

*New York City. Finding that Laurie is too fond of her, Jo spends some time working in New York, where she lives in a rooming house in which she meets Professor Bhaer, to whom she becomes engaged near the end of the novel.

*Europe. Amy's visit to Europe signifies the girls' coming of age. Laurie visits her in southern France and Switzerland, while she is traveling with a rich aunt and is intent on improving her drawings. Laurie and Amy fall in love in Europe and marry there before returning to America. The marriage of the youngest of the March girls indicates that the March girls have indeed come of age.

— *Charles S. Pierce, Jr.*

LOLITA

Author: Vladimir Nabokov (1899-1977)
Type of work: Novel
Type of plot: Satire

Time of plot: 1910-1952
First published: 1955

An essential element of this novel is its depiction of the American landscape as seen through the European eyes of Humbert Humbert, a middle-aged intellectual who is doomed by his romantic obsession for Dolores (Lolita) Haze, a cheerfully vulgar comic-book-reading adolescent American girl.

*United States. In the course of the novel, the narrator, Humbert traverses the highways, towns, roadside attractions, hotels, motels, and tourist camps of most, if not all, of the forty-eight states of the United States, from Maine to California, as well as Alaska (which was not yet a state at the time the story is set). He does this first with Lolita, then alone, in search of her, after she is taken away from him. Humbert contrasts the canvas of America, with its natural landscapes of true beauty, dotted with garish billboards, gift shops, and gas stations, with what he calls "sweet, mellow, rotting Europe."

Early in his narrative, Humbert outlines his first journey with Lolita, from east to west and back again, through New England, past "corn belts and cotton belts," caverns and cabins, through mountains and deserts, and the "pale lilac fluff or flowering shrubs along forest roads" of the Pacific Northwest, and back to New England.

Their second trip, several years later, begins at Beardsley and takes them slowly through the Midwest and West, with stops in Kasbeam, where Humbert first becomes aware that they are being followed, and Wace, where they attend a summer theater with a play by Humbert's rival, Clare Quilty, another pedophile who is following their trail through the West, and finally to Elphinstone, a western town "on the flat floor of a seven-thousand-foot-high valley." There, Lolita falls ill, is hospitalized, and leaves the hospital with Quilty. Maddened with grief, Humbert follows their trail, stopping at hundreds of hotels, motels, and tourist homes, checking registers for the clues, which he finds in the form of mocking false names left by Quilty.

While the ironic vision and mocking voice of the novel's European narrator are turned upon many aspects of twentieth century American civilization to comic effect, Humbert does not mock when he describes the epic beauty of the American wilderness—a beauty to which native-born Lolita, who is bored by "scenery," is blind.

Hotel Mirana. Luxurious, palm-shaded hotel on the French Riviera owned by Humbert's father and the place where Humbert, at thirteen, met his first love, Annabel Leigh, the precursor to Lolita. The hotel remains, for Humbert, an enchanted childhood memory, a world of "clean sand, orange trees, friendly dogs, sea vistas and smiling faces." He searches for its twin in America but never finds it. The closest he comes is in a picture postcard in a museum devoted to hobbies at a Mississippi resort. The Mirana is a lost, graceful world that can never be regained, representing both Humbert's lost innocence and pre-World War II Europe.

Ramsdale. New England town, the "gem" of an unnamed eastern state, where Humbert meets Lolita and her mother. Through a series of chance referrals, Humbert rents a room there from the widow Charlotte Haze and meets her twelve-year-old daughter, Lolita. Humbert initially finds the **Haze house**, at 342 Lawn Street, unappealing; it is a shabby, grayish white-framed suburban house with mismatched furniture and a rubber tube attached to the tub faucet instead of a shower. However, the moment he glimpses the pubescent Lolita in the garden, he decides to stay—a decision ultimately fatal to all.

Vladimir Nabokov's descriptions of Ramsdale, its citizens, and its social life are satirical, highlighting the pretentiousness, snobbery, and cultural vacuity of the American middle-class suburb. From the fuzzy pink cozy covering the toilet seat in Charlotte's house to disparaging remarks her friends make about Italian tradesmen, Nabokov skewers with perfect, telling detail the false gentility and provincialism of suburban life.

Hourglass Lake. Lake near Ramsdale, whose name Humbert mishears as "Our Glass Lake." Humbert contemplates using the lake to drown Charlotte, whom he marries in order to be near Lolita, but cannot do it. Ironically, Charlotte dies shortly after his failed murder attempt when, blinded by tears after learning of Humbert's true reason for marrying her, she rushes into the street, where she is struck by a car and killed.

Beardsley. Sleepy New England town where Humbert resettles with Lolita after her mother dies. The town is home to Beardsley College, where Humbert teaches. Lolita attends the Beardsley School for Girls, as she and her lover, Humbert, pretend to be a normal daughter and father.

Enchanted Hunters. New England country inn to which Humbert takes Lolita after her mother dies and where, he claims, Lolita seduces him. Located in **Briceland**, a secluded town of "phony colonial architecture, curiosity shops and imported shade trees," the inn plays an important role in the fatalistic twistings of the novel's plot. On its dark veranda Humbert first encounters Clare Quilty, the decadent playwright who later takes Lolita away from him. Quilty also later writes a play called *The Enchanted Hunters*, in which Lolita is to star at her school.

Murals in the inn's dining room depict a fantasy scene of hunters and dryads in a forest. Later, Humbert notices similarities between the unknown muralist's work and the plot of Quilty's play; however, he imagines them both to be based on some common New England legend. It is not until the novel's end that he learns of Quilty's earlier presence at the inn and his role in Lolita's disappearance.

Gray Star. Settlement in Alaska, described as "the remotest Northwest," where eighteen-year-old Dolores Haze, now Mrs. Richard Schiller, dies in childbirth on Christmas Day in 1952, a little more than a month after Humbert dies in prison.

— *Kathryn Kulpa*

A LONG AND HAPPY LIFE

Author: Reynolds Price (1933-   )
Type of work: Novel
Type of plot: Domestic realism

Time of plot: 1957
First published: 1962

Rural north-central North Carolina is the setting for this novel, whose action revolves around white and African American churches, a thick wood holding a hidden spring within, and the homes of its characters. Services in the two churches—a funeral and a nativity play—dramatize the beginning and completion of the heroine's emotional journey.

Mount Moriah Church. African American church in a rural North Carolina community at which the novel opens with the funeral of Mildred Sutton, a childhood friend of the novel's white protagonist, Rosacoke Mustian.

Alston's woods. Wooded area owned by the community's oldest member, Mr. Isaac Alston, once a relatively powerful resident of the area, now nearly helpless after a stroke, that is the scene of Rosacoke and Wesley's first encounter. The woods contain a pecan grove. The autumn leaves are gone from its trees, but nuts are still hanging on the branches. Sitting high in a tree, the handsome self-contained young Wesley shakes down handfuls of nuts to Rosacoke and also imprints her forever. Within the woods in a broomstraw field, beyond Alton's hidden spring, Rosacoke gives herself to Wesley. He is gentle, but does not seem to value the magnitude of her gift nor understand the depth of her sorrow at feeling so lonely afterward.

Mason's Lake. Private pleasure lake, with a bathhouse, a tin slide, and a diving platform, but only a few trees, most of them having been bulldozed when the owner created the swimming facility. At the Delight Baptist Church picnic Rosacoke watches her brother Milo and Wesley at play in the leech-infested water as she sits with her widowed mother, her younger sister, and her brother's pregnant wife, Sissie. Also on the shore is Marise Gupton, prematurely aged from constant childbearing.

Mustian house. Simple home in which Rosacoke, Milo, Rato (now in the army), and Baby Sister have grown up. The house has a black tin roof that absorbs the sun, making Rosacoke's bedroom directly under the eaves hot and oppressive and leaving a yellow rust stain on her ceiling. There is a wood stove in the kitchen and not much privacy for Milo and his wife as Sissie's home delivery date approaches, and later, her long painful labor that will result in a stillborn boy.

Delight Baptist Church. Community church to which Rosacoke's family belongs. While Rosacoke is secretly pregnant and more lonely than ever, she is pushed into playing the part of Mary in the traditional Christmas Eve pageant. Wesley plays one of the Three Wise Men.

— *Nan C. L. Scott*

LONG DAY'S JOURNEY INTO NIGHT

Author: Eugene O'Neill (1888-1953)
Type of work: Drama
Type of plot: Psychological realism

Time of plot: August, 1912
First performed: 1956; first published, 1956

The Tyrone family's summer home in New London, Connecticut, is the setting of this play. Specifically, four family members in the living room of that home on a summer day wrestle with the extreme dysfunction of their intertwined lives. Ironically, it is the very lack of a proper, permanent, and respectable home that Mrs. Tyrone suggests may be at the root of their problems.

*New London. Connecticut town that was both the boyhood and young-adult home of Eugene O'Neill, who employs it as the setting of this markedly autobiographical drama. The family's summer home is modestly furnished with items of lesser value than one would expect for a wealthy, successful actor. His modest rooms are also dimly lit in the night scenes, because Mr. Tyrone wishes to save money on the electric bill.

One feature of this house that plays a prominent, almost haunting role in each scene is the spare room upstairs. There it is that Mrs. Tyrone withdraws from the rest of the family to give herself shots of morphine, to which she is addicted. An eerie aura also surrounds this house because of the dense fog, which rolls in from Long Island Sound and enshrouds it.

Another aspect of New London and the Tyrone family's interaction with its citizens is important to the meaning of the play. The family is not the social equal of the prominent families in this ocean-side city. Mr. Tyrone has made his fortune by acting, a profession of some disrepute in his day. The addictions which afflict his wife and two sons (morphine, alcohol, and dissolute lifestyles) further isolate the Tyrones from the more substantial and well-respected residents of New London. The social isolation of the Tyrones is mirrored symbolically in their fog-enshrouded house.

*Broadway. Great theater district of New York City in which Mr. Tyrone makes his fortune. It is also referred to disparagingly throughout the play as a place of frivolous adult playtime. It is a place where Jamie Tyrone, a reprobate in his father's eyes, idles away his time drinking and womanizing.

*Hilltown Sanatorium. Mentioned in the last act of the play as Edmund's destination, where he goes for six months to cure his tuberculosis. It is a climactic point in the drama when it is revealed that Edmund's father is sending him to a state-run facility usually reserved for charity cases. Mr. Tyrone, ever fearful of poverty, will even sacrifice his young son to possible death at an ill-equipped sanatorium rather than pay for a more expensive, private facility.

While Hilltown is a fictitious name, it was based on an actual Connecticut public sanatorium. This real place was a wood-frame farmhouse in an isolated, hilly town about ten miles west of New Haven, in which terminal tubercular patients were housed. The sanatorium itself was named "Laurel Heights." O'Neill actually stayed there for less than forty-eight hours, while the physician in charge contacted the playwright's father and forced him to transfer O'Neill to a more appropriate, private sanatorium.

— *Patricia E. Sweeney*

THE LONG JOURNEY

Author: Johannes V. Jensen (1873-1950)
Type of work: Novels
Type of plot: Epic
Time of plot: Prehistoric to historic

First published: Den lange rejse, 1908-1922,
   6 volumes (English translations, 1922-1924,
   3 volumes: *Fire and Ice*, 1922; *The Cimbrians*,
   1923; *Christopher Columbus*, 1924)

This six-volume epic describes the colonizing exploits of a branch of the human race who thrive in northern latitudes by virtue of their domestication of fire. The epic's incompatibility with modern palaeontological accounts of human prehistory has consigned it to the company of the creation-myths it attempts to account for, but its metaphorical map of the journey from Stone Age tribalism to modern civilization retains a defiant lyrical grandeur.

Gunung Api. Volcano in whose vicinity the Forest Folk first domesticate fire in *Fire and Ice*. Its exact location is unspecified, but it lies on the far side of the Baltic Sea from Sealand. Its slopes are surrounded by the vast and richly populated Forest of Change: a paradise whose memory gives rise to the myths of Eden, the Isles of the Blest, and the world-tree Ygdrasil, while Gunung Api itself is the archetype of Loki and Lucifer. Gunung Api's ultimate fate is to be ground down by glaciation and deposited as shingle in the Baltic, but the fire it provides allows a distinctive people—formed by an intermingling of the Forest Folk and the Ice Folk—to thrive in Scandinavia. They follow a nomadic existence as hunter-gatherers, whose legacy is a hereditary restlessness, until the crucial inventions of agriculture and animal husbandry permit a further diversification of folkways.

*Sealand. Major eastern landmass of what is now Denmark; part of an archipelago separating the Baltic Sea from the Cattegat channel. A Sealand fjord is the birthplace of Norna Gest, the immortal hero of *The Cimbrians* and rediscoverer of the technological rudiments of seafaring. The development of sailing ships allows Gest's family to colonize Sweden before he embarks on a world-encompassing odyssey in search of the Land of the Dead.

Migration routes. Gest's fellows institute a great Stone Age migration, crossing the Baltic and penetrating the heart of continental Europe, then proceeding across Asia, eventually moving across the land bridge, where the Bering Strait now is, into the Americas (where Gest is long remembered in Tenochtitlán as Quetzalcoatl). Some move south from Asia into the South Seas, while others meet up again with the descendants of the Forest Folk who have remained in southern Europe, Asia Minor, and Africa all the while. Further waves of migration continually reiterate the elements of this pattern, including the one taking place in the early centuries of the Common Era, which brings Christophorus and the Longobards southward from the Gothic homeland in the first part of *Christopher Columbus*.

*Jutland. Continental part of Denmark, to which Gest frequently returns as a *scald*. Cimberland, the doomed heartland of the pagan culture featured in the second part of *The Cimbrians*, is a hilly tableland in the northern region, bounded by the Limfjord.

*Rome. Center of the Mediterranean empire disrupted by the descendants of the displaced Cimbrians and the allies they make on their trek through Gaul. Rome's slave-market, through which the women of the defeated Cimbrians are sold, becomes the principal conduit by which the spirit of the north reinfects the world formulated by the descendants of the ancient Forest Folk. In the garden of the sculptor Cheiron, beside the river Tiber, Vedis is immortalized in her own way.

*St. George's Church. Church in Palos, Spain, in which a service is held in August, 1492, for the crews of the three departing ships commanded by the eponymous hero of *Christopher Columbus*. Its appearance is momentary, but carries tremendous symbolic significance because the preceding section of the narrative has established a key metaphor by which the architectural design of actual churches, and the Roman Catholic Church as an institution, recapitulate the image of a ship akin to that which carried Norna Gest away from Sealand and began the first great migration.

*Santa Maria. Columbus's flagship, whose actual historical significance is further increased by its symbolic identification with the Church—an association which permits Columbus's arrival in the Americas to broaden out almost immediately into a wide-ranging synoptic account of the European colonization of the continent. The *Santa Maria* continues as a phantom; her course intersects that of the HMS *Beagle*—the ship that centuries later carries Charles Darwin on his epoch-making journey of discovery to the Americas—en route to the stars.

— Brian Stableford

THE LONGEST JOURNEY

Author: E. M. Forster (1879-1970)
Type of work: Novel
Type of plot: Social realism

Time of plot: Early twentieth century
First published: 1907

The tripartite division of this novel follows place designations—Cambridge, Sawston, and Wiltshire, locations that serve as metaphors for several things. Among other things they represent the three stages in Richard (Rickie) Elliot's evolution on his "longest journey" of life. By the same token. Cambridge represents truth; Sawston, crassness; and Wiltshire, recovery and rebirth.

*Cambridge University. Prestigious English institution of higher learning at which Rickie is studying through the first part of the novel. Rickie's rooms at one of the colleges are closely identified with a happy and inquiring frame of mind, all the more so as his intellectual hero, student-philosopher Steward Ansell, is nearby. Rickie's drawing room has a fireplace, a sofa, a table, chairs, a piano, and a painting on a wall. The opening scene set here keynotes the entire novel inasmuch as Rickie and his fellow students, led by Ansell, are having a philosophical discussion on the nature of reality.

With no permanent home since he was orphaned at fifteen, and crippled by a congenital foot deformity, Rickie regards Cambridge as a secluded shelter between the stormy seas of his unhappy childhood and the uncertain world awaiting him in the future. Cambridge stands for friendliness, sensitivity, and mutual consideration. As he does with people, Rickie endows places with absolute beauty and goodness.

Sawston School. Boarding and day school for boys in an unspecified suburban community where Rickie goes to teach. There, he lives with his new wife, Agnes, and her brother, Herbert Pembroke, the master of Dunwood House, the school's largest building. There, Rickie shares a study with Herbert. The house's large saffron drawing room is full of cozy corners and dumpy chairs that receive parents. Nothing in the house is accidental. Everything is planned, contrasting with Rickie's rooms at Cambridge, with their casual jumble of items, which find their way to Sawston and are placed hither and yon.

Modeled on E. M. Forster's own Tonbridge School, Sawston is a modern complex with classrooms, dormitories, cubicles, studies, a preparation room, a dining room, hot-air pipes, and parquet floors. Sawston is also a symbol of some of the negative aspects of British middle-class values, with their emphasis on conformity and deadening conventions. It is also a representation of Great Britain's imperial past and presumed imperial future, with portraits of empire-builders all around. Sawston worships success, not truth; it promotes personal power, not close human relationships. It seeks to develop *esprit de corps*, not brotherhood. In short, it is a regulated and hierarchical world.

At Sawston, Rickie is stuck in a dreary marriage to a scheming gold-digger after his inheritance, and his daughter dies soon after her birth. Sawston is thus not only the site of his nightmare but also the setting for a contagious emotional and spiritual deterioration.

Cadover. Estate in Wiltshire of the unlovely, spiteful and sardonic Mrs. Emily Failing, Rickie's aunt on his father's side. Her residence—which Forster modeled on Acton House near Felton, Northumberland—was built around 1800 in the Roman style of architecture highlighted by several pilasters stretching from its top to its bottom. There, her ward, Stephen Wonham (who is eventually revealed as Rickie's half-brother), lives in an attic room illuminated by a single round window above eye level.

Cadover includes a railroad crossing, the scene of the novel's denouement in which the drunken Stephen, lying on the tracks, is rescued from an oncoming train by Rickie, who is nevertheless killed by it.

*Wiltshire. County in southern England to which references occur throughout the novel. It is represented as the place where the "fibres of England unite"—a place where one gets a sense of historic continuity. To Rickie, Wiltshire offers a happier alternative way of life. While Sawston represents competition and worldly success, Wiltshire stands for a mode of life in which instinct and direct physical experience rank above both the practical rationality of Sawston and the intellectualism of Cambridge.

— Peter B. Heller

LOOK BACK IN ANGER

Author: John Osborne (1929-1994)
Type of work: Drama
Type of plot: Protest drama

Time of plot: 1950's
First performed: 1956; first published, 1957

This play's simple setting of a one-room flat in an industrial city in the English Midlands was an innovative setting for the contemporary theater of its time. The shabbiness of its interior stood in marked contrast to the upper- and middle-class settings of most then-popular drama.

English Midlands. Central region of England in which the play is set. Midlands counties contain the country's major industrial cities, such as Manchester, Birmingham, Liverpool, Sheffield, and Leeds. Factories dominate their urban landscapes, and their residents are largely working-class. Historically, the Midlands have often been viewed with condescension by more cosmopolitan residents of London, Oxford, and Cambridge. Relatively few literary works prior to the 1950's were set in the Midlands, and the distinctive northern accent was rarely heard on stage.

Porters' flat. Described as "a fairly large attic room, at the top of a large Victorian house," the one-room apartment of Jimmy and Alison Porter is an example of the trend derided as "kitchen-sink realism" by some critics during the 1950's and 1960's. In stark contrast to the stylish and elegant upper- and middle-class settings of then-popular plays by Noël Coward and others, Osborne's setting is economically downscale. Its furniture is "simple and rather old," including two "shabby" armchairs. A double bed takes up much of the space along the back wall.

As in plays by Tennessee Williams, the mere presence of the young married couple's bed on stage connotes a certain frankness about sexuality that was considered daring for its time—as does Alison's being seen wearing only a slip during the second act. Books crowd the shelves and cover the chest of drawers, indicating that Jimmy Porter, though of working-class background, is educated, in contrast to virtually all working-class characters depicted in literature earlier. The fact that on Sundays he reads the "only two posh papers," which are strewn about the room, also indicates his level of intelligence and interest in the larger world, though he complains that the London-based book reviews all sound the same. The ironing-board symbolizes Alison's unfortunate status in the marriage and the domestic subordination of women in the 1950's, though her parents are more middle-class than her husband's.

University. Unnamed institution of higher learning that Jimmy apparently attended but left early. He alludes to a university that is "not even red brick, but white tile." In contrast to Oxford and Cambridge, where England's social and intellectual elites are educated amid buildings of centuries-old gray stone, "red brick" universities were primarily twentieth century institutions that were more accessible to the public. White tiles are associated with public toilets.

— *William Hutchings*

LOOK HOMEWARD, ANGEL: A Story of the Buried Life

Author: Thomas Wolfe (1900-1938)
Type of work: Novel
Type of plot: Impressionistic realism

Time of plot: 1900 to early 1920's
First published: 1929

An autobiographical account of the author's struggles to escape from his family and the provincialism of the South, this novel is a fictionalized account of his early life in North Carolina.

Altamont. North Carolina town in which most of the action takes place. Modeled on Thomas Wolfe's own hometown, Asheville, in western North Carolina, Altamont is a mountain resort town that serves as a frequent stopover for travelers commuting between eastern Tennessee and Charleston, South Carolina.

Gant often visits his sister at her home in the state capital of North Carolina. Eventually, she returns to Altamont to care for their dying father. Her experiences serve as a vivid reminder of how Altamont retains a hold on all of its inhabitants—a hold that author Thomas Wolfe—in the fictional guise of Eugene Gant—was determined to escape.

Dixieland. Altamont boardinghouse owned by Eliza Gant, protagonist Eugene Gant's mother, in which Gant spends most of his childhood. There he develops a deep disdain for boarders. Described as "America's Switzerland" by his mother, Eliza, who owns the house, it is situated in a bustling and growing section of Altamont. The house contains at least twenty rooms; throughout the novel, additions are made to include additional living and dining spaces for the family, bathrooms, a sleeping porch, and a larger dining room for the boarders.

As in many family-owned boardinghouses, members of the Gant family are relegated to small, often damp and dark, living quarters, leaving the finest rooms for paying guests. The house is often not used in winter seasons, and the young Gant prefers to spend time at his father's home because it is smaller, more intimate, and always has a roaring fireplace. Throughout the entire novel, Eliza Gant is obsessed with the acquisition of property, and while she continues to reside at Dixieland, several scenes unfold around her burgeoning real estate business.

Pulpit Hill. North Carolina town that is home to the state's leading university serves as the primary setting for part three of the novel. Its name is an obvious play on Chapel Hill, site of the University of North Carolina. Located in the central part of the state, the university stands in an area of remote pastoral wilderness. The center of Pulpit Hill itself is dominated by faculty houses and university buildings that reflect some of the excesses associated with post-American Revolution neo-Greek archi-tecture, with oversized columns and pillars. Gant often compares Pulpit Hill to an outpost of the Roman Empire, but amid its ivied walls, ancient trees, and gallantly decorated fraternity houses, the town is a tangible reminder of state power and authority in the South.

At age fifteen, Gant, now an articulate gifted student, enters the university filled with romantic notions of academic life. However, these are quickly shattered by abusive older classmates. This setting plays a pivotal role in Gant's growing desire for a life of isolation and contemplation after experiencing the brutal harshness of peer pressure and the social caste system at Pulpit Hill.

As World War I escalates and the United States is drawn in, the university setting reveals the nation being captivated by patriotism and the heroic pageantry often associated with war.

Norfolk. Virginia port city to which Gant goes to seek work after the United States enters World War I. This setting is filled with character sketches of men who fascinate Gant. The bustle of the piers, the movement of ships, and the forbidden nature of brothels contrast sharply with the places Gant is previously familiar with. Streets strewn with military materiel and the rustling trucks commandeered by stevedores provide scenes suggesting great wealth, large-scale spending, and forbidden pleasures.

While in Norfolk, Gant lives in cheap hotels, heat-infested boardinghouses, and the YMCA, where he shares sleeping quarters with forty drunken sailors. After exhausting his savings, he attempts to find work as a carpenter or mason, but because he possesses no skills, he eventually works as a numbers checker for work gangs that clear land of tree stumps and fill swamps. Perhaps predictably, he blows his earnings during a week of debauchery in Norfolk and again finds himself penniless.

Although eras of wartime production are often depicted as prosperous periods in American history, Gant's experiences in wartime Norfolk are filled with horrific scenes of poverty, hunger, and despair. In the end, Gant uses these experiences to justify his rejection of politics, moving him to forsake materialism and utopian causes for a solitary life of literary pursuits.

— *Robert D. Ubriaco, Jr.*

LOOKING BACKWARD: 2000-1887

Author: Edward Bellamy (1850-1898)
Type of work: Novel
Type of plot: Utopian

Time of plot: 1887 and 2000
First published: 1888

After the insomniac narrator of this novel, Julian West, pays a hypnotist to help him fall asleep in 1887, he awakens in Boston in the year 2000, where he finds the utopian society that his narrative describes.

Leete house. Private residence of the retired physician and scientist Dr. Leete in which Julian awakens. At first the Leete home appears so similar to the private homes to which Julian is accustomed that he does not perceive that any appreciable time has elapsed. He thinks he is in the home of some contemporary who is his social equal and a member of the educated middle class. In 1887 members of the middle class signaled their status with possessions. This fact suggests that when he awakens, he finds himself within a typical Victorian home, with heavy draperies, dark and ornate wooden furniture, and an abundance of bric-a-brac and works of art. The most dramatic changes are ones that to West are not immediately apparent, such as delivery of music to homes via the telephone system and the absence of household servants. It is not until West sees the city outside Leete's house that he recognizes that he really did sleep through the twentieth century.

Boston (2000). The future Boston is a city startling to Julian in its orderliness, cleanliness, and quiet. From the roof of the Leete home he sees the city laid out in neat blocks with wide tree-lined streets and numerous park areas. The only features he recognizes from his own time are geological, such as the Charles River, which separates Boston from Cambridge. Islands in Boston Harbor confirm that he is indeed in his native city. When he explores the city on his own, he is baffled by its lack of shops. The numerous small stores with display windows that lined nineteenth century Boston streets are gone, as are the taverns once common to city neighborhoods. Anonymous monumental buildings have taken their place. Bostonians still shop, but in buildings remarkably akin to what twenty-first century readers know as discount stores; exteriors of these buildings provide no clues as to their functions. Inside, customers may examine goods and compare products without the help of clerks, merchants do not haggle, products all bear clearly labeled set prices, and customers pay with debit cards issued by the government.

***Boston (1887).** The Boston of Julian's own time is a noisy, smelly, and crowded city. Its streets are lined with shops in which customers have no direct contact with merchandise. When they enter they see counters behind which the proprietors stand, and they must ask clerks to show them products and tell them their prices. Boston's streets are narrow, filthy, and winding, still reflecting the original foot paths from colonial times, and the air is thick with industrial pollution and coal smoke. Soot and grime coat everything. Pedestrians crossing streets must dodge mud and horse dung. Although Boston had public parks in 1887, Edward Bellamy does not mention them. Instead, his narrator's native Boston is a rough and dangerous city, one that is changing and not for the better.

Julian West's house. Narrator's home in nineteenth century Boston. The neighborhood around his house is filled with squalid tenement buildings and factories. His family has owned his house for generations, but he plans to build a new house in a better neighborhood before getting married, as his old family home is no longer suitable for a middle-class family. The nearby tenements are populated by poor people and recent immigrants, two groups of people to whom middle-class women should never be exposed. Street noises are so noisome and pervasive at all hours of the night and day that Julian had to construct a sound-proof room in his cellar for sleeping The Boston of 1887 is a most unpleasant city in which to live.

— *Nancy Farm Mannikko*

LORD JIM

Author: Joseph Conrad (Jósef Teodor Konrad Nałęcz
   Korzeniowski, 1857-1924)
Type of work: Novel

Type of plot: Psychological realism
Time of plot: Late nineteenth century
First published: 1900

*Seaports and jungles of South and East Asia, from the Indian Ocean to the Malaysian archipelago, form the set-
ting for an Englishman's voyage of self-discovery and redemption.*

Veranda. Porch with comfortable chairs and side tables located somewhere in the East—apparently in one of Great Britain's colonial territories—where men gather into the tropical evening for long conversations. Throughout the night they listen as Marlowe, the narrator of the novel, recounts the story of a man named Jim. In the darkness, Marlowe's words alone must carry the narrative.

Patna. Old steamer on which Jim serves as chief mate during an ill-fated voyage. A rusty, ill-tended vessel, the *Patna* sails from an unnamed port—most likely on the west coast of India—carrying Muslims on their pilgrimage to Mecca in Saudi Arabia. During the transit described in the novel, some eight hundred pilgrims are aboard the dangerously overcrowded ship; many sleep on deck and in the holds below.

Little more than a derelict, the *Patna* has rusty bulkheads and antiquated engines. The only place of comfort is its bridge, which catches some breezes as the ship steams through the night. Jim is on duty on the bridge when the ship collides with some unknown object in the water. Because the ship appears on the verge of sinking, the captain and his European crew—including Jim— abandon both it and their passengers. However, despite the damage it sustains, the *Patna* does not sink and is later taken under tow by a French vessel. The resulting inquiry and Jim's search for redemption for his own cowardice provide the mainspring for what follows in the novel.

Courtroom. Colonial administrative building, probably in India, where a panel investigates the *Patna* incident. There Jim is the only member of the ship's crew to testify and accept responsibility for deserting the ship's passengers. For no particular reason, Marlowe attends this hearing and it is there that he first comes to know Jim. Afterward, he and Jim encounter one another in the street and strike up a friendship. Stripped of his certification as a chief mate, Jim afterward moves about in the Orient, seeking redemption for his act of cowardice.

Patusan. Remote district of a native-ruled state in the Malay archipelago. About forty miles inland from the sea, it is located on a river between two prominent hills with a deep fissure between them—a geographical fact that may be interpreted as a symbolic reference to Jim's own divided nature. Patusan is nominally ruled by a corrupt rajah who allows his subjects to be robbed and extorted by a series of local strongmen. This situation is possible because Patusan is dominated by an old European fort whose rusty cannon can easily overwhelm the local residents. Sent to Patusan as a trading agent by Marlowe, Jim restores order to the community, whose people gratefully dub him "Tuan (Lord) Jim." Jim thereby achieves some peace of mind but when his well-intentioned actions in a later crisis cost the lives of villagers, he willingly allows himself to be shot as an act of penance.

Malabar House. Social club at an unspecific location that is frequented by English and other Europeans doing business in the East. There, amid wicker chairs, potted plants, and little octagonal tables with candles shielded in glass globes, Jim first tells Marlowe his story in a long and sometimes excited oral narrative. The gulf between Jim's experience on the rusty steamer *Patna* and the background and expectations of the European settlers and merchants is highlighted by the setting, which attempts to re-create, as much as possible, the atmosphere of a conventional English club.

*Asian port cities. After losing his certification as a ship's mate, Jim moves about among such cities as Bombay, Calcutta, Rangoon, Penang, and Batavia, working as a water-clerk. As a water-clerk, he acts as advance salesperson for ships' chandlers that sell nautical goods and supplies. It is his job to solicit business from ships newly arrived in port and steer their captains to do business with his employers. Although he is an outstanding

water-clerk he continues to move eastward, leaving each job as word of his connection with the *Patna* affair reaches the port. Marlowe sometimes encounters Jim in these ports, while at other times he hears of the man's restless journey ever eastward.

— *Michael Witkoski*

LORD OF THE FLIES

Author: William Golding (1911-1993)
Type of work: Novel
Type of plot: Fable

Time of plot: The future, during a nuclear war
First published: 1954

In this novel, a tropical Pacific island with lush vegetation and a pristine beach provides unrestrained freedom for a group of British schoolboys stranded when their airliner goes down and leaves them the only survivors. Their idealized island playground becomes a war zone for the boys until a British cruiser finds and rescues them.

Pacific island. Unnamed tropical island on which the novel is mainly set. The island serves as a metaphor for society in general, providing the setting for the boys' trials and adventures. Through the use of the only symbol of authority they have, a conch shell, they try to re-create British civilized society. The conch, like a whistle, yields an assembly of older boys and "littluns." Throughout the novel, the group who identify themselves as choir boys, and are under the leadership of Jack, progressively stray from the civilized behavior of the assembly area and into irresponsible anarchy.

The Scar. Meeting place where the boys, led by Ralph, hold assemblies in imitation of Great Britain's Parliament. Created by the plane crash, free of tropical vegetation, and level and sandy, it is the site of three crude huts. It is also the site of the docking of the rescue cutter that comes ashore from the cruiser.

Mountain. Site selected by Piggy and Ralph as the most obvious place to build a signal fire for smoke, the means of attracting rescuers. Irresponsibility by the littluns allows the fire to get out of control, taking the life of a littlun. Jack's hunters cause the keepers of the fire to abandon it for the joy of hunting. The fire goes out; the

possible rescue ship passes without seeing the smoke. The mountain is also the place of "the beast" that Simon sees.

Castle Rock. Headquarters of Jack's gang, this place is unlike the rest of the island. This piece of rock, barren of vegetation, is slightly set apart from the main part of the island. Easily defended, this rocky place is the site of the violent death first of Simon, then of Piggy, and the planned site of Ralph's violent death. However, Ralph escapes to the thick tropical vegetation of the main island.

Altar of the "lord of the flies." Sacrificial site, located in the tropical forest, at which a slaughtered sow's head stuck on a sharp stick drips with blood and is covered with flies. This is also the site of Simon's hallucination or conversation with the beast, wherein he recognizes that this beast is the evil within all humanity, not an external force or form. Instead of creating fear in Simon, as it does in the hunters, this beast seems able to communicate with Simon.

Tropical jungle. Simon's place, where he goes to observe nature and contemplate the evil and violence within each of the boys. This is also the place where Ralph finds sanctuary when the hunters set the island on fire, hoping to smoke him out and use his severed head in sacrificial ritual.

Latrine. Communal toilet area, away from fresh water and huts, that allows a vestige of British civilization until it is abandoned by the boys in favor of irresponsible freedom.

Cruiser. British warship that represents safety, comfort, rescue, and civilized society, even though it may be headed into unsafe water in wartime conditions. To the boys, however, it is salvation.

— *Anna Hollingsworth Hovater*

LORNA DOONE: A Romance of Exmoor

Author: R. D. Blackmore (1825-1900)
Type of work: Novel
Type of plot: Adventure

Time of plot: Late seventeenth century
First published: 1869

Set in mostly real places during the midst of real historical events, this long-popular adventure novel features dramatic moorland settings.

*****Exmoor.** Moorland in southern England overlapping the counties of Somerset and Devon. The flat sweep of moorland south of Plover's Barrows farm has bogs here and there with brushy areas around them. Deep ravines run inland from the sea. The fertile valleys are either wooded or farmed.

Exmoor has changed little since the time in which *Lorna Doone* is set. From his childhood home in nearby Newton, Glamorganshire, R. D. Blackmore could see the heights of Exmoor. The roads across the moors are often deep in mud and prone to being covered with dense fog. Dulverton, the home town of John Ridd's great-uncle Reuben Huckaback lies at the southern edge of the moor.

Plover's Barrows. Farm of the protagonist and narrator, John Ridd. Located in the East Lynn River valley, it is the largest of three farms in the valley and is the closest to the coast. The farmyard is surrounded by outbuildings—a barn, a corn-chamber, a cider press, a cow house, and stables—and orchards lie beyond. The farm's rooms are underground so that both people and animals are warmer in winter and cooler in summer. The farmhouse has a kitchen and parlor downstairs and several rooms upstairs. John Ridd's room, under the rafters, faces east and from the latticed window he can see the yard, the wood-rick, and the church in the village of Oare in the distance.

Doone Valley. Home of the outlaw Doone clan; an oval-shaped green valley surrounded by eighty- to one-hundred-foot cliffs of sheer black rock. The valley is traversed by a winding stream, on the banks of which are fourteen one-story square houses built of stone and wood. Sir Ensor Doone's house is closest to the Doone-gate. Carver Doone's house is lowest in the valley.

Doone-gate. Entrance to Doone Valley. Approached along a straight track, it has three archways, above which a huge tree trunk is suspended, ready to be dropped to bar entrance to the valley. A ledge twenty feet above the road provides a good defensive position. Inside the central archway, a crude cannon guards the entrance. Sentries are posted in a niche part way along the passage.

Another approach to the valley lies hidden in an ash wood. A wooden door leads to a low, narrow passage which comes out at the top of Doone valley.

*****Bagworthy Water** (BADJ-wer-thee). Called "Badgworthy Water" on modern maps, a stream that flows two miles below Plover's Barrow, into the Lynn River Valley. On either side of Bagworthy Water lies dense Bagworthy Wood. Following the water upstream through the wood, it opens into a pool. At one side water cascades over a cliff as a water slide.

At the top of the cliff is the secluded area of Doone Valley in which John Ridd meets Lorna Doone, an ostensible member of the outlaw family. At the top of the slide, Lorna's bower is reached by stone steps leading to a narrow ivy-covered crevice. The chamber, open to the sky, is eighteen or twenty feet across, and its walls are adorned with living ferns, moss and lichens. Grass and moss cover the floor, around the edge of which are seats of living stone.

*London. Great Britain's capital city, which John Ridd first visits in 1683. In contrast to Exmoor, London is a hideous and dirty place, although some of its shops and their signs are very fine. Its streets are very noisy, filled with coaches and people and footmen rushing about. John takes lodgings in the house of a fellmonger abutting the Strand. which runs from Temple Bar to Charing (then a village surrounded by fields). The house of Earl Brandir, Lorna's guardian, is at Kensington. It is approached along a lane between fields from Charing Cross.

Wizard's Slough. Mire in Exmoor in which Carver Doone dies. Located at the end of a gully south of Black Barrow Down, the slough is a black, bubbling bog ringed by yellow reeds. Bright green watergrass hides it from the unwary. On the margins grow plants such as campanula, sundew, and forget-me-not. The surrounding hillsides are dotted with tufts of rush, flag (water iris), and marestail, and a few alder-trees. No birds dwell here. On the far side of the mire is the vertical shaft of the entrance to the gold mine exploited by Reuben Huckaback. There is a path between the cliff and the slough, but it is not easy to find.

— *Pauline Morgan*

LOST HORIZON

Author: James Hilton (1900-1954)
Type of work: Novel
Type of plot: Adventure

Time of plot: 1931
First published: 1933

This story describes a refuge from the social and political ills of the world. The refuge is defined almost entirely by what it is not, being sharply contrasted with the other locations in the novel, such as Peking (Beijing), Macao, Shanghai, Yokohama, and Honolulu. These real places map out a journey through various regions of the real world, while the imaginary covert of Shangri-La is the kind of earthly paradise that such heroes as Conway truly deserve.

Shangri-La. Lamasery in the Karakoram mountains of Tibet, situated on the lower slopes of a peak called Karakal ("Blue Moon"), whose elevation of 28,000 feet makes it nearly the equal of Mount Everest. The lamasery consists of a group of blue-roofed pavilions, delicately poised on the mountainside above a fertile valley. The lamasery is rich in decorative Chinoiserie but it also has an excellent library. Although it is on the site of a much older Buddhist lamasery, its present construction dates from 1734, when Father Perrault—then a Capuchin friar—took up residence prior to developing his own syncretic amalgam of Eastern and Western religious ideas. It is, therefore, a hybrid erection, grafting modern Christian ideals onto a Buddhist base, looking up all the while at an unscalable peak.

Shangri-La reminds Conway, just a little, of Oxford University. Having been deeply disillusioned and spiritually wounded by World War I and its aftermath, Conway naturally looks back to his college days with deep nostalgia. Common parlance calls Oxford a "city of dreaming spires" and a collage of "ivory towers," and Shangri-La's architecture and elevation are presented in similar terms. Its loftiness is, however, associated with a particular kind of atmosphere: clean, refined, and exceedingly beneficial to the health. The text carefully points out that "la" is the Tibetan word for a mountain pass, emphasizing that the lamasery is also a metaphorical gateway, offering a passage to a way of being that is far superior to anything available in the modern, civilized world.

The valley below the lamasery is a peaceful utopia whose citizens are happy to submit to the benevolent dictatorship of the lamas. Laws are unnecessary to ensure order because the valley's inhabitants are so carefully schooled in courtesy that disputes never become violent. All this is part of a legacy, an estate, in both senses of the word, which Perrault now desires to leave to a suitable heir. If Conway were an aristocrat he would probably have an estate awaiting him at home, but he is not, and his sense of duty is oriented toward the grandiose political institutions and ambitions of the British Empire rather than to the stewardship of a tract of land. It is not until he has forsaken his estate that he realizes its true value.

Baskul. Remote outpost of the British Empire on the northwest frontier of the Indian subcontinent, to the northeast of Peshawur (Peshawar). Baskul represents the furthest edge of the decaying empire, beset by rebellious confusion. To its south lies the most troubled region, while the untracked wilderness of the Himalayas lies to the north. It is an obvious backwater, beyond the control or influence of any diplomatic presence.

— *Brian Stableford*

LOST ILLUSIONS

Author: Honoré de Balzac (1799-1850)
Type of work: Novel
Type of plot: Realism

Time of plot: 1821-1822
First published: Illusions perdues, 1837-1843 (English translation, 1893)

This novel is set primarily in Paris and the provincial town of Angoulême. A central theme of the novel is the contrasts between Paris and Angoulême. However, by the novel's end, these contrasts are less clear than they initially appear to be.

*****Paris.** France's capital and leading city, which in the first part of the novel is a place of fantasy, an ideal. At the beginning of the second part of the novel, when Lucien and Madame de Bargeton actually arrive in the capital, it initially seems to live up to its promise. In fact, it seems so luxurious, magnificent, and bustling that both Lucien and Madame de Bargeton feel like backward provincials. Soon, however, Lucien finds himself in sordid lodgings that seem little different from what he has left behind in L'Houmeau. Later still he discovers that behind its glittering facade Paris is full of corruption and intrigue. This seems different from the world he left behind, but not necessarily better.

One of the first things Lucien notices in Paris is the disparity between rich and poor, and in general Paris seems a place of extremes: Lucien, for instance, swings from giddy success to misery in Paris while his sister Eve, back in Angoulême, leads a much more stable life. However, this may say more about the two characters than the two locations.

*****Angoulême** (ahn-gew-LEHM). Town in southwestern France. Two of the central characters, Lucien Chardon and Madame de Bargeton, feel restricted here and yearn to escape to Paris. Lucien feels that only in Paris can he fulfill his promise as a writer. Madame de Bargeton yearns to be among the geniuses and fashionable people of the capital, and the narrator agrees that provincial life has narrowed her, forced her to focus on trivial matters, and led her to become extravagant and eccentric.

In Angoulême, Madame de Bargeton attempts to re-create Paris by establishing a Parisian-style salon in her house to which she invites the leading aristocratic figures in the old part of town (the Upper Town). However, after she finally visits the real Paris, she discovers that Angoulême is not Paris.

At the end of the novel, the Paris-Angoulême dichotomy seems less clear. Although Angoulême is obviously less elegant and magnificent than Paris, the corrupt intrigues that are revealed in the capital city find an echo in Angoulême, notably in the way the Cointet brothers manipulate the honest local printer, David Séchard, and arrange to send him to jail.

*L'Houmeau (lew-MOH). Prosperous business district of Angoulême; also called the Lower Town. The aristocrats of the Upper Town in Angoulême look down on L'Houmeau. L'Houmeau is to them as Angoulême is to Paris. Lucien lives in L'Houmeau in a shabby attic room above the pharmacy his father used to own. It is a major accomplishment for him to rise above his humble roots and become a regular frequenter of Madame de Bargeton's aristocratic salon in the Upper Town as a promising young man of genius and her recognized favorite.

Angoulême printing house. Belonging originally to David Séchard's father, the printing house is dirty, dangerous, and full of antiquated equipment, reflecting the miserliness and backwardness of David's father and perhaps more generally the backwardness of the provinces.

Flicoteaux (flee-koh-TOH). Restaurant in Paris's Latin Quarter that is frequented by students and artists. There, Lucien meets other struggling writers during his early days in the capital. Among these people is the saintly d'Arthez, who pushes him to be serious about his art, and the cynical Lousteau, who tells him that the way to get ahead is by intrigue and writing journalistic articles to order.

*Wooden Galleries.** Row of shops found in Paris until 1826. The area has an unsavory atmosphere, full of conspirators and prostitutes. There, Lucien makes the contacts that lead to his briefly successful journalistic career, in which he abandons principles for money, as do prostitutes.

*Panorama-Dramatique.** Paris theater that Lucien visits. He goes behind the scenes and sees all the dirt and ugliness behind the glitter, a symbolic depiction of Paris in general. There, Lucien meets the actress Coralie, who becomes his mistress even though she is already the mistress of a wealthy merchant.

Coralie's apartment. Lucien moves into Coralie's opulent apartment. However, the opulence has shaky foundations and does not last, reflecting the fact that Lucien has established himself only among an unstable section of the population—the city's journalists and theater people.

*Faubourg Saint-Germain** (FOH-bur san-zhur-MAYN). Aristocratic suburb of Paris where Lucien meets residents whose wealth and standing are much more solid than his, and who in fact skillfully maneuver things to destroy his wealth and standing.

— *Sheldon Goldfarb*

A LOST LADY

Author: Willa Cather (1873-1947)
Type of work: Novel
Type of plot: Domestic realism

Time of plot: Late nineteenth century
First published: 1923

This novel is both a collection of character studies and a portrait of a declining small Nebraska town. Each of its principal characters has a different relationship to community and region based on personal history, ethics, and ambition, and each displays a distinct response to the limitations of life in a place that was once a heroic frontier but is now a backwater.

Sweet Water. Small Nebraska town in which the story is set. In describing Sweet Water, Willa Cather drew upon memories of her own youth in Red Cloud, Nebraska; however, it should be noted that Nebraska once had a town called "Sweetwater" several counties to the north that may have provided a literal source, if not the inspiration, for Cather's name for her fictional town.

The historical Sweetwater, Nebraska, shared the decline of a host of similar small towns in the region. Like the town of the novel, but unlike Cather's Red Cloud, it was on a railroad route leading to the Black Hills of South Dakota, the destination of some of Captain Forrester's road-building.

Whatever Cather's precise geographical inspirations,

her understanding of her home region was precise, almost scientific. *A Lost Lady* provides her with an occasion to describe the physical and social character of rural Nebraska in a relatively early phase of European American settlement. Nevertheless, Cather's description of the town and its physical surroundings is secondary to her portraits of Sweet Water's inhabitants. For example, Niel Herbert, whose point of view is foremost in the novel, is a local boy whose widowed father is obliged to work in Denver after the collapse of the local family farm. Niel no longer lives in his "frail egg-shell house" but instead in a room behind his uncle's law office. He has a special affinity for Captain Forrester's home, with its aura of both social authority and feminine grace. His eventual departure from Sweet Water to study architecture reflects the formative role of the civilized spaces of the Forrester home and his desire to escape the lawyer's career that seems ordained for him.

By leaving for Boston to study architecture, Niel sets himself apart from his near-contemporary, Ivy Peters, who as Mrs. Forrester's tenant plows her meadows to plant wheat and who as her lawyer invests her money in Wyoming land schemes. Marian Forrester advises Niel that Peters gets splendid land from Indians for next to nothing, but not to tell his uncle, as she suspects his schemes are crooked. By the novel's end, the author's endorsement of Niel's love of the western prairie becomes paired with her scorn for Peters's cynical materialism.

Forrester home. Sweet Water home of Marian Forrester (the "lost lady" of the title) and her husband, Daniel Forrester, known in the region as "Captain" Forrester for his earlier work as an important builder of railroad lines. Their home is a legacy of the captain's early years on the prairies after the Civil War, when he was taken with the location while it was still intermittently an Indian encampment. Forrester's relation to the land predates the railroad-building era that is the source of his prosperity. His initial claim to the land consisted simply of a willow stake that he drove into the ground on a low hill. On his return years later, he finds that the stake has sprouted roots and become a tree. There, Forrester himself takes root by building a warm, though not lavish, home in which he can offer hospitality to prominent friends passing through on the railroad line between Omaha, Nebraska, and Denver, Colorado.

The house is surrounded by groves of poplar trees and marshy meadows along a meandering creek that separates the Forresters' land from the nearby town. Captain Forrester has a garden and he plants rows of stately Lombardy poplars on each side of the lane approaching the house; however, he refuses to plow his rich meadows to plant wheat. Having directly participated in the introduction of industrial culture into a region that he first knew as a grass sea six hundred miles wide, he possesses a sense of the proper balance between the amenities of civilization and the spiritual comforts of nature.

Although Mrs. Forrester treasures her modest but celebrated home, under the surface she is restless for the refined life of the city. Her experience is an instance of Cather's concern with the contrasting values of the country and the city, with the notable variation that she is not from the East—the captain brought her to Nebraska from California some years earlier as a bride twenty-five years his junior.

*****California.** Pacific state from which Marian Forrester comes. The novel descries her earlier life in California only indirectly, through brief stories told later in the novel, but Cather depicts California as colorful and alluring to her middle-aged heroine. Several years after her husband's death, Marian returns to California to try to live the life that she has imagined as she lived on the Nebraska prairie.

— *Clyde S. McConnell*

THE LOST WEEKEND

Author: Charles Reginald Jackson (1903-1968)
Type of work: Novel
Type of plot: Psychological realism

Time of plot: October, 1936
First published: 1944

Set in Depression-era New York City, this story is primarily a novel of interiors. Except for a single nightmarish trek through city streets in search of a pawnshop, most scenes take place inside: in bars, a hospital, an apartment, and within Don Birnam's alcohol-haunted mind, as he goes from daydreams of grandeur to remorseful ruminations on the past to the agonies of delirium tremens.

Birnam's apartment. Home of Don Birnam, at 311 East Fifty-fifth Street in Manhattan, where the novel begins and where Don spends a long weekend on a drinking binge. He lives with his brother, who pays the rent, but, tellingly, it is Don who sleeps in the one bedroom, while his brother sleeps on the living-room couch. The apartment is in midtown Manhattan but has a small garden, an indication of the middle-class comfort Don enjoys despite his unemployment. The apartment is both his refuge and his prison. It is a prison of boredom and frustration when he is sober and faces the empty hours to be filled; it is a refuge when, after it is too late to drink in bars, he returns home with a bottle, locks the door, and allows the phone to ring unanswered.

Bars. Once free of his brother's company, Don's first destination is his neighborhood bar, Sam's, dark and cheap and quiet; here he is known and enjoys a kind of friendship with Sam the bartender and the barmaid Gloria. He has less pleasant experiences in other bars, notably Jack's, a former speakeasy in Greenwich Village, where he attempts to steal a woman's purse as a drunken prank and is caught and humiliated. When drinking in public, he imagines himself aloof, superior, apart from the crowd. He is apt to fictionalize his life, as he does to Gloria, inventing an imaginary unhappy marriage. Although he drinks heavily in bars, he does his most serious and most dangerous drinking when he is alone at home.

*****Manhattan.** Borough of New York City in which Don lives. In part 3 of the novel, Don Birnam, moneyless, hung over, and in desperate need of a drink, carries his typewriter sixty-five city blocks up Manhattan, to an unfamiliar neighborhood on 120th Street, where two Jewish men he meets inform him that all pawnshops are closed in honor of Yom Kippur. "Don Birnam's Rhine-Journey," he calls it sarcastically, and indeed his journey has an epic quality, despite its absurdity and pointlessness. The description of Manhattan in this section is vivid and surreal, with passages that read almost like a catalog of commercial life, with milk bars, orange-juice stands, weighing machines, linoleum and bedding, cut-rates, remnants, watch repairers, barber poles, and so on. Fixated on his goal, Don walks through this urban jumble in a state of detachment, never a part of the life he observes, not even sure that the journey itself is not another dream or a story he might tell someday.

Hospital. City hospital in whose alcoholic ward Don lands after falling downstairs in his apartment building. There he observes the other patients, ranging from derelicts to a successful advertising man, in various states of derangement. There, also, he himself is observed by doctors on their rounds, who discuss him and the other patients casually and impersonally. Don recognizes his degradation as he is treated like an inanimate object, yet he finds a freedom in his anonymity at the hospital, in being merely another nameless alcoholic.

University. Unnamed university from which Don withdrew or was expelled fifteen years earlier, in an early failure that continues to haunt him. That failure is emblematic of his life's pattern: early promise followed by some fatal error. Several references are made to this incident, in which Don was asked to leave his fraternity because of a suspected homosexual crush on an upperclassman; however, the university appears only in a long dream sequence in part 4. Don dreams of himself in a large auditorium set up with gymnasium equipment and packed with young men, listening to a lecture, then finds himself running across the campus, past familiar buildings, at the center of a lynch mob of angry students searching for him. The dream sequence shows the significance the university incident still has for him. More than fifteen years later, he still avoids meeting anyone who might have known him at the university. Don's world has become a kind of minefield, filled with places and people to be avoided: a bar from which he was once thrown out, cab drivers who witness his shame, the delicatessen owner on Fifty-sixth Street from whom he borrowed and never repaid ten dollars. Don is really at home nowhere except in his own inner world of liquor-inspired fantasy, and the novel's ending suggests that it is to this world he will always return.

— *Kathryn Kulpa*

THE LOST WORLD

Author: Randall Jarrell (1914-1965)   *First published:* 1965
Type of work: Poetry

The largely autobiographical poems in this collection, most notably the title poem, recall not only a lost world of Hollywood images, but also the lost time of Randall Jarrell's childhood, when he lived with his grandparents in Hollywood during the 1920's.

Hollywood. Southern California home of the young movie industry, as well as of Randall Jarrell's grandparents. In 1926 Jarrell's parents separated and sent Jarrell to live with his grandparents and great-grandmother in Hollywood. In 1962 Jarrell's mother returned to him the letters he had written to her during that period, and they opened a world of memory—a lost world that became the subject of this series of poems.

The opening lines of "The Lost World" recall a "camera man on a platform on the bumper of a car," a movie lot that used wind machines to create a blizzard, and the papier-mâché dinosaurs used in the making of the fantasy film *The Lost World* (1925). Another poem recalls a friend of Jarrell's aunt whom Jarrell visited often who owned the famous Metro-Goldwyn-Mayer lion.

The poems' juxtaposition of Hollywood images and Jarrell's childhood memories reminds readers that the past, like the movies, is a strange compilation of image, memory, imagination, and symbol. A movie is a way of representing a world that exists nowhere but in the filmmaker's mind. Likewise, a poem about an event from childhood is a way of representing a world that exists nowhere but in the poet's mind. Thus, the past is truly the "lost world" Jarrell traverses in these poems, made particularly potent by the connection with the illusion and reality of Hollywood.

— *Diane Andrews Henningfeld*

LOVE IN THE TIME OF CHOLERA

Author: Gabriel García Márquez (1928-   )
Type of work: Novel
Type of plot: Psychological realism

Time of plot: 1880's and 1920's
First published: El amor en los tiempos del cólera,
    1985 (English translation, 1988)

This novel is a long, meandering story about the love affair between a dreamy poet, Florentino Ariza, and Fermina Daza, a beautiful young lady of the upper classes. Yet this is no ordinary love affair since it blossoms during their adolescent years, fades during the fifty or so years when Fermina Daza is married to Juvenal Urbino, a well-connected local doctor, and then resumes after the latter's tragicomic death.

Cartagena. Colombian port city on the Caribbean Sea that forms the backdrop to the novel. Gabriel García Márquez never names the city within the novel; however, the clues he provides are sufficient to ensure that the city is, in fact, Cartagena. Details about the novel's city include the fact that it was the most prosperous city in the Caribbean during the eighteenth century, that it once possessed the largest slave market in the Americas, and that it was the traditional residence of the viceroys of the Spanish colonial Kingdom of New Granada. The capital of the Bolívar region in northern Colombia, Cartagena was founded in 1533 and became important in the mid-sixteenth century, when Spain's great mercantile ships began stopping there annually to load up with gold and other products for transport back to Spain. In the process, Cartagena also became a center for the burgeoning slave trade.

García Márquez doubtless does not mention the name

of the city in order to keep it firmly within the realm of the imagination and brings his fictional city alive in a variety of ways. He provides detailed descriptions of the grand colonial houses in the downtown district, where Juvenal Urbino's family lives, and contrasts these houses with the rudimentary hovels where the descendants of the black slaves live on the outskirts of the city, near the swamp.

Contrasts between these two areas of the city are brought home to the reader when Urbino visits the outskirts; his carriage driver gets lost repeatedly, and the children stand in the street laughing at the driver's clothes. This is clearly a different world from the upper-class, professional world that Urbino inhabits, and yet he eventually falls prey to its charms since he ends up having an extramarital affair with a mulatto woman, Barbara Lynch, who comes from the other side of the tracks. The novel thereby uses geography in order to structure its message.

The cholera outbreak that forms a central part of the backdrop to the action is known to have originated in the swamps on the outskirts of the city. Dr. Juvenal Urbino, like his father before him, is involved as part of his professional duties in attempting to stop the spread of the disease; however, he is as powerless to stop its onslaught as he is to resist the temptation of Barbara Lynch's love. The connection is not a casual one; García Márquez is suggesting that love, far from being nothing but joy, is like a disease. Indeed, the love that Florentino Ariza experiences for Fermina Daza—essentially turning him into a love-sick admirer from a distance when she decides to marry someone else—is something that upsets his sleeping patterns, makes him lose his appetite, and causes him to break out in rashes so severe that his mother thinks it is actually cholera from which he is suffering.

Magdalena River. Colombian river flowing northward from the Andes Mountains to the Caribbean Sea that provides a central symbol in the novel. The river echoes the ebb and flow of the characters' lives. When Florentino and Fermina go on a boat-ride on the river together, the river, like them, shows signs of its age. However, it also functions as the setting for their twilight love. Fermina and Florentino ask the captain of the ship—the *New Fidelity*—on which they are journeying if they can simply go on a trip by themselves. Against all the odds he agrees, and the yellow flag normally used to indicate cholera is hoisted, guaranteeing that they will be left undisturbed. The ship subsequently sails off into the sunset to a destination which is no more specific than "straight on, straight on, to La Dorada." In this last scene of the novel, various geographic leitmotifs—such as the river, travel, and the association between cholera and love—are brought triumphantly together. Florentino has been waiting for this moment for more than fifty years.

— *Stephen M. Hart*

THE LOVE SUICIDES AT SONEZAKI

Author: Chikamatsu Monzaemon (Sugimori Nobumori, 1653-1725)
Type of work: Drama
Type of plot: Tragedy

Time of plot: Eighteenth century
First performed: Sonezaki shinjū, 1703 (English translation, 1961)

Regarded as Chikamatsu's masterpiece in Bunraku, *or puppet theater—a genre that he developed, this tragedy is a "domestic play," in which a young clerk and a prostitute in Osaka have a doomed love affair.*

Ikutama Shrine (ih-kew-tah-mah). Place where Tokubei meets the courtesan Ohatsu by chance while making deliveries to his customers. According to legend, the shrine's origin dates back to when Emperor Jinmu arrived in Osaka and built the shrine. Even after the Tokugawa period, the government protected the shrine's extensive grounds and magnificent architecture. It is said to have been popular with worshipers and regarded as one of the grand Shinto shrines in Japan.

Temma House (teh-muh). Brothel in which Ohatsu

works. Located in a disreputable neighborhood, the house is purposefully inconspicuous in architecture in order to keep its patrons anonymous. Tokubei and Ohatsu hold each other and cry under the porch of the house, and Tokubei tells her that the only option left for him is suicide.

Sonezaki Wood (soh-neh-zah-kee). On their journey to Sonezaki Wood, Tokubei and Ohatsu speak of their love, and a lyrical passage spoken by the narrator comments on the transience of life. The surrounding woods are lonely and deserted and leading to their graveyard. Tokubei apologizes to his uncle, and Ohatsu to her parents, for the trouble they are causing. Chanting an invocation to Buddha, Tokubei stabs Ohatsu and then himself.

— *Jonathan L. Thorndike*

THE LOVER

Author: Marguerite Duras (1914-1996)
Type of work: Novel
Type of plot: New Novel

Time of plot: Late 1920's through 1940's
First published: L'Amant, 1984 (English translation, 1985)

Set in Vietnam during the declining years of French colonial rule in Southeast Asia, this novel is a woman's memoir of her teenage love affair with a Chinese man twice her age. The narrator weaves her story through the lyrical, immediate, and sometimes raw and seedy, descriptions of the places where she and her lover meet.

*Saigon. City in Cochin China (now Ho Chi Minh City in Vietnam), near which the author, Marguerite Duras, was born and raised. During the prewar era of French colonization, Saigon was dubbed Paris of the Far East; it was a city of lights and pleasures in which all things exotic and decadent lurked within opium dens, rented housing complexes, market squares at night, alleyways, hidden flats, or under scorching afternoons of tropical heat. The city is a center of colonial wealth built on the labor of disenfranchised Vietnamese and enjoyed by the country's French occupiers and immigrant Chinese businessmen.

The unnamed narrator looks back on the time when she was a teenage daughter of a poor French family in Saigon, recalling her adolescence and the forbidden affair she enjoyed with her wealthy Chinese lover, when she succumbed to the seductive, shimmering limelight of the city, with its tropical heat. She and her lover are both strangers and yet natives to Saigon: strangers because she is French and he is Chinese, natives because they live, tread, and breathe each and every place of Saigon: its mercantile commotions and rickshaws, its Chi-

nese and French eateries, its stagnant water, its bodies in the market squares and city sidewalks.

In Saigon the girl attends an all-girl boarding school, and her lover takes her to his bachelor flat in the Chinese part of the city. There he introduces her to material luxury and his wealth. His black limousine usually waits for her outside her boarding school to take her to his flat or wherever she desires to go. Eventually, however, their interracial affair becomes a scandal.

Bachelor flat. Home of the narrator's lover, located in a housing complex in Cholon, the Chinese part of Saigon where the narrator loses her virginity. The flat is the physical representation of sordid and covetous lust and love between the doomed lovers.

Family home. Located in Sadec and inhabited by the schoolgirl, her mother, and two brothers. This house is the epitome of familial inequity, sibling rivalry, enmity, bitterness, domestic violence, sadness, occasional laughter, and always poverty. What the girl lacks in this house she seeks and gets from her Chinese lover.

— *Hanh N. Nguyen*

LOVE'S LABOUR'S LOST

Author: William Shakespeare (1564-1616)
Type of work: Drama
Type of plot: Comedy of manners

Time of plot: Sixteenth century
First performed: c. 1594-1595; revised presentation, 1597; first published, 1598

The setting encompasses different areas of "a park with a palace in it" in Navarre, whose King Frederick, along with his three gentlemen, have sworn oaths to dedicate themselves to scholarship and ascetics—a utopian dream that excludes life's social pleasures, including the company of women. The absurdity of their contract surfaces upon the arrival of the princess of France and her three ladies.

*Navarre. Historical kingdom in northern Spain, along the French border. In this early play, William Shakespeare depicts a conception of an ideal commonwealth. Setting the play within the king's park underscores the struggle between man's natural will to enjoy and society's desire to restrict that will. The palace—which is never actually entered on stage—symbolizes the rules of the community to which the king and his gentlemen have chosen to retreat. The park itself is a representation of nature, not Rosalind's forest of Arden, but rather a landscaped sculpture of that world designed to unite the beauty of what is natural for people to savor with the practicality of proper behavior. The king and his men swear off revelry, feasting, and women, as though these were moral deficiencies. Setting the reconciliation between their passions and their social inhibitions in this park signifies the possibility of living a life that is full both spiritually and intellectually. This understanding is appropriately brought home to them by women, nature's consorts, and it is poetically fitting that the king and his men must take what they have learned and demonstrate it in the world for a year before they are permitted to return to the garden and reunite with their new lovers.

— *Erskine Carter*

LOVING

Author: Henry Green (Henry Vincent Yorke, 1905-1973)
Type of work: Novel

Type of plot: Domestic
Time of plot: World War II
First published: 1945

This novel has strong overtones of a fairy tale, complete with the castle in Ireland in which the story unfolds. The action takes place completely within the walls of the castle, which is a remnant of a bygone age and a living monument of conformity to customs and fashions with no living vitality. Against this backdrop, two servants in the castle struggle to fulfill their romantic relationship. Unable to do this within the sterile castle, they eventually flee to England.

Kinalty Castle. Ancient Irish castle surrounded by a wall that is somehow symbolic of "neutral" Ireland. While the rest of the world is being sucked into the horrors of World War II, Ireland clings to bygone days and refuses to become engaged in the changing world. The castle is the epitome of old forms, with a rigid social separation of owner and servants. Also a museum of artful decoration with no meaning, it contains a facade with a pseudo-Greek temple and a deliberately ruined wall to give it an appearance of antique authenticity.

Castle interiors. Many upstairs rooms in the castle are closed and filled with dusty sheeted furniture; however, the maids Edith and Kate open the rooms every few weeks to air them out. One day while they play a gramophone and waltz in one of these rooms, Charley Raunce, the former footman, now butler, hears the music, interrupts them, and turns it off. All Edith's attempts to bring living forms into the castle are stifled. Seeking shelter from the rain one day, Edith and Mrs. Jack Tennant's children and the pantry boy enter the Greek Temple lit only by dark skylights. There, the little group plays a game of blindman's bluff, infusing life and joy among the bronze and marble statues, symbols of lives now cold and dead. Raunce interrupts this scene and coldly breaks up the game because he has not yet been transformed by Edith's love and still feels it necessary to protect the old forms.

The servants go upstairs to take care of Mrs. Tennant, the owner, and her daughter-in-law, Mrs. Jack. Edith, an underhousemaid, finds Mrs. Jack naked in bed with Captain Davenport. This leads to both hilarity and scandal in the quarters of the servants, who hold themselves to a higher standard of morality. Although the flame of erotic love burns high between Raunce and Edith, they restrain themselves until they are safely married in England.

When Mrs. Tennant ventures downstairs to the kitchen to talk to Mrs. Welch, the cook, they hardly understand each other. The social division is so great that they seem to speak unrelated languages. The cook speaks with ambiguity and deviousness to the end in view, mindful of all the traditional taboos, while Mrs. Tennant speaks with direction and overemphasis. When she finishes the conversation in the kitchen she has difficulty breathing and her face is congested.

Castle grounds. Doves and noisy peacocks inhabit the castle grounds, exhibiting more vitality than the human inhabitants of the castle. Raunce, the character who changes the most, is so removed from real life that he becomes ill when, for the first time in years, he leaves the castle and ventures outdoors. The elevated dovecote—a miniature replica of the Leaning Tower of Pisa with small balconies to each tier of windows—is another of the castle's fake adornments. However, the doves that inhabit it are real creatures. One day Nanny takes the children to the dovecote to tell them a story about baby doves, but while she is talking, the children are mesmerized by the activities of the doves themselves, busy fighting, mating, and pushing fledglings out of their nests. In the final scene of the book, Raunce is so completely overcome with pleasure by the vision of Edith feeding birds while iridescent peacocks circle her skirt and doves settle on her shoulders that he experiences almost painful delight.

— *Sheila Golburgh Johnson*

THE LOWER DEPTHS

Author: Maxim Gorky (Aleksey Maksimovich Peshkov, 1868-1936)
Type of work: Drama
Type of plot: Naturalism

Time of plot: Late nineteenth century
First performed: 1902; first published, 1902 as *Na dne* (English translation, 1912)

First presented by the Moscow Arts Theater, known for the extreme realism of its productions, this play depicts the terrible living conditions of working Russians at the turn of the twentieth century, focusing attention on the plight of the poor and oppressed.

Tenement basement. Cellarlike rooming house accommodating a varied group of inhabitants, located in an unspecified Russian town along the Volga River. Representative of the kind of living conditions for a large percentage of Russia's population in the early twentieth century, the setting of the play is a further statement in protest against inequalities.

The play's stage set represented a combination of elements actually present in slum apartments, of which there were many. Russia was not a nation of great wealth, natural resources, or manufacturing, and its short growing season further increased its poverty. Many citizens considered themselves fortunate to find shelter even in such conditions as those depicted in the play's damp, dim, sooty, cavernlike communal living area. Privacy, such as it was, occurred only when residents hung blankets or curtains to form cubicles. The setting reminds the audience of a den or a lair where harried and exhausted animals hole up to regain their strength. The setting has the impact of a purgatory in which the denizens wait, caught between life and death, for whatever happens next. At the same time, the residents must pay dearly for their shelter, so that nearly every penny that they make must go to pay their greedy landlords, leaving little money for anything else.

— *H. Alan Pickrell*

LUCKY JIM

Author: Kingsley Amis (1922-1995)
Type of work: Novel
Type of plot: Social satire

Time of plot: Mid-twentieth century
First published: 1954

This novel's unspecified provincial university in which Jim Dixon undergoes his trials and achieves eventual victory stands for all the so-called redbrick universities that became important in post-World War II England, even though some considered them inferior versions of the otherwise unattainable Oxford and Cambridge Universities.

Redbrick university. Unnamed provincial university at which Dixon lectures in history. Kingsley Amis first conceived the idea for *Lucky Jim* while visiting his friend Philip Larkin at the University of Leicester. He realized that the fictional portrayal of such an insular and parochial community had not previously been attempted. Before *Lucky Jim*, novelistic treatments of English university life had involved either Oxford or Cambridge, but with the return of so many soldiers after World War II, both as pupils and teachers, provincial universities, commonly referred to by their construction of red brick (as opposed to the dreaming, granite spires of "Oxbridge"), became much more significant in the intellectual life of the country.

Originally called Hamberton, Jim's unnamed university is fairly generic, as is the city in which it is placed, unspecified by region and minimally described. Amis borrowed one symbolic detail from the University of Leicester: its location across the street from a cemetery. Otherwise, the campus is strictly portrayed in functional terms; it has a library, common rooms, laboratories, but nothing seemingly worth describing in anything but generalities. At the end of the novel, the campus does not even inspire Jim to take one last look when he leaves. Although the university is a fitting location for the "crappy culture" that Amis later noted as an important element in the novel, it must be kept in mind that many of these judgments are Jim's and not necessarily Amis's.

Interestingly, the only rooms that are described in detail are those in which the Summer Ball takes place. These walls are decorated with historical, martial illustrations that Jim, a reluctantly aspiring professor of history, cannot (or will not) identify. However, these murals are fitting, in a mock epic sort of way, since the Summer Ball marks the first important battle between Jim and Bertrand Welch for the favor of Christine. It also brings Jim to the attention of his "fairy-godfather," Gore-Urquhart.

Welch home. Suburban dwelling of Professor Welch, the head of the university's history department. Also never completely described, it seems full of culturally pretentious bric-a-brac and trashy, trendy artworks. A statue of Buddha that adorns Jim's guest room so disgusts him that he cannot name it but can only describe it ("a small china effigy, . . . in a squatting position, of a well-known Oriental religious figure"). Although Jim hates the place, particularly after suffering through an unpleasant weekend there, he finds himself drawn to it because of Welch's importance to his future and the presence there of Christine Callaghan.

*London. Great Britain's capital city is Jim's ultimate goal in his dream of escape, which he achieves upon becoming Gore-Urquhart's secretary. Jim's own name (Dixon sounds like "Dick's son") contains a partial allusion to a previous young man from the prov-inces, Dick Whittington, who dreamed of going to London and succeeding. Curiously, London is never fully visualized in Jim's thoughts, although he admits having gone there perhaps a dozen times; it appears only as a strangely two-dimensional vision of chimney pots surmounted by a bank of clouds. This deflationary image is in keeping with the general tone of the book. At the end of the novel, Jim admits that the one section of London he will not live in is Chelsea, presumably because of its reputation as a neighborhood of artists.

— *William Laskowski*

THE LUSIADS

Author: Luís de Camões (c. 1524-1580)
Type of work: Poetry
Type of plot: Epic

Time of plot: Fifteenth century
First published: Os Lusíades, 1572 (English translation, 1655)

This stirring tale of exploration and adventure is Portugal's national poetic saga. The voyages of Vasco da Gama are the framework upon which Luís de Camões erects an epic account of his country's origins and aspirations, with the gods and goddesses of the Greeks and Romans brought in to acknowledge his reliance on Virgil's Aeneid *(19 B.C.E.) as a major source of inspiration. Like the latter, this is a narrative that blends the glamorization of the past, the exaltation of the present, and the forecast of a successful future into the celebration of a distinct national identity.*

*Portugal. Fledgling country in Camões's time to whose remarkable history *The Lusiads* is dedicated. Camões identifies Portugal as the "crown" on the head of Europe, the nation that has taken the lead in exploring the world and bringing true religion to primitive races. Approximately one quarter of his poem is devoted to a recounting of how his tiny country, long an obscure province of other nations' empires, eventually became the world's foremost naval power. In the process of accomplishing this task, the narrative often makes direct connections between dramatic events in the past and aspects of the country's natural landscape that would be familiar to sixteenth century readers: A famous King's victorious military strategy is likened to a fierce guard dog's attack on a bull, and this ruler's death causes Portugal's hills to weep for him and its rivers to overflow in sorrow. Camões's technique of infusing the everyday present with the atmosphere of a glorious past makes poetry out of the prosaic and flatters his contemporary readers by suggesting that they are the worthy heirs of a distinguished tradition.

*Mombasa (mohm-BAH-sah). City on the east coast of Africa in what is now Kenya. Although da Gama and his crew have considerable contact with the city's predominantly Muslim residents, *The Lusiads* treat the Mombasans merely as a backdrop for the evil plotting of Bacchus, the Roman god of wine who is the most powerful enemy of the Portuguese explorers. The poem's only glimpse of Mombasa's interior occurs at a house in which Bacchus has created what appears to be a Christian shrine; however, this is in fact a ruse aimed at convincing the Portuguese that Mombasa's king is well disposed toward them; the complicity of local Muslims in this charade is treated as evidence of their essential deceitfulness.

*Malindi (mah-leen-DEE). Port city about one hundred miles northeast of Mombasa, also now in Kenya. Unable to find a reliable pilot in Mombasa, da Gama backtracks to Malindi after being informed that it is the likeliest place to hire one. Malindi's inhabitants, also Muslims, are depicted as being much friendlier than the Mombasans, although their city goes similarly undescribed by the text.

The explorers' apparent lack of interest in sights they have never seen before implies that places such as Mombasa and Malindi are not worthy of anyone's notice. An even stronger indication of this attitude is provided by the fact that the narrative devotes more attention to what the mariners wear when going ashore than it does to the alien societies in whose midst they find themselves. This is very much in keeping with *The Lusiads'* primary concern of celebrating the expansion of Portugal's global influence and is also a forecast of the elitist prejudices that European nations would subsequently use to justify the oppressive treatment of their colonial possessions.

*Calicut (Calcutta). Indian city that is the most distant destination of da Gama's voyage. This bustling metropolis is the capital of a Hindu kingdom whose ruler initially welcomes the Portuguese as worthy and distinguished visitors. In contrast to Camões's treatment of Mombasa and Malindi, Calicut is described in some detail; an account of the interior of a Hindu temple, in particular, offers one of *The Lusiads'* few portraits of a non-Western culture, even though the emphasis is on the heathen barbarity of its contents rather than any worthwhile characteristics that the religion might possess.

Once again, however, it is the anti-Portuguese machinations of the god Bacchus, now as before aided by devious Muslim collaborators, that take over the plot and push any consideration of the actual location of these events to the sidelines. Although the narrative's relatively favorable treatment of Hindus vis-á-vis Muslims probably stems more from the contemporary fear of the latter as a menace to Christendom than from any belief in the positive qualities of Hinduism, it does indicate that Camões is capable of making distinctions among alien cultures. On the whole, however, *The Lusiads* treats all non-Western peoples as inferior and largely uninteresting segments of humanity, and denies them either voice or representation.

Olympus. Mountain home of the Greek and Roman gods. As is characteristic of the classical epics that Camões employs as his models, the gods are conceptualized as possessing supernatural powers and recognizably human personality traits. Mount Olympus is depicted as a place of opulent furnishings on which the gods debate the fate of the Portuguese in a manner similar to that of an earthly legislative assembly, and the victorious speeches of those deities who support the explorers provides Camões with many additional opportunities for the rhetorical exaltation of his country's national aspirations.

Neptune's court. Underwater palace of the god of the sea and his cohorts. Bacchus is more successful at inciting some of the marine deities to assail the Portuguese, and the ensuing scene of the expedition's ships battered by an ocean storm is exciting, as well as one of the few passages in which nature is realistically depicted.

Isle of Love. Island created by Venus to reward the voyagers for their efforts. This luxuriant paradise, where an abundance of fabulously beautiful nymphs is ready to indulge the voyagers' every desire, represents the text's vision of Eden come down to earth: delicious fruits, beautiful flowers, and the ultimate in sexual gratification.

— *Paul Stuewe*

THE LUTE

Author: Gao Ming (c. 1303-c. 1370)
Type of work: Drama
Type of plot: Opera

Time of plot: c. 200
First performed: c. 1367; first published, c. 1367 as *Pi-pa ji* (English translation, 1980)

A work of Chinese classical opera, this drama concerns Zhao Wuniang, a beautiful young woman given in marriage to Cai Bojie, an outstanding scholar. The couple is blissfully happy until Bojie's father urges him to take the difficult Confucian imperial examinations used to choose government officials. After Bojie earns the highest score, the prime minister compels him to marry his daughter and keeps him in the capital for six years, during which time his parents die, and his first wife pawns her possessions to stay alive. Eventually, she reaches the capital, remaining ever faithful to his memory.

Caijiazhuang (tsi-geeah-JWANG). Rural village in eastern China that is the home to the young scholar Bojie, who enjoys reading books in the garden surrounded by rivers, winding paths, and peach and pear trees spreading in the sky. Wonderful flowers, herbs, and chirping birds create scenes of rich pastoral abundance. At the end of the opera, Zhao Wuniang's plight moves the heart of the prime minister's daughter, and she, Zhao Wuniang, and Bojie settle down as a family in Caijiazhuang, where they pay respect to their ancestors.

Luoyang (Loo-YAHNG). Capital of China under the Han Dynasty where Bojie reluctantly goes to take a competitive examination. On his way to the city, he meets three other examination candidates with whom he forms a partnership. Along their way, they discuss scholastic matters, drink wine, and recite poetry. The capital city is filled with magnificent towers and terraces, rows of willow trees, ornamental bridges, beaded curtains, and embroidered screens in the aristocratic homes. When he goes to meet the prime minister, Bojie is impressed with the opulence of his court. Bojie plays a lute in Luoyang to express his homesickness and yearning for the wife and parents he has left behind. Under orders of the emperor, he marries the prime minister's daughter and cannot leave the capital city.

Apricot Garden. Garden in Luoyang to which Bojie is invited to attend a lavish feast after he earns the highest score on the Confucian examinations. The Apricot Garden is a scenic paradise with yellow flags flapping in the breeze, bunches of flowers and brocades hanging everywhere, and fragrant apricot blossoms. Bojie enjoys a celebratory feast on tables inlaid with coral and turtle shells but greatly misses his wife back in his home village.

— *Jonathan L. Thorndike*

LYSISTRATA

Author: Aristophanes (c. 450-c. 385 B.C.E.)
Type of work: Drama
Type of plot: Satire

Time of plot: Fifth century B.C.E.
First performed: Lysistratē, 411 B.C.E. (English translation, 1812)

This play is set in Athens at a moment when the ancient Greek city-state reached its lowest ebb during its long war with Sparta following a disastrous defeat. The play uses Athens to project an antiwar theme that pleads for peace and the needed unity of all Greek city-states. Aristophanes wrote it for Athenian audiences during the midst of the very war he describes. The play's location is organic to its action; its title character, an Athenian woman sick of war, conceives and effectively organizes a sex strike among the women of Greece forcing the men to make peace.

*****Athens.** Capital and city-state of the peninsula of Attica, a province of east central Greece. Firmly established as a cultural, political, and commercial center by 429 B.C.E., Athens became an imperialistic empire and naval power. In 431 B.C.E. it began its war with Sparta, the powerful city-state of southern Greece's Peloponnesian Peninsula. Aristophanes depicts Athens at a time when it was suffering naval and military disasters and undergoing chaotic political and social conditions, which he uses to give Athenian women a motivation for striking. It is significant that the play's women consist of the strong and weak-willed, suggestive of the city's fickle population. Their strike ends the war. (The historical Athens surrendered in 404 B.C.E. and lost its empire and military power.)

Acropolis. Citadel and highest point in Athens, and the place containing the city's treasury and the Parthenon, a temple significantly holding a statue of Athena, goddess of wisdom, arts, and the preserver of the state. On the Acropolis Lysistrata has the women seize the treasury that finances Athens's war. They are aided by Athenian old women and repel an attacking group of Athenian old men and male officials trying to oust them. Suffering the effects of sexual abstinence, warriors throughout Greece come to the Acropolis, where they agree to make peace on the women's terms, and reunite with them for a joyous celebration.

Greece. In addition to Athens, Lysistrata's female company come from other Greek city-states that represent Athens's most bitter enemies whose defecting women signify the theme of antiwar Panhellenism. These cities also bear features that characterize superior Athenian attitudes toward their inhabitants. Sparta is the Peloponnesian capital known for its military prowess and physically fit women, such as the play's Lampito. Corinth, noted for general dissoluteness produces a full-figured lass of possibly easy virtue; and from Boeotia a fertile east central Grecian land with people reputedly dulled by plenty, comes a pretty, well-fed girl.

— *Christian H. Moe*

M

THE MABINOGION

Author: Unknown
Type of work: Novel
Type of plot: Folklore
Time of plot: Middle Ages

First published: 1838-1849 (tales from *The White Book of Rhydderch*, 1300-1325 and *The Red Book of Hergest*, 1375-1425)

This collection contains Welsh tales reflecting the Celtic culture's interest in history, folktale, and mythology. Their geography likewise reflects both reality and fantasy. Because no narrative line or unified authorship creates continuity among the tales, each has its own stage and boundaries. However, many of the tales are set in common places.

***British Isles.** European island group comprising Great Britain, Ireland, and smaller surrounding islands whose early inhabitants spoke Celtic languages. Celtic culture once extended throughout Europe. By the time period in which most of the tales in *The Mabinogion* are set—perhaps the sixth or seventh century C.E.—continental Celts held only Brittany in western France, and Germanic Anglo-Saxons controlled the parts of southeastern and central Britain previously ruled by the Roman Empire.

The Celtic "fringe" lands of Wales, Cornwall, and Ireland provide the setting for most of *The Mabinogion*'s tales. Its characters also traverse parts of England, however, and places like London (King Lludd's favorite court) and Oxford appear as Celtic towns, while the father of Peredur the knight seems to hail from York. Ireland is a place to be visited, and at least in "Branwen" is associated with otherworldly powers, while Britain is the "Island of the Mighty."

Otherworldly places. Among the pagan Celts the connection of specific locations with gods or spirits was common and may emerge in these Christianized stories as spiritually charged spots, like **Gorsedd Arberth** or the oxhide cot in the "Dream of Rhonabwy." More spectacular are mystic kingdoms like that of Annwvyn in

"Pwyll," which produced the shape-shifting King Arawn, or Heveydd the Old's court. These places seem to dot the landscape without need of fantastic journeys. They provide a constant tension between the real and imagined, the possible and the unlikely.

Castles and courts. The authors of the tales are constantly concerned with the life and customs of the royal courts through which their characters move. These are generally places of refuge and, especially, hospitality, in which rank and honor are carefully noted and taken into consideration. Food, drink, entertainment (including sex), and conversation dominate the feasts that seem so common. When provision is scanty or begrudged, as at the home of Heilyn the Red in "Dream of Rhonabwy," the sneer of the author comes through on the page. When it simply disappears, as do the folk of Arberth, or the supplies of King Lludd's courts, enchantment alone may be the cause.

At the royal courts wandering knights and nobles find shelter, spare armor, and women to love. Court rules and rituals are also evident, as means for controlling what could easily become drunken, unruly crowds. The granting of requests, which was a form of generosity, gets some noble characters in trouble when they fail to realize that promising "anything" may lead to disaster or a loss of face. Courts are also places of great beauty, both natural and man-made, and rich descriptions of clothing and decorations cause several narratives to pause.

King Arthur's court. Courts of the legendary King Arthur have various names and locations. The **Camelot** familiar to many modern readers disappears behind the Celtic **Kelli Wig** and **Caer Llion ar Wysg** (Caerleon on Usk). Arthur is not only the most famous and powerful ruler (sometimes called "emperor") in the tales, he also presides over the ideal royal court as a paragon of generosity and gentility. Nonetheless, it is at his court that some characters are offended (Peredur) or even assaulted (Gwenhwyvar), in clear violations of what would elsewhere be called courtesy. Arthur's courts also provide convenient starting points for several of the tales, including "Culhwch," "Owein," and "Gereint and Enid."

*Countryside. Most of *The Mabinogion*'s stories entail travel for one purpose or another. While concrete routes can rarely be traced, the authors clearly associate certain types of terrain with certain moods. As might be expected, forests provide the greatest mystery and danger, as in "Gereint and Enid," while lovely valleys, flowing rivers, and views of fine cities either contrast with characters' black moods or accentuate the lightheartedness of the moment. The authors present these settings and details in a spare but effective way.

Cities. Neither Celtic culture nor these Welsh authors are comfortable with urban areas. London, for example, is depicted as a court rather than a town, and the towns in which the refugees of "Manawydan" seek a livelihood are hotbeds of conspiracy against the young "craftsmen." This suggests a hint of fourteenth century mutual animosity between the bourgeois and nobles, as well as between the Welsh and English.

— *Joseph P. Byrne*

MAC FLECKNOE

Author: John Dryden (1631-1700)
Type of work: Poetry
Type of plot: Mock-heroic

Time of plot: Late 1670's
First published: 1682

Although this poem describes how the imaginary writer Thomas Shadwell comes to rule over the realms of Nonsense, its setting abounds with allusions to John Dryden's own London, especially its districts of brothels, theaters, and publishing houses. These references help build metaphorical connections between the literary and political domains.

*River Thames (tehmz). River running through London where the fictional poet, Mac Flecknoe, first catches sight of Shadwell, his true heir in literary ineptitude. Flecknoe beholds the ample form of Shadwell rowing a small boat in the river that reflects his relative unimportance in the currents of literary history.

Augusta. Alternative name for London that stresses its connection to the cultural flowering of ancient Augustan Rome. A part of the inflated description of Shadwell's surroundings that contrasts sharply with their vulgar reality.

*Barbican. Ancient watchtower, near the Roman wall surrounding the old City of London, that has deteriorated into nonexistence by the seventeenth century. Only the name remains to describe a neighborhood full of brothels and frequented by fledgling actors and prostitutes. Ironically, the vigilance and security symbolized by the tall fortification has lapsed into a world of lowlife. Flecknoe chooses this site for the coronation of his successor, Shadwell.

*Ireland. Island in the British Isles that fell under English rule several decades before Dryden wrote *Mac Flecknoe.* Dryden cites it as one of two places over which Shadwell might reign. Both Ireland and Barbados had reputations for savagery, which make them appropriate for Shadwell's lack of civilized talent.

Barbados. Island in the West Indies whose seventeenth century sugar industry was based on slave labor. The poet adds that Irish lawbreakers might be "barbadoe'd"—transported to the New World to serve as slave labor. Shadwell, the poem implies, has transgressed against the rules of writing and churns out his hack work like one condemned to a fate of drudgery.

— *Jennifer Preston Wilson*

MACBETH

Author: William Shakespeare (1564-1616)
Type of work: Drama
Type of plot: Tragedy

Time of plot: Eleventh century
First performed: 1606; first published, 1623

Scotland's history and terrain are organic to this early Jacobean tragedy, not only influencing William Shakespeare's choice of topical contemporary subject matter, in tribute to the new Stuart British king, James I, but also enabling him to construct an exotic but recognizable atmosphere of violence and superstition. Adapting freely from a popular history of Britain, Shakespeare creates a nonrepresentational world in which history, reality, and fantasy freely alternate, commingle, and collide.

Scotland. British country north of England that historically had its own language, monarchy, parliament, and culture. In the period in which *Macbeth* is set, 1040 to 1057, Scotland was beginning to form as a nation, building on its Viking and Saxon tribal nucleus, while constantly wracked by bloody internal disputes and wars with England. Shakespeare's choice of this period in Scottish history is far from accidental, as it pertains to the origin of the two Scottish lineages—those of Malcolm and Banquo—through which James I constructed his successful claims to the thrones of both England and Scotland. Shakespeare even stages the constitutional shift from feudal elective monarchy to patrilineal inheritance and the construction of "divine right" (to which James constantly referred), when Duncan names Malcolm as heir and prince of Cumberland.

By the seventeenth century, Scotland was usually described in the English cultural imagination as wild and ungovernable because of its difficult topography, harsh weather, and uncivilized people. Images of Scotland, like those of Ireland and Wales, suffered from English Tudor nation-building—that is, "England" was constructed negatively, by defining what it was *not*. Hence, Shakespeare's Scotland becomes England's antithetical Other, a nightmarish land of barren heaths and misty crags, populated not only by aggressive clansmen and regicides but also by supernatural forces and demoniac spirits. The play's "England," on the other hand, is depicted as graciously ruled by a "good king," the saintly Edward the Confessor, who heals with a royal touch and possesses a "heavenly gift of prophecy."

This imaginary rugged Scottish landscape, with its crags, hollows, and storms, is symbolically central to Shakespeare's depiction of a turbulent political structure. Consequently, in the play's denouement, as the nation is returned to "natural" order, the wild countryside itself seems to rise up against the murderous Macbeth, as Birnam Wood comes toward Dunsinane, in the shape of Malcolm's camouflaged troops and in accordance with the weird (or wyrd) sisters' prophecy. Simultaneously, the disruptions of the natural world, the "hours dreadful and things strange" with cannibalistic horses and "strange screams of death," which accompany Macbeth's regicide and rule, are apparently purged as health is restored to the "sickly weal." However, the replacement of one regicide by another reveals the similarities between the regimes, staging the play's equivocal wordplay and eliding the differences, as each term becomes "what is not," both "fair" and "foul," like the landscape itself.

Heath. Fictional Scottish wasteland of uncontrollable natural and supernatural forces. As inhabited by the three weird sisters, the "blasted heath" is a symbolically liminal site of transformation and equivocal multi-vocality, in which weather is both "foul and fair," where the sisters are both "women" and bearded males, who can appear and disappear, and where prophecy is both "ill" and "good" as language subverts sight and meaning. In addition, the sisters' presence gives Scotland gender as (super-)naturally "female" in its uncontrollable wildness throughout the play, in contrast to Scotland's strongly masculine warrior culture.

*Scone. Ancient castle and holy site, immediately north of Perth and thirty miles north of Edinburgh. The Pictish capital of the early Scots, Scone became the traditional site for the "investment" or crowning of new monarchs, who sat on the Stone of Scone, a legendary symbol of nationalism that traces back to the eighth century. The stone was seized by England's Edward I in 1296 and removed to London, where it remained for many centuries.

*Inverness. Scottish town on the Moray Firth, at Loch Ness, about thirty miles west of Forres and about ninety miles north of Fife. Inverness is the site of the Macbeths' feudal castle, located on the northern edge of Duncan's territory and strategically placed to guard against incursions from northern Europe. However, this distant frontier also makes it an ideal place for rebellion against a centralized government, as evidenced by Cawdor's insurrection. The town of Cawdor is only ten miles east of Inverness.

*Dunsinane Hill. Thousand-foot-high crag, part of the Sidlaw hills and less than ten miles north of Scone. The site of Macbeth's military fortress and last stand, the daunting hill faces a forested area which stretches twelve miles northwest to the town of Birnam. It is through this "wood" that Malcolm and Siward make their final, disguised attack.

— *Nicolas Pullin*

MCTEAGUE: A Story of San Francisco

Author: Frank Norris (1870-1902)
Type of work: Novel
Type of plot: Naturalism

Time of plot: 1890's
First published: 1899

Although primarily compressed to a single avenue in the heart of San Francisco, this novel offers a panoramic view of California's topographical diversity. Through that diversity, Frank Norris presages a changing California that moves from raw vigor to greater social sophistication.

*Polk Street. Service street in the heart of San Francisco, which was California's largest and most prosperous city during the period in which this novel is set. Most of the novel takes place around the turn of the twentieth century, and much of the action centers around a specific neighborhood. On the one hand, the Polk Street passages reveal the naturalist's attempts to document reality by incorporating numerous details concerning place, occupations, and customs. The sheer weight of data was believed to create a total, objective rendering of the subject. On the other hand, Polk Street operates a demimonde, a microcosm of something larger, and the narrator often refers to it as the "little world of Polk Street."

Gazing out his window early in the novel, McTeague beholds the spectacle of Polk Street, which is described as an "accommodation" street, a place where people journey to do their marketing or seek other services. As McTeague watches the parade of life, the narrator notes that few of the passersby actually live on Polk Street, and those that do stand in bold relief to the sophistication of the visiting shoppers. Frequent references are made to the "great avenue" (Van Ness) a block away, which at that time was home to some of the city's elite. Thus the descriptions of Polk Street accentuate the social class distinctions which are so significant to an understanding of the novel and its vision of a changing California.

While the street bristles with activity, McTeague's boardinghouse stands in mute contrast. On the surface it is a quiet retreat to which the hapless dentist repairs after his brief forays to a nearby café. The building itself is another mirror of the social stratification found on the street. Those with the greatest financial means occupy the top floor, while McTeague, who both lives and works in his dental parlor, resides roughly in the middle of building. On the bottom floor is a squalid hovel where a ragman eventually murders his delusional lover.

Once stripped of his job and at loose ends, McTeague begins to journey about the city, visiting a construction site for a mansion being built on Van Ness and marveling at its size and intricacy. On other days he enjoys hiking the full width of the city to arrive eventually at the Cliff House, the Presidio, and a beach displaying "the full sweep of the Pacific." There, the dentist lingers and for once feels at ease in a surrounding that for the most part has overwhelmed him. He begins to return to an earlier condition—that of a rough, simple boy from the mines who had been hurled into the complexities of urban life. The wild freedom of the Pacific becomes metaphoric of the wild freedom to which McTeague will return after murdering his wife.

*Sierra foothills. California's gold country. Once McTeague kills Trina and loses any hope of assimilating back into urban life, he returns to the only life that seems natural and instinctive, that of mining in the hills of California. The contrast between the urban and rural McTeague is striking and ironic. The man who could not find a seat in a theater can invariably discover the best trails through the mountains. An unlucky dentist transforms himself into the luckiest of miners, and the strength and coarseness which appear perverted in the city become fitting attributes for a creature in the wilderness. It would seem that McTeague has finally found his place, but an encounter with the Native American, Big Jim, who solicits charity from the miner, signals McTeague's fate. McTeague, like Big Jim, is an immense, solitary, obsolete figure who will also be swallowed into the white blur of the desert. Big Jim stands as an anachronism signaling the end of the frontier and the possibilities for rural rejuvenation and rehabilitation one finds in so much American literature.

*Death Valley. Arid, low-altitude region of southeastern California that is the state's hottest and least hospitable area. When his urban past in the figure of his former friend and now bounty-hunter, Marcus Schouler, catches up with him, McTeague flees, racing across the California desert in a desperate attempt at escape. Often criticized as extraneous, the death in the desert episode is integral to the plot and the novel's themes. On the one hand, the movement from city to desert concludes the tension between interior, restrictive space and open, free space that defines many of the city episodes.

More important, though, the scene concludes a narrative pattern dominating all action: As McTeague moves steadily backward, the atavism inherent in his genes is given physical expression. These changes in setting thus represent not only a decline in personal fortune but also, more significant, McTeague's deterioration to a final beastly state. Ultimately, his fate in Death Valley is also foreshadowed in the lines of one of the songs he often sings, "No one to love, none to caress,/ Left all alone in this world's wilderness."

— *David W. Madden*

MADAME BOVARY

Author: Gustave Flaubert (1821-1880)
Type of work: Novel
Type of plot: Psychological realism

Time of plot: Mid-nineteenth century
First published: 1857 (English translation, 1886)

This story is founded upon a woman's quest for happiness through three different French cities, Rouen, Tostes, and Yonville-l'Abbaye. The novel's original subtitle, "Provincial Customs," implicitly contrasts these provincial cities with the central place in the French imagination: Paris. The exclusion of France's capital city for the heroine thus prefigures the unhappy life that will be hers in this journey from farm to a regional city.

*Rouen (rew-AN). City in Normandy where Emma Bovary is educated in a convent school. The home of Gustave Flaubert in his youth, Rouen represents Emma's first moment of happiness—one that she later regrets. After her first lover abandons her, she returns to Rouen to attend an opera that she hopes will distract her and be a source of healing. This visit to Rouen serves as a transition between the second and third parts of the novel. At the opera Emma again meets the young Léon Dupuis, whom she met in Tostes. The affair they conduct in Rouen effectively replaces the spectacle they have both come to see. However, Rouen proves to be no different for Emma than Tostes, as Léon, too, abandons her.

*Tostes (tahst). Town south of Rouen that proves to be an ideal place for Dr. Charles Bovary to set up his medical practice and live a married life with his first wife, Héloïse, who soon dies. Emma Rouault marries him—and becomes "Madame Bovary"—but finds life in Tostes to be boring. Her only moment of relief comes when she is invited to a ball at a nearby château that symbolizes her ideal. This interval of happiness only serves to emphasize the general tedium that Emma experiences in Tostes and the disappointment she feels in her married state. To make her happy, her husband leaves his medical practice in Tostes and goes to Yonville-l'Abbaye, which he hopes will become their promised land.

*Yonville-l'Abbaye (YAHN-veel lah-BAY). Town near Tostes to which the Bovarys move in the hope of finding a better life for Emma Bovary. After entering the town and meeting its leading residents, who gather at the town inn to greet their new doctor and his wife, Emma spends most of her time talking about literature with the young Léon Dupuis and the life they have seen idealized in their readings. However, this romantic ideal is in strong contrast to the reality of Yonville. Described in great detail at the beginning of the second part of the novel, Yonville is situated in the region where Normandy, Picardy, and the Ile-de-France meet, a region characterized by poor soil and a people resistant to change. It is said to be a bastard part of France. This description echoes the meeting of the three main places of the novel and its three parts.

Flaubert describes Yonville in far more detail than he does Tostes and singles out the town's civil and religious authorities for criticism. Yonville's church, for example, uncharacteristically bears no proper name, and although it has been recently renovated, it remains in a state of disrepair. Just as Emma replaces Héloïse and Yonville replaces Tostes in the narrative, so does the pharmacy replace the church as the center of community activity, and its pharmacist becomes the town's new priest and doctor. For this reason, Yonville turns out not to be a good place for Charles to practice medicine. As a solution to Emma's boredom, the town offers Emma distraction in the form of two men who will become her lovers, Léon with whom she will eventually carry on an affair in Rouen, and Rodolphe Boulanger, who enters her life only because he has sought out the new Yonville doctor to care for one of his workers.

Yonville, thus introduced as a solution to Emma's discontent in Tostes, will itself be replaced by Rouen in the third part of her search for a place in which to satisfy her desire.

— *Peter S. Rogers*

MADEMOISELLE DE MAUPIN

Author: Théophile Gautier (1811-1872)
Type of work: Novel
Type of plot: Sentimental

Time of plot: Early nineteenth century
First published: 1835-1836 (English translation, 1889)

Few novels deploy environmental information in a fashion as strange as this one does. Most of the French landscapes it describes are remembered or imagined rather than actually experienced, and information about real settings is usually unrecorded or imaginatively distorted; this is because descriptions of place within the novel always serve to reflect and elaborate the erotic emotions and unattainable ambitions of the characters.

Rosette's house. Home of Monsieur d'Albert's mistress, Rosette. Little is revealed about the location or contents of this house, save for the fact that Rosette's bath is a large marble tub, and that an odor of lime trees drifts in from the garden. Readers are never told the name of the town in which it is situated.

Avenue of elms. First location significant to d'Albert's affair with Rosette that is described. Significantly, it is only there that d'Albert imagines, for one brief moment, that he loves Rosette. The avenue's elms are very tall, sifting the light of the setting Sun in such a way as to create strange and striking chromatic effects in the sky and the surrounding terrain.

Mansion. House selected for a love nest by Rosette, located twenty miles from d'Albert's hometown. The mansion is elaborately described, in terms of its quaint surroundings—including the quasi-magical oak forest, in which Rosette and Théodore de Sérannes (who is really Mademoiselle Madelaine de Maupin) go hunting, its eccentrically ornamented architecture, and its internal decoration. There, again Théophile Gautier's emphasis is on fanciful chromatic effects, and he makes symbolic use of flowers. The mansion's surroundings are strongly contrasted with the remembered environment in which d'Albert grew up, which is described in terms redolent of severity and gloom. When "Théodore" arrives there at the end of her journey of discovery, her approach and arrival are described in a similar manner, although more particular attention is paid to the scenery depicted in its tapestries.

Gothic tower. Edifice that features in an allegory offered to Rosette by "Théodore" in chapter 6. Human life is likened to a pilgrim ascending a serpentine staircase within the tower's dark interior, toward heights from which dazzling vistas can be glimpsed, albeit through narrow windows.

Red Lion. Hostelry at which Mademoiselle de Maupin, as "Théodore," winds up after her mad ride in chapter 10. In its dining room, whose oak-beamed ceiling is blackened by smoke, she listens to male guests bawdily discussing women, and in the bed which she has to share with one of these men she first realizes the extent of her confusion regarding her own sexuality.

Theater. Most bizarre of all the imaginary environments featured in the story, a representative model of d'Albert's hectic and seemingly perverse desires after he has fallen in love with "Théodore," still mistakenly believing "him" to be a man. The theater's apparatus and orchestra are made up of insects, while the souls of poets are accommodated in its mother-of-pearl stalls, using dewdrops as opera glasses. The scenery is utterly exotic—even the sky is striped—and the theater's players wear the most fantastic costumes imaginable. The characters they play are not from any known place or period of history, and their actions do not display any comprehensible motives. The plots through which they move defy causality, and their dialogue is chaotic. The unusually extended description of a world turned upside down dissolves into a supplementary vision in which d'Albert represents his soul as an equally fabulous continent, lush and splendid but haunted by decay. Although these flights of the imagination are prompted by a plan to mount a production of William Shakespeare's *As You Like It* (1599-1600)—a play whose plot hinges on mistakes caused by characters' cross-dressing—they are a uniquely extreme depiction of sexual confusion, quite unparalleled in method or extravagance.

— *Brian Stableford*

THE MADWOMAN OF CHAILLOT

Author: Jean Giraudoux (1882-1944)
Type of work: Drama
Type of plot: Parable

Time of plot: A little before noon in the spring of next year
First performed: 1945; first published, 1945 as *La Folle de Chaillot* (English translation, 1947)

In this parable, a powerful syndicate tries to exploit suspected riches under the streets of Paris, ignoring humanity, beauty, and truth in the process. The free souls of Paris oppose them and eventually triumph by literally removing the syndicate from the scene. Paris represents all that history and culture have deposited in the French capital, being a meeting place of writers and artists for centuries.

Chaillot (shay-loh). District of Paris between the Champs Élysées and the Seine River, directly opposite the Eiffel Tower. In this district is located the Café Terrace of Chez Francis on the **Place de l'Alma**, where the Madwoman and her allies meet. The imaginary Chaillot seems to be a timeless place. There are few references to everyday life, and little appears on stage to suggest any specific part of the actual neighborhood. The play lacks any authentic sense of geography: This Chaillot is a charming, bustling neighborhood filled with funny and interesting people who seem to come and go quite freely. Most of the characters are referred to not by name but by who they are or what they do—the Ragpicker, the Baron, and the Policeman, for example. Against the fantastical backdrop, only a few characters stand out as genuine individuals, notably the Madwomen, who claim particular Paris neighborhoods as their domains: Madame Constance of Passy; Mademoiselle Gabrielle of St. Sulpice; Madame Josephine of La Concorde; and the Countess Aurelia, the Madwoman of Chaillot.

*Paris. Capital of France, which suffered under German occupation during World War II. Jean Giraudoux

was deeply disturbed by the fact that some French citizens collaborated with the Germans during their occupation. Illegal financial activities and fraudulent business practices enabled unscrupulous citizens to profit mightily at the great expense of their fellow countrymen. In his play, Paris is a literary symbol for all the cities that experienced the tragedy and destruction of World War II. It is also a symbol for the purity, simplicity, beauty, and culture destroyed by profiteers. The play's story revolves around a scheme of the president to drill for oil that he believes lies below the city, even though doing so would destroy the beauty and charm of the city.

In this allegory of human purity and human corruption Giraudoux uses the threat to destroy the city as a way to attack modern capitalism. The Madwoman and her friends represent the citizens of Paris just as the profiteers represent the Nazis and their French collaborators. Ultimately, the Madwoman sends the profiteers to the bottomless pit, symbolically ridding the world of greedy exploitation and restoring the city to its former beauty and purity.

— *Rhona Justice-Malloy*

MAGGIE: A Girl of the Streets

Author: Stephen Crane (1871-1900)
Type of work: Novel
Type of plot: Naturalism

Time of plot: Late nineteenth century
First published: 1893

This short novel is set in the tenement housing of New York City in the 1890's, but it could have been set in almost any large American city of that period. The primary conflicts in the novel accompany the places in the novel; Maggie's hellish home life is set against an even more difficult existence on the streets of impoverished immigrant society where Maggie is at the mercy of social and environmental forces that eventually cause her demise.

Maggie's home. Apartment in Manhattan's Rum Alley in which Maggie lives with her parents and brother. Her father and mother are both alcoholics, and her mother, despite her piety, is particularly given to violence. Stephen Crane often describes the shambles of the troubled home: bloody fights, broken items, loud, vulgar language, and drunken stupors. Maggie's father, though

mostly absent in Maggie's life, describes their home as "reg'lar livin' hell! Damndes' place!" The abuse that Maggie and her brother Jimmy experience causes Maggie to fantasize about places beyond the interior of her home. She is thus easily attracted to a flamboyant barkeep, Pete, who can take her to places outside the misery of her home's four walls.

Maggie's relationship with Pete eventually results in her expulsion from her home. In her subsequent aimless wandering she finally confronts Pete with the haunting question, "where kin I go?" This question epitomizes the tragic and futile relationship of Maggie to the places of this novel. Pete's answer, "go teh hell," pushes her to the point of desperation. She is eventually found in the gloomy districts near the river. In other words her descent has reached its social and moral nadir.

After it is clear that Maggie is dead, the final scene of the novel returns to the interior of her home where her mother, in pitiful self-indulgence and brazen denial of reality, forgives her. Thus, readers are brought full circle to see how the family environment into which Maggie was born is part of a larger social system that destroys innocent and unsuspecting flowers like Maggie.

Rum Alley. Street in Manhattan's impoverished Bowery district on which Maggie's family lives, along with many other Irish immigrant families. The neighborhood is used symbolically to portray not only the dismal nature of Maggie's world, but also to emphasize the extent of environmental forces that Maggie and others in her neighborhood must overcome just to survive.

The novel opens with a description of a fight between gangs of young boys from Devil's Row and Rum Alley (including Maggie's brother Jimmy). The names of these fictitious Manhattan streets suggest the fatalism that Crane attaches to this novel, in which even very young children are caught in the ironic struggles of defending places that are not worth defending. In fact, these slums are responsible for the dysfunctional behavior of the citizens of these places, places where "deh moon looks like hell" and where Maggie "blossomed in a mud puddle."

Shirt factory. Sweatshop in which Maggie works long hours as a seamstress before she meets Pete. This place in the novel reinforces the poverty that immigrants faced, where women and children experienced horrible working conditions. Such sweatshops were usually insufficiently heated in winter, beastly hot in summer, and poorly lighted year round. Crane uses the shop to underscore the futility of Maggie's life.

Manhattan nightclubs. After Maggie meets Pete, an arrogant bartender and friend of her brother Jimmy, Pete takes her to a variety of nightclubs. At first Maggie regards Pete as the "beau ideal of a man," and the places of his world provide a pleasant contrast with her limited and oppressive home. In reality, however, the clubs that Maggie visits are merely cheap imitations of the nightlife spots that wealthy New Yorkers frequent. They seem brilliant to Maggie, but their presence in the novel only underscores the deprivation of Maggie's existence.

The clubs appear in the narrative in an approximately descending order of taste. Pete first takes Maggie to cheap theaters and music halls. Next comes a visit to the Bowery, a carnival-like atmosphere where immigrants of various ethnic origins mingle in "phantasies of the aristocratic theatre-going public, at reduced rates." This is followed by an evening at the hall of irregular shape where two painted women are in the crowd. Finally, Maggie is taken to a hall in which prostitutes are stationed at every table. There, Pete abandons Maggie for Nell, a "woman of brilliance and audacity."

— *Kenneth Hada*

THE MAGIC MOUNTAIN

Author: Thomas Mann (1875-1955)
Type of work: Novel
Type of plot: Philosophical

Time of plot: 1907-1914
First published: Der Zauberberg, 1924 (English translation, 1927)

This novel is set high in the eastern Swiss Alps, at a sanatorium for people with lung disease. The patients' illnesses and their great distance from the workaday world below predispose them to seek transcendence and explore metaphysical ideas. Hans Castorp's excursions into the mountains bring encounters that promote educa-

tion and self-discovery. The snow and ice of the chill mountain winter, associated with solitude and death, lead to altered perceptions of space and time.

Berghof Sanatorium. Health-care institution at Davos-Platz in the mountains of Switzerland. Primary setting of the novel. Thomas Mann's visit to his wife while she was at a sanatorium near Davos was the inspiration for the novel and the source of many descriptions of place. Private rooms where patients lie for hours alone on their balconies as well as the monotony of the spa routine make the time pass quickly. What was to be a two-week sojourn for Castorp lasts seven years. Illness brings out the extraordinary even in a mundane person like Castorp. The unusual proximity to mortality sparks the genius in Castorp and other characters; it also stimulates their intellect and heightens their emotions. The detailed attention to the body that comes with constant physical exams, regular massage, and discussions of individual illnesses contributes to the basic conflict in the novel between the mind and nature, the material and the spiritual worlds—a conflict that preoccupies Mann in many of his works.

*Davos. Swiss resort area that includes a lake and the enclaves Davos-Dorf and Davos-Platz in the river valley, all places that the characters frequent and that constitute the view from the sanatorium, high on the mountain. As was true historically, Davos in the novel is a playground for the idle rich at the turn of the twentieth century. Stylishly dressed people wile away their leisure with outdoor band music, shopping in elegant stores, going to the movies (a new entertainment in those days), or winter sports. In view of World War I, which thunders into the novel at its close, these people and their pastimes look irresponsible or shallow. The more profound experiences of Castorp take place in the mountain wilderness or in the solitude of his room at the sanatorium.

Dining room. Cheerful room in the sanatorium with bands of color on the vaulted walls, brass chandeliers, and glass doors. Sanatorium guests look forward to mealtime, where they socialize at their seven tables and enjoy countless delicacies described in detail and consumed lovingly throughout the novel. This room is also the scene of Dr. Krokowski's evening lecture series on topics such as love as a cause of illness or sexual drives and the reasons these may be inhibited. Polite dining involves sensual enjoyment which is at the same time kept in check by various restraints of table manners. The conflict between social propriety and elemental needs is important in the novel and is developed in dining-room scenes.

Snow. An important chapter is devoted to Castorp's solitary excursion on skis into the mountains, where he is surprised by a snowstorm. The driving snow makes him unable to distinguish the land from the sky and causes him to lose his sense of direction; the cold exhausts and numbs him. He fears he will be found dead the next morning. The extremity of this setting, which is disorienting morally and metaphysically as well as physically, forces Castorp to contemplate the meaning of life and death. The vision he has as he leans against a locked barn, trying to shelter himself from the storm, contrasts completely with his real surroundings. He experiences an archetypal sunny Greek landscape with a classical temple and serene people. In the inner sanctum of the temple, however, is a terrifying scene of cannibalism, which hints at the hidden side of civilized life.

*Flüela Valley. Valley containing a powerful waterfall along the Flüela River, not far from Davos, that is the goal of a picnic excursion led by Mynheer Peeperkorn. The forest on the way, which contains exotic hanging moss and parasitic plants that make the trees seem diseased, echoes the novel's general fascination with illness. While the deafening thunder of the falls makes all speech comically inaudible, the scene also points to the possible profundity of things beyond that which language can express. When Peeperkorn, obviously drunk, raises his cup in a speech drowned out by the waterfall, he resembles a pagan holy man celebrating life. He enjoys the rapt attention of the group as they eat.

— Julie D. Prandi

THE MAGICIAN OF LUBLIN

Author: Isaac Bashevis Singer (1904-1991)
Type of work: Novel
Type of plot: Psychological realism

Time of plot: Late nineteenth century
First published: Der Kuntsnmakher fun Lublin, 1959
(English translation, 1960)

Yasha Mazur, a Polish stage magician and tightrope walker, has affairs with several women and plans to leave his wife. An attempt to steal running-away money misfires, and he loses everything material. In an attempt to atone, he returns to his Jewish faith as a hermit.

*Warsaw. Capital of Poland. Isaac Bashevis Singer's evocation of the city's atmosphere around 1880 is one of his novel's major achievements. At the time in which the novel is set, Warsaw is a large city with palaces and slum housing, served by railways, interior plumbing, and new gas lighting in some streets. Some affluent residents and businesses have telephones installed. There is culture in the shape of theaters and opera houses, high fashion, bookshops, and café society. Yasha is to appear at the Alhambra Theatre. The air smells of "fresh baking, coffee, horse manure, smoke from the trains and factories." It is a bustling, noisy metropolis.

Singer mentions many of the city's real streets, including Avenue Dluga, Marshalkowska Boulevard, Alexander Place, and Nalevsky Street. Yasha keeps a small apartment on Freta Street, containing books, antiques, and "his collection of billboards, newspaper clippings and reviews." It is just large enough for him and his mistress, Magda. Kroleska Street has the apartment in which Yasha's principal love, the widowed Emilia, lives with her daughter in genteel poverty. Though poor, they keep a servant, own a piano on which the daughter practices daily, have good-quality furnishings, as Emilia's late husband was a university professor. Singer draws the sharp contrast between her home and that of Zeftel in Piask.

One night, Yasha attempts to burglarize the apartment of a rich landowner on Marshalkowska Boulevard but fails to open the owner's safe in the dark and hurts his foot while descending from the apartment's balcony. His failure costs him his girlfriends, profession, and self-respect.

Synagogues. Jewish houses of worship in which several important scenes are set. While traveling by horse-cart to Warsaw, Yasha and Magda are caught in a rainstorm and forced to take shelter in a synagogue. Yasha is

Jewish but has not visited a synagogue for years and can scarcely remember the ceremonies, the prayer-shawls, the phylacteries. He takes away a damaged copy of a holy book, then pretends not to be Jewish.

Later, after Yasha bungles his burglary attempt, he again takes shelter in a synagogue. This time he is more humble, noting some familiarity when he sees young men in sidelocks, skullcaps, and sashes studying the Talmud and hears the cantor intoning. He accepts help in donning a prayer-shawl and recalls his promise to his father to remain a Jew.

*Lublin. Rural town in eastern Poland where Yasha owns a house, in which the novel opens and closes. The description suggests a small farm or smallholding, with barns, stables, and fruit trees. Yasha keeps chickens; he is considered a rich man. He has a loving and faithful wife; all he lacks is children.

At the end of the novel Yasha is living in a tiny shed in the courtyard in which he has had himself bricked up; he can communicate with the outside world only through a tiny shuttered window. With no space for a bed, Yasha lies on a straw pallet. He has a chair and a small table but little else; he has not emerged from this cell for three years.

*Piask. Small town on the road to Warsaw from Lublin that is home to two of Yasha's girlfriends. Magda lives in a house just outside the town with her mother and younger brother. The mother accepts the fact of Magda's affair with a married man. She welcomes Yasha's presents of food, and makes no objection to Yasha and Magda sharing a bed in her house. Zeftel's home is in the town. She is the widow or abandoned wife of a thief who has escaped from prison. She lives in poor circumstances behind the town slaughterhouses.

— *Chris Morgan*

THE MAGNIFICENT AMBERSONS

Author: Booth Tarkington (1869-1946)
Type of work: Novel
Type of plot: Social realism

Time of plot: 1873-early twentieth century
First published: 1918

This early twentieth century novel about the passage of an old way of life in the Midwest deals with urban problems commonly associated with later periods: urban sprawl, inner-city decay, pollution, the impersonality and alienation in urban life, and other social and environmental problems.

Midland town. Midwestern city modeled on Indianapolis, Indiana, Booth Tarkington's birthplace and hometown. The town offers a physical representation of the novel's theme: changes in values and even the kinds of corruption that arrive in the wake of progress. The novel conveys the idea that while change is inevitable—in the town, in class structure, in the economy—it also exacts a high cost in aesthetic and moral values.

The novel's Midland town is in transition. Its center of population is moving away from its former downtown area as new generations build their homes on the town's outskirts. Additions and subdivisions and roads multiply. However, as the town's economy becomes more reliant on manufacturing and as gas and electricity are more commonly used, the town also acquires grime, soot, and polluted air.

Tensions between the past and the future are incarnated in the novel's two antagonists, George Minafer, scion of the wealthy, upper-crust Amberson family, and Eugene Morgan—an inventor, particularly of automobiles. George hates automobiles and intensely dislikes Eugene for both personal and cultural reasons. It is clear that George wants the present and the future to be identical to the past. Eugene, on the other hand, knows that the future must bring change and finds the future exciting. To resist change—personal, cultural, and economic—George goes to extremes that are painful for him and for other members of his family. Ultimately, however, the theme of change, as seen in motifs of place, becomes manifest in George's learning about the very contingency of life itself. In one of the novel's cruelest ironies, George is seriously injured when he is struck by an automobile while crossing the street.

Amberson mansion. Midland home of several generations of the Amberson family. The great house reflects both the Ambersons' prosperity early in the novel and their later decline. The house is a masterpiece of late Victorian architecture and furnishing. In an early scene, the Ambersons give a ball in the house in honor of George's return home from school. The ball is presented as a symbol of the end of an era; there will be no more displays of such elegance.

George and Eugene, voices of the past and of the future, meet for the first time at the ball. Their personal confrontation begins, against the background of the clash between nineteenth century upper-class society, on one hand, and entrepreneurship, adventure, and confidence in the future on the other hand. Also at the mansion's ball, Eugene resumes his courtship of Isabel, George's mother, while George himself is smitten with Eugene's daughter Lucy.

Later, the neighborhood around the mansion deteriorates as old families sell their homes and move out or rent them; property values decline, and eventually the mansion itself is demolished.

Boardinghouse. Place where George and his aunt Fanny share rooms after the Amberson family fortune is gone after the death of patriarch Major Amberson, and George must go to work for a living. The boardinghouse is a concrete representation of the depths to which George falls, and there he learns to deal with insults to his pride.

— *Gordon Walters*

MAGNIFICENT OBSESSION

Author: Lloyd C. Douglas (1877-1951)
Type of work: Novel
Type of plot: Domestic realism

Time of plot: Early twentieth century
First published: 1929

The events of this novel revolve around a Michigan hospital and the homes of its characters. Other important scenes take place in various towns or cities in Europe, especially Italy, known as a land of lovers.

Brightwood Hospital. Fictional Detroit hospital sometimes called Hudson's Clinic in honor of Dr. Wayne Hudson, whose brilliant brain surgery has made the place famous. The hospital is described as being white, neat, and having a variety of well-lighted rooms; however, it also harbors a dark mystery concerning Hudson's life and work. Hudson is strongly driven by secrets he learned from an artist who drew his ideas for gaining creative power from Christ's Sermon on the Mount. In the mysteries of brain surgery, the inescapable connection between the physical and the spiritual forms a hinge that holds together the novel's central drama. Hudson's work at Brightwood is symbolic of the modern struggle of humans to understand themselves as more than machines.

The rich playboy Robert Merrick is taken to Brightwood Hospital after a boating accident. There, he not only recovers, but also discovers his vocational calling to become a brain surgeon in order to atone for his inadvertent part in Hudson's death.

Lake Saginack. Lake overlooked by Dr. Hudson's Flintridge home. Its black waters and steep sides sym-bolize the depths of life and death into which Hudson perpetually dives in spite of his fears. For Robert Merrick and his grandfather Nicholas Merrick, this lake is a place of leisure—for swimming and sailing. Ironically, when young Merrick has a sailing accident and is saved from drowning by a resuscitation apparatus belonging to Hudson, Hudson himself drowns in the lake and cannot be saved because his apparatus is not available. Thus, his life ends in the same waters where the younger man's life is renewed.

*Paris. France's capital city is the home of Merrick's widowed mother. To Merrick, the city represents a world of posturing and pretense that he avoids as much as possible, even as he tries to avoid memories of his very unpleasant childhood at home with two parents who hated each other.

Gordon's Gardens. Cabaret in Detroit where young people, such as Tom Masterson and Joyce Hudson, go for wild parties and heavy drinking. Merrick rescues Joyce from an incident there with an acrobat who uses her as a stage display, even though she has passed out.

— *Daven M. Kari*

THE MAGUS

Author: John Fowles (1926-   )
Type of work: Novel
Type of plot: Psychological realism

Time of plot: 1953
First published: 1965; revised, 1977

A novel in which the magic of the eastern Mediterranean has a liberating effect upon a young Englishman afraid of emotional commitment; here the magic is expressed in the curious psychological experiments of a rich recluse on a remote Greek island.

Waiting Room. Facetious name that the wealthy Greek-English philosopher Maurice Conchis gives to his villa, where the novel's narrator, Nicholas Urfe, finds himself the subject—or perhaps victim—of a series of shifting realities orchestrated by Conchis. At first the experiments seem like a strange game, but it is one that eventually comes to have a more sinister cast. The isolation of the villa is emphasized in several ways. It is on the southern tip of the island of Phraxos, with no other human habitation anywhere near. It is surrounded by barbed wire, left over from World War II, it has its own private beach, and only its rooftop is visible from the forest outside the estate.

The character of the villa itself seems to change as the nature of Conchis's experiments on Urfe change; at times the novel emphasizes the richness of the villa's furnishings, which include original paintings by Amedeo Modigliani and Pierre Bonnard. At other times, the novel focuses on the plainness and simplicity of the villa's fittings. Readers quickly understand that the Waiting Room—whose name comes from a *salle d'attente* sign from a French railway station, left behind by German occupation troops after the war—is a stage set whose different features are emphasized depending on each new mystery that is played out there.

The appearance of attractive English twins, June and Julia, turns the villa into a place of sexual attraction, even though their roles within Conchis's ever-shifting drama make it difficult to get the measure of them. The villa is a place whose mysteries constantly befuddle and bedazzle visitors. It also becomes the embodiment of the warm and liberal atmosphere that makes the eastern Mediterranean so attractive to the buttoned-up English: "It was Greece again, the Alexandrian Greece of Cavafy; there were only degrees of aesthetic pleasure; of beauty in decadence. Morality was a North European lie."

Lord Byron School. Private school on the island of Phraxos at which Urfe is a replacement teacher; it is modeled on the Anargyrios and Korgialenios College on Spetsai, where Fowles taught in 1952. Named after the great English poet who died in Greece while supporting the country's struggle against its Turkish master, Lord Byron School is run along the lines of an English school. Its atmosphere is suffocating; only one other teacher speaks any English, and Urfe initially speaks no Greek. Although Fowles has elsewhere stated that his fictional school is nowhere near as grotesque as its real-life counterpart, he clearly presents it as a place from which to escape—in contrast to which even the mysteries of Conchis's villa seem attractive and liberating.

The school's island is also described in terms of its lack of amenity. All its tiny village has is a bar where Urfe can drink with his fellow teachers and a woodland where, for much of the year, there are not even goatherds tending their flocks. The island's loneliness is evoked constantly.

*****Athens.** Capital of Greece, where Urfe attempts to discover the sexual liberty he dreams of finding in Greece during his periodic excursions from the school. However, the actual city is depicted as a crowded, bustling city of unlovely aspect where, on one occasion, Urfe thinks he has contracted syphilis from a prostitute. The true liberty he seeks is to be found only by threading through the maze of Conchis's mysteries on Phraxos.

*****London.** Great Britain's capital city appears twice in the novel. At the beginning of the book it is the impersonal city that ideally suits Urfe's selfishness. There he starts a relationship with Alison, little understanding what a cold and uncaring person he really is. At the end of the novel, he finds that he must return to reality in London, where he again meets Alison and hence realizes the degree to which he has been changed by his experiences in Greece.

— *Paul Kincaid*

THE MAHABHARATA

Author: Unknown
Type of work: Poetry
Type of plot: Epic

Time of plot: Antiquity
First transcribed: Mahābhārata, c. 400 B.C.E.-200 C.E.
   (English translation, 1834)

Set in remote antiquity in northern India, this complex epic poem is a mythical tale about the civil wars fought between the descendants of King Bharata, the Pandavas, and the Kauravas. Places in the poem—many of which are filled with supernatural beings—are often designated as sacred, and natural elements are often personified.

Kurukshetra. Plain of the Kurus (another name for the Bharatas); the battlefield on which the two factions meet. Just before the battle, Krishna outlines a philosophy of life and theological truths to Arjuna—a long commentary that is often printed separately as the *Bhagavad Gita* (song of the lord), a sacred Hindu religious text. Considering Krishna's spiritual message, the plain might be seen as the battlefield of life, on which one's nobler self must fight against one's baser self.

Hastinapur. Capital of the Bharata Kingdom in which the five Pandavas and one hundred Kauravas grow up together and site of the inheritance over which they fight.

Indraprastha. Capital of the Pandavas' part of the Bharata Kingdom after King Dhritarashtra divide the kingdom in an attempt to prevent civil war between the Pandavas and the Kauravas.

Assembly hall. Grand hall built especially for the occasion of a dice game, in which the Pandavas lose everything and agree to go into exile in a forest.

Kingdom of Matsya. King Virata's court, at which the Pandavas spend the thirteenth year of their exile incognito. The Kauravas' invasion of Matsya during the last year of the Pandavas' exile precipitates the latter's involvement in the struggle and the consequent premature revelation of Arjuna's true identity and the Kauravas' subsequent refusal to return the kingdom as promised.

Indra's heaven. Final resting place for brave warriors who die in battle; one of many heavens mentioned in the epic. During the Pandavas' exile in the forest, Arjuna departs to find divine weapons and eventually visits Indra's heaven for years while learning to use the weapons. At the end of the epic, Yudhishthera realizes that all is illusion, including heaven and hell.

*Ganges River (GAN-jeez). River in the northeast part of the Indian subcontinent that Hindus consider to be sacred. In the epic, the Ganges is a river goddess, Bhishma's mother.

— *Kathryn A. Walterscheid*

MAIN STREET: The Story of Carol Kennicott

Author: Sinclair Lewis (1885-1951)
Type of work: Novel
Type of plot: Social satire

Time of plot: c. 1910-1920
First published: 1920

This blistering satire on life in small-town America is set in a typical midwestern town, which is viewed through the eyes of young urbanite who marries a local doctor.

Gopher Prairie. Fictional Minnesota town that is the novel's primary setting and target of its satire. Lewis begins with a prologue describing Gopher Prairie's **Main Street** as the "continuation of Main Streets everywhere. . . . the climax of civilization. . . . Our railway station is the final aspiration of architecture."

Lewis modeled Gopher Prairie on the similarly sized town of Sauk Centre, Minnesota, in which he grew up. Each is a wheat town of about three thousand residents,

situated at the edge of an endless prairie, but within easy reach of Minnesota's many lakes. In a thirty-two-minute walk, Carol Kennicott, the newly arrived bride of Dr. Will Kennicott, completely explores the town. She hopes to find a village of the sort described in sentimental novels, with hollyhocks and quiet lanes and quaint inhabitants. Instead, she is overwhelmed by the ugliness that greets her as she walks down Main Street. The town's three-story hotel is shabby; its dining room a sea of stained tablecloths. The drug store features a greasy marble soda fountain and shelves of dubious patent medicines. A grocery story has overripe fruit in its window. The meat market reeks of blood. The saloons stink of stale beer. The clock in front of the jewelry store does not work. There is no park or courthouse with shady grounds where she can rest her eyes. Only two buildings please her. The Bon Ton Store, the largest in town, is at least clean, and the Farmers' National Bank is housed in an Ionic temple.

The people of Main Street match the buildings. The clerk raising an awning before his store has dirty hands, and none of the men appears to have shaved in the last three days. The Gopher Prairie elite, who gather in the evening to welcome Carol, disappoint her. Lewis defines the village aristocracy as composed of all persons engaged in professions, or earning over twenty-five hundred dollars a year, or having grandparents born in America. However, to Carol they appear uncouth, lacking in culture, and deficient in style.

Lewis displays some ambivalence in his attitude toward Gopher Prairie, softening his satire as the novel continues. As Main Street becomes more familiar territory, its blemishes become less irritating to Carol. She learns to discriminate among the inhabitants of the town, finding virtues even in people who seem crude and uninteresting when she first meets them.

*Minnesota countryside. Brief passages throughout the novel contrast the beauty of Minnesota's rural landscape with the shabbiness of Gopher Prairie. While walking down the railroad track to Plover Lake, Carol marvels at the wildflowers she finds in bloom, and is enchanted with a pasture near the lake, likening it to a rare old Persian carpet of cream and gold. On a hunting trip with her husband, Carol admires Minnesota's lakes and wheat fields, seeing in them the dignity and greatness of style she cannot find on Main Street.

Lake Minniemashie. Minnesota resort area where Dr. Kennicott buys a summer cottage. Although the lake's cottages are mere shacks, clustered too close to one another, Carol enjoys her summers at the cottage. Majestic elms and linden trees shade the dwellings; across the lake, fields of ripe wheat slope up to green for-

ests. Soothed by the gentle landscape at the lake, Carol finds it easy to get along with the same women who irritate her in town. To her regret, she cannot persuade her neighbors to use the cottages after their customary September closing. A rare winter sledding trip to the lake reveals the beauty of Minnesota's scenery under snow and ice.

*Chicago. Although Lewis uses Carol to dramatize his critique of village life, he does not elaborate on her city life. The narrative of Carol's experiences while in a Chicago library school is little more than a list of features that no rural town can offer—the Art Institute, symphony concerts, theater, and professional ballet. Likewise, while she is a librarian in St. Paul, Minnesota, she reads widely, socializes briefly, and meets her future husband.

*Minneapolis. Minnesota's largest city. After Carol settles in Gopher Prairie, Minneapolis functions as a place of cultural refuge; the sound of a passing train's whistle holding out hope of escape from village limitations. However, when her husband takes her to Minneapolis for a week, she feels like a country bumpkin, confused by the crowds in the railroad station, shy and hesitant in the grandiose lobby of their hotel, and amazed by the conveniences offered in the hotel's bathroom.

*Washington, D.C. National capital where, during World War I, Carol escapes from Gopher Prairie for an extended period by working as a clerk in a government bureaucracy. Lewis uses the city and Carol's experiences to elaborate on his own ambivalence toward small-town life. Washington offers Carol vast parks and splendid buildings whose absence disturbs her on her first encounter with Gopher Prairie. She particularly values lively political and cultural discussions with her new friends. However, she also soon discovers that two-thirds of her Washington acquaintances come from small towns. When Gopher Prairie residents visit, she welcomes them to Washington and shows them its many sights. Experiencing urban life as a mature woman, Carol becomes more sympathetic to Gopher Prairie, accepting the raw new settlement's uncouthness. Eventually, she returns to her life within it.

— *Milton Berman*

MAJOR BARBARA

Author: George Bernard Shaw (1856-1950)
Type of work: Drama
Type of plot: Play of ideas

Time of plot: January, 1906
First performed: 1905; first published, 1907

George Bernard Shaw described this play as a "discussion in three acts," and its three settings, in Middlesex and London's East and West Ends, establish not only context and mood but also serve as visual evidence for the main characters during their debates about money, religion, and power.

Wilton Crescent. Fashionable section of London's upscale West End. Act 1 is set in the library of Lady Britomart Undershaft's house, which she has tastefully decorated with money from her husband, who has become wealthy by manufacturing arms. Although the pictures, books, and music portfolios identified in stage directions suggest the Undershaft family will be gathering in an enlightened environment conducive to liberal thinking, Lady Britomart steps forward as a Victorian relic of upper-class materialism. Thus, the library's rich decor calls attention to Lady Britomart's insistence upon money as the panacea for whatever problems she and her adult children confront.

West Ham. Location of the newly whitewashed Salvation Army shelter in London's impoverished East End in which the play's second act is set. Seen through Barbara Undershaft's eyes, the shelter represents charitable compassion. Conversely, for the destitute who seek refuge here from the January cold, it represents food as bribery. Barbara has devoted herself to saving souls within these bleak surroundings, but she is no match for her intruding millionaire father who proves

that her means for rescuing the downtrodden are hollow. After Undershaft purchases her religious idealism by donating five thousand pounds to the shelter, Barbara walks away under a leaden sky, knowing that her illusions have been as thin as the whitewash on the slum warehouse.

Perivale St. Andrews. Location of Andrew Undershaft's munitions foundry set amid the hills of Middlesex. The fictitious Perivale St. Andrews of act 3 is a frighteningly perfect utopian community made up of churches, libraries, schools, banquet chambers, and nursing homes. Not to be overlooked, however, the dummy soldiers strewn under a high explosives shed testify to the ghastly effects produced by the bombshells on display at this "triumph of modern industry." The foundry clearly symbolizes the entrepreneur's right to spread destruction; however, from among the clutter of props in the closing scene, Barbara emerges as an energetic life force who intends to use her inherited money and power to fight the evils of war.

— *Joe Nordgren*

THE MAKING OF AMERICANS: Being a History of a Family's Progress

Author: Gertrude Stein (1874-1946)
Type of work: Novel
Type of plot: Psychological realism

Time of plot: Late nineteenth and early twentieth centuries
First published: 1925; abridged, 1934

Gertrude Stein's conception and utilization of place, like other elements of her work, was purposely designed to deviate from traditional literary practice, even to encourage readers to reconsider the customary meaning of the term itself. While this long, amorphous novel about the history of two American families is one of her earliest works, its narrative method arises from her conviction that psychological reality can be effectively expressed as an ongoing stream of consciousness. Consequently, most of the novel is set within the narrator's mind, and its characters are rarely grounded in tangible physical places.

Gossols. Town in the western United States that is home to the Herslands, one of the novel's two central families. Stein wanted to establish a basic difference between the places where the two families were primarily located, contrasting East and West, coastal city and heartland settlement, old European culture and developing American social values. The Herslands are described as "really western," since David Hersland as a young man had gone far into new country. A sense of community is conveyed by Stein's description of the people from Gossols picking roses from the Hersland's hedge to make sweet-scented jars.

The Hersland family is substantially more prosperous than most of their neighbors, whom Stein repeatedly refers to as a "poor queer kind of people." The Herslands are shown in contact with a multicultural population quite different from the social class that their family fortune makes available. The interchange and friction between the first-generation immigrants of Gossols and the social strata toward which David Hersland inclines provides part of the tension that energizes and unsettles the members of the Hersland family.

Hersland house. Gossols home of the Herslands. The house is a relic from the days when Gossols was beginning. Built of wood, it is of medium size, standing on rising ground, surrounded by grass that becomes dry in summer. A vegetable garden, fruit trees, and hay fields provide sustenance. One of Stein's infrequent descriptive passages evokes the essence of the Herslands' life with a lyric effusion that celebrates the pleasures of eating radishes with soil still sticking to them, of

planting seeds, and of running fully into a strong wind.

Bridgepoint. Atlantic coastal town that represents the old Eastern establishment that controlled the social and cultural norms of the United States through the nineteenth century. Stein's second primary family, the Dehnings, is an exemplar of this, as its members have been born and reared in Bridgepoint; they all also have both city and country homes.

Dehning houses. The Dehnings' country house is a large and commodious house, with spacious lawns, great meadows, and open marshes leading down to salt water, where the Dehnings ride horses, sail, and fish. Their city house itself is an emblem of their prosperity, although a "nervous restlessness of luxury" runs through it. Stein likens the house to a "splendid canvas" painted over but full of empty space. The house's decor is redolent of an older time, of confidence and affluence, with a parlor filled with ornate marbles on onyx stands. These and other details of acquisition link American life with an older European refinement. Stein summarizes this aspect of the Dehning family by saying of Julia Dehning that "Eastern living was natural to her being," and that when she is in Gossols, she is "cut off from Eastern living."

Farnham College. Liberal arts college for women somewhere in the western United States at which Martha Hersland's husband, Philip Redfern, teaches. Born in a small southwestern town, Redfern is a representative of rural America, and Farnham College is depicted as a "democratic community," a reflection of Stein's experiences at Radcliffe and at Johns Hopkins.

— *Leon Lewis*

THE MALCONTENT

Author: John Marston (1576-1634)
Type of work: Drama
Type of plot: Tragicomedy

Time of plot: Thirteenth century
First performed: 1604; first published, 1604

In common with much Elizabethan and Jacobean drama, this play requires minimal staging: A few doors, drapes, and benches suffice. The sense of place the play conveys, therefore, lies largely in its audiences' imagi-

nation. Genoa, Italy, is ostensibly the play's setting, but it is not a Genoa that has any geographical reality. Thirteenth century Genoa, historically, was the center of a huge commercial maritime enterprise, rivaling that of Venice. None of this is apparent in the play. All that matters to John Marston is his Italian setting, wherein the political philosophy of Niccolò Machiavelli, combined with the hot-blooded lusts, supposedly, of southern Europe, created an other world for his northern European Protestant audiences.

*Genoa.** Northwestern Italian city-state and mercantile center around whose palace and court of Duke Altofronto the play centers. Within the palace building only the duchess's bedchamber has special significance, for its sexual intrigues and adulterous relationships. Marston never shows the inside of the bedroom, only its outside. At its door, the young courtier Ferneze is stabbed, so though sexuality is promised, only violence is delivered. However, the general atmosphere is one of promiscuity; the lack of borders in the staging reinforces this.

Citadel. At some location near the Palace lies the citadel, in which Maria lies imprisoned through most of the drama. Act 5, scene 2 presumably takes place there, though this is never stated as such. The citadel symbolizes the chastity of the duke's wife, Maria, which has a stronghold even in a corrupt court, thereby making some sort of comic resolution possible.

Countryside. A hunting scene in act 3 is the only other scene not taking place in court. Hunting is a feature of tragicomedy, derived from the pastoral, but here denoting the sexual chase.

*Florence.** Powerful city-state in north-central Italy that was a rival of Genoa. Although no scene in the play is set there, the duke of Florence is a manipulative force in the play; he helps usurp Altofronto and through Bilioso seeks to reinstate him. Florence therefore represents a rival power base and the source of a complicating corruption.

— *David Barratt*

MALONE DIES

Author: Samuel Beckett (1906-1989)
Type of work: Novel
Type of plot: Absurdist

Time of plot: 1940's
First published: Malone meurt, 1951 (English translation, 1956)

The title character of this novel finds himself in a bed in a hospital or asylum of some kind during the last few days or weeks of his life—perhaps in the spring of the year—and struggles to come to terms with his own pending death, first by cataloging his surroundings, then by creating stories, some of fiction and some of fact.

Asylum or hospital. Malone does not know where he is or how he got here, and since he is alone, no one else can answer his questions. All he can know for sure is that he is alone, disoriented, and baffled. Most immediately he is reliant on information his senses can provide, but since he is no longer capable of negotiating the world under his own power, what he can tell readers must come first of all from a fixed position. That he is in a room of spare furnishings is obvious enough simply from glancing around, and there is at least *prima facie* information that this room is in an institution of some kind, most likely an asylum. It is in any case the last stop on the train line, a home for the wretched.

Both the personal experiences Malone recounts and the tales he relates to amuse himself blur fiction with fact. Yet Samuel Beckett's most careful readers have speculated where Malone is by taking clues from geographical details that his uttered memories contain. Given these memories, one speculation is that Malone is somewhere south of Dublin, Ireland, where Beckett spent time as a boy. For example, Malone recalls listening as a child to the barking of dogs at night in nearby hills. It has been suggested that this allusion is Beckett himself recalling hearing dogs from the hills west of Carrickmine, a pastoral area outside Dublin.

The primary "place" of the novel is inside Malone's own mind, and that is central to what the novel is about. It is probably futile to expect fully to understand *Malone Dies* in terms of conventional notions of time and space. Try as Malone does to accept his fate, try as he does to surrender to the way of all flesh, Malone's mind will not relent. This, above all, is what *Malone Dies* is about: the relentless struggle of human consciousness to sort through sensory data independent of whether or not that data are reliable, its struggle to organize, to find a pattern that makes sense of experience.

— *Jay Boyer*

THE MALTESE FALCON

Author: Dashiell Hammett (1894-1961)
Type of work: Novel
Type of plot: Detective and mystery

Time of plot: 1928
First published: 1930

This novel is set entirely in San Francisco, as is much of Dashiell Hammett's other fiction. Hammett himself worked as both a detective and a writer in San Francisco and knew the city well. Placing the corrupt action and characters of this novel on the far western shore of the United States underscores the westward movement of the failure of the American Dream.

*San Francisco.** California port city in which the novel is set. San Francisco is depicted as a dark and corrupt place, one in which protagonist and unsentimental private detective Sam Spade says that most things in San Francisco "can be bought or taken." To emphasize the connection between the characters, particularly Spade, and the corrupt city setting, Spade refers to San Francisco as his "burg." The fact that most of the story's action occurs at night further emphasizes the dark side of society and human nature.

Spade's apartment. Home of Sam Spade on San Francisco's Post Street, a well-appointed bachelor's apartment with a sitting room, a kitchen, a bathroom, a bedroom, and a separate entry foyer. Many significant scenes are set in the apartment. For example, Spade is there when he learns of his partner's death through a late-night phone call and is later visited there by the police.

Spade appears to be comfortable and at ease when he is in his apartment, but it cannot be considered a completely safe haven. The police repeatedly appear there to harass him, and in one scene, a fight breaks out there between Brigid O'Shaughnessy and Joel Cairo. It is also the apartment in which Spade turns in Brigid, the woman he says he loves, to the police.

Spade's office. Private detective office on San Francisco's Sutter Street in which many of the novel's daytime scenes take place. Setting daylight scenes in the office suggests that Spade's professional headquarters may be more above board, perhaps more moral, than his apartment or the hotel rooms of other characters. Effie Perine, Spade's secretary and the most consistently upright character in the story, is also always seen at the office. The office contains an outer room, in which Effie's desk is located, and an inner room that Spade shared with his partner, Miles Archer, until the latter is killed at the beginning of the novel.

Coronet Hotel. Hotel on San Francisco's California Street at which Brigid O'Shaughnessy stays after she leaves the St. Mark's Hotel, where someone has searched her room. Later, her room at the Coronet is searched—another indication of the difficulty of finding safety in Hammett's San Francisco.

Archer's murder spot. Bush Street location at which Spade's partner, Miles Archer, is gunned down. The murder occurs at night while Archer is tailing Floyd Thursby while working for Brigid O'Shaughnessy. Dark and lonely, the murder scene borders **Chinatown**, which

Hammett often depicts as a frightening, duplicitous place. The nighttime setting intensifies the dread and danger of this spot.

Alexandria Hotel. San Francisco hotel in which Casper Gutman, the leader of those seeking the falcon statue that gives the novel its title, is staying. Spade visits the Alexandria twice. On his first visit, Gutman drugs him. The Alexandria is another location filled with both danger and lies.

— *Bonnie C. Plummer*

THE MAMBO KINGS PLAY SONGS OF LOVE

Author: Oscar Hijuelos (1951-   )
Type of work: Novel
Type of plot: Social realism

Time of plot: 1930's-1980's
First published: 1989

The Castillo brothers play their music under more modest names until they arrive in New York and become the "Mambo Kings," but they pay a high price for their brief reign that no other city in the world could provide—and neither brother can entirely escape the Cuba they have left behind, which continues to haunt them in different ways.

Hotel Splendour. Flophouse on New York City's 125th Street and Lenox Avenue in which Cesar Castillo drinks himself to death, chosen for that purpose so that he can recollect much happier times, when it was a regular venue for fervent bouts of love-making with Vanna Vane. The name is ironically symbolic: for Cesar (unlike Nestor) New York is—at least to begin with—all splendor: a prolific well of sexual and other delights that shows no indication of running dry until Nestor's death.

*****Las Piñas.** Village in Cuba's Oriente Province that is near the farm on which the Castillo brothers are born and raised. Three miles from town, the farm is approached by a dirt road which runs alongside the river. It is in the "concert hall" of the local sugar-mill that Cesar first encounters the music that shapes his life and soul and makes contact with bandleader Ernesto Lecuona. Unlike Nestor, the young Cesar is harshly treated by his father, subsequently remembering the farm primarily as a place where he suffered frequent undeserved beatings.

La Salle Street tenement. Six-story tenement building west of 124th Street that becomes the Castillo brothers' New York residence. Their fourth-floor apartment is initially rented by Pablo, the cousin with whom they lodge on first arriving in New York, but it becomes theirs when Pablo moves his family to Queens. Following Nestor's death, when Cesar joins the merchant marines, it becomes the home of Delores, her children, and her second husband; after his return, Cesar obtains the job of building superintendent, with his own apartment on a lower floor and a workroom in the basement. The building—which is home to a rich assortment of ethnicities, is two minutes from the 125th Street El and offers a view from its roof of the Hudson River and Grant's Tomb—is the foundation-stone of the brothers' New York experience. Cesar's changing relationship with it maps the financial and emotional trajectory of his life.

*****Havana.** Cuba's capital and leading city, where Cesar and Nestor serve the latter part of their "apprenticeship" as professional musicians, while working by day at the Havana Explorer's Club. Havana serves as a staging ground for their two principal homes, facilitating the break-up of Cesar's marriage as well as providing a practice-ground for life in the city, compared to which prerevolutionary Havana seems merely a pale echo. It is in Havana's red-light district, La Marina, that Nestor's fateful meeting with Maria takes place. Although Cesar marries Luisa in Santiago de Cuba, and first abandons her there, it is in Havana that she remarries; thus Cesar retains a connection to Havana via his daughter Mariela—although that tie is far weaker than the one that binds Nestor inescapably to his homeland. The neurotic nostalgia encapsulated in Nestor's song "Beautiful Maria of My Soul" wears a romantic disguise, but its subject is as much a symbol of a forsaken home as of a lost love; it is as significant that Nestor's wife Delores also originates from Havana as it is that his mother is also named Maria.

Park Palace Ballroom. Ballroom on New York's 110th Street and Fifth Avenue that is Cesar's favorite among the many pickup joints he frequents in his heyday. Its exceptionally luxurious rest rooms accommodate bookies, dealers in magazines, flowers, condoms, and reefers, and shoeshine boys as well as the usual facilities—everything that a Mambo King could possibly desire, save for the women awaiting his reemergence on the dance floor.

*Hollywood. Section of Los Angeles that is the center of the television and motion picture industries and the place at which the brothers' career reaches its zenith, when they are befriended by bandleader-actor Desi Arnaz and make a guest appearance on an episode of his *I Love Lucy* television show. Hollywood's reward—a few minutes of universal fame and a kind of immortality—is one that even New York cannot grant.

Fan Sagrada. Village in Spain's Galicia region from which the Castillo brothers' father emigrated to Cuba and toward which his own life-blighting nostalgia is directed.

— *Brian Stableford*

MAN AND SUPERMAN: A Comedy and a Philosophy

Author: George Bernard Shaw (1856-1950)
Type of work: Drama
Type of plot: Play of ideas

Time of plot: c. 1900
First published: 1903; first performed, 1905

Uncharacteristically, George Bernard Shaw changes the setting of each act of this play, moving from a stodgy London office to suburban Richmond, and then to Spain's Sierra Nevada, where an atmosphere of historic adventure inspires a dream sequence. The final act is set in romantic Granada, with references to the Alhambra and the "air of the Sierra" complementing the breakdown of British reserve by Ann Whitefield and of self-control by Tanner, who finally recognize themselves as destined lovers and twentieth century heirs of characters from Wolfgang Amadeus Mozart's opera Don Giovanni *(1787).*

Ramsden's office. London workplace in which Jack Tanner works. As a bastion of ossified conservatism, the office becomes a symbol of Victorian social morality and an arena for Tanner's ferocious assault on conventional values in act 1. Its stuffy respectability provides an obvious motive for Ann Whitefield's display of her determination to subvert convention in pursuit of her aims.

Whitefield house. Suburban home in Richmond, near London, used for an outdoor setting in act 2, that establishes the importance of the automobile for subsequent action and introduces the pragmatic outlook of the modern technological man, Henry Straker.

*Sierra Nevada. Spanish mountain range in which Mendoza's comic opera bandits hide out in act 3. It evokes the atmosphere of Spain's cultural Golden Age and inspires the "Don Juan in Hell" dream sequence, embodying Tanner's vision of a philosophical Don Juan.

Hell. Act 3 is set either in an empty void in Hell or on Hell's border. This austere setting presents Shaw's new version of Hell, a forum for elegant philosophical debate by bodiless spirits outside of time.

*Granada. Province in southern Spain, where act 4 is set in the garden of a villa within sight of the famous Alhambra ruins of early Moorish occupation. Granada's exotic ambience seems to inspire the emotional power of scenes that reveal the truth about Violet's secret marriage and present the dramatic climax of Ann's protracted pursuit of Tanner. The aura of Moorish Spain makes the passionate conflict of Ann and Tanner's final scene, counterpointed by Shavian comedy, more credible.

— *Edgar L. Chapman*

A MAN FOR ALL SEASONS

Author: Robert Bolt (1924-1995)
Type of work: Drama
Type of plot: Historical

Time of plot: 1530-1535
First performed: 1954, as a radio play; first published, 1960

Based on real historical events, this play is set in London during the reign of England's King Henry VIII. Its specific locations include the royal court, Sir Thomas More's home, and the Tower of London—all of which are evoked onstage by simple wooden sets that echo the style of theater during the sixteenth century, when locales were evoked through language rather than realistic stage sets.

*London. Capital city of England that was torn by religious controversy during the reign of King Henry VIII. After defying the Roman Catholic pope, the king established the Church of England, with himself as head, and in so doing severed ties with the Roman Catholic Church. Although Sir Thomas More had long served Henry loyally as lord chancellor, he remained a staunch Catholic and refused to accept the English king as head of his church.

*Tower of London. Famous prison by the River Thames in central London, with roots going back to the reign of William the Conqueror in the eleventh century. More was imprisoned there for refusing to take an oath to acknowledge the supremacy of Henry VIII over all other foreign kings, including the pope. In 1535 he was executed in the tower, whose cells are the location of the play's scenes depicting his final days.

Stage set. Like the Globe Theater where William Shakespeare's plays were first performed, and like other Renaissance theaters, the stage set for *A Man for All Sea-* sons is divided into three primary acting areas. Playwright Robert Bolt visualized the set as "two galleries of flattened Tudor arches, one above the other, able to be entered from off-stage" and "a projection which can suggest an alcove or closet, with a tapestry curtain to be drawn across it." A stairway connects the upper and lower acting areas, and a table and heavy chairs are the only permanent props on stage. As in Shakespeare's plays, the stage space is used quite flexibly, and specific locations are defined by the actors' language and props brought on for each scene. The style of the production has strong affinities with the history plays of Bertolt Brecht, whose works were particularly influential in England in the 1950's and 1960's.

The much-acclaimed film adaptation of *A Man for All Seasons*, directed by Fred Zinnemann (1962), abandoned all of the play's Brechtian devices and was notable for its elegant costumes, historic locales, and spectacle.

— *William Hutchings*

THE MAN OF FEELING

Author: Henry Mackenzie (1745-1831)
Type of work: Novel
Type of plot: Sentimental

Time of plot: Mid-eighteenth century
First published: 1771

As sketchy and fragmentary as its text, the novel's geography becomes detailed only when its hero is at the greatest remove from his home, engaged in an ultimately pointless excursion to London, a city which—like everything else that he encounters—loses no opportunity to move him to tears of pity.

Harley's home. Village in which Harley's home is situated; it lies some way beyond a stagecoach terminus, though not as far north of London as the border of author Henry Mackenzie's native Scotland. The only detail confided to the reader is that Harley's aunt lives with him and looks after him. Harley is not the local squire but has an estate that includes a few tenant farms, one of which he eventually lets to Edwards.

London. Capital of Great Britain, to which Harley journeys in the hope of obtaining the lease of **Bancroft Manor.** The "great man" whom he goes to see for help lives in Grosvenor Square in Mayfair, London's richest district. While awaiting his reception, Harley spends a good deal of time in and around Hyde Park, on Mayfair's western boundary. While there he attempts to exercise his supposed skill in the science of physiognomy (reading character in the facial features), but a typical misjudgment leads him to a taproom where he loses a considerable sum of money playing piquet; it is his fellow victim of that deception who informs him, after a chance meeting, that the lease has been dishonestly awarded, after which he resolves to go home.

Among the excursions Harley takes during his fruitless wait is one to Bedlam, a notorious hospital for the insane then located in Moorfields. Although Harley disapproves of making a spectacle out of suffering, he goes with a party to witness the anguish of the enchained patients deemed incurably mad and the silly projects of patients not deemed dangerous; he hears tales of woe in the female quarters. He also visits the house of a "Misanthropist" in order that he may contrast the madness of Bedlam with a cynical and distinctively modern species of wisdom. A more significant encounter takes place in the Strand, when he is accosted near Somerset House by one of many prostitutes loitering there. Taking pity on her, he takes her to a room in a nearby tavern, where she faints from hunger, and then visits her lodgings, where he hears her dismal tale of elopement, betrayal, abandonment, miscarriage, and ruination before her father arrives to save her.

On the road. Harley has several moving encounters while traveling to and from London; on his outward journey he meets an itinerant beggar, while his homeward journey—most of which he travels by stagecoach—offers him further scope for the exercise of his supposed skill in physiognomy upon his fellow passengers. These include Ben Silton of **Silton Hall,** one of the few places outside London named in the story. After leaving the inn at the end of the stagecoach's route, on foot again, he meets an old soldier returned from India, who turns out to be Edwards, the one-time tenant of **South Hill**—a farm near Harley's home—whose loss to a landlord's greed precipitates yet another catalog of disasters. Harley's distress on hearing Edwards's tale is exacerbated when he discovers that his old schoolhouse has also been pulled down by order of Squire Walton, and Edwards's grandchildren are delivered as orphans into the care of the schoolmaster's widow.

Milan. Italian city that is the setting of yet another tale of man's inhumanity to man, told in an interpolated fragment in which two Englishmen come to the aid of a family victimized by Count Respino.

Harley's grave. Burial-place near the grave of Harley's mother, in the only part of the churchyard shaded by a tree. Every time the narrator visits it he is moved to feelings of pity for the contemporary human condition by the "air of gentleness" around it, having evidently been converted by Harley's noble example to the then-fashionable "cult of sensibility"—inspired by the philosophy of Jean-Jacques Rousseau—which deemed emotion more trustworthy, as a source of moral integrity, than reason.

— *Brian Stableford*

THE MAN OF MODE: Or, Sir Fopling Flutter

Author: Sir George Etherege (1635?-1691)
Type of work: Drama
Type of plot: Comedy of manners

Time of plot: 1670's
First performed: 1676; first published, 1676

This play is one of the earliest comedies of manners, plays in which fashion consciousness and social concerns determine behavior. The fact that this play is set in fashionable seventeenth century London matters greatly to understanding the play, for in it, London represents the world of fashion and society.

*London. Fashionable capital of Great Britain in which the play is set during the seventeenth century. The characters move easily through this world of fine society, a world of playhouses, parks, and drawing rooms. Original audiences of upper-class gentlemen and ladies, many of whom would be from the court, would be familiar with the common places of London that are mentioned in the play. They would be familiar with the fashionable shops on the Exchange, mentioned in act 1, as well as the Inns of Court, where the lawyers practice, mentioned in act 3. The vision of London in the play excludes most of the real London of the day, which would in reality be dominated by the merchant middle class and large areas of poverty-stricken dwellings and shops.

English countryside. Contrasting with fashionable London in the play is the world of the "country," essentially anywhere outside London. The city represents all that is fashionable and modern; the country represents the unsophisticated and out-of-date lives of such characters as Lady Woodvill and Old Bellair. Harriet, accompanying her mother to town, sees her only hope for a satisfactory life in making a marriage that will assure her a residence in London. Dorimant, in act 5, vows to move to the country if that is what it would take to marry Harriet. This vow shows the sincerity of his intentions toward her.

*St. James Park. Much of the play occurs out of doors in the fashionable Mall area of St. James Park. The Mall was a long tract in St. James formerly used for playing pall-mall. By the time of this play it was known as a fashionable park used for walking, for meeting lovers, and for displaying the latest fashions. In this play the Mall is contrasted with Hyde Park, another, much more fashionable area of leisure.

— *Paul Varner*

THE MAN WHO CAME TO DINNER

Authors: George S. Kaufman (1889-1961) and Moss
   Hart (1904-1961)
Type of work: Drama

Type of plot: Comedy
Time of plot: Christmas season, late 1930's
First performed: 1939; first published, 1939

This play is set entirely within the living room of a small-town midwestern home that is commandeered by an overbearing big-city celebrity confined to the house after being injured in a fall. The conflict of and contrast between two vastly different American lifestyles are the instruments for the inherent comedy of this work.

Stanley home. Moderately affluent home of the Stanley family in a small, unnamed Ohio town. Representing a kind of normalcy or upper-middle-class standard, the house is furnished tastefully. The play is set during the 1930's, when the living room was the center of the typical American home; callers were greeted and entertained there, and families relaxed together there. *The Man Who Came to Dinner* is about an invasion and transformation of a typical American living room.

Soon after the larger-than-life Sheridan Whiteside is confined to the Stanleys' house because of his accident, he takes over the room to broadcast his weekly radio show and conduct his business as if he were living in New York. The generous proportions of the living room and its gracious furnishings and decorations soon become a shambles, overrun by exotic and famous visitors and strange gifts—such as penguins and a mummy case.

George S. Kaufman's play exaggerates the bizarre and exotic and juxtaposes them against the middle-class environment in which they are presented. This juxtaposition creates the play's comedy, as Whiteside fills the Stanley's living room to overflowing, and the identities of the Stanleys themselves are absorbed as their possessions are relegated to other places in their home, replaced by an avalanche of objects and artifacts pouring in from Whiteside's friends and admirers.

— *H. Alan Pickrell*

THE MAN WITH THE GOLDEN ARM

Author: Nelson Algren (Nelson Ahlgren Abraham, 1909-1981)

Type of work: Novel

Type of plot: Social realism

Time of plot: Late 1940's

First published: 1949

This novel unfolds within the enclosed world of Chicago's Division Street, an urban jungle from which escape is impossible. Nelson Algren's protagonist, "Frankie Machine," returns there after World War II and struggles to change his life, which is being ruined by drugs, alcohol, and crime. An overpowering feeling of entrapment pervades the novel, which concludes with Frankie's attempting to flee the police, who want him on a murder charge. The novel's concluding words, "the last dark wall of all," articulate the entrapment motif that culminates with Frankie's suicide.

Division Street. Violent, crime-ridden neighborhood of Chicago that provides the novel's primary setting. There, drugs, alcohol, gambling, and theft are a way of life. Algren's protagonist, Francis Majcinek—nicknamed Frankie Machine—works as a card dealer in an illicit upstairs gambling den at the Club Safari and is known as the "man with the golden arm" because of his skill. Algren modeled the neighborhood on Chicago's real Wabansia Street, where he briefly lived.

Club Safari. Sleazy Division Street nightclub in which Frankie deals cards in illegal games. There Nifty Louie also gives community junkies their fixes, adjusting dosages to ensure that addicts keep returning, and paying, for ever-stronger and more expensive hits. Frankie himself also gets his fixes from Louie and needs them to deal cards with a steady hand. As the source of both his employment and his ever-strengthening drug habit, the club entraps Frankie in a way of life that he cannot escape.

Division Arms Hotel. Frankie's Chicago residence, in which he is initially trapped with his psychosomatically crippled wife, Sophie, who also trapped him into marriage by faking a pregnancy. She has also faked her disability, which she attributes to an accident caused by Frankie. Sophie uses Frankie's guilt to draw "the knot so fiercely that she felt he could never be free of her again."

Tug and Maul Bar. Aptly named zoolike bar whose animal-like patrons gather to keep up on neighborhood news. The most offensive of the patrons is Blind Pig (called Piggy-O), who would seem to be more at home in a refuse bin.

Jail. Chicago police station in which Frankie is held. It is here that the walls begin closing in on him more tightly than ever before. For Frankie, who wants to kick his drug habit, the jail becomes an "iron sanctuary"—a concept that at once suggests both imprisonment and safety. The jail is the only place where he can be free of the debilitating influences of Division Street; a red metal tag labels his cell as a "deadlock," meaning he has no privileges. Frankie himself is in another kind of "deadlock," a psychological one just "one bit lighter than the deadlocks of the cells with the red metal tag." There, time seems to stand still for the prisoners, since all the clocks permanently, and symbolically, read twelve o'clock.

When Frankie is released from jail, he attempts to stay free of drugs but again becomes quickly addicted. Since Record Head Bednar, a police investigator, suspects Frankie of Louie's murder, Frankie is only temporarily and theoretically "free." Bednar employs Piggy-O to set up Frankie and Sparrow, Frankie's friend and a witness to the murder, on a drug charge. Frankie is freed, but Sparrow is taken to the "query room" at several police stations, in which he is interrogated and threatened until he implicates Frankie.

The walls of these rooms are places where men literally have their "backs to the wall." Algren writes of the inevitability of the confessions: "Indeed, your query room is your only true house of worship, for it is here that men are brought to their deepest confession." After Sparrow testifies against him, Frankie—who is ironically described as "the fair-haired boy"—flees. He is sheltered by the faithful Molly, turned in by Drunkie John, and wounded, like Achilles (an ironic twist of Algren's), in the heel, before he hangs himself. His death by suffocation is particularly appropriate since it also suggests entrapment and enclosure.

— *Thomas L. Erskine*

THE MAN WITHOUT A COUNTRY

Author: Edward Everett Hale (1822-1909)
Type of work: Short fiction
Type of plot: Historical

Time of plot: Nineteenth century
First published: 1863

In this short story, a U.S. Army officer involved in Aaron Burr's plot against the U.S. government is convicted of treason and sentenced to spend the rest of his life aboard naval vessels at sea so that he will achieve his ill-considered wish never to hear the name of his country again.

Sea. The open seas provide the primary setting for the novel. After the protagonist, U.S. Army lieutenant Philip Nolan is convicted of treason in 1807, he is sentenced never to hear the name of his country again. To carry out this unusual sentence, he is put aboard a series of naval vessels that keep him perpetually away from the United States, and the naval officers with whom he comes into contact are instructed never to utter "United States" in his presence or allow him to come into contact with any printed material containing those words. Witnesses say that "he must have been in every sea, and yet almost never on land." Among the distant places to which the ships take him are the Cape of Good Hope, the Indian Ocean, the Windward Islands, the Mediterranean Sea, the South Atlantic, and Argentina. After Nolan dies, the sea becomes his burial place, his final home, and his only country.

Navy ships. Through the fifty-five years remaining in Nolan's life, he is moved through a succession of twenty-one U.S. naval ships that serve as his floating prisons. Whenever he is aboard a homeward-bound vessel that nears any American coast, he is transferred to an outward-bound vessel. Eventually, he spends time on half of the U.S. Navy's finest ships, including the *Nautilus*, the *Intrepid*, the *Warren*, the *George Washington*, and the *Levant*, on which he dies.

While the United States is fighting Great Britain during the War of 1812, Nolan gets caught up in a sea battle aboard the unnamed American ship of the line on which he is a prisoner. When a gun officer is killed, Nolan takes charge of the gun and directs a successful action that earns the captain's praise.

USS *Levant.* U.S. naval vessel that is Nolan's last home. Aboard this ship, he converts his stateroom into a shrine celebrating the United States. Framing a portrait of George Washington is the current flag of the United States. It has thirty-four stars, fourteen of which represent new states about whose names he is unclear. He paints a picture of a proud eagle, with bolts of lightning in its beak and wings overshadowing the talons of one foot grasping the entire globe. At the foot of his bed is a map of the United States, beautifully drawn from memory. On it are letters indicating Indian, Mississippi, and Louisiana Territories and a patch showing Texas extending west to the undefined Pacific coast.

As Nolan lies dying in 1863, an officer visits him and updates the map by penciling in Texas, California, and Oregon. Also present in Nolan's stateroom are his note-books and scrapbooks, some with his own drawings, evidence of his reading about historical events and aspects of science, in censored books and newspapers. These touching accoutrements convert Nolan's final cell into a kind of living history museum and its captive's mini-autobiography.

— *Robert L. Gale*

MANFRED

Author: George Gordon, Lord Byron (1788-1824)
Type of work: Drama
Type of plot: Poetic

Time of plot: Indeterminate
First published: 1817

The title character of this play, a noble prince, isolates himself in his castle in a remote part of the Alps, where he calls on supernatural beings to aid his quest for forgetfulness. Alienated not only from civilization but also from himself, he seeks a place that will release him from his self-torment. Manfred's ascent to mountains, his descent to valleys, and his incarceration in his castle reflect his inability to soar or sink to any place that might relieve his suffering.

Gothic gallery. The play begins by evoking mystery and the supernatural. The gallery is not described, but its Gothic nature suggests pointed arches and ribbed vaults which emphasize Manfred's towering sense of being oppressed by "a continuance of enduring thought." As immortal beings the spirits cannot cope with his quest for "self-oblivion" and his rejection of being "coop'd in clay."

*****Jungfrau** (YEWNG-frow). Peak in Switzerland's Bernese Alps on whose cliffs Manfred is ready to end his life, even though he does not know if death will end his suffering. Prevented from jumping off the cliffs by a chamois hunter, who simply cannot accept suicide as a response to suffering, Manfred is led to safety in a cottage in the Bernese Alps. Finding no comfort in this domestic setting, Manfred explains why he is unfit to live among other people.

At the summit of Jungfrau the Destinies discuss Manfred's plight, observing that "his aspirations/ Have been beyond the dwellers of the earth." They cannot help him because they can only ratify what he has learned: "Knowledge is not happiness."

*****Alpine valley.** Manfred encounters the Witch of the Alps and explains that he has always identified with the wilderness, felt estranged from human beings, and even caused the death of his beloved, Astarte. However, he refuses the witch's request that he swear obedience to her as the price of relieving his mortal consciousness.

Manfred's castle. In his castle Manfred expresses his continuing desolation. He refuses the abbot's appeal to return to the church. Manfred is "self-condemn'd" and has made, as he earlier remarks, a hell of his own life. Then he withdraws to another chamber, a more private room, to watch the brilliance of the setting sun and to declare that he will end his life.

Mountains. In the distance can be seen Manfred's castle. He stands on a terrace before a tower remembering how he alienated his beloved, who had been the "sole companion of his wanderings." Moving even farther away from others in the interior of the tower, Manfred vows to die as he has lived: alone. He has made a desert of his life. The abbot watches Manfred will himself to death, having enclosed himself in the tower of his own suffering.

— *Carl Rollyson*

MANHATTAN TRANSFER

Author: John Dos Passos (1896-1970)   *Time of plot:* 1920's
Type of work: Novel   *First published:* 1925
Type of plot: Impressionistic realism

This novel of life in the big city contrasts the aspirations with the realities of life for the hordes of people who seek fortune's smile in New York City in the early twentieth century. The tall buildings of Manhattan's skyline and up-scale apartment houses symbolize the dreams and expectations of immigrants who populate the city, while the squalid tenements, bars, and dirty streets show the disappointing reality that pervades the lives of urban dwellers who walk the teeming streets and ride the ferry and elevated trains that both connect and separate the two halves of the same world.

*New York City. Largest city in the United States and the second largest city in the world during the 1920's, the period in which the novel is set. In the first section of the novel, John Dos Passos places New York among some of the great cities of history: While Babylon and Nineveh were made of brick, Athens had gold marble columns, and Constantinople's minarets were like candle flames around the Golden Horn, New York City's stark pyramids are made of steel, glass, tile, and concrete.

Setting his novel in the 1920's, when American mores and values are changing, Dos Passos uses the city both as a symbol of the possibilities and dreams of those who left failure behind, and as a realistic environment that is either hostile or indifferent to their dreams and aspirations. The novel uses the city as a character, an architect that molds and shapes the strong, or a mechanical monster that crunches and consumes the weak. The one-word titles of the chapters—"Metropolis," "Tracks," "Steamroller," "Fire Engine," "Rollercoaster," "Revolving Doors," "Skyscraper"—give the major role in the novel to the city and the steel parts that bring it to life.

New York City's streets, docksides, and tenements are peopled with thousands of migrants from America's rural farmlands and hundreds of thousands of immigrants who have fled the old cities of Europe for the land of opportunity. People appearing in the novel's snapshots and vignettes are much like stock characters who show *types*, rather than individuals with whom readers can develop intimate acquaintances. They seem as programmed in their movements as the mechanized metropolis they inhabit. Some characters, like an old immigrant playing a violin on the ferry and a homeless derelict weeping in the street, seem to illustrate an anonymous class of city dwellers forgotten by both fellow human beings and the city.

Some characters appear in a few scenes but seem to be disconnected from the lives of other characters. For example, Bud Korpenning, who eventually commits suicide, demonstrates the life that goes steadily down to defeat in the city. Other types—a banker, a lawyer, a broker, an actor, a bootlegger, a labor leader, an architect, and an arsonist—connect in passing with the lives of two exceptional characters, Ellen Thatcher and Jimmy Herf, who appear in successive scenes throughout the novel and give it continuity. Ellen, often frightened by the city but determined never to show that fear, becomes a hardened and self-centered "Elaine" or "Helena," depending upon her aspirations of the moment. She has no qualms about using people to get what she wants.

Jimmy Herf may be an incomplete projection of Dos Passos himself. Herf is a fatherless boy orphaned at sixteen when his mother dies. He returns to New York after a sojourn in Europe and serves in the Red Cross during World War I. He functions in the novel almost as a counterculture to the city's dehumanizing environment. He is sensitive and caring, and seeks to maintain a value system that rejects compromises in order to gain wealth or social success in the urban, industrialized world. In the end, the uncompromising Herf abandons the city that rejects him and his kind.

By presenting the characters in impressionistic images, in brief scenes that show them in combat with the elements, disastrous illnesses, and accidents, swayed by fragments of songs, the roar of the elevated trains, spoken words, or silent gestures, Dos Passos shows New

York as a symbol that has betrayed the promises of the land of opportunity. The novel moves from the attraction of the city that brings the hopeful characters to it, through their desperate battles to survive within the steel and concrete jungle, to an almost frantic desire to get away from it. Its bigness attracts, then dehumanizes with indifference and an environment ruinous of health, and finally becomes an evil monster that destroys or spits out its human cargo.

— *Marguerite R. Plummer*

MANON LESCAUT

Author: Abbé Prévost (Antoine-François Prévost d'Exiles, 1697-1763)
Type of work: Novel
Type of plot: Sentimental

Time of plot: 1700
First published: Histoire du chevalier des Grieux et de Manon Lescaut, 1731 (English translation, 1734); revised, 1753 (English translation, 1786)

This novel deals with the inherent fatality of passion and the conflicts of individual will and the organized social group. Paris, colonial New Orleans, and the desert are the ideal settings for Prévost to develop his theses and his plot. The use of real places helps to give the novel authenticity.

***Paris.** Capital city and center of all activity—political, social and cultural—in eighteenth century France. The Paris of Abbé Prévost's novel is the real Paris of the period. At the time he was writing, the novel was not accepted as a literary genre. The novels of the seventeenth century had become so fantastic that the novelists of the eighteenth century were particularly concerned with portraying contemporary times as realistically as possible to avoid criticism of their works as frivolous, absurd, and unworthy of consideration. By setting the novel in Paris and in actual places and institutions found in the Paris of the time, Prévost created a sense of authenticity. By choosing Paris, Prévost also satisfied the interests of his readers because it was the city where everyone wanted to be and about which everyone wanted to read. The provinces and provincialism were not in vogue.

Paris contained all of the elements Prévost needed to develop his plot. The population was composed of people from all social classes, and Parisian society was one strictly controlled by class distinction. Inequality of class is one of the major problems faced by Manon Lescaut and her lover the Chevalier des Grieux. He is of noble birth and belongs to a social stratum that has no place for her. Paris has a social milieu eager to accept her, but unsuitable for him. The world of the demimonde offers Manon all of the materials things that she desires: jewels, money, elegant lodgings, and entertainment. Manon is well suited to this world, as she proves early in the novel. Once des Grieux joins her, everything turns to disaster.

***New Orleans.** Leading city of what was then France's North American Mississippi territory. Situated in the New World, New Orleans symbolizes a second chance for the ill-fated couple, the possibility of finding a simpler society not fettered by class distinction. These hopes soon fade for them. Although the colony, heavily populated by people deported from France, is free of the strict observance of class found in Paris, it is governed by an established system of rules. Manon and des Grieux are not free to marry. The selection of a husband for a woman newly arrived in the colony is allocated to the governor. The governor's nephew Synnelet will marry Manon. The couple Manon/des Grieux is unacceptable to this social community. There is no place for them.

Desert. Imaginary region immediately east of New Orleans in the direction of the English colonies. Prévost's knowledge of the geography of the American colonies was undoubtedly imperfect, but so was that of most of his readers. The desert is the ideal place for Manon and des Grieux's final moments together and for her death. It symbolizes both the impossibility of happiness for the couple and also des Grieux's total loss of everything. Alone in the desert, at her graveside, des Grieux is stripped of everything.

*Havre-de-Grace (ha-vahr-deh-grays). Seaport in northern France from which Manon is deported to the American colonies. Havre-de-Grace was one of the ports from which people were sent to the French colonies. Prévost repeatedly anchors his novel in the reality of his time. Havre-de-Grace is also the place in which Prévost introduces his narrator, the Man of Quality. There and later at Calais (another seaport), des Grieux, recounts his story to him. It is in turn the Man of Quality who tells the reader des Grieux's story. Prévost uses a reliable narrator and gives more credence to his novel.

Cart. Means of transporting Manon and her unfortunate companions to the point of deportation. Open carts served this purpose during the period. Although the cart is not an actual geographic location, it is important place in the novel. It is a place of confinement and of exhibition. The degradation of the cart is the final blow, which, coupled with des Grieux's fidelity, transforms Manon.

Pacy Inn. Manon and des Grieux meet here. Inns are important in Prévost's novel because they are places of anonymity for people and places where few questions are asked. It is also here that the fatal passion between Manon and des Grieux begins.

— *Shawncey Webb*

MAN'S FATE

Author: André Malraux (1901-1976)
Type of work: Novel
Type of plot: Social realism

Time of plot: 1927
First published: La Condition humaine, 1933 (English translation, 1934)

This, André Malraux's best-known novel—like his other novels—is set in Asia. More precisely, the bulk of the events in the novel are set in Shanghai, China, whose cosmopolitan population during the 1920's makes it an apt site for Malraux to dramatize and foreshadow the rise of international communism.

*Shanghai. Port city at the mouth of the Yangtze River that was—and still is—the most populous city of China, housing an estimated three million people in 1927, thirty-five thousand of them foreigners. Shanghai then was also uniquely international, made so by European imperialism. Europeans in China enjoyed extraterritorial rights and were beyond the jurisdiction of Chinese law. Hence, although Shanghai was a Chinese city, it was actually divided into three administrative and juridical sectors: the Chinese sector, the British sector (known as the "international settlement"), and the French sector (or "concession"). In each sector, Chinese inhabitants were in the majority. Shanghai in 1927 was a divided city somewhat like Berlin, Germany, following World War II.

Although Malraux had lived in Asia, it is doubtful that he knew Shanghai firsthand in 1927; his descriptions therefore resemble a newsreel. More important, because of Shanghai's international nature, Malraux could assemble a multinational cast for his epic—French, Germans, Russians, Chinese, and mixed-race characters. Malraux's Shanghai can thus be seen as a political microcosm of his contemporary world during an existentialist moment of history when the communist revolution was challenging capitalist imperialism as a global ideology.

Hotel room. Setting of the opening scene, in which Ch'en, a Chinese communist leader, assassinates an arms dealer. Malraux transforms this room into a metaphoric place with metaphysical significance. Beginning here, Malraux divides his novel's places (also characters, actions, ideas) into two dialectical opposites: the absolute versus the relative, the essentialist versus the existentialist, the static versus the evolving. Through Ch'en's narrative point of view, this dark room becomes an absolutist place where he will bring death (the absolute, essentialist, and static experience) into being. Outside the room, it is brightly lit Shanghai by night, a relativist place with human beings in relationships—existential, changing.

Black Cat nightclub. Baron de Clappique's favorite hangout. It is another absolutist and essentialist site because its patrons escape relatedness and existential responsibility through liquor and sensuality. There also, Clappique indulges in mythomania, escaping into an absolutist fantasy world by spinning tall tales about himself.

Gisors' house. Located in Shanghai's French section, this is home to Gisors, a French Marxist sociology professor; his part-Japanese son Kyo, a Chinese Communist Party leader; and Kyo's wife May, a German communist doctor. There, Kyo experiences an absolute of isolation as he realizes that his relationship with May is not founded on reality and that his identity is split between his inner sense of himself (essentialist, absolute) and others' sense of him (existentialist, relative). There also, Ch'en visits Gisors, his professor, after the assassination, hoping to communicate and exorcise his angst; instead, Gisors becomes aware of the essential isolation of each individual and retreats into an absolutist world by smoking opium.

*****Hankow (Hangzhou).** City near Shanghai. Malraux identifies it as the Chinese Communist Party's strong-

hold, where the Russian advisers are headquartered. He also makes Hankow a metaphor for ideological essentialism and absolutism. Kyo and Ch'en go there to seek advice on what to do when General Chiang Kai-shek's Kuomintang Party (supported by capitalists and Western imperialists) begins persecuting communists. The Russians fall back on Lenin's writings, trusting them like absolute and essentialist (fundamentalist) scripture and refusing the Chinese Communists permission to evolve their own revolution.

Prison yard. Schoolyard that has been converted into a prison for communists sentenced to death. Although death is the ultimate absolute and the essentialist isolation of an individual, Kyo transforms his death into an existential act by committing suicide with his cyanide pill. His Russian comrade Katov is even more heroic. He gives his own cyanide to two other terrified condemned men, then he accepts immolation alive in a furnace. In Malraux's metaphoric use of the schoolyard, the nationalists (capitalists and imperialists) are in this former schoolyard to teach a lesson about the absolute certainty of futility for humans in death, while the communists are there to teach a lesson about the relative possibilities of meaningfulness and utility to humans, even in death.

— *C. L. Chua*

MANSFIELD PARK

Author: Jane Austen (1775-1817)
Type of work: Novel
Type of plot: Domestic realism

Time of plot: Early nineteenth century
First published: 1814

This, Jane Austen's most austere novel, uses three principal settings to ground its characters and pursue its themes of personal integrity and social order.

Mansfield Park. Estate of Sir Thomas Bertram; an elegant, well-maintained English country house set amid formal shrubberies and bridle paths. Although Lady Bertram is congenitally idle, the estate's servants keep the large house running smoothly. Fanny Price, a young niece and poor relation, is quartered in a "little white attic near the old nurseries." Across the park is the Mansfield parsonage, the home of Mrs. Norris,

Lady Bertram's overbearing sister, whose husband is the rector.

While Sir Thomas is in residence, the estate is a model of order and dignity, the beau ideal of a noble family seat. However, a flaw appears when the death of Mr. Norris coincides with the extravagant behavior of Tom, Sir Thomas's older son. To cover this son's debts, Sir Thomas must dispose of the estate to outsiders, the

Grants, instead of holding it until his younger son is ordained. The Grants' arrival opens the rectory doors (and hence, those of Mansfield) to their young relatives, the Crawfords. As this attractive but fundamentally cynical and corrupt pair begin to destabilize Mansfield Park, Sir Thomas must travel to Antigua to see to his properties there. An offstage presence in the story, Antigua hints at further disturbance of a basically conservative social order.

The Mansfield young people are talked into converting a room of the manor into a stage for amateur theatricals. Only Fanny is convinced that Sir Thomas would find this unacceptable; even Edmund, the most moral of the Bertram children, is swayed by the enthusiasm of the teasing Mary Crawford. Mrs. Norris, in charge owing to Lady Bertram's indolence, indulges her nieces in rehearsing a play that encourages dangerous flirtations.

Sotherton. Family estate of Mr. Rushworth, Maria Bertram's dull but wealthy fiancé, which is visited by a party from Mansfield Park. Approached through a long avenue of oak trees, the house, which has its own family chapel, is substantial but fairly modern and not very interesting. Its grounds include a bowling green and a long terraced walk, but beyond the formal parkland lies "a nice little wood," in which shady serpentine paths overlook a sunken fence. There, a tired Fanny is forgotten as Edmund and Mary explore among the trees and Maria disappears with Henry Crawford. While Austen's writings are rarely heavily symbolic, this lo-

cale surely underlines the moral wilderness into which most of the principal characters are plunging.

*Portsmouth. Port city on England's southern coast to which Fanny is sent to stay at her parents' home after she rejects Henry Crawford's proposal of marriage. Sir Thomas hopes the contrast between the serenity and order of Mansfield Park and the squalor of a lower-middle-class home in the great naval port city will cause her to rethink her decision.

Price house. Portsmouth home of Fanny's parents. The house is small, untidy, and full of ragged, dirty, and rude children. Its walls are thin, and it is an "abode of noise, disorder, and impropriety." Austen makes no simplistic pairing of wealth with corruption and poverty with innocence. If Mansfield Park has become somewhat tainted, Portsmouth is altogether coarse and gross, failing even to recognize standards of harmony and restraint that one may be unable to meet perfectly. Although the Price house is disagreeable physically and disappointing emotionally, Fanny is able to control her desire to return to Mansfield Park until all the social couplings have been sorted out appropriately, and she is in a strong position to refuse Henry Crawford again. She eventually marries her cousin Edmund and installs the most trainable of her younger sisters as Lady Bertram's resident niece and errand girl at the estate, which will be in good hands in the future.

— *Nan C. L. Scott*

THE MANSION

Author: William Faulkner (1897-1962)
Type of work: Novel
Type of plot: Social realism

Time of plot: 1908-1948
First published: 1959

The residence of Flem Snopes after he becomes president of the bank in Jefferson, Mississippi, the "mansion" of this novel's title is the main setting of a story in which the real subject is neither the mansion itself, nor the town, nor the Old South, but humanity collectively. Geography abets theme in order to describe changes to the society.

Mansion. Antebellum Mississippi mansion that is the residence of Flem Snopes and later his daughter Linda. The mansion is the overarching symbol of the novel. Gaudy and materialistic and furnished tastelessly with

objects imported from New York and Europe, the oversized, conspicuous, and centrally located house exhibits the best that poor white trash can do in the Old South (and, this, by hiring what would later be called "home decorators"). Snopes can buy the semblances and symbols of power and respectability and he can move within the town's upper social echelons, but he can never be the real thing. Appropriately, Snopes's murder occurs here to indicate that he can never be fully assimilated into the community.

***Jefferson.** Northern Mississippi town that is home to descendants of the old Southern aristocrats who come to blend indistinguishably with the poor white trash (primarily the Snopes family), who move in and gradually take over the town. The population of Jefferson comes to be an amalgam of illiterate sharecroppers transplanted from the countryside and the last remnants of the old European highbrows. As such, William Faulkner intends the town to be typical and normal and therefore representative of all such towns in the American South in the first half of the twentieth century.

Frenchman's Bend. Village that is the source and wellspring of the Snopes family. Also the setting for Faulkner's *The Hamlet* (1940), Frenchman's Bend is important here because it is near the farms owned by Mink Snopes and the man he murders, Jack Houston. Moreover, Will Varner conducts magistrate's court here and finds against Mink in a legal matter. Though not a town, Frenchman's Bend is important as the place where most Snopes family members originate.

Parchman. Fictional name of the Mississippi state penitentiary, in which Mink Snopes spends thirty-eight years of his life as punishment for the murder of Jack Houston. It is here that he plans with great deliberation the vengeful murder of his cousin Flem Snopes. When the prison is visited by Gavin Stevens and Linda Snopes, it provides a backdrop for showing that the superficially moral of the community (Linda Snopes representing purity and the lawyer Stevens representing justice) are truly collaborating with each other.

***Memphis.** Tennessee city that serves as the cosmopolitan cultural center of the region that encompasses northern Mississippi. From Frenchman's Bend and Jefferson the Snopeses and the upper classes alike go to Memphis to relax, shop, and conduct other matters of business. Of primary importance in *The Mansion* is Madame Reba's brothel, visited not only by members of the Snopes clan but also by men from the upper class of Jefferson. It is here that Madame Reba herself first pronounces what is commonly considered the most important theme of the novel: "Mankind. The poor sons of bitches." In this novel about morality and justice, it is fitting that a whorehouse provides the setting for its most important point.

— *Carl Singleton*

MARAT/SADE

Author: Peter Weiss (1916-1982)
Type of work: Drama
Type of plot: Social morality
Time of plot: 1808
First performed: 1964; first published, 1964 as *Die Verfolgung und Ermordung Jean Paul Marats dargestellt durch die Schauspielgruppe des Hospizes zu Charenton unter der Anleitung des Herrn de Sade* (*Marat/Sade: The Persecution and Assassination of Jean-Paul Marat as Performed by the Inmates of the Asylum of Charenton Under the Direction of the Marquis de Sade*, 1965)

The setting of this play is a therapeutic bath serving as a theater inside the asylum of Charenton in early nineteenth century Paris. However, the physical setting quickly becomes an allegorical one, expressing the theme that the entire world is a madhouse. Weiss's unusual use of literary place helped him create one of the most important plays of the 1960's.

***Charenton** (shar-in-TON). Mental institution in Paris that provides the play's main setting. Although the action of the drama is centered on a series of violent encounters between the political radical Jean-Paul Marat and the then-infamous Marquis de Sade, in the madhouse of Charenton, this encounter was entirely imaginary. Jean-Paul Marat, one of the architects of the French Revolution, was never incarcerated at Charenton, he never met the Marquis de Sade, and he was assassinated in 1793—fifteen years before the year in which the play is set. However, de Sade was, in fact, incarcerated there from 1801 until his death in 1814. He was imprisoned not for political crimes but for a variety of acts of violence so shocking that the word *sadism* has derived from his name. While de Sade was a prisoner, he frequently staged plays that he wrote in Charenton.

Placing infamous Marat and de Sade together in a mental institution in which they converse about important social questions allows the author to improvise short, rapidly shifting and changing scenarios, in which the actors, miming the thoughts and actions of sane people, are actually madmen and women who are, time and again, overcome by their various psychoses. They frequently forget de Sade's scripted words and discourse wildly and violently on social issues. That they are incarcerated lunatics is a subtle touch, for it allows playwright Peter Weiss to insert social commentaries on everything from the futility of political revolution to the immoral, indeed criminal, mistreatment of society's poor in ways that are, seemingly paradoxically, both distressing and funny at the same time.

The idea that all the world may be mad is made by an ingenious use of literary place. *Marat/Sade* is actually a play-within-a play: The "outer action" involves the bourgeois director of the asylum, Coulmier, and his guests, the elite of Parisian society, who have been invited to witness one of de Sade's plays. The "inner action," or core of the drama, consists of de Sade, playing himself, and some patients who play the roles of various "normal" people. The reader becomes part of the audience watching, and ironically commenting on, the action of both the outer and inner dramas. This device draws readers in, suggesting that they, too, continue to engage in the horrors of war, of social injustice, and of personal delusion.

— *Ronald Foust*

THE MARBLE FAUN: Or, The Romance of Monte Beni

Author: Nathaniel Hawthorne (1804-1864)
Type of work: Novel
Type of plot: Psychological realism

Time of plot: Mid-nineteenth century
First published: 1860

This novel is the story of two Americans, Hilda and Kenyon, living in Italy, whose moral and aesthetic education is enlarged through their encounter with two Italians, Miriam and Donatello, and the latters' country and its pagan and Christian cultures.

*Rome. Italy's capital city, in which the novel's opening and closing chapters are set. These chapters feature extensive descriptions of the tourist attractions prominent during Nathaniel Hawthorne's 1858-1859 sojourn in Florence and Rome. As the center of both Western Christendom and an older pagan civilization, the locale helps to fuse together two of the major cultural elements of the novel. Roman history is deeply layered and provides the symbolic background against which to place the two Americans, who come from a New World culture that is thinner and less confident than that of Rome, but also one that is less encumbered by time and therefore freer of intellectual and emotional constraints.

*Capitol sculpture gallery. Roman museum in which the novel opens with the two Americans and their two Italian friends exploring the collected art treasures. Among their discoveries is a marble faun that is believed to have been sculpted by the ancient Greek Praxiteles. The friends decide that the faun bears a striking resemblance to Donatello. With its ancient associations, the faun becomes the central symbol for the novel, one through which Hawthorne develops his clash of cultures and conflict among his characters.

*Roman catacombs. Subterranean Roman burial and worship center of the early Christians that Miriam visits with her friends. There she encounters a mysterious figure who follows her throughout the early pages of the story. Symbolically, this figure suggests that she is dogged by her past, one intimately associated with both the pagan and Christian histories of Rome that distinguishes her from the American Hilda.

*Roman Colosseum. Arena that was the scene of ancient Rome's greatest public entertainments—gladiatorial contests, Christian sacrifice, and other spectacles. Its history brings together the two leading cultural elements of the novel. There, pagan Rome tried to eradicate Christianity, which was threatening to replace classical culture.

*Tarpeian Rock (tar-PEE-yahn). Located on the Capitoline Hill beside the Forum, the Tarpeian rock was the site from which traitors were hurled to their deaths during ancient times. There, separated from the others, Donatello, with the apparent consent of Miriam, pushes the mysterious stranger to his death. This act of murder sets the stage for the rest of the novel and symbolically replaces the enigmatic stranger with a concrete act of violence that eventually severs the ties among the four principal characters and frees the Americans from their thrall to the past.

Monte Beni. Fictional ancestral home of Donatello in Tuscany, which Kenyon visits in order to sculpt a bust of its owner. There he learns of the history of Donatello's family, now living on the faded memory of past glories.

*Perugia. Central Italian city standing on a hill overlooking the Tiber River north of Rome. On his return to Rome, Kenyon stops to see the celebrated frescos by the town's native son, Perugino. There he meets Miriam and Donatello and in a memorable scene witnesses them kneeling before the statue of Pope Julius III in the central piazza to receive his blessing. This act of contrition sets the stage for Miriam's fate at the end of the narrative.

*St. Peter's Basilica. Chief church of Roman Catholicism and principal building complex in Vatican City, which was part of Rome in Hawthorne's time. While wandering among the splendors of St. Peter's, Hilda, distraught by her knowledge of the murder, goes to confession even though she is not a Catholic, and for the first time admits her secret. Her sense of guilt over the murder and her waning attachment to Donatello is developed further in this scene.

*Appian Way. One of the main thoroughfares of ancient Rome, the Appian Way is lined with the memorials to the dead. On a walk along the road, Kenyon happens on an excavation of a buried statue. With the introduction of this second ancient statue, Hawthorne stylistically brings his narrative full circle.

— *Charles L. P. Silet*

MARDI, AND A VOYAGE THITHER

Author: Herman Melville (1819-1891)
Type of work: Novel
Type of plot: Allegory

Time of plot: Mid-nineteenth century
First published: 1849

In contrast to Melville's realistic novels set in the South Seas, this novel is a genre-defying exercise that combines elements of the action adventure tale, political allegory, and religious vision. Mardi is a fictional archipelago of islands located in the Pacific Ocean, previously undiscovered by European explorers. While some of the islands are clearly allegorical representations of European nations, others take on more complicated moral and philosophical significance.

Mardi. Fictional archipelago located in the west-central Pacific Ocean. Melville's narrator Taji places the islands about sixty degrees west of the Galápagos Islands and to the north of the Ellice, Marshall, and Kingsmill Islands of what is now Kiribati. Taji happens upon the previously undiscovered islands after jumping ship from a whaler and experiencing a series of increasingly improbable high seas adventures. Eventually, he lands on an island ruled by Media, a philosopher-king who represents Herman Melville's ideal platonic ruler. A search for the abducted maiden Yillah takes Taji and Media throughout the islands, on which they observe the variety of "Mardian" customs and discourse at length upon the philosophic, aesthetic, and moral implications of what they see. Mardi serves as a microcosm of world cultures and a convenient mechanism for Melville to sally forth on ideas ranging from such political questions as New World slavery to such philosophic issues as free will versus determinism. By the end of the novel, with a deconstructive stroke, Melville identifies the seemingly endless fictional Mardi islands with his own vast, unfolding fictional text *Mardi*.

*Pacific Ocean. Despite its allegorical structure, the novel is often realistic in tone. Melville cannot refrain from incorporating highly detailed descriptions of South Seas flora, fauna, and customs into his otherwise fanciful description of the Mardi Islands. For example, early in the work he pauses in his adventure plot to lavish upon the reader a fascinating catalog of the various species of shark encountered in the Pacific. A later dissertation on the swordfish is equally impressive. Similarly, his sharp eye for Polynesian architecture is evident in his realistic description of the wood-carved palace in the otherwise fanciful island of Juam. The fictional island of Yammo contains stone idols of the Mardians' supreme god, reminiscent of the striking stone sculptures of Easter Island.

Vivenza. Island in the Mardi archipelago that is a representation of the contemporary United States. Melville skewers his native country's mix of self-congratulatory idealism and rampant materialism. The U.S. Congress becomes a "Temple of Freedom" known more for windy monologues than for effective action to solve problems such as the slavery issue. An arch before the temple has a quotation in hieroglyphics that translates "In-this-republican-land-all-men-are-born-free-and-equal"— to which is added the deflating graffiti, "except the tribes of Hammo." A sojourn to South Vivenza lays bare both the cruelties of the "peculiar institution" and inhumane pseudo-philosophy used to support it. A caricature of John C. Calhoun as the slavery-defending chieftain "Nulli" caps this episode.

Dominora. Island ruled by the warlike King Bello, who dominates Mardi through a combination of naval supremacy and cultural imperialism. An allegorical representation of Victorian England, Dominora reveals Melville's anglophilia in literature and politics. While he satirically reveals the economic underpinning of Great Britain's "glorious" empire, he too easily apologizes for its harsh treatment of the Irish (whose island is here called **Verdanna**), culminating in the effective genocide of the potato famine.

Serenia. Island that owes more to Melville's uneasy flirtation with American Transcendentalism than to contemporary political allegory. Devoted to the "true teachings" of Alma (the Mardian equivalent of Jesus), the Serenians seek unity based upon the mystic reception of divine love rather than shared intellectual dogma. One of Taji's companions, a skeptical philosopher, decides to remain on this island after having a dream reminiscent of a beatific vision. However, in a move that prefigures Melville's own rejection of Transcendentalism in *Moby Dick* (1851), Taji leaves the island to continue his unfulfilled quest to rescue Yillah.

— *Luke A. Powers*

MARIUS THE EPICUREAN: His Sensations and Ideas

Author: Walter Pater (1839-1894)
Type of work: Novel
Type of plot: Philosophical

Time of plot: Second century
First published: 1885

The life-story of Marius and the geography of the novel lead inexorably to Rome, in the period when it enjoyed its last brief burst of grandeur during the reign of Marcus Aurelius (161-180). The image of Rome presented in the novel is dominated by the ideas of irreversible decline—from the time of Hadrian—and impending fall.

*Rome. Center of the Roman Empire. When Marius first looks out upon Rome it appears to him as a "vast intellectual museum," and that colors his view of all its various components—not merely its many pagan shrines, its multilayered tombs, and its many ruins, but its functioning institutions: the Forum, where the body

of Aurelius's brother Lucius Verus is set to lie in state before the tribunal before being conveyed to its funeral pyre in the Campus Martius; the Marmorata, where precious marbles are accumulated; the Appian Way, more cemetery than thoroughfare; the Field-of-Mars, colonized by public buildings that have reduced its grassy playgrounds to mere enclaves; and, most important, the Temple of Peace, part college and part club, in whose library the Diurnal (a primitive newspaper) is posted. Even the Arena, notorious throughout history as a public slaughterhouse, does not strike Marius immediately as a place of vulgar spectacle but as a religiously significant stage set for the contrivance of marvels and illusions. When Marius visits the imperial palace it is to receive the emperor's manuscripts for copying and revision: the kind of journeywork which will, albeit at several centuries' remove, provide the foundations of Europe's Renaissance.

It is significant that Marius is happiest when he is able to remove himself temporarily from the hubbub of Rome itself to the clean air, clear light, and serenity of the Alban and Sabine hills. Two locations are of particular significance: the house near Cicero's "haunted" villa at Tusculum where, as a fellow guest of the emperor's son Commodus, he watches a satire of Socrates by Lucian; and the secluded house of Cecilia, two miles outside the city, where he obtains his first intimations of the Christian faith. Cecilia's villa is the only place whose architecture and garden, though only superficially different from his old home, seem to him symbolic of nascence rather than senility.

*Pisa. Italian city in which Marius attends school. Although somewhat decayed from its former splendor, it fills Marius with dreams of Rome. The school is an imitation of Plato's Academy, with its own cypress grove; it is there that Marius meets Flavian and reads the "golden book" (Lucius Apuleius's *Metamorphoses*, better known as *The Golden Ass*), whose interpolated tale of Cupid and Psyche, paraphrased in Walter Pater's text, is a powerful influence on him. After watching the symbolic launching of the Ship of Isis from Pisa's harbor, Flavian dies of the plague, prompting a new phase of Marius's philosophical self-education.

White-nights. Pater's version of the name of Marius's boyhood home, to which he returns in the final chapter. It comprises a villa surrounded by farmland, whose extent has shrunk while the family's fortunes have declined. The establishment is run-down, but it preserves a residual dignity appropriate to a kind of farming that was never more than an "elegant diversion." The house lies well away from the road, on raised ground above a marsh. The main building is constructed of pink and yellow marble, now mellowed by age and encrusted with moss. The pavement of the hall is decorated with mosaics, and there are ancestral masks in cedar chests at each corner. An oval chamber contains artworks collected by its founder, Marcellus, including a famous head of Medusa. There is also a two-story prospect-tower topped by a pigeon-house. Its windows look out on the crags of Carrara and the coast, dominated by the lighthouse-temple of Venus Speciosa.

Temple of Aesculapius. Temple in the Etrurian Hills beyond the Arnus Valley, to which Marius is taken as a boy when he falls ill. The temple provides facilities for patients to sleep, so that the priests may deduce the causes of their illness and appropriate treatments from the imagery of their dreams—although its clear air and pure water supply must have been its primary curative agents. Its garden is flanked by the Houses of Birth and Death, set apart for the use of mothers-to-be and the dying.

— *Brian Stableford*

THE MARRIAGE OF FIGARO

Author: Pierre-Augustin Caron de Beaumarchais (1732-1799)
Type of work: Drama
Type of plot: Comedy

Time of plot: Eighteenth century
First performed: 1784; first published, 1785 as *La Folle Journée: Ou, Le Mariage de Figaro* (English translation, 1784)

Comic theater generally does not maintain the unity of place that characterizes tragedy; however, Pierre-Augustin Caron de Beaumarchais limits the action of this comedy to the château and grounds of Count Almaviva, located near Seville, Spain. The immediate setting varies, however, with the differing emphases of each act.

Figaro and Suzanne's bedroom. Room that Figaro and Suzanne hope to share after their marriage. The minimal furniture reflects the fact that the marriage has not yet taken place. It also emphasizes the poverty of the couple, which makes them susceptible to Marceline's machinations.

Countess's bedroom. The luxurious appointments emphasize the differences of class that separate the characters and cause Figaro's struggles. The use of bedrooms, private places linked to secrecy, also coincides with the numerous plots in which the characters engage.

Throne room. This setting further stresses the power of the count with the portrait of the king representing his aristocratic connections. A secondary scene involving the count and Figaro's proposed trip to England serves both to mock the English and to show how Figaro's trickery will aid him.

Gallery. Public room that allows the characters to spy on one another, creating new problems. The festive decorations reflect the joy of Figaro and Suzanne, who seem to have overcome the obstacles to their marriage.

Park. Outdoor setting that functions as the location of Figaro's famous revolutionary monologue. This is especially appropriate in that, outside the château, Figaro seems to gain increased freedom.

— *Dorothy M. Betz*

MARTIN CHUZZLEWIT

Author: Charles Dickens (1812-1870)
Type of work: Novel
Type of plot: Social realism

Time of plot: Nineteenth century
First published: serial, 1843-1844; book, 1844

This novel is lengthy and complex, but only three basic settings focus its action and themes: Salisbury, England, where the consummate hypocrite Mr. Pecksniff is headquartered; America, where young Martin Chuzzlewit assumes he can gain wealth and independence; and London, to which everyone goes, where paths cross, and where the final unveiling occurs.

***Wiltshire.** District in southern England in which Mr. Pecksniff runs an architectural school out of his home in an unnamed village near Salisbury. From this base, Pecksniff plots to secure the money from his aging cousin old Martin Chuzzlewit, ultimately reducing him from house-guest to helpless dependent. When old Chuzzlewit's repentant grandson, young Martin, poses a threat to Pecksniff's power, Pecksniff smugly dismisses the young man from his home, secure in his power over the grandfather. Pecksniff also invites old Martin's companion, Mary Graham, planning to take advantage of her proximity to seduce her into marrying him.

Apprentices John Westlock, young Martin, and Tom Pinch, all victims of Pecksniff's hypocrisy, leave Pecksniff's architectural school. Finally, this home also provides staged scenes of family harmony when needed, but when convenient, both daughters are sent from the family hearth, Mercy to wed the despicable Jonas Chuzzlewit and Charity to fend for herself in London at Todgers's boardinghouse.

Blue Dragon. Inn in Wiltshire where old Martin is first introduced, ill and pursued by an expectant horde of scavenging relatives. Mrs. Lupin, the model landlady is especially welcoming to young Martin and Mark Tapley when they return from their disastrous trip to America. At her fireside, they hear of Pecksniff's latest machinations. The Blue Dragon is also the place where Tigg Montague and Jonas Chuzzlewit invite Pecksniff to invest in the Anglo-Bengalee Loan Company, which leads to disastrous consequences for all three.

Village church. Church in which the saintly Tom Pinch plays the organ and first sees Mary Graham as she quietly listens to his music. One of the novel's comic scenes later takes place here when Tom and Mary converse seriously about their concerns, and Pecksniff despicably eavesdrops, popping up and down behind a pew like the puppet Punch.

*United States. Indignant at his grandfather's rejection of his wish to marry Mary Graham, young Martin goes to America hoping to make an easy fortune so he can return to England and claim Mary. However, he finds the country a nation of bores and boors. After Martin and his faithful assistant, Mark Tapley, arrive in New York City, they encounter snobbery, hypocrisy, and rudeness. Through young Martin, Dickens takes aim at American English, ignorant politicians, the press, and American complacency about the still-legal institution of slavery.

Dickens evidently decided to send his hero to North America because readership of his serial novels was falling, and he hoped these adventures would spur his readers' interest.

Eden. Fraudulent land-development in New York in which young Martin and Mark Tapley buy shares. On their arrival, they find only rude cabins in a swamp. Eden has malnourished children, dying parents, decomposing slime, and fatal maladies. Martin falls ill with fever, and when he recovers, Mark becomes sick. While he nurses his friend, Martin ponders the faults of his own character and the true reasons for the failure of his hopes. At Eden, Martin is transformed: "So low had Eden brought him down. So high had Eden raised him up." After a nightmarish year, Martin and Mark board ship and return to England.

Todgers's. Boardinghouse for commercial gentlemen in the heart of London to which Pecksniff and his daughters make their way, as through a maze, groping, distracted, backtracking. "Surely there never was in any other borough, city, or hamlet in the world such a singular sort of place as Todgers's." Part gritty reality, part imaginative fantasy, Todgers's is a stage for Charity's and Mercy's flirtations, for their father's more senior-style coquetry, and for Pecksniff to tighten his grip on the rich old man.

Anglo-Bengalee Disinterested Loan and Life Assurance Company. The British parallel to the American Eden land speculation scam; it appears overnight, "grown up," and running at a great pace, resplendent in stucco and plate glass. Everything is new, substantial, and expensive, designed to impress the visitor with its security, solidity, and profitability. This facade, plus the home of the director, Tigg Montague, in London's St. James Square, all serve to dupe the public. Jonas Chuzzlewit ungraciously approaches, suspicious of the fine exterior, but through Tigg's blackmail and pressure, he not only invests his money but is forced to promise to deliver Pecksniff as another investor.

*Islington. District of London in which Tom Pinch settles with his sister Ruth after he exposes Pecksniff and leaves Wiltshire. They choose Islington after having heard no more about it than it is said to be "merry." Their modest triangular parlor witnesses many innocent and happy scenes as Ruth and John Westlock fall in love, and also poignant scenes, as Tom watches the happiness of young Martin and Mary Graham.

Library. Office near Temple Gate on London's Fleet Street in which Tom Pinch works for an unspecific employer. There, in a dusty, lumber-filled upper flat, he cleans and orders books and organizes papers, faithfully and quietly earning his wages until he discovers that his employer is old Martin Chuzzlewit, now liberated from Pecksniff's manipulation and shedding his false dementia. In a highly orchestrated denouement, old Martin summons characters to this library, one by one, to offer blessings and mete out justice. Tom is praised and honored for his steadfast goodness and loyalty. Ruth Pinch is joyously joined to John Westlock, who has been handling arrangements in old Martin's name. Mark Tapley is to wed Mrs. Lupin of the Blue Boar. Young Martin is forgiven, embraced, and united with Mary Graham. After a brief and ineffectual chastisement of Sairy Gamp's excesses, Martin announces judgment on Pecksniff, revealing the latter's hypocrisy and sending him away penniless.

— *Marie J. K. Brenner*

MARY BARTON

Author: Mrs. Elizabeth Gaskell (1810-1865)
Type of work: Novel
Type of plot: Social realism

Time of plot: 1840's
First published: 1848

Unusual for its time in having all working-class characters, this novel sets a love story in Manchester, England, against a background of the struggles of trade unionists to secure living wages.

*Green Heys Fields. Open area several miles from the center of the city of Manchester. With its fields, village, and half-timbered buildings surviving, Green Heys symbolizes the life left behind by Manchester's factory workers—a world to which they hope to return. This is particularly expressed by Alice Wilson throughout the book. All her life she aspires to return to the farm where she lived as a child but never manages to do so. In her final illness, she believes she has returned to the country.

Barton house. Home of John Barton in central Manchester, amid an area of half-finished houses erected to accommodate factory workers. The house looks onto a small paved court—in which the washing is hung—a typical arrangement in Victorian towns. Its central gutter indicates that no drainage has been laid. The house is small, with one main room in which the family lives and cooks and a small sculler-cum-pantry leading off it, and also a coal-hole. Upstairs are two small bedrooms. The downstairs room is crowded with furniture that would normally be regarded as a sign of prosperity; however, it is clear that much of the furniture is for show rather than use. The house is clean and bright, an indication that the family, though poor, is respectable.

Alice Wilson's cellar. Home of the washerwoman, sick nurse, and herbalist Alice Wilson; a basement room at 14 Barber Street in Manchester. Her single room serves as both bedroom and workroom. Like the Bartons' house, it is clean and whitewashed, but it is also damp. Alice has fewer possessions than the Bartons, so there is a stark contrast between her bare room and their crowded house.

Legh's house. Home of Job Legh and his granddaughter Mary Barton, in a Barber Street apartment above Alice Wilson's cellar. Legh is an amateur entomologist, and his room is like a "wizard's dwelling," crowded with display cases, books, and scientific instruments.

*Manchester. Industrial city in central England. Central Manchester, the oldest part of the town, is the site of Carson's mill, which is located on a street consisting of public houses, pawnbrokers' shops, rag and bone warehouses, poor grocery shops, and crowded alleys and back streets. It is a rundown area susceptible to fire.

Davenport's cellar. Home of Ben Davenport, a man thrown out of work by the fire at Carson's mill, on Berry Street. His court is not paved, and the central gutter on his building does not drain as well as that in the Bartons' court. His cellar is dark, dirty, and not whitewashed, and its windows are broken. The cellar is damp and cold. Davenport, his wife, and several children live in the cellar, and Davenport is dying of typhoid brought on by the place's unhealthy conditions. His cellar is a stark contrast to Alice Wilson's cellar.

Carson's house. Home of Mr. Carson, the owner of the mill. Located far from the mill, almost in the country, the large house is well decorated and staffed by servants. When Jem Wilson is sent to Carson's house to get an infirmary order for Davenport, he waits in a kitchen, wherein the life of the house is laid open to him. Even the servants live luxurious lives in comparison to his own, and they are at first unaware that he is starving. Wilson is received by the Carsons at the breakfast table in the well-appointed library, which acts as a counterpoint to his own much less comfortable house.

*Liverpool. Major English port city on the west coast to which Mary goes to find an alibi for Jem Wilson when he is accused of murder. Liverpool is a seafaring city, with the docks in the center of the city. Manchester is compared unfavorably with Liverpool as a "nasty, smoky hole."

Sturgis's house. Home of Ben Sturgis in which Mary Barton takes refuge after she is taken out by boat to catch Will Wilson's ship before it sails; there she recuperates after an illness. The old-fashioned house was built long before the rest of the houses on its street and looks as though it belongs to a country town. The house represents a return to an older, better time, and emphasis is laid once again on light and on cleanliness, with hints of the exotic in the objects brought back from a foreign country by the sailor.

— *Maureen Speller*

THE MASTER AND MARGARITA

Author: Mikhail Bulgakov (1891-1940)
Type of work: Novel
Type of plot: Satire
Time of plot: 30 C.E. and 1920

First published: Master i Margarita, expurgated, 1966-1967; unexpurgated, 1973 (English translation, 1967)

This novel's attack on cowardice, materialism, personal and institutional corruption, and atheism is structured around two cities: Moscow in the 1920's and Jerusalem in the time of Jesus Christ. Like Christ's ancient confrontation with Pontius Pilate, the Devil's descent upon twentieth century Moscow tests moral responsibility and demonstrates worldly power's weakness in the face of eternity. Persistent sun and moon imagery associated with divine providence links the two settings across time.

*Moscow. Capital of Russia around the time the Soviet Union is being formed. Appropriately, this novel about spiritual values opens at Patriarch's Pond in Old Moscow, named after the Patriarch of the Russian Orthodox Church. Thereafter, the capital city combines recognizable topography from Moscow's center—Spiridonovka Street, the Kiev Railway Station, the Aleksandrovsky Gardens, Skaterny Lane—with occasional arbitrary changes in street locations and other details. Ultimately, most facets of the Devil's visit to the city reveal how communism under the Bolsheviks reduces its citizens to hypocrisy, bribery, blackmail, spying, and denunciation by thwarting their "normal desire to live a decent, human existence."

Griboyedov house (gree-bo-YE-dof). Home of the literary organization MASSOLIT, apparently Mikhail Bulgakov's version of an actual literary headquarters of the 1920's-1930's called Herzen House. Bureaucratic inequities, envy, and self-interest dominate the scene. MASSOLIT's members enjoy such perks as summerhouses and fine meals at the gourmet restaurant.

Dramlit house. Eight-floor dwelling trimmed with black marble and gold letters in which Margarita destroys the apartment of the unscrupulous critic who ruins the Master, a Soviet writer who has written a novel about Jesus and Pontius Pilate.

Variety Theater. Theater on Moscow's Sadovaya Street that is the site of a magic spectacle hosted by the Devil and his crew to probe the audience's spiritual state. The Devil concludes that modern Muscovites are ordinary humans, weak yet compassionate, whom the housing shortage has "soured."

Devil's headquarters. Apartment number 50 at 302A Sadovaya Street in Moscow that is initially a home shared by the MASSOLIT chairman and the manager of the Variety Theater. It becomes the Devil's center of operations for tempting and testing Moscow inhabitants. As the site of visits from covetous citizens and of inexplicable disappearances, the apartment is central to Bulgakov's satire of the Soviet housing shortage as well as of the secret arrests favored by dictator Joseph Stalin. In a crucial chapter, the Devil's transformation of the apartment into the site for his annual ball (whose extravagance is possibly modeled on a ball given at the American embassy in Moscow in 1935) shows the ordinary dimensions of time and space yielding to cosmic infinity.

Bulgakov modeled the apartment on an actual housing block in Moscow in which he once lived with his wife.

From the roof of another building, described as the most beautiful in Moscow, the Devil surveys the city at sunset. This unnamed building can be identified as an eighteenth century mansion in downtown Moscow called Pashkov House. The Devil's view includes the city's "vast panorama of palaces, huge blocks of apartments and condemned slum dwellings."

Stravinsky's insane asylum. Famous psychiatric clinic in the suburbs, on the bank of the Moscow River, that becomes home to the Master after his breakdown. The asylum takes in the many characters smitten with a "mad" belief in the Devil's presence.

*****Pushkin statue.** Metal statue of Russia's greatest writer, Alexander Pushkin, in Pushkin Square in the center of Moscow. There, Pushkin represents the quintessential artist in his defiance of censorship and his immortality through his work.

*****Torgsin store.** Store in Smolensk Market that is one of many nationwide stores carrying specialty items available only for hard cash (preferably in foreign currency), precious metals, or gems. There, as at Griboyedov's, the restriction of such "luxury" edibles as chocolates, herring, and tangerines to the moneyed elite indicts communist socialism.

Master's apartment. Humble two-room basement apartment near the Arbat in which the Master takes refuge before his arrest. Located off a square near one of Moscow's most picturesque and bustling old streets, the lowly apartment with its garden full of lilacs, limes, and maple trees and its simple comforts represents the Master and Margarita's benign withdrawal from society into art, love, and nature.

*****Sparrow Hills.** Site with a splendid view of Moscow from which the Devil and his crew ascend into eternity. As at Patriarch's Pond and in other scenes, the city's west windows glitter with fragmented sunset reflections that suggest the Devil's refraction of God's powers. This time the rainbow arching over the city further stresses nature's link to the metaphysical world.

*****Jerusalem.** City in ancient Judaea that appears in the novel as Yershalaim—from the Aramaic language spoken alongside Greek and Latin in the ancient Middle East. Similarly, Judas's town, Iscariot, becomes Kerioth. Bulgakov further demythologizes the holy city through his evocation of such mundane specifics as a bread store at the Hebron Gate, the Lower City's labyrinthine streets, the acacia and myrtles trees growing in the Gethsemane fields, and the smell of leather and sweat filling the palace of Herod the Great. Although Bulgakov fantasizes Moscow while evoking Jerusalem realistically, he shows both cities oppressed by totalitarian systems that despise spirituality and thrive on deadly bureaucracy, spies, coercion, and violence.

— *Margaret Bozenna Goscilo*

THE MASTER BUILDER

Author: Henrik Ibsen (1828-1906)
Type of work: Drama
Type of plot: Psychological realism

Time of plot: Nineteenth century
First published: Bygmester Solness, 1892; first performed, 1893 (English translation, 1893)

The first two acts of this play take place in the interior of the Solness home, which is apparently located in Norway; the third takes place outside. The psychological relations of the characters are developed in the interior scenes; the active consequences of these relationships, chiefly, the death of Halvard Solness, the master builder, as he falls to his death from his newly built home, are presented in the exterior ones.

Solness home. The town, or village, in which the home is located is not named but may be envisaged as within the vicinity of Trondheim, which lies on the west coast of Norway. Slightly northeast of Trondheim lies Størdalshansen, which could be the actual setting of the play. West of this town, on the other side of the fjord, is Stranda; and well northeast of this town on the upper part of the fjord is Levanger. Løvstrand, representing the future, is where the master builder wants to build a villa. Lysanger, the past, is the scene of triumph: There, ten years earlier, against extreme odds, he crowned with a wreath the highest point of the tower of a building he had constructed. The thirteen-year-old Hilde Wangel, who witnessed this event with transcendent pleasure, comes to the Solness home to exact from Solness the fulfillment of a promise she claims he made at that time, namely, to make her a princess and build her a castle. The promise is translated into Solness's wreathing the tower of his newly built home. He wreathes the tower at Hilde's insistence and to her joy but then falls to his death. The location of the home, below the mountains and below, or south of, the scene of his past triumph, comports with Solness's situation as a relatively successful man (a master builder but not an architect) who will die attempting the impossible, that is, to repeat his triumph, rather than go on to old age while younger professionals surpass him.

— *Roy Arthur Swanson*

"MASTER HAROLD" . . . AND THE BOYS

Author: Athol Fugard (1932-   )
Type of work: Drama
Type of plot: Political realism

Time of plot: 1950
First performed: 1982; first published, 1982

Like much social and political writing, this play has a setting that is important as the location for the specific social ills being addressed—in this case, South Africa's old apartheid system of racial segregation. But the play works equally well in this post-apartheid age as a drama about the conflicts between fathers and sons, between employers and employees, and between different social classes in any country.

*Port Elizabeth. City on the southern coast of South Africa. A strictly segregated city at the time of the play, Port Elizabeth is inhabited only by white families like the family of seventeen-year-old South African boy Harold (Hally), by a small merchant class of Indian origin, and by the black servants of these groups. Most black workers like Willie, who is employed in the tearoom owned by Hally's parents, might have jobs in Port Elizabeth, but they come into the city by bus from black townships and neighborhoods including New Brighton, Kingwilliamstown, and the other localities represented in Willie's blacks-only dance competition. Hally has lived so long as one of the privileged whites in segregated areas that he is usually unaware that others' movements are more restricted than his own. Until Sam tells him near the end of the play, he goes for years without realizing that the reason Sam did not stay on the park bench and fly the kite with Hally is that the bench was restricted to whites only.

St. George's Park tearoom. Shop owned by Hally's mother. Like most South African businesses in white areas, the owners and customers are white, but the employees are black. The play takes place in the tearoom, where Hally enjoys the power and privilege of being the owner's son, lording his position over the employees. The dynamic added by the tearoom itself allows the play to resonate beyond the themes of history and race.

— *Cynthia A. Bily*

THE MASTERS

Author: C. P. Snow (1905-1980)
Type of work: Novel
Type of plot: Psychological realism

Time of plot: Mid-twentieth century
First published: 1951

This is the fifth novel of the Strangers and Brothers series, which C. P. Snow wrote to chronicle life in twentieth century Great Britain. This volume examines university life as it was lived at Cambridge during the 1930's. Set in a fictional college, the novel revolves around the election of a new master carried out over several months, while the current master is slowly dying.

***Cambridge.** Seat of one of England's great universities, along with Oxford. Cambridge itself figures little in the novel and is presented as an adjunct to the university rather than an entity in its own right. The novel unfolds largely within the confines of the college itself, but from time to time, characters go into the city to visit friends, shop along its various streets, or visit the market place with its church, Great St. Mary's, whose bells echo over the college walls tolling the passing time.

***Cambridge University.** One of England's two great universities, Cambridge is made up of various colleges, in which students and many faculty members live. However, it also exists apart from them, offering lectures, providing laboratories for research, a university library, and a senate, and finally granting degrees. Snow looks at the university primarily as it has an impact on his novel's unnamed college, as when the university supplements the income of the college through the academic work its fellows undertake outside the college.

Students of Cambridge, along with those of Oxford University, produced most of prewar Britain's leaders: its captains of industry, bankers, diplomats, and other functionaries who ran the government and maintained what was left of the empire. Unlike educational systems in most other countries, Cambridge and Oxford exerted considerable power throughout Great Britain. Because Snow is writing about the relationship among various segments of British society, he portrays the university as a testing ground for the values and codes experienced elsewhere in British society.

College. Unnamed college of Cambridge University in which the novel is set. Snow's coda to the novel, "Reflections on the College Past," explains that he did not supply a fictional name for his college but deliberately left it anonymous, although it clearly reflects the college system present at Cambridge at the time. Because the novel is meant to be a study of character and of how power was maintained and transferred in British society, even within this circumscribed environment, Snow opted for this claustrophobic locale within which to set his fiction.

The various components of an Oxbridge college are all present: the master's lodge, the hall for dining, the fellows' common room, the individual studies and living quarters of instructors and students. They all have a place in the unfolding of the novel's themes. Because the locale is so limited, Snow can concentrate on the various personalities of his characters, whom he uses as types to indicate the various ways within the university that decisions are made and what influences such decisions—economic, political, and social—so that the college becomes a microcosm of the contending forces at work in British society. This is particularly true in the subtle conflict between the college's scientists and the humanists, a theme that Snow returned to in his famous series of lectures published as *The Two Cultures* (1959). As one who moved within both cultures, Snow was especially well situated to comment on the conflicts arising from what he perceived as a growing gulf between the two ways of comprehending the world.

***London.** Although Great Britain's capital city does not play a direct role in the novel, it represents the world to which the college, through its graduates and fellows, is connected. The location of the government, the Houses of Parliament, the Home and Foreign Office, and the Royal Society, London mirrors the local structure of the college and provides a connection with the wider world of events and power.

— *Charles L. P. Silet*

MAURICE

Author: E. M. Forster (1879-1970)
Type of work: Novel
Type of plot: Bildungsroman

Time of plot: 1903-1913
First published: 1971

As is the case with other novels by E. M. Forster, place is symbolic in this work. There, places, especially homes and the rooms within, are intricately connected with class status. Suburban London is the habitat of the middle classes, and country estates are the provenance of the upper classes.

***London.** Great Britain's capital city, in which Maurice Hall grows up and works. His suburban house is "near London, in a comfortable villa among some pines." The location may well be southwest of London in Weybridge, in Surrey, where Forster lived with his mother from 1904 to 1924. Surrey is also the location of Windy Corner, the home of the Honeychurches in *A Room with a View* (1908). London suburbs are growing rapidly in the early twentieth century, particularly in middle-class detached houses. Mr. Hall is able to commute easily by train to his job in the city, as Maurice will do after him. As Forster says, Maurice's suburban surroundings are exasperating in their very normality. Maurice works in the area of London known simply as the City, which is the oldest part of London and its financial center. The offices of Hill and Hall are here, and this location stands in stark contrast to Cambridge and even suburbia. The values of the City are symbolized by money, and it is no accident that Maurice and Clive's relationship suffers once they leave Cambridge and that Maurice and Alec have trouble making a connection in the City and in the British Museum, that warehouse of empire.

***Cambridge.** City north of London that is the home of Cambridge University, one of England's two great "ancient universities." In the early twentieth century, the city had a mix of medieval and classical architecture. Cambridge was Forster's alma mater, and he lived there for several years at the end of his life. Maurice attends Cambridge following attendance at his public school, Sunnington. Both Cambridge and Oxford were bastions of middle- and upper-class men, although each had a college for women. Cambridge is located on the River Cam, and the image of male undergraduates punting (propelling a flat-bottomed boat with a long pole) on the Cam is a familiar one in the English academic novel. The surrounding countryside is rural and provides an opportunity for Maurice and Clive to escape from the confines of their rooms within the college walls for their grand day out.

Penge. Country manor that is the home of the Durham family. Located in the west of England on the border between the counties of Wiltshire and Somerset, the house has been in the family for four generations. Penge is a symbol of the English gentry and their economic situation in the early twentieth century. The Durhams' fortune has dwindled, needing to be replenished by a wealthy bride, and the estate is in a stage of "immobility" preceding decay. The house itself stands in the midst of a vast park, the former common lands of the village, and a wood. The estate also includes an array of indoor and outdoor servants, tenant farmers, and responsibilities for the squire. It is here that Maurice meets Alec, the estate's under-gamekeeper.

The Greenwood. Edenic spot in a mythical England where Maurice believes he and Alec might live together in peace. Maurice connects his classical education, relating to the Greeks, with the English myth of Robin Hood and his merry band of men. Forster explained in his concluding "Terminal Note" that the image of the greenwood is necessary for Maurice and Alec to have a happy ending. The greenwood is a place of liberation, and as such it is related to Forster's treatment of the English countryside in *Howards End* (1910) and, especially, the Cadbury Rings in *The Longest Journey* (1907).

— *James J. Berg*

THE MAYOR OF CASTERBRIDGE: The Life and Death of a Man of Character

Author: Thomas Hardy (1840-1928)
Type of work: Novel
Type of plot: Psychological realism

Time of plot: Nineteenth century
First published: 1886

Unlike most of Thomas Hardy's other Wessex novels, this one focuses on a single urban setting—Casterbridge. By concentrating on one place, Hardy's complex interweaving of destiny and character takes on sharper focus. The instability of the title character's fortune is set ironically against the stability of community, symbolized by the solidity and historical continuity of Casterbridge itself.

Casterbridge. Bustling market town in Hardy's fictional Wessex countryside in southern England. Its origins date back to Roman times, and several of its features remain from that era: a Roman amphitheater, a graveyard, and the straight roads connecting Casterbridge with adjacent towns. Hardy describes Casterbridge from two opposite perspectives. On one hand, from Yalbury Hill a mile away, it appears a well-defined urban community, set square in rolling, open countryside, sharply divided from the country by a wall, tree-lined avenues, and a river. On the other hand, from a worm's-eye view, it seems to be a sprawling, confusing set of streets in which boundaries are constantly eroded. Market stalls cover sidewalks; carts jostle for right-of-way; smart private residences abut commercial premises. Secret back alleys lead to houses and pubs.

This double perspective of the town symbolizes the ambiguity of protagonist Michael Henchard's own rise and fall. From one perspective his downfall seems to be brought about by a cruel but clear-cut fate; from another, by the muddle of his own character and choices. The tensions created by these opposite perspectives create the power of the novel.

Recurring geographical features of the town include High Street; St. Peter's Church; the market house; the town hall, in which magistrates preside over the police court; two inns, the Mariner's Arms and the King's Arms Hotel; and the Bull Stake, an open area. The buildings are typically either timber houses with overhanging stories dating from Tudor times, or stone Georgian structures. Stores serve a variety of agricultural needs. The houses have no front yards, opening straight onto sidewalks, though they often have long rear courtyards and gardens.

Casterbridge corresponds to the real Dorchester in the county of Dorset in southwestern England. Hardy knew the town intimately, for it was there he received his high school education, practiced as an architect, and built his own house, Max Gate.

Henchard's house. Home of Michael Henchard on Casterbridge's Corn Street—a suitable address for the town's official corn factor. The house's change of ownership from Henchard to the grain merchant Donald Farfrae marks the decisive change of balance of power between the men.

High-Place Hall. Old stone house near Casterbridge's market that Lucetta Le Sueur leases on her departure from Jersey, one of the British Channel Islands off the French coast. The hall is built in the fashion of a country mansion but sits in the center of town, thereby symbolizing the ambiguity of Lucetta's position. From its windows, Lucetta and Elizabeth-Jane Newson watch the commercial transactions of Henchard and Farfrae. The hidden relationships of these four characters is suggested by the hidden entrance to the house.

The Ring. Old Roman amphitheater immediately outside Casterbridge's southern boundary, just off the Budmouth (Weymouth) road. The amphitheater is described as being as large as the Colosseum in Rome; what goes on inside it is hidden, but such secretiveness does little good: It is a "dismal privacy," as if ghosts were watching it. Likewise, Henchard's first meeting with Susan, his later meeting with Lucetta, his spying on Farfrae's meeting with Elizabeth-Jane, and his observing Newson's return never lead to anything open and healthful, and contribute only to the continuation of the secrets and lies that finally enmesh him.

Durnover. Casterbridge's only suburb, located to the east and northeast of the town, along the river. The river itself embodies "mournful phases" of Casterbridge life, and the slum area of Mixen Lane abuts it. A form of public humiliation known as a skimmity ride is planned in Durnovers' low-class pub, Peter's Finger; Henchard finds lodgings with Jopp in Durnover when both are down on their luck; the "chorus of yokels" lives in Durnover.

Bridges. Casterbridge's two bridges symbolize the town's social class divisions and tragedies. The brick bridge at the end of High Street is frequented by low-class characters down on their luck, while the stone bridge, situated in the meadows, is a more secluded place, one to which the better classes go when in misfortune. People occasionally jump off the bridges to com-

mit suicide, and their bodies end up in Blackwater Pool or Ten Hatches Hole, which is where Henchard sees his straw effigy or double after the skimmity ride, a ghastly omen of his own impending death.

Weydon Priors. Village in Upper Wessex, some six days' walk from Casterbridge, that is the only important location outside Casterbridge in the novel. Weydon Priors is in economic decline, marked by the decline of its annual fair and individualized in the downfall of the Furmity woman, who knows Henchard's dark secret. Her arrest in Casterbridge, where their fated paths cross, precipitates Henchard's downfall.

— *David Barratt*

MEASURE FOR MEASURE

Author: William Shakespeare (1564-1616)
Type of work: Drama
Type of plot: Tragicomedy

Time of plot: Sixteenth century
First performed: c. 1604; first published, 1623

Although there are numerous settings—some high and austere, others low and bawdy—the prevailing ambience is achieved by the city of Vienna itself, for William Shakespeare is concerned with probing deep into the dark places of society and the human mind in order to expose the corruption that often lies beneath outer virtue and rigid conduct.

*Vienna. Great Austrian city ruled by Duke Vincentio. As the duke himself realizes, Vienna is a moral morass, and bawdry and licentiousness of all sorts are rampant. The duke accepts responsibility for having been lax in enforcing the law. Corruption seethes throughout society from the nobility down to the base characters who are engaged less in a comic subplot than in a series of vulgar exemplifications of the pervasive moral decay. Concerned by the city's deterioration, the duke devises a scheme to revive civic authority: Pretending to go to Poland, he puts the administration of the city in the charge of his trusted, and presumably virtuous, deputy, Angelo, and remains in Vienna disguised as a friar. While staying in a friary, he spies on Angelo. The friary, which

should ordinarily be a place of quiet contemplation and prayer, thus becomes a den of intrigue.

Shakespeare's Vienna is no joyous café society or waltz-and-chandelier ballroom for the aristocracy. Rife with pimps, prostitutes, lechers, violated virgins, and murderers, it is not ready to be overrun by the wave of puritanism set in motion by Angelo. Scenes set on a street provide a microcosm of Viennese society, especially its smart men-about-town, such as Lucio; low-life figures such as Pompey the bawdy clown, and the syphilitic Mistress Overdone. Even Angelo proves to be corrupt, and in the privacy of his own abode, he reveals his hypocritical dissembling and hidden lust.

— *Keith Garebian*

MEDEA

Author: Euripides (c. 485-406 B.C.E.)
Type of work: Drama
Type of plot: Tragedy

Time of plot: Antiquity
First performed: *Mēdeia*, 431 B.C.E. (English translation, 1781)

In this play about the vengeance of a wronged woman, the Greek setting creates a tension between Greek and barbarian, male and female. Both main characters are displaced persons: The Greek Jason is living in exile in Corinth; his estranged wife, Medea, is living as an alien in Greece, where her foreign birth also labels her as a barbarian. As exile and alien, neither character has any legal status in Corinth.

*Corinth. Rich and powerful city in ancient Greece, located on the northeastern portion of the Peloponnesian Peninsula, that is the setting for Euripides' play.

House of Medea. Corinth home in which Jason and Medea live in exile with their young sons. All the play's action takes place in front of this house. Jason and Medea's precarious position in Corinth is underscored by this building, which lacks the power and status of a king's palace. Concerned about his status in Corinth as a noncitizen, Jason abandons Medea and his children in this house, where Medea kills the children to punish Jason for his unfaithfulness.

Creon's palace. Home of Corinth's King Creon. Located offstage in the play, the palace is the focus of Jason's ambition and of Medea's vengeance. Jason seeks the power of the palace in his plans to marry the daughter of Creon. Medea sends her sons to this palace with a gift of a poisonous cloak, which kills both Creon and his daughter.

*Athens. City to which Medea flees with the bodies of her dead sons in a fiery chariot after obtaining a promise of protection from Aegeus, the king of Athens. Euripides' Athenian audiences would have understood these events in the context of Athens's role as a place of sanctuary and as the enlightened protector of the oppressed.

— *Thomas J. Sienkewicz*

MELMOTH THE WANDERER

Author: Charles Robert Maturin (1780-1824)
Type of work: Novel
Type of plot: Gothic

Time of plot: Early nineteenth century
First published: 1820

This masterpiece of the gothic novel is set mostly in Spain, with brief glimpses of India and London: Each place emphasizes the generic themes of entrapment and religious hypocrisy.

*Spain. Charles Robert Maturin's Spain is typically gothic, a bleak landscape of rough hillsides and poor and superstitious inhabitants lorded over by proud noblemen and hypocritical clergy. Several characters in the novel, including the titular character, traverse Spain; an English traveler tours the monasteries in Spain during the seventeenth century; Melmoth himself travels throughout Spain pursuing his unholy schemes; and a young Spanish lord travels throughout Spain trying to escape from incarceration in a monastery and from the dungeons of the Inquisition.

In each case, Spain figures as a place in which the characters are trapped by powers greater than themselves. For instance, the Spanish lord finds himself in the dungeons of the Inquisition, a setting that itself is highly attractive to writers of gothic literature. Narrating his characters through dark and terrifying prisons gives Maturin the opportunity to perpetuate a familiar English concept of Roman Catholicism. Many of the English gothic writers represented Roman Catholicism as a system of control, not of devotion. This novel gives this representation a highly powerful twist. The young Spaniard, for instance, is first locked in a monastery and is manipulated almost to the point of accepting religious vows. The monastery is at first presented as a place of peace and devotion. However, when he decides to refuse the forced vocation, the monastery becomes a place of imprisonment and torture. In one scene, set in the monastery, the Spaniard is subjected to psychological and physical torture.

Later, when he escapes the monastery with the aid of his younger brother, the Spaniard is pursued by the agents of the Inquisition and is eventually caught. Once again he escapes, this time when he is just about to be burned alive, and makes his way to Ireland in pursuit of the villain Melmoth.

Indian Ocean island. Unnamed edenic island populated only by a young princess, Immalee, and a satanic tempter, Melmoth. This setting is introduced in the middle of the novel and breaks the Spaniard's narrative into two halves. It repeats the representation of the Spanish monastery by first appearing as a place of beauty and peace, which later turns terrifying. Although the island is edenic and deserted, it is close enough to the mainland to allow Immalee to watch the various goings-on of the Indian people.

As he does with his fictional Spaniards, Maturin represents the Indian people as superstitious to the point of stupidity and depicts their religion as little more than superstition. For instance, Immalee watches Indian worshipers willingly being crushed beneath the wheels of a cart that carries the image of the god Juggertha. As is the case with the young Spaniard's progress through the dungeons of the Inquisition, this setting implies that most religions are systems of mental and physical force crushing the spirit and sometimes the body of the worshiper.

*Bedlam. Famous London insane asylum used to show Melmoth's power to entrap and crush those who would oppose him. This setting twists the familiar gothic anti-Catholicism and xenophobia by introducing a domestic version. Like few other English gothic novels, this part of Maturin's novel shows that England can also be a place in which religious madness has run amok. In this case, an Englishman who has learned of Melmoth while traveling in Spain finds himself locked in a madhouse in London. There, he is trapped between a maddened Anglican and an insane Puritan; the two engage in pointless and tiresome dogmatic arguments, thereby, the novel seems to suggest, proving their madness and extending Maturin's argument of religious madness to the heart of England and not simply the margins of Europe.

Limbo. Desolate and dark cliff that serves in this novel as a brief stopping point before the soul of the departed goes on to its eventual destination. This setting is presented in the final chapter, after Melmoth has lived out his period of lengthened life and must fulfill the terms of his satanic pact. In the midst of the desolation, Melmoth perceives the souls of those he has wronged ascending to an eternity of bliss, even as his own soul sinks to a place of eternal torment. This setting is important because it shows that Melmoth is himself at the mercy of a higher power and has been trapped despite his own attempts to escape the consequences of his choices.

— *Michael R. Meyers*

THE MEMBER OF THE WEDDING

Author: Carson McCullers (1917-1967)
Type of work: Novel
Type of plot: Impressionistic realism

Time of plot: 1945
First published: 1946

Places in this novel help to reinforce the feelings of Frankie Addams, a confident yet naïve tomboy, who feels caught in the midst of her own development. She feels trapped in her small southern town during this endless summer of her twelfth year.

Georgia town. Unnamed and typically southern community that is Frankie's hometown. Frankie spends much of this hot August weekend walking to town, downtown to her father's jewelry store just off the main street, for example, and later to Sugarville, the Black section of town where Berenice Sadie Brown and her mother live, and to the Blue Moon, a bar where Frankie has her adventures with the red-haired soldier.

Addams home. Small house on 124 Grove Street, some blocks from the main section of town. Frankie, her cousin John Henry West, aged six, and the Addams's cook Berenice have spent the summer sitting in the Addams's kitchen, playing cards and talking. If Frankie feels stuck between childhood and adolescence, this house, with John Henry's childlike drawings on the kitchen walls, and Frankie's sleeping-porch bedroom, perfectly reflects her condition. At the end of the novel, Frankie's father decides to move her to another house on the outskirts of town with relatives, which signals the changes that have occurred in Frankie.

Winter Hill. Georgia site of the wedding of Frankie's brother Jarvis and Janice Evans, and the goal of all Frankie's dreams. Frankie plans to break out of her preadolescent jail by joining Jarvis and Janice on their honeymoon; after the wedding her father has to drag her out of their car. Winter Hill (like much of the novel's imagery) thus symbolizes the freedom that maturity will bring, in contrast to Frankie's hot, last summer of childhood.

— *David Peck*

MEMED, MY HAWK

Author: Yashar Kemal (Yaşar Kemal Gökçeli, 1923-   )
Type of work: Novel
Type of plot: Folklore

Time of plot: Early twentieth century
First published: İnce Memed, 1955 (English translation, 1961)

This novel depicts Turkish mountain village life in what the author himself characterized as a "world by itself." The lives of its many characters represent archetypes ranging from simple peasants through important rural figures who are all involved in the saga of the outlaw hero Memed—nicknamed the Hawk—who while fleeing from mountain region to mountain region becomes a symbol of freedom to the mountain villagers.

*Dikenli Plateau. Highland plain nestled beneath the rugged peaks of Turkey's Alidagh Mountains in the Taurus chain; tiny villages on the plateau, such as Kinalitepe, provide the main setting for the novel. The novel devotes considerable attention to the various natural images offered to the viewer of Dikenli. Because of its high altitude, it is often cloaked in a cloudy mist and is barely visible. In the season of intense sun, the whiteness of an extensive blanket of thistles make it appear as a field of snow. Kemal speaks also of the strong aroma of soil which, although not fully fertile, symbolizes the earthiness of village existence.

*Alidagh Mountain. Most prominent peak in the region in which the novel is set. Its vegetation ceases at a certain height, and the rocky crags around its summit provide a multitude of refuges in which Slim Memed hides during his flight. His last refuge before he is captured is in a cave on Alidagh. The mountain's summit commands a view of the Seyhan River as it runs its most rapid course through the mountains, and at the end of its descent from the mountain, the beginnings of the open plains of Cilicia.

*Taurus. Major mountain range that separates southeastern Turkey from northeastern Syria. Known to the Turks as Aladaghlar, the range forms an arc around the rich agricultural plain of Cilicia. The novel paints a vivid picture of the separation between rugged mountain village life and the plains life in Cilicia proper. Indeed, the story revolves around the concept of the mountains as a refuge from governmental agents of control in the plains.

Cilicia. Agricultural plains of southeast Turkey (formerly known as Asia Minor) that have always been richly productive. Settled life of villagers on the plains contrasts markedly with the more marginal village life in the surrounding mountains. Despite their determination to remain independent of government authority, some of Kemal's Dikenli Plateau villagers say they might eventually come down to the plains, where life is easier, but only after the time of troubles depicted in the story is past.

Adana. Main city of the Cilician region, located centrally on the agricultural plains, that owes its life-blood to the Seyhan River, which flows out of the Taurus Mountains. Older Turks remember Adana under its older name, Seyhan, symbolizing its debt to the river.

Saurun River. One of several rivers that flow out of the Taurus Mountains onto the Cilician plains. Where the Saurun empties onto the flatlands a shallow lake sometimes appears, depending on runoff amounts. The novel describes a particularly swampy region known as Aghdjasas where, again, the author's keen sense of contrasting colors and aromas allow him to offer a verbal tableau very much like a painting.

— *Byron D. Cannon*

MEMENTO MORI

Author: Muriel Spark (1918-   )
Type of work: Novel
Type of plot: Psychological realism

Time of plot: 1950's
First published: 1959

The characters in this novel live in London boroughs that indicate their interests and upper-middle-class status. Their advanced ages mark them as members of another community, one in which each receives an anonymous telephone call, saying "Remember, you must die," as the supernatural world becomes real.

London. Capital city with many different areas determined by wealth and social position. For example, the successful novelist Charmian Colston and her husband, Godfrey, live in Vicarage Gardens, off Kensington Church Street. Godfrey's sister Dame Lettie Colston, a pioneer penal reformer, has a house in Hampstead, where Lisa Brooke had a small brick studio house until her death. When the blackmailer Mrs. Mabel Pettigrew secures Lisa Brook's inheritance, she moves to a hotel in South Kensington near Harrod's department store. Alec Warner has a flat off St. James Street, and Guy Leet's flat was in Hyde Park. Olive Mannering, parasitic granddaughter of the poet Percy Mannering, lives in a basement flat in Tite Street in Chelsea.

Spark records complex interlacings among these characters—the sexual affairs, blackmail, literary debates, jealousies, quarrels, and gossip that are part of living in the city all their lives, apart from holidays abroad. The specified places indicate a close community in which everyone knows everyone else, and each person knows someone else's dark secrets.

Removed from the group, but sometimes visited, is Jean Taylor, for many years Charmian's companion, now confined to her bed at the Maud Long Medical Ward, part of a state hospital with limited amenities. A nice comparison is made when Charmian decides to go to an elegant private nursing home in Surrey, although both are Roman Catholics with a sense of detachment from the immediate present. Associated with the geriatrics, but distanced for several reasons, is Henry Mortimer, a retired police inspector, who has a home at Kingston-upon-Thames, outside London.

Supernatural world. Unearthly realm that is represented by a voice that speaks to each member of the community of old people, most frequently by telephone. This is Spark's brilliant modernization of the medieval convention of the coming of Death. In an age of scientific rationalism the disembodied voice from a telephone, a product of technology, evokes feelings of fear—or acceptance—that were familiar during the Middle Ages.

Closer to this older vision is Jean Taylor, whose own reminder of death (*memento mori*) is not a telephone caller but other elderly women waiting to die in her hospital ward. She is the first to identify the caller. While those in the flow of London are terrified, Taylor is detached, quietly analytical, pleased to be alone yet still caring of others. She is essentially a contemplative, closer to God than to other human beings. Knowing that the caller is Death does not disturb her, since she accepts Death as she accepts suffering, part of her devout Roman Catholic faith. Her belief is in sharp contrast to the scientific rationalism and agnosticism of Alex Warner, a sociologist who writes down details about his aging friends, who are of interest to him primarily as facts on his note cards.

— *Velma Bourgeois Richmond*

MEMOIRS OF A PHYSICIAN

Authors: Alexandre Dumas, *père* (1802-1870), with Auguste Maquet (1813-1888)
Type of work: Novel
Type of plot: Historical

Time of plot: 1770-1774
First published: Mémoires d'un médecin, 1846-1848 (English translation, 1846)

The principal stage and focal point of this novel is France's capital city, Paris. The early chapters are mapped out by the road that leads there from Strasbourg; once the destination is attained, the story unwinds in the city and its various supplementary royal residences.

Mont Tonnerre (toh-NAYR). Also known as Mount Thunder, a mountain on the left bank of the Rhine River near Worms, topped by a ruined feudal castle, where Balsamo receives his commission after confronting three hundred sword-bearing phantoms and revealing himself to their chiefs as their long-awaited messiah, the Great Copt.

Taverney château (ta-ver-NAY). Comparatively humble abode reflecting the reduced circumstances of the Taverney family, whose grander castle of **Maison-Rouge** lies in ruins nearby. It is situated between Saint Mihiel and Bar-le-Duc on the road from Strasbourg to Paris. There, the narrative begins to take shape, as a fateful storm interrupts Balsamo's progress, forcing him to seek shelter in the château.

Lachaussée (lah-koh-SAY). Village farther along the road, between Vitry and Chalons, where Philip fights Jean Dubarry after Chon attempts to commandeer Marie Antoinette's horses.

*Paris. Principal locations within the city featured in the plot are philosopher Jean-Jacques Rousseau's house in the rue de Plâtrière, where Gilbert finds refuge after meeting the philosopher in the woods at Meudon; the Hôtel d'Armenonville, the Taverney family's townhouse in the rue Coq-Heron, where the family is lodged in Paris; and Balsamo's exotically furnished house in a cul-de-sac off the rue St. Claude. Other key scenes are enacted at the Carmelite convent of St. Denis, where Lorenza seeks refuge with Princess Louise before Balsamo reclaims her, and the various locations in which the Comtesse de Bearn is duped and manipulated: the house of the lawyer Flageot in the rue du Petit-Lion-Saint-Sauveur; the Coq Chantant inn in the rue de Saint-Germain-de-Prés; and Comtesse Dubarry's house in the rue de Valois.

At the Place Louis XV, the celebration of the marriage of the Dauphin to Marie-Antoinette turns to disaster during the fireworks display. This scene is a crucial turning point in the plot, offering the first glimpse of the surgeon and revolutionary-to-be Jean-Paul Marat—who subsequently accompanies Balsamo to the Hôtel Dieu, where the magician demonstrates his medical skills. The house of the lieutenant of police, Monsieur de Sartines, in the Faubourg St. Germain and the Hôtel d'Aiguillon, residence of the duc de Richelieu's nephew, also serve as significant settings.

As in many *romans feuilletons*—novels serialized in the Paris newspapers—the effect of this range of settings is to forge a strong link between contemporary readers' knowledge of the city and the supposed secrets of its pre-

Revolutionary past. The novel trades heavily on presumed hindsight, not merely on the fate of King Louis XVI and Marie-Antoinette after the French Revolution but on the scandalous appearance in their court of the self-advertised magician Cagliostro (whose real name, Giuseppe Balsamo, Alexandre Dumas appropriated for his oft-reincarnated villain).

*Versailles (ver-SI). Royal palace west-southwest of Paris built in the mid-seventeenth century. Of the various royal residences featured in *Memoirs of a Physician*, the most celebrated is Versailles, whose splendor and luxury in the era of Louis XIV were legendary. Although several key scenes take place there—notably a symbolically loaded scene in a salon full of clocks, one of which the future Louis XVI restarts—the narrative continually emphasizes the fact that Louis XV prefers humbler surroundings.

Although Comtesse Dubarry has a suite at Versailles, Louis prefers to see her at Luciennes, near the woods of Chatou, where he is quite content to feed the carp in its lake when she keeps him waiting. It is there that de Sartines presents him with lettres de cachet for Rousseau and Voltaire. He holds his court at Marly, where he plays cards in the blue drawing room and hunts in the surrounding forest; it is there that Richelieu is introduced into the plot. The most important royal residence in the story is, however, Trianon, great pains being taken to point out that while Louis XIV had built Grand Trianon as a miniature of Versailles, Louis XV had commissioned Gabriel to build him a Petit Trianon—a mere pavilion, sixty feet square—connected to it by a path over a wooden bridge; it is here that the key events of the story's climax take place.

— *Brian Stableford*

MEMOIRS OF HADRIAN

Author: Marguerite Yourcenar (Marguerite de Crayencour, 1903-1987)
Type of work: Novel
Type of plot: Historical realism

Time of plot: 76-138 C.E.
First published: Mémoires d'Hadrien, 1951 (English translation, 1954)

Places play an important part in the reminiscences of the dying Publius Aelius Hadrianus. His experiences as student, soldier, quaestor, tribune, praetor, and emperor took place throughout the Roman Empire, from Britain to Judaea and from Germany to Egypt, but his most profound life lessons were learned in Rome, Athens, Nicomedia and Phrygia in Asia Minor, and Canopus in northern Egypt.

*Tibur (Tivoli). As Hadrian waits for death at his villa in central Italy, places haunt his thoughts. He sees his life "like dismantled rooms of a palace too vast for an impoverished owner to occupy in its entirety." He thinks about the places that brought him joy—the Spanish forests where hunting acquainted him with suffering and death, and the Mauretanian savannas in northwest Africa where he killed lions. But he also thinks of places that caused him pain—Rome whose public debaucheries sickened him, whose delight was in moderation.

Italica. Obscure town in the southern part of the Iberian Peninsula, where Hadrian was born. Despite his Spanish origins, Hadrian felt that his true homeland was

schools and books. Educated in Spain and, after the death of his father, in Rome, he returned to his homeland where, with the Seventh Legion in a wild region of the Pyrenees, he learned, through hunting and rough living, to judge the courage of men.

*Athens. Intellectual center of ancient Greece. Having mastered Greek in Rome, Hadrian continued his education in Athens, which seemed to him "slumbering in a haze of ideas" compared to Rome, where the world's business was being done and undone. Athens, with its rich intellectual history, appealed to Hadrian's scholarly side, but his appetite for power drew him back to Rome, where decisions could determine the fate of the world.

Roman Empire. Before and during Trajan's reign, Hadrian held a succession of administrative and military appointments that prepared him to become emperor. By participating in Rome's battles with the Germanic tribes, he learned to love this northern region, which contrasted so sharply with the dry and sunny Mediterranean lands he had previously known. Though a kind of umbilical cord attached him to Rome, he liked the harsh Germanic terrain, for he had a passion for privation and discipline.

These early experiences set the pattern of his life: periodic stays in Rome (to advance his career) and extensive travels throughout the empire (to bring order to an increasingly disordered society). For Hadrian, Greece was the place where civilizers had separated themselves from the monstrous by creating rational politics and ennobling art. He thus saw his task as Hellenizing the barbaric lands and Atticizing Rome.

The empire's eastern lands, which had troubled Rome for centuries, would also trouble Hadrian both before and after he was emperor. He compared the empire that he inherited from Trajan to a man who had survived a serious illness. For Hadrian, Rome was no longer confined to Rome, and he believed that Rome had to identify herself with her conquered countries, or be conquered by them. He restored order in Egypt, Mauretania, and Britain. He saw all these places, even those precariously held, as Romes-to-be. On all these different nations Hadrian wanted to superpose an enduring unity. In contrast, he himself never had a genuinely fixed abode in his twenty years of rule.

The dominating passion in his personal life was for Antinous, a handsome youth he had met at Nicomedia in the province of Bithynia in northwest Asia Minor. Hadrian's love for Antinous led him to see places as he never had before. Now he delighted in the pine forests of Bithynia, the wine-rose hills of Attica, and the volcanic heights of Mount Aetna. In Phrygia, where Greece melds into Asia, he had, with Antinous, his most complete experience of happiness. However, after trips to Jerusalem and Alexandria, Antinous, in Hadrian's absence, traveled to Canopus where, in a basin near a bend in the Nile, he killed himself to secure favor from the gods for the man he had loved and the emperor he had worshipped.

Following Antinous's death, places that Hadrian had formerly loved he now abhorred. He commanded that a city, Antinoöpolis, be built with an encircling wall, a triumphal arch, and a tomb, but he sensed that this ideal city would soon become just another place to shelter commercial fraud, prostitution, and political corruption. He traveled through the eastern empire, but he was everywhere faced with anarchy. For example, the Jews were in rebellion against the Romans, and though Hadrian was able to pacify Judaea, he came to see this war as one of his failures.

On his return to Rome he encountered a criminality that was infecting politicians, lawyers, even ordinary people. He chose to build, away from Rome, a villa as a place of refuge, where the books that he had collected in his travels would be his source of comfort. After arranging for his successor and his mausoleum, he died at Baiae, near the sea, where he found it easier to breathe.

— *Robert J. Paradowski*

THE MENAECHMI

Author: Plautus (c. 254-184 B.C.E.)
Type of work: Drama
Type of plot: Farce

Time of plot: Third century B.C.E.
First performed: Menaechmi, second century B.C.E.

The primary setting of this farce is a street in Epidamnus, a typical ancient Roman town. All five acts are staged on a street between two houses, with two exit streets to the Forum and the harbor, and an alleyway convenient for eavesdropping. As the comic case of mistaken identity involving identical twins is played out in Epidamnus, Plautus reveals insightful slices of family life and society in the Roman world.

Epidamnus (ihp-ah-DAHM-nahs). Roman port on Greece's Macedonian coast (also known as Dyrrhachium). Epidamnus is home to the merchant who kidnapped Menaechmus, one of the twins, raised him as his son, bought him a suitable wife, made him his heir, and then suddenly died. As Plautus sets the stage in his prologue, he reveals that Menaechmus's dwelling could be anybody's house in the Roman world. Menaechmus himself prefers the house across the street, where his mistress lives; her house is the place where he entertains his guests. When the other twin, renamed by his grandfather "Menaechmus," to honor the name of the stolen twin, arrives in Epidamnus on a quest to find his brother, the farce begins, hilarious encounters revolve around confusion over the two "Menaechmi."

Tarentum (tah-rehn-tahm). Roman port in southern Italy. In the prologue, Plautus uses cargo ships to move his characters from Syracuse to Tarentum to Epidamnus. It is to Tarentum that Moschus takes Menaechmus along with a shipload of merchandise. When the boy is lost, the father dies of grief and is buried in Tarentum. Plautus thus removes the scene of tragedy from both the family's hometown and from the scene of the comedy in Epidamnus.

Syracuse. Sicilian port city that is home of the merchant Moschus and his wife, to whom the Menaechmi are born. It is also of the grandfather who renames the remaining brother Menaechmus in honor of the one that is lost. That the brothers leave for Syracuse after they are reunited speaks to the tenuous hold that Roman society had on the hearts of its subjects, and the strong sense of place identified as home.

— *Marguerite R. Plummer*

THE MERCHANT OF VENICE

Author: William Shakespeare (1564-1616)
Type of work: Drama
Type of plot: Tragicomedy

Time of plot: Sixteenth century
First performed: c. 1596-1597; first published, 1600

The primary settings in this tragicomic fable about love, generosity, revenge, and justice are Venice and Belmont, towns in northeastern Italy that represent contrasting social and moral worlds.

Venice. Major Italian port whose commercial activities are the play's focus. William Shakespeare's Venice is a busy mercantile center, in which businessmen are concerned about their cargoes at sea and who are often at the mercy of usurious moneylenders, such as Shylock. A wealthy Jew, Shylock has a deep-rooted animosity toward Christians, who chronically insult him and his religion. Although Venice is dominated by money, with its foundations resting on commerce, trade, and family inheritances, there is a society of exclusiveness under its busy mercantile surface—which is symbolized by the Rialto Bridge, a common meeting place for businessmen. Venice's people include reviled Jews and anti-Semitic Christians, and Venetian law has the inveterate power to turn individuals into scapegoats.

Belmont. Town near Venice in which the wealthy young Portia lives. In contrast with Venice, Belmont is a place of beautiful material luxury and pleasure. Portia's beauty, wit, and grace distinguish her home, but it is actually a world of idleness, frivolity, music, and romance. Portia and her waiting-maid Nerissa seem to do little but gossip about Portia's eager suitors and show much anxiety about Bassanio's chances at winning her hand. A scene in which Portia's suitors must choose among treasure caskets to win her hand in marriage is pregnant with the symbolism of wealth and moral implications.

Shylock's house. Venetian home of Shylock the moneylender. Shylock's daughter Jessica and his servant Launcelot Gobbo complain about the hellishness of the place, where thrift is practiced, where doors and windows are shut against the masked Christian revelers whom Shylock regards as threats to his religion and his property.

Shakespeare also uses generalized street scenes or scenes in front of Shylock's to demonstrate the anti-Semitism of Solario, Salerio, and Gratiano, and to contrast the shallowness of these men and of Launcelot Gobbo with the wisdom of Portia and the considered judgment of Antonio, the rich and generous merchant of the play's title.

Court. Venetian court of justice that is the setting for the all-important trial scene, in which the problem of Shylock's bond is resolved by Portia's ingenious cleverness and a bargain that Shylock is forced to make with Venetian law in a crystallization of opposite forces: lofty Jewish concept of right and Christian "mercy."

— *Keith Garebian*

THE MERRY WIVES OF WINDSOR

Author: William Shakespeare (1564-1616)
Type of work: Drama
Type of plot: Comedy

Time of plot: Sixteenth century
First performed: 1597; first published, 1602

It is fitting that this comedy concerned primarily with business and domestic matters should have the bourgeois setting of Windsor, a small country town well known to William Shakespeare and his audiences. The play reflects the topography and social life of Windsor in great detail while celebrating the values of this society.

*Windsor.** Town on the River Thames that is the play's principal setting. Windsor is also the site of Windsor Castle, about twenty miles west of the center of London. Landmarks in the town include the great park and the castle, Datchet Mead, the road to Frogmore, the Garter Inn, the great oak in the forest, the nearby sawpit, and the castle ditch, in which Thomas Page conceals himself with Justice Shallow and Shallow's simple-minded nephew, Slender. The play's Windsor is a solid, comfortable community that takes pride in itself. Apart from the decadent knight Sir John Falstaff, Master Fenton, Justice Shallow, and Slender, all the characters in the play are citizens of Windsor.

*Garter Inn.** Windsor meeting place of Falstaff and his cohorts. The setting provides another perspective of Windsor society and affords Falstaff a place in which to hatch his scheme to replenish his finances by wooing Mistress Ford and Mistress Page, the wives of two substantial citizens.

Caius's house. Home of the stupid French doctor Caius that is the scene of sheer farce, in which the eccentric Frenchman is satirized. Production designers avail themselves of the opportunity to embellish the set with extra doors and paraphernalia that add to the scene's zaniness.

Herne's oak. Site of Falstaff's third adventure, where he appears at midnight, disguised as Herne the Hunter with antlers on his head. The forest is appropriate for the references to Diana and Actaeon, with Falstaff's becoming a parodic Actaeon figure.

— *Keith Garebian*

THE METAMORPHOSIS

Author: Franz Kafka (1883-1924)
Type of work: Novella
Type of plot: Allegory

Time of plot: Early twentieth century
First published: *Die Verwandlung*, 1915 (English translation, 1936)

Franz Kafka's masterful story of human alienation is set primarily inside Gregor Samsa's bedroom, emphasizing the total isolation from his family and the rest of the world that is created by his transformation into an insect. Kafka separated the story into three parts, each beginning in Gregor's bedroom and describing one of his attempts to reclaim his place within the family—and, by doing so, a part of his former self. Each attempt ends in failure, leaving Gregor confined to his decaying room.

Samsa apartment. Dwelling, in no particular city, of Gregor Samsa and his family. Comfortable and spacious, the apartment signifies Gregor's success in providing for his family, which fell on hard times after his father's business failure. Gregor's exhausting work as a traveling salesman keeps the family in respectable circumstances. After his metamorphosis, however, the apartment proves to be too big and expensive to maintain. In a sense, it has always been a burden. Gregor selected it, and his support of the family has stimulated a growing lethargy among them. His mother coughs incessantly, his sister is losing her youth to extreme fatigue, and his father has abandoned his role as the head of the family. All of this changes as Gregor changes, and after his death, the family is liberated from the apartment and from Gregor.

Gregor's bedroom. Room in which the story begins, with Gregor's metamorphosis into a giant insect already an accomplished fact. Though initially alarmed, he soon takes comfort in the familiarity of his bedroom. The room itself changes through the course of the story, in ways that mirror Gregor's own decline. His furniture is removed to provide him with more space to crawl. After his sister neglects to clean the room, filth begins to accumulate. Eventually, the room becomes a storage space for useless household items—much like Gregor himself. Once a refuge from the toils of his job, the room becomes his cell and ultimately his tomb.

Living/dining room. Social center of the family, where Gregor's father once read the newspaper aloud to the family and where Grete played her violin. Immediately after revealing his altered self to the family, Gregor is cut off from this space. Grete keeps the door to his room locked. Each time he ventures out among the family, his father drives him away. Late in the story, the family relents and allows his door to stand ajar in the evening, allowing Gregor a distant view of the family from which he has been excluded. Drawn by the music from Grete's violin, Gregor enters the living room a final time, to the horror of the three boarders who have taken rooms with the Samsas. Amid the turmoil his presence creates, he finds that his sister, in whom he has placed the last hope of any understanding and future happiness, can no longer stand his presence in the apartment. Without needing to be forced, he retreats to his room, and Grete locks him in. His position within the family is irrecoverable, and his transformation is complete.

Tram car. Conveyance on which members of Gregor's family travel from the apartment to the country in the story's final scene. They are the only passengers, and the car is filled with warm, morning sunlight. The tram moves quietly into the peaceful countryside, and with it the Samsas discover that their prospects for the future are brighter than anticipated. Gregor's death has lifted an enormous burden from them, and as his parents watch their young daughter, they see that, despite the recent hardships, she has blossomed into a beautiful woman. With Gregor gone, the family moves, like the tram, toward a peaceful future.

— *Philip Bader*

METAMORPHOSIS

Author: Edith Sitwell (1887-1964)
Type of work: Poetry

First published: 1933, in *Five Variations on a Theme*

Edith Sitwell published "Metamorphosis" in two versions. The earlier, longer version alludes to a wide variety of places; however, the later and shorter version presents a more concise and unified set of images that clarifies a sense of place. Both versions allude to African, Far Eastern, Greco-Roman, Judeo-Christian, and South

American cultures, lending their verses an ageless, universal setting. As its title suggests, the poem deals with transformation, particularly transformations from life to death and then from beyond death to life again.

Time. Although Time is not a place, it can be seen as a dimension of all life, and for Sitwell it is also a symbol of destruction and decay. For example, for Athens's Parthenon—mentioned in her poem's opening line—Time is the destroyer that extinguishes beauty and life, leaving ruins, skeletons, and rags.

Death. In contrast to Time, Death is a place of rest and respite from the ravages of Time. In keeping with the theme of metamorphosis, Time is like a caterpillar and Death is like a cocoon. The grave then becomes a welcome home for those wearied by the trials of life only because Death marks the end of Time.

Sun. Often paralleled with Death in this poem, the Sun burns away the body but also illuminates the beauty of what remains of life, like gems among the bones. Sitwell completes her poem by referring to the conquering of Death by Christ, punning on the word "Sun" and "Son" of God. Christ the Sun brings a new spring that melts away the ice of Death and the crusts of Time. The final transformation is through the fire of spring, an eternal state of life beyond Death and Time.

*Ethiopia. Modern country in Northeast Africa; also, biblical name for tropical Africa. In comparing Death and the Sun, Sitwell often alludes to "Ethiopia," which is perhaps best understood here in its biblical sense as a broad name for tropical Africa, as a place of the hot Sun and of beauty. Since the modern nation of Ethiopia is also a home of the early Christian church, references to Ethiopia anticipate those to Heavenly Love or Christ, who is finally connected with the metamorphosis beyond death.

— *Daven M. Kari*

MIDAQ ALLEY

Author: Naguib Mahfouz (1911-   )
Type of work: Novel
Type of plot: Historical realism

Time of plot: 1940's
First published: Zuqaq al-Midaqq, 1947 (English translation, 1966, 1975)

This novel is set in and around a Cairo back alley whose inhabitants' efforts to escape the alley end with unfulfilled dreams. The setting provides a vivid picture of a cross-section of life in Cairo in the early twentieth century. Relying on the best techniques of realism and naturalism, Naguib Mahfouz allows the events of everyday life in the alley and the philosophies and obsessions of its residents to depict a bleak picture of urban Cairo that reveals Egypt's political, social, religious, and intellectual turmoil.

Midaq Alley. Small, dead-end street in the ancient Gamaliyya section of Cairo. The ancient stone-surfaced alley leads to historic Santadiquiya Street in the heavily populated urban quarters of Cairo. Among the odoriferous shops and houses lining the alley's three isolating walls, the sociopolitical ills of Egyptian society, familiar to Mahfouz from his boyhood homes in the Egyptian districts of al-Jamaliya and al-Abbasiya, are revealed through this intimate look into the lives of Uncle Kamil, Sheikh Darwish, and the other residents of the alley.

Within the alley, Egypt's past and present mingle like the aromas from Kirsha's café, with its crumbling multicolored arabesques, and permeate the voices of the residents as they go about their daily activities. Midaq Alley is a place of contrasts, a place where the recitations of an old poet who has frequented the café for twenty years are now met with protests from the owner who reminds the poet that things have changed. His customers want to listen to a radio, not to a poet. As the story opens, workers busily install the voice of the modern world into the otherwise isolated alley.

One side of the alley houses a shop and a bakery; on the other side sits a second shop and an office, while two adjoining three-story houses, filled with luckless tenants—including the marriage broker Umm Hamida and her scheming foster daughter—constitute the alley's literal and symbolic dead end. Just outside the alley's entrance sits a sweets shop to the right and a barbershop to the left. Within the cramped, dark confines of the alley, into which the warming light of the sun reaches only a few hours each day, details of the interconnected lives of the inhabitants are revealed as they move from place to familiar place. Conversations within the shabby houses, at the barbershop with its shiny instruments and mirrors, and among the café's patrons reflect the material and spiritual ties that bind persons to each other and to the alley.

In their contacts with the world outside the alley, the characters struggle to reconcile the disparity of their hopelessness in a time of rapid modernization; the presence of the British army in Cairo, in the midst of wartime campaigns, continues the economic exploitation of Egypt's colonial past while providing much needed work for local men. The contrast, for example, between the luxurious life flaunted by Husain Kirsha, son of the café's owner, who has a job in the British camps during the day, and the lives of the other residents of the alley, creates a wide gulf of envy between Husain and his boyhood friends. In the world of the alley, no lasting good can come of these outside alliances, and the tragic murder of the barber Abbas Hilu—whom Husain encouraged to leave the alley—by British soldiers reinforces the theme that satisfaction can never be found in pursuit of seductive materialistic passions.

In the end, life in the alley subsides to its lakelike surface; the alley absorbs its losses and the addition of a new family of tenants in an unwavering state of indifference and forgetfulness. Kirsha's proclamations of spiritual acceptance remind readers of the cycle of life reflected by the alley: God gives and takes all things. Sheikh Darwish's fitting comment that all things have their end closes the story, and the alley, with its narrow scope and inevitable end, stands as a timeless symbol of the struggles and disappointments that make up human life and the spiritual acceptance that is the only real consolation.

— *Kathleen M. Bartlett*

MIDDLEMARCH: A Study of Provincial Life

Author: George Eliot (Mary Ann Evans, 1819-1880)
Type of work: Novel
Type of plot: Psychological realism

Time of plot: Mid-nineteenth century
First published: 1871-1872

An exploration of a nineteenth century provincial village, George Eliot's novel shows how residents are affected by the environment whose manners and customs rule their lives. The novel is set on the eve of enactment of Great Britain's Reform Bill of 1832 and examines a rising manufacturing town and the country gentry reacting to social pressures. At center stage a young physician, Tertius Lydgate, seeks to bend the opinion of Middlemarchers toward his scientific reforms. Sharing the stage is the youthful heroine, Dorothea, who attempts to aspire beyond her ordained role as a woman and reform the social scene of poverty on the wealthy estate of her inheritance, going against the grain of the village inhabitants.

Middlemarch. Fictional English village in which much of the novel's action is centered. The book opens on the Middlemarch estate of the Brooke family, **Tipton Grange**, home to the orphaned sisters, Dorothea and Celia Brooke, and their uncle. The adjoining estate of Sir James Chettam, **Freshitt Hall**, whose land lies close to Tipton Grange, attaches property and money to the novel's purpose. For this reason, Sir James is the logical suitor for the elder sister, Dorothea. Her interest lies, however, in the scholarly Reverend Edward Casaubon, of **Lowick**, five miles away. Again, property and prosperity make Lowick significant, insofar as no reform is needed in this affluent neighborhood. The novel's action, however, moves skillfully to nearby Middlemarch as well as abroad, always returning to Middlemarch as the heart of the tale.

The moral center of the novel is located in the rambling, homely house with an orchard in front of it, a little way outside the town, where the Garth family resides. They are of the kind and quality that Eliot considered the true source of Britain's strength. Their farmhouses, their family, and their family relationships play a significant role in shaping the atmosphere and tone of this novel.

Stone Court. Estate near the center of Middlemarch in which another drama of money and property is played out by the miserly uncle Featherstone, who holds the purse strings of many relatives and affects the lives of Mayor Vincy's son and daughter.

Houndsley. Town just outside Middlemarch. In this "unsanitary" town, gambling and bad faith dealings are carried on, where horses are bought and sold, many of them deficient in quality. There, the mayor's son incurs debts that soon have a rippling effect in the novel. This undercurrent of bad debts and bad faith spills over into the lives of the major and minor characters, again underscoring the importance that Eliot gives to money and property.

*****Rome.** Leading Italian city that provides a symbolic setting for the brief honeymoon of the poorly matched couple, Dorothea and Casaubon. The strong contrast between the lush, warm art works in this sensuous city and the couple's cold relationship reveals serious shortcomings in Dorothea's scholarly husband and foreshadows the failure of their marriage.

*****Paris.** France's capital and leading city, in which the youthful medical student Tertius Lydgate is shown in a flashback that demonstrates his weakness for the wrong kind of woman—a young actor. Eliot uses the Paris incident to prepare readers for Lydgate's next misstep, when he chooses Middlemarch's town beauty, Rosamond, for his wife.

*****Bath.** English resort town, where Lydgate retires with his demanding wife to treat wealthy patients with gout after being spurned by the town of Middlemarch. Bath provides a plush setting to signify the loss of aspirations for medical reform.

*****London.** Capital of Great Britain where Dorothea lives after her first husband, Casaubon, dies, and she marries Will Ladislaw, who pursues a political career. The more anonymous location of London allows Dorothea to leave behind the censorious Middlemarch. To the Middlemarchers, London meant living "in a street," giving up the luxury of an estate, living among poverty and crime.

— *Esther K. Labovitz*

A MIDSUMMER NIGHT'S DREAM

Author: William Shakespeare (1564-1616)
Type of work: Drama
Type of plot: Comedy

Time of plot: Antiquity
First performed: c. 1595-1596; first published, 1600

The Greek palace and woods that provide the principal settings in this play evoke images of holiday license and merriment, an atmosphere of marvelous magic and madness. The play's concern with dream, play, art, love, and imagination is rehearsed in settings that span social classes and both human and supernatural worlds.

Theseus's palace. Home of Theseus, the "duke of Athens," in which the play opens, shortly after Theseus has militarily subdued the Amazon queen Hippolyta, whom he plans to marry in the evening. Theseus is an important figure in ancient Greek mythology, but the Athens of William Shakespeare is partly classical and partly medieval, hence Theseus's title as a "duke." The Athens of the play mirrors a courtly world with inflexible codes of conduct that become oppressive to the quartet of young lovers.

At the end of the play, all the characters who have appeared in the play reappear at Theseus's palace for the marriage festivities, on which the Fairies bestow a final blessing. By this point, the palace resembles an Elizabethan great house.

Woods. Forested region close to the palace that is the setting for most of the play. Woodlands are familiar English locales with their beautiful moonlit glades and common English insects and flowers. However, the woods are also mysterious and alien, with fairies and spirits. Within these woods, confusions about love and imagination crystallize. The play's woodland fairyland has its own laws of time and space. For example, the king of the Fairies, Oberon, appears in an instant from India, and the mischievous fairy Puck circles the earth in forty minutes. The woods' rhythms are those of sleeping, dreaming, and awaking. Dangers lurk—not only those of hunting but the bafflements of reason, illusion, random desires, and shifting identities.

— *Keith Garebian*

THE MIGHTY AND THEIR FALL

Author: Ivy Compton-Burnett (1884-1969)
Type of work: Novel
Type of plot: Domestic realism

Time of plot: Mid-twentieth century
First published: 1961

The deepest secrets of an outwardly happy and close-knit English family are revealed when its widower father remarries and introduces his new wife into the household that is this novel's principal setting. Although the house is never described in any detail, its claustrophobic nature is central to the story.

Ninian Middleton's house. Upper-class home in an unspecified English town of Ninian Middleton, a self-righteous widower who wants to take a new wife and provide his children with a stepmother. Most of the novel is set within this house, but the novel is nearly 90 percent dialogue that never describes it or any other place in any detail. Thus, while it is clear that the house has rooms, descriptions of them are limited to labels of their functions. For example, the house has a downstairs kitchen, a dining room, a hall, a cloak room, a school room, and at least one bedroom; other rooms can only be assumed to exist. The text contains occasional references to furniture, such as a table, a wastebasket, and a bed, but nothing else is described beyond the fact that the house stands in a garden, which is also not described. In any case, no significant action takes place in the garden, in which only Middleton's youngest children play.

There is a village somewhere beyond the house, where Miss Starkie, the children's governess and keenest observer of the family's activities, lives. Only she and Ninian Middleton himself regularly leave the house.

In many respects, Middleton's home is a cipher, simply a container for his family that seems to have little existence in its own right. Indeed, from the ways in which author Ivy Compton-Burnett opens chapters with little or no indication of their individual settings, or how much time has passed since previous chapters, readers might almost see the home as a dollhouse, whose front is open to view and whose characters are randomly moved from room to room like dolls, without regard for conventional human ways of moving around within a house. Significantly, however, many key moments in the narrative occur as characters enter or leave rooms, and the movement of the plot relies heavily on snatches of conversation overheard and then questioned through family discussion.

The Middleton house and Middleton family would seem to be synonymous, at least to Ninian Middleton, the head of the family. As his relationship with his children approaches a crisis point, he says to his mother, almost plaintively, that he should know the "temper of the house"; however, his frequent absence from the house either suggests that he does not know the house and its occupants, or that if he does recognize that the house is more of a prison than a home—particularly to his eldest daughter, Lavinia—he is content with the situation. Indeed, much of the book's narrative, a merciless dissection of a claustrophobic and dysfunctional family, rests on Middleton's complacent view of his family as his possession and consequent failure to see its constituent members as individuals, each with individual needs. To him his children can be treated as easily as models in a dollhouse.

Ransom Middleton's house. Home of Ninian's brother, Ransom Middleton, who has lived away from the rest of the family for many years for unspecified reasons. When he returns home to die, he chooses not to return to the family house but to a separate house that he has bought with the proceeds of his life's work. This idea is novel to the Middleton family, whose members are accustomed to existing on income from their estate, dwindling though it is. Ransom Middleton recognizes, as does Miss Starkie and Teresa Chilton, Ninian Middleton's new wife, that Ninian's house is claustrophobic and inimical to a fully developed life. On learning that Lavinia tried to stop her father's marriage by hiding letters from Teresa, Ransom takes Lavinia into his own house and makes provision for her future by rewriting his will in her favor, leaving her his house. Ransom's house represents an escape for Lavinia, who will attempt to build a future for herself, including marriage to her adoptive uncle, Hugo. However, her father, Ninian, cannot accept this situation and attempts to destroy his brother's will to ensure that Ransom's house goes to him and is absorbed into his estate so that he can keep his family together, despite Lavinia's wish to break free.

Like Ninian's house, Ransom's house is not described except by room function. Lavinia appears briefly in the house's garden, but this scene is not described in detail.

— *Maureen Speller*

THE MIKADO: Or, The Town of Titipu

Author: W. S. Gilbert (1836-1911)
Type of work: Drama (opera libretto)
Type of plot: Satire

Time of plot: Middle Ages
First performed: 1885; first published, 1885

Although this play is set primarily in the courtyard and garden of Ko-Ko, the lord high executioner of Titipu, the action of the play includes everyone of consequence in the town of Titipu, including the august Mikado of Japan.

Titipu. Medieval court and government of the emperor of Japan. Titipu represents a microcosm of Japan. Its officials and functionaries are myriad and coexist in a Byzantine complexity of rules and regulations; this milieu is meant to satirize the Victorian bureaucracy of Great Britain during the era in which the play was first produced. The settings are stereotyped to resemble the many Japanese decorative objects being imported into Britain at that time. Examples of high Japanese art were also on display in London museums and had created a craze for Japanese things in the moneyed middle and upper classes. The two scenes set in Titipu reflect these Japanese influences, both paying homage to and satirizing them as the temporary passions of the wealthy.

Ko-Ko's palace. The palace courtyard, appearing in the opening act of the play, is magnificent, as befits the Lord High Executioner of Titipu. It thus satirizes the needless largesse expended on government functionaries in the Victorian era.

Ko-Ko's garden. The garden scene of act 2 provides the backdrop for the heroine Yum-Yum's preparation for her wedding to the wandering minstrel Nanki-Poo, who is really the Mikado's son in disguise. The garden is also the scene of the Mikado's magnificent entrance, which paves the way for a happy marriage. The wedding occurs after Nanki-Poo is threatened with execution and Ko-Ko is married to the odious Katisha, who wanted to marry Nanki-Poo herself. All ends happily in a setting straight from a book of Japanese fairy tales.

— *Isabel Bonnyman Stanley*

THE MILL ON THE FLOSS

Author: George Eliot (Mary Ann Evans, 1819-1880)
Type of work: Novel
Type of plot: Domestic realism

Time of plot: Nineteenth century
First published: 1860

Plot, character, and theme are all closely tied to the setting of this novel, a rural area in England's Midlands, where George Eliot herself spent her childhood. The natural setting and the community living there provide a home that nurtures the characters' humanity but also brings about the tragedy that engulfs the heroine.

***English Midlands.** Central region of England. The novel is set in what seems like an idyllic country setting, modeled on Warwickshire, in the English Midlands, where George Eliot grew up as the child Mary Ann Evans. Eliot's protagonist, Maggie Tulliver, and her brother Tom (Evans had a beloved brother named Isaac) love the river and the countryside. There they pick flowers, fish in the Round Pond, and romp with their dog Yap. Eliot suggests that human beings are nurtured by living close to nature, and that people are, in many important ways, a part of nature: Eliot often uses analogies drawn from nature, as in the comparison of Tom and Maggie to friendly ponies shaking their manes at each other.

In the novel, nature is not an entirely benign force. The reader sees conflicts arising between Maggie and Tom, owing to their different dispositions and exacerbated by the misogynist climate of the times. Nature can also be the source of destruction, as seen in the flood that kills Maggie and Tom. In introducing the **Floss River** into the landscape, Eliot made one alteration to her geographical model. She needed a tidal river to make the flood possible. The configuration of the river and the flood basin suggests the Trent River in Lincolnshire.

Tulliver home. The precise setting is drawn from Eliot's childhood memories of growing up in Griff House, on the Arbury estate, where her father managed the property for the landowner. Griff House has survived the years and was converted into an inn. Even the Round Pond has an exact prototype in Griff House Pond. The pond, perfectly round and of unknown depth, suggests the mystery and magic of natural places. The Tullivers' house is spacious and comfortable, and Maggie's life there would be perfect were it not for her intelligent and passionate nature, which makes it difficult for her to conform to the confining gender role prescribed for female children in the Victorian age. When her mother reprimands her for losing her sunbonnet, allowing her hair to become disheveled, or running and jumping too boisterously, she retreats to the large attic to nurse her doll and shed tears of frustration. Her self-seclusion in the attic suggests her distance from conventional Victorian society.

A stultifying society puts a curb on her natural desires and abilities. Only her father can be depended on to take her side, frequently taking her on his lap to comfort her. He is the owner of **Dorlcote Mill**, and a significant person in the web of relationships that surrounds Maggie. The mill, based on Arbury Mill, with its piles of grain and floury spiders is a wonderland for the imaginative child. As Maggie matures, her life becomes more difficult. Her father goes through bankruptcy and is in conflict with the lawyer whom he feels deprived him of the mill. Maggie gains some consolation from meeting her lover, Philip (ironically the lawyer's son), and they take long walks in the **Red Deeps**. A lovely spot, again based on a real model, its trees and natural beauties provide consolation, offering a romantic conception of nature. Griff House is close to the town of Nuneaton.

***St. Oggs.** Town noteworthy for its provincial mindset and puritanical attitudes. St. Oggs is a representative river town, larger than Nuneaton. The values that define St. Oggs—wealth, social standing, rigid conformity to social rules—put Maggie at odds with her surroundings when, as a young woman, she spends some time there. She cannot be forgiven for an inadvertent social indiscretion. She must struggle against an immovable wall of hostility, and Eliot ends the novel with her drowning in the course of her attempted rescue of Tom from the flood.

— *Charlotte Templin*

MILTON

Author: William Blake (1757-1827)
Type of work: Poetry

First published: 1804-1808

The whole universe is the poem's setting, conceived by William Blake as an extended human form evolving from a fall through struggle and redemption to apocalypse, which is precipitated by Milton's descent through regions of the compass governed by spirits corresponding to four aspects of humanity: western Tharmas (body), eastern Luvah (emotions), southern Urizen (reason), and northern Urthona (imagination).

Golgonooza (gol-goh-NEWS-ah). William Blake's holy City of Art, a spiritual form of London encompassing all Britain, like the biblical New Jerusalem. There at his seven furnaces Urthona's manifestation Los melts all of nature into gold for the City of God and gives form to uncreated things. His labor is the imaginative creation of all that can be redeemed. The architecture of the city therefore unites it with the four levels of human existence: Ulro, hellish nature untamed by humans; Generation, love's struggle to rise above savagery; Beulah, the subconscious realm of recovered innocence, a sleepy place of respite from the fury of creative inspiration; and Eden, a paradise where reason has been dominated by imagination.

Brooks of Arnon. Tributaries of the Arnon River in Jordan, where Milton struggles with the satanic spirit of reason, Urizen. These are biblical places where Jacob wrestled with God to gain a blessing for Israel, where the Jews escaped from bondage in Egypt, and where Moses was buried. Thus, symbolically, Blake connects his myth with the religious journey of God's chosen people into liberty, nationhood, and deliverance from the tyranny of law. Urizen baptizes Milton with the icy river water (religious dogma). Milton uses the living red clay to make a human form for Urizen. Thus their struggle ends in a victory of imagination over reason.

— *John L. McLean*

THE MINISTRY OF FEAR

Author: Graham Greene (1904-1991)
Type of work: Novel
Type of plot: Psychological realism

Time of plot: 1941
First published: 1943

Graham Greene's literary genius inspired him to adapt a conventional thriller plot—about a fugitive wanted for a murder he did not commit—as a device enabling him to paint a word-mural of London being devastated by the nightly German air raids of 1941, a turning point in history when Germany's air force tried to bomb Britain into submission.

*****London.** Great Britain's capital city, which faced the brunt of the heavy German air attacks in 1941. German chancellor Adolf Hitler launched the air attacks on Britain because he was afraid to risk ferrying his troops across the English Channel in open barges, subject to bombardment from ships, planes, and shore batteries and always in danger of hitting underwater mines. Instead, he gambled on Hermann Göring's promise to force Britain to surrender through relentless bombing. London eventually became the prime target of the powerful German Luftwaffe. During the period the British called the "Blitz," masses of German planes arrived every night on schedule. Air raid sirens would begin their mournful wailing, as if they were mourning the end of civilization. Londoners hurried to shelters carrying their bedding and valued possessions.

Up above the blacked-out city the sky was pierced with searchlights trying to pick out planes for the antiaircraft gunners to shoot at. When the bombs began to fall, the fire fighters would aim their hoses at the burning buildings, but the little streams of water seemed pitifully ineffective against the blazing chaos. In the morning, the Londoners would go off to work in their shops, offices, warehouses, and factories, trying to conduct business as usual, although every morning saw numbers of dead and wounded being trucked away in makeshift ambulances. It was the first time in history that the civilian population of a major city had witnessed such sights—staircases leading to upper stories that no longer existed, burnt-out vehicles blocking streets, human limbs protruding from piles of rubble, detours around enormous craters holding unexploded bombs, broken glass everywhere, children shouting for joy after discovering their schools had disappeared overnight. Greene realized that all this made a magnificent setting for a novel about fear and alienation.

In *The Ministry of Fear*, the external reality reflects the mood, the internal reality, of the protagonist Arthur Rowe, whom Greene introduces as the "Unhappy Man." His life is a microcosm within a macrocosm, a nightmare within a nightmare. Just as London is being demolished block by block and brick by brick, so too Rowe's life seems to be falling apart. But it should be noted that Rowe retains a quirky, fatalistic sense of humor, just as many embattled Londoners maintained good cheer in the midst of chaos.

Greene's masterful novel is sprinkled with characteristically whimsical, tragic, and funny thumbnail descriptions of London under siege. An example:

> The stairs were at the back of the flats looking toward Chelsea, and as you climbed above the second floor and your view lifted, the war came back into sight. Most of the church spires seemed to have been snapped off two-thirds up like sugar-sticks, and there was an appearance of slum clearance, where there hadn't really been any slums.

No history book can give as graphic an impression of London at this critical turning point in human history as Greene's dramatic "entertainment," *The Ministry of Fear*. Arthur Rowe may have been a creature of his imagination, but the setting in which his story is played out was very real indeed. The great Battle of Britain, which ended only after the Hitler took the fatal misstep of throwing all of his military forces against the Soviet Union, inspired Greene's tragicomic thriller, and burning, embattled, heroic London was integral to the plot.

— *Bill Delaney*

THE MIRACLE WORKER

Author: William Gibson (1914-   )
Type of work: Drama
Type of plot: Psychological realism

Time of plot: 1880's
First performed: Television play, 1957; stage play, 1960; first published, 1959

This play dramatizes the true-life story of how a woman taught a blind and deaf child to behave and to communicate through language. William Gibson's staging instructions call for an exceptionally simple set, whose essential qualities "are fluidity and spacial counterpoint." Directions for scene changes are given using lights and distant belfry chimes. The simplicity and low costs of the sets have long made the play a popular one for schools and colleges to perform.

*Keller house.** Two-story farmhouse located near Tuscumbia, Alabama, that was Helen Keller's birthplace and the home in which she grew up. Gibson's script calls for a set consisting of two areas divided by a diagonal line. The area behind the line represents the Keller house and includes two rooms and a porch area.

The other area accommodates a variety of other settings as needed. Audiences can best appreciate the simple setting by trying to imagine how a blind and deaf child who initially has no concept of human language would interact with surroundings that she can neither see nor hear.

Angry and full of incomprehension of the world outside her body, Helen lashes out at those around her until Annie Sullivan forces her to settle down, behave civilly, and begin to learn how to understand the world in terms of language, which she teaches Helen through hand movements. Shortly after Annie arrives, she and Helen have a fight, which Helen wins by locking Annie in her room and hiding the key. Annie wins the next big fight by forcing Helen to eat off her own plate with a spoon. Afterward, she takes Helen from the main house to live with her in a detached garden house, where she can exercise complete control over Helen to break her of her almost feral habits. The play's "miracle" occurs when Annie makes Helen pump water into a pitcher, and Helen finally grasps the connection between Annie's hand movements and water, thus discovering the concept of language. The play thus ends with her on the threshhold of full entry into human society.

— *Christopher E. Kent*

THE MISANTHROPE

Author: Molière (Jean-Baptiste Poquelin, 1622-1673)
Type of work: Drama
Type of plot: Comedy of manners

Time of plot: Seventeenth century
First performed: 1666; first published, 1667 as *Le Misanthrope* (English translation, 1709)

This comedy takes place in the salon of a young Parisian widow named Célimène. In order to avoid being overwhelmed by her grief, she receives into her home a variety of people who help her pass the time. Audiences expect rather frivolous topics to be treated in such an artificial setting; however, such is not the case in this complex comedy of manners.

Célimène's salon. Parisian apartment in which the wealthy widow Célimène holds receptions to which she invites distinguished guests, in the custom of wealthy Parisian women of the seventeenth century. At first, audiences assume that Célimène is merely another frivolous rich woman who passes her time hosting fancy parties and engaging in vapid conversations. However, she invites not merely superficial people, such as Philinte and Oronte, but also the rigidly outspoken young Alceste (the "misanthrope" of the play's title), who is in love with her.

In the formal setting of the salon, Alceste discusses serious moral questions, such as honesty and ethics, while at the same time courting Célimène in a manner surprising for such a rich suitor. Instead of paying her traditional compliments, Alceste criticizes her for the types of guests whom she invites to her home and suggests that she should banish from her apartment men whose behavior is not becoming a woman as serious as herself. Célimène appreciates his unexpected frankness but is surprised when he insists that she leave her Paris to follow him to his country estate. She is unwilling to make such a sudden decision to leave her Parisian apartment. Alceste's inflexibility causes this comedy to end in an unhappy ending for both characters. Alceste does not understand that he should be more sensitive to Célimène's emotional needs and not simply expect her to abandon everything for him. The salon in which this comedy takes place creates specific expectations that create numerous surprises in the minds of Molière's audiences.

— *Edmund J. Campion*

THE MISER

Author: Molière (Jean-Baptiste Poquelin, 1622-1673)
Type of work: Drama
Type of plot: Comedy

Time of plot: Seventeenth century
First performed: 1668; first published, 1669 as
  L'Avare (English translation, 1672)

This comedy of manners takes place in the Parisian house of a wealthy miser who loves his money above all else. Molière did not provide many stage directions, but the dialogue of his characters testifies to the shabbiness of Harpagon's house and clothing that exemplifies his greed and insensitivity to the feelings of others.

Harpagon's house (AR-pa-gon). Parisian home of the miser Harpagon, a widower without a wife to restrain his obsession with accumulating money while spending as little as possible on his two adult children and his house. He tells others that he has transformed his house into a makeshift hiding place for his money. Fearful of being robbed and killed for his wealth, he buries his money in his garden and suspects even his own children of planning to rob him. He believes that anyone who seeks entry to his house must be a thief, and this makes life so miserable for the children, Cléante and Elise, that they both wish to marry as quickly as possible in order to get away from him.

With its tacky furniture, Harpagon's house is an en-tirely inappropriate home for a wealthy businessman. As a member of the upper class, Harpagon is expected to maintain a comfortable house in which he and his children enjoy a comfortable lifestyle. However, his children are humiliated whenever friends visit their house, and guests are shocked to see Harpagon beat his cook, Master Jacques, for spending too much money on food. Harpagon thinks that he can impress guests by serving them sparse and unappetizing meals. The shabbiness of his house, with its extremely old and dilapidated furnishings, exemplifies his moral insensitivity and his complete indifference to his children's feelings.

— *Edmund J. Campion*

LES MISÉRABLES

Author: Victor Hugo (1802-1885)
Type of work: Novel
Type of plot: Social realism

Time of plot: c. 1815-1835
First published: 1862 (English translation, 1862)

For the most part, Victor Hugo uses actual geographical towns and Paris, France, streets in order to make his novel all the more realistic in terms of place and time. Each place or street serves as a location for an important event such as a suicide, a couple falling in love, a secret society meeting, or a battleground where soldiers and rebels fight.

*Paris. Capital of France in whose mean—and mainly unknown—neighborhoods most of the novel is set. In setting most of his action in these neighborhoods, Hugo emphasizes how a great majority of honest and hard-working people ("les misérables") live in overcrowded and dilapidated conditions. His criticism does not originate in class warfare but rather out of a desire to help improve their unbearable situation. Many streets mentioned in the novel were destroyed or absorbed in other wider arteries during various urban renewals, especially under the Second Empire in the 1850's and 1860's—and later. Some simply have changed names to new appellations: For example, rue Plumet has become rue Oudinot.

Rue Plumet house. Jean Valjean and Cosette's new rented home in a good neighborhood. The furnished townhouse, with its solidly enclosed garden, is not only vast and almost elegant, it has a secret passageway offering escape if necessary. Since they want to be unnoticed, Valjean and Cosette never use the entrance on rue Plumet, but use a side door to a back street. After discovering her address, however, Marius visits the sixteen-year-old girl, and both confess their love for each other as they kiss. The untended garden, which symbolizes the naïveté and free-spiritedness of Cosette, is now transformed into a wondrous place, alive with sheltering trees and perfuming flowers, that welcomes their innocent "idyll."

*__Rue des Filles-du-Calvaire__ (rew day feey-doo-kal-VEHR). Street in upper-class district. Mr. Gillenormand (Marius's grandfather) owns a mansion and private garden at No. 6. Beautifully furnished and appointed, it is the residence of a wealthy bourgeois who appreciates fine art and good books but who is reactionary in his politics. The mansion is so large that it can house seven people quite easily along with Marius's office. (Valjean, though urged to move in, refuses.)

"Bowels of Leviathan." Hugo's metaphor for the sewers of Paris. Beside their utilitarian purpose, the underground sewers hide Marius, who is being rescued by Valjean. They must wade through long tunnels filled with sleaze and slime, as the latter intelligently follows the mazelike topographical pattern to secure their safe exit. In comparing the sewers to a Dantesque hell, Hugo stresses the subterranean presence of vice and of moral decadence in society and, thus, the need to redeem one's soul (never an easy task, witness Valjean's several struggles with his conscience) through goodness toward others and self-sacrifice.

*__Rue de la Chanvrerie__ (rew deh lah shan-vrer-ee). Area of anti-Louis-Philippe insurrection (June 5-6, 1832). This Parisian street in the St. Denis district is the setting for the battle between the well-armed king's soldiers and the poorly supplied democratic rebels fighting behind makeshift barricades. No wonder so many of them die (gloriously) and Marius is gravely wounded.

*__Montreuil-sur-mer__ (mon-TROEY-sur-mehr). Town in northern France. Jean Valjean (alias Monsieur Madeleine) runs a glass bead factory that gives employment to many, including Fantine. Its distant location from Toulon, the naval port city on the Mediterranean and home of prison ships, also offers him a better chance to hide from the police. However, his past eventually catches up with him and he is sent back to Toulon, from where he later escapes.

*__Digne__ (deen). Small city in southern France. Instead of a luxurious episcopal palace, Bishop Myriel's house is small and modest and well reflects the prelate's own modesty. Moreover, even the name of the city (*digne* means "worthy") underlines the charity, generosity, and saintliness of Monsignor Bienvenu.

*__Waterloo.__ Town in Belgium that was the site of Napoleon Bonaparte's famous final defeat on June 18, 1815. Hugo shows a deep understanding and knowledge of both the strategy and tactics employed by the French and Anglo-Prussian armies. Thénardier allegedly performed an unselfish deed by rescuing Colonel Pontmercy during the battle.

*__Rue de l'Homme-Armé__ (rew deh luh-MAR-may). Another apartment (at No. 7) used by Valjean and Cosette. Since it is to be a hideaway/refuge for the escaped convict, it contains only the furnishings necessary for him and his young charge.

Gorbeau hovel (GOR-boh). One of Jean Valjean and Cosette's numerous homes as they flee across Paris; later the Thénardiers and Marius will live there. As a typical tenement, it acts as a microcosm of lower-class French society, from criminals, young orphans, and prisoners on the run to neglected adolescents and impoverished students.

*__Montfermeil__ (mon-fer-MAYL). Town east of Paris, where the Thénardiers operate an unsavory and ramshackle inn. Cosette, a foster-child in their care and Cinderella-like heroine, lives there, too. Valjean buries his treasure in the forest on the outskirts of this town.

Petit-Picpus convent (peh-tee peek-PUH). Estate inhabited by nuns. Although given a specific address (62, Petite rue Picpus), this fictional religious community, containing large gardens, a school, and a nunnery, represents a haven for Valjean and Cosette. For five years he is employed as gardener and general handyman, while she attends its school.

*__Père-Lachaise__ (pehr lah-SHAYZ). Famous cemetery in eastern Paris. Valjean is buried here away from the plots of the rich and powerful, his unkempt and nameless tombstone further accenting the anonymous character of this tragic Everyman.

Notre-Dame Bridge. Bridge across the Seine River, which is here at its most tortuous and fast-flowing. A so-called deranged Javert, unable to comprehend Valjean's merciful generosity, purposely chooses this site to commit suicide.

Luxembourg Gardens. Parisian park with beautiful grounds and a promenade. It is here that Marius and Cosette see each other for the first time and fall in love from afar.

Café Musain (kah-FAY mew-SAYN). Latin-Quarter drinking establishment whose back room serves as a meeting place for the ABC secret society.

— *Pierre L. Horn*

MISS JULIE

Author: August Strindberg (1849-1912)
Type of work: Drama
Type of plot: Naturalism

Time of plot: Nineteenth century
First published: Fröken Julie, 1888 (English
   translation, 1912); first performed, 1889

August Strindberg's venture into naturalism is set in rural central Sweden, with its single act confined to a manor house kitchen. The social hierarchy and the rights of tradition and class are challenged from beyond this scene, in debates on Darwinism, gender roles, and the parts of nature and nurture in shaping personality.

Country estate. Grand home of an unnamed Swedish count. A silent but prominent symbol of the unseen count's authority in his manor house's kitchen is a pair of his riding boots. Julie is his unmarried daughter of twenty-five, whose engagement has recently been broken off. With its community of tenant farmers, the estate could well lie near Stockholm, a region Strindberg knew well.

It is Midsummer Eve, an occasion for carousing by the rural population. In traditional Scandinavian culture, the shortest night of the year was an interstice in normal time, when social lines might be crossed. The farmers sing off-color songs to satirize their "betters," and the aristocratic Julie invites, even commands, her father's servant to dance on the village green that is only hinted at by lilacs in bloom beyond the kitchen door.

As Julie explains her mixed aversion and attraction to men, she reveals her family past. Her mother was not well born, and Jean knows that even the count's supposed aristocratic background has little historical depth. The manor house itself had been destroyed by arson, then rebuilt under questionable financial circumstances dictated by the likely arsonist, Julie's mother. Until the count restored patriarchal order to the chaos of the estate, Julie's mother had raised her as a tomboy. She learned to ride and shoot but not manage a house. As an adult in this house of dubious origin, she is helplessly stranded between age and gender roles, and the conflicting demands of awakening sexuality and constraining social order.

Jean's tree. Image in a recurrent dream of the count's valet, who is Julie's lover. Kristin's kitchen is set in ordinary space, although the scene has an intentionally skewed quality explicitly stated in the dramatist's stage directions that suggests the areas beyond it. Vertical space is also important as the dimension of social hierarchy, the medium of personal rise and fall. Jean had a childhood experience and a recurrent dream, both articulated vertically. As a boy he had been called to help his mother weed onion beds near the count's manor house. Attracted to a decorated pavilion, he explored it, only to discover that it was an outhouse (privy), and his only means of escape was through the hole and out the back. Filthy after this "descent to Hades," he saw the young Julie and was struck with her beauty, as well as by her higher social station and its privileges. His more mature dream is of climbing a great tree that would lead him up to the clouds among the birds of prey, if only he could reach the first branch.

Julie's column. Miss Julie's corresponding dream is of being trapped at the top of a pillar and then of inevitable downward motion, both feared and desired: subjecting men to her will but being personally degraded as well. After alienating her fiancé, this movement continues with her yielding to sexual urges on Midsummer Eve, an occasion already culturally identified for this purpose.

Kitchen and side-rooms. When commoners from the rustic celebration approach the manor house, Julie and Jean wish to avoid being seen together and leave the kitchen. The revelers enter, drink, sing, and dance. This lightly scornful pantomime provides enough time for Julie and Jean to make love off stage. When they return to the stage, everything has changed—except the time and place. In Julie's mind, no future is possible on the estate: She and Jean cannot marry because of class distinctions, and she is unwilling to continue as Jean's casual mistress.

The play has only one scene. The seemingly cozy farm kitchen, invaded by the intoxicating smell of summer flowers, is a place where a woman of Julie's rank and age would normally enter only to give orders. It is too constraining a place for positive change to occur. Instead, it becomes a crucible where social qualities and character attributes are broken down but do not fuse into a stronger new alloy. Rigid as the setting is, the significant acts of sexual union and self-destruction can only occur beyond it.

*Ticino. Resort town in southern Switzerland where Julie and Jean fantasize about going to open a hotel. This utopian fantasy is alternately scorned and promoted by Julie, who at one point even tries to rope in the reluctant cook, Kristin. However, the cook immediately senses the social shift taking place around her: Jean's transgression—which she forgives as the act of an ambitious male—and Julie's defloration—which she judges willful self-abasement and cannot excuse. In her eyes, the manor house has again been brought low.

— *William Sayers*

MISS LONELYHEARTS

Author: Nathanael West (Nathan Weinstein, 1903-1940)

Type of work: Novel

Type of plot: Social satire
Time of plot: Late 1920's
First published: 1933

Most of the settings in this novel are barren landscapes; however, the protagonist's bed serves as the mode of transportation for some dream sequences. In each location, Miss Lonelyhearts tries to establish meaningful contact with another human being but is killed while trying to rescue a physical and emotional cripple.

Miss Lonelyhearts' home. Home of the newspaper advice columnist whose pseudonym is "Miss Lonelyhearts." It is an apartment with little furniture and bare walls except for an ivory Christ figure nailed to the wall with large spikes, a calmly decorative symbol that plays a crucial role in Miss Lonelyhearts' regeneration. Early in his quest to assuage the grief and misery of his readers and vent his frustration, Miss Lonelyhearts accepts a proposal of seduction by Fay Doyle, one of his letter writers. Fay is repelled physically and in every other way by her husband, the physically challenged Peter

Doyle. Miss Lonelyhearts' room is also the setting of some reciprocal visits by Betty, his innocent, loyal, but not-too-bright girlfriend, to whom he had earlier proposed marriage.

Park. Public park near the newspaper office that is presumably a little nook in Central Park, given the reference to a Mexican War obelisk at one end. This location provides the occasion for a scene in which Miss Lonelyhearts and a colleague, Ned Gates, find a man, who they believe to be a homosexual, sitting on a turned-down toilet cover in a comfort station. Miss Lonelyhearts, in whose mind the stranger represents all the desperate, broken-hearted, disillusioned letter writers who seek his advice, decides to brutalize the old man. The park, then, in addition to being a refuge for him, is also a place of turmoil.

***Post-Dispatch* city room.** Miss Lonelyhearts' workplace, where some thirty letters from readers await his reply daily. It is not a particularly congenial place, not only because of the steady dose of his readers' misery but also because his superior, Willie Shrike, orchestrates many practical jokes at Miss Lonelyhearts' expense.

Delehanty's speakeasy. Prohibition-era bar that is a gathering place for the lonely; located close to the newspaper office and small park where Miss Lonelyhearts frequently stops to escape the concrete jungle of New York. The speakeasy is located in the cellar of a brownstone building, which differs from its neighbors in that it has an armored door. It is a gathering place for other news reporters from the *Post-Dispatch*. Willie Shrike, who derides Miss Lonelyhearts' advice but nevertheless urges him to try to increase the paper's circulation with his piece, is a frequent visitor. It is also the setting where Peter Doyle—an advice seeker like his wife Fay—is introduced to Miss Lonelyhearts. In the end, it is on the stairs leading to Miss Lonelyhearts' room that the gun in Doyle's hands explodes, and both roll part of the way down, the Christ-obsessed Miss Lonelyhearts and the nearly redeemed Doyle caught in deadly embrace.

Although New York City does not appear to be quite as sordid as Los Angeles is in Nathaniel West's *The Day of the Locust* (1939), the picture of Peter Doyle dragging his lame foot up and down stairways as he reads gas meters is a reminder that the American Dream was not for everyone, even during the so-called Roaring Twenties.

— *Peter B. Heller*

MISTER ROBERTS

Author: Thomas Heggen (1919-1949)
Type of work: Novel
Type of plot: Satire

Time of plot: Last months of World War II
First published: 1946

With the exception of one brief episode ashore, this story takes place entirely aboard a U.S. Navy cargo ship during the last days of World War II. The geographical location of the ship is not nearly as important as the fictional names the author gives the islands where the ship drops anchor. The names are allegorical, each one representing the isolation and mind-numbing boredom of the crew.

USS *Reluctant*. Navy cargo ship operating in the Pacific Ocean during the last months of World War II. It is a typically dull, navy blue color, with the same lettering, equipment, and rigging as any other cargo ship listed in the navy's register. The name of the ship is the first of several clues to the inhabitants on board. The crew is even reluctant to call the ship by name, referring to it as a "bucket."

The *Reluctant* could be any ship sailing to any number of islands in the Pacific Ocean. The author has also chosen fictional names for the islands that are indicative of the general state of mind and attitude of the crew, for example, Tedium, Apathy, Monotony, and Ennui. This helps the author to illustrate the boredom and isolation the men feel. This also lends some insight into the behavior of the crew.

Deck. Main deck of the ship where the crew carries out its dreary purpose of loading and unloading cargo, performing routine maintenance, and standing watch against an enemy which will never be close enough to encounter. It is because they have no real enemy to fight that the crew has unanimously nominated the captain as their sworn enemy. They spend much of their time on deck planning, like bored children, various schemes to aggravate him. When the tedium becomes unbearable, they also are not above taking jabs at each other.

When the ship is in port, Mister Roberts spends most of his time on deck, supervising the activities of the crew and dealing with the captain. In describing the activities of the crew while on deck, the author is able to demonstrate Mister Roberts's unique relationship with the crew. He can be stern when he needs to be, but he is fair, and he has the respect and unfailing admiration of his men.

The deck is also a place of solitude and reflection for Mister Roberts. His turns on the watch give him ample opportunity to fixate on his desire to be transferred to a fighting ship and be part of the action.

Ensign Pulver's cabin. Double room occupied only by Ensign Pulver, who is Mister Roberts's most ardent admirer. The bottom bunk is used for sleeping, and the top bunk is a general storage space for everything from soiled clothes to old magazines. Pulver spends most of his time in this room, lying in his bunk, planning elaborate acts of revenge against the captain, which he never carries out.

Doc's cabin. Also a gathering place for Mister Roberts and his small band of friends. It is here with Doc that Mister Roberts can be completely honest about his feelings about being on the ship and the real reasons he wants to be in the middle of the action.

Ward room. Below-deck space is used by the ship's officers as a place in which to gather, enjoy cold drinks or coffee, play friendly games of checkers or cards, and relax. There is usually a good-natured atmosphere in this room, and for a brief time the men can forget their boredom and frustration.

Elysium. Island whose name represents the joy and anticipation the crew feels at the prospect of going ashore for liberty. It could be any island along the ship's route. The landscape or inhabitants are immaterial to the story. The only thing that makes this particular island any different from Tedium, Apathy, and the others is the fact that the crew will actually get to go ashore. They have been cooped up on the ship for so long, that when they are finally allowed on the island, they run wild, expressing their happiness and excitement by getting into all sorts of mischief. Their behavior causes the captain to revoke any future visits ashore, but the crew, for a while at least, assumes an attitude that reflects the happiness and contentment of Elysium.

— *Molly M. Dean*

MITHRIDATES

Author: Jean Baptiste Racine (1639-1699)
Type of work: Drama
Type of plot: Tragedy

Time of plot: First century B.C.E.
First performed: 1673; first published, 1673 as
    Mithridate (English translation, 1926)

The variety of geographical references and frequency with which they are mentioned in this play, which is set in the first century B.C.E., *serve to underline the vast extent of the Roman Empire, the size of the challenge facing King Mithridates, and the breadth of his own kingdom.*

*****Pontus.** Historical kingdom in Asia Minor (now part of Turkey) whose independence from Rome King Mithridates the Great fought long, but ultimately unsuccessfully, to preserve. In the play, Pontus and nearby Colchis are the power bases of his sons, Xiphares and Pharnace. Since they have traveled to Nymphaeum, neither is on home territory and each must calculate what he can and cannot achieve against the advancing Romans, the forces of his brother, and those of Mithridates who, believed dead, suddenly returns alive to the city.

*****Nymphaeum** (nihm-FI-um). City in the Crimea to which Mithridates flees after his army is defeated by the Romans at the Euphrates River. The city's principal significance is that it lies at the easternmost extent of the Roman Empire in the period before Julius Caesar. From Nymphaeum, Mithridates proposes to march to Rome, passing through numerous countries and enlisting support from other rulers. His references to Spain, Gaul,

Germany, Greece, Italy, the Black Sea, the Danube River, and other places propel the imaginations of the audience outside and away from the palace in which Mithridates speaks.

*Ephesus (EF-uh-sus). Ancient Greek city in Ionia, the Aegean Sea. Once part of Mithridates' kingdom, Ephesus was Queen Monime's home when he first saw her. Several allusions to Ephesus and Greece in the play recall Monime's childhood, suggesting Monime's innocence in the rough world of power politics and sexual rivalries in which she finds herself.

*Rome. Capital of the Roman Empire and symbol of all that Mithridates loathes. Thirty mentions of Rome in the play demonstrate its importance in the scenes relating to military ambition. These contrast strongly with scenes featuring Monime, who is betrothed to Mithridates but loves, and is loved by, his son Xiphares. When characters speak of their love, they forget their territorial agendas. Conversely, when Monime accuses the treacherous Pharnace, Mithridates' other son, of being in thrall to the Romans, her rejection of him is both personal and political. When she believes Xiphares to be dead, her references to the enmity of Rome underline his filial honor and the poignant recognition that she has caused his downfall.

— *William Brooks*

MOBY DICK: Or, The Whale

Author: Herman Melville (1819-1891)
Type of work: Novel
Type of plot: Adventure

Time of plot: Early nineteenth century
First published: 1851

This complex novel traces the long voyage of a whaling ship from Massachusetts around Africa into the Indian Ocean and beyond. Herman Melville, who sailed in those regions himself, weaves long asides on whaling, the South Seas, and other subjects into his narrative.

*New Bedford. Massachusetts fishing community and seaport about sixty-five miles southeast of Boston, where the novel begins when its narrator, Ishmael, arrives to sign onto a whaling ship. He first stays at the Spouter Inn, where the only accommodation available is a room with one bed that he must share with the forbidding-looking harpooner Queequeg, a "heathen" from an uncharted South Seas island. During a storm, Ishmael seeks shelter in the Whaleman's Chapel, where he is deeply moved by the sermon of the retired harpooner Father Mapple on the biblical story of Jonah and the whale.

*Nantucket. Massachusetts island, about thirty miles south of Cape Cod, that was the center of the New England whaling industry in the early nineteenth century. There, Ishmael and Queequeg join the crew of the *Pequod* and begin their voyage.

Pequod. Whaling ship commanded by Captain Ahab on which Ishmael and Queequeg sign. It is one of three well-equipped whaling vessels they find anchored at Nantucket, preparing to undertake three-year expeditions. When the *Pequod* begins its long voyage on Christmas Day, its mysterious captain remains in his cabin, a small, private world into which he retreats.

The repeated play of light and dark while the ship is at sea reflects the light and dark of the personalities aboard the whaler. Looming high above the ship's decks, the tops of masts are important lookout stations from which Ishmael and other crew members watch for whales.

*Oceans. The first leg of the *Pequod*'s voyage takes the ship southeast from Nantucket, across the Atlantic Ocean to the west coast of Africa, which it follows across the equator to the Cape of Good Hope. The ship reaches the Cape of Good Hope, near the southern tip of Africa, before heading east into the Indian Ocean. In that ocean, the ship reaps a rich harvest of sperm whales but continues east into the Pacific Ocean, where it makes its way to the Japanese Sea. The ship eventually confronts Moby Dick in the Pacific, near the equator.

*Japanese Sea (Sea of Japan).** Branch of the Pacific Ocean enclosed by Japan, Korea, and Siberia which, during the early nineteenth century, had large numbers of sperm whales. There, the obsessed Captain Ahab hopes to find the great white whale he calls Moby Dick, to which he once lost one of his legs. The captain's monomaniacal quest to find Moby Dick alarms the ship's mates, but other members of the crew take his quest as a challenge and encourage him.

Rachel. Whaling ship that the *Pequod* encounters after it, the *Rachel*, has recently encountered Moby Dick, to which it has lost an entire boat crew, which includes the captain's own son. Still obsessed with his personal quest to kill Moby Dick, Ahab declines the other captain's appeal to help search for the lost boat—a decision that members of his own ship's crew view as a bad omen.

Ahab's boat. Whaleboat on which Ahab pursues Moby Dick after the great white whale is finally sighted. His boat is one of three that chase the whale in a struggle that lasts for three days. On the third day, Ahab's own harpoon inflicts a severe injury on the whale, and Ahab orders the other two boats back to the *Pequod*, so his own boat alone can make the kill. This boat becomes the crucible in which Captain Ahab plays out the final stages of his quest. Mad with pain, Moby Dick rams the *Pequod* with its huge head, shattering the ship's bow. When Ahab launches another harpoon at the whale, its line wraps around his own neck, pulling him to his death. As the *Pequod* sinks, Moby Dick surfaces and dives, with Ahab's lifeless body held tightly to its side by the harpoon lines.

— *R. Baird Shuman*

A MODERN INSTANCE

Author: William Dean Howells (1837-1920)
Type of work: Novel
Type of plot: Domestic realism

Time of plot: Nineteenth century
First published: 1882

The two main locales of this novel are a small Maine town and Boston, the largest city of New England. The relationship of its two principal characters commences in Maine, where the wife is thoroughly at home, and continues in Boston, to which the woman cannot adjust at all, while her conniving husband finds it an opportune place to enrich himself at others' expense.

Equity. Small town in Maine in which the novel opens on a picturesque winter scene. The town initially seems attractive and in harmony with its natural surroundings. However, several variant meanings of the word "equity" suggests that W. D. Howells had ambivalent thoughts about the town. Equity is a place that fosters the basically simple and provincial outlook of a woman like Marcia Gaylord and constrains an ambitious and unscrupulous man like Bartley Hubbard, whom she marries. Human nature is not morally more pure in Equity; it merely faces less varied temptations there. Bartley is the kind of person who takes mean advantage of others wherever he is, but Equity, where transgressions of laws and mores quickly become generally known, offers only limited scope for his selfishness and arrogant disregard of others. This conservative community also imposes restrictions on him as a journalist and seeker of an interesting social life. In short, Equity cannot hold Bartley, and because Marcia is infatuated with him, she departs also, although it is the sort of place that suits her temperament.

Logging camp. Simple place, close to nature, where Bartley visits Kinney, a man of gentle nature and ingenuous admiration for the philosophy of Ralph Waldo Emerson. Bartley himself acknowledges that only a person in what he calls "first-rate spiritual condition" can safely commune so closely with nature, but he is far less interested in nature than in the sort of "copy" Kinney, the camp's cook, can provide him. This man, at home in such surroundings, later becomes the easiest of all Bartley Hubbard's victims.

*Boston. New England's largest city, where Bartley takes Marcia after they marry. At first, she is overwhelmed by the fixtures and furnishings of the first-class hotel at which they stay but is appalled by the expense, when she learns of it. Soon they find more modest quarters and settle into big-city life. To Bartley's friend from college days, Ben Halleck, Boston is "more authentic" and more "municipal" than any other modern city.

Boston is a city of multiple newspapers and thus of numerous outlets for Bartley's writing. Bartley readily "takes on" the city, as one editor remarks, but Marcia remains an uncomfortable country person. When they attend the theater, the unsophisticated Marcia cannot take it in; Bartley enjoys it, but in the superficial way of a man unattuned to aesthetic values yet happy to be among the "swells" who patronize such entertainments. Boston cannot change either Bartley or Marcia, as Ben Halleck's sister learns when she tries unsuccessfully to create a social life for them.

After Bartley eventually deserts his wife, another friend obtains another "country" woman to stay with Marcia and their infant son as the only solace available to this inflexibly countrified woman. Not even Marcia's father, a crafty attorney in his own small town, can be of much service to her when he visits, for he loses his identity in the big city.

It is clear that Howells, who spent a considerable portion of his own literary and journalistic career in Boston, did not regard it as a city of sin. The Hallecks live a highly civilized life there, but both Hubbards, in their distinct ways, are immune to civilities. Bartley cannily profits from the weaknesses of Boston's honest newspapermen and sells tasteless material to less respectable ones. Through much of the nineteenth century Boston had reigned as the literary capital of the United States. But by the 1870's it was becoming a commercial center, the implication being that a man like Bartley Hubbard could not have thrived there in the time when Kinney's hero Emerson had lived while composing his earliest works.

— *Robert P. Ellis*

MOLL FLANDERS

Author: Daniel Defoe (1660-1731)
Type of work: Novel
Type of plot: Picaresque
Time of plot: Seventeenth century
First published: The Fortunes and Misfortunes of the Famous Moll Flanders, Who Was Born in Newgate, and During a Life of Continued Variety, for

Threescore Years, Besides Her Childhood, Was Twelve Years a Whore, Five Times a Wife (Thereof Once to Her Own Brother), Twelve Years a Thief, Eight Years a Transported Felon in Virginia, at Last Grew Rich, Lived Honest, and Died a Penitent. Written from Her Own Memorandums, 1722

This novel employs six primary settings, each of which corresponds to a stage in Moll Flanders's development as an independent, mercantile figure. The tale she relates in her own words begins in the modest, conservative English countryside of Essex, moves to London, to Britain's North American colonies, then back to the English countryside and London before ending back on American soil.

*Colchester. Town in southeastern England's Essex district, in which Moll's narrative begins by moving quickly through her early years. After being orphaned, she is taken into a home in Colchester in which she first

is seduced by one brother and then married by the other, in a loveless relationship.

*London. England's capital city and mercantile center, to which Moll goes after her husband dies. Now wiser about the ways of the world, she schemes to make a rich match for herself, only to connect with a gentleman-tradesman who proves to be as much a fraud as she is. Moll takes a greater hand in determining her own fate in London, where, as she learns, everything is business.

After having brief relationships with men in the countryside, Moll returns to London on her own and becomes a prostitute and a thief. The bulk of the book concerns her second sojourn in London, where, from her point of view as a storyteller, she is near to full-bloom.

*Virginia. British North American colony where Moll lives for eight years with her third husband, a gentleman-planter whom she marries after her second marriage fails. She is initially content in this new situation, but when she is given reason to believe that she may have a blood-relationship to her husband, she is aghast at the possibility of having committed incest and returns to England on her own.

After another sojourn in England—where she lives in Bath—Moll comes back to North America, finds that her third husband has died, and inherits his land. She thus returns to Virginia a landowner. Although it is doubtful the local courts would uphold her claim if someone were to challenge it, Moll knows that she has a better chance to own land in America than she could ever have in Europe. The novel ends with her making a formal claim to the Virginia land, thereby declaring to her readers that she has, at last, substantially the same rights as a man.

— *Jay Boyer*

MOLLOY

Author: Samuel Beckett (1906-1989)
Type of work: Novel
Type of plot: Absurdist

Time of plot: Mid-twentieth century
First published: 1951 (English translation, 1955)

An experimental stream-of-consciousness novel that could be set almost anywhere, Samuel Beckett's book tells the story of the disordered and hallucinatory journeys of two mysterious Irishmen, Molloy and Moran. As the fastidious Moran follows in the footsteps of the troubled derelict Molloy, the distinction between the two men dissolves.

Forest. Unnamed forest in which most of the story is set. Although its location is never identified, the fact that the novel's two main characters have Irish names suggests that the forest is in Ireland, Beckett's homeland. However, other clues in the play suggest that the forest could as easily be in France, Beckett's adopted country. In any case, the forest is probably in northern Europe.

Like the enchanted forest of traditional fairy tales, Beckett's forest is a powerful agent that acts upon both the body and soul of any person who enters it. In this regard, the forest is more symbolic than specific and may even be said to represent a state of mind or a metaphysical situation rather than an actual location. However, although the forest is nonspecific, its character is bleak and unwelcoming, occasioning a profound sense of homelessness and despair for those who enter it. In this regard, the forest can be said to echo the "dark forest" Dante enters at the beginning of *The Divine Comedy* (c. 1320). It is in this forest that the hobo Molloy gives up his apparently fruitless quest for his mother; instead, time grinds to a halt, and becomes filled with anxiety and a sense of pointlessness. Ultimately, Molloy irrationally assaults a charcoal burner who apparently lives in the forest, and then sinks helplessly to the bottom of a ditch, from which he is somehow rescued and returned to his room.

It is also in this forest that the dapper detective Moran gives up his quest for the fugitive Molloy. While in the forest, Moran quarrels with his son, loses his bicycle, and is forced to live on roots and berries. He finds the forest even more disorienting than does Molloy, but, like

Molloy, he also kills a man there—a man who closely resembles Moran himself, or at least the Moran he used to be. Although their time in the desolate forest does include some activity on the part of Molloy and Moran, in the end they seem to have been walking in circles, so that each quest is only ambiguously successful, or succeeds only if one assumes that the unconscious motive for each man's journey was to seek his own personal disintegration.

Molloy's room. This room, like this novel's settings of the forest, the sea, and the town, is denuded of any specificity. Typical of all Beckett's work, this setting is deliberately presented so that it evokes no particular time or place—it is an archetypal room. The most important thing about this room is that it was originally Molloy's mother's room, to which he (and possibly Moran) has been brought after his disastrous experiences in the forest, returning the narrative to the novel's beginning, in which Molloy is in his room writing his report.

Moran's house. Located in an unnamed town, Moran's house is typically bourgeois and is run according to scrupulous domestic requirements. Moran must leave this little haven when he is assigned the task of tracking down the mysterious Molloy. After disintegrating emotionally and physically in the forest, Moran wends his way back to his house, where he begins to write a report on what has happened to him.

Lousse's garden. This is a garden in an unnamed town belonging to an old widow called Lousse, who adopts Molloy as a replacement for the pet dog Molloy accidentally runs over with his bicycle. Rather than seeing the garden as a haven, however, Molloy feels that the garden hinders him from his true journey, which requires him to wander disconsolately into the forest.

Seacoast. Just as the unnamed forest seems vaguely Irish, the unnamed sea suggests one of the coasts of Ireland—in each case, however, the impression is of a bleak and uninviting setting. It is by the sea that Molloy renews the stock of sucking stones he keeps so that he never suffers from hunger pangs. Actually, Molloy barely notices the sea, instead spending much time obsessing over a mathematical order for the carrying and sucking of the stones.

— *Margaret Boe Birns*

THE MONK

Author: Matthew Gregory Lewis (1775-1818)
Type of work: Novel
Type of plot: Gothic

Time of plot: The Spanish Inquisition
First published: 1796

One of the most powerful and terrifying gothic novels, this work introduced Spain as the epitome of gothic settings: a country in which social institutions serve only to control the minds and bodies of the young and innocent; and a place in which religious devotion and sexuality coalesce into perversion.

Church of the Capuchins. Elaborate religious complex in Spain's capital city, Madrid, with multiple interconnected institutions. Typical of churches in gothic fiction, this one has a monastery with secret tunnels that lead to a nearby convent, which is itself built over top of a deep catacomb that serves as a burial ground and a prison. This novel made significant changes to the gothic novel genre. In the first place, most novels before this one were set in either France or Italy; this one, however, made use of Spain and was thus able to tap into longstanding English hostility to Spain and to Roman Catholicism. For instance, Matthew Gregory Lewis chose a cathedral as the centerpiece setting of his novel and linked various other institutions to it: The villain, Ambrosio, is the abbot of a nearby monastery; his female counterpart, a tyrannical mother superior, dominates a linked convent. With the use of this setting, Lewis presents Spain as a country in which "superstition reigns with . . . despotic sway." Everything about Spain, from the point of view of this novel, revolves around either repressed sexuality or religious hypocrisy.

Nowhere is this more true, according to Lewis, than

in the main monastery. Ambrosio is represented as the archetype of repressed sexuality, and the setting is to blame. As Lewis puts it, Ambrosio's naturally powerful character might have led him to virtue and greatness in society; however, the monks "[rooted] out his virtues, and . . . allowed every vice which had fallen to his share, to arrive at full perfection." Thus the monastery serves in this novel to thwart natural feelings and channel them in unhealthy directions. Instead of being a place of devotion, it is a place of resentment and perversion. Predictably, the monastery is the setting for other vices—including various forms of repressed sexuality and black magic.

Convent of Saint Clare. Place of living death and of barbarous incarceration for the female characters of the novel. The novel explores female and male religious devotion, and the convent serves as a counterpart setting to Church of the Capuchins. Like the latter, the convent is represented as a place in which the emotions and human drives are sublimated not into religious devotion but into cruelty and vice. The female characters suffer intensely under the tyranny of various religious figures, none so barbaric as the sister who is in charge of the convent. The suffering they undergo is extreme, as, for instance, one character is bound to the corpse of her stillborn infant and locked into an underground chamber. Although scenes like this one earned Lewis a considerable amount of critical condemnation, they were highly believable to many English readers and were copied by later gothic writers.

Monastery garden. Place of natural beauty and hidden temptation. As in other gothic novels, Lewis's work introduces a garden that replays and transforms the biblical story of Eden. In this novel Adam is represented by the titular character, Ambrosio, whose life in the monastery has not prepared him to resist temptation; representing Eve is a young woman who has disguised herself as a monk in order to be close to Ambrosio, whom she claims to love. As is typical of gothic settings, however, the tempter is never far away. In this case, the young woman is in reality a demon who has taken on human form in order to lead Ambrosio into damnation.

— *Michael R. Meyers*

MONSIEUR LECOQ

Author: Émile Gaboriau (1832-1873)
Type of work: Novel
Type of plot: Detective and mystery

Time of plot: Nineteenth century
First published: 1869 (English translation, 1879)

This foundational work in the mystery and detective genre is set entirely within Paris. Focusing narrowly on the processes of investigation and interrogation, the novel portrays the city as a corrupt and complex place that makes justice difficult or impossible to attain.

*****Paris.** Although the French capital is the country's political, cultural, and artistic center, none of these attributes appears to matter in *Monsieur Lecoq*, except insofar as they contribute to the quest for justice, or, more likely, to crime. The only time that one of Paris's famous cathedrals appears is when its bell wakes Lecoq; the only allusion to the city's arts is made when Lecoq visits theaters investigating the identity of a man suspected of a triple homicide. Likewise, no private or public Parisian venue exists except as it relates to the investigation. Émile Gaboriau, who worked in Paris as a journalist, describes the living quarters of the very rich and the very poor; crime and justice are all that unite them. This is emphasized when Lecoq visits the morgue, which many Parisians of the period visited for entertainment.

A great deal of Lecoq's expertise is his knowledge of Paris. There, Gaboriau draws on his own knowledge of the city, learned as a journalist. This knowledge extends beyond the official maps of the city; Lecoq trails his murder suspects out of a garden and into the unmarked wasteland beyond; he can track suspects even down unnamed streets.

Locales outside Paris are important primarily as they influence Paris, symbolizing European anxiety over a shifting sense of place in the nineteenth century. Some places produce known characters, such as a coachman who volunteers his help in the investigation in part because he is a Breton. However, unnamed places are threats. When the murder suspect May tells of being found as an infant by the side of the road, Lecoq is at a loss as to know his character.

Poivriere (pwah-vree-ehr). Fictional Parisian saloon in which the murder occurs. The saloon takes its name from the fact that it is a place where men get "peppered" (drunk). While Lecoq studies the saloon in sufficient detail to draw it as part of his police report, the only descriptions given are those that contribute to his investigation, such as knowing the sight lines between levels. Because the saloon represents any lower-class public meeting house, the crime itself could have been committed anywhere.

Palais de Justice. Official building housing judges. Lecoq's investigation divides into three interwoven approaches. First, information gathering happens throughout Paris. The bulk of the novel follows Lecoq through its streets. Second, that information is sorted at the Palais de Justice, where the magistrate (or judge of instruction) responsible for rendering a verdict in the case has his of-

fices. The Palais is described in enough detail to seem threatening, but the description is still sketchy. Gaboriau keeps the focus on the judge's interrogation of suspects and witnesses. When Lecoq fails to obtain justice through his work at the official Palais, he visits its symbolic counterpart: the home of Papa Tarabet, a consulting amateur detective who prefigures Sherlock Holmes in his use of logic.

Prison. Parisian jail in which Lecoq takes a cell next to the suspect May's in order to observe him in secret, thereby undertaking the third approach to his investigation: observation. Like the novel's descriptions of the morgue, descriptions of the prison demonstrate the novel's link to the nineteenth century sensational novel. However, the act of observing the prisoner is a necessary step in confirming his guilt. Like Lecoq's ultimate failure to convict May, the inability of the officials to keep criminals from communicating symbolizes modern society's inability to keep any place safe from crime and corruption. Likewise, May's refusal to drop his guard in his cell gestures toward an erosion of the belief in a private space; May, and perhaps readers, must treat all places as public.

— *Greg Beatty*

MONT-ORIOL

Author: Guy de Maupassant (1850-1893)
Type of work: Novel
Type of plot: Satire

Time of plot: Mid-nineteenth century
First published: 1887 (English translation, 1891)

The setting of this novel is the Auvergne of south-central France, a region noted for its impressive chain of extinct volcanos and foul-smelling, foul-tasting sulphurous springs thought to be therapeutic. This setting, picturesque and exciting, on one hand, and a potential source of lucrative exploitation, on the other, dramatically changes all the principal characters, both urbane upper- and middle-class visitors from the outside world and the ignorant, impecunious locals. It fosters greed, lust, malice, and deceit, as well as pernicious romantic illusions and heartbreak, all of which are symbolized by the haunting alien landscape.

***Enval.** French resort in which the novel opens with a description that creates a mood of the overpowering force of nature that persists throughout *Mont-Oriol*: "the charm of the little village, amid the shadow of gigantic trees, whose gnarled trunks seemed as large as the houses. Besides this they were drawn there by the fame

of the gorges at the end of the weird valley, which opens on the great plain of Auvergne and ends abruptly, at the foot of a high mountain studded with ancient craters, in a wild rift filled with fallen and overhanging rocks."

Enval is the site of a natural spring that William Andermatt buys from a peasant named Oriol and develops into a health spa that he calls **Mont-Oriol**, after Oriol's lovely daughters.

***Auvergne** (oh-VERN). Historical region of southern France that plays a dominant role in the novel, not only because Guy de Maupassant's descriptions of the unique environment maintain a haunting mood, but because the unique setting is essential to the plot. The love-starved Christiane Andermatt is carried away by the hypnotic spell of nature, and Paul Bretigny, the fop who becomes her lover, is captivated by her refreshingly genuine emotions. Her money-hungry husband William is captivated by the opportunity to make a fortune by investing in a new resort that will exploit the newly discovered mineral spring. His business dealings force him to make return trips to Paris, thus providing Christiane and Bretigny ample opportunities to be alone together and to consummate their adulterous passions under the spell of nature. Their first sexual liaison, which ultimately leads to the birth of a bastard child, is the emotional high point of the novel. There, Maupassant makes explicit his thesis that environment shapes character and behavior:

> If they had lived in a city, their passion, no doubt, would have been different, more cautious, more sensuous, less airy and less romantic. But there, in that green country, whose horizon widened the emotions of the soul, alone, with nothing to distract, to diminish their wakened instinct of love, they had thrown themselves suddenly into a wildly poetic tenderness of ecstasy and fancy. The landscapes around them, the warm breeze, the woods, the fragrant odors of this country, sang to them through all the days and the nights the music of their love.

When Maupassant first visited this region in 1885, he realized that it offered an ideal background for a novel because it could bring together a cross section of French society—aristocrats, bourgeois, professionals represented by doctors and nurses, working class types who catered to the tourist trade, and the peasants who were the original inhabitants of a region being "gentrified" because of its exploitable resources—mineral water, cheap land, and scenic beauty. It would have been difficult for Maupassant to have found anywhere else in France a setting that would bring together as broad an assortment of contrasting characters.

By contrast with the romanticizing Paul and Christiane, Father Oriol's character is shaped by the environment in quite a different way. He is unable to appreciate the beauty in the land where he has lived all his life. To him, as to Christiane's husband the banker, nature is only something to be exploited for cash. This hard-bargaining, unscrupulous, chronically and justifiably suspicious rustic is one of Maupassant's typical French peasants. Oriol's character is shaped by poverty and the heavy labor required to wrest a living from the land for himself and his family. The discovery of the gushing mineral spring on his property not only makes him rich but also offers his daughters opportunities to marry higher. It is only because of the unique character of this specific geographical location that any of these events could have transpired.

Throughout his novel, Maupassant makes it clear that he regards the Auvergne as a sort of natural stage upon which human beings play out their tragicomic roles. The landscape is the main "character" in Maupassant's *Mont-Oriol*. It existed in splendid solitude long before any of these people ever came there, and it will continue to exist long after their foolish, selfish, ephemeral lives have ended. Like all great artists, Maupassant understood the effect of contrast. His masterful descriptions of the pristine environment make the reader conscious of the paltriness of human aspirations in comparison with nature's grandeur and the perspective of eternity.

— *Bill Delaney*

A MONTH IN THE COUNTRY

Author: Ivan Turgenev (1818-1883)
Type of work: Drama
Type of plot: Psychological realism

Time of plot: 1840's
First published: Mesyats v derevne, 1855; first performed, 1872 (English translation, 1924)

Although the setting of this play is merely a country estate in a Russian province, it serves the author as a springboard for a far-reaching psychological probe of his characters and a general comment on Russian society in the middle of the nineteenth century.

Islaev estate (ees-LA-ev). Country estate of a rich landowner, Arkady Islaev, located in an unspecified part of Russia. Ivan Turgenev uses a tranquil country setting because he is familiar with it, despite his frequent world travels, and also because he wants to contrast it with the emotional turmoil within practically all the characters. Although the play is subtitled a comedy, it depicts serious conflicts of several love relationships, mostly unrequited, that belie the quiet and beautiful settings of nature. Drawing rooms, a card table, the ballroom, the gardens, a shady pavilion—all point to a leisurely life in the country.

It is ironic that, when love's passions reach a boiling point, "like a sudden storm on a fine day," several char-

acters leave for Moscow, as if fleeing from rustic country life. This seems to confirm the critic Georg Brandes's seeing nature in Turgenev's works as *la grande indifférente*. After several characters leave the estate, the quiet life returns. Those that remain, especially Islaev's wife Natalia Petrovna, who had caused most of the turmoil with her infatuation with the young student Belaev, her jealousy and her desire to break the monotony of her life, are forced to find a rapport with nature again. With its lyrical mood and scarcity of action, *A Month in the Country* is a forerunner of Anton Chekhov's plays.

— *Vasa D. Mihailovich*

THE MOON AND SIXPENCE

Author: W. Somerset Maugham (1874-1965)
Type of work: Novel
Type of plot: Biographical

Time of plot: c. 1897-1917
First published: 1919

Inspired by the life of Paul Gauguin, this novel follows the fictional Charles Strickland's transformation from London stockbroker to great painter. Strickland moves through several stages as a painter, at each stage moving farther from his London origins, both geographically and metaphorically. The early London scenes are narrated at first hand, but the later scenes are at second hand, re-created from several sources or simply projected outward as an extension of the narrator's views on art and life.

***London.** Capital of Great Britain in which the novel opens with several chapters satirizing the city's domestic and literary worlds. Except for chance encounters in the streets, all the novel's scenes are set in middle-class living rooms. Maugham's London is a completely known world, in which original vision is impossible because everyone knows how they are supposed to behave, and, for the most part, do. Even the threats of the world— dullness, sarcastic insults, infidelity—are known, and may be dealt with. When Charles Strickland decides that he wants to paint and abandons his London home to do so, it is a scandal. Strickland goes to Paris, and the narrator is dispatched to bring him back, and to get rid of the

supposed "other woman" his wife insists must have led him astray.

Strickland home. London home of Charles Strickland and his first wife, Amy, who attempts to advance her own ambitions as a hostess who supports the arts by hosting luncheon and dinner parties for rising writers. When the narrator visits Strickland's home, he finds it "chaste, artistic, and dull" and reflects that there must be five hundred homes in London decorated exactly the same.

***Paris.** Capital of France where Strickland settles in the Hôtel des Belges, a flophouse in which he lives in squalor. This place shows Strickland's contradictory character. Although he spends his hours painting, seeking beauty, he does not care if he lives in filth. It is as if all settings are the same to him, because he sees the world differently. Nevertheless, Strickland's Paris is recognizably romantic compared to London. Strickland and the narrator meet in cheap hotels, sidewalk cafés, and bars frequented by prostitutes, and here Strickland's work first receives attention from other painters and gallery owners.

Strickland would not even enter a recognizable domestic space if he did not fall ill, a sign that for him these domestic spaces are for the weak. When Strickland is sick, another painter and his wife (Dirk and Blanche Stroeve) take him into their home to nurse him to health. Strickland destroys their home, and, as he recovers, he literally drives Stroeve from his own studio. When Stroeve finally asks him to leave, his wife Blanche says that she loves Strickland and wants to leave with him. Stroeve then abandons his studio to them. Blanche later commits suicide when she realizes that Strickland's demoniac urge to paint will always keep her at a distance, almost worthless to him. These chapters indicate the essential split between artistic genius, which is wild, and the domestic, which is tame and familiar.

The narrator avoids Strickland after this, then meets him on the street. Strickland takes the narrator to his apartment; he is the only character other than Strickland or one of his lovers to be taken into Strickland's space. The narrator spends pages both describing Strickland's paintings and his own reactions to them and explaining to Strickland why he thinks Blanche's love makes him so uncomfortable. Strickland calls him a "dreadful sentimentalist," but within a week he leaves for Marseilles, indicating that he was waiting for this final recognition before he could move on to his next location, and next level of artistic development.

*Marseilles (mar-SAY). Port city in the south of France where Strickland goes after leaving Paris. The narrator himself never sees Strickland again after their Paris meeting; however, while later traveling through the South Pacific, he meets several people who knew Strickland. All accounts of Marseilles come from Captain Nichols, a sailor who knocked around Marseilles with Strickland. Strickland never entered a private home in Marseilles, but lived on the street or in shelters for the homeless. The impersonality and violence of Marseilles stripped away the trappings of civilization that had limited Strickland's artistic vision, reducing Strickland to nothing more than his desire to paint. Since Marseilles is also the oldest city in France, Strickland is also moving backward through time, trying to reach a place as pure and original as his vision of the world.

*Tahiti. French Polynesian colony, the largest of the Society Islands in the South Pacific, that is Strickland's last home. During one of his talks with the narrator in Paris, Strickland said that he longed for an island in a "boundless sea" where he could find what he sought. Though he begins his time on the island with regular visits to the capital city of Papeete, Strickland eventually marries a Tahitian woman and moves into the bush, completely giving up on Western civilization. Though he is still considered odd in Papeete, Strickland fits in more fully on this beautiful island than anywhere else he has lived, and, accordingly, there are more people who appreciate his art. Maugham blends observations from his own travels with descriptions of paintings done by Gauguin. However, as in all places in the novel, he focuses almost entirely on only three types of Tahitian locations: places where people come together to talk, such as bars and restaurants; domestic settings; and places seen through Strickland's art.

Strickland's hut. Tiny hut in which Strickland lives with his Tahitian wife, Ata. The novel begins and ends in domestic spaces, but the dramatic difference between the first and last communicates Maugham's views on the power of art. In London, Strickland is dying spiritually and has to abandon a home that almost everyone would regard as beautiful. In Tahiti, he contracts leprosy. Now feared by the Tahitians, Strickland lives out his final years in ecstasy as he paints his own vision of paradise into being. He eventually covers every inch of his hut's walls with portraits of his own re-creation of the Garden of Eden, re-creating that mythic place in Polynesia. Because he is bringing his vision of the world into being, Strickland dies happy within his crumbling jungle hut.

— *Greg Beatty*

THE MOONSTONE

Author: Wilkie Collins (1824-1889)
Type of work: Novel
Type of plot: Detective and mystery

Time of plot: 1799-1849
First published: 1868

British society and customs, including the concept of "seasons," are imperative to the workings of this novel and its mystery. Repeated back-and-forth journeys between the mysterious, secluded, and dangerous shores of Yorkshire and the civilized, staid, solid London are integral to the plot and atmosphere.

*Seringapatam (se-rihn-guh-puh-TAM). Capital of southern India's Mysore under the reign of Sultan Tipu Sahib in the late eighteenth century. The novel opens with the storming of Seringapatam by the British, during which John Herncastle steals the fabulous sacred Hindu diamond known as the "Moonstone." As a land of mystics, mystery, and fabled gems, a land known as the "jewel" in the British crown, India provides an appropriate setting for the opening of this mystery novel.

*Yorkshire. Region in northern England in which Lady Verinder has an estate on the shore of the North Sea. Yorkshire provides atmosphere; its moors and the wildness of the North Sea serve as a forbidding and oppressive setting for many Victorian novels, providing loneliness and desolation as a background. The Verinder estate, at some distance from Frizinghall, the nearest town, stands in isolation, adding to the mysterious nature of the novel. There are a few other farms some miles distant, and the tiny fishing village of Cobb's Hill marks the boundaries of the estate to prevent a sense of total isolation, even though the manor stands alone in its environment.

Echoing the intensity of the plot, the location rapidly changes back and forth from the deserted estate to London. The trips become more and more frenetic, giving a sense of breathlessness to the atmosphere.

One of the most ominous features of the estate, a large, deep stretch of quicksand locally known as the **Shivering Sands**, lies along the beach front of the grounds of the manor. The danger of the shoreline itself with its hidden rocks and reefs adds to the ominous nature of the surroundings. In addition to providing an at-

mosphere of terror and horror, the sea and the quicksand become metaphors for being caught in a mire of overwhelming circumstances beyond human control and reinforce the content of the novel. In this deserted spot, the supernatural curse carried by the stolen diamond and its Indian origins are frequently recalled, causing the foreboding and danger to be amplified by the isolation. An additional benefit to this rural setting can be found in the characterization, as the people are more natural and themselves here than when bound by the rigid social conventions in London.

*London. Capital city of Great Britain, in which Lady Verinder owns a house on Montague Square. Many wealthy and titled people of the novel's period lived in country houses during the spring and summer seasons and in London homes during the fall and winter seasons. When the novel's characters are living in London, they find their lives becoming more formal and artificial. London has always been known for its entertainments, society, and royal court.

In contrast, London has another side that is characterized by squalid poverty and crime. This contrast in environments is essential to the progress of the novel, which culminates in London's slums.

*Brighton. Popular seaside resort in the south of England to which the novel's setting shifts from London. Brighton has always been a popular retreat because of its climate and healthful atmosphere. In *The Moonstone*, however, Brighton's balmy climate is a foil to emotional tempest and cannot sustain its healthful effects.

— *H. Alan Pickrell*

LE MORTE D'ARTHUR

Author: Sir Thomas Malory (1400?-1471)
Type of work: Chronicle
Type of plot: Arthurian romance

Time of plot: Age of chivalry
First transcribed: c. 1469; first printed, 1485

While the roots of the Arthurian legend are more often Celtic or French than English, Thomas Malory's vast synthesis of the earlier versions remakes the legend into a specifically and emphatically English national epic.

Camelot. King Arthur's primary residence and most important seat of power, home of the Round Table. Malory identifies Camelot as Winchester, though his sources had offered a range of other locations, mostly in southern England. William Caxton, for example, Malory's first editor and publisher, writes an important preface to the work in which he concedes that the Round Table is indeed kept at Winchester but claims that Camelot itself is in Wales. Descriptions of the city and of the castle are as vague as those of its geographical location, and the image of Camelot seems to have been a rather fluid one, which each generation of writers and readers would visualize in terms of the cities and castles most familiar to them, whether from observation or from reading other romances.

Forest. Generic setting for many of the adventures of Arthur's knights. The forest functions as the site of conflict and disorder in opposition to the civilized order and decorum represented by Camelot. By the end of the epic, Camelot itself has declined into a state of chaos and hostility. These forests function both as empty stages upon which the errant knights encounter perils (frequently in the form of other wandering knights) and as enchanted worlds in which the supernatural emerges more readily than in the comparatively realistic world of the court. Characters like Lancelot and Tristram go to the forest when they are driven temporarily mad. Although the forests are depicted as wildernesses where the laws of society are suspended, they are somewhat paradoxically well provided with abbeys, hermitages, and priories at which the knights can obtain food and lodging and hear mass. The forest also contains numerous massive castles built literally in the middle of nowhere.

*Glastonbury. Small English town that is the site of one of the most ancient British Christian communities and a major Benedictine abbey. Glastonbury is cited in a number of Arthurian contexts. By the early twelfth century it became the place to which Guenevere is taken when she is kidnapped. In 1190 to 1191, the monks of the monastery announced that they had found the remains of King Arthur and Queen Guenevere in their cemetery under a cross bearing an inscription that conveniently identified them. Caxton's preface to his edition of Malory also locates his sepulchre there. A legend was soon popularized that the religious site had been founded by Joseph of Arimathea, who is supposed to have brought the Holy Grail to the Isle of Avalon, putatively located near Glastonbury. At the end of Malory's work, Sir Bedivere, the only survivor of the final battle between Arthur and Mordred, becomes a hermit in a chapel beside Glastonbury. Lancelot and seven other knights join him as hermits, and Lancelot dies there.

*Salisbury. Town in southern England that is the site of the climactic battle between the forces of Arthur and his nephew/son Mordred, in which the Knights of the Round Table are virtually all killed. Arthur himself is mortally wounded and sent off in a mysterious barge to the vale of Avalon to be healed.

Avalon. In most versions of the legend, the magical valley or island to which Arthur is taken after his final battle to be healed, and from which he shall one day return to lead the English people again. Malory himself does not support this part of the story.

*Rome. Arthur's military campaign against the Roman emperor Lucius, which results in Arthur's being named emperor of Rome, makes up one of the few sustained military operations in the work and one of the few in which Arthur himself is a primary participant. Notable among the battles along the way is Arthur's combat with a giant at La Mont-Saint-Michel. Popular legend claimed that Britain had been founded by (and named after) Brutus, great-grandson of Aeneas, who had paved the way for the founding of Rome after fleeing Troy. This cultural myth of the *translatio imperium* saw the history of the world as a progress west from Troy to

Rome to England, the third great world power after the empires of Greece and Rome.

Joyous Gard. Lancelot's castle in England, usually located in the northern part of the country, perhaps in Northumberland. He brings Guenevere here for protection after rescuing her from Arthur's knights when she is about to be executed for treason. Arthur and Gawain besiege the castle to recover her, but even though the pope intervenes to impose peace, the alliance of Lancelot with Arthur's court is effectively ended. Lancelot renames the castle Dolorous Gard after his split with Arthur. Lancelot is taken there for burial after his death at Glastonbury. Malory locates the castle and the associated town in Alnwick or Bamburgh.

*****Tintagel Castle.** Castle in which Arthur is conceived by his father, Uther, and his mother, Ygerna, at that time the wife of Duke Gorlois of Cornwall. Tintagel is also the primary castle of King Mark in the legend of Tristram. Ruins in the area have suggested to some that there may have been a historical basis for the location of a stronghold there.

Logres. One of the names for Arthur's realm. A near-synonym for England for Malory and other English writers, much less precisely located for most French writers. Depending upon the context, Logres may comprise large expanses of Europe, up to and including the Roman Empire, to which Arthur lays claim and then conquers. It also covers such imaginary countries as Lyonesse, the home kingdom of Tristram, who typifies the internationalism of Arthurian legend: He is born in Lyonesse, raised in Cornwall, educated in France, married in Brittany, and serves in Ireland, Scotland, and Wales, besides being one of Arthur's knights in Camelot.

— *William Nelles*

MORTE D'URBAN

Author: J. F. Powers (1917-1999)
Type of work: Novel
Type of plot: Social realism

Time of plot: Late 1950's
First published: 1962

Father Urban Roche's impressive fund-raising skills are put to the test when he is transferred by his order, the Clementines, from metropolitan Chicago to remote St. Clement's Hill, a run-down retreat house located in the hinterlands of Minnesota where secular and spiritual values are more stringently drawn. J. F. Powers utilizes the striking contrasts between the two settings to underscore the competing worldly and religious demands made upon the priest.

St. Clement's Hill. White elephant of a retreat house located near the fictional town of **Duesterhaus**, Minnesota, and a symbol of the Clementine order's struggle for survival. In Father Urban's mind, the central question confronting the Clementines is whether St. Clement's Hill will end up "as one more spot where the good seed of its zeal had fallen and flourished, or as another where the order had lost out?" In a practical sense the task handed Father Urban primarily involves his being able to apply his entrepreneurial talents to his new environs. It is a switch rich in irony. Chicago had provided for him a market he had become accustomed to, a vast commercial landscape upon which he could wheel and deal with a unique mix of business insight and

religious devotion. He had been the order's star performer. Then suddenly and without clear cause, he is banished to a backwater retreat house where a devoted priest's view is expected to turn within, especially to the direction his life is taking. However, Father Urban's entrepreneurial instincts are still on display immediately upon his arrival at St. Clement's Hill. One of his first reactions to the facility is to the welcoming signboard whose "lettering was sharp and elegant, worthy of a tombstone" but whose colors "didn't do much for each other" and had the overall effect of stating "fresh eggs for sale."

*****Chicago.** Major midwestern city in Illinois where Father Urban is able to roam with confidence between church rectories, chancelleries, and corporate offices in pursuit of the latest fund-raising opportunity that might benefit the Clementines. The city represents one of the great centers of twentieth century Catholicism during a period when the church was undergoing a major transformation as a result of the flight of great segments of the population from the cities to the suburbs.

St. Clement's Golf Course. Course that Father Urban arranges to build near the retreat house as a fundraising vehicle. To Father Urban the course represents the common ground on which the sacred and secular can meet in a mutually beneficial manner. He views it as an inroad to the Minnesota rich. Powers utilizes the course as a kind of demarcation line that underscores the incompatibilities between the modern and spiritual world. He does so in the most satiric manner, when he has Father Urban struck in the head by his own bishop's errant golf shot. The incident immediately drains the bishop of his enthusiasm for proprietary projects and Father Urban of his customary zeal.

Thwaite estate. Rural home of Mrs. Thwaite, a wealthy and invalid benefactress of the Clementine order, where Father Urban convalesces. Once he is outside the confining environment of St. Clement's Hill and ensconced in the estate's palatial surroundings, his thoughts turn to more worldly matters, particularly his fondness for fashionable office space. His stay at Mrs. Thwaite's estate allows him time to ponder where he might have been—"in some kind of business you could breathe in, perhaps heavy machinery, much of it going overseas—operating out of a spacious office on Michigan Avenue—with a view of the lake." Earlier in the novel, a prestigious office site had been donated to the Clementines as a result of Father Urban's efforts. However, his idea to decorate it with luxurious furnishings as a lure to wealthy visitors is squelched by his superior. The office as a dual symbol of commercial success and unbridled greed is effectively utilized by Powers to demonstrate the recurring theme of conflicting priorities.

— *William Hoffman*

THE MOTHER

Author: Grazia Deledda (1871-1936)
Type of work: Novel
Type of plot: Psychological realism

Time of plot: Early twentieth century
First published: La madre, 1920 (English translation, 1922)

This novel's significant action unfolds in the tiny Sardinian village of Aar, a mountainous gathering of humble abodes and humanity constantly buffeted by strong winds. The claustrophobic setting of the novel—a spooky presbytery in a remote village on a lonely island—lends credibility to the compulsive actions leading to the devastation of three human beings, a priest named Paul, his mother Maria, and Agnes, the young woman for whom he yearns.

*Sardinia. Italian island that is the second largest island of the Mediterranean Sea and one of the most ancient of European lands, with remnants of human habitation dating from 6000 B.C.E. Until well into the twentieth century, it remained one of the most isolated of Italian regions, maintaining its own languages and tribal customs. The literary revelation of Sardinia was the work of Grazia Deledda, who won the Nobel Prize in Literature in 1926, with special praise by the Swedish Academy for her skilled descriptions of splendidly rugged and desolate landscapes. In the Sardinia of Deledda's novels the

vendetta remain, bandits are admired, loss of chastity is horribly punished, and emotions are always raw. Her characters are not Rousseauistic noble savages, but they are also not yet corrupted by the more subtle vices of the European mainland. As in a Homeric epic, fate broods over the landscape, which, like the weather, seems to mirror the emotions of the people.

Presbytery. Primitive Sardinian home designed for the ascetic life of a priest and a female housekeeper of "a certain age." Paul's housekeeper is his own widowed mother, who functions as his conscience and jailor as well. She listens to his every movement and shadows him on his pastoral rounds. The austerity of the home and its keeper serves daily to remind the young priest of the life he has been forced to renounce; no youthful frivolity or sensual pleasure is to be his. Ordered by his bishop to show deference to his mother, this woman who has chosen for him this vocation, and to frequently kiss her hand, Paul has a frightening vision of her lying on the altar, like a mysterious pagan idol whose cold hand he is forced to kiss.

Aar. Fictional Sardinian village, typical of the island's villages in the Nuoro region in the early twentieth century, long before developers and tourists arrived. The nearby mountains are the lairs of bandits; in the sur-

rounding fields, shepherds tend their flocks. Peasants, petty craftsmen, small landowners, and priests are the neighbors. Life is especially lonely for women, shrouded in their long black garments. Older women such as Maria may live through their children, who are themselves condemned to limited, deprived existences, but younger women like Agnes, especially when they are alone, are constantly watched and judged. Only the church calendar, with its cycle of fasts and feast days, slightly relieves the monotony of the lives that pass here from birth to death without even the respite of a trip to the island's cities, Cagliari and Sassari.

— *Allene Phy-Olsen*

MOTHER

Author: Maxim Gorky (Aleksey Maksimovich Peshkov, 1868-1936)
Type of work: Novel
Type of plot: Naturalism

Time of plot: First decade of the twentieth century
First published: Mat, serial, 1906; book, 1907 (English translation, 1906)

In this novel, a heroic Russian revolutionary mother joins with her son and a variety of young and old political activists to battle against the institutionalized injustices of czarist Russia in the early years of the twentieth century. Although the event is not mentioned by name, the action relates to the events leading up to and transpiring shortly after the 1902 May Day demonstrations of workers in Sormovo. Most places mentioned in the novel are generic. The stress is on the thoughts and actions of the characters.

Vlasov house (VLAH-sof). Home of protagonist Pavel Vlasov located on the outskirts of an unnamed Russian town. In the main room of the small gray house, Pavel gathers together his ever changing circle of radicals, and a feeling of affinity with the suffering workers of the world is born. There also, Pavel's mother, Pelagueya Vlasova, is slowly drawn into the lives and work of the revolutionaries. The house becomes a center of radical activity as well as the focus of observation by police spies and is the target of several police raids.

Factory. The unnamed town is dominated by the tall black smokestacks of the factory, in which grime-faced workers have their life force sucked out of them through working in horrid conditions for sub-subsistence wages. Disguised as a food vendor, Pelagueya goes to the factory's yard secretly to distribute literature to sympa-

thetic workers in order to foment labor strikes. Led by Pavel, workers in the factory refuse to work and instead join a parade that assembles in the churchyard to celebrate May Day. Their parade is stopped by a gray wall of soldiers with fixed bayonets who charge the marchers and arrest Pavel and nineteen other demonstrators.

Ivanovich's house. Secluded home of Nikolay Ivanovich, a revolutionary friend of Pavel, to which Pelagueya goes to stay after Pavel is arrested. Strategy meetings continue there as Pelagueya helps tidy the bachelor's simple one-story shack, which is typical of those of simple workmen. Nikolay is in revolt against the type of life led by his father, a factory manager in Vyataka. Before Pavel's trial, Nikolay's house is ransacked by police investigators.

Woods. Forested area outside the town that contain

what little beauty can be found in the workers' lives, such as sunrises and birdsongs. Whatever personal or deeply reflective thinking in which the major characters engage takes place in the woods.

Nikolskoye (nih-kohl-SKOY-ah). Small town to which Pelagueya goes secretly to distribute literature to workers. There she sees Pavel's friend Rybin being beaten by the chief of police for distributing literature. Rybin had earlier gone to Yegildeyevo (one of the few specific towns mentioned in the novel) to take revolutionary literature to the peasants.

Courthouse. Government building in which Pavel and his associates are tried before judges suffering from boredom and ill health. Pavel and Andrey denounce private property and czarism, and Pavel predicts that socialism will rebuild the land that czarist greed has destroyed. Pavel's conviction is a foregone conclusion, and he is exiled to Siberia. Afterward, his words are printed in leaflets that his mother carries to a train station, where police intercept her and beat her.

— *Irwin Halfond*

MOTHER AND SON

Author: Ivy Compton-Burnett (1884-1969)
Type of work: Novel
Type of plot: Satire

Time of plot: End of the nineteenth century
First published: 1955

This satiric look at a large, dysfunctional Victorian family concentrates especially on the twisted relationship between a domineering mother and her intimidated son. Much of the narrative is located in a large old English mansion, which is ruled with an iron hand by its matriarch, who implicitly uses the weight of tradition and convention suggested by the house itself to bolster her power.

Miranda Hume's house. Typical of Ivy Compton-Burnett's work, this novel is set in an old Victorian manor house in a respectable suburban British enclave. These large and ancestral estates represent the economic and social power usually associated with the south of England. But for all their solidity and security, the mansions in Compton-Burnett's work inevitably isolate those who live within them.

Staffed by domestic servants who all sleep under the mansions' roofs, run to rigid timetables, and organized into hierarchies over which parental figures have absolute control, these traditional stately homes reflect Victorian family life at its most crushing. While this world is modeled on that of Compton-Burnett's own large and troubled Victorian family, the houses of her fiction are even larger and more traditional than the house in which the author herself lived. The enlargement and enhancement of her own childhood house enabled Compton-Burnett to use her mansions symbolically rather than literally—they became microcosms of Victorian society. This is particularly the case because Compton-Burnett

almost completely dispenses with description, instead preferring dialogue to further her narrative.

In *Mother and Son*, a large Victorian household is presided over by the typically autocratic matriarch Miranda Hume. The presence of easily cowed servants in the house and the imperious manner of Miranda suggest that she feels that she is entitled by a kind of natural law to her present position of power. That Miranda is the unassailable mistress of an intimidated and discontented group of family and servants is, for Miranda, part of the Victorian way of life and is not subject to question.

The solidity and prosperity of the house itself gives Miranda a status that makes it impossible for those who live there to interpret her behavior as psychopathic or criminal. Instead, Miranda successfully represents herself as a model of Victorian probity, whose severity should be an occasion for praise rather than interrogation. Because of her domestic tyranny, the house gives an impression of complete discomfort—an atmosphere of fear, anxiety, and even madness prevails, punctuated only by the malicious teasing of the younger children, whose satiric jibes are the only defense they have against Miranda and her rigid domestic rule.

Ultimately, the house stands for the hypocritical and authoritarian social structure of Victorian society, and especially the Victorian family. As the parental authority, Miranda bullies and intimidates her family remorselessly, especially her own son Rosebery. Believing utterly in her godlike powers of omniscience, Miranda actually dies of shock when she is confronted with family secrets of which she has been previously unaware. These concern her husband's sexual activities, which resulted in the birth of three illegitimate children who also live in the household. When Miranda's husband tells her about his sex life, one could say that he literally murders his wife with the truth. A further devastating disclosure reveals the secret, illegitimate parentage of Rosebery himself. Driven by biological imperatives and instincts, Miranda from the start forges a twisted bond between herself and her son that deliberately excludes Rosebery's ostensible father. In the end, the real nature of Miranda and her family cannot be covered over by its surface of Victorian domestic respectability.

Emma Greatheart's house. This neighboring house in which Emma Greatheart lives is of secondary importance in the narrative. In contrast with Miranda's house, Emma's home is more welcoming. Although also a traditional Victorian home, it is a happy one precisely because it is free of the family structure imposed by Miranda and of the weight of Victorian tradition. Emma and her two friends live happily free of marriage and family, in contradistinction to the Hume household, which is exposed as a venue for loveless power struggles in which humanity's darker instincts are given free reign.

— *Margaret Boe Birns*

MOTHER COURAGE AND HER CHILDREN

Author: Bertolt Brecht (1898-1956)
Type of work: Drama
Type of plot: Play of ideas
Time of plot: 1624-1648

First performed: 1941 (in German); first published, 1941 (in English); German original, 1949 as *Mutter Courage und ihre Kinder*

A protest against war, this play is ostensibly set in Europe during the Thirty Years' War of the early seventeenth century; however, almost nothing in the play actually relates to that period, as the play could be set almost anywhere. A life-long pacifist, Bertolt Brecht attempts to show that there are no victors, only losers, in the game of war.

*Sweden, *Germany, and *Poland. European countries in which the play is ostensibly set during the Thirty Years' War of the early seventeenth century. Settings for the play are accomplished via legends displayed or projected for the audience to read, along with small or suggestive bits of scenery or stage properties. The play, with the exception of Mother Courage's canteen wagon, could easily be performed without any scenery or setting. Brecht's time frame also creates anachronisms, as he makes no concession to the diction or costuming of the seventeenth century. The play's apparently modern characters are vital if the audience is to understand that the drama is not actually about the Thirty Years' War, but about wars in general. The play is universal and timeless in its appeal.

Known for his creation of Epic Theatre, Brecht seeks to alienate his audience by his use of the V effect, thereby destroying the illusion of reality. It is necessary that the audience always remember that they are viewing a performance so that the play's message can get through to them. If the audience is alienated, it is objective; therefore, the working components of the stage must always show through to the audience, and the appearance of reality must be avoided. Throughout the twelve brief scenes of the play, even though the locales may change, the emphasis is never on the place but rather on the characters and their actions.

— *H. Alan Pickrell*

MOURNING BECOMES ELECTRA

Author: Eugene O'Neill (1888-1953)
Type of work: Drama
Type of plot: Tragedy

Time of plot: 1860's
First performed: 1931; first published, 1931

Perhaps Eugene O'Neill's most ambitious experiment in theater, this play is actually a trilogy in thirteen acts that parallels the ancient Greek Oresteia, *Aeschylus's fifth century* B.C.E. *trio of tragedies. O'Neill sets his own work in the period following the U.S. Civil War, while the Greek original concerned the aftermath of the Trojan War. O'Neill's three tragedies parallel the three parts of the* Oresteia. *The story of the vengeance of Electra and Orestes on their mother for the murder of their father is transformed into a dramatization of the life of the family of General Ezra Mannon and his unfaithful wife and the two children who avenge his murder by his wife and her lover.*

Mannon mansion. Home of the Mannon family, on the outskirts of a small, unnamed New England village near the sea, that is the setting for twelve of the thirteen acts of the trilogy. As each of the three plays progresses from act to act, the settings move from the mansion's exterior to its interior. Gradually, the house's study, Ezra's bedroom, and the sitting room are revealed. O'Neill's description of the surrounding area, with its woods, orchard, garden, lawn, and greenhouse, are carefully detailed. The position of the mansion on a hill above the town suggests the assumed power and assumed superiority of the Mannon family. O'Neill describes the house in such detail that it is clear he considers it integral to the action of his plot.

Clipper ship. The only setting other than the exterior and interior of the Mannon mansion is the stern of a ship and the wharf to which it is moored. This is used only in the fourth act of *The Hunter*, the second play in O'Neill's trilogy, when General Mannon's son, Orin, kills the ship's captain.

— *W. Kenneth Holditch*

THE MOUSETRAP

Author: Agatha Christie (1890-1976)
Type of work: Drama
Type of plot: Detective and mystery

Time of plot: Mid-twentieth century
First performed: 1952; first published, 1954

This play, probably the most famous closed-room story, focuses on universal anxieties associated with unfamiliar surroundings, unknown people, and a feeling of being trapped when a severe snowstorm isolates eight people in an old country inn.

Monkswell Manor. Guest house located thirty miles west of London, in Berkshire County, in which the play is set. The stage is set as one large room with tall windows. A door and two arched openings lead off to numerous other rooms, hidden spaces beneath staircases, and a basement, which was perhaps once a crypt. Snowbound, the owners and guests feel cut off from the world; even the telephone stops working. Detective Sergeant Trotter startles them when he raps on the big window. A murder was committed the previous day in Paddington, an area of London, and he says two more intended victims may be at Monkswell Manor. Soon the lights in the room go out, and one of the guests is found strangled to death.

Constant entrances and exits from the room enhance the confusion about where passages lead and what other characters are doing. "Suspect everybody" was a dictum of mystery writer Dorothy L. Sayers, Agatha Christie's contemporary, and Christie makes it credible that even husband and wife suspect each other. The representative British character types, such as the naïve young couple on their first day as guest house managers or the aging woman who demands her creature comforts, are familiar types anywhere. However, appearances deceive. Everyone is a stranger, isolated in separate pasts and self-interests. Literally located together in this communal room, the characters also inhabit, along with the audience, the realm of the imagination, where suspicions and fears know no boundaries.

— *Lois A. Marchino*

THE MOVIEGOER

Author: Walker Percy (1916-1990)
Type of work: Novel
Type of plot: Social realism

Time of plot: Early 1960's
First published: 1961

Although the primary setting of this novel is New Orleans, the alienation and modern malaise of the central characters is a universal theme. While the characters attempt to conquer their condition by changing their physical location, they carry their malaise with them from place to place.

***New Orleans.** Louisiana's biggest city, in whose Garden District Aunt Emily and Uncle Jules Cutrer live in a large house with their African American servants and their daughter Kate, Binx Bolling's cousin. Frequently Aunt Emily, Binx's great aunt, attempts to convince him to embrace her patrician and stoical attitudes, symbolized in her life in this home.

Binx has chosen to work as a stockbroker in a branch of Uncle Jules's brokerage firm and to live in Elysian Fields in Gentilly, a middle-class suburb. His basement apartment in Mrs. Schexnaydre's bungalow, which he furnishes with the latest appliances, contrasts sharply with the more formal living arrangements of Aunt Emily, with her antique furniture and uniformed servants, and with the Bolling's ancestral home in Feliciana Parish. In Greek and Roman mythology Elysium, or the Elysian Fields, were where the souls of heroes resided after death. In this land of sunshine and fragrant flowers, souls existed joyously. Binx prefers the sameness of Gentilly to the old world humor of the French Quarter, where he lived for two years, and the genteel charm of the Garden District, where Aunt Emily lives. The movie theaters Binx visits for escape from everydayness are also located in Gentilly.

Bayou des Allemonds (BI-yew dehz-ah-leh-MAWN). Summer fishing camp for Binx's mother, stepfather, and their children. Binx spent summers here in his youth, but when he and his girlfriend Sharon unexpectedly visit the Smiths after a weekend trip to the Gulf Coast near Biloxi, Mississippi, he learns that the everydayness he seeks to escape through nature has spread from the cities to even the swamps. Walker Percy uses the evening supper with the middle-class Smiths, as they crack crabs and suck the shells, to contrast with the more formal meals served at Aunt Emily's home. Binx cannot escape his depression at either place.

Feliciana Parish. Fictional Louisiana parish outside New Orleans. Percy acknowledges in a prefatory paragraph to the novel that East Feliciana and West Feliciana parishes do exist, but he has altered the geography of New Orleans. His later novels are also set in Feliciana Parish. The Bollings' ancestral home, Lynwood, is here and represents the southern aristocracy's false approach to life through its reliance on social class, custom, tradition, and race, an approach that Binx rejects.

***Chicago.** Illinois city to which Binx and Kate go, after Kate's attempted suicide, to attend a professional meeting of stockbrokers and to seek a new approach to life. Like New Orleans, the city is dominated by an adjoining lake, but amid the tall buildings and the lake-driven winds Binx experiences the harsh malaise of urban existence and decides to return to New Orleans with Kate. On this trip Binx and Kate also visit Harold Graebner, who saved Binx's life during the Korean War. While lying in a ditch after being wounded in the shoulder, Binx had become fully conscious of the death-in-life in which individuals exist. Because Harold is now a successful businessman with a wife and newborn son, Binx's godson, Harold does not understand the malaise Binx and Kate are attempting to escape.

Eufaula (yew-FAWL-uh). Alabama home of Sharon Kincaid, Binx's secretary. In contrast to Kate, Binx's cousin and eventual wife, Sharon does not suffer from the same psychological depression experienced by Kate and Binx. Her small-town southern background keeps her immune to seeing existence through Binx's depression-filled eyes.

— *Alan T. Belsches*

MR. SAMMLER'S PLANET

Author: Saul Bellow (1915-   )
Type of work: Novel
Type of plot: Social realism

Time of plot: Mid-twentieth century
First published: 1970

The city of New York as it comes reeling out of the 1960's is the microcosm for Artur Sammler, intellectual and Jewish Holocaust survivor, who wonders if all of Earth and the destructive creatures who inhabit it have any future at all.

New York City. Like many of Bellow's protagonists, Sammler functions chiefly as an eye and a brain, and audiences see New York through his eyes. The city is, to use a phrase of Saul Bellow's that he got from Wyndham Lewis, a "moronic inferno," a metropolis ridden with detritus, broken objects and wrecked people, reduced to the level of a Third World capital. Its parks are full of dog excrement, and their flowers are soiled with pollution almost immediately after blooming. The X's painted on the windowpanes of a building marked for demolition loom in Sammler's mind as portents of the end of time. In a notorious scene, an African American pickpocket whom Sammler observes threatens retribution by physically exposing himself to Sammler in the run-down lobby of his own apartment building.

In Sammler's mind, this decay is the result of Western civilization's surrender to the philosophies of the Enlightenment, the concrete aftereffects of the dreams of nineteenth century Romantic poets. His images for the city's denizens are based in literature; at one point they are spider monkeys, throwing their excrement at passersby—in other words, Yahoos. Later, the zonked-out youths lounging in the city's parks remind Sammler of H. G. Wells's effete Eloi race of the distant future in *The Time Machine* (1895); they are almost feral, tinged

with a decadent grace. Outside the city, even the flora can be ominous; like the ancient Roman poet Juvenal, Sammler views the plant life as providing hiding spaces for thieves, robbers, or even worse. "Great cities are whores," he concludes.

Yet even in this metropolitan circle of hell, Sammler can find pleasure—"Bliss from his surroundings!" as he calls it. There is a hint that Sammler resists such delights as the city can provide him, the resistance symbolically expressed by his injured eye. His own personal history, so intertwined with the worst aspects of twentieth century history in the Holocaust, limit the pleasures he can take from his milieu. Nevertheless, near the end of the novel he can exult: "To see was delicious."

Poland. Eastern European country in which Sammler is born and where he experiences the horrors of the Holocaust. In Poland's Zamosht Forest he returns to a state of nature and kills a German soldier, and later must hide in a mausoleum: Both locations are obviously symbolic.

London. Capital of Great Britain in whose Bloomsbury district Sammler lives before World War II. Britain's greatest city is a fitting location for an Anglophile who loves the life of the mind and who, like the early twentieth century writers of London's Bloomsbury

Group were accused of doing, has not yet confronted the problem of evil in the modern world.

*Israel.** Modern Middle Eastern homeland of the Jews, which Sammler visits twice; both times are marked by incongruities of place and time. During his first visit, he encounters an Argentine gaucho in Galilee and notes that William Blake's verdant imagery in "Jerusalem" (1820) does not tally with the arid landscape before him. Later, during his visit when Israel is fighting the Six-Day War, his observation of a tank battle is invaded by an irruption of modernity as several photographers, accompanied by uncomprehending models, come to photograph it. In Gaza, Sammler sees a group of Bedouin tents made not out of fabric, but pieced together out of the detritus of modern civilization—plastic, styrofoam, and cellulose. Even the famous biblical sites of the Holy Land are not immune from the disease of modern life, a disease that leaves eternal remnants of itself.

*Earth.** Mr. Sammler's planet. As the title of the novel suggests, Sammler is forced to consider the entire globe because of the imminent landing on the Moon and Dr. Govinda Lal's manuscript about humanity's settling there. Sammler is initially not sanguine about the prospect of humanity's surviving on Earth, let alone its Moon. Having seen the world nearly collapse during the Holocaust, he is afraid of its happening again. The extraterrestrial perspective inspired by Lal's writing allows Sammler to see Earth not as one big, blue ball, the home of life, but as one huge grave. Yet at the end of the novel, Sammler holds out a glimmer of hope: "We will die. Nevertheless there is a bond." Whether that bond has the strength to allow people, to use the epigraph of a famous Bloomsbury novel, to "only connect," is outside the province of the narrative.

— *William Laskowski*

MRS. DALLOWAY

Author: Virginia Woolf (1882-1941)
Type of work: Novel
Type of plot: Psychological realism

Time of plot: 1923
First published: 1925

Set on a single day in mid-June, 1923, this novel focuses on activities in London. The London locations represent post-World War I political issues and their effects on English society, such as the disintegration of the British colonies, women's suffrage, and socialism.

*London.** Capital of Great Britain whose diversity of life is characterized by the city's commercial life, its social order, and national politics. As characters walk through the streets of London, they encounter famous locations and monuments—Whitehall, Westminster, the parks, Big Ben, and St. Paul's Cathedral. London's diversity suggests the potential for harmony in society on at least two levels: a union between public and private, epitomized in the characters of Clarissa and Septimus, and among all the diverse social and political factions found in English society.

*Westminster.** This upper-class London neighborhood houses many government officials and politicians. The Dalloways' life in Westminster symbolizes their upper-class social status. Richard Dalloway is a member of Parliament and Elizabeth considers the possibility of membership in Parliament as a career.

*Whitehall.** Section of London stretching from Trafalgar Square to the Westminster Bridge that gives its name to the area where the Houses of Parliament stand. Downing Street, the official address of the British prime minister, is off Whitehall, as are many government offices. In the 1920's, Whitehall was associated with war and government. In Whitehall, Peter Walsh is overtaken by a parade of boys marching to lay a wreath at the Cenotaph, a World War I memorial erected in 1920. Septimus Smith, a soldier, encounters the glory of war heroes' statues and government sites, and questions the patriotism and nationalism that promoted the death and destruction of World War I. Ultimately Walsh's musings and Smith's devastating reflections contrast with the privileged existence of Clarissa.

***Bourton-on-the-Water.** Gloucestershire town in the heart of the Cotswolds, west of London, close to the River Windrush, Bourton epitomizes country living; its quaint village atmosphere exudes luxury of the upper middle class. The fact that Clarissa's family home is located here suggests expectations for her future in the upper class. Throughout the novel Clarissa recalls a summer at Bourton more than thirty years earlier, during which she decided not to marry Peter Walsh and shared confidences with Sally Seton. The freedom of youth at Bourton is contrasted with the social protocols of adult society in London.

***Regent's Park.** Large London park with gently undulating hills with a steep rise in the north from which Westminster and the city can be viewed. Predominantly open parkland with numerous benches, it is a place of rest and relaxation for all Londoners. Regent's Park reinforces the novel's theme of creating harmony amid diversity; it provides a place where all the social classes come together: Septimus and Reiza Smith, Maisie Johnson, Mrs. Dempster, an elderly nurse, children, and Peter Walsh. This park is also the location where Septimus

Smith hallucinates about his witnessing the death of a friend in battle. The contrast between the idyllic setting and the horrors of war symbolizes the conflicted position of British society at this time.

***Big Ben.** Great bell in a Westminster clock tower that is one of London's best-known landmarks. Big Ben acts as an organizing device as it chimes throughout *Mrs. Dalloway* signaling the passing of time. Bloomsbury, the neighborhood where Septimus and Reiza Smith live, where Dr. Holmes's office is located, and where Peter Walsh stays at Bedford Place, is associated with artists, intellectuals, and a bohemian lifestyle. The British Museum, London University, and the Slade School of Art are located in the Bloomsbury area.

***St. Paul's Cathedral.** Late seventeenth century church that is mentioned as a hallowed place in London. Its historical value rests in its being the first English cathedral built after the creation of the Church of England in 1534. It is not merely a religious site but also the site of numerous tombs and memorials that speak of heroism and bravery and the tragedy of war. Elizabeth Dalloway ventures by bus, then on foot, toward the cathedral after tea with Miss Kilman. Though she never makes it to the cathedral, she is drawn to it, feeling that it will provide a sense of direction in her life.

— *Kathryn N. Benzel*

MUCH ADO ABOUT NOTHING

Author: William Shakespeare (1564-1616)
Type of work: Drama
Type of plot: Comedy

Time of plot: Thirteenth century
First performed: c. 1598-1599; first published, 1600

The primary setting for this play is the house and gardens of Leonato, governor of the Sicilian port city of Messina. Because of its great distance from William Shakespeare's English audiences, Messina provided a suitable venue for satirizing the manners of the English aristocracy. Tales of the opulence of Italian life circulated throughout sixteenth century Europe, giving Shakespeare the opportunity, without impunity, to ridicule the behavior of the English court by replacing its equivalent with Italian characters.

Leonato's house. Home of Leonato, the governor of Messina on the island of Sicily, which during the thirteenth century in which the play is set was an important European cultural center. The governor would have had

rooms enough in his house lavishly to entertain and host nobles from the artistic and intellectual Italian cities of Florence and Padua, as well as the one of the most powerful independent kingdoms in medieval Spain, Aragon.

Although most of the governor's guests are Italians, they are regarded as foreigners in Messina, and as such, are easily duped.

The grounds around the house contain an elaborate orchard described in act 1, scene 2, as having a "thick-pleached alley" or an arched walkway lined with trees whose boughs are interwoven. The thickness of the boughs would hide anyone who wanted to overhear a conversation; in this way, Shakespeare could present secrecy and comedic intrigue.

— *Ginger Jones*

MUMBO JUMBO

Author: Ishmael Reed (1938-   )
Type of work: Novel
Type of plot: Satire

Time of plot: 1920's
First published: 1972

This postmodern novel is set immediately after World War I, from which America has emerged as a world power. What kind of power it will become remains to be seen. Meanwhile, a battle is going on for the soul of the nation. As the country rushes into a high-tech age, a countermovement is beginning to sweep through the country as ancient longings of the soul and spirit cry out for satisfaction. These longings are manifesting themselves in New Orleans, Harlem, and elsewhere in jazz music, a small part of the HooDoo movement. Protagonist Papa LaBas seeks to recover the sacred text of HooDooism before the Neo-Atonists in Washington, D.C., can destroy it.

*Harlem. District of New York City at the north end of New York City's Manhattan Island. Harlem has long been known as a center of African American culture, but at the time in which the novel is set, most of New York's African American residents are living to the south in Lower Manhattan. However, Harlem's black population is steadily increasing and white residents are moving out. Meanwhile, the influx of newcomers to New York is creating a rich cultural mix, one of the most outstanding manifestations of which is music. Clustered between Harlem's 125th and 135th Streets and between Lennox and Seventh Avenues are clubs in which New Orleans Dixieland music is evolving into jazz.

*New Orleans. Louisiana's largest city, in which the African musical heritage of the region's former slaves has developed into what becomes known as Dixieland jazz, a uniquely American form based upon the melodic lines and tempos of African American funeral processions and parades. New Orleans is the principal setting of *Mumbo Jumbo* and an important venue throughout Ishmael Reed's fiction, poetry, and essays. Reed is concerned with the African American tradition of the supernatural known as "HooDoo," and New Orleans is its home. There, what appears to white people to be the devil's work is in effect something else. There and elsewhere HooDoo steps aside a white, Anglo-Saxon, Christian tradition and looks to a different set of deities predating Christianity, extending back at least as far as the African god Osiris and the Atonists. With its wellsprings in New Orleans, HooDoo is a movement that recognizes that America is on a path that will turn it into a spiritual wasteland, and the movement means to turn that around.

*Washington, D.C. As the capital of the United States of America, Washington is virtually synonymous with the federal government. The land on which it is built was initially ground held sacred by local Native Americans. Building the young nation's capital was an undertaking of gargantuan proportions that needed cheap labor. One advantage of its location is that it was set between Maryland and Virginia—states with large numbers of slaves. Thus, Washington has at its historical heart the dominance of powerful white men over people of color. Reed picks up on this in *Mumbo Jumbo*, which associates the city with Reed's version of the military-industrial complex and the Neo-Atonists, the Bokors. These forces can only remain in power if they can destroy the sacred text of HooDoo, thereby limiting its spread to the masses. The competition to control the sacred text drives the novel's complex plot.

— *Jay Boyer*

MURDER IN THE CATHEDRAL

Author: T. S. Eliot (1888-1965)
Type of work: Drama
Type of plot: Historical

Time of plot: 1170
First performed: 1935; first published, 1935

Cathedrals are generally considered places for communion and worship. However, in this play—which is based on the assassination of Archbishop Thomas à Becket in 1170—England's Canterbury Cathedral becomes a place of temptation, murder, and rationalization. The cathedral here is essentially a place of conflict. Worldly power in the form of King Henry II's knights pits itself against God's power manifested through the church and its archbishop.

*Canterbury Cathedral. Church in southeast England that was the seat of the archbishop of Canterbury and the center of Roman Catholic power in England during the period in which T. S. Eliot's play is set. In the play, the cathedral quickly becomes a place of temptation. Each of four tempters offers Becket a course of action supposedly intended to save his life. In his resistance the cathedral is shown to be a place of anxiety and confrontation. However, in the process it also becomes a place of strength. Becket's rejection of the tempters' invitations underscores an important Eliot theme: Religion's place in the world is not to secure for its adherents automatic safety, but faith gives direction for decisive action.

In the second part of the play the theme of the cathedral as a place of violence is intensified. Becket's priests try to protect him from the murderous knights. His instructions to them to open the doors and not make the cathedral into a fortress constitutes a key Eliot theme about the role of place. Even after violence enters the house of prayer, Becket will not allow the barring of the doors. The unbarred doors allow the knights to enter and kill him, but his martyrdom shows that the cathedral is not simply a place of sanctuary, but also a place where one may suffer for the good of all.

After the assassination, each of the four knights attempts to justify the murder of Thomas Becket. Their rationalizations make the cathedral a place where, finally, the audience must bear the burden of the world's false attempts at justification of its power against faith in God.

— *Scott Samuelson*

MUTINY ON THE BOUNTY

Authors: Charles Nordhoff (1887-1947) and James Norman Hall (1887-1951)
Type of work: Novel

Type of plot: Adventure
Time of plot: 1787-1792
First published: 1932

A fictionalized account of the ill-fated historical voyage of the British naval vessel Bounty *into the South Seas to collect breadfruit trees for planting in the West Indies in the late eighteenth century, this novel uses far-ranging settings to test the human limits of justice, tolerance, and decency.*

*Withycombe. Village in western England's Somerset district that is the ancestral home of Roger Byam, the novel's fictional narrator. Writing from Withycombe at age seventy-three, Byam recounts his initiation to life at sea when he was a midshipman on HMS *Bounty* in the late 1780's.

*Spithead. British naval base near southern England's Portsmouth Harbour, where Byam reports for duty aboard the *Bounty* in 1787. While the ship's sailing is delayed for a month, Byam becomes acquainted with his shipmates and gets his first taste of the severity of naval discipline when he witnesses a sailor being flogged

around the fleet—an incident that foreshadows Captain William Bligh's severe treatment of the *Bounty*'s crew.

*HMS *Bounty*. Historical British warship about half of whose crewmen mutinied on April 28, 1789. With a length of only ninety feet and a displacement of only 215 tons, the *Bounty* was a cramped vessel for the long mission on which it was sent, and the special provisions made to accommodate the breadfruit plants make conditions for the crew even worse. After the ship goes to sea, Captain Bligh places the men on short, often inedible, rations, has both seamen and officers flogged, and is suspected of stealing from the ship's stores himself for his own profit. Meanwhile, a rift develops between Bligh and Fletcher Christian, his second-in-command. After suffering the rigors of a long and exhausting voyage, as well as Bligh's discipline, the crewmen enjoy a long respite on Tahiti—a tropical paradise whose conditions are polar opposites of those aboard the *Bounty*. However, after the ship departs from the island, Bligh returns to his former autocratic self and even confiscates gifts his men received on Tahiti. After First Mate Christian leads the mutiny, he takes command of the ship and becomes as autocratic as Bligh. Not being one of the mutineers, the narrator Byam is a among a handful of men whom the mutineers return to Tahiti. The later fate of the *Bounty* is related by a different narrator in the authors' sequel to this novel, *Pitcairn's Island* (1934).

*Tenerriffe. Main port in the Canary Islands, about one hundred miles off the west coast of Africa, where the *Bounty* stops during its outward voyage. Byam notes that the seeds of discontent that are destined to ruin the voyage are sown here.

*Cape Horn. Southern tip of South America, where the *Bounty* spends thirty days battling gale-force winds and freezing weather, trying unsuccessfully to cross from the Atlantic to the Pacific Ocean. After the seams of the ship nearly give way, Bligh charts a new course for the Cape of Good Hope, to reach Tahiti on an easterly course.

*Cape of Good Hope. Headland on the peninsula separating the waters of the Atlantic from those of the Indian Ocean on the southwest coast of South Africa. The *Bounty* spends thirty-eight days in False Bay, near the cape, having its keel caulked and the damage that its sails and rigging sustained at Cape Horn repaired. From there, the ship sails across the Indian Ocean to Tahiti.

*Tahiti. Largest island of the Windward group of Society Islands in the central South Pacific. The *Bounty* reaches Tahiti after having sailed over 27,000 miles during ten months at sea.

For the next six months, its crewmen collect and prepare for transport about one thousand young breadfruit plants. Meanwhile, many crewmen develop amorous relationships with Tahitian women and become spoiled by the island's easy living and exotic pleasures. Byam describes Tahiti as a "Mohammedan paradise," on which the British sailors enjoy physical leisure, abundant fresh food, and compliant women. The warmth, beauty, and sensuality of Tahiti make the British seamen resent their miserable existence aboard the *Bounty* enough for many of them to mutiny.

After the mutiny, Byam is among the loyal crewmen whom the mutineers return to Tahiti, where he marries a local woman and has a daughter. After another British ship forcibly returns him to England, he returns to Tahiti for a final time in 1810, as the captain of his own ship, and finds that the island has been ravaged by war and disease. His wife is dead, and he cannot make himself known to his daughter, so he leaves Tahiti without telling her that he is her father. To him, the beautiful green island is a place filled with ghosts of younger men, and his younger self is one of them.

*HMS *Pandora*. British frigate on which Byam and the other British sailors left on Tahiti are returned to England. Byam and the other loyal officers are treated like criminals on the voyage and suffer unspeakable cruelties. When the ship sinks after striking a reef in the Great Barrier Reef, the *Pandora*'s captain delays releasing the prisoners from their irons until the last possible moment, an act that costs the life of Byam's friend Stewart, who drowns. The captain, Byam, and other survivors patch together three boats and head for distant Timor. Byam eventually reaches England, where he is condemned to be hanged for mutiny but is exonerated at the last minute.

*Tupai. Small island in the Leeward group of Society Islands on which Christian and the other mutineers attempt to establish a settlement. After constantly fending off attacks from islanders, they abandon Tupai to search for an uninhabited island.

— *Joe Nordgren*

MY ÁNTONIA

Author: Willa Cather (1873-1947)
Type of work: Novel
Type of plot: Regional

Time of plot: Late nineteenth and early twentieth centuries
First published: 1918

Few works evoke the vast American prairie as stunningly as this novel by Willa Cather, who finds it a source of strength among the people who work it and a source of disappointment and alienation for those who abandon it.

Burden farm. Ranch in pioneer Nebraska owned by Jim Burden's grandparents. It is to this farm that the ten-year-old Jim Burden is brought from Virginia after his parents die, and it is here that he learns to love the prairie. It is also here that he meets the Shimerdas, a Bohemian family (immigrants from Bohemia) who are distant neighbors struggling to survive in this harsh new land.

Shimerda home. Sod cave, built into a hillside, that is home to Ántonia and her family. The Burdens help out their Bohemian neighbors, who live in isolation and deprivation in their first year in America. The Shimerdas survive the brutal winter, but the father, homesick for the old country, kills himself. When the church refuses to bury Mr. Shimerda in the cemetery, he is laid to rest in a corner of his property. In the spring, the Shimerdas build a log house, and through hard work and economy begin to make their farm prosper.

Black Hawk. Small town that is the center of this farming region (probably based on Red Cloud, Nebraska, where Cather grew up). When the farm gets too much for them, the Burdens rent it out and buy a house in town, where Jim can start school. Ántonia also moves to town to work for the people who live next door to the Burdens. Jim feels a loss of freedom in the move from the prairie to Black Hawk and becomes "moody and restless," but life is made better by the presence of Ántonia and the other "hired girls" (immigrants from Europe like Ántonia) who work in town. Certainly, Cather shows, they have an energy and love for life missing in many of their neighbors. At the town dances, it is Ántonia and her friends who show the most spirit. Jim graduates from high school, dedicating his commencement oration to Ántonia's father.

*Lincoln. Nebraska's state capital, largest city, and home to the university where Jim starts his separation from his family and the prairie life. After succeeding at the university, he goes on to Harvard Law School. Jim hears about Ántonia and her family during his years away but visits her only once before starting his legal career.

*New York City. Center of American financial and cultural life by the end of the nineteenth century. Jim becomes a lawyer for the railroads in New York and marries. It is clear from Cather's fictional introduction to *My Ántonia*, however, that his marriage is loveless and produces no children. In the greatest city in the country, he has lost something of what he had as a young man growing up with Ántonia on the American prairie.

Cuzak farm. Farm where Ántonia, her husband, and their many children live. In the last scene of the novel, Jim visits this farm years later and discovers the richness and happiness of immigrant life on the prairie. Ántonia has aged, but she has "not lost the fire of life." With Ántonia and her family, Jim feels at home again, and the novel has circled back to the prairie. It is the land, Cather implies, and the immigrants who bring their dreams and energy to it, which sustains this country. Jim Burden no longer shares either the dreams or the land, but he personally understands the prairie's power and the heroism of people like "my Ántonia."

— David Peck

MY BRILLIANT CAREER

Author: Miles Franklin (1879-1954)
Type of work: Novel
Type of plot: Psychological realism

Time of plot: 1890's
First published: 1901

Considered to be uniquely Australian in tone and style, this novel effectively uses various Australian settings to represent the economic and social strata through which Sybylla Melvyn, the protagonist and narrator, moves during this story. Although the author publicly discouraged readers from interpreting this novel as biographical, it is nonetheless clear that the settings are strongly rooted in the places of her girlhood.

Caddagat. Name of the homestead belonging to Sybylla's grandmother, near the fictional town of **Gool-Gool** in Australia's New South Wales state. Modeled on Talbingo, the home of Miles Franklin's grandmother. Caddagat exemplifies everything that Sybylla loves in life: art, music, literature, education, and congenial companionship. Sybylla relates that she was born in this house and that her earliest and fondest memories lie within. At sixteen, Sybylla rejoices when her grandmother invites her to live at Caddagat for a while, because Caddagat represents a respite from the constant drudgery of hard work that Sybylla performs while her father squanders money on bad stock market investments and alcohol.

Initially, Sybylla expects to be treated as an unwelcome poor relation, but she is immediately installed in a small, pretty bedroom of her own and made the pet of the household, which includes her sympathetic Aunt Helen. Much description is given to the details of Caddagat's physical environment, including books, artwork, and comfortable furnishings, all of which reassure Sybylla that she is no longer entrapped by the mean poverty of her parents' home.

The land surrounding Caddagat similarly provides Sybylla with a soothing environment; it is not only beautiful, but also capable of supporting the horses and livestock indispensable to life in the Australian Bush. Sybylla is easily accepted into the circle of gracious and genteel friends on neighboring stations, and, most important, she finds at Caddagat the type of mentally stimulating environment that she craves.

Barney's Gap. Small homestead near the fictional town of **Yarung**, New South Wales. Barney's Gap clearly symbolizes the opposite of everything that Caddagat means to Sybylla. Her pleasant stay with her grandmother is cut short when her father arranges for her to work as a servant and governess in order to pay the interest on a loan on which he would otherwise default. Sybylla dreads leaving Caddagat, and Barney's Gap is every bit as horrible as she expects, with no music or literature and nobody with whom to discuss such subjects. The house is filthy and the M'Swat children slovenly and uneducated. Sybylla cannot abide the sheer dirtiness of her surroundings, yet Barney's Gap seems less intended to represent abject poverty than the dangers of intellectual starvation—indeed, Sybylla falls into such despair that she becomes ill and is finally sent back to her parents' home.

Possum Gully. One-thousand-acre farm near the fictional town of **Goulburn**, New South Wales. This location provides a comparative framework for the novel. When the book opens, Sybylla is about to move to Possum Gully at age nine with her parents and siblings, and she returns there from Barney's Gap at the end of the novel. Figuratively, Possum Gully lies somewhere between the easy luxury of Caddagat and the mean, dirty ignorance of Barney's Gap. Sybylla does not find life at Possum Gully as terrible as that at Barney's Gap, but the dairy farming, which her family has been forced to take up, consists of hard physical labor with little reward. Upon first arriving, Sybylla observes that the flat, monotonous landscape seems dreary after the mountains near her first childhood home. Similarly, Goulburn is socially barren because most of the young people leave for better prospects elsewhere as soon as they are able. Just before Sybylla leaves for Caddagat to stay with her grandmother, a severe drought renders the landscape even more desolate.

Bruggabrong. Large cattle station leased by Sybylla's father before he moves to Possum Gully. With its fellow stations, Bin-Bin East and Bin-Bin West, Bruggabrong totals nearly 200,000 acres among the Timlinbilly Ranges in New South Wales, representing the vastness of Australian stations, or ranches. Sybylla remembers her early years at Bruggabrong as a prosperous and happy time.

— *Amy Sisson*

MY NAME IS ASHER LEV

Author: Chaim Potok (1929-   )
Type of work: Novel
Type of plot: Domestic realism

Time of plot: Mid-twentieth century
First published: 1972

This novel begins and ends in a Jewish community in Brooklyn, New York, a setting that serves as the reference point for the title character's journey from childhood in a Ladover Hasidic community to his eventual expulsion from this home as he comes to terms with his gifts as an artist that are not fully accepted by his religious community.

*Brooklyn. New York City borough in whose Crown Heights neighborhood Asher Lev and his family live. Asher's home is a small, two-bedroom apartment not far from Brooklyn Parkway and a collection of Jewish establishments. A block and a half from this home stands the three-story, Gothic-style building in which his father, Reb Aryeh Lev, works for the Ladover headquarters of his Hasidic community. From this place the Rebbe, or spiritual leader of the community, sends Reb Aryeh Lev on journeys across the country and to Europe.

The Jewish community in which Asher grows up is populated with a jewelry shop owned by Asher's Uncle Yitzchok Lev, Reb Yudel Krinsky's stationery store where Asher buys art supplies and learns about persecution of the Jews in Russia, a yeshiva where Asher attends school, and a synagogue where the family worships. This part of Brooklyn is filled with the people whom Asher first learns to draw and admire. In this place his talents begin to emerge, and he feels his future is tied to this community. When given the opportunity to travel to Vienna with his parents, ten-year-old Asher fights to stay in Brooklyn, where he knows the parks and people.

While his father is away, Asher's mother takes him to the Parkway Museum for the first time. There, he learns about painting and also encounters scenes depicting the crucifixion of Christ. Although Asher is cautioned by his father against looking at such paintings, he sees in these crucifixion themes a curious portrayal of profound suffering and love, a theme Asher ultimately incorporates into his own painting of his parents and himself.

Lev home. Because Asher's mother, Rivkeh Lev, loses her brother in an automobile accident while he is traveling for the Rebbe, she is constantly filled with anxiety about her husband's travels and her son's delays in returning from school. She often stands by the window of the small apartment and watches for the return of her family. The window frame around her becomes symbolic of Asher's artistic vision of his mother's anxiety over life. This window figures prominently in what become Asher's crucifixion paintings of his family.

*Manhattan. New York City borough to which Asher Lev goes to study art with Jacob Kahn. By the age of thirteen, Asher is identified by the Rebbe as a young man destined to be a great artist, even though Asher's father cannot accept art as something more than foolishness in his son's life. The Rebbe assigns Asher to Jacob Kahn as a mentor for teaching the young Asher how to develop his gifts. Kahn's studio is on the fifth floor of an Upper Manhattan loft building with an excellent skylight and serves as a meeting place for learning art, as well as arranging shows through Anna Schaeffer, Kahn's sponsor and art agent. There, Asher is initiated into the world of modern art, especially abstract expressionism, and the painting of nudes, which his father has taught him to shun. Asher's first show is given at Anna

Schaeffer's gallery on Manhattan's Madison Avenue, and he learns to deal with the highly varied criticisms of newspaper reviewers.

*Provincetown. Massachusetts coastal town in Cape Cod to which Jacob Kahn takes Asher to stay in a beach cottage during several summers. There, the two artists study light and sand and paint. Asher comes to understand the light as seen by Edward Hopper, Paul Cézanne, and other great artists. Kahn also introduces Asher to a variety of artists in this community that has not yet become a tourist town. In this new setting Asher begins to discover the value of traveling to new places to improve his ability to see creatively.

*Paris. French capital city in which Asher reaches his maturity as an artist. After a second successful show, Asher travels to Florence, Italy, to develop new ideas. He especially studies Michelangelo's *David* and his Duomo *Pietà*. This *Pietà* profoundly shapes Asher's imagination and later becomes the inspiration for his own crucifixion paintings, which include him and his parents. After a trip to Rome, Asher returns to Paris to continue painting and studying art, not realizing that this city is to become his home after his parents and their Ladover Hasidic community reject his artwork and the Rebbe banishes him from his Brooklyn community.

— *Daven M. Kari*

MYRA BRECKINRIDGE

Author: Gore Vidal (1925-   )
Type of work: Novel
Type of plot: Social realism

Time of plot: 1968
First published: 1968

Drawing on his own experiences in Hollywood during the 1950's and 1960's, when he wrote screenplays for the film industry, Gore Vidal wrote this story of obsession to probe the boundaries of society's sexual tolerance and to present a picture at once both realistic and grotesque of Hollywood and the not-quite-ordinary people who live there.

*Hollywood. Southern California city and capital of the American movie industry that to Myra is important as the place where the "classic" movies of the 1930's and 1940's were made. To her, Hollywood is the source of all the century's legends. However, by the late 1960's—when this story takes place—Hollywood has turned to low-budget movies in order to compete with television and has lost much of the magic Myra associates with it. Along with Hollywood's legendary cachet, Myra looks for, and expects to find there, her inheritance from a relative. To her surprise, she actually does find the kind of "true" love she so enjoys seeing in movies.

Academy of Dramatic Arts. Acting school belonging to Myra's "Uncle" Buck Loner, located on about fifty acres of a Westwood residential property, half of which has been bequeathed to Myra's dead husband, Myron. The academy is a place where young hopefuls go to learn about acting with the expectation that they

will get jobs in movies and even become stars. Myra sees the school as a place that will give her financial security after her husband's mother's will has been properly executed. After she has had a chance to examine the school, it becomes even more significant as a place where she can avenge herself on "men" for the abuses her husband suffered. Buck reaps an excellent income from the academy and is loathe to give even a small share of it to Myra, who believes the school may be worth millions. Activities at the school proceed with little or no disruption, even as Myra does everything in her power to interfere with the lives of two students, Mary-Ann Pringle and Rusty Godowsky, and Uncle Buck.

Academy infirmary. Clinic on the academy campus; a small, antiseptic, white room with cabinets full of drugs and instruments, an examination table, scales, and other instruments for measuring height and body width. An orderly place, it is an odd scene for Myra's ruthless emasculation of the young man Rusty. Yet it is exactly because it is the school infirmary that Myra can get the young man to be alone with her.

Myra's room. Furnished room above the Hollywood Strip that is Myra's first residence after her arrival in Hollywood. During one of his own stays in Hollywood, Gore Vidal lived in a room in the Château Marmont and could see a rotating statue of a woman with a sombrero from his window. Myra's room provides a similar view of the revolving "plastic chorus girl" with a sombrero in one hand. This room seems to hold a special significance for Myra as she looks out over the Strip and other Hollywood sights that remind her of the classic "old" Hollywood. However, the room takes on another significance when a distraught Mary-Ann finds sanctuary there with Myra after her affair with Rusty falls apart.

Letitia's home. Beach house in Malibu, an arty, upscale community in the coastal region northwest of Los Angeles that runs along Pacific Coast Highway. The home of Hollywood agent Letitia Van Allen, it is a gray clapboard Provincetown-style house. During one of Vidal's Hollywood sojourns, he lived in a similar beach house off the same highway. Although Letitia's beach house is not a major setting in Vidal's novel, it figures into the story as part of Myra's plot to break up the affair between Rusty and Mary-Ann.

Uncle Buck's office. Richly appointed office at the Academy of Dramatic Arts. Myra and Buck have interesting encounters in this room, which Myra believes is electronically bugged, like everyplace else in Hollywood. Buck feels in control within his sumptuous office, but he rarely gets the upper hand with Myra. This is the one place where Buck and Myra skirmish as Buck seeks to retain total control of the administration and the money of the academy, and Myra shoots him down each time. It is here where Buck finally capitulates and hands over the money for Myra's inherited share of the property.

— *Jane L. Ball*

THE MYSTERIES OF PARIS

Author: Eugène Sue (1804-1857)
Type of work: Novel
Type of plot: Melodrama

Time of plot: 1838-1841
First published: Les Mystères de Paris, 1842-1843
(English translation, 1843)

This novel established an important template for romans feuilletons *(novels serialized in Parisian newspapers), distributing its plot across a "cross section" of France's capital city, drawing connections between its richest houses and its meanest districts, its places of business and its prisons.*

***Paris.** Capital of France. In the worldview of the* roman feuilleton, *Paris is not a* city but rather *the* city—the archetype of modern civilization. As well as providing a rich spectrum of individual settings for the plot, Paris is, in a sense, the main character in the story: both a human hive buzzing with progressive industry and a cauldron of corruption in which civilization is coming to the boil.

Mint. Network of narrow streets, profusely supplied with dens of vice, distributed between the Palais de Justice and Notre Dame Cathedral (the principal landmark of Paris-set popular fiction, thanks to Victor Hugo). It is here, in the "White Rabbit" in the rue aux Fèves, that

Eugène Sue's story begins with the symbolic meeting of several not-so-distinct worlds, represented by various exemplary characters whose fates are inextricably entangled. The heavy irony which Sue deploys in naming his characters (such as La Chouette—the Screech-Owl—and the Schoolmaster), drinking-dens featured (such as the Bleeding Heart and the Dredger's Arms), and imaginary streets (such as the Allée des Veuves—Widows' Alley—and Brasserie Passage) echoes a tacit irony in certain real Parisian place-names, which he gleefully appropriates, especially the Champs Élysées [Elysian Fields].

Bouqueval (bew-kay-val). Village outside Paris, east of the woodlands surrounding the Château Ecouen. It functions within Sue's scheme as the great city's humble antithesis, a kind of rustic paradise. It is the site of the farm in which Rudolph establishes La Goualeuse after removing her from the power of the Ogress.

Faubourg Saint-Germain (foh-bur san zhur-mayn). Prosperous Parisian suburb (now the heart of the Left Bank), where Rudolph's mansion is located at the junction of the rue Plumet and the boulevard des Invalides. It is here that Rudolph lives the other half of his double life, dealing with aristocrats and diplomats. The Lucenays' town house is not far away. The most prestigious residences, however, are on the other side of the river, in the city itself. The d'Harville town house, where Clémence lives surrounded by splendid décor and fine works of art, is in the rue Saint-Dominique, at the corner of the rue Belle Chasse. Viscount Saint-Rémy lives in the rue de Chaillot, close to the Champs Élysées.

Temple. Enormous marketplace—Sue terms it a bazaar—in the heart of the commercial district of Paris. It is in the rue du Temple that Rudolph acquires another home-away-from-home while searching for clues as to the whereabouts of François Germain. The house is home to the honest and industrious Mademoiselle Dimpleton and the unfortunate Morels, and it yields abundant evidence of visitors from higher and lower social strata, who have employed it as intermediate ground. The rue du Sentier, the location of the house of the crooked lawyer Jacques Ferrand, is not far away.

Saint Lazare (san lah-zahr). Women's prison situated in the rue de Faubourg Saint Denis, which Clémence visits for charitable purposes, and where La Goualeuse is confined. The boulevard Saint Denis, where Germain resides before his imprisonment, is in the same neighborhood.

La Force. Nickname of the Conciergerie, the principal prison of Paris, where Germain is confined. Along with Saint Lazare, La Force figures prominently in the social protest element of Sue's novel, which indicts the entire criminal justice system on the grounds of inefficiency and ineffectiveness. La Force is also the setting of a remarkable essay on the narrative politics of popular fiction surrounding the suspenseful story with which Pique-Vinaigre must distract his fellow inmates, in order to save Germain from assassination.

Gerolstein. Grand Duchy to which Rudolph is heir: an imaginary element of the Germanic Confederation (Germany was not yet a nation-state in the early nineteenth century, and most of its fragments retained strong links with Paris by virtue of having been temporarily integrated into Napoleon Bonaparte's short-lived empire). Rudolph met Sarah there before departing for Paris filled with romantic notions, and he returns there at the end of the story, accompanied by his long-lost daughter.

— *Brian Stableford*

THE MYSTERIES OF UDOLPHO

Author: Ann Radcliffe (1764-1823)
Type of work: Novel
Type of plot: Gothic

Time of plot: 1584
First published: 1794

In a tale whose settings are often outward expressions of the moral character of persons associated with them, virtuous heroine Emily St. Aubert is forced by her evil guardian Montoni to move from her beloved home in the French countryside to the gloomy Gothic castle Udolpho, where her life and fortunes seem constantly imperiled by mortal and possibly supernatural dangers.

La Vallee (lah vah-YAY). Château in the Languedoc region of France, home to the St. Aubert family. The château is part of a larger family estate which, since childhood, has held fondly nostalgic associations for Monsieur St. Aubert. Once a cottage, the château has been renovated and expanded to harmonize with the surrounding rural landscape. The interior is furnished in "chaste simplicity," with simple furniture and a library filled with good books. Its attached greenhouse supports St. Aubert's interest in botany and bespeaks his sympathy with nature. Ann Radcliffe portrays the château as a place of comfort, tranquillity, and spiritual fulfillment.

La Vallee is a physical symbol of the domestic virtues practiced by the St. Aubert family. Its ideal character as a pastoral retreat is emphasized by its contrast with the adjoining estate, which St. Aubert sold to Monsieur Quesnel to settle his father's debts. Quesnel prefers the city life of Paris to life in the country, and his proposed extravagant renovations, which will entail destroying the natural beauty of the grounds and planting foliage incongruously out of step with the setting, affirm the insensitivity of those not attuned to nature.

For Emily St. Aubert, La Vallee is a reservoir for memories of the last happy days spent with her family. The château symbolizes an innocence that is threatened when her guardian, the villainous Count Montoni, schemes to sell it and pay off his debts.

*Languedoc (lang-gah-DAHK). Mostly wild region in southern France, favored by St. Aubert and Emily. Its vivid colors and breathtaking vistas give rise to spiritual thoughts and veneration of the Great Creator by those sensitive to its sublime beauty. Throughout the novel, Radcliffe contrasts the wholesomeness of this natural world with the artifice of the city and human-made dwellings, most notably the castle Udolpho. Places that look upon the landscape, such as La Vallee and the Château-le-Blanc, are portrayed as serene and free. People who prefer the city to its natural splendor are depicted as insincere and superficial. In this setting Emily enjoys her final moments with her father and meets Valancourt, who proves to be her savior.

Udolpho (oo-DOHLF-oh). Castle in the Apennine Mountains to which Montoni moves Emily, her aunt, and the rest of his entourage following their brief sojourn in Venice. Emily first glimpses it as a "gloomy and sublime object" that seems to absorb ambient light and plunge the surrounding woods into darkness. That gloom is so intense that Emily can only discern parts of the castle in outline, as though Udolpho is partly made of shadow. The castle's immense dimensions suggest great strength, but are more grotesque than reassuring. Parts of the castle are in disrepair, hinting at a former glory that is long past. Udolpho was once a formidable fortress, but the evil Montoni exploits its remoteness and inaccessibility to protect his band of marauding condottieri.

Aging castles and buildings are common props in gothic fiction, and Udolpho is among the most famous because it magnificently manifests the spirit of menace associated with the literature. The castle is poorly illuminated, and Radcliffe describes its gloom as a contagion capable of infecting those who stay there. In contrast to the interior furnishings of La Vallee, which are minimal yet suited to the simple tastes of its residents, the furnishings of Udolpho are austere and suggest an absence of basic comforts. Hallways that trail off into darkness and illusions of both sound and sight, created by the castle's vast interior, all contribute to its aura of supernatural peril. Above all, Udolpho conveys a sense of entrapment and imprisonment. Emily's removal to the castle is tantamount to an abduction, and Montoni does not allow her to leave its premises. Each night, she is locked in a bedroom set apart from other rooms in the castle.

Typical of gothic fiction, the castle serves as a physical manifestation of the states of mind of its inhabitants. The deterioration of parts of Udolpho and reclamation of some of its grounds by the wild natural world express the moral decline of its owner, Montoni, a nobleman who indulges in thievery and murder. The secret passages that honeycomb the walls of its rooms are as tortuous and labyrinthine as Montoni's evil schemes. Emily sees a grim portent of her own fate in a legend associated with the castle: Udolpho is supposedly haunted by the ghost of its former owner, a woman who refused to acquiesce to Montoni's will.

— *Stefan Dziemianowicz*

THE MYSTERIOUS ISLAND

Author: Jules Verne (1828-1905)
Type of work: Novel
Type of plot: Adventure

Time of plot: 1865-1869
First published: L'Île mystérieuse, 1874-1875 (English translation, 1875)

The impact on human characters who are cast away on isolated islands is a familiar theme in world literature. This novel, a loose sequel to Jules Verne's Twenty Thousand Leagues Under the Sea *(1870), explores how five resourceful Americans stranded on a Pacific island use technology to transform it from a wilderness to a garden.*

*Richmond. Virginia capital of the Confederate States of America during the Civil War at the time this novel is set. Although Verne was fond of the United States, he never visited it. His creation of American places, such as Richmond, is based entirely on his reading and imagination. This adventure starts during the last days of the Civil War. The idea of place as prison is encountered in the novel's initial location, Richmond, shortly before the South surrendered to the North to end the war. Under siege when the novel opens, Richmond becomes a Confederate "island" inside a Yankee ocean. Within the rebel island are five Northern prisoners who escape to begin their adventure.

Balloon. Hijacked Confederate balloon that the escaping Northern prisoners use to get out of Richmond. The unfamiliar balloon craft becomes as real a prison to the Northerners as Richmond was, for they are caught for five days in the worst hurricane of the century, which carries them across North America and the Pacific Ocean.

Lincoln Island. Uninhabited island in the Pacific Ocean on which the escaping Northerners' balloon lands. There, they become castaways on a deserted island and are once again prisoners. Trapped without much hope of rescue, they determine to make the place a "Little America" and transform it through Yankee ingenuity and technology. They christen the island "Lincoln" in honor of Abraham Lincoln, president of the United States through the Civil War. Their choice of names is ironic, as Lincoln was known as the Great Liberator.

Verne, who loved history as much as geography, watches the five castaways transform a wilderness into a near-paradise, replicating in a short period the entire spectrum of human cultural evolution, starting with the domestication of animals, the introduction of agriculture, the invention of pottery, the development of tex-

tiles, and invention of stone tools. Eventually, the castaways find iron, pyrite, coal, clay, and lime, and create a "tiny Pittsburgh." Steel supplements wood and stone for tools and weapons. A steam engine augments the wind and water power and the muscle power of animals and humans. The men build machinery and even install a telegraph line. Comfort and security characterize Granite House, a home in a cave on the side of a steep cliff. Verne suggests that earth, like Lincoln Island, is a place of profound ambiguity—ripe with opportunity and rife with danger.

Nautilus. Submarine under the command of Captain Nemo (previously introduced in *Twenty Thousand Leagues Under the Sea*), who rescues the castaways from the island. Some 232 feet long and 26 feet wide, the submarine is a composite product of the world's highest technology—its keel is from France, its shaft from London, its iron plates from Liverpool, its screws from Glasgow, and its engine from Prussia. This "Anonymous Giant" embodies for Verne both the positive and negative sides of science in its mission to free humanity from physical oppression. The profound ambiguity of Earth and its species is revealed in the self-willed destruction of the *Nautilus*, in the nature-caused annihilation of the colonists' own escape ship. The survivors are later rescued by a U.S. naval ship.

*Iowa. Midwestern state in which the castaways settle after returning to the United States. Verne's fascination with the American West, evident in *Around the World in Eighty Days* (1873), surfaces in his conclusion to this novel. Iowa becomes for the castaways both an escape and an opportunity for a new life in a new land. Symbolically it, like the entire West in the American mythos, is a place of new beginnings—the note on which Verne concludes his novel.

— *C. George Fry*

THE MYSTERY OF EDWIN DROOD

Author: Charles Dickens (1812-1870)
Type of work: Novel
Type of plot: Detective and mystery

Time of plot: Mid-nineteenth century
First published: 1870

This unfinished novel, Charles Dickens's last, returns to the locale of his first novel, Pickwick Papers *(1836-1837)—the English cathedral town of Rochester. However, unlike the bright Rochester depicted in that first novel, the Rochester in* The Mystery of Edwin Drood *is called Cloisterham, and it is a dark and brooding place, overhung by secrets, death, and deception. Appearances deceive, duplicity is rampant, and death is imminent.*

Cloisterham. Fictional cathedral town in southern England in which the novel is primarily set. The orphaned young Edwin Drood's work as an apprentice engineer takes him all over the world, but he returns to Cloisterham at every opportunity to see his fiancé, Rosa Bud, also an orphan, who is attending a finishing school in Cloisterham, and his guardian and uncle, Jasper, who is the novel's central figure. Dark themes of death, violence, and obsession pervade the novel, and the town's cathedral is a forbidding and relentless presence that foreshadows the end of life—just as Dickens was prematurely coming to the end of his own life as he was writing this book. Dickens contrasts the setting of a cathedral town with the vastly different setting of London's East End opium dens to point up the moral lassitude of Uncle Jasper—a choirmaster who is addicted to opium, obsessed with Rosa, and the probable murderer of Edwin.

The past betrays the present: All the dead in the cathedral's crypt are part of the chain tying the orphans to each other. The fact that the last wishes of Edwin's and Rosa's dead fathers was that their children should marry each other gives Jasper a motive to get rid of his nephew to clear the way for himself with Rosa. Ironically, however, he is unaware that Edwin and Rosa have secretly decided to stay friends but not to marry each other.

Even the sacred resting grounds of the monastic orders in the cathedral are used to evil purposes by Jasper, who tours the crypt with the stonemason to learn how bodies decay with quicklime. Nothing is as it seems: Even Christmas, a Dickens scene typically symbolizing new beginnings and great joy, is herein the time when Drood vanishes, in the middle of a Christmas Eve storm.

Dickens modeled Cloisterham on Rochester, near Chatham in Kent, where he lived for five years when he was a child. Cloisterham's cathedral is based on that of Rochester, and its Nuns' House is based on Rochester's East Gate House.

*London. Great Britain's capital city, in which the novel opens, is, for Dickens, often a place demonstrating the ravages of industrialism on the English people, as well as the indifference of societal structures such as the law. In *The Mystery of Edwin Drood*, Dickens's only full-length murder mystery, London shows its evil side by the prevalence of the Eastern curse of opium. However, London is too variegated a place to signify only one evil or one good.

— *Holly Dworken Cooley*

THE NAKED AND THE DEAD

Author: Norman Mailer (1923-   )
Type of work: Novel
Type of plot: Social realism

Time of plot: World War II
First published: 1948

Set on an island in the Pacific Ocean, Norman Mailer's novel recounts a long, difficult, and ultimately failed patrol undertaken by American soldiers in the final months of World War II. General Cummings, who sends the patrol on its mission, expects its commanding officer, Hearn, to be killed and thereby hopes to eliminate a threat to his own career, as he fears that Hearn suspects that he is a homosexual. The distinction between the reasonable and the primal, the rational and the unconscious, is one Mailer employs throughout the novel, focusing attention on Mount Anaka and the jungle out of which it seems to rise.

Anapopei. Imaginary island in the South Pacific on which the novel is set. The island's dense jungle terrain is itself almost a character in the novel—a constant reminder of how primal Nature is when seen in the raw. From the novel's earliest sections, Mailer uses the jungle to remind readers that this is also true of human beings. One of the foot soldiers thinks that the jungle looks like the Garden of Eden, and there is, in some sense, a parallel. However, this is a post-Fall Eden, not Paradise. Anapopei's jungle is primal, a force unto itself, and it stirs some ancient, atavistic recognition in the men who try to survive it.

Another soldier feels a deep excitement, "as if he were witnessing creation"—a feeling that seems to typify the soldiers' reactions to the jungle. Their experience in the jungle is instinctive, pre-verbal, almost visceral in many cases. The experience precedes what the rational mind can codify, what the reasonable mind can articulate.

Not even a mind as reasonable and as fine as that of General Cummings can quite put into words what the jungle means; however, he comes closest. He is obsessed with bringing order to the primal world in which he finds himself, ordering the land cleared and a world

of officers' tents set out in a neat alignment of ninety-degree designs, only to have the clearing overgrown in a few days or to have an unexpected storm play havoc with his plans and labors. The jungle itself seems to be his one unconquerable enemy: Heat licks at everything; foliage grows to prodigious sizes; the jungle is never silent. After a week of fumbling through the jungle, the "military concept of connected lines seemed no more than a concept."

Mount Anaka. Peak on Anapopei that Hearn's platoon is to climb across so that it can attack the enemy position from its rear. The mission is a fool's errand at best, and at worst it is suicidal, as Hearn comes to realize. Nevertheless, he feels compelled to proceed. He feels a primal attraction to the mountain, almost as if it were a woman. He feels a desire to assault the mountain, capture, dominate, and subdue it. However, he also knows that these thoughts are ridiculous.

Sergeant Croft's reaction is not quite so easily harnessed. The jungle and an enemy ambush awaken a dark place in his soul. Killing, being on the brink of being killed, being part of a jungle ecosystem completely beyond the boundaries of anything civilized and ordered arouses in Croft an erotic desire of tangible dimensions.

Croft can not articulate this, not with ease, at least; all he knows is that something primal within him is responding to the jungle itself. He can almost put this into words the first time he sees the mountain through his field glasses:

He feels a thrill of anticipation at the thought that the patrol might be at its peak by the following night. He feels a "crude ecstasy."

— *Jay Boyer*

NAKED LUNCH

Author: William S. Burroughs (1914-1997)
Type of work: Novel
Type of plot: Fantasy

Time of plot: Mid-twentieth century
First published: 1959

Although including references to real places, such as New York and Chicago, William S. Burroughs's novel is a surrealistic interpretation of place that horrifies readers and obliges them to reconsider reality.

*Subway. New York City's subway system is a dirty underground environment where criminals and drug addicts mix with the citizenry. The stairs, turnstiles, platforms, and closing doors of trains afford opportunities for criminals to elude police. One can emerge from the subway in one place and quickly descend into another, catching a train in another direction. In the subway system, especially late at night, hustlers and thieves take advantage of drunks, robbing them after they have passed out; however, in some stations, such as Queens Plaza, a station with various levels, the police cleverly conceal themselves and make criminal activity risky for the criminals. Burroughs makes the subway stand as a metaphor for the wretchedness and corruption of society.

Freeland Republic and **Annexia.** Dr. Benway arrives from Annexia, a quagmire of bureaucratic requirements, where people are constantly stopped and made to validate themselves by presenting documents. Now Benway is an adviser to the Freeland Republic, a place devoted to free love. In Freeland, Benway takes William Lee, the narrator, on a tour of the Reconditioning Center. In Drag Alley, Benway shows Lee victims of Irreversible Neural Damage. One patient has no apparent awareness but does, as a reflex, bark like a dog and salivate when taunted with chocolate. In the next ward, Benway shows Lee drug addicts waiting for their fixes. An iron shutter opens, and responding to a hog call, the addicts receiving their narcotics make the noises of pigs. Next, Benway reveals the ward housing the mild deviants and

criminals. Calling homosexuality a political crime rather than deviancy, Benway remarks that his homosexual patients showed strong unconscious heterosexual drives, while his heterosexual patients showed strong unconscious homosexual drives. Later, as Lee and Benway have lunch, Benway gets a phone message that all the ward subjects have been erroneously released. A horrible general madness occurs, and tourists rush to escape Freeland.

Hassan's rumpus room. This surreal environment combines promiscuity, perversion, excretion, orgasm, torture, and execution. On one hand, the environment seems elegant and luxurious, with people dressed in evening wear. However, a Mugwump sexually abuses and executes a boy. The scene, according to some critics, is a satire of the death penalty.

Interzone. Sometimes simply called "the Zone," the Interzone is a nightmare world. At Interzone University, the classroom is disrupted by animals and carts between the lecture platform and the students, who sit on makeshift seats, consume narcotics, and read comics. The professor arrives on a bicycle and declares that he has severe back pain caused by a sexual attack. The lecture apparently focuses on Samuel Taylor Coleridge's *The Rime of the Ancient Mariner* (1798), but the students draw knives and attack. A train roars through, and the professor appeases the class by filling a trough with pearls and allowing pigs to feed. The political parties of the Interzone include the Divisionists, who produce replicas of themselves and aim at world domination through self-replication. The Liquefactionists, in contrast, seek the eventual merging of everyone into one person. The Senders engage in obligatory outgoing telepathy until exhaustion, followed by conversion into centipedes. Factualists oppose all the groups named above, especially the Senders. The narrator reveals that the Zone is one vast building. Whether drunk or not, people regularly fall unconscious. People are forced through walls from one bed to another; all business is conducted in bed. Opposite the Zone is the Island, which is under British military control. In the Zone, peddlers sell most of the merchandise, but transactions become mired in paperwork. The Zone is Burroughs's most complex satire of politics and business.

— *William T. Lawlor*

THE NAKED YEAR

Author: Boris Pilnyak (Boris Andreyevich Vogau, 1894-1937?)
Type of work: Novel
Type of plot: Regional

Time of plot: Early twentieth century
First published: Goly god, 1922 (English translation, 1928)

This novel about Russia's Bolshevik Revolution and its aftermath lacks a unifying and well-developed plot. However, in its totality it offers a powerful picture of the most important event in modern Russian history. It also offers the author's unique interpretation of it, rejected by all sides but colorful nevertheless.

***Russia.** Country in which the entire novel is set. In numerous vignettes, an almost fragmentary procession of interconnected scenes, the action moves from one (often fictitious) place to another, as if in passing, underscoring the whirlwind nature of the Russian Revolution. The narrative opens in the town of Ordynin and is generally centered there, but the overall stage is much larger than that.

While the fragmented plot does not allow for a unifying picture, it reflects the fragmentary nature of the happenings in various parts of the country. What gradually becomes clear is that Boris Pilnyak is not attempting to describe the revolution so much as voice his own views about it. He welcomes the revolution but in his own, unorthodox way. He was one of those considered "fellow travelers"—those who sympathized with the revolution without supporting it wholeheartedly or who had rather personal and often misguided understandings of it. Pilnyak saw the revolution as a clash between East and West in Russia, with Bolshevism, by getting rid of autocratic rule, bringing Russia back to its roots. Thus, his novel pits the spiritual culture of Russia against the mechanical culture of the West. The Old Russia of religious fervor and spiritualism, closeness to Mother Nature, and almost pagan adherence to the peasant way of life was almost obliterated by the West-leaning leaders, beginning with Peter the Great. Pilnyak failed to understand, or chose to ignore, the fact that the ideology of communism adopted by the revolutionaries was itself a product of the West.

The novel's dynamic, fleeting, and impressionistic picture of the revolution often borders on chaos, not only in the absence of a defined plot, but also in its fragmented syntax, frequent repetitions, hectic pace, and telegraphic narrative with truncated sentences. However, Pilnyak uses this narrative technique to underline the inherently chaotic nature of the events themselves. What delights him is the revolution's primitive, elemental, vigorous, and passionate side, as reflected in the actions of most of his characters. He approaches the revolution as a romantic, emotional experience, presenting it as a powerful elemental force of nature—like a blizzard or a flood. This romantic, almost mystical, notion of the revolution was popular among some Russian writers at the time, and Pilnyak is the best example. *The Naked Year* does not overlook the disease, famine, dislocation, and other calamities brought by the revolution, and its mood is sometimes pessimistic; however, in Pilnyak's view, that also is a part of the experience.

Ordynin (ohr-DEW-nihn). Fictitious Russian town, somewhere between Moscow and Asia, in which the aristocratic Ordynin family lives. Ordynin serves Pilnyak as a springboard for advancing further his theses about the Russian society and the revolution. Various members of the Ordynin family mirror the degeneration of the aristocracy. They are either impotent, aimless, deranged, or syphilitic. The only exceptions are a son. who is a religious fanatic seeing Russia's salvation in a return to its past, and a daughter who embraces Bolshevism. These two represent the two warring sides in the rev-

olution. Faithful to his understanding of it, Pilnyak strangely sees both of these sides winning. This incongruence reflects Pilnyak's unique interpretation of the revolution or, perhaps, his desire to see Russia return to its spiritual, Christian, almost pagan past.

"China Town." Term that Pilnyak uses several times in the novel as representative of the East. He stresses the point that Russia belongs to the East, straddling the border line between Europe and Asia. There are no further explanations of this reference.

— *Vasa D. Mihailovich*

THE NAME OF THE ROSE

Author: Umberto Eco (1932-   )
Type of work: Novel
Type of plot: Detective and mystery

Time of plot: 1327
First published: Il nome della rosa, 1980 (English translation, 1983)

Many cities and abbeys in many European countries are mentioned in this mystery novel, but the narrative is confined to a single Roman Catholic abbey and its immediate surroundings. The mysterious atmosphere of this story is heightened by the abbey's setting among mountain cliffs, its enclosing walls, its imposing octagonal building, and its obvious link with religious—and therefore supernatural—powers.

Abbey. Unnamed Catholic abbey in northern Italy that provides the novel's setting. The abbey is modeled on abbeys of the thirteenth and fourteenth centuries. Besides the central area of action—the library—the abbey includes a church, an infirmary, a chapter house, a cloister with dormitory, pilgrim quarters, stables, a smithy, mills, oil presses, granaries, pigpens, gardens, and a cemetery.

Library. Forbidden and mysterious area of the abbey, located in the Aedificium, a large octagonal building housing the kitchen and refectory on its lower floor and the library and scriptorium on its upper floor. The scriptorium is a writing room in the abbey that leads to the main entrance to the library. As was usual in medieval times, the scriptorium is located near the kitchens so that the warmth from cooking fires would help keep the monks warm as they worked.

Most medieval monasteries had libraries because their monks were engaged in religious study and had to undertake daily reading. The abbey's library serves to preserve manuscripts and provide income and power for the abbey

when nobles pay for handwritten copies of manuscripts. Significantly, at this abbey, only the librarian and his assistant are allowed to enter the library itself; they decide who may or may not see certain manuscripts, and only they understand the complex structure of the library.

The labyrinthine design of the library connects it with the medieval mazes often built into cathedrals. The library is designed much like the maze on the floor of the Rheims Cathedral in France. In church symbolism, the maze would be the world, and walking the maze would be a way of reenacting the complex and distracting obstacles in life.

The ossarium, a bone vault leading to a secret entrance into the library, serves a practical purpose as a cemetery and a spiritual purpose as a "memento mori," reminding all that they will die (and frightening them away from the secret entrance to the library).

Sections of the library are coded according to geographical areas on a medieval map. For example, the *finis Africae* houses forbidden books—those written by pagan authors that Jorge of Burgos (the former head librarian) considers most dangerous; therefore, it is protected by distorting mirrors and hallucinatory drugs. Aristotle's *Comedy* is lodged in the *finis Africae* because it is the book that Jorge most feared would lead the world astray; this manuscript includes both Arabic and Syriac texts, which indicate that the *Comedy* was transmitted to the Christian world through infidels.

Church. The abbey's sturdy church is, like many medieval churches, decorated with carvings intended to inspire religious feeling in the illiterate peasant. When the narrator Adso, a Benedictine novice assigned as William's scribe, first beholds the church's carvings, they prompt in him a vision instructing him to write down what he sees; this vision is an allusion to the seven trumpets of the Apocalypse, a theme that permeates the novel.

*Abbey of Melk. Benedictine abbey on the banks of the Danube in Austria. Adso is from this monastery, which, like the fictional abbey, had a library that was gutted by fire.

Baskerville. Fictional English town from which the amateur detective Brother William comes. This place is important for its symbolic name, which connects Brother William to Arthur Conan Doyle's fictional detective Sherlock Holmes, who solved a famous murder mystery at the equally fictional Baskerville Hall.

*Abbey of Cluny. Benedictine abbey in France that was one of the most important centers of Christianity in the fourteenth century. Bernard of Cluny wrote a poem from which the title of the novel is taken. The long poem is a denunciation of immoral clergymen and of the wickedness of the world. While the meaning of the "rose" of the novel's title may be debated, to Bernard, the rose symbolized the brevity and sadness of mortal life.

*Avignon (a-vee-nyo[n]). City on the east bank of France's Rhône River that was the temporary seat of the papacy during the period in which the novel is set. It is from Avignon that Pope John XXII promulgates papal bulls against the Franciscans.

— *Kathryn A. Walterscheid*

NANA

Author: Émile Zola (1840-1902)
Type of work: Novel
Type of plot: Naturalism

Time of plot: 1860's
First published: 1880 (English translation, 1880)

The fundamental theme of this novel is the moral, social, and political decadence of France's Second Empire before its fall in 1870. The novel's settings complement and comment upon the its main characters and events. From the beginning of the novel, the courtesan Nana Coupeau and the cross-section of Parisian society that lusts after her represent the decay that spells the downfall of the country.

*Paris. Capital of France in which, apart from a brief section early in the novel, the entire novel is set. The initial action takes place in the cultural and social heart of the city during the 1860's, in the section known as the "boulevards." However, if *Nana* is a story of the fall of France, it is also the tale of the courtesan Nana's rise and fall, ups and downs—literal and figurative. Nana moves widely in Paris during her career, in her pursuit of power, lost innocence, and material success.

Zola is also concerned with the ways in which traditional social distinctions have been blurred in France, how the country's ruling classes have adopted the morality of the gutter. He frequently presents literary coun-

terpoints, moving from places such as the swank home of the Countess Sabine on the rue de Miromesnil to Nana's apartment. The Count Muffat de Beuville, who serves in the government, and his wife are known in Paris society as devout, virtuous Roman Catholics; however, while Muffat lusts after Nana, his wife sleeps with a theater critic. In consecutive chapters, the countess receives her elegant social circle; later, Nana presides at a drunken dinner party in her apartment. Still later, the same chapter that visits the countess in her country estate reveals that Nana has been set up in her own country place—quite nearby—by a wealthy Paris banker.

Early in the novel, Nana has an apartment on the boulevard Haussmann, not far from the home of the Countess Sabine and Muffat. Later, when she goes broke, she lives in shabby Montmartre—and still later, when she stages a spectacular triumph over men, she lives in the new, fashionable area around the Parc Monceau.

*__Théâtre des Variétés__ (tay-at-treh day vehr-ee-ay-tay). Vaudeville theater located on Paris's boulevard de Montmartre, on the southeast side of the Right Bank of the River Seine. There, the novel examines a topsy-turvy society in which many people are not what they seem—respectable people are guilty of gross immorality; some are people who have sprung from the gutter to rise to positions of power. As Émile Zola focuses on hypocrisy, he deals at some length with theater—in which deliberate illusion is the rule.

The setting of the novel's first chapter, the Variétés is the scene of Nana's stunning rise to fame, fortune, and destructive power. There, she gives her breathtaking sensual performances before audiences comprising all social classes, including men who have positions of power in the French government. Sex is what attracts all of these men.

Outside the Variétés is the teeming boulevard itself, with its nighttime crowds and their constant movement and potential violence. Inside the theater, in its dressing rooms, is an inferno smelling of sex and sweat. It is a hell in which at least one character, the Count de Muffat de Beuville, lucidly and shamelessly gives up his soul in exchange for Nana's attentions. When Muffat first visits Nana's dressing room, he has to climb a spiral staircase—on which his ascent is the reverse of his figurative fall. The colors that dominate the descriptions in the novel's opening chapter, red and yellow, prefigure the flames seen at its end.

*__Montmartre__ (mon-MAR-treh). Area in the northern section of Paris located on a steep butte. After Nana has a falling out with Muffat and Steiner, her banker lover, she also falls into slums—landing first in Montmartre, a moral abyss. Nana had grown up on the east side of Montmartre, in the Goutte d'Or section, where she began her working life as a prostitute. After leaving Muffat, she returns to prostitution in Montmartre.

__Country estates.__ In the French countryside Nana sees the imposing estate of Irma d'Anglars, a former courtesan who has become so rich in her old age that she lives in a château once inhabited by a king. When d'Anglars attends church on Sundays, she is treated with the utmost respect by people who live in her village. Once again, those who seem respectable are not; those with shady pasts successfully dupe others. Deeply impressed with Irma's stature, Nana vows to achieve the same success. Eventually she succeeds—by destroying the men for whom she has contempt. However, she dies of smallpox at the same moment France finds itself on the brink of war with Prussia.

— *Gordon Walters*

THE NARRATIVE OF ARTHUR GORDON PYM

Author: Edgar Allan Poe (1809-1849)
Type of work: Novel
Type of plot: Adventure

Time of plot: Early nineteenth century
First published: 1838

This, Edgar Allan Poe's only finished novel, uses authentic geographical and scientific data from other sources to make its readers accept the authenticity of narrator Arthur Gordon Pym's fantastic voyages on four different vessels. Meanwhile, Pym's zigzag routes into the southern oceans display landscapes, waters, events, and beings that become increasingly symbolic, surrealistic, mystical, metafictional, and fantastic.

*__Nantucket.__ Major whaling port on an island south of Cape Cod in southern Massachusetts. While all the place-names are real, one senses a certain amount of biographical and metafictional game-playing and hoaxing. For example, sixteen-year-old Pym initially reports that he was born in Nantucket and that his grandfather (his guardian) has speculated successfully in the stocks of the Edgarton New Bank. This rather placid, matter-of-fact beginning—strewn with descriptions of ships and docks—is abruptly followed by a harrowing escape from a shipwreck in a sailboat, complete with a thoroughly unbelievable return to breakfast the next morning, as if nothing has happened, even though Pym has been pierced through the neck by a bolt of the ship that saves him. Pym then deceives his family into believing that he is going to visit a relative in New Bedford, while he is actually stowing away on the whaling ship *Grampus* with the help of his friend Augustus. The grounding in the everyday reality of Nantucket soon veers into nightmarish horror as Pym hides in the hold of the *Grampus*, ready for more near disasters.

*Antarctic Circle. South Polar region in which the novel concludes. Poe's yearning for an actual expedition to be sent to explore the South Pole may have led him to color the descriptions of the Antarctic environment with enticing, imaginative anomalies. For example, a canoe carries Pym and Dirk Peters into warmer, milky water as they venture farther south. Eventually, they see a strange white-haired mammal with red teeth and claws float by. In the novel's final scene, as their canoe rushes into a cataract, a huge "shrouded human figure" with perfectly white skin appears before them. No explanation is provided after the journal stops short.

The appearance of the strange figure at the end of the novel has been variously explained as being almost everything from a divinity, to a Titan guarding the hole at the South Pole, to a sail or figurehead from a ship seen by a deluded Pym. The incident has been explained as the ultimate metaphysical enigma or as an emblem of epistemological questioning of perception, reality, or language itself. Perhaps Poe succeeded in this "hodge-podge" novel of mixed descriptions, tones of voice, styles, genres, and intentions in making what he once described as the "ludicrous heightened into the grotesque."

Grampus. Whaling ship captained by the father of Pym's friend Augustus Barnard in which Pym becomes a stowaway. The secret compartment in the hold that Augustus prepares for Pym seems to have all the comforts of home. However, the labyrinthine snug space quickly turns into a premature burial, a nightmarish coffin, filled only with rotten food and a threatening dog, lacking fresh water, and leaving Pym confined and cut off for a long time from communication with Augustus or the ship's crew.

Once aboard the *Grampus*, Pym observes butchery, mutiny, murder, a Dutch "death" ship of rotting corpses,

starvation, and, eventually, cannibalism. However, each description of nightmarish despair on the ship is suddenly followed by one of hopeful salvation. For example, when the ship rolls over at sea, it reveals barnacles on its hull that the starving members of its crew can eat. Descriptions of the *Grampus* reveal the endless oscillations of despair and hope, of torture and release, of near destruction and salvation that allow Pym to feel the perverse pleasures of suffering and despair that early in the novel he says he desires to experience.

Tsalal Island. Lush wooded island, full of plants, streams, and game, that is discovered within the Antarctic Circle by the crew of the *Jane Guy* as it sails toward the South Pole. The island is inhabited by people who are completely black—including the color of their teeth—and who are frightened by everything white. On the island, members of the ship's crew discover a variety of odd creatures, such as black albatrosses and black-wooled animals. Pym and Dirk Peters are the only members of the crew left alive after the islanders kill all their companions.

After earlier chapters provide documentary-like descriptions of nature, the novel suddenly infuses the strange island of black and white polarities with elements of symbolism and surrealism that emphasize the temptation of the forbiddingly mysterious and the inaccessibly sublime. For example, a rocky ledge is described as looking like "corded bales of cotton." The water appears to be in "layers," colored like silk, with distinct purplish "veins."

*Kergulen's or Desolation Islands. Group of islands in the southern Indian Ocean located near Southern Africa. Chapters describing the actual history of exploration of these islands are mostly lifted from published accounts, primarily those of Captain James Cook. Pym's extensive descriptions of birds and other animals on the islands can be found in other sources. Poe's heavy reliance upon these sources also helps explain the gaps in Pym's journal and the erratic, zigzag course Pym takes around the Cape of Good Hope to Kergulen's or Desolation Islands, back to the Islands of Tristan da Cunha in the South Atlantic, and then southward in the Antarctic Circle to the Island of Tsalal and finally toward the South Pole. The overall effect is to hoax the reader by making the voyages seem credible with an overload of details, facts, nautical terms, and verifiable history.

— *Joseph Francavilla*

THE NARROW ROAD TO THE DEEP NORTH

Author: Matsuo Bashō (Matsuo Munefusa, 1644-1694)
Type of work: Poetry

First published: Oku no hosomichi, 1694 (English translation, 1933)

Places in Matsuo Bashō's book of brief haiku poems are locations that the poet visited during a five-month journey to the north of Japan, through the rural interior of his country, and then south again along Japan's western coast. Believing that traveling would provide a means of broadening the scope of his life and his poetry, he eventually made four journeys that can be considered spiritual pilgrimages as well as physical journeys to seek the ultimate in beauty.

*Fukagawa (foo-kah-gah-wah). Suburb on the outskirts of Tokyo, when it was known as Edo, that was the poet Matsuo Bashō's home. After selling his home, he set out on a journey to the provinces of the far north of Honshū, the central and largest island of Japan. Several of his closest friends and students accompanied him a few miles up the Sumida River. There, they left him and he set out walking with one companion, Kawai Sora.

*Oshukaidō (oh-shew-ki-doh). Great north road that stretches up the eastern coastal plain of Honshū. Oshukaidō led to the remote province of Oshu, at the northeastern end of the island of Honshū. Bashō followed this road for six weeks.

*Shirakawa barrier (shee-rah-kah-wah). Checkpoint along the north road where all travelers had to stop. The barrier marked the boundary between the cultured world dominated by Edo and the wild lands of the north.

*Ichinoseki (ee-chee-noh-seh-kee). Village in Oshu Province where Bashō turned inland to travel west into the rugged mountains and forests. In the mountains, he met the Yamabushi, hermit priests, and spent a week in their sanctuary.

*Hokurikudō (hoh-kew-ree-kew-doh). Highway along the western Japan Sea coast of Honshū. Bashō walked this road back toward the south for two and half months.

*Ogaki (oh-gah-kee). The town in Mino Province, in southern Honshū, where Bashō finished his journey in October, 1689.

— *Carl L. Bankston III*

NATHAN THE WISE

Author: Gotthold Ephraim Lessing (1729-1781)
Type of work: Drama
Type of plot: Philosophical

Time of plot: Twelfth century
First published: Nathan der Weise, 1779 (English translation, 1781); first performed, 1783

The setting is Jerusalem during the Crusades, when the historical sultan Saladin ruled the area known as Palestine. Each of the play's three settings represents a contending religion: Nathan's house represents Judaism; the Holy Sepulcher, Christianity; and the Sultan's palace, Islam. Subtle connections among these settings hint at interdependence and the possibility for common ground among the three faiths, which are locked in enmity at the outset.

Nathan's House. Jerusalem home of the play's central Jewish character. In addition to indicating that he is a merchant, a common occupation for Jews in the Middle Ages, the goods piled up in front of Nathan's house when he returns from a business trip are emblems of his most precious possession, his foster daughter Recha, as well as an occasion for him to show his generosity. Nathan offers sumptuous cloth and jewelry, which he spreads out on stage, freely as gifts, not only for his household, but also for Conrad von Stauffen, a young knight templar who has rescued his daughter, and for the sultan, who needs ready cash. Visits by the templar and Al-Hafi the dervish provide opportunities for contact among the faiths.

*Holy Sepulcher Square. Purported burial place of Jesus Christ and site of other Christian shrines. Under the palm trees on this square, the templar is pictured repeatedly pacing back and forth, as if to illustrate his awkward position. For he is a Christian knight who has rescued a Jew's daughter and has been inexplicably pardoned by another sworn enemy, the Muslim ruler Saladin. Nathan seeks out the templar here to express his gratitude to his daughter's rescuer. The monastery on the square serves as the backdrop for the Christian patri-

arch, a fat prelate dressed ostentatiously, whose patent intolerance is echoed by his confinement to this area and refusal to interact with people of other faiths.

Saladin's palace. Lavishly furnished, the palace rooms speak of Saladin's wealth, although like Nathan, Saladin indicates he could be content with much less. The bags of money piled onto the floor, courtesy of Nathan, indicate the budding friendship between the Jewish trader and the Muslim ruler. Later, the delivery of Egyptian tribute enables Saladin to return Nathan's gift and exhibits wealth that matches Nathan's own. Shown playing chess with his sister, Saladin is again linked to Nathan, whose chess partner is a dervish in Saladin's service. The templar and Nathan come freely to Saladin for the play's culmination, which shows the three faiths brought under one roof and into one family.

— *Julie D. Prandi*

NATIVE SON

Author: Richard Wright (1908-1960)
Type of work: Novel
Type of plot: Social realism

Time of plot: 1930's
First published: 1940

Set during the Great Depression of the 1930's and the Great Migration of African Americans from the South to the industrial cities of the North, this novel reflects the author's belief in environmental and economic determinism as influences on man's character. The main character, Bigger Thomas, reacts in predictably violent ways to the brutalizing physical and social realities in which he exists.

*Chicago. Illinois's largest city and the industrial center of the Midwest. Richard Wright's family was one of thousands of southern black families that migrated to Chicago between 1916 and 1920 and eventually settled in the South Side ghetto, where Wright grew up. His protagonist, Bigger Thomas, has the same Chicago background. Wright's novel depicts the city as a virtual prison of brick and concrete walls and narrow streets that shut out the light in his corner of the world. The physical limits of Bigger's world reflect the limited opportunities for black men in the white-controlled world. Bigger feels constricted by his limited space, as though he is on "the outside of the world peeping through a knot-hole in the fence."

Three major scenes of violence show Bigger's progressive dehumanization: his killing of a huge rat, his attack on Gus in a poolroom, and his accidental killing of Mary Dalton in her bedroom. Denied space and privacy by being forced to live in one room, Bigger's entire family is dehumanized. There, the young Bigger corners and kills the huge rat that terrorizes the family. The room is a death trap for both Bigger and the rat, with whom he identifies. He admires the rat's strength and defiance even as he beats it to death.

After Bigger kills Mary, his view of the city mirrors his inner chaos. Avoiding the police, he heads for his mistress, Bessie's, place along streets that are but "paths through a dense jungle" of black, empty buildings with "black windows like blind eyes"—a surrealistic landscape over which street lamps cast a ghostly sheen. In Bigger's eyes, the city is filled with rotting, tumbledown buildings that symbolize his own disintegration into guilt and fear. After involving Bessie in a plot to extort money from the Daltons, he and Bessie drive through a howling blizzard that symbolizes Bigger's inner tumult. When he realizes that Bessie's knowledge could send him to prison, he rapes and kills her. Now on the run, he experiences the city as a labyrinth in which the police are closing all means of exit. When the police find him in the ghetto, he is on a water tower on a rooftop, paralyzed by the cold jets of water that the police use to immobilize him.

Chicago's South Side. Even when the family moves from its one-room apartment to the larger world of Chicago's South Side, Bigger still feels trapped in his environment. As he struggles to fit in with his black cohorts, he finds himself trapped by fear again. He is afraid to join his street gang in robbing the white-owned grocery but is also afraid to confess his fears to his companions. To cover his fear, he fights with Gus in a poolroom and terrifies him with a knife.

Dalton home. Mary Dalton's family home, located at 4605 Drexel Boulevard. Her home symbolizes the white man's world that Bigger covets and fears. Her house is surrounded by a black iron picket fence that both constricts and excludes Bigger after he becomes the Daltons' family chauffeur. When he drives Mary and a friend to Ernie's Chicken Shack, he is invited to join them. Inebriated by heavy drinking at Ernie's, Bigger loses his grip on reality. As he drives the girls back home through Washington Park, he becomes increasingly excited and follows Mary through the "dark and silent" house to her bedroom. When Mrs. Dalton enters the room as Bigger is about to make love to Mary, he accidentally smothers Mary while trying to keep her silent. Faced with his fear that he has killed Mary, Bigger loses his grip on reality. He sees the house as haunted, the room filled with hazy blue light, and the whole scene dissolving into a "vast city" of angry whites seeking vengeance.

Prison. Place where Bigger awaits execution after being convicted of his crimes. The prison becomes his place of transformation. Only when he faces the truth that he has built his own traps by his violent acts can he discover his innate sense of humanity and displace his killer instinct with acts of friendship and concern for others.

— *Marguerite R. Plummer*

THE NATURAL

Author: Bernard Malamud (1914-1986)
Type of work: Novel
Type of plot: Fable

Time of plot: 1930's-1940's
First published: 1952

Roy Hobbs, the protagonist of this novel, is a baseball player of extraordinary ability whose early life is shrouded in darkness and obscurity. From somewhere in rural America, he comes to New York City to revive a moribund professional team but is confronted with the vice and corruption pervading a metropolitan corporation. Hobbs follows a perilous course between the hellish lair of the team's evil owner and the vice dens of urban iniquity and the redeeming possibilities of the natural world that are represented by a good woman from the heartland who loves him.

*New York City. City in which Hobbs's major league baseball team, the Knights, is based. Bernard Malamud's mixture of affection for and displeasure with New York City is at the source of Hobbs's experiences with the Knights. The energy, sophistication, variety, and ethnic diversity of the city form a fascinating background for the narrative, and Hobbs's American heartland perspective makes him a somewhat daunted, but nonetheless fascinated, observer of the city's allure and dangers.

Baseball stadium. Stadium in which the New York Knights play. Local landmarks, such as Grant's Tomb, the Empire State Building, and the prominent Sardi's supper club, project an aura of importance over the actions of the characters, but it is the Knights' stadium— a simulacrum for society at large—that is the most significant setting in the book. There, Malamud presents the compelling diversity of urban life—casual spectators, rabid fans, gamblers, and bizarre and eccentric ticket-holders react to the games and the players with emotions running the gamut from adoration to contempt. The stadium is a kind of sacred ground, the rituals of the game akin to religious rites, the behavior of the crowd an expression of a shifting *Zeitgeist* that Malamud uses as a commentary on American life.

American heartland. Broad, nonspecific region of the United States from which Hobbs comes; the term is more symbolic than tangible. Hobbs's background and origins are vague, his roots somewhere in the Northwest, his years of travail in minor league baseball outposts described as places he has "bummed around in," slop-joints, third-rate hotels, boxing gyms, and so on. When he arrives in Chicago for a tryout with the Cubs, he is astonished to see so many people living together in one place. His reaction to the size of the hotel he stays in is similar.

While the novel depicts the cities of baseball's old National League circuit realistically, rural America is drawn with a blend of evocative naturalism and semi-mystical fabulism. Malamud's purpose here is twofold. He is contrasting the redemptive powers of the natural world—particularly symbolized by Iris Lemon, whose name implies fertility and new growth—with the psychological ruin and decay of a blighted wasteland. In addition, Hobbs is troubled by dreams in which he is engulfed by the dark forces of a surreal landscape, lost in the wilderness or submerged in swirling waters. The shift between the relatively realistic and the fantastic enables Malamud to extend his narrative from strong social satire toward allegory and myth, and Hobbs's rootlessness is made tangible by his inability to become comfortable in any of the book's settings.

*****Long Island.** Island off the southeast coast of New York State where Hobbs spends time with his temptress, Memo Paris. As a corollary to the scenes in which Hobbs sinks into the mental turmoil occasioned by a sign or signal that reminds him of an incident of dismay in his past, he has several episodes of fear and uncertainty in which he is revisited by some of the demons inhabiting his subconscious. One of the most significant involves his sojourn with Memo, a woman he desires, at the ocean's edge beyond the limits of New York City. This location, situated between the natural world and the edge of urban temptation, gives Malamud the opportunity to show how Hobbs is riven by positive and negative impulses—light and darkness; clear water and pollution; a straight road and a winding trail—features of the geophysical world aligned with memory and desire.

— *Leon Lewis*

NAUSEA

Author: Jean-Paul Sartre (1905-1980)
Type of work: Novel
Type of plot: Philosophical realism

Time of plot: 1930's
First published: La Nausée, 1938 (English translation, 1949)

Many readers are put off by Nausea*'s grimness. But Jean-Paul Sartre wants his readers to see the ugliness of reality—so that they can make the right philosophical choice. This book is a great novel in part because of the ways in which Sartre's settings and descriptions of objects establish the necessary dark tone. The novel is set in grim, ugly, confining Bouville, France, the site of hero Antoine Roquentin's personal quest to escape the darkness and see the existentialist light.*

Bouville (boo-VEEL). Dark, cold, rainy, and foggy coastal city, which, in its ambience, stimulates the historian Antoine Roquentin's growing despair and anger. Bouville is Sartre's fictional version of the western French port Le Havre. However, Sartre makes an immediately bitter satirical point by setting *Nausea* in "Bouville." In French, "la boue" is "mud"—*Nausea* therefore takes place in gloomy, viscous "Mudville."

Nausea is essentially Roquentin's journal of his experiences in Bouville. As Roquentin sees the city, it is dominated by a narrow-minded, self-satisfied, intolerant, oppressive bourgeoisie devoid of culture. Bouville and its people create, then, an appropriate backdrop for Roquentin's effort to move out of figurative as well as literal darkness into the light of personal truth.

Bouville train station. The first passages in Roquentin's diary concern his experience in the city's railroad station. The trains and their schedules, exercises in strict regularity and predictability, save Roquentin during one of his first crises of contingency. At the beginning of this opening passage, Roquentin is terrified that there is no security in the universe—that anything can happen at any time. This fear is driving him crazy, he thinks. However, when he later considers, from the perspective of the window of his nearby room, the arrival in the station and the departure of the same trains at the same time every day, carrying and delivering the same people, he puts his anxiety to rest—temporarily. Life, he now thinks, is orderly, something one can count on.

Café. Unnamed neighborhood café (known only as "the café") that Roquentin often frequents. A dull, shabby, working-class milieu, the place is thoroughly typical, with its smoke, mirrors, booths, friendly female proprietress, and men playing cards. What is most important about the café is that it contains a jukebox, which in turn contains a recording of "Some of These Days," sung by an anonymous African American woman. The recording offers yet another example of new ideas that attract Roquentin's attention. Like the trains that always run on time, Roquentin observes, the notes of the song follow each other predictably and coherently. The song is always the same, one always knows what to expect;

there are no surprises. Indeed, the café is the scene of Roquentin's definitive enlightenment, and the numerous exemplary qualities of the recording provide a model for his future.

Bouville museum. Museum containing a portrait gallery that glorifies great citizens of Bouville's past and their way of life. Roquentin tours the museum occasionally and bitterly comments on the subjects of the portraits. He imagines biographies that seem to match the expressions of the portraits he sees of doctors, businessmen, generals. Such men are Roquentin's enemies—smug, satisfied, powerful, merciless, anti-Semitic people with only one idea, as Roquentin thinks, by which he means that they were as dead and like things as their portraits are now—and, confident and complacent as they were, they had no sense of contingency. People who never think, in Roquentin's eyes, believe that Nature is composed of inalterable laws. Roquentin knows better; he knows not to take life for granted.

Park. Roquentin's final existential crisis takes place in a Bouville park. Before this point in his story, he has had a number of hints regarding the true state of Nature—that things are never what they seem, that people cannot control things any more than they can control events. In the park, Roquentin is stunned by what he calls a vision.

He contemplates the root of a chestnut tree. It is black and ugly, just as the faces in the museum portraits are ugly, as Bouville itself is dark and hideous; brutal, deceptive reality is not pretty. Roquentin sees that he cannot affect the root, that it exists on its own, independent of him or anything else, as pure reality. The root thus clarifies for him the real meaning of "contingency"—that there is no transcendent reason (such as God) why anything (or anyone) exists or ceases to exist. Everything and everyone is terribly, frighteningly free. The importance of this discovery in the park—of humankind's burden of freedom—is that Roquentin is ultimately converted to taking responsibility for his own life, accepting the fact that he alone can create his own identity.

— *Gordon Walters*

A NEST OF SIMPLE FOLK

Author: Seán O'Faoláin (John Francis Whelan, 1900-1991)

Type of work: Novel

Type of plot: Regional

Time of plot: 1854-1916

First published: 1933

Seán O'Faoláin uses three settings in this novel—the country, the town, and the city—to convey how they all influenced one another during Ireland's bitter fight for independence from Great Britain, and how the actions of one generation reverberated into the future. The novel culminates in Ireland's Easter Rebellion of 1916, in which one character, who represents Ireland's slumbering Gaelic pride, becomes a heroic figure, and another, a policeman who represents British authority, is exposed as a spy and a traitor.

*County Limerick. County in southwest Ireland, four farms of which are central to O'Faoláin's family saga, which centers on the age-old struggle to control land. O'Faoláin demonstrates how land, or a lack of land, really, can cause deep family strife because it remains central to Irish survival. The underlying historical cause of contention, which turns family members into enemies, results from Great Britain's historical colonization of Ireland. As the cultivation of large estates by British landowners left fewer acres for Ireland's own people to cultivate, and as the Irish population increased, families were pushed to the breaking point to survive.

Bawnrea. Farm into which the novel's central character, Leo Foxe-Donnel, is born. When his mother, Judith Foxe, marries his father, Long John O'Donnell, she marries down socially from the local estate house, **Foxehall**. While Long John welcomes his new bride, he welcomes her land, **Ahill Farm**, even more and mortgages it immediately so he can buy a third farm, **New Plot**. Ignoring his older brother's birthright, his mother makes sure that her youngest son, Leo, will inherit the best land. Leo, however, squanders his chances at education, preferring to drink, chase women, and father illegitimate children. Because Leo is privileged, he makes enemies of his brothers, who must spend their life on poorer land, barely scraping out subsistence livings to provide dowries for their seven sisters. While Leo spreads his wild oats, they must postpone marriage until they are in their fifties or sixties. Leo is saved as a character because he harbors a deep resentment against Britain. During the Fenian uprising, he shoots a man, spends ten years in jail, and thereby loses his land to his hardworking brother.

*Rathkeale. Town in County Limerick to which the older Leo gravitates after he has lost his land. There, O'Faoláin demonstrates that even though it might not seem related, occurrences on the land deeply influence events in the town. The parish priest forces Leo to marry Julie from Ahill Farm, with whom he has fathered two illegitimate children and started a shop in Rathkeale. In the town, the man from the country clandestinely continues his rebel activities. His wife's sister Bid becomes involved with an Irish policeman, Johnny Hussey, employed under the jurisdiction of the British crown. All have been forced off the land in County Limerick, and although they get along well on the surface, political conflict arises between Leo, who represents victimized Ireland, and Johnny who represents imperial England. Intent on moving up by becoming a sergeant, Johnny spies upon Leo's patriotic activities, informs his superiors, and has him returned to prison.

*Cork. Irish city in which the family settles after Johnny is transferred from Rathkeale. His wife's sister Julie and Leo move there after Leo's release from prison. Now old and seemingly enfeebled, Leo starts another shop and becomes a bookie, which aids him ultimately in revenge against his traitor brother-in-law, who illegally plays horses. The family's agony in its efforts to reconcile the past on the land is passed down to the third generation: Leo's illegitimate son, another Irish patriot, and Johnny's artistic-hearted son, Denis. Johnny and Bid, intent at any cost to forget their peasant beginnings on the land, relentlessly force Denis to enter the priesthood, or to rise financially in the world.

— *M. Casey Diana*

NEW GRUB STREET

Author: George Gissing (1857-1903)
Type of work: Novel
Type of plot: Naturalism

Time of plot: 1880's
First published: 1891

An early exponent of realism, George Gissing understood London and Londoners from painful personal experience. He set his scenes on real streets, in real districts, and in real places that heighten verisimilitude. This method enhances the impression that the principal characters represent common types encountered in the literary world and provides further interest by creating the illusion of a guided tour through Victorian London. Staging his drama in real places highlights his thesis that the literary profession entails a struggle for survival of the fittest—though not always the most deserving. The comfortable dwellings enjoyed by those who ultimately survive reiterate this thesis with graphic images.

Milvain home. English provincial home of Jasper Milvain's mother, where the novel opens in a peaceful English scene. There, the self-centered Jasper dominates conversations with his mother and sisters, expounding his cynical principles and materialistic values. Gissing intends to depict cold, foggy London in all its dirt, noise, and competition for living space, but he employs the venerable artistic device of contrast by devoting several opening chapters to a bucolic setting, which is the diametrical opposite of the narrow, unsanitary streets and grim, overshadowing buildings of the city. Throughout the novel, escape to the English countryside remains an impossible dream to literary toilers like Edwin Reardon, Alfred Yule, and Harold Biffen, who cannot afford vacations and dread losing their precarious footholds in the literary marketplace.

Reardon home. London home of Edwin Reardon and his wife, Amy, located in a respectable neighborhood near St. James Park. Like many characters in *New Grub Street*, they aspire to middle-class status even though their income level should make them lower class. Their shabby genteel lifestyle requires a minimum of several hundred pounds per year to maintain; however, Edwin can only earn about half that much from his writing. The description of their tiny flat tells a great deal about Amy's social aspirations and Edwin's ambitions. It is respectable enough, but they have to climb eight flights of stairs to get to it. Edwin has to use the sitting room as his study, forcing Amy to sit in the kitchen. They share the only bedroom with their infant, whose crying torments Edwin while he tries desperately to write. The rent is more than they can afford, but Amy requires a middle-class standard of living and Edwin feels duty bound to provide it. Though poor, Edwin owns hundreds of tattered books in English, Latin, Greek, and French. While lying sleepless, Edwin can hear the clock of the Marylebone Workhouse chiming the hours, seemingly threatening him with disgrace and disaster if he ceases to write for a single day.

*British Museum reading room. Reading room of London's great national library, which Gissing uses as a setting for several important scenes, including one in which Marian Yule falls in love with Milvain. This cavernous room with walls covered with books is the very nucleus of the literary world. Writers gather here, not only because it offers the reference materials they need, but because it offers them a haven from their nagging landlords, threatening creditors, squalling babies, and anxious spouses.

The reading room is a meeting place in which writers exchange malicious gossip motivated by the dog-eat-dog competition of their trade. Marian, whose father has been a permanent fixture in the reading room for many years, sees the place from Gissing's viewpoint. Jasper Milvain, the cynical opportunist, calls the reading room "the valley of the shadow of books," echoing words from the Bible's Twenty-third Psalm: "Yea, though I walk through the valley of the shadow of death." Many freelance writers live close to the British Museum because they depend on its reading room. Therefore, the setting provides a center of gravity around which Gissing's characters orbit.

Yule home. Home in which Marian lives with her parents on St. Paul's Crescent, a street consisting of "small, decent homes." By working through the day and halfway through the night, Yule manages to achieve a respectable middle-class lifestyle, but his home is a stark, cheerless place in which meals are eaten in silence, and his wife and daughter are afraid to disturb the master of the house when he retires to his study to do more literary hackwork by lamplight. Gissing uses this grim setting to symbolize the life of a certain type of writer who discovers too late that he lacks the talent to realize his youthful dreams. It is worth noting that Gissing, the modern realist, describes this setting objectively and dispassionately, in contrast to the seriocomic manner in which such a place would certainly have been handled by the flamboyant Charles Dickens.

Biffen home. Home of Harold Biffen, located in a respectable London neighborhood on Clipstone Street between Portland Place and Tottenham Court Road. Biffen is an educated man with middle-class aspirations, but his home is a drafty garret in which he lives while writing books that will never get published, while eking out a living by tutoring dullards for sixpence an hour.

Gissing characteristically describes the place in objective terms: "It was a very small room, with a ceiling so low that the tall lodger could only just stand upright with safety; perhaps three inches intervened between his head and the plaster, which was cracked, grimy, cobwebby. A small scrap of weedy carpet lay in front of the fireplace; elsewhere the chinky boards were unconcealed." It is ironic that Biffen, the most idealistic of the writers portrayed in the novel, should be forced to endure the worst living conditions. There, Gissing uses place to underscore the fact that conscientious, gifted artists freeze, starve, and perish while plagiarists and empty-headed scribblers thrive in this modern literary marketplace he calls **New Grub Street**.

*****Bayswater.** Fashionable district of London, where Jasper Milvain and his wife, Amy—the two most materialistic and selfish characters in the novel—are ensconced at the end of the novel. There, they entertain small and select parties of friends. Their comfortably appointed home is a tangible illustration of Gissing's cynical thesis that in the real world, as opposed to the world of romantic literature, Philistines prosper while dreamers and idealists get trampled underfoot.

— *Bill Delaney*

THE NEW HÉLOÏSE

Author: Jean-Jacques Rousseau (1712-1778)
Type of work: Novel
Type of plot: Philosophical

Time of plot: Early eighteenth century
First published: Julie: Ou, La Nouvelle Héloïse, 1761
(*Julie: Or, The New Héloïse,* 1761)

Jean-Jacques Rousseau's philosophical novel, which examines the relationship between passion and reason, is actually two novels in one. It is the story of Julie d'Etange and Julie de Wolmar. The settings of the d'Etange and Clarens estates divide and, at the same time, unite these two narratives.

Clarens. Fictional estate of Monsieur de Wolmar, located in Switzerland. Clarens is a rational utopia based on Monsieur de Wolmar's philosophical ideas. It is isolated and has no political or social connections to any exterior groups or institutions. Wolmar leads the little community assembled there with benevolent paternal authority. Life at Clarens is the ideal life admired by the economically ordered middle class. Order and reasonableness are the bases for all activity and for relationships between people. Clarens is imbued with happiness, order, and peace based on devotion to virtue. The Julie whom the reader meets at Clarens is a different Julie than the passionate young woman of the early parts of the novel. She is a model of virtue and marital fidelity. Julie de Wolmar, wife and mother, is the center of life at Clarens, where there are no disquieting thoughts or happenings. Reason and religion exist in harmony in the little community. Although Wolmar is not a believer, he respects and encourages religious devotion.

Clarens is also a place for healing. It is the scene of Wolmar's great experiment. In this idyllic setting, where reason and virtue reign supreme, Saint-Preux is to be cured of his passion. The husband, the wife, and the lover are to live in harmony founded on virtue. Reason is to prevail and devotion to virtue is to be the guide. However, Saint-Preux's presence changes Clarens. Clarens is little by little transformed into the home of not only Julie de Wolmar but also Julie d'Etange. The utopia of reason is no longer viable; it is in danger of collapse. Clarens has been transformed from a place of healing and safety to a place of danger and disaster.

D'Etange estate (day-TAHNZH). Fictional place created by Rousseau. It is here that the passionate love affair between Julie and Saint-Preux begins. The family home is also the scene of Julie's seduction by Saint-Preux and of her marriage to Monsieur de Wolmar.

***Paris.** France's capital city is the center of French society. Rousseau found never-ending fault with French manners and morals. Saint-Preux's sojourn in Paris provides Rousseau with the opportunity to criticize and condemn this lifestyle, which he detested. In Paris, Saint-Preux discovers all sorts of vices and the most dissolute ways of living—the theater, gambling houses, illicit sexual activity. Rousseau devotes a considerable amount of his novel to castigating the French.

Nature settings. Woods, groves, lakes, mountains, gardens. Nature has a powerful effect on the characters. Their emotional states are always heightened by views of the natural world. Julie kisses Saint-Preux for the first time in the grove at the d'Etange estate. Saint-Preux writes in his letters to Julie of his intense pleasure in seeing the mountains.

Lake at Clarens. Saint-Preux is tempted to kill himself and Julie on a sailing excursion. Rousseau foreshadows Julie's death; she will sacrifice herself to save her son Marcellin from drowning.

— *Shawncey Webb*

THE NEW LIFE

Author: Dante Alighieri (1265-1321)
Type of work: Poetry with prose comments
Time of plot: 1274-1292

First transcribed: La vita nuova, c. 1292 (English translation, 1861)

Unlike Dante's more widely known Divine Comedy, *this poem describes the everyday realities of late thirteenth century Florence. Places are always identified vaguely; geography in* The New Life, *then, is emotional. The places in which Dante meets Beatrice are light, airy, and delightful. When he is in the grip of despair, he is always found in his narrow room.*

***Florence.** North-central Italian city that in Dante's day was a medieval walled fortress enclosing about thirty thousand people, making for little privacy. Everyone would have known everyone else's business in Dante's Florence. Thus, the image of Dante at nine, and later at eighteen, being struck motionless and speechless by the sight of a beautiful girl on the streets of the city is not only effective emotionally but also plausible literally. The loci of Dante's sightings of Beatrice are never made specific. Even a scene obviously set in a church is described only as a place in which people are praying to the Virgin Mary. Dante's response to his glimpses of Beatrice always involves a change of place: He goes to his room, he is obliged to travel to another city, he finds a solitary place, or he walks down a path by a clear stream. Yet his focus always comes back to the streets of Florence, not because Florence is his home, but because it is Beatrice's.

— *John R. Holmes*

THE NEWCOMES: Memoirs of a Most Respectable Family

Author: William Makepeace Thackeray (1811-1863)
Type of work: Novel
Type of plot: Social morality

Time of plot: Early nineteenth century
First published: 1853-1855

As their name indicates, the members of the Newcome family are archetypal arrivistes, *descendants of a self-made man who came to London from England's industrial north. While two brothers, who comprise the more self-aggrandizing branch, put down roots in Mayfair, their half-brother makes his own fortune—which proves disastrously precarious—in India before returning with his son to search unsuccessfully for a secure place in a fast-evolving social world.*

*London. Great Britain's capital and leading city, where members of the Newcome family live. The various addresses cited in the text provide a map of the Newcomes' social positions and shifting fortunes. For example, the colonel's half-brothers establish their families in Park Lane, Queen Street, and the slightly less fashionable Bryanstone Square to the north. The living acquired by the Reverend Charles Honeyman, the colonel's brother-in-law, is also in Mayfair, on Denmark Street, while his lodgings are in Walpole Street. The colonel himself resides for a time at 120 Fitzroy Square, on the edge of Marylebone, which is considerably farther north than Bryanstone Square; however, Clive contrives to live for a while in Hanover Square on the east edge of Mayfair. After the colonel's financial disaster, however, Clive settles in Howland Street, which is close to Fitzroy Square but considerably less grand.

*Clapham. Village near London in which the colonel's father settles on first arriving in London. He lives in a cottage with his first wife, but moves into the Hobson family "mansion" when he marries his employer's daughter and heiress, Sophia Alethea Hobson—after whom, according to the story's fictitious claims, several local terraces and minor roads are named. When the novel was written, Clapham was in the process of being devoured by Greater London's expansion, because it had become the site of a major railway junction.

Newcome. Manufacturing town situated between Liverpool and Manchester in the north of England. It is the senior Thomas's native town, but the junior Thomas finds a cold welcome when he visits (his still-resident brother is nicknamed Screwcome). The town becomes significant late in the story when one of Clive's cousins attempts to use his family connection to become the town's member of Parliament. It eventually evolves into Newcome New Town, characterized by a great railway viaduct, and swallows up the nearby village of Rosebury, where Madame de Florac, née Higg, eventually settles (the Higgs hail from Manchester).

Grey Friars. School in the City of London where the notional author first meets Clive. The school plays a key role in a heavily nostalgic scene near the end of the novel, when the colonel attends its founder's day celebration. The fictional school's situation corresponds with that of the real Bluecoat School, on the site of Christ's Hospital, where the Grey Friars (members of the contemplative monastic order also known as the Cistercians) established their abbey in 1223; that abbey was confiscated by Henry VIII in the 1530's and destroyed by the great London fire of 1666.

*Paris. France's capital city plays an important role in the plot because the elder Thomas's beloved Léonore settles there after becoming the comtesse de Florac. Clive becomes re-entangled with the family because he stays in the rue de Rivoli, where the Hôtel de Florac is located, on his first trip to Paris. After experiencing his financial disaster, the colonel—following the fashion of English exiles of the period—takes up residence in Normandy, in Boulogne-sur-Mer.

*Rome. Italy's capital city is the destination of Clive's grand tour; the enthusiastic description of the city—where Clive spends his happiest days—is the most detailed in the book, reflecting the fact that William Makepeace Thackeray based Clive on the painter Frederick Leighton, whom he met there. Clive also visits Pompeii in southern Italy and runs into the Kews again at nearby Naples.

Baden-Baden. Spa town in southern Germany that was a favorite resort of English aristocrats. It is an important setting in the novel. Clive stays there while on tour, running into Lord Kew and the vicomte de Florac before their duel.

Brighton. Resort town on the south coast of England, where Clive's aunt has a lodging-house at 110 Steyne Gardens. Clive visits it several times, and other characters occasionally stay there.

— *Brian Stableford*

NEWS FROM NOWHERE

Author: William Morris (1834-1896)
Type of work: Novel
Type of plot: Utopian
Time of plot: Late nineteenth century; twenty-first century

First published: News from Nowhere: Or, An Epoch of Rest, Being Some Chapters from a Utopian Romance, 1891

The nineteenth century narrator of this novel awakens to find himself in a future London, radically changed by civil war and a new philosophy of life—one that is in accord with author William Morris's own views—that lays great emphasis on removal of ugly buildings and reclamation of natural landscapes. The story ends as the narrator again awakens—this time from his dream.

Guest house. Home of the narrator, William Guest, in London's Hammersmith district, where Morris himself lived in a late eighteenth century brick Georgian town house that he called Kelmscott House. Guest's house stands on the very site of Morris's house, which Morris regarded as merely a convenient place in which to live and store his belongings. Guest's home echoes Morris's own taste in architecture and ornamentation. However, in the novel the surrounding area is greatly changed for the better: The nearby River Thames is cleaner, all signs of industry are removed, and Hammersmith Bridge has been replaced by something similar to the old London Bridge.

London. After Guest awakens in the twenty-first century, he visits central London with Dick Hammond, the weaver, and compares the future city with the London of his own time. Most of the nineteenth century buildings with which Guest was familiar in his own time have been replaced by buildings that are more beautiful. These buildings embrace the best qualities of Morris's favorite architectural styles, including the Gothic and the Byzantine. Public buildings are designed according to function and there are fewer of them—mostly meetinghouses, market halls, and guest houses for a population that is remarkably mobile. At the same time,

much of London has reverted to woodlands and pastures, and Guest learns that this is true for all of England. Many towns have disappeared altogether, particularly those concerned primarily with manufacturing.

Many old London streets have disappeared, but the main roads still exist, among them Piccadilly, which has become a short street of shops with Italian-style arcades, close to elegant houses, each with a garden. The Houses of Parliament, however, are now known as the Dung Market, reflecting Morris's own strong distaste for the work carried out by nineteenth century British architects, such as George Gilbert Scott and Augustus Welby Northmore Pugin. Trafalgar Square, however, has become an orchard and Covent Garden once more lives up to its name. The British Museum survives, although some people would like to see it pulled down, a notion that others reject because of the historical importance of the collections contained in it.

River Thames (tehmz). River running through London up which Guest agrees to travel with Dick to a haymaking in Oxfordshire. This further enables Morris to draw comparisons between his present and the future. Guest sees further examples of areas that have reverted to their original, natural states, with fewer houses and more woods and parklands, which are used for recreation. Grand houses such as Hampton Court have become guest houses, and many churches are regularly used for purposes other than worship.

The travelers stay at guest houses and in the homes of private individuals who without exception welcome them. As the journey continues, Guest sees the Thames valley as Morris recalled it, before the rapid expansion of towns began during the late nineteenth century. Villages retain their distinct character while towns have shrunk in size. The new houses now being built are designed to fit harmoniously into the landscape.

*Kelmscott Manor. Oxfordshire estate at which Guest's journey and the novel end. This is the only building in the novel that seems to be entirely unchanged in its appearance since the nineteenth century. The house is modeled on the real Kelmscott Manor that Morris jointly leased with Dante Gabriel Rossetti. To Morris, the house was a haven from the world for which he felt so much distaste. It is significant that once this haven is reached in what is revealed to be Guest's dream, Guest cannot remain there but must awaken.

— *Maureen Speller*

THE NIBELUNGENLIED

Author: Unknown
Type of work: Poetry
Type of plot: Epic

Time of plot: c. 437
First transcribed: Nibelungenlied, c. 1200 (English verse translation, 1848; prose translation, 1877)

This heroic epic centers upon the love, loss, and revenge of Kriemhild, a woman who has been wronged by her own kinsmen. Although somewhat ambiguous and vague in certain places in the text, localities serve to clarify the boundaries of armies and those thresholds that may, or may not be crossed. Many places mentioned in the poem are real.

*Castle of Worms. Castle by the Rhine River in northern France's historic Burgundy region. It is the home of Kriemhild and her family, who face much hardship and death as a result of Kriemhild's great love for Siegfried. This place represents the unmarred beauty and happiness of a young woman, while it also symbolizes her maturity and the bitterness that follows betrayal, which eventually leads to death and destruction—her own and those of innumerable others.

*Netherlands. Homeland of Siegfried that signifies his power, as well as his own evanescent nature. In certain instances within the poem, Norway and Nibelungenland seem to be synonymous with the Netherlands, which is analogous to the relationship that Siegfried has with his own people and those of other nations—that of a known origin, but of an indistinct nature.

Isenstein. Location of Brunhild's court. For a long while, this place was thought to be in Iceland because it is described as having been along the coast. However, that is no longer considered the case. Brunhild may also correspond with her place of origin, for just as she has enormous power that is eventually taken from her by an act of betrayal, so is her court.

Nibelungenland. Mythical setting in which Siegfried is believed to have won his cloak of invisibility and the gold hoard. It represents that which is inscrutable for humans, unknown power and wealth, and those possessions to which everyone in this epic aspires but never attains.

*Hungary. Homeland of King Etzel, the heathen. Although Etzel himself is not portrayed in a negative light, Hungary is associated with the dark deeds of Kriemhild, who remains there until her death for the sole purpose of revenge.

— *Adriana C. Tomasino*

NICHOLAS NICKLEBY

Author: Charles Dickens (1812-1870)
Type of work: Novel
Type of plot: Social realism

Time of plot: Early nineteenth century
First published: 1838-1839

Publication of this novel revealed Charles Dickens to be a writer of extraordinary promise—a development evident in his psychological treatment of place, which became one of his creative trademarks. There, Dickens transforms places into psychological domains that reflect the fetters and freedoms that bind their occupants to, or emancipate them from, the worlds of reality and imagination.

*London. Capital and leading city of Great Britain. After his father dies, Nicholas takes his mother and sister to London to seek assistance from his uncle Ralph. A misanthropic miser, Ralph arranges for the Nicklebys to leave their pleasant lodgings and take up squalid ones, while Nicholas goes to Yorkshire to teach at Dotheboys Hall. The novel presents London initially as a heartless place of illusion and deprivation, which underscores Ralph's deceptions and machinations.

Dickens's gloomy depictions of such London locations as Snow Hill and the Manchester Buildings—the residence of corrupt politicians—serve to deepen the atmosphere of despair and mistrust that smothers the hapless Nicklebys. Despite his wealth, Ralph Nickleby resides in the shabby and ironically named Golden Square. In contrast, the offices of the Cheeryble Brothers and the cottage they provide for the Nicklebys underscore their warmth, compassion, and belief in the essential goodness of the human spirit. It is through this tangled web of misery and hope that Nicholas must hack a way for his family and himself, indeed to save their very souls from the darkness that threatens to engulf them.

Dotheboys Hall. Yorkshire boarding school at which Nicholas teaches under the supervision of the vicious schoolmaster, Wackford Squeers. The northern England county of Yorkshire was notorious for its unpleasant boarding schools, and Dickens depicts Squeers's school as a hell on earth. Filthy, ruined, and desolate, it provides an apt metaphor for the psychological and physical nightmare that each boy sent to the school endures. Dickens's satire is savage, indignant, and unsparing, but the possibility of redemption is alive in the cheer and warmth of the nearby farm of John Browdie, who helps Nicholas bring down Squeers.

*Portsmouth. Southern English port city. While on the run from Squeers and Ralph, Nicholas and Smike travel to Portsmouth with Vincent Crummles, whose acting troupe they join. Nicholas discovers in Crummles's theater a freedom and creativity he has never before experienced. With the freewheeling seaport of Portsmouth a haven of safety and discretion, Nicholas hones his acting abilities and matures as an independent man responsible for others. The world of the theater is seductive, but Nicholas recognizes the false comfort in such illusions, and he departs this crucial training ground to return to London to unravel the knots that await him there.

*Dawlish. Coastal town in southern England's Devonshire, where Nicholas grows up. Dawlish frames the novel, beginning with the Nicklebys' exile in bankruptcy and ending with their triumphant return and repurchase of the family home. Dawlish symbolizes the possibility of paradise regained, of the eventual triumph of goodness over evil, but not without suffering and loss, as emblematized by Smike's grave, tended in the years to come by innocent children who weep and mourn over his tragic tale.

— *Erskine Carter*

NICK OF THE WOODS: Or, The Jibbenainosay, a Tale of Kentucky

Author: Robert Montgomery Bird (1806-1854)
Type of work: Novel
Type of plot: Adventure

Time of plot: 1782
First published: 1837

Wilderness scenes constitute a sizable number of this novel's settings. Although the forest is described occasionally in favorable terms such as "noble" and "wild but beautiful," it is much more often depicted as a claustrophobic, gloomy, lonely, difficult, and dangerous maze. It primarily represents an obstacle to white progress, as symbolized by white settlements like Bruce's Station, and a dangerous mire for the spiritual values of white civilization, as "white Indian" villains like Abel Doe who take to the woods make clear.

Bruce's Station. Large Kentucky fort in which the novel opens. The fort is protected by a blockhouse at each corner of its walls. In addition to serving as a barometer of settler-Indian relations, the station stands in stark symbolic opposition to the forest itself, with its Shawnee threat, since the fort's occupants have destroyed the forest near it to plant fields of corn, although still "all beyond and around was a dark and solemn wilderness." The settlement's attempt to push back that wilderness by girdling, or cutting broad swaths of bark away from the trunks of the trees to slowly kill them, leaving them "girdled and leafless, but not yet fallen," is evocative of their hatred for the lurking Shawnee, as well as symbolic of the supposedly doomed status of the American Indians themselves.

Beech grove. As Captain Roland and his cousin Edith leave the station, they begin to journey toward the river ford through the forests. As strange cries begin to echo through the forest, the result of Ralph Stackpole's attempt to summon someone to free him from his lynching, the author deliberately builds suspense in a decidedly theatrical and overtly gothic fashion, as the forests grow even darker, an effect "peculiarly fitted to add double effect to sights and sounds of a melancholy or fearful character."

Ashburn cabin. Small family fort on a cliff overlooking a river where Captain Roland's party takes refuge while fleeing from a Shawnee war party. The cabin is a smaller, shoddily built version of Bruce's Station, "carelessly and feebly constructed," and almost worthless for defense. The gothic mood emphasized at the thick grove of beeches is heightened even more here, with the "truly cheerless and forbidding" ruined cabin and the "hoarse and dismal rush of the river below" adding "double horror to its appearance." The setting thus establishes a mood of despair to foreshadow the desperate siege yet to come. After Bloody Nathan is sent to find help, the Shawnee set fire to the cabin, and Captain Roland's party tries to ford the raging river rapids on their horses, with mixed success.

Hollow vale. Valley surrounded by stunted shrubs and parched grasses where Roland's party is finally captured by the Shawnee. The vale exhibits a physical desolation that mirrors the mood of the captives themselves. The river Roland and the others have been trying to cross glimmers tauntingly in the distance. The Shawnees' separation of their captives in the vale sets up later attempts to rescue Edith.

Forest glade. Clearing whose "spring of sweet water" bubbling up through the grass contrasts with the hollow vale and its mockingly distant river. The refreshment that the glade offers to the captured Captain Roland foreshadows his eventual rescue and contrasts with the whiskey-drunkenness of Piankeshaw. The edenic description of the "wild but beautiful little valley," in which Bloody Nathan and Captain Roland next rescue Ralph Stackpole from Shawnee torturers, likewise echoes and reinforces the jubilant mood of Stackpole upon his release.

Wenonga's village. Settlement of the Shawnee leader Wenonga, who is also known as the Black-Vulture. The novel returns to an overtly ironic use of setting here, as Captain Roland goes in search of the kidnapped Edith, describing the Shawnee village as sitting in a river valley with "an air of tender beauty" ill-suited to "the wild and warlike children of the wilderness."

Wenonga's wigwam in the village is a busy setting, offering a quick succession of scenes. Telie Doe begs Edith's forgiveness here, after which it becomes a site for potential miscegenation via sexual threats, as Braxley tells Edith she will only emerge from it as his wife or that of a Shawnee. Finally, the wigwam serves as the backdrop for Bloody Nathan's intensely bloody revenge, as he hacks apart Wenonga.

— *Michael T. Wilson*

THE NIGGER OF THE "NARCISSUS": A Tale of the Sea

Author: Joseph Conrad (Jósef Teodor Konrad Nałęcz Korzeniowski, 1857-1924)
Type of work: Novel

Type of plot: Symbolic realism
Time of plot: Nineteenth century
First published: 1897

As with many ships in Joseph Conrad's works, the sailing ship Narcissus *in this novel is a microcosm of the world. There, Conrad draws on the Greek myth of Narcissus, the distinct areas of the ship itself, and the ship's journey southward around Africa's Cape of Good Hope before turning north to England to highlight the theme of the literal and figurative journey to self-awareness.*

Narcissus. Freighter on which the novel's action takes place, as the ship sails from India to Britain, going around Southern Africa. The *Narcissus* is modeled on a real ship on which Conrad worked in 1884. A light/dark, white/black, life/death motif begins within the ship's forecastle even before the arrival on board of the black sailor, Wait. The narrator notes how the light there illuminates the white of the berths and only the heads of the men, whose bodies "were lost in the gloom of those places, that resembled narrow niches for coffins in a whitewashed and lighted mortuary," and takes on a new dimension with Wait's boarding the ship. With Wait confined there at the beginning of the voyage because of his mysterious illness, the forecastle becomes the focal point for the crew's emotional life and id-like underworld in which the men respond in various ways, according to their beliefs and temperaments, to the shadow of their own mortality.

The above-deck section of the ship represents the visible ego-like area, a place illuminated by the light of day and controlled by the captain, whose elevated "Olympian" position on the poop deck suggests the hierarchical position and the role of the superego. The dark, emotional turmoil of the forecastle moves above deck when Wait is moved into the deckhouse, an effort intended to quell the mutinous spirit arising from Wait's impossible demands on crew's time and emotions and Donkin's ceaseless shirking and grumbling about mistreatment. The inner storm is externalized not only by the movement of Wait into the light of day and reason but also by a strong gale that the ship encounters at this point.

*Cape of Good Hope. Peninsula near the southern tip of Africa separating the Indian Ocean from the Atlantic Ocean. Conrad selected this location—the literal turning point of his novel's journey—to draw together several of the novel's themes: the early modernist sense of isolation and alienation alluded to by the description of the ship as a lone, minuscule, foundering object tossed about by enormously powerful forces in contrast to the men's teamwork; the saving dignity of good, hard, honest labor in spite of the facts that it will neither be noticed nor prevent the inevitable end to life; and the hope to be found both in wise, attentive, self-sacrificing leaders and in men willing to set aside their private desires when so demanded by higher authority for a greater good than any one individual's satisfaction.

The men's ability to survive the storm is due primarily to their knowledge of ships and seamen, and the watchfulness, the concern, and the devotion of Captain Allistoun. After traveling far southward both geographically and psychically, facing the traditional hero's three major trials, in this case a gale, a near mutiny, and the death of Jim Wait after the storm—the crewmen demonstrate, by the spirit with which they approach their work, a better understanding of themselves and a rebirth in spirits as they travel northward. All except Donkin are united for that time before landfall by a sense of solidarity.

***Bombay.** City in west central India that is now called Mumbai. Bombay is the exotic East of seamen's romantic dreams, the symbolic dawning place of the journey, and a representative example of the darkness and corruption that Conrad associates with the land: the men are not happy until well out to sea and into their normal work routine. The darkest elements emerging from the land of Bombay are two new seamen, Donkin, an agitator, and Jim Wait, late to come aboard and thereby necessitating a "wait" for his arrival. Wait is the only black member of the crew, and a dying man whose process of decline and whose attitudes toward death and his fellow crewmen become a nearly unbearable "weight" on the rest of the men.

***London.** Capital city of Great Britain and the journey's end in the novel. Once the men are ashore, the land exerts its influence, drawing to its corrupt bosom the ill-natured Donkin (despising the sea, he takes a job on land) even as the wilderness appears to have patted the head of its child Kurtz, in Conrad's novel *Heart of Darkness* (1899), and scattering to the winds the men who once sailed together on the *Narcissus*.

— Daryl Holmes

NIGHT

Author: Elie Wiesel (1928-   )
Type of work: Novel
Type of plot: Autobiographical

Time of plot: 1941-1945
First published: *Un di Velt hot geshvign*, 1956; *La Nuit*, 1958 (English translation, 1960)

This fictionalized memoir of Elie Wiesel's confinement in the German concentration camps at Auschwitz and Buchenwald follows the deportation of the Jews from his native Sighet, Transylvania. Only under the conditions and in the places described in this work could Wiesel, as the creator, narrator, and protagonist, convey the horrors he witnessed.

Sighet (SEE-get). Transylvanian village in which the novel's opening section is set. Scenes in Sighet provide an introduction to life in the Jewish community by focusing on Wiesel's introduction to his Jewish heritage and religion. The invading Nazi troops establish two ghettoes into which the village's Jews are herded after being forced to give up all but what they can carry with them.

Birkenau. Polish town that is the site of the first concentration camp in which the Wiesel family is imprisoned. Following their stay in the ghetto, the family, along with their neighbors, are put onto trains and sent to concentration camps. Their first stop is Birkenau, where they are introduced to the horrors that follow. There they see families separated, mothers and children going in one direction and fathers and working-age sons in another. Wiesel's mother and sister are taken from him and, as he learns later, murdered. At Birkenau young Wiesel witnesses people giving up on life and willing themselves to die. In fact, Wiesel himself contemplates suicide, but the religious teachings he receives at home and the dogged determination of his father keep him from killing himself.

Auschwitz. Polish city that is the site of another concentration camp to which Wiesel, his father, and numerous workers from their first camp are later sent. There, Wiesel is briefly separated from his father. Although he is still in a concentration camp, Wiesel finds Auschwitz much more attractive than his previous prison because it is cleaner. Even though his job as a factory worker allows him to prove that he should be allowed to live, Wiesel becomes jaded and numb to the beatings he ex-

periences and the deaths of those around him. About the time he becomes acclimated to his new surroundings, Wiesel is sent to Buna with his father.

The greatest adjustment that Wiesel makes at the new camp is to the smell of burning bodies. There, too, Wiesel undergoes surgery on a seriously injured foot. Acquaintances warn him that he must not remain in the hospital too long or he will be killed. At one point, while still recovering, Wiesel is forced to march in the prison yard with other prisoners to prevent Russian planes from bombing the camp. In fact, the weak and wounded prisoners are forced to make a forty-two mile march to another concentration camp, Buchenwald.

Upon reaching this camp, the prisoners are allowed to rest. However, as a result of their long march and a serious case of dysentery, Wiesel's father dies, leaving his son to survive on his own. Elie is eventually among the few prisoners who are finally liberated from Buchenwald.

Scenes in the concentration camps become even more focused when Wiesel takes readers into the barracks, factories, hospitals, and death chambers that become the scenes of horror. He survived in part because of the strong religious faith that he had developed through his early education and the examples of his parents.

— *Tom Frazier*

NIGHT FLIGHT

Author: Antoine de Saint-Exupéry (1900-1944)
Type of work: Novel
Type of plot: Psychological realism

Time of plot: Early 1930's
First published: Vol de nuit, 1931 (English translation, 1932)

The skies over Argentina and the offices of a postal air service are the principal locales of this battle between ambitious humans and intractable nature. The narrative—which covers only a few hours—shifts between the cockpit of an airplane that eventually crashes in a storm and an office in Buenos Aires that directs both pilots and ground crew. Since the struggle of the chief of the airmail service to prove that night flights are worth risking is largely psychological, the narrative focuses on his psyche, in which his principles of duty and leadership are tested by the turmoil in the skies, that parallels the turmoil in his mind. Eventually, he comes to understand his place, and that of all humans, in the universal struggle between the forces of darkness and human destiny, and his principles are reaffirmed.

***Buenos Aires.** Capital city of Argentina, whose offices of the airmail service are the nerve center of air operations and of the central drama of the narrative. These offices are the command post from which Rivière, the operations chief, wages a war against the darkness of night, severe weather, and other hazards to aviation. In this heroic struggle, Rivière stations himself in Buenos Aires, the nerve center of an epic struggle. He feels that he must do away with the mystery, symbolized by such natural elements as the night, the ocean, the vast forces that constantly threaten to overwhelm and defeat humans. This mission is a moral one that challenges him to command events rather than be commanded by them. To do so is to become a creator of humanity's future. This struggle imbues this outpost of humanity's progress with universal significance, and Argentina symbolizes one of the last frontiers of human endeavor.

Night sky. Saint-Exupéry's metaphors repeatedly depict the night sky as an ocean traversed by the pilots in their airplanes, ships heading to port and weathering the storms. The airmail pilots are depicted as sea divers who descend to the sea floor in search of the sea's mysteries, then make their way back to the surface, but the principal arena of their battle is the night sky above South America, symbol of humanity's reach into the unknown.

In the sea of darkness that the pilots confront in their journey to and from Buenos Aires, the chief enemies are the darkness itself, which blinds them and threatens always to lead them off course, and the weather, whose powerful squalls, wind currents, and sudden changes constantly challenge pilots to perform heroically. The central issue of the narrative is whether humans can prevail against nature in their quest to extend the range of their activities, expand their presence in nature, and enlarge their significance in the universe. In the sky, especially the night sky, these heroic warriors are opposed by nature, which represents death, ignorance, and weakness.

The pilots represent the human struggle to advance against the darkness, and one of them, Fabien, gives his life in the struggle, waging war against a cyclone from his cockpit in the dark sky above Patagonia. His death demonstrates not only the hazards of night flight but the tremendous power of a natural force to overwhelm a mere mortal. The storm and the dark sky are his field of battle, which stands for any place in which humans struggle to survive in a noble cause.

Fabien's home. As he prepares for one of his night flights, Fabien is depicted as a warrior suiting up for battle, his wife in admiring attendance. This homely scene balances the heroic drama taking place in the pilot's cockpit and Rivière's offices. This location symbolizes domesticity, motherhood, marriage, and personal happiness. To Rivière, it represents a truth that he cannot deny but, at the same time, cannot allow to enter his world, which places the struggle against nature above personal happiness.

The brief scene inside Fabien's home contrasts sharply with the solitary, hard, unforgiving world of the pilot. This place is especially important, for it represents the powerful forces that home and family represent and shows that they are not diminished by the heroic battle in the night sky. One of the dominant images in the book is that of a solitary plane, deep in an ocean of stars and darkness, journeying toward home.

— *Bernard E. Morris*

'NIGHT, MOTHER

Author: Marsha Norman (1947-   )
Type of work: Drama
Type of plot: Psychological realism

Time of plot: Late twentieth century
First performed: 1982; first published, 1983

The ranch-style, remotely located American house in which two women live in this play is an area of confinement and duty for the daughter, but a comfortable, lovely place for the mother who owns it. The daughter's bedroom door is open and visible throughout the play, suggesting a private and quiet place of escape for her.

House. Typical ranch house built at the end of a country road. No name is given to a town here, but the rather isolated nature of the house is important, as it symbolizes the lonely life that Jessie lives in it. In contrast to Jessie, her mother is happily ensconced in her cozy living room. It is filled with nice products of her needlework that are all pleasantly attractive. Since Jessie is ill with epilepsy, she seldom leaves her house, in which she is increasingly becoming a prisoner as she ages.

On the land abutting the house, Jessie's father had once had a farm, described as existing almost totally independent of the house. The realm of the farm belonged to the father almost exclusively, just as the realm of the house belonged to the mother.

Small house. House that Jessie's husband, a carpenter, built for her in earlier years. It was a small and cozy house, in which she seems to have been happy.

— *Patricia E. Sweeney*

THE NIGHT OF THE IGUANA

Author: Tennessee Williams (Thomas Lanier Williams, 1911-1983)

Type of work: Drama

Type of plot: Psychological realism

Time of plot: Late summer, 1940

First performed: 1961; first published, 1961

In this searching and often painful play, Tennessee Williams uses a run-down hotel on the coast of Mexico as a vehicle for exploring the problem of evil. Although on the surface it seems picaresque, even charming, the Costa Verde proves to be a place of festering pain, where the defrocked and tormented preacher T. Lawrence Shannon (openly admitted to be a representation of the playwright himself) seeks the comfort of an old friend. Instead, he finds only more misery and despair after his faith-shaking experience of seeing people in appalling poverty searching through a manure pile for morsels of undigested food.

Costa Verde. Hotel in Mexico, its name literally means "green coast" in Spanish. Williams describes it as rustic and bohemian, situated at the crest of a hill that overlooks a beach. He also notes that it is important to recognize that this is not the Mexican coast of his present, but of the early 1940's—the temporal setting is as important as the spatial, given the important role of the German tourists and their blatant Nazi attitudes.

The entire play takes place on the roofed veranda at the front of the hotel. The rest of the setting is presented only as hints: background noises, glimpses of light and motion, shouts by the principal characters to unseen servants. Behind this wide veranda upon which folding tables are placed for supper, there is a row of small cubicles, each shrouded with mosquito netting. During the night scenes, they are lighted from within and serve as miniature interior stages within the main stage. Williams masterfully uses this constrained setting to keep the focus of his story tightly on the problems of the tormented characters.

— *Leigh Husband Kimmel*

NIGHT RIDER

Author: Robert Penn Warren (1905-1989)

Type of work: Novel

Type of plot: Social morality

Time of plot: 1904-1905

First published: 1939

Warren used territory he knew at first hand, the tobacco farming region of southwestern Kentucky, for this tragic novel of the conflict between tobacco growers and buyers. To reconstruct the violent historical clash known as the Black Patch War, he drew on oral tales as well as historical research to depict the tragic irony of an idealistic cause corrupted by violence. Drawing on memories and personal experience, Warren describes the landscape in concrete detail and portrays scenes of violence with authentic realism.

*Southwestern Kentucky. Region of Kentucky stretching from Bowling Green to the Mississippi River, containing valleys and rolling hills; an intense agricultural region that long depended heavily on tobacco production. The region contrasts greatly with the Appalachian regions of eastern Kentucky, with their mountain culture and troubled history of coal mining, and the region also differs sharply from the traditionally genteel "blue grass" and bourbon areas of the state's northern section, around Lexington and Louisville. Despite being intensely agricultural, southwestern Kentucky and northeastern Tennessee comprise an area of independent farms of varying sizes quite different from the plantation economy of the Deep South's cotton industry. The intense individualism of the tobacco farmers tended to make the formation of the tobacco growers' association somewhat difficult, creating differences of opinion about methods of protest. As Warren's novel reveals, these philosophical differences erupted into violence against tobacco growers who failed to cooperate with the association—a fictional event suggested by regional history.

In addition to describing the events that led to the conflict known as the Black Patch War, Warren provides memorable descriptions of the physical terrain of this area, describing it as a plateau of wooded hills and arable valleys, with hardwood forests and inspiring ridge-top vistas. However, Warren also realistically depicts the region's propensity for violence, resulting in part from its memories of the Civil War and ranging from acts of racial hatred to the barn burnings and midnight murders of the tobacco growers' association.

Bardsville. Fictional town where the tobacco growers in the novel form their first association, debate political and economic issues, and hold public trials. Warren based the town partly on his personal memories of Clarksville, Tennessee, a major commercial center on the Cumberland River, across the state border from southwestern Kentucky. Bardsville may also have elements of Warren's native Guthrie, Kentucky, where the historical tobacco growers' association was formed in 1904.

Warren tended to make the fictional Bardsville a kind of archetypal symbol of southern agricultural towns at the turn of the twentieth century. In contrast to what he did in *Night Rider*, he used the real name of Clarksville in "Prime Leaf" his first published treatment of the conflict in 1931. In yet another famous novella, "The Circus in the Attic" (1948), Warren depicts another Bardsville, which has even more of the character of a self-satisfied village, sketching its historical development through World War II as this history was reflected in the frustrated experience of Bolton Lovehart.

Monclair. Kentucky senator Tolliver's mansion, in reality an enormous farmhouse commanding a view of the nearby hills that serves as one of the headquarters of the tobacco growers' political program. The mansion is an ironic representation of Tolliver's spurious leadership and dubious gentility. Its eventual destruction symbolizes the declining fortunes of the tobacco growers' movement.

Proudfit's cabin. Home of the independent farmer Willie Proudfit. In contrast to Monclair, which the gentleman farmer and lawyer Percy Munn envies early in the novel, Proudfit's rough-hewn cabin serves as both a refuge from the law and an opportunity for Munn to gain a more realistic perspective on his flawed crusade and his own identity. There, too, the elemental countryside and the backwoods Proudfit family offer a common-sense contrast to the exalted social status he has sought.

American West. Broadly defined section of the western United States depicted as a region of aimless violence and moral chaos in Proudfit's narrative of his past as a buffalo hunter, plainsman, and Indian fighter. Although Proudfit returned to southwestern Kentucky, his original home, with its seeming tranquillity because he came to experience a personal revulsion against the destructive world of the frontier days on the Great Plains of the West, his story suggests—through an unromantic description of the destruction of the buffalo and the eruption of wars with Native Americans—that in the midst of turmoil, he discovered the futility of violence and the importance of self-understanding. His narrative describing the crucible of violence he has endured provides an ironic commentary on the process of moral disintegration that takes place within Percy Munn, as he drifts from bourgeois passivity to idealistic passion and finally to a surrender to self-destructive outlawry and violence.

— *Edgar L. Chapman*

NIGHTMARE ABBEY

Author: Thomas Love Peacock (1785-1866)
Type of work: Novel
Type of plot: Fiction of manners

Time of plot: Early nineteenth century
First published: 1818

Although this novel is haunted only in a metaphorical sense, its setting might be reckoned the most comprehensively and coherently haunted house in the annals of English literature. Nightmare Abbey stands symbolically on the edge of civilization, its halls and corridors carefully reflecting every form of human unhappiness to which they play host—and they play host to every kind there is, ranging from the everyday distress of a loveless family to the gloomy abstractions of philosophical pessimism.

Nightmare Abbey. Dilapidated mansion in England's Lincolnshire County; a former monastery whose state of sad disrepair reflects the plight of its residents, the deeply dysfunctional Glowry family. The house is not far from the sea, being separated therefrom by a tract of low-lying fenland dotted with windmills.

There is nothing unrealistic about an early nineteenth century English family living in what once had been an abbey; many English religious houses became secular residences following King Henry VIII's dissolution of England's Roman Catholic monasteries in the sixteenth century. The abbey's address reveals something about the Glowry family's problematic social status—they are products of social upheavals that were still considered recent by the English landed aristocracy—but its real significance is that Nightmare Abbey is symbolic of a nation and a world whose secularization has left it uncomfortable and desolate. The road that connects the abbey to the nearest town, Claydyke, is a narrow causeway raised above the fen, from which carriages are all too easily dislodged.

The abbey itself is square in shape, its four walls facing the four points of the compass. It has a tower at each corner, and is surrounded on every side but the south by a moat. The northwestern tower is the domain of Christopher Glowry, the abbey's owner. The southeastern tower, which is home to Christopher's son, Scythrop, opens up onto a terrace which is called the garden, but nothing grows there except weeds. The abbey's southwestern tower is in ruins, inhabited only by owls. The northeastern tower houses the servants, who have all been chosen for the lugubrious quality of their names and faces. The main body of the building contains numerous reception rooms, dining rooms, and guest bedrooms, all of which are underused. The rare guests entertained there are well fitted to the surroundings, especially the connoisseur of the macabre, Mr. Flosky, and the Manichean Millenarian, Mr. Toobad.

Scythrop Glowry longs to transform this doom-laden scenery with the aid of "transcendental technology," but his father is a considerable obstacle to this ambition, as is the place itself—whose distinctive atmosphere is explicitly identified in chapter 9 as "the spirit of black melancholy." Scythrop's cause is not greatly advanced by his romantic association with his formidable cousin Marionetta O'Carroll. When he secretly offers sanctuary to the mysterious Stella—who is briefly mistaken for a mermaid by the ichthyologist Mr. Asterias—the life-enhancing presence that gradually begins to transform his apartments soon turns out to have been an illusion. Fortunately or unfortunately, he is saved from the necessity of marrying either woman, and is thus liberated to return his full attention to his progressive plans for the regeneration of Nightmare Abbey—and hence, symbolically if not actually, the redemption of human nature.

At the end of the novel, Scythrop is still alone in his dreary tower, having failed to make the least material difference to his surroundings—which strongly suggests that readers should not be optimistic about the future reconstruction of Nightmare Abbey.

*London. Great Britain's capital city is not featured as a setting in the novel; however, there are repeated references to it in the text. For example, when Christopher Glowry is absent from the abbey, it is because he has gone to London, and it is from London that most of the guests featured in the story have come. There, London is not an opposite extreme of English life, to be contrasted with the lonely abbey, but a macrocosm symbolically embodied in the microcosm of the abbey: the same collation of nightmares, writ slightly larger. The city offers no possibility of escape, to either the complacently gloomy Christopher or his ambitiously disaffected son. If any salvation is to be found, it has to begin within the abbey's nightmarish heart and grow outward; the causeway to Claydyke is no highway to Heaven.

— *Brian Stableford*

NIGHTWOOD

Author: Djuna Barnes (1892-1982)
Type of work: Novel
Type of plot: Psychological surrealism

Time of plot: 1920's
First published: 1936

While a number of geographical and cultural places figure in this surrealist masterpiece, they are all essentially the same place. Rather than merely describe physical reality in the usual picturesque way, the novel uses places to suggest the "sur-reality" created in readers' minds by the text's ubiquitous thematic paradoxes, its "mythopoeic" method, and its highly polished, sometimes perplexing, but always intriguing, experimental style.

Vienna. Capital city of Austria, in which the novel opens with a flashback from 1920 to 1880, when one of its central characters, Felix Volkbein, is born. The very first paragraph describes Felix's mother, Hedvig, giving birth while "lying upon a canopied bed of a rich spectacular crimson, the valance stamped with the bifurcated wings of the House of Hapsburg, the feather coverlet an envelope of satin on which, in massive and tarnished gold threads, stood the Volkbein arms." The ornate richness and highly self-conscious quality of the language of this passage, perhaps the most accessible of the novel's many physical descriptions, is indicative of the novel's style.

Opening the story in Vienna serves two related purposes. Since Vienna was psychologist Sigmund Freud's city, it serves to prefigure the most important of the novel's Surrealist themes—the primacy of sleep and dreams over reason and waking "reality"—and it announces the author's "mythopoeic" intention. For Felix, readers soon learn, is not simply one person, a historical being, among others cast in a realistic drama of human passion. Rather, he is a modern embodiment of a mythic archetype—he is once called a "wandering Jew"—and so are all the other characters.

Berlin circus. Subject of a brief flashback within the Vienna section of the novel that introduces a circus performer, the duchess of Broadback. This woman is also known as Frau Mann, a mannish woman whose name announces the subtheme of the paradoxes of gender. Her purpose is to allow a discussion of one of the favored surrealist themes: the superiority of circus life to "normal" life.

A favored subject of many then avant-garde artists of Djuna Barnes's era, such as painter Pablo Picasso, the circus is associated with the illicit life of the night and particularly with sexual license. In this regard, it contrasts with the falsity and "bad faith" of the lives of the comfortable bourgeoisie audience that it entertains.

The Berlin flashback also introduces the formidable Dr. Matthew O'Connor, an Irish American expatriate who, as a homosexual and a self-styled gynecologist, is one of the novel's many "outsiders." Through his extraordinary talent for talk, O'Connor becomes the story's chief moral intelligence. Berlin seems very much like Vienna, and serves to introduce a number of highly eccentric characters, all of whom suggest the theme of the polyglot quality of modern urban life.

Paris. France's capital city is the novel's central setting, but it, too, is wrapped in surrealist eccentricity. For example, readers never meet a French person there, but only a variety of expatriates. While a number of real landmarks and streets are named, none is ever given a detailed description. As the novel's title suggests, Barnes is interested in the psychological and cultural implications of the metaphor of "night," and especially the myths about it that her Surrealist predecessors (notably Andre Breton, the founder of the Surrealist movement) had invented.

Paris seems to be the central literary place in the novel primarily because it was the center of the European avant-garde at the time. The novel's central event—the meeting and the lesbian love affair between the American expatriates, Robin Vote and Nora Flood—happens here. Robin's chapter is titled "La Somnambule" and she is a fictional projection of that favored Surrealist figure, the sleepwalker. Perpetually bewildered by consciousness, truly alive only within the mysterious folds of night, Robin is the novel's emblem of intrigue and almost unfathomable sexual attraction to the novel's other female characters, Nora Flood and Jenny Petherbridge.

Robin is also a tragic figure, an archetype of the lost soul who will be destroyed by her own psychological contradictions. Paris is a place that, due to its great age, has created a complex and decadent culture that alone can sustain the lives of characters, like Robin, who are so eccentric as to be irredeemably outside the bourgeois norm. Famous as the City of Light, Paris is also the city of night; in its acceptance of all the mystery, paradox, and abnormality that the human race can produce, it is the antithesis of the puritanical American possessiveness and mania for regularity and for soul-denying clarity that is symbolized by New York City.

New York City. The story ends with Robin and Jenny, now her lover, in New York City, where Robin aimlessly wanders the nighttime streets, haunting train terminals and out-of-the-way Roman Catholic chapels. Like the novel's other cities, New York is another symbol of the night, a dark landscape of somnambulant wandering in which sensual desire predominates over conscious self-control.

A sudden leap—typical of the novel's effort to create the sense of life's essential lack of logic, no transition from one place to another is provided—finds Robin suddenly wandering the rural New York countryside. She is unconsciously winding her way, slowly and tortuously, toward Nora's country home. There she enters the estate's decaying chapel—a place of candlelight and flickering shadow reminiscent of T. S. Eliot's use of the same image in his poem *The Waste Land* (1922)—and descends into madness in a scene that is one of the strangest and most interesting, if disturbing, conclusions to a novel in literature. The countryside is no more realistically described than the city—they are indistinguishable as physical places since neither is treated in any detail—but Barnes's unique style creates an eerie sense that life is most fully lived at night and in the dark, that "surreality" is more important than daylight "reality" or consciousness. Barnes's treatment of place in *Nightwood*, like the other aspects of plot and character development, is at the service of the novel's dark and deeply ambiguous, but ultimately quite moral, theme: that "Man was born damned and innocent from the start, and wretchedly—as he must—on those two themes—whistles his tune."

— *Ronald Foust*

NINETEEN EIGHTY-FOUR

Author: George Orwell (Eric Arthur Blair, 1903-1950)
Type of work: Novel
Type of plot: Science fiction

Time of plot: 1984
First published: 1949

This novel uses aspects of place to suggest the direction and scope of change in a future dystopian London. Place names are emblematic and ironic; locale both influences and reflects characters' behaviors and states of mind. The general conditions and maintenance of buildings and neighborhood infrastructures correspond to a hierarchy of importance reflecting the changes in values and ideology of the grotesque world order, whose evolution the novel depicts.

London. Capital of a future (from the perspective of 1949, when George Orwell wrote the book) political unit called **Airstrip One** in the superstate Oceania that is the setting for the novel. London's skyline is dominated by four government ministries, whose enormous bulk and tasteless architecture distinguish them from the surviving historical structures surrounding them. Residential sectors of the city segregate members of the unnamed Party from proles ("proletarians"), but both Proles and Outer Party members live in crumbling tenement buildings that are unsanitary, crowded, and poorly maintained. Police patrols are highly visible; posters of Big Brother—the ever-present, seemingly loving personification of the state—are ubiquitous.

The city's squalor is symptomatic of the Ingsoc government's disdain for the welfare of its own citizens.

This is the result of a change in the fundamental principles and core values of the society; human rights are nonexistent, and all available resources support building and maintaining government structures that administer and preserve the collective. The life of the individual is barren; this barrenness is suggested by lack of luxury, beauty, and privacy.

Inner Party member Winston Smith has a fascination with the past that he acts out by paying clandestine visits to the oldest and meanest areas of the city, where the proles live and work. Because the proles are considered by Inner Party leaders to be beneath concern, their sectors are largely ignored by the government and have become *de facto* museums of prerevolutionary culture, customs, and mores. Only within the prole neighborhoods can Winston enjoy the smell of real coffee, the sounds of unconstrained conversation and songs, and the sights of uninhibited children playing and adults gathering to talk—all of which reminds Winston of his own childhood and suggest the complexity and fullness of prerevolutionary life.

Victory Mansions. Run-down London building in which Winston has a flat on the seventh floor. The building has bad plumbing, no heat, a broken elevator, and the inescapable stench of rancid cabbage. The one thing in the building that works flawlessly is its network of telescreens, which broadcast ceaseless propaganda and, in turn, watch residents through television cameras.

Charrington's shop. Cramped, dilapidated antique store in a prole sector of London that Winston frequents. He sees the shop as a microcosmic remnant of the past, but it is, in fact, a carefully maintained surveillance tool. Its upstairs apartment, which Winston rents for trysts with Julia, becomes the place of their downfall. Though infested by biting bedbugs and large, aggressive rats, the room also has a private entrance to facilitate Winston and Julia's secret meetings. There they abandon themselves to sensuality only because they think the room has no telescreen. However, it does have a telescreen, which, ironically, is obscured by something that would never be found in the home of a Party member—an engraving of a medieval church. The illusion of privacy leads Winston and Julia to incriminate themselves, and furthermore leads Winston inadvertently to betray his abject horror of rats to the Thought Police watching him and Julia through the telescreen.

Ministry of Truth. Government ministry building in which Winston is one of many writers who revise historical records to match the government's constantly changing definitions of reality. Each time Oceania's military alliances shift, history must be rewritten to show that Oceania has always had the same allies and same enemies. Winston often rewrites the same news stories many times, making something different happen each time, and he comes to appreciate the power of the government precept that whoever controls the past controls the future.

Ministry of Love. Site of Winston and Julia's detention, torture, and reintegration into the Party. One of four enormous pyramidal steel and concrete structures that dominate the London skyline, "Miniluv" has no windows. Standing behind heavily guarded barricades, it is protected by barbed wire and automatic gun pods. Inside, brilliant lights gleam on sparkling clean white walls, which Winston comes to think of as "the place where there is no darkness," a phrase he remembers either from a prescient dream or from his confused memory. The absence of clocks and windows creates a sense that time is suspended or has no influence, an impression rendered more powerful by the contrast with life outside, where all activities are maintained on a rigorous schedule. Thus Miniluv becomes a mockery of heaven, and by extension, Winston's indoctrination and reintegration into the Party by O'Brien become a mockery of the loving inclusion into Paradise and communion with God promised by the saints.

Golden Country. Place about which Winston dreams frequently. It is an abandoned pasture that, although once hedged, is being reclaimed by nature. Winston associates it at first with the distant past, and early in the novel, dreams of having a sexual encounter with Julia here; after this dream, he awakens speaking the word "Shakespeare." Less than a month later, Winston and Julia have their first sexual experience in a rural spot outside London that Winston realizes is almost identical to the place of his dreams. In the midst of his first encounter with Julia, the Golden Country comes to represent for him an animal sensuality unburdened by reason, the antithesis of calculation and cold restraint. Such freedom, for Winston, is possible only in a place largely untainted not just by Ingsoc, but also by the political and philosophical milieu from which it has arisen. The disappearing traces of human domination and the return of the pasture to an idyllic state suggest perhaps not just a yearning for the past, but also a hope for the future. Nevertheless, it is a hope so wild that Winston can hardly allow himself to indulge it except in dream.

Chestnut Tree Café. Sidewalk coffeehouse associated with Party members who have been reintegrated and subsequently targeted for vaporization. Early in the novel, Winston destroys an exculpatory newspaper photograph of three enemies of Big Brother whom he later sees at the café, *before* their disappearances but *after* their much-publicized but false confessions. A year later, in the novel's final episode, Winston himself, now a doomed outcast, again sits at the café, drinking sweetened clove-flavored gin, the café specialty, and solving newspaper chess problems. As the telescreen announces a military victory for Oceania's armies, Winston, who throughout the novel has reacted to such questionable government claims with cynical skepticism, can no longer resist proclaiming his joy and his love for Big Brother.

Oceania. One of three superstates that cover most of the globe. The superstates are conglomerates of nations and regions that first formed alliances then annealed into new entities under the pressures of revolution. The three states are engaged in a constant state of war and shifting alliances, on which Ingsoc broadcasts interminable news bulletins through the telescreens. Oceania itself comprises the lands of the Western Hemisphere, Australia and its surrounding islands, the British Islands, and part of Southern Africa. The easternmost province of Oceania is **Airstrip One**, which corresponds to what had once been the United Kingdom.

Eastasia. Superstate that comprises China, Southeast Asia, Japan and its surrounding islands, and varying portions of Manchuria, Mongolia, and Tibet.

Eurasia. Superstate that comprises most of Europe and northern Asia, from Portugal to eastern Siberia. When the novel opens, Oceania is at war with Eurasia; when it ends, Eurasia is Oceania's ally.

— *Andrew B. Preslar*

NO EXIT

Author: Jean-Paul Sartre (1905-1980)
Type of work: Drama
Type of plot: Existentialism

Time of plot: Twentieth century
First performed: 1944; first published, 1945 as *Huis clos* (English translation, 1946)

*The setting of this play is ostensibly an ordinary room in the real world; however, it is actually a room in Hell, in which three people are locked for eternity, hence the play's title—*No Exit.

Hell. As the play opens, a man is being ushered into an ordinary-looking room by a valet. It appears at first to be a hotel or the guest room of some country mansion. The man notices that the furniture is French Second Empire, an elaborately decorative pastiche of earlier styles, which makes the furniture appear to transcend history. There are three sofas: one claret red, another vivid green, and the third a more neutral color. The guest, Garcin, also notices a bronze statuette by Ferdinand Barbedienne, known for his copies of famous originals. Again, this implies that nothing in the room is authentic or real. Garcin also remarks on the absence of mirrors and ob-

serves that the only domestic tool in the room is a letter opener. He inquires of the valet about its purpose and is assured that its purpose will soon be revealed. As the valet exits, he indicates that the door will be locked behind him and that the servants' bell does not always function.

Two women are then let into the room by the valet. After some intense conflicts and confessions, it becomes obvious to the three people that they are in Hell, locked together for eternity. They pound on the door to no avail. Committing suicide with the letter opener only intensifies their agony since they are already dead. They are their own devils. There are some intense exchanges between the characters in this tiny room, and it becomes clear that this torture will last forever. The setting, a room in Hell, is Jean-Paul Sartre's metaphor for his belief in existentialism, the philosophy that states that out-side circumstances have no power to affect human beings' lives. Humans are responsible for their own destiny and cannot escape that responsibility.

— *August W. Staub*

NO-NO BOY

Author: John Okada (1923-1971)
Type of work: Novel
Type of plot: Historical realism

Time of plot: Shortly after the end of World War II
First published: 1957

Whether America is a country in which the Japanese American protagonist can continue to live and prosper is this novel's central question. By law, Ichiro Yamada's birth in the United States makes him an American citizen. However, his Japanese background leads to his internment and eventual incarceration when he refuses to serve in the U.S. military on principle. After he is released when the war ends, he wonders whether his life belongs to the land of his birth or the distant land of his parents and ancestors.

*Seattle. Pacific Northwest city in Washington State that is hometown to Ichiro Yamada. Described realistically and with a keen eye for detail, Seattle's **Japan town** struggles to come back to life after most of its residents return from internment camps after World War II. Rising above the harbor, with Jackson Street as its central thoroughfare, this district lies between the city's Fifth and Twelfth Avenues, and borders Chinatown.

Through the eyes of Ichiro, readers learn of the changes that political upheavals bring to his old neighborhood. Before the eviction and internment of its Japanese and Japanese American residents in 1942, the neighborhood was home to a community that harbored strong ties to the land and culture of their ancestors: Japan. After the war, the returning residents struggle with the influx of African Americans, and the effects of a pleasure-seeking, relatively affluent postwar society that turns clothing stores into pool parlors. There, young Japanese American men who have fought in the U.S. Army participate in the raucous nightlife, feeling they have earned their place in American society. They despise those who—like Ichiro—did not fight. Yet Ichiro remains skeptical whether this place will really accept these men.

Ozaki's grocery store. Seattle store run by Ichiro's parents. A familiar feature of prewar Japan town, the operation is a cramped and marginal enterprise. Separated from the small shop by a curtain, the family's living quarters are in the back. Four people share a kitchen, a bathroom, and one bedroom. With its typical bell to alert the family to each entering customer, the grocery is a place indicative of the fate of so many Japanese immigrants.

Instead of striking it rich quickly and returning to Japan as they had hoped to do when they came to America, Ichiro's parents find themselves living in a place they still consider alien territory after thirty-five years. With frugality and persistence, they have made a modest living while their children have grown up and adopted American ways. The wartime internment, however, serves as brutal reminder that the place of one's birth may turn against one. To Ichiro, the family grocery store represents both the cultural insularity of his parents' generation and their meek acceptance of America's social and economic order. While his mother believes the Japanese will eventually win the war, she nevertheless works hard to keep her store afloat. She commits suicide after realizing that Japan has lost the war.

Akimoto's apartment. Run-down home of Fred Akimoto, another "no-no boy" who is carrying on an affair with his married neighbor, a young plump Japanese American mother. Fred's shabby apartment mirrors his mental torment at being ostracized by his fellow Japanese Americans for having refused to enlist in the army.

His affair with the woman next door reflects the nihilistic recklessness that ultimately leads to his death.

*University of Washington. Because Ichiro has refused to fight for the United States, he believes he has no right to return to this idyllic Seattle campus. His departure after visiting his old professor is described in terms that invite an allusion to Adam's banishment from the Garden of Eden, with Ichiro passing his expulsion on himself.

Club Oriental. Nightclub on King Street in Seattle's Chinatown that serves a Japanese American clientele, some of whom bring white girlfriends. The intended harmony of the place is destroyed when the club becomes flashpoint for the tensions generated by the majority of Japanese Americans, who feel that their army service has earned them a place in American society. They hate those like Ichiro who refused to serve, and the club sees violent altercations.

Emi's house. Home of a young married woman with whom Ichiro has an affair, located south of Seattle.

Since Emi's husband refuses to leave the army and prefers to stay in Germany, she lives alone and invites Ichiro to share her bed. Emi's house represents a comforting shelter that Ichiro continually denies to himself.

Kumasaka house. Home owned by a Japanese American family. In Ichiro's eyes, buying a home in Seattle makes the Kumasakas Americanized. Unlike Ichiro's mother, the Kumasakas have let go of the dream of returning to Japan and embraced America as their own— the land for which their son Bob dies in the war.

*Portland. Oregon city to which Ichiro goes to see his friend Kenji, who is dying from a war wound. While he is there, he refuses a job offer because he feels guilty about taking the place of a Japanese American man who fought in the war. However, Kenji tells him that soon the United States will not honor these veterans and again discriminate against them. Before Kenji dies, Ichiro follows his advice by returning to Seattle to make his peace with himself, the city, and the United States.

— *R. C. Lutz*

NORTH AND SOUTH

Author: Elizabeth Bishop (1911-1979)　　　　　　*First published:* 1946
Type of work: Poetry

Elizabeth Bishop's poetry treats locale as an intellectual experience. In this collection of poems, place has an element of allegory. The North is sometimes represented as cold, intellectual, and severe, for example, and the South is sometimes represented as warm, sensual, and mild. This allegory, however, is only a minor part of Bishop's larger poetic goal, which is to comprehend the essence of a place, even as this comprehension is, by necessity, entirely limited to the perceptions of one witness at one time. In many poems, the speaker's physical experience of a place is the essence of her understanding of not only the place but also her place in it.

Map. Appropriately enough, the explorations of *North and South* begin with an examination of a map. In "The Map," the first poem of the collection, the speaker examines a map of the North Atlantic area. The map is tangible evidence to her of the riddles of human perception, whereby she sees real things as if they were symbolic and—more important in the poem—understands symbols as if they were real. The poem begins with a question of perception: How can the map, which is flat, represent something as three-dimensional as land and ocean? The second stanza offers examples of how the speaker (and, by implication, anyone) can translate the abstractions of a map into the vivid, sensual perceptions to which her understanding is attached. The speaker imagines peninsulas as women's fingers, feeling the water between them as women's fingers would feel cloth. In her imagination, the lines on the paper are like women's fingers. This simile is presented simply as the means by which people make symbols understandable. This poem argues one of Bishop's central themes about place—people understand it only as much as they experience it with their senses.

Paris. Capital of France and ostensible setting of Bishop's poem titled "Paris, 7 A.M." Its speaker draws general conclusions from the immediate particulars of her environment, as she wanders from room to room setting clocks in an apartment. She looks out a window and sees a courtyard and pigeons. She notes the details of her apartment building—ornamental urns, mansard roof, a slice of sky, and gray and yellow stones. This is framed by the rectangle of the window. Using these details as the starting place of an imaginative association game, she strives to understand her own place in this city. By recognizing what these details make her think of, she comes to understand how she is feeling.

In poetry, when something tangible and outside the speaker is implicitly compared with the thoughts and moods within the speaker, it is called an objective correlative. In this poem, the clocks are an example. The speaker calls them "histrionic," which a clock cannot be but a person can be. Throughout the poem, the imagery implies disorientation and vulnerability and thus that the speaker is feeling disoriented and vulnerable.

The solidly built apartment building, for example, is made of a light-colored stone. The stone reminds her, because of its color, of something fragile, ephemeral, and gone—the snow forts and snowballs of her youth. Bishop is making a sly allusion to one of the most common themes of poetry, one that is usually cited by asking a question: "Where are the snows of yesteryear?" (This question comes from a French poem, so her allusion to it in a poem set in Paris is quite apt.) The answer to the question is that they are gone. The speaker, looking out the window while worried about time (she is setting clocks), considers how time will quickly erase even something as seemingly solid as the stones of her apartment. She is reminded of how fragile and ephemeral all things are, including herself. From the particulars of a place and time she discovers not only a general truth but the particular truth that underlies her experience of that place and time.

— *Eric Howard*

NORTH AND SOUTH

Author: Elizabeth Gaskell (1810-1865)
Type of work: Novel
Type of plot: Social realism

Time of plot: Mid-nineteenth century
First published: 1854-1855

This story about a romance between a girl from southern England forced to move to a northern mill town, and a young northern mill owner focuses on their differing attitudes toward urban life and industry.

*Harley Street. London street on which Margaret Hale has spent nine years living in a town house as a companion to her cousin Edith, who is about to be married as the novel opens. The house is to be shut up as Edith, her husband, and her mother, go abroad, and Margaret is to return home to the country parsonage where her parents live. The novel reveals little about the house at 96 Harley Street, other than a series of public and private rooms and, at the top of the house, a nursery, where Margaret spent much of her early life. The life of the house has been formal, with children eating apart from their parents.

Helstone vicarage. Home of Margaret's parents in New Forest, Hampshire, that Margaret regards as her true home, despite having been away from it for many years. There she is happy to live an outdoor life, visiting local people and walking in the forest. Her mother, however, is discontented; she regards Helstone as one of England's most out-of-the-way places and would rather live at 96 Harley Street. She dislikes the trees and lack of nearby society and yearns for everything her daughter has happily given up.

The interior of the vicarage house is not seen from Margaret's point of view. It has a drawing room, a dining room, a library, and other rooms not seen. Readers see the drawing room from the point of view of Henry Lennox, a visitor, who sees that the family is not well off, noting the room's old carpets and faded chintzes. Readers later see the vicarage from the point of view of the next incumbent and his wife, who are renovating and expanding the house to accommodate a growing family. Elizabeth Gaskell does, however, offer several lyrical descriptions of the vicarage's garden, which supports fruit trees and flowers.

Milton-Northern. Fictional town to which the Hales travel when the Reverend Mr. Hale feels obliged to resign his living because of his religious doubts. Hale has been able to establish himself as a tutor through the good offices of an Oxford friend, Mr. Bell, who owns property in Milton-Northern but remains in Oxford. Milton is a growing industrial town and property is rising in value, making it difficult for the family to rent the kind of house to which they aspire. They are obliged to settle in a suburb, Crampton, subject to dampness and fog. The emphasis of Gaskell's description of Milton is of straight lines, small houses built of brick rather than stone, and with great factories dominating the landscape.

Canute Street. Street in Milton's Crampton district on which the Hales live in a cramped house. It is initially decorated in what they consider to be a vulgar style, but this is altered before they move in, thanks to the intervention of John Thornton, owner of a local mill and one of Mr. Hale's pupils. Impressed by Margaret's demeanor, Thornton endeavors to have the house altered to suit her.

Higgins house. Home of the working class Higgins family, who become Margaret's friends, at 9 Frances Street. It is a small house off a squalid street. The house is ill kept, as Bessie Higgins cannot work and her sister, Mary, while good-natured, is rough and clumsy and not adept at housework.

Thornton's house. Home of John Thornton on Milton's Marlborough Street, When Margaret Hale and her father call on Thornton, they learn first that his house is adjacent to the mill, unlike other mill owners, who prefer to live in the country, away from the noise and dirt of their own factories. In the drawing rooms of the houses, they find that the furniture is covered, as though it has not been used for a long time, though this is as much to keep everything clean of the dirt from the yard. The dining room is also described as "grim." This contrasts with a later visit when the Hales dine with the Thorntons at an elaborate party, when the covers are taken off and the chandelier is lighted. Gaskell particularly notes a lack of books in the public rooms.

— *Maureen Speller*

NORTH OF BOSTON

Author: Robert Frost (1874-1963)   *First published:* 1914
Type of work: Poetry

Settings in these collections of poems are the farms, towns, and villages of Vermont and New Hampshire. Although most of the poems do not specify locales, they are rich in natural description and sometimes refer to neighboring farms and local landmarks. In many of the poems Robert Frost develops natural images into metaphors and symbols of the psychological state of a character.

Lunenburg. Small Vermont township, appearing in "The Mountain," that is made up of farms scattered around the foot of Mount Hor, near the western New Hampshire border town of Lancaster. The mountain's name alludes to the biblical Mount Hor, and Frost may have intended the reader to associate the present mountain's remote summit with the tops of Mount Hor and Mount Sinai, where God spoke to Aaron and Moses. In the poem, however, the man with the oxcart, to whom the narrator speaks, is uncertain of the mountain's name. In any event the allusion is ironic, since neither the narrator nor the oxcart driver has been to the mountain's top.

*New Hampshire.** New England state containing the small towns Lancaster, Woodsville Junction, and Bow, mentioned in "A Hundred Collars." Lancaster, near the Vermont border, in the northern part of the state, is the hometown of Dr. Magoon, a professor who is returning to town. Traveling by train, he stays in the hotel in Woodsville Junction (present-day Woodsville), where he shares a room with Lafe, a large, talkative man who drives around the countryside collecting for the Bow *Weekly News.* Bow, located about ten miles south of Concord, is the scene of the Stark family reunion in "The Generations of Men."

*Lake Willoughby.** Large body of water in the northeastern corner of Vermont that is the setting of "A Servant to Servants." The lake's isolation and natural beauty provide an objective correlative for the woman speaker's fears that her loneliness and overwork have made her vulnerable to the insanity that runs in her family.

— *Roy Scheele*

NORTHANGER ABBEY

Author: Jane Austen (1775-1817)
Type of work: Novel
Type of plot: Domestic realism

Time of plot: Early nineteenth century
First published: 1818

A strong sense of place pervades this earliest of Jane Austen's novels, which parodies the popular reading matter of the late eighteenth century, such as Ann Radcliffe's 1794 novel The Mysteries of Udolpho. *Austen's unsophisticated protagonist, Catherine Morland, has an imagination supercharged with events, persons, and places in the books she reads, and she must learn—while experiencing some humiliation—the difference between fictional worlds and the world in which she lives. Eventually, she does learn, becoming much wiser in the ways of the world and the people about her.*

Fullerton. English parsonage in Wiltshire, about eight miles from Salisbury, that is home to seventeen-year-old Catherine, whose father is the local rector. The family is relatively prosperous, and Catherine is introduced as rather attractive, but "ignorant and uninformed."

*Bath.** Resort city in western England famous for its hot springs and Roman ruins. Catherine visits Bath for several weeks at the invitation of the Allens, owners of Fullerton. At first, Catherine experiences the discomfort of being in such a crowded place without knowing anyone else there; however, she has Ann Radcliffe's gothic novel to occupy her mind as she begins to meet people. A whole new world opens to her at Bath; she is delighted with the social life of the colony. There, she meets the more worldly Isabella Thorpe, who takes it upon herself to instruct Catherine in the ways of society. Isabella also introduces Catherine to her brother, John Thorpe.

Northanger Abbey. Old country home of the Tilneys, who invite Catherine to come for a visit. Catherine is thrilled because reading Radcliffe's novel makes her expect to find subterranean tunnels, haunted rooms, and medieval furnishings in the abbey. Her overnourished imagination moves her to begin her stay by trying to open old cabinets in her room and imagining the medieval manuscripts she may find. Her host, General Tilney, is a widower and an unsympathetic character, and Catherine builds a fantasy of the unhappy life of his former wife, leading her to suspect that the woman died under painful circumstances—perhaps even that the general himself did away with her. Catherine also imagines that Tilney's wife may still be living—imprisoned somewhere within the abbey. However, when Catherine actually visits the former Mrs. Tilney's bedroom, she is surprised to discover how pleasant and modern it is; indeed, it is one of the most attractive rooms in the abbey. She subsequently learns the prosaic truth about Mrs. Tilney's illness and death and is embarrassed by her own wild imaginings. The truth destroys most of her fantasy-based ideas about Northanger Abbey.

Northanger Abbey is an amusing parody of gothic novels, with their mysterious castles and abbeys, gloomy villains, incredibly accomplished heroines, sublime landscapes, and supernatural claptrap. Austen's satire is not, however, pointed only at such novels; the exaggerated romantic sensibility of the gothic enthusiast is also a target. *Northanger Abbey* is a comic study of the ironic

discrepancies between the prosaic world in which Catherine lives and the fantastic shapes that her imagination, fed by gothic novels, gives to that world. Throughout the novel, the author holds up the contrast between the heroine's real situation and the gothic world she fantasizes.

— *Carolyn Dickinson*

NOSTROMO: A Tale of the Seaboard

Author: Joseph Conrad (Jósef Teodor Konrad Nałęcz Korzeniowski, 1857-1924)
Type of work: Novel

Type of plot: Psychological realism
Time of plot: Early twentieth century
First published: 1904

Joseph Conrad uses place realistically in Nostromo, *but also to symbolize states of being and of mind. In this respect, he follows in the tradition of the great nineteenth century novelists, especially that of his older contemporary, Thomas Hardy. The corruption of a South American country politically and physically symbolizes the corrupting power of undistributed material wealth even over the most morally upright.*

Costaguana. Imaginary South American republic vaguely located on the continent's west coast, with the bulk of the country over the mountains, or *cordillera*, where is situated its capital, **Santa Marta**. Costaguana suffers under political corruption and instability, and its people live in great poverty.

Sulaco (province; suh-LAH-koh). Only maritime province of Costaguana and the only province in the country with a sound economy, thanks to its silver industry. The province has tried to gain its independence several times. After various military reversals, its independence is once again established by the end of the novel, with some degree of economic stability guaranteed by the mining of its silver resources.

Sulaco (town). Provincial capital. European civilization exists here, but only as a thin veneer. The town's main features are a cathedral, plaza, the *Intendencia*—later to become the presidential palace—and the **Amarillo Club**, where separatist leaders meet. The town bears the brunt of the damage done by the factional fighting that rages intermittently, and constantly reinvents itself. The **Casa Gould**, the town house of the British owner of the silver mine, represents some degree of continuity. Its English forms and customs survive the

corrupting power of local politics. The corrupting force of the silver mine operates at a much deeper level.

Sulaco (port). As the town of Sulaco lies a few miles inland, there is a small port, which plays a significant part in the communications network. In Costaguana, "communications" reduces itself to revolutionary expeditions and shipping out silver, the country's only export. The railway runs from the port inland toward the mountains but seems not to extend beyond to the rest of the country. Its only significant destination is the branch line to the mine. The railway is financed by American capital attracted to the mineral wealth.

Casa Viola (kah-sah vee-OH-lah). Italian restaurant run by Giorgio Viola located between the town and the port. The establishment is frequented by Nostromo (the nickname of Gian' Battista), a fellow Italian and foreman of the dockers. Its in-between location signifies the placelessness and lack of identity of Nostromo, who is neither a sailor (rover) nor a citizen of the town. His lack of identity allows him to be corrupted.

Gould Concession. Silver mine located about ten miles from the town, that has been run by the Gould family for three generations. Not only has the mine been a curse to Charles Gould's father, it is the cause of much bloodshed, bribery, and political maneuvering. However "pure" its silver, and however efficiently the mine is run, Conrad uses this notion to question whether material wealth can ever be a civilizing force of itself, or only ever a corrupting, sapping one. The novel's central dialogue over the nature of imperialism focuses on the mine.

Isabella Islands. Three islands off the coast of Sulaco port, set in the gulf. Only one, Great Isabel, is inhabitable. It is here that Nostromo and Decoud hide a cargo of silver ingots on behalf of the Gould Concession, to protect them from the revolutionaries. Later, a lighthouse is built on the island near where the treasure lies hidden. Nostromo's physical death on the island is anticipated by his moral death, as he fails to surrender the treasure to its rightful owners. He is morally marooned, shipwrecked.

Golfo Placido. Great semicircular bay on which the port of Sulaco lies. The only other ports are sixty miles distant to the north and south. The seaboard is described as iron-bound. The gulf itself has a tangible heaviness and weight about it that press down. At night, its darkness is profound. Its isolating effect on Decoud is similar to that on Kurtz in Joseph Conrad's novel *Heart of Darkness* (1899), which uses a similar technique of equating physical and moral darkness. In *Nostromo*, the isolating darkness and soul-destroying silence are formed by the mountains, framed by their highest peak, Higuerota, ensuring a constant cloud-cover over the gulf.

— *David Barratt*

NUNS AND SOLDIERS

Author: Iris Murdoch (1919-1999)
Type of work: Novel
Type of plot: Psychological realism

Time of plot: 1970's
First published: 1980

This novel is set primarily in two homes of Gertrude Openshaw—her flat on Ebury Street in London and her country house outside Provence in France. The contrasting ambiances of these two places are carefully developed, and the main characters are deeply influenced by the differences between the traditionally decorated town flat and the natural world of southern France. The rational side of human nature runs things at Ebury Street, while Eros, the god of love, holds sway in France.

Ebury Street flat. Home of Gertrude Openshaw and her husband, Guy, an administrator in the British Home Office. Located on London's fashionable Ebury Street, the tastefully decorated flat has a drawing room that is elegant and warmly furnished, complete with three tall windows overlooking the street, and a fireplace. A picture of Guy's paternal grandmother hangs over the mantel; other pictures depict powerful men, dogs, and expensive houses. The room reflects the accomplished, wealthy, Openshaw family, whose present-day descendants gather in the flat to comfort Gertrude while her husband, Guy, lies dying in the bedroom. The guest room, where Gertrude's friend, Anne, stays when she comes to help, is also elegantly furnished, with china knickknacks on the mantel and Victorian family silhouettes on the wall.

In this orderly and spotless flat, Gertrude is not her own person. She is dominated by Guy's extended family and a few others who gather regularly. Peter Szczepanski, who is known as the "Count, is not a real count but a disappointed Polish emigre; he is a good friend of Guy's and has been accepted in the Openshaw circle. His role in the London flat is that of Guy's admirer and pupil, although they are of the same generation. He is painfully formal in all his relationships. Guy dies in the flat, and together with Anne, Gertrude changes the pictures and ornaments which have not been moved for years.

Tim's studio. Studio apartment over a garage on London's Chiswick High Road in which Guy's protégé, the unsuccessful artist Tim Reede, lives. From the studio can be heard the frequent hum of motors from downstairs; a sloping roof and gray boards hold the mattress upon which Tim sleeps. The studio contains stores of wood and painting material, as well as Tim's own favorite drawings: crucifixion pictures, old men, young men drinking, and painted girls waiting. Tim wakes up in his studio every morning knowing he is free.

Les Grandes Saules (lay grahnd sohl). Gertrude's towered gray stone house in southern France. The house stands over a valley through which runs a stream bordered by olive trees and large silvery willows, for which the house is named. Beyond these are a vineyard, undulating rocks, a cliff with a rock that resembles an awful human face, and at the foot of the cliff a circular, clear pool that seems to have no source. Tim and Gertrude fall in love with each other at the place and spend three days lost in a dream of planning their future and making love. However, Tim cannot see how they could establish a life together at Ebury Street.

Later, after Tim and Gertrude have a falling out in London, they marry, only to have another falling out. Tim later tries to catch up with Gertrude and her friends in France. When he approaches her house from the valley and sees her sitting with the Count, he flees. He then falls into the canal, which sweeps him through a drainage pipe and deposits him on a sandy bank. Battered, tired, and hungry, Tim creeps back to the house, where Gertrude welcomes him with joy.

— *Sheila Golburgh Johnson*

O

O PIONEERS!

Author: Willa Cather (1873-1947)
Type of work: Novel
Type of plot: Regional

Time of plot: 1880-1910
First published: 1913

This novel is set on the plains of southern Nebraska where Willa Cather lived from 1883 until she left for college in 1890. Farmers from many different ethnic groups settled in this harsh climate and learned to deal with other cultures and religions that they did not fully understand. O Pioneers! emphasizes themes such as the importance of the land, which plays a major role in motivation and plot development. Alexandra, for example, feels she is a part of the land. Through her endurance and ability to farm the land—while others leave it—she achieves success and riches. The American legend of European immigrants coming to the New World to seek their fortunes through land ownership figures heavily. The immigrants turn the wilderness along the frontier into farms and ranches and thereby profit. Alexandra Bergson lives this American legend.

Hanover. Fictional southern Nebraska town on a windblown plain closely modeled on Cather's Nebraska hometown of Red Cloud, that provides a focal point for this novel. Cather spent her formative years on Nebraska's plains. Although she moved away from Nebraska in 1896 to pursue careers in journalism and writing, she never lost her love of the plains, on which she set six of her novels. She wrote lyrically about the beauty of its plains and the challenges of the simple people who struggled to survive in an inhospitable climate.

Bergson farm. Nebraska home of the Bergson family near Hanover. As this novel begins, a Swedish immigrant couple named Bergson have recently arrived in Nebraska, where the eldest child and only daughter, Alexandra, becomes the head of the family after the father dies. Despite financial problems, she refuses to sell the small family farm because of her devotion to the land. A shrewd businesswoman, she purchases land at depressed prices from farmers who move into town, and through great physical labor she not only saves the fam-

ily farm but earns enough money to buy her brother Oscar a farm for his own family.

Roman Catholic church. Local church with which Alexandra becomes affiliated. Norwegians, the Bergsons are Lutherans, and at first Alexandra attends a local Lutheran church. However, after her fellow Lutherans shun her because of her proposed marriage plans, she begins attending the local Catholic church, whose parishioners are mostly French immigrants. Although she does not convert to Catholicism, she is much happier in the Catholic parish because its services and social activities seem full of joy. For the first time in her life, Alexandra understands that religion and joy can coexist. She is amazed that the Catholics accept her with open arms although they know that she does not desire to convert to their faith. They do not judge or shun her.

*Lincoln.** Nebraska town that is home to the University of Nebraska and the state prison to which the murderer of Alexandra's brother Emil is sent.

— Edmund J. Campion

OBASAN

Author: Joy Kogawa (1935-   )
Type of work: Novel
Type of plot: Historical realism

Time of plot: 1972, with flashbacks to the 1940's
First published: 1981

Place in Joy Kogawa's poignant novel about Japanese Canadians raises questions of nationality: What it means to " belong" to a country, what it mean to be a citizen, and where one's native land is within a country that arrests its own citizens merely because of their ethnicity.

*Vancouver. Largest city in British Columbia that was home to many Japanese Canadians before World War II. Schoolteacher Naomi Nakane's grandparents came to Canada from Japan in 1893, and she herself was born in Vancouver in 1936 and has lived there happily through her first six years in a large and beautiful house on West 64th Avenue in the Marpole district.

In 1972—the time present of *Obasan*—the thirty-six-year-old Naomi remembers the house vividly: its living and music rooms, her father's study, the kitchen, the playroom, the backyard. She also remembers exploring Vancouver with her family, from Kitsilano Beach to the zoo at Stanley Park. She recalls as well the exhibition grounds at Hastings Park, however, where in 1942 many of the twenty-three thousand Japanese Canadians living along the British Columbia coast "were herded into the grounds and kept there like animals until they were shipped off to roadwork camps and concentration camps in the interior of the province."

Slocan. Ghost town in British Columbia's interior to which Naomi and her extended family are sent. In this former mining settlement, they spend three years living in an abandoned two-room shack. Aside from their shack, Naomi and other internees spend some of their time at the Odd Fellows Hall in town, where they watch movies every Saturday night, and in the public bathhouse. (The original Native American name for this village was "Slow-can-go," meaning "If you go slow . . . you can go.")

Granton. Small town in southern Alberta, not far from the city of Lethbridge. From 1945 to 1951, Naomi, her brother, her Uncle Isamu, and her Aunt Aya (the "Obasan" or "aunt" of the novel's title) live in a hut on the Barker farm, some seven miles outside of Granton. Prohibited by the Canadian government from returning to Vancouver (where their home has been confiscated) after the war, Naomi and her makeshift family live in "a small hut, like a toolshed, smaller even than the one we lived in Slocan." Naomi's father, who has been hospitalized for years, dies of tuberculosis in 1949. In 1951, Naomi and Stephen and their uncle and aunt finally move into a house in Granton itself. It is on a bluff a half mile from the Barker farm to which Naomi and her uncle go, at the beginning and end of the novel, to stand at the edge of the Canadian prairie that reminds Uncle Isamu of the Pacific coast, where he worked as a master shipbuilder and fisherman before the war. It is to this house that Naomi returns to be with Aunt Aya when her uncle dies in 1972.

Cecil. Small rural town some 150 miles northeast of Granton, where Naomi Nakane is a single school teacher in the time present of the novel.

*Nagasaki. Japanese city on which the United States dropped an atom bomb in 1945. After the war ends, Naomi learns that her mother died a horrible death as a result of that atomic attack.

Her mother had returned to Japan in 1939 to nurse her mother and was trapped in Nagasaki by the war. The novel personalizes the bombing, but, even more directly, questions the internment of loyal Canadian citizens who were uprooted from their coastal homes and forced to spend the remainder of their lives in internal provincial exile. At the end of the novel, in a metaphor that taps the earthy imagery used throughout *Obasan*, Naomi muses:

Where do any of us come from in this cold country? Oh, Canada, whether it is admitted or not, we come from you we come from you. From the same soil, the slugs and slime and bogs and twigs and roots. We come from the country that plucks its people out like weeds and flings them into the roadside. . . . We come from Canada, this land that is like every land, filled with the wise, the fearful, the compassionate, the corrupt.

— *David Peck*

OBLOMOV

Author: Ivan Alexandrovich Goncharov (1812-1891)
Type of work: Novel
Type of plot: Social realism

Time of plot: First half of the nineteenth century
First published: 1859 (English translation, 1915)

This novel's Ilya Oblomov is what critics would call the ultimate superfluous man—a character type found in Russian literature—so alienated from society that he cannot engage in any fulfilling activity. Oblomov takes this type to absurd lengths, having become so consumed with lethargy and ennui that he cannot even bestir himself from his bed. As a consequence, he seems to exist outside the society in which he lives.

Oblomov's apartment. Residence of Ilya Ilyitch Oblomov on St. Petersburg's Gorokhovaya Street. Oblomov has settled in so tightly that his apartment has become a prison of his own making. He spends most of each day lying in bed, wrapped in a robe of Asian style, without any hint of the European character Czar Peter the Great had tried to impose upon the Russian aristocracy. Even Oblomov's manservant, Zakhar, has slipped into the thrall of his master's lassitude, and the entire apartment has become covered by a layer of dust. Books lie open wherever Oblomov has lost interest in reading them, dusty and often yellowed by exposure to light.

*St. Petersburg. Capital of Imperial Russia, whose northern location is so close to the Arctic Circle that it is subject to extreme variations in the lengths of its days and nights. During the winter, the sun hardly rises before it vanishes again beneath the horizon. Near the summer solstice, the sun hardly sets, creating the "white nights" for which the city is famous. Because of this, St. Petersburg is seen in literature as a city where reality is tenuous at best, where extraordinary things can happen. Although Oblomov lives in the city, he has little contact with the social life of the imperial capital. Occasionally his visitors may mention various activities they plan to attend at prestigious places, but Oblomov cannot find the energy or initiative to leave his bed, let alone go out on the town.

Oblomov's house. Home in the Vyburg District where Oblomov settles with the landlady who becomes his wife. This dwelling, on the opposite side of the Neva River from the apartment where he lives earlier, is a model of domestic simplicity, in contrast to the high-society dwelling in which his former teacher Scholtz settles with Olga Sergeevna. At first Oblomov's move represents a break from his former lassitude, and he begins to take initiative in his life once more. However, he eventually has a relapse to his former self and ultimately dies of a stroke in his sleep.

Oblomovka (oh-BLOH-mov-kah). Oblomov's rural estate, a rather plain, quiet place in eastern Russia, near the border of Asia, and quite Asian in nature. It is seen only in Oblomov's lengthy, dreamlike reminiscences and imaginings. There, Oblomov grew up, tended by a peasant nurse who told him fairy tales about a magical ideal bride, tales he came to prefer to practical reality. Oblomovka is also said to be the origin of the malady from which Oblomov suffers, the *Oblomovshchina* (the *-shchina* suffix is frequently used in Russian to describe an ill associated with a particular person, place, or thing, for instance: *gruppovshchina*, ethnic bullying, or *Yezhovshchina*, the Great Terror, after secret police chief Nikolai Yezhov).

Verklevo (ver-KLEH-voh). Location of Scholtz's school. Although not far from Oblomovka, the school is utterly unlike the aimless Asiatic idleness of the Oblomov family's estate. Scholtz, a German, insists upon industry and activity from his pupils, and gives them a broad-based education.

— *Leigh Husband Kimmel*

THE OBSCENE BIRD OF NIGHT

Author: José Donoso (1924-1996)
Type of work: Novel
Type of plot: Magical Realism

Time of plot: Mid-twentieth century
First published: El obsceno pájaro de la noche, 1970
   (English translation, 1973)

Surreal fantasies dominating this novel's plot are depicted as both real and metaphorical labyrinths, within which the human capacity to think rationally is continually led astray by unconscious fears and desires. Humberto Peñaloza, the protagonist, narrates the story of a wealthy Chilean family's attempts to turn its properties into places that will be socially beneficial, rather than mere reflections of the family's aristocratic status. However, their plans are undermined by the anarchic forces that their efforts unleash, and what initially seems only the bizarre material of fantasy becomes the all-too-real basis of a world in which society's breakdown is symbolized by the loss of control over its traditional institutions.

Casa de Ejercicios Espirituales de la Encarnación. Home for elderly women in the fictional Chilean city of La Chimba. A large, rambling structure, the Casa has over the years become a labyrinth through two different but complementary processes of growth. Externally, additions of varying sizes and architectural styles have proliferated to the point that no one remembers what the original building looked like; internally, rooms have been divided and subdivided until even Humberto Peñaloza, the Casa's caretaker, no longer comprehends its overall layout.

The Casa is variously depicted as a magic kingdom, a beehive, a prison, and a place to which both people and things go when they have outlived their usefulness. Clearly, it is a world of its own that is nonetheless intended to have some metaphorical relationship to the world as a whole. Its complex and labyrinthine character is further emphasized by the narrative's frequent references to its many nooks and crannies, and to secret recesses in which witchcraft and other mysterious rites are practiced by its residents. Although it is supposed to be an institution that benevolently looks after those who live within, it is the inmates who have in fact taken control of the asylum, as the novel continues to develop its theme of the unpredictable and often irrational outcomes of human action.

La Rinconada. Country estate of the de Azcoitía family. When Don Jerónimo de Azcoitía's wife, Inés, gives birth to a monstrously deformed baby, the father decides to shield the boy from reality by fabricating an artificial world in which the abnormal will seem normal. La Rinconada is transformed into a haven for those usually identified as freaks, as once again readers encounter a world that has produced its own labyrinthine complexity in the process of creating an alternative to the conventional treatment of society's underprivileged classes.

Because of its almost complete isolation from the mainstream world, La Rinconada becomes even more detached from mundane reality than does the Casa. Life within its well-guarded walls is portrayed as subverting conventional social structures. There, the very idea of the normal has been abolished, as Don Jerónimo strives to create a culture in which people are not classified in terms of any systems or generalizations, but are instead treated as unique individuals who will be accepted regardless of whatever each happens to be. Like the Casa, however, La Rinconada invents a future for itself in a way unforeseen by the de Azcoitías, as its inhabitants' decision to murder Don Jerónimo represents their complete rejection of any degree of social control.

La Chimba. Major city of the region in which the novel takes place, situated near the real locations of the Maule River and the towns of Cauquenes, San Javier, and Villa Alegre in north-central Chile. Whenever the inhabitants of the Casa venture out into the surrounding city, they encounter another kind of labyrinth in which a rapidly growing urban community's network of streets and buildings spills over into the adjacent countryside.

La Chimba hospital. Site of Humberto's operation for a stomach disorder. The narrative's emphasis on labyrinths as the fundamental organizing principles of human nature is further elaborated when both the hospital and Humberto's body are depicted as complex, proliferating networks characterized by multiple passageways and ultimate incomprehensibility.

— Paul Stuewe

THE OCTOPUS

Author: Frank Norris (1870-1902)
Type of work: Novel
Type of plot: Naturalism

Time of plot: Late nineteenth century
First published: 1901

This novel reveals the interconnectedness among wheat farmers, their dependence on railroads, and the ultimately triumphant bounty of wheat as a crop in a setting revolving around four prosperous wheat farms in California's San Joaquin Valley. Although several towns and a mission play key roles in the novel, the four farms are its central concern. A great railroad—the "octopus" of the novel's title—controls the commercial destiny of the farms, entangling every element of their operations in its tentacles, suffocating unnecessary components—particularly people—in the process. The novel's denouement illustrates Frank Norris's conviction that land is the most primal and prominent element in the book.

El Rancho de los Muertos. Largest ranch of the four San Joaquin Valley ranches in which the novel is set. Containing ten thousand acres of land, it is run by Magnus Derrick and his son, Harran. It consists of the home ranch, nestled in the north end in a grove of eucalyptus, oak, and cypress trees; two division houses; a tenant farmer's house; and the house of Hooven, a German immigrant who farms a section of the ranch. The Derrick ranch home is a stately structure, containing many bedrooms, a large kitchen, an expansive dining room, a hallway with a glass ceiling, and an office—the center of the operation, in which telephones, a stock market ticker, and record books are kept. The house's lawn is as well groomed as any city garden. The property also has a summer house Derrick has constructed for his mother.

The ranch reveals Derrick's deep concern for respectability, integrity, and family. The dispersal of the family's belongings onto the lawn reveals the great loss and fragmentation that result from the railroad's seizure of the property at the novel's end. At Hooven's house, the farmers make a stand against the railroad's occupation of the farms, resulting in the deaths of several farmers, including Hooven and Harran Derrick.

Quien Sabe Ranch. Farm run by young, contrary Buck Annixter, lying north of the Derrick ranch. It comprises Annixter's ranch house and barns, and an artesian well that feeds the irrigation ditch. Annixter raises a new barn on the place in which he holds a dance, the most significant social event occurring on any of the ranches during the course of the book. His hard-driving ways are softened by his love for Hilma Tree, daughter of the family who operates Annixter's dairy farm. Annixter's compassion and benevolence extend far beyond his own interests, as after his wedding to Hilma, they take in the dispossessed Dyke family. The Quien Sabe becomes the warmest and most harmonious ranch of the four, epitomizing the novel's vision of the powers of love and close connection to the land.

Osterman and **Broderson ranches.** These ranches, which play less prominent roles than the other two, occupy the northwest sections of the novel's wide, interconnected region of wheat farms. Both are given little treatment and do not serve as settings for any significant scenes. Nevertheless, they illustrate the vast sweep of the wheat-farming community. Osterman, a young, brash "poser," does not live on the ranch but in a house in Bonneville. He farms simply as a way of making a living. Broderson, on the other hand, is an aging man, slipping into the twilight years with his wife on the farm they love and cherish. With these ranches, Norris reveals the diversity of farmers and farming life, and the interdependence of all wheat farms, regardless of their size or vitality.

San Juan Mission. Old Franciscan mission station run by Father Sarria, containing a bell tower and red-tiled roof. The interior consists of a great oblong of whitewashed adobe with a flat ceiling, lit by sanctuary lamps hung from three long chains. The walls bear pictures of the Stations of the Cross. A graveyard and garden are on the grounds. In the garden, Father Sarria grows vegetables and wheat and maintains a vineyard. The produce of his gardening provides for communion and sustenance for downtrodden inhabitants of the valley.

The mission's nurturing of the land connects the church with the wheat farmers in a fundamental manner, and reveals Norris's ultimate vision of the sanctity of the earth's natural abundance. In the mission's garden, the wanderer Vanamee first met his only love, Angéle, who was killed by a murderer never identified. When he returns to the garden after years of long and sorrowful wandering, Vanamee receives a vision of Angéle. Through these scenes, Norris again creates an inseparable link between human spirituality and nature, sanctifying both in the process.

Guadalajara (gwah-thah-lah-HAH-rah). Fictional California town that was vibrant in the days of Spanish and Mexican rule. Now dying, it was constructed when the novel's wheat farms were part of a Spanish land grant. The quiet town has a drug store, two saloons, a hotel, and a few shops for tourists who come to visit the mission. The inhabitants are relics of a former generation whose way of life is slipping away as the town loses commerce to Bonneville and the railroad. Through Guadalajara, Norris reveals the railroad's capacity to ruin the lives of people other than the farmers.

Bonneville. Burgeoning California railroad town between San Francisco and Fresno that has three newspapers, numerous commercial buildings, a train station, and a city opera house. One of the newspapers, the *Mercury*, is manipulated by the railroad and blackmails Magnus Derrick. At the opera house, farmers hold a town meeting after their violent conflict with the railroad. There, Derrick is shouted down and disgraced by accusations of bribery printed in the *Mercury*. Although the accusations are true, Magnus and the other wheat farmers view winning control of the railroad commission as their only hope of survival, an attitude approved by the novel. This attack, following the deaths of his neighbors and son, is the final devastation for Derrick, so completely defeating him that he later takes a job with the railroad.

San Francisco. Northern California port city that is home to Lyman Derrick, eldest son of Magnus, who leaves farming to become a lawyer. His political aspirations encourage him to conspire with the railroad against the interests of his own family, demonstrating the power of cities to corrupt people removed from the land. The city is also home to the Cedarquists, ineffectual supporters of the arts, who are also so removed from the land and reality that while their artistic tastes may be refined, their human sympathy and understanding are significantly deficient.

Port Costa. California port city twenty miles from San Francisco, where the corrupt railroad agent S. Behrman boards a ship hauling wheat, slips into its hold, and is suffocated to death. This ironic ending provides the novel with a measure of poetic justice, despite its naturalistic tendencies.

Caraher's Saloon. Saloon outside Bonneville operated by Caraher, a pronounced anarchist, who encourages Dyke to take action against the railroad that has fired him. Dyke robs a train of its gold but is eventually caught and sentenced to life in jail, another indication of the strength of the railroad.

— *Mark Walling*

THE ODD COUPLE

Author: Neil Simon (1927-   )
Type of work: Drama
Type of plot: Comedy

Time of plot: Mid-1960's
First performed: 1965; first published, 1966

All the action in this stage play takes place in the living room of the large eight-room apartment of sports writer Oscar Madison on New York City's Riverside Drive. The appearance of this living room embodies the comic conflict between the play's two main characters—the sloppy and easy-going Oscar and his best friend, the fussy and obsessively tidy Felix Ungar. The condition of the living room alters as the characters alternate in gaining control over the living space.

*New York City. A native of New York City's Bronx, playwright Neil Simon placed most of his early plays in New York apartments, and his critics often suggest that these largely uniform urban settings limit his appeal. Others suggest that Simon's comedy transcends place, and the enduring success of *The Odd Couple* in its many manifestations (stage plays, male and female versions, film, and television) would seem to prove this.

Oscar's apartment. In the play's initial stage directions, Simon indicates that Oscar's Riverside Drive address suggests a certain gentility and that the grotesquely untidy state of the apartment seems a recent development given the stylish furnishings of Oscar's wife, who has been away for three months. This subtle visual impression is only reinforced in the dialogue by Oscar's quip in the first scene that the maid quit (after his wife and children left) because cleaning up after him became too difficult. However, Oscar's comic messiness is explicitly contrasted in the play's second act with the extreme tidiness introduced by Felix after he moves in, takes over the housekeeping, and creates the incompatible "marriage." At the end of the play, Felix relinquishes control over the appearance of the apartment and moves out. Oscar's last words imply that he will be tidier in the future.

— *Terry Nienhuis*

ODES

Author: Pindar (c. 518-c. 438 B.C.E.)
Type of work: Poetry

First transcribed: Epinikia, 498-446 B.C.E. (English translation, 1656)

During the fifth century B.C.E., Pindar wrote victory odes to praise victorious athletes and their patrons in the various athletic events, including the original Olympic games. Victory in any event of the games, which were holy gatherings held in consecrated places, offered Pindar a subject for a poem that not only retold religious stories, but also presented his vision of how human beings should conduct their lives. Categorized by the location of the games, Pindar's odes project the view that the physical perfection required of victors is similar to the spiritual perfection to which human beings aspire.

*Olympia. Sacred Greek city, near the Ionian Sea on the western side of the Peloponnesian Peninsula, that was dedicated to Zeus, king of the gods, and named after his home, Mt. Olympus. Held every four years from the eighth century until the end of the fourth century B.C.E., the Games at Olympia took precedence over all wars, which were suspended so that warring factions and their leaders could attend and participate.

*Pytho. Greek city renamed Delphi in honor of the oracle sacred to Apollo. The Pythian Games, in honor of Apollo, were held on the southern slope of Mount Parnassus on the mainland of Greece.

*Nemea (NEE-mee-ah). This shrine to Zeus was located in the Nemean Valley, southeast of Olympia, near present-day Argos. Games held here included musical contests, whose winners were crowned with ivy.

*Isthmus of Corinth.** Held in the shadow of a shrine sacred to the sea god Poseidon, the Isthmian Games were conducted on the narrow strip of land that joined the Peloponnesian Peninsula to the Greek mainland. The modern towns of Isthmus and Corinth are near where these ancient Games were held.

— *Ginger Jones*

THE ODYSSEY

Author: Homer (c. ninth century B.C.E.)
Type of work: Poetry
Type of plot: Epic

Time of plot: Years immediately following the Trojan War

First transcribed: c. 800 B.C.E. (English translation, 1616)

Odysseus's circuitous ten-year voyage from Troy to his home on the island of Ithaca leads him through a range of real and imaginary places in and around the Mediterranean. Homer's geography is, however, notoriously inexact, and many of the real places are used in a largely symbolic way. Many of the places function as representations of the gulf between civilized and savage behavior, one of the primary themes of the poem.

*Ithaca. Odysseus's home, a mountainous island to the west of mainland Greece, and the primary setting of the first two and last twelve books of the twenty-four-book poem. The two key locations on Ithaca are the palace of Odysseus and the hut of the swineherd Eumaeus. Odysseus's twenty-year absence has finally resulted in the palace being overrun by 108 suitors for the hand of his wife and supposed widow, Penelope. Ironically, while the greedy and disrespectful suitors have turned the formerly noble palace into a place of lawlessness and disorder, the humble hut of the apparently lowly Eumaeus exemplifies the courtesy and hospitality that the suitors fail to observe.

*Troy. City on the west coast of Asia Minor (now part of Turkey) and the site of the Trojan War, where Odysseus and the Greek armies spend ten years fighting the Trojans to recover Helen, the wife of the Greek leader Menelaus. The final year of that war serves as the focus of *The Iliad* (c. 800 B.C.E.; English translation, 1616), the narrative of life during wartime that serves as a companion piece to *The Odyssey*.

*Pylos and *Sparta. Greek kingdoms visited by Odysseus's son, Telemachus, in books 3, 4, and 15 of the poem, which constitute a sort of miniature, parallel version of Odysseus's much longer journey. These kingdoms also offer a contrast to Ithaca in that they are models of the proper observance of social decorum and order. Pylos is ruled by Nestor, the wisest of the Greeks, and Sparta is ruled by Menelaus, the husband of Helen, whose abduction by Paris had begun the war. His introduction to these men, both great heroes of the Trojan War, and his ability to win their approval, serve as symbolic markers of the young man's psychological and social "voyage" from adolescence to maturity. While the

"Telemachia," as it is sometimes called, has a relatively minor plot function, it does allow for considerable exposition, as the rulers inform Telemachus about key sections of the story of Troy and Odysseus's wanderings.

*Argos (AR-gohs). Greek home of Agamemnon, brother of Menelaus and leader of the Greek armies in the Trojan War. Agamemnon's own homecoming from the war, which results in his murder by Aigisthos, lover of his unfaithful wife, Clytemnestra, is frequently mentioned in the poem as a contrast to the homecoming of Odysseus to his own faithful wife, Penelope. A further parallel is developed between Orestes, the son of Agamemnon, who revenges him by killing Aigisthos and Clytemnestra, and Telemachus, who will assist his own father in the massacre of the suitors.

Skheria (skeh-REE-ah). Land of the Phaeacians, where Odysseus arrives after having been freed from Ogygia. There, Odysseus relates the full story of his ten-year journey to the Phaeacians, who then provide him with gifts and transportation to Ithaca. The Phaeacians, identified as kin of the gods, are distinguished by their respect for established custom, hospitality, and generosity, and Odysseus pointedly contrasts their civilized behavior with the barbaric treatment he receives at several places he visits on his journey.

Cave of the Cyclops. Island dwelling of Polyphemos, a member of the race of Cyclopes—giant cannibals who exemplify the dystopian world of savagery and barbarism that the poem frequently juxtaposes with examples of civilized societies. The Cyclopes dwell in caves rather than crafted structures and do not farm their land or build ships. Odysseus and ten companions find themselves trapped within the cave of the Cyclops Polyphemos, who eats his guests rather than providing them with aid and gifts as is the custom at such exemplars of civilized behavior as Pylos, Sparta, and Skheria. Odysseus and some of his men escape after blinding Polyphemos. Polyphemos's request that his father, the sea god Poseidon, revenge him against Odysseus, results in Odysseus's ten years of forced wandering.

Aiaia (ay-EE-ah). Home of the enchantress Circe, a place of seductive beauty and ease, in which Odysseus is detained for more than a year on his journey home. Circe's custom is to turn visitors into wolves, lions, and swine, in a symbolic reversal of proper hospitality, which makes the proper treatment of guests one of the highest attributes of true humanity. Even though he is not literally transformed into an animal, Odysseus is seduced by Circe's hospitality into forgetting his mission to return home. As always, however, Odysseus chooses the hardships of the return home over the temptations of an easy life away from society and his duty.

Nekuia (neh-kew-ee-ah). Underworld home of the dead. It is presented somewhat inconsistently as a remote northern location on the earth's surface and as an underground realm. Odysseus journeys there in book 11 to get instructions from the prophet Tiresias and meets the shades, or ghosts, of several figures from his past and from Greek mythology. The shades of the dead suitors appear there at the end of the poem as well.

Island of the Sirens. Home of the Sirens, whose irresistible songs enchant sailors into running their ships ashore, with usually disastrous results.

Scylla and **Charybdis.** Mythical monsters that guard a strait through which Olysseus's ship must pass. Scylla, a monster with twelve legs and six heads, and Charybdis, a gigantic whirlpool, flank a narrow strait between headlands. Their significance lies in the idea that Odysseus cannot possibly get home without passing between them and losing some of his crew. In modern parlance, their names have come to signify any dilemma in which a person is forced to choose between two unavoidable yet thoroughly unpleasant alternatives.

Thrinakia (THREE-nah-kee-ah). Island of the cattle of Helios, lord of the sun. Odysseus's men unwisely slaughter some of the sacred cattle, for which transgression Zeus hits their ship with a thunderbolt. Odysseus is the only survivor.

Ogygia (OH-gee-jee-uh). Edenic island of the nymph Calypso, on which Odysseus is shipwrecked after the destruction of his ship by Zeus. This episode constitutes Odysseus's most powerful temptation to abandon his journey home, as Calypso offers him not only worldly pleasure and luxury, but immortality: He will neither die nor grow old if he stays.

Olympus. Mountain in northern Greece traditionally believed to be the home of the gods. The poem narrates several meetings the gods have to discuss and direct Odysseus's fate. The civilized societies and customs depicted in the poem are always in some sense versions of this Olympian society.

— *William Nelles*

OEDIPUS AT COLONUS

Author: Sophocles (c. 496-406 B.C.E.)
Type of work: Drama
Type of plot: Tragedy

Time of plot: Antiquity
First performed: Oidipous epi Kolōnōi, 401 B.C.E.
(English translation, 1729)

The principal setting of this tragedy is a wooded grove outside Colonus. It is the final resting place of the Theban hero Oedipus, but a further significance perhaps is that it is the birthplace of the author, Sophocles. In fact, a tale told shortly after Sophocles' death attributes his vindication in a court trial to his beautiful lyric description of Colonus in the play.

***Colonus.** Ancient Greek city near Athens. In a beautiful grove outside Colonus, Oedipus and his daughter Antigone rest while fleeing from Thebes, from which

Oedipus has been banished. Sophocles' play opens with Antigone describing the grove in detail. She establishes its distance from Athens by observing that the great city's towers are far off, though visible. The shaded grove is thick with laurel and olive trees, as well as grape vines. This grove might convey a calm to the fugitive Oedipus, but Antigone suspects that the place is sacred to some deity. As it turns out, the grove is dedicated to the Furies, who seek to punish Oedipus for killing his father.

The most famous passage in the play is a portion that Sophocles is said to have read at his trial: a lyrical choral ode in praise of Colonus that appears in the middle of the tragedy. The chorus emphasizes the peaceful nature of the protective grove, the facts that no wind disturbs it, and that it harbors the sweet-singing nightingales. The clear-running spring represents the purity of the place, and the olive trees its dedication to peace. Flowers, particularly narcissus and crocus, also beautify Colonus. The entire description is calculated to convey a sense of wonder and peace, which contributes to Colonus's role as Oedipus's final resting place.

— *John R. Holmes*

OEDIPUS TYRANNUS

Author: Sophocles (c. 496-406 B.C.E.)
Type of work: Drama
Type of plot: Tragedy

Time of plot: Antiquity
First performed: Oidipous Tyrannos, c. 429 B.C.E. (English translation, 1729)

The principal setting of this play is ancient Thebes, where all its action takes place. However, background events leading up to the action of the play have carried Oedipus from his confinement on Mount Cithaeron as an infant, to his early life at Corinth, to Delphi where he learns of his inescapable fate, then to the meeting place of three roads, where he kills King Laius in self-defense, and finally to Thebes, where he is crowned king after saving the Thebans from the monstrous Sphinx.

*Thebes (theebz). Ancient city in east-central Greece, northwest of Athens, where all the action in Sophocles' play takes place. As the seat of power of King Oedipus, Thebes represents civil power, though as Oedipus comes to realize, his royal power must be subservient to the divine power of Apollo, whose temple is nearby.

*Mount Cithaeron (si-THE-ron). Mountain in southern Greece on which Oedipus was chained and abandoned as an infant. The image of the mountain as the mysterious "parent" of the king whose parentage is clouded continually recurs throughout the choral odes.

*Trivia. Crossroad where the roads from Daulia, Delphi, and Thebes meet. At this auspicious location Oedipus kills, in self-defense, a man who he later learns was his father. The converging of the roads echoes the intertwining threads of Oedipus's fate.

*Delphi. Oracle at the Temple of Apollo that is the source of all divine wisdom for the ancient Greeks. To Oedipus, it represents the place where he learns the truth about his past.

*Corinth. Distant Greek city from which a messenger arrives at the end of the play to announce the death of King Polybus, who Oedipus mistakenly believes is his father. Corinth represents the untroubled home of the only parents Oedipus ever knew.

— *John R. Holmes*

OF HUMAN BONDAGE

Author: W. Somerset Maugham (1874-1965)
Type of work: Novel
Type of plot: Naturalism

Time of plot: Early twentieth century
First published: 1915

W. Somerset Maugham's most autobiographical novel follows Philip in England as he wanders restlessly from place to place and occupation to occupation in search of purpose and identity. Each place in which Philip lives represents a distinct and important stage in his search, and he eventually comes to believe that each place and experience is an integral part of the inevitable pattern of his life.

Blackstable. Small town in Kent, about sixty miles southeast of London, based upon the real town of Whitstable, where Philip goes at a young age to live with his aunt and uncle, the town vicar, after his mother dies. Life in this environment is so rigid and monotonous that Philip is forced to seek release in his uncle's large collection of books, which sets the stage for his later desire to travel extensively.

King's School. Public school (the British equivalent of an American private school) for boys that Philip attends in the fictional town of **Tercanbury**, believed to be based on a school of the same name that Maugham attended in the real town of Canterbury. The boarding school setting, typical of British schools of the time, is to Philip a place of misery, where he is first tormented about his clubfoot, a physical deformity that prevents him from participating in most athletic activities. In addition, the lack of privacy associated with a boarding school is difficult for Philip to endure, and he longs to escape.

*Heidelberg. Picturesque German city on the Rhine River in which Philip spends a year learning French and German after leaving public school. As Paris represents the art world, Heidelberg seems to Philip the seat of philosophy and intellectualism. In addition, Heidelberg represents Philip's first chance at freedom and independence. There, much as Maugham did in real life, Philip lives in a boardinghouse with professors and students from many different countries; this setting gives him his first real opportunity to examine his religious beliefs and philosophy of life, and he ultimately concludes that he does not believe in God.

*Paris. France's leading city and the heart of the painters' world, to which Philip escapes after spending a dreary year in London working as an articled (apprenticed) clerk. At first, Philip is enamored of the bohemian lifestyle that Paris represents: the run-down studios in which the poverty-stricken art students both live and paint, the good-natured arguments about art over meals in cheap cafés, and the proximity to museums housing many of the world's greatest works of art. However, realizing that his talent is only mediocre, Philip eventually decides to give up painting rather than become a second-rate artist. In spite of this painful decision, Philip remembers his time in Paris with fondness.

*London. Great Britain's capital city, where Philip spends a year as a clerk after leaving Heidelberg and to which he returns, after his time in Paris, to become a medical student. Philip generally views his time in London as something to get through as quickly as possible so he can attain the financial freedom necessary to travel to exotic places. In addition, England's involvement in World War I brings about a period of high unemployment at the same time Philip is forced to leave medical school for lack of funds. His difficulty in finding work, the grim realities of working long hours for very low wages at a department store, and a disastrous love affair all taint London in his mind as an uncompromising and humiliating place; however, London also makes Philip realize that class barriers are perhaps not as insurmountable as he had supposed.

Farnley. Fictional fishing village on the south coast of England, where Philip substitutes as a medical assistant immediately after qualifying as a doctor. Philip initially considers his time in Farnley to be nothing more than a temporary assignment that may lead to better jobs in the future; he is surprised, however, by how well he gets along with Dr. South, the crusty old doctor he is assisting, and the townspeople. Dr. South offers Philip a partnership, which Philip at first refuses because he still intends to work and travel to exotic places. When Philip later decides to marry Sally, a girl whom he believes he has gotten pregnant, he accepts Dr. South's offer and is utterly astounded at how happy the prospect of marriage and life in this small fishing village makes him. Even when it develops that Sally is not pregnant after all, Philip proposes to her, because he has now come to believe that life in Farnley represents the simplest and most beautiful life pattern to which a man can aspire.

— *Amy Sisson*

OF MICE AND MEN

Author: John Steinbeck (1902-1968)
Type of work: Novel
Type of plot: Impressionistic realism

Time of plot: Mid-twentieth century
First published: 1937

This brief novel—a rehearsal for John Steinbeck's The Grapes of Wrath *(1939)—is a story about rootlessness and futile quests for permanent homes in which the characters can control their own destinies and live off the fruits of their own labor. Like* The Grapes of Wrath, *it is set in the rich agricultural lands of California during the Great Depression—a region that provides riches to the landowners but only backbreaking labor and disappointment to their workers.*

*****Salinas Valley** (sah-LEE-nas). Rich agricultural region along north-central California's Pacific coast in which the novel is set. Steinbeck grew up in the Salinas Valley and set much of his important fiction there and in the surrounding areas. In this short novel, his focus is comparatively narrow: All its action unfolds between the Salinas River, a single ranch, and the nearby town of Soledad. Although the backdrop of the story hints at social discontent—which is manifest in the dream of itinerant farmworkers George Milton and Lennie Small to own their own land—the book's drama centers on the personal problems of the giant Lennie, who has a history of stumbling into serious trouble wherever he and George go.

*****Salinas River.** Stream next to which the story begins and ends. The novel opens as itinerant farmworkers George and Lennie are hunkering down beside the pleasant river, discussing the new ranch to which they are headed. They also talk about a little ranch they hope to buy for themselves, and the pastoral riverside location evokes Lennie's wistful yearnings to raise rabbits and live "off the fatta the lan'."

Fearing that the simple Lennie may get into trouble with their new employers, George makes him promise to return to this same spot by the river if something happens that forces them to flee the ranch. Later, Lennie accidentally kills a woman and comes back to the river, where George finds him before the rest of the ranch hands catch up with him. There, Lennie has a vision and then with George's help, imagines the little place with rabbits, where there is no trouble. As George instructs him to gaze across the river and see the place with no trouble, he shoots Lennie with a pistol to prevent his being lynched by others.

Ranch. Salinas Valley farm on which George and Lennie take jobs as hands. George hopes only that he and Lennie can keep their jobs long enough to build up a cash stake that will help them buy a small farm for themselves. There is little description of the farm beyond its barn and the bunkhouse in which George and Lennie are quartered. They arrive during what appears to be a barley harvest—work at which the powerful Lennie excels. George and Lennie establish a pleasant camaraderie with some of their bunkmates, so their immediate prospects seem favorable. Such trouble as arises comes from the owner's family: his belligerent son who unwisely taunts Lennie into a pointless physical confrontation, and the son's wife, whose coquettish flirtation with the man who humiliates her husband results in both her and Lennie's deaths. Although George and Lennie's troubles have nothing to do with broader labor problems, it is significant that their downfall is brought on by representatives of landowners.

Crooks's room. Quarters of Crooks, the ranch's African American cook, who has been living apart from the main bunkhouse through the many years he has worked on the ranch. Although forced to live alone because he is black, he has the ironic privilege of being the only hand on the ranch to enjoy true privacy. He hungers for company other than his books but has never admitted another hand into his room before the night in which Lennie wanders in to pay a friendly call. When another veteran ranch hand, Candy, soon follows, Crooks grudgingly allows the intrusions but secretly relishes having human company, even if it consists only of two fellow pariahs—a dimwit and a crippled amputee. Crooks's hunger for companionship comes to the surface when he begs to be allowed to join Lennie, Candy, and George's plan to live on a ranch of their own. In another of the book's little ironies, its sole African American character also appears to be the ranch's only hand who was once a member of a family that owned its own land.

*Weed. Small Northern California farming town, about 330 miles north of Salinas, from which Lennie and George were run out immediately before the narrative begins. Although George is afraid that he and Lennie will lose their new jobs if anyone at the Salinas ranch finds out why they left Weed, he tells his guilty secret to the skinner Slim. Mentioned several times throughout the novel, Weed is an icon of George and Lennie's perpetual failure to find stable work and homes, as well as an example of the great distances farm hands must travel to find work.

Imaginary farm. Ten-acre plot of farmland that George hopes to buy for himself and Lennie from an elderly couple whom he knows. Though a real place, the farm is appropriately at an unspecified remote location—a place "you couldn't find in hundred years." The chances of George and Lennie ever actually owning the place are so slim that it may as well be the farm existing in Lennie's simple imagination: an idyllic place with abundant crops, rabbits, and other animals that Lennie will tend, and no trouble.

So as not to jeopardize their employment on the Salinas ranch, George repeatedly instructs Lennie not to mention the farm to anyone else. However, Lennie can not stay silent, and each ranch hand whom he tells about the farm wants to be a part of it. George and Lennie's quest to live on a place of their own is the dominant motif through the novel, so it is fitting that Lennie is imagining life on the farm at the moment George shoots him, thereby ending that dream for everyone.

— *R. Kent Rasmussen*

OF TIME AND THE RIVER: A Legend of Man's Hunger in His Youth

Author: Thomas Wolfe (1900-1938)
Type of work: Novel
Type of plot: Impressionistic realism

Time of plot: 1920's
First published: 1935

This partly autobiographical novel follows Eugene Gant, a young man seemingly obsessed with devouring all of life, as he leaves his southern country town for northern cities, exchanges family life for university life, and goes from America to Europe. Each place in this novel represents a stage of growth and development in Eugene's life as he seeks self-knowledge and fulfillment.

Altamont. Small North Carolina town in which Eugene grows up. Annoyed with his mother's gossiping and his sister's complaining, frustrated with his family's financial problems and the general static superficiality of the town, he longs to leave. He is revolted by the constriction and triviality of what he regards as the paltry lives around him. He desires to escape these constraints and the hopeless location of his childhood. Hoping for a pilgrimage of discovery and escape, he resolves to travel to a northern land of promise where he can achieve understanding and satisfaction. Altamont stands for the beginning, the departure point; it is the place that Eugene works against but is also the place he works from.

*Harvard University. Venerable New England center of learning in which Eugene enrolls. There, removed from the stifling elements of his youth, he grows enamored with the possibilities of his new life. His hunger for knowledge and intellectual growth make him open to learning from books and from life experience. He continues to develop his sharp eye for the peculiarities and inconsistencies of human nature. In a writing class, he becomes inspired and dreams of earning fame as a playwright. He believes that an answer to the loneliness and despair he has always been prey to might be found in a vast outpouring of language. He has begun to see his world expand, and he desires to engage an even larger world. Harvard and nearby Boston symbolize early hope, the seeds of education and the beginnings of a perspective from which Eugene can write about his experience.

*New York City. Great northern city in which Eugene settles after finishing college. With his extravagant hunger for new experiences, he approaches the city's energy, wealth, and possibilities with high expectations. He hopes for success in playwriting, relationships, and self-knowledge. At first, he succeeds in expanding his circle of acquaintances, sensing the deep bonds that unite him with his fellow man. However, he eventually becomes disillusioned. Teaching college English gives him little sense of accomplishment. His writing career does not take off; his idea of the glamour of the wealthy life is hollow; and his hopes for meaningful relationships fall flat. He seems to sense that to reach his true destiny, his life must be linked to a woman, so he is inclined toward romantic hopes and adventures, but these too lead nowhere. Eugene's life in New York becomes one of frustration and disappointment. At the same time, however, the city symbolizes a key place for his obsession with processing all experience.

*France. Eugene continues his restless wanderings as he hopes to find in Europe the inspiration and purpose that have eluded him in America. In Paris he encounters Starwick, Ann, and Elinor—friends from America. He visits the sites of the city with them, feeling a paradoxical mixture of appeal and revulsion for them. He comes to realize how void and unpromising are his relationships.

Eugene also visits other cities in France—Chartres, Orleans, Tours, Lyons, Marseilles, and Cherbourg,—but what once seemed exciting with its possibilities now fills him with weariness and distaste. For example, he comes to believe that the notions of class and caste governing society are vastly mistaken. His personal hopes come to naught, but he begins to realize that he must return to America to discover himself. As he boards the ship for home, he hears the voice of a woman named Esther who, he feels, will be his true love and a key to his future. Thus, France, for all of its disappointment, yet proves to be a place where Eugene begins to get a grip on the nameless fury that drives him.

— *Scott Samuelson*

THE OLD CURIOSITY SHOP

Author: Charles Dickens (1812-1870)
Type of work: Novel
Type of plot: Social realism

Time of plot: Early nineteenth century
First published: serial, 1840-1841; book, 1841

This novel opens in London, from whose corruption young Nell Trent and her grandfather flee, seeking refuge in the more wholesome countryside, where their journey takes on the form of John Bunyan's The Pilgrim's Progress.

Old Curiosity Shop. Curio shop in an unspecified part of London that is owned by Nell's grandfather when the novel opens. The old man's only source of livelihood, the shop provides a meager income that the grandfather tries to supplement with careless gambling ventures. When his gambling losses leave him in debt, he loses the shop to the avaricious dwarf Quilp. After Quilp dies at the end of the novel, the shop is destroyed to make way for a new building.

Dickens originally intended to make this novel a story about a lovely child surrounded by grotesque objects and remnants of ancient times in her grandfather's shop. However, the story and the character caught Dickens's imagination, and he extended his vision to contrast the lovely child with the grotesque images that surrounded and followed her wherever she went.

*London. Dickens does not provide specific sections of the city or addresses for the most part, leaving readers to use their own imaginations to advantage and to place characters' homes and businesses in even worse places than Dickens might suggest. However, Dickens does mention some vicinities—such as the malicious grotesque Quilp's residence on Tower Hill and Dick Swiveller's rooms near Drury Lane.

Dickens hoped to effect social reform in the treatment of children of the poor. His novel's preoccupation with the child Nell Trent and her surroundings calls attention to the plights of such children. For this reason, other child characters, ever more wild and outlandish, are juxtaposed against Nell, making a kind of environment and setting in themselves. Likewise, Nell's increasing visits to churchyards and her concern for the dead are at once setting and literary foreboding and show an image from a gothic vision: Death and the Maiden.

*English countryside. After Nell and her grandfather flee London to live in the country, the novel becomes even less specific about locations. Readers know only that they are headed west. At that point, Dickens lets readers know that the rest of the story will follow John Bunyan's *The Pilgrim's Progress* (1678, 1684) a Christian allegory about human beings struggling to make their way to the Celestial City.

Nell's journey begins with a visit to the horse races. Possibly these are the famous Ascot Races, but within the text of the story, the races are Dickens's version of Bunyan's Vanity Fair, which tempts travelers to stay by providing them with comforts and pleasures. At the horse races, Nell is surrounded by grotesque people. Later, while working for a traveling waxwork, Nell sleeps among the cadaver-like dummies at night to guard them. The city in which she and her grandfather stay seems to be a haven, but it is the equivalent of Bunyan's castle of the giant, Despair. In despair, Nell flees, still pursued, figuratively, by the evils of urban life.

One of Dickens's most memorable descriptions and locations is that of coke-fired furnaces in a large iron-manufacturing town. At night, the fires leap like fires in Ghenna and turn human beings into demon silhouettes. Smoke and soot rain down and cover and kill living things and souls of the people who live there. Struggling onward through the hellish landscape, Nell makes slow progress, and this setting becomes her Slough of Despond.

Eventually, Nell reaches what becomes her Celestial City, a small country town with an ancient church and graveyard. At last, the exploitation ends and the rural life offers its blessings to the travelers. Within this natural setting, there is respite and spiritual healing and a quiet place. This point is reinforced in the conclusion of the novel when other characters find the country life and settle there in contentment. This quiet life enables them to overcome even wrongful imprisonment in Old Bailey, the most infamous prison of its time. The urban life destroys and blights souls; the country life blesses its adherents and makes them whole.

— *H. Alan Pickrell*

THE OLD MAID

Author: Edith Wharton (1862-1937)
Type of work: Novella
Type of plot: Social realism

Time of plot: 1850's
First published: 1924

The second of four novellas published under the title Old New York, *this story reveals the shallowness and superficiality of New York City's high society through a close examination of its narrow rules and etiquette.*

*New York City. Setting for the entire story. Delia has married well into the Ralston family and enjoys all the wealth and privileges the name Ralston affords—especially within Manhattan's post Gramercy Park neighborhood. As Delia wakes up each morning, she looks out toward the city, appreciating what surrounds her, and then slowly considers that what surrounds her is actually the banality of the everyday life of the well to do. Although she has some regrets, feeling trapped in Ralston wealth and privileges, she is happy to be spared the fate that has befallen her unmarried cousin, Charlotte Lovell, who had a baby out of wedlock that she gave up to an orphanage.

During the period in which this story is set, the 1850's, New York high society had no tolerance for any digression from what were perceived to be a woman's virtues. Thus, Delia and Charlotte must keep Charlotte's dark secret, and this Charlotte can best do by remaining unmarried. As a consequence, the unmarried Charlotte becomes a stereotype of an old maid and lives deprived of the good life to which she otherwise would be entitled. However, Charlotte recognizes the consequences of her transgression and accepts her fate.

— *Hanh N. Nguyen*

THE OLD MAN AND THE SEA

Author: Ernest Hemingway (1899-1961)
Type of work: Novella
Type of plot: Symbolic realism

Time of plot: Mid-twentieth century
First published: 1952

The symbolism of this plot occurs in the vast waters off the coast of Cuba, where an old fisherman risks his life when he catches the greatest fish of his life. The boundless expanse of the sea is a striking place in which to set a solitary and reflective character.

*Caribbean Sea. Branch of the North Atlantic Ocean that surrounds Cuba. The sea contributes to the sense of fatalism in the primary character. Alone on the vast expanses of the sea, Santiago, the "old man" of the title, suggests a symbolic understanding of human alienation amid an indifferent world. The sea functions as a backdrop for his reflections of his interior being, thus reinforcing themes of loneliness, struggle, and courage. Ernest Hemingway says of Santiago, "He looked across the sea and knew how alone he was now." His loneliness, however, is also comforted by the sea, as he knows that no man is ever completely alone on the sea.

The desolation of the open sea overwhelms the character, suggesting man's relative insignificance, yet in this vast space, a courageous man finds beauty and solace by understanding his relationship to the environment. For Santiago, this relationship is like that of a man and woman (again reinforcing the man's solitary existence). He understands the sea as *la mar*, a feminine noun in Spanish, something to be loved, something that gives or withholds great favors. In contrast, others understand the sea to be masculine, *el mar*, a rival or even an enemy.

Despite Santiago's understanding of the aesthetic nature of his relationship to the sea, the sea itself is ultimately a violent, dangerous place on which survival becomes a primary goal and the ability to survive is the cardinal virtue. It is a place where predators feed on lesser forms of life, and Santiago's struggle with the fish and with the sharks who feed on it illustrates that man also participates within this vicious cycle. Human existence is about surviving in a beautiful but hostile environment.

Santiago's shack. This place reveals the man's poverty. Symbolically, it functions as a place where he retreats each night in humility before going out at daylight to fish and survive. It is a returning to the womb, demonstrating man's longed for comfort in stark contrast to the hostilities on the sea.

*Havana. Capital and principal city of Cuba, in sight of which Santiago has long done his fishing. Its opulent urban setting contrasts with Santiago's simple village and his daily struggle to catch and sell fish.

— *Kenneth Hada*

OLD MORTALITY

Author: Sir Walter Scott (1771-1832)
Type of work: Novel
Type of plot: Historical

Time of plot: 1679
First published: 1816

Placed mostly in the western county of Lanarkshire, this novel focuses on an area along the Clyde River between the towns of Lanark and Bothwell. For Walter Scott, this region was of special historical interest because of its having been the center of the radical Presbyterian Covenanter uprising against the English government in 1679. In all of the major places in this novel, both the real and the fictional, Scott dramatizes and symbolizes the passions and tensions that lay behind that uprising.

*Western Scotland. The main backdrop of the novel. For Scott, this region of Scotland was the geographical heart of the radical Covenanter tradition in Scottish history, and he was intensely interested in and deeply knowledgeable about this area, its people, and its history. Most of the places in the novel illuminate aspects of western Scotland and of the Covenanter rebellion which grew out of the west country of Scotland and which tore the country apart in 1679. On a more specifically symbolic level, Scott describes western Scotland as divided between bleak and empty moorland to the north and a fertile and richly productive valley to the south. For Scott, these two areas of western Scotland symbolize the fanaticism and violent division of the Scottish past and the order and rationality of Scotland's future in the eighteenth century. The novel is about the place where these two forces clash at the end of the seventeenth century.

Tillietudlem (TIHL-ee-TUHD-lehm). Ancient Scottish castle characterized by its great central tower and sturdy battlements that is the home of the Bellendens. Scott based Tillietudlem mainly on his firsthand knowledge of the ruined castle of Craignethan. Although Tillietudlem is itself fictional, the popularity of Scott's novel was so great that the Caledonian Railway established a station called Tillietudlem in the 1860's to accommodate those passengers who insisted on seeing the "real" Tillietudlem. In the novel itself, the castle is in part a symbol of the deeply felt Royalist faith of the Bellenden family. For Lady Bellenden, Tillietudlem is a holy place because Charles II once had breakfast there. Tillietudlem stands in the novel with its proud tower looking down, in every sense, on the wild Covenanters whose fanatical Presbyterianism leads them to rebel against Charles II. Despite this, Tillietudlem and the feudal faith it represents are surrounded by conflict and rebellion, and throughout the novel it is a place caught in the middle of strife, under siege, and threatened by both war and legal fraud. The trials of Tillietudlem become Scott's main way of showing the cost of civil unrest.

Milnewood. Home of Henry Morton, the novel's protagonist. Whereas Tillietudlem represents the Royalist cause, Milnewood is a symbol of moderate Presbyterianism and moderate Scottish nationalism. Relative to Henry Morton, Milnewood has other symbolic values. Early in the novel, he lives at Milnewood, but more or less as a poor relation. For Henry, Milnewood is scarcely more than a prison of frustrated potential. In the last chapters of the novel, Henry returns from exile to his old home, and Scott explains that even after his marriage to Edith Bellenden, when he has in essence outgrown his home, he celebrates an annual feast at Milnewood. Morton's frustrations and achievements as a maturing character are reflected in his relationship to Milnewood.

*Loudon Hill (LOWD-en). Scene of the Covenanter victory over the Royalist forces of Claverhouse. This battle represents the finest qualities of the Covenanter rebels, in part because their knowledge of and military skill in using the landscape, their sense of fighting for their own country, and the contrasting failure of the Royalist forces to understand either the place of battle or the country in which they are fighting, dramatize the Covenanter rebellion as a nationalist struggle.

*Bothwell Bridge. Scene of the greatest battle in the Covenanter uprising, in which the rebels are decisively defeated. Scott describes the battle and its aftermath with great power, revealing the brutality and cruelty of both Covenanters and Royalists, and of war in general.

At the end of the novel, Henry Morton returns to Bothwell Bridge ten years after the battle to find it a place of peace and rural beauty. Scott thus uses Bothwell Bridge in 1679 and 1689 to symbolize his central theme of the horrors of war and the joys of peace.

Black Linn of Linklater. Hiding place of the insanely fanatical and violent John Balfour of Burley. This strange, secret, and eerie place is a perfect reflection of Balfour himself. Its dark and secret cave, its raging waterfall, and its frightening and gloomy chasm mirror the inner torments and fierce depths of one of the novel's greatest characters.

— *Phillip B. Anderson*

THE OLD WIVES' TALE

Author: Arnold Bennett (1867-1931)
Type of work: Novel
Type of plot: Naturalism

Time of plot: Nineteenth century
First published: 1908

Through the story of two sisters, Constance and Sophia Baines, Arnold Bennett explores the influence of an English region on his characters' personalities and personifies the story's central place, Bursley, with characteristic phrases, attitudes, and social expectations.

Bursley. English town in which the Baines sisters live and die. Arnold Bennett adapted the name "Bursley" from that of the real town of Burslem, which is located in Staffordshire in the English Midlands, between Liverpool and London—the region in which he was born. The area around Bennett's Stoke-on-Trent birthplace was known as the Potteries because its towns were famous for producing the clay and craft associated with the production of fine Wedgewood and Staffordshire china and earthenware. Such other Bennett novels as *Anna of the Five Towns* (1902) and *The Clayhanger* (1910) also use Bursley as their primary locations. Known collectively as the "**Five Towns**" novels, these books gave Bennett's London readers a sense that they were being exposed to life in a place and a town that they would never visit. This gives the novel a documentary quality as well as a strong sense of regional realism.

In *The Old Wives' Tale*, the central goal of the Baines sisters, who are teenagers when the novel opens, is to leave Bursley. Constance, however, does not leave; instead, she marries Samuel Povey, becomes a mother of sons and inherits and manages the family dry goods store. Sophia elopes with a traveling salesman, Gerald Scales, who abandons her in Paris. At the end of their lives, they reunite in Bursley, live together in their family's home, and die there within a brief time.

When Sophia finally returns to Bursley from Paris, she finds her hometown dirtier, smaller, smokier, and more insular than she remembers it to have been. In contrast, her sister "Constance did not appear to realize the awful conditions of dirt, decay and provinciality in which she was living." Sophia feels that it would kill her to have to live there again: "It's deadening. It weighs on you." At the same time, however, Sophia realizes that she has been haunted by Bursley her whole life as "she had always compared France disadvantageously with England," and thus, missed the uniqueness and beauty of Paris until she was once again in Bursley, subject to her old feelings of being trapped in a place where the inhabitants "probably never realized that the whole rest of the world was not more or less like Bursley."

Almost nothing ever changes in Bursley, which, as a town, has an uneasy relationship with the adjacent countryside. Its industrial works seem to be superimposed on the natural beauty of the place. Bennett used his "Five Towns" novels to examine how people living in industrial regions tend not to find any beauty in their lives, while showing how beauty and aesthetic value can exist in such places. Bennett depicts Bursley as possessing a synthesis of opinions, limited experience of the outside world, and a general air of self-satisfaction. Constance's domestic life, for example, though not happy, attests to the economic value of hard work, respectability within a community, and a stable marriage. Because of the centrality of pottery to civilization, the Potteries is symbolic of the reach of industry across all of England, as almost every English cook and homemaker had Potteries wares in kitchens and dining rooms.

*Paris. Capital of France, in which Sophia spends much of her life after eloping with Gerald Scales. Bennett moved to Paris in 1903 and finished writing *The Old Wives' Tale* there. While he was there, he came to realize that England's Midlands region meant much to him, both personally and as a source of literary inspiration. Sophia's character is the vehicle for the exploration of how people carry influences of the past into their present lives, and what it feels like to return "home" after many years away. When Sophia returns, she is an alien to her sister's affection, to Bursley, and to herself, as she is not really attached to either her hometown or to Paris, where she transforms herself from an abandoned wife into a successful businesswoman.

When Sophia first arrives in Paris, Gerald Scales takes her to an art exhibit of prints by the French artist Gustave Doré, who was popular in the Five Towns. During their first few months in Paris, both Sophia and Gerald try to overcome how "the locality was not one to correspond with the ideal" of Paris. After Scales leaves her, Sophia makes her own way, respectably, and acquires a small hotel, the **Pension Frensham** on the rue Lord Byron—which is named after the English poet. She hopes to hear news of the Five Towns from some of the thousands of guests who stay under her roof. However, not one of them ever mentions Bursley or anyone Sophia knew there until Matthew Peel-Swynnerton, a young employee of the Peels stores of the Five Towns, and a friend of her nephew, Cyril Povey, takes rooms in her hotel. He eventually arranges for Sophia to reunite with Constance and moves her back to Bursley.

— *Beverly Schneller*

THE OLD WIVES' TALE

Author: George Peele (1556-1596?)
Type of work: Drama
Type of plot: Comedy

Time of plot: Indeterminate
First performed: c. 1591-1594; first published, 1595

The setting of this comedic play is rural England, where harvest-men sing reaping songs and nightingales sing evening songs. The frame takes place in a blacksmith's cottage near an English forest, where the weary Frolic and Fantastic listen to a magical fantasy story told by their hostess, Madge, around the evening fire. Normalcy yields to fantasy. The story of magic and magicians constituting the main body of the play moves through magical locations that transform people and things until day breaks. Listeners lulled asleep by the story awaken, and the old woman whose story the play dramatizes begins her morning chores. The descriptions of place are limited to brief phrases to be filled out by the dramatic company, but given the Elizabethan theater's lack of focus on props and scenery, most scenes must be filled out in the imagination of audiences.

English forest. Unspecified woodlawn; it may be in or near Devonshire, in southwestern England, but its precise location probably does not matter. There, the three pages, Antic, Forth, and Fantastic, lose their way in the dark, amid owl hoots and hobgoblins, until they encounter the rustic but hospitable blacksmith Clunch, who guides them to his cottage. There, his wife, Madge,

entertains them with the merry tale that becomes the basis for George Peele's play.

Crossroads. Junction of two roads that is a center of magic dominated by the enchanted man Erestus, whose advice, offered in rhyming riddles, aids some and punishes others. There also, Calypha and Thelia, who have come to England to find their lost sister, Delia, come to the aid of Erestus, whose betrothed, Venelia, has been stolen by the sorcerer Sacrapant.

Sacrapant's castle (SAK-ruh-pant). Great stone castle in which the magician Sacrapant holds his prisoners. Fortified against assault by armed forces, it can only be penetrated by magic: a recitation of a riddle predicting that only a dead man can destroy Sacrapant. Sacrapant keeps the princess Delia prisoner in his study, where he converses with her and provides her magic feasts served by a friar. When Delia's brothers, Calypha and Thelia, arrive to rescue her, Sacrapant captures them and puts them in the castle's dungeon, forcing them to do hard manual labor in the enchanted grounds surrounding the castle. After the knight Eumenides, assisted by the ghost of the pauper Jack, finds the source of Sacrapant's power buried in the castle grounds, Sacrapant's magic spells are broken.

Well of Life. Enchanted pool of water where the beautiful but proud and vociferous Zantippa, Lampriscus's daughter, breaks her mother's water pot on a head she sees in the water, thereby breaking the enchantment of the braggart Huanstango, whom Sacrapant has made deaf. There a peasant, blinded by Sacrapant and unable to see the deformity of Lampriscus's gentle daughter Celanta, falls in love with Celanta and helps her to a pot of gold. There too, the ghost of Jack, appreciative of his body's burial, makes a pact to assist Eumenides, first at the inn, and later at Sacrapant's stronghold.

— *Gina Macdonald*

OLDTOWN FOLKS

Author: Harriet Beecher Stowe (1811-1896)
Type of work: Novel
Type of plot: Regional

Time of plot: Late eighteenth century
First published: 1869

Despite its weak plot, this book ranks among Harriet Beecher Stowe's most successful novels because of its realistic depiction of a vital, although theocratic New England "old town" as it, and particularly its young people, come into conflict with the less constricted culture of the emerging American republic. Her skillful rendering of the colloquial speech and mannerisms of Oldtown's inhabitants establishes her as one of the earliest successful practitioners of local color in American fiction.

Oldtown. New England town modeled on Natick, Massachusetts, the hometown of Stowe's husband. More of the action takes place in the homes of the Oldtowners than in church, but a keen religious consciousness characterizes most Oldtowners. In the early Federalist years in which the novel is set, villagers ponder religious changes more often than civic ones. The daughter and sister of clergymen and wife of a biblical scholar, Stowe makes her characters think hard and often, not only on the nature of religious observance and duty but on difficult theological issues such as those distinguishing the strict Calvinism that dominated early New England from the more liberal versions of Protestantism that were making headway in the late eighteenth century.

Oldtown is not merely a refashioned Natick but Stowe's typical New England small town, a place in which people must choose among competing orthodoxies, as well as the rationalism provoked by the new nation's Founders. Stowe's characters reflect her conviction that the descendants of the Puritans at their best led reflective, but not gloomy, lives. An often anthologized chapter shows them celebrating Thanksgiving in a light-hearted evening of eating, singing, and dancing. Sam Lawson, the "do-nothing" of the community, is not scorned as idle but redeemed by his cheerful disposition and folksy wisdom.

Given their preoccupation with maintaining an authentic religious life, Oldtown villagers only vaguely recognize the dangers of the growing secularism. One of the three young principals of the novel, Tina Percival, is allowed to meet Ellery Davenport, a skeptical scoffer patterned upon Aaron Burr, in Stowe's mind a man who disgraced the heritage of his grandfather, Jonathan Edwards, the great eighteenth century divine. Thus Oldtown is a community teetering between the security of the old pieties and the perils of the new independence.

Because Stowe was an acute observer, not merely of the mores, but of the linguistic habits of New England village life, her portrayals of Oldtown's denizens, particularly Sam Lawson, also qualify her as a literary pioneer in the realistic rendering of the speech and mannerisms of ordinary people and confirm her importance as an early exponent of local color fiction.

Meetinghouse. Oldtown church used for community meetings that Stowe modeled on the Natick meetinghouse established by Reverend John Eliot to minister to Native Americans of the area. In the novel the central seating area of the church contains not the pews for white parishioners that one might expect, but benches for the remnants of the local Indian tribe a century after the establishment of this "praying town." In another link with history, Oldtown's magistrate for Indians, Judge Waban, bears the name of a real Native American who became a civic leader in early Natick. Also prominent in the congregation, though segregated like Waban's people had been, are African Americans. Stowe's narrator, Horace Holyoke, frequently a spokesman for the author,

holds that the weekly assembling of worshipers of all its races and classes is a civilizing influence.

*****Boston.** Massachusetts town that is not yet a true city is nevertheless a place of "grandeur" when Mrs. Lothrop, the wife of Oldtown's village minister, takes children there for a visit. They worship in the famous Old North Church, visit shops, and learn of the possibility of education beyond the scope of village schools. Boston is, in short, a place where their horizons are widened; however, it is also a place where they are more often exposed to libertines like Ellery Davenport. Later in the novel, much to the chagrin of family and friends, Tina Percival marries Davenport there.

Cloudland. Town patterned on Litchfield, Connecticut, where Stowe was born and spent her earliest years. There Tina, her brother Harry, and their friend Horace attend the local academy. Cloudland reflects its minister, the Reverend Mr. Avery, whose "reasonable" version of Calvinism permitting undoubted freedom of the will and personal responsibility, contrasts sharply with that of his Oldtown counterpart. Under the influence of Mr. Avery's less stringent theology, the relatively relaxed moral atmosphere of the town makes it easier for Ellery Davenport to charm Tina into what is destined to be an unhappy marriage.

— *Robert P. Ellis*

OLIVER TWIST: Or, The Parish Boy's Progress

Author: Charles Dickens (1812-1870)
Type of work: Novel
Type of plot: Social realism

Time of plot: Early nineteenth century
First published: serial, 1837-1839; book, 1838

Different parts of nineteenth century England act as symbols for the levels of progression in Oliver Twist's life, from poverty and extreme hardship to eventual comfort and happiness.

Workhouse. Orphanage in which Oliver Twist is confined when the novel opens. Located approximately seventy-five miles north of London, the workhouse plays an important role in the mood, atmosphere, and plot of the story. The dingy, poor, hard-edged conditions of the workhouse and town make these places appear to be characters in their own right. Oliver spends many of his early years in the workhouse as a frail, malnourished lad

in worn work clothes. His condition represents the conditions in the workhouse and the town. In English society, the workhouse and its inhabitants were at the lower end of the class scale.

The caretakers of the workhouse, Mrs. Mann and Bumble, are above the workhouse children in status. They are oblivious to the hardships and death around them in the workhouse. Alcoholism, a part of the life of poor English people, is rampant in the workhouse. Furthermore, the weather in the town is very dramatic, ranging from hail, freezing rain, snow, and bracing winds to the occasional bright sunshine. These extremes symbolize the changes that occur in Oliver's life. Because of the adverse conditions of the workhouse, Oliver finally runs away and walks for seven days before reaching the outskirts of London.

*London. Capital and greatest city of Great Britain. After arriving in a suburb of London, Oliver meets Jack Dawkins, known as the Artful Dodger, who leads Oliver to the east side of London. Before long, Oliver finds himself part of the London underworld, a world overseen by the sinister Fagin. The deserted streets, alleys, old dirty buildings, dark back streets, dim rooms, smoke, fog, and pitch-black nights of east London provide the proper atmosphere for Fagin's gang of thieves. They lurk in the crumbling ruins, which are symbolic of the political injustices of English society. The numerous evidences of neglect and decay in the surroundings closely correspond to the decadent human qualities that were running rampant in the hearts of the people. As in the workhouse environment, slime and filth prevail in much of London.

The general mood of terror and extreme brutality that exists in London can be directly correlated with the frequent rain and extremely cold weather. Rooftops and corridors that interconnect the dirty, crumbling buildings provide Fagin's thieves with escape routes that reflect the squalor of their occupation. Bill Sikes, the leader of Fagin's band of trained pickpockets, is a lower-class alcoholic, who makes his living by robbing people at night. A significant portion of the action in the novel occurs during the nighttime, a time for darkness, criminals, and corruption.

*Chertsey. Quiet village along the River Thames. Oliver is exposed to a completely different world when he is rescued, first by Mr. Brownlow, and later by Mrs. Maylie and her adopted daughter. It is only in these settings that brightness and sunlight occur for any length of time in the novel. This setting expresses hope in moral values that make a positive difference in the quality of human life. Mr. Brownlow and Mrs. Maylie live in country homes in Chertsey, a community providing a pleasant, mellow atmosphere, where well-heeled members of English society lived. When Oliver moves to Mr. Brownlow's home, his worn, tattered, second-hand clothing is exchanged for a new woolen suit. The transition represents the progress Oliver has made from a harsh, unpleasant life of poverty to a comfortable, peaceful lifestyle. From the abuse and social injustice of the workhouse and the world of Fagin, Oliver has escaped, having relied on his moral character to bring him up from dire circumstances to find happiness and peace in Chertsey.

— *Alvin K. Benson*

OMENSETTER'S LUCK

Author: William H. Gass (1924-   )
Type of work: Novel
Type of plot: Symbolic realism

Time of plot: 1890's
First published: 1966

This novel of loneliness and self-consciousness is set in a backwater Ohio town that emphasizes its themes of the divorce of humanity from nature and the difficulties faced by self-conscious, civilized beings even when they live quiet lives. The woods of the valley surrounding the town symbolize the original home of humanity from which townsfolk have been cut off and from which Brackett Omensetter, an Adam figure, emerges. Omensetter's secret is his wholeness, revealed through his connection with nature and his natural inhabitation of his own body. This naturalness provokes a variety of responses from other townspeople, to whom the woods are a place of chaos and decay. Throughout the novel, William H. Gass depicts the grappling of preconscious and self-conscious states, described by numerous commentators on the book as pre- and post-Fall states of being, by the main characters through their relationship with the woods and the town.

*Ohio River Valley. Region lush with wild game and vegetation, yet also the domain of animal struggle, the uncontrollable river, and dense growth of weeds and thorns. There, the woods are home to Brackett Omensetter, who can whistle like a cardinal. When he and his family first arrive in Gilean in a horse-drawn wagon, he finds a house to rent owned by Henry Pimber down the South Road near the river, where the woods are dense with trees. Gass depicts nature as the original home of humanity before the onset of rationality and self-consciousness.

Gilean townsfolk, such as Pimber and Jethro Furber, know better than to live there, yet the separation they feel from the natural environment creates significant distress in both. Shamed by the naturalness of Omensetter—who heals Pimber's lockjaw at one point with a beet poultice—Pimber hangs himself in a white oak, seventy feet above ground, representing the pain of his separation from nature. Pimber's suicide, coupled with the death of Omensetter's son Amos from illness, causes the townspeople to blame Omensetter's lack of reason, introducing him to the pangs of conscience, causing his "fall" from natural grace which is signaled by his family's departure from the woods.

Gilean. Imaginary Ohio town in which the novel is principally set. Gass does not describe the town in detail, but it is clearly a backwater settlement near the Ohio River and not far from Columbus. The town contains a Methodist church, to which Furber ministers, Matthew Watson's blacksmith shop, where Omensetter works after arriving in town, and numerous houses, including Henry Pimber's.

In a novel of consciousness and intense metaphysical reflection, the town represents civilized human community, in which church, law, and medicine—the voices of reason—preside. However, consciousness in this novel separates humanity from the world of natural action. The three primary narrative reflectors in the book—Furber, Pimber, and Israbestis Tott—are men of the community, and their perceptions are densely packed with the relentless voices of consciousness—which breed envy, fear, and suspicion of both the woods and Omensetter.

By utilizing a rural backwater for his setting, Gass reveals the innate struggle of the civilized world. The townspeople are not plagued by civic problems but simply by the separation of civilized life from nature. Thematically, the novel reveals the possibility of human redemption through a reconciliation of spirit and body, reason and intuition, and experience and innocence. Some commentators argue that Furber's character achieves such a redemption, yoking pre- and post-Fall states of being, and that his departure from Gilean suggests that he will locate a new place of being where such harmony may occur communally as well as privately.

Omensetter's house. Home of Brackett Omensetter; an old wood house in the woods near the river that Omensetter rents from Pimber. In a location susceptible to seasonal flooding, the house's exterior reveals water lines of past floods, signaling the capacity of nature to overwhelm humanity. Omensetter lives there peacefully with his family until Pimber's suicide and the death of his own son.

An abandoned well at the house becomes a trap for a fox that kills one of Omensetter's chickens. With no sign of enmity or anger, Omensetter tells Pimber to let the fox be and allow nature to have its way. Such an acceptance of nature, with its indifferent and often fatal struggles, distresses Pimber. Omensetter's later departure from the house signals his fall from grace but also reveals the novel's complex vision: That humanity cannot go back to a primal state and must find a reconciliation that admits, rather than denies, reason and conscience.

Pimber's house. Home of Henry Pimber; a broad house with a shaded porch, Pimber's home contains vases, silver spoons, handmade quilts, china cups, bubbled colored glass, painted plates, and wood-framed beds. A barn and cellar are also present on the lot. At the beginning of the novel, which opens in the early twentieth century, although most of the narrative that follows unfolds during the 1890's, an auctioneer is selling off the items of the property, signaling the dismantling of a life that abounded in creature comforts but was too removed from nature to achieve peace.

— *Mark Walling*

OMOO: A Narrative of Adventures in the South Seas

Author: Herman Melville (1819-1891)

Type of work: Novel

Type of plot: Adventure

Time of plot: Early 1840's

First published: 1847

This novel mixes elements of an adventure story with the travel narrative in an examination of the effects of European colonization upon the Polynesian islands, particularly Tahiti. While ostensibly the story of a pair of vagabond sailors roving episodically from one island to another, the novel's real theme is the quest for a glimpse of a fast-vanishing "true" Polynesia unadulterated by Western religion and culture.

*Papeetee (pah-pay-AY-tay). Principal city and colonial capital of Tahiti. Papeetee (now generally spelled Papeete) provides the setting for the first half of *Omoo*. Its deep, spacious harbor is well protected by reefs, making it one of the South Pacific's most valuable anchorages for both commercial and military purposes. Melville's narrator duly notes the harbor's activity in a steady stream of whaling ships and trading brigs. He also delineates the city's role as a colonial catspaw, or pawn, used by the British and French.

*Tahiti. Major island in the South Pacific's French-occupied Society Islands. At the time in which the narrative is set, the island group had been unofficially ceded by the British to the French; however, the British presence in Papeetee is still maintained in the form of its chief consul. His corrupt administration exemplifies the self-delusory arrogance inherent in colonial systems that purport to "civilize" colonized peoples but in fact exploit and debase them. For instance, the narrator contrasts the simple beauty and usefulness of the native barkcloth (tapa) with the European fripperies ridiculously adopted by some Tahitians. Moreover, he provides an insightful analysis of the cycle of dependency and idleness engendered in a colonized people who abandon traditional economies (such as tapa-making, canoe-building, and even coconut harvesting) to accept handouts from colonial authorities. Yet, the narrator reserves his greatest scorn for the European missionaries, both Protestant and Roman Catholic, who seem more interested in establishing the dominion of their own narrow creeds than in sharing the common message of Christianity. These "mickonarees," as they are called in the island's pidgin English, have effectively eradicated Tahitian culture—from the innocent pleasures of its traditional sports to the profound spectacle of its ritual dances.

Imeeo (ee-MAY-ay-oh). Small remote island in the Tahitian group offering a view of more purely traditional Tahitian culture that contrasts with the decadence of Papeetee. The narrator first goes to this island to work as a day laborer on a plantation. However, he soon wearies of the tropical, mosquito-infested climate, and sets out for the highlands on a hunt for bullocks, wild descendants of animals left by the explorer George Vancouver fifty years earlier. The increasing wildness of his trek culminates in a walking tour into the interior. In the solitary village of Tamai, he experiences the old Tahitian hospitality that welcomes him as an honored guest in the first house he approaches. Unlike his friendships with parasitic Tahitians in Papeetee, the friendships he forms with his Imeeo hosts are real, and he effectively becomes part of their family.

The narrator offers many ethnographic details on traditional Tahitian food, drink, and architecture. He recounts both the food served in a traditional Tahitian feast and the complicated seating arrangement dictated by the laws of hospitality and family lineage. In one passage that presages the epic catalogs in *Moby Dick* (1851), he provides an exhaustive list of myriad uses of the coconut tree—its fruit for food, its leaves for thatch, its nuts for cups, its fibers for cord, its oil for embalming, and so on. He also informs on taboo subjects such as the intoxicating kava drink and the girls' ritual dance that has been suppressed by missionaries in Papeetee.

Partoowye. Royal village of hereditary Tahitian queen Pomaree that is the narrator's final destination on Imeeo. There, he glimpses the once-glorious past of the Polynesian court with its strict protocol and rigid hierarchy. Compared to the sickly, degenerate Tahitians of Papeetee, the inhabitants of Partoowye live up to the physical and spiritual ideal of the "noble savage" that the narrator has sought. Pomaree herself is almost the caricature of the unpredictable Polynesian who is mild one moment, passionate the next. Ultimately, though, he portrays these "true" Tahitians as a doomed culture without the focus or resources to defend themselves from the overwhelming forces of European imperialism.

— *Luke A. Powers*

ON THE ROAD

Author: Jack Kerouac (1922-1969)
Type of work: Novel
Type of plot: Autobiographical

Time of plot: 1947-1950
First published: 1957

Although this novel's narrator, Sal Paradise, visits many places in the United States and Mexico, the book is really about North American life as a whole. Places serve to substantiate Jack Kerouac's central theme that life on the road promises excitement, thrills, and satisfaction, although in the end it is shrouded in gloom.

*Denver.** Colorado's capital and largest city. In Denver, Sal ventures to the apartment of Carlo Marx, which is in a brick boardinghouse near a church. To get to Carlo's door, he must walk down an alley, descend stairs, open an old door, and pass through a cellar. Within the apartment, the walls are damp, and the scant furnishings include a candle, a bed, and a homemade icon. A meeting between Carlo and Dean Moriarity sets off the events in Colorado, and Sal soon finds himself embarked on a trip to Central City, where a performance of an opera is staged in a renovated opera house. The day starts well when an empty miner's shack becomes available, and Sal and his friends dress formally for the performance. Later, back at the shack, they throw a party. When troublesome young visitors ruin the party, Sal and his friends go to the local bars, where they get drunk and begin shouting. Unfortunately, drunkenness leads to fights in the bars, but Sal and his friends escape before the violence escalates. At the shack, the friends cannot sleep well on the dusty bed. Breakfast is stale beer. In the car, the descent to Denver is depressing.

*Southern California.** Upon his arrival in Los Angeles, Sal declares that Los Angeles is the loneliest city in America. Traveling with Terry, his Mexican lover, Sal walks down a main street, where there is a carnival atmosphere. Short of funds and finding no employment, Sal and Terry journey to Bakersfield to earn money by picking grapes. Finally, near Sabinal, they find work as cotton pickers. They rent a tent for a dollar, and though Sal's wages provide only for day-to-day subsistence, Sal is wonderfully in love and feels happy that he is living off the earth, as he always dreamed he would be. Nevertheless, the chill of October arrives, and Sal has the restless desire to leave. Sal and Terry promise to meet in New York, but each knows the meeting will never come to pass. Getting a ride to Los Angeles, Sal stops at Columbia Pictures, where his rejected manuscript awaits him. Instead of embarking on a Hollywood career, Sal finds himself making baloney sandwiches in a parking lot, waiting for the departure of his bus.

*New Orleans.** Louisiana's largest and most cosmopolitan city. As Dean, Sal, and others drive along, they are thrilled to hear jazz playing on the radio. New Orleans appears ahead of them, and they anticipate the excitement of the city. The women on the streets are stunningly beautiful. On the ferry across the Mississippi River, Sal appreciates the great American river.

*Algiers.** District of New Orleans. Arriving in Algiers, the traveling band finds the dilapidated house of Old Bull Lee. Sal and Dean hope to visit exciting bars in New Orleans, but Bull insists that the bars are all dreary and takes his friends to the dullest places. Later, when Sal wants to look at the Mississippi, he finds that a fence blocks his view. As days go by, Bull reveals his eccentricities and distrust of bureaucracy, and they begin to weary of one another's company. Finally, in the dusky light, Dean, Marylou, and Sal get in their car and head to California.

*Mexico.** Sal, Dean, and Stan drive into Mexico, and Sal takes the wheel. He notices the surrounding jungle and the road that rises into the mountains. In Gregoria, a young Mexican named Victor approaches and provides marijuana and prostitutes. A wild night of intoxication, sex, music, and dancing ensues, making Sal feel that he is experiencing the end of the world. Nevertheless, as soon as Sal and Dean leave Gregoria, the road slopes downward.

The night is dark and steamy hot, with bugs swarming and biting. On the map, the men see that they have crossed the Tropic of Cancer. Caked with dead bugs and stinking in their sweaty shirts, they proceed to Ciudad Mante. After refueling there, Sal, Dean, and Stan begin another ascent. At an elevation of more than one mile, they discover a tiny thatched hut. They meet some native children, whose eyes are like those of the Virgin Mary. Sal is especially impressed that these native people are oblivious to atomic weaponry and its power to destroy everything. Their old Ford rolls on, and soon the men are immersed in the frantic pace of Mexico City. Sal becomes delirious after contracting dysentery, and Dean, having secured his Mexican divorce papers, abandons Sal to make his return trip.

— *William T. Lawlor*

THE ONCE AND FUTURE KING

Author: T. H. White (1906-1964)
Type of work: Novel
Type of plot: Arthurian romance
Time of plot: Middle Ages

First published: 1958 (as tetralogy): *The Sword in the Stone*, 1938; *The Witch in the Wood*, 1939 (also known as *The Queen of Air and Darkness*); *The Ill-Made Knight*, 1940; *The Candle in the Wind*, 1958

For T. H. White, Arthur's England is in many ways both like modern England, and unlike popular preconceived notions of medieval, "merry" England.

*England.** The England of the legendary King Arthur, often called **Gramarye**, is a totally imaginary realm. T. H. White's narrator refers to the historical kings of England as mythical, and other real and imaginary characters such as John Ball and Robin Hood (here called Robin Wood) are anachronistically jumbled into Arthur's time period.

White's mythical kingdom can be divided into two periods: before and after Arthur's succession. Before Arthur, England is a savage realm, "without civilization," in which might makes right. The narrator is careful to point out that the feudal system was not inherently bad; under good lords, such as Sir Ector, the peasants are well treated. Indeed, at times the narrator's descriptions of lower-class life resemble the romantic imaginings of the Merrie England school of English history, represented by writers such as G. K. Chesterton and Hilaire Belloc. Even England's weather is tame. According to the narrator, the greatest modern fault in imagining life in the Middle Ages is to base one's views on the pale and bare ruins of the era that remain in modern times. Arthur's England was, according to the narrator, an almost inconceivable riot of colors.

During Arthur's reign, England becomes a much safer place after the abolition of Fort Mayne, the force of might. Lawyers and legalisms take over, and the realm begins to resemble the one described by Thomas Carlyle in *Past and Present* (1843), where a child with a sack of gold could walk from one end of England to another without being accosted. But even justice has its limits, and Arthur's England is already crumbling when the novel ends.

Camelot. Mythical seat of King Court's court. Both Camelot and London are frequently mentioned in White's narrative, but it is difficult to tell which of them is England's primary city.

Castle of the Forest Sauvage. Castle of Arthur's foster father, Sir Ector, where Arthur (who is called "Wart" as a boy) is raised under the tutelage of Merlin. There and in the surrounding forest, he is taught by being transformed into different beasts. Although his surroundings themselves seem typical (such as the moat in which he is a fish), his lessons are definitely not. In the ant farm, for example, he encounters a society not far removed from the totalitarian human society depicted in George Orwell's *Nineteen Eighty-Four* (1949).

The Forest Sauvage itself, like Sherwood Forest, is described as being incomparably larger and wilder than modern forests; however, during Wart's adventures there (finding Merlin, rescuing the prisoners from the Castle Chariot), the forest does not seem much harsher than those of modern times.

Castles. Descriptions of the various castles throughout the novel stress the vibrant and rich colors with which they were adorned, both inside and out. The stained glass windows, for example, that form so prominent a part of their construction, make their interiors glow: "They were in a magic world of gems, a glade under trees whose leaves were jewels."

Castle Chariot and Dunlothian Castle, the homes of Arthur's half-sisters Morgan le Fay and Morgause, are surmounted by towers with weather-cocks of carrion crows. Castle Chariot, in its enchanted form, is made entirely of food, the total effect of which is nauseating, rather than tempting. Dunlothian Castle, home to Sir Gawaine and his brothers, is run-down and dilapidated, emblematic of the passing of power from the older Celts to the newer invaders, symbolized by Arthur and his father.

Merlin's cottage. Home of the court magician Merlin. As befits a wizard, Merlin's dwellings are crammed full of unusual and abstruse objects, some of which do not belong to his time period, such as a gun case, an encyclopedia, and a set of cigarette cards.

Justice Roome. One of the few interior locations described in any detail, this room is where Arthur is forced to pass judgment on Lancelot and Guinevere. Its boxlike walls are covered with tapestries that illustrate stories of justice from the Old Testament. However, as Arthur discovers at the end of the novel, justice is not enough to overcome the human ills he first sees illustrated during his youthful animal transformations: "Suspicion and fear: possessiveness and greed: resentment for ancestral wrong." The cures for these ills lies far beyond the ken of Camelot.

— *William Laskowski*

ONE DAY IN THE LIFE OF IVAN DENISOVICH

Author: Aleksandr Solzhenitsyn (1918-   )
Type of work: Novel
Type of plot: Historical realism

Time of plot: 1951
First published: Odin den Ivana Denisovicha, 1962
   (English translation, 1963)

The setting of this novel is in an unnamed forced labor camp in Siberia. The novel marks the beginning of a series of Aleksandr Solzhenitsyn's works about Soviet concentration camps and has a special meaning for the author, who spent eight years in one of those camps. Besides being an autobiographical account of the inhumane policies of an oppressive regime at its worst, the novel indirectly started the rebellion against the tyranny that eventually led to the Soviet Union's downfall.

*Siberian labor camp. Concentration camp located somewhere in eastern Russia's vast Siberian wastes. The novel accurately depicts a single full day in the camp, using the words of one of its inmates, Shukhov, who is Solzhenitsyn's alter ego. The grim eleven-hour workday in labor gangs subjects camp inmates to a stern test of character. In a situation where everyone fights for oneself, all human beings show what they are made of. Selfishness, cunning, cowardice, anger, hope against hope, and animalistic will to survive are some of the character traits that dominate life in the camp.

Although the individual inmates are named, they

seem to exist only as badge numbers, as props in this human tragedy. Their practical anonymity fits the nature of an archipelago (as Solzhenitsyn would call the prison camps with which Siberia was dotted in his later set of novels, titled *Gulag Archipelago*, 1974-1978). The camps are filled with people sentenced on trumped-up charges. Shukhov himself, for example, after escaping capture by the Germans, is accused of spying for the Germans and is serving a ten-year sentence for treason, even though no one could prove what he was supposed to have done. He signed his own confession, for if he had not, he would have been as good as buried. It is only in a place like the prison camp that the protagonist's character is fully revealed. He is humble, helpful, polite, forgiving, thinking of others, conscientious, meticulous even at slave labor, and grateful for every day he survives. For example, after finishing the wall of a nonsensical building the prisoners are erecting in the subfreezing weather, he returns once more to check whether he has aligned the bricks properly. The cathartic experience he, like others, is forced to endure makes him stronger. He also seems to indicate that only with such attitudes can the evil be conquered and life returned to normalcy. The day depicted in the novel, January 1, serves also as a symbol of a new, hopeful beginning.

The fact that the location of the camp is not named underscores the universality of the experience. Literally millions of Soviet citizens were herded through similar camps, and many of them did not survive. The sheer enormity of the state's crime against its people makes it unnecessary to restrict the novel's location to a single place. Instead, the whole country identifies with Siberia and, in reality, becomes Siberia during the Soviet period.

Solzhenitsyn's depiction of the camp is extremely realistic, though most Soviet labor camps looked alike. To be sure, Solzhenitsyn was less interested in its description, preoccupied as he was with the conditions under which the inmates lived and suffered. This approach added to the universality of this experience. Perhaps for that reason, he did not deem it necessary to pinpoint the exact geographical location of the camp. By the same token, the camp could have been located anywhere in this huge archipelago of human sorrow, and the impact upon the reader would have been the same.

— *Vasa D. Mihailovich*

ONE FLEW OVER THE CUCKOO'S NEST

Author: Ken Kesey (1935-2001)
Type of work: Novel
Type of plot: Psychological realism

Time of plot: 1960
First published: 1962

Set in a mental hospital for men near Portland, Oregon, this novel addresses various issues of conformity, authority, and individuality in Cold War American life. It ultimately served as one of the literary cornerstones for activists in the 1960's counterculture movement and helped inspire many to question the legitimacy of government control.

Mental hospital. Government institution for mental patients somewhere in Oregon, that is the novel's primary setting. Organized as an efficient machine that eliminates any opportunity for choice or individual decision making, the hospital has staff members to take meticulous care of all the patients' needs. In the mornings, ward residents are herded into a shaving and tub room where they are forced to shower and prepare for the day's activities.

The patient ward itself is filled with a system of locks and keys that help the supervisor, Nurse Ratched, manage all of her affairs. She is usually positioned behind a locked glass door, from which she dispenses daily doses of medication that dull each patient's senses. Ratched easily dominates the inmates, but when Randle McMurphy, a free-spirited outdoorsman, enters the ward, a classic confrontation unfolds as he challenges the neatly ordered world constructed by the nurse.

Day room. Common area in the patient ward in which many activities occur. Amid a scattering of tables and chairs, the men are expected to spend the day listening to a radio or participating in board games. As music blares from speakers throughout the day, the fog machine, an apparatus of fictitious wires, compressors, and vacuums, dulls the men into accepting their mundane daily routine.

McMurphy explodes into this environment and attempts to dismantle both the fog machine and the hospital's tight-fisted management of everyone's affairs. He immediately organizes a blackjack game in which he inevitably wins everyone's cigarettes. During these card games, many of the more intricate and complex issues affiliated with the novel are explored. Through various conversations, it is revealed that few of these men are suffering from any real form of mental illness, and the real problem appears to be the state's desire to eliminate all forms of individual expression.

Group therapy meetings also occur quite regularly in the day room. Run with a firm hand by Nurse Ratched, the men are forced to sit in a circle of chairs and reveal their deepest and darkest secrets. They are also encouraged to spy on one another and then expose each other's weaknesses. During these meetings McMurphy discovers that the overall aim of the institution is to frighten patients into believing that they can recover only if they shed all remnants of their individuality.

Shock Shop. Place in which Ratched and her staff eradicate negative behavior of rebellious inmates. Behind an unmarked metal door, men are dragged into a room full of tubes, electronic machinery, wires, and a bare mattress. There they are strapped onto a table—on which they assume crucifixion poses—as electricity is shot through their brains. Most of the men in the ward have had this experience at least once and none of them wants to repeat it. Those who fail to respond to electroshock therapy, like McMurphy, are escorted to the surgical wing of the hospital, where they receive lobotomies.

Fishing boat. In an act of rebellion, McMurphy persuades other patients to disregard Ratched's gloomy warnings about wrecks, drownings, and hurricanes by participating in a deep-sea fishing expedition for salmon off the Pacific coast. During the outing, the men successfully fix up reels and lines, attach poles to their harnesses properly, and systematically troll for fish. The tranquil ocean swells, the hum of the boat's engine, and the scenic view of high flying birds provide the patients with an unprecedented sense of calm and temporary confidence. With the benefit of an ample supply of beer, they erupt into laughter as they catch fish. McMurphy also arranges for two women to join the expedition, and they flirt with the men throughout the trip. Despite rough seas, the men navigate safely back to port. Their success clearly reveals that the mental hospital is hindering, not aiding, their recoveries and ultimate return to life outside the institution.

Columbia River. River that forms the border between Oregon and Washington before emptying into the Pacific Ocean. Although none of the novel's action takes place on the river, there are frequent references to it throughout. In earlier times, Native Americans erected wood scaffolding on the river from which to spear salmon and built tree stands to hunt birds. Several times in the novel one of the patients, Chief Bromden, dreams of his youth on the river before hydroelectric dams and government agencies destroyed his tribe's land—like the mental hospital, an example of how government often undermines, rather than serves, the interests of people.

— *Robert D. Ubriaco, Jr.*

ONE HUNDRED YEARS OF SOLITUDE

Author: Gabriel García Márquez (1928-   )
Type of work: Novel
Type of plot: Magical Realism

Time of plot: 1820's to 1920's
First published: Cien años de soledad, 1967 (English translation, 1970)

This novel uses fantasy, fiction, and Magical Realism in its setting, one that nonetheless reveals the historical, political, and cultural underpinnings of contemporary Colombia, while also tracing the one-hundred-year legacy of the Buendía family. The novel accomplishes this by detailing the founding, the struggles, the prosperity, the decline, and the eventual annihilation of the village of Macondo.

Macondo (ma-COHN-doh). Fictional inland town in Colombia that is not far from the coast. Critics generally agree that Macondo is modeled after Gabriel García Márquez's hometown of Aracataca, Colombia. Indeed, a nearby banana plantation was named Macondo. In the novel, Macondo is founded by an expedition led by the Buendía family who, after crossing mountains and looking for a new outlet to the sea, finally decide to simply stop and settle. The novel describes the town in terms reminiscent of Eden: It is a town so young that no one is older than thirty and no one has died. The town of Macondo is isolated from the outside world, except for the band of gypsies led by Melquíades, who ride through the air on carpets and bring the wonders of the world to the townspeople.

The novel is organized around the development of the town. The first five chapters detail the founding and early years of Macondo. This is then followed by four chapters describing military uprisings, civil wars, and revolutions. The next five chapters represent a period of prosperity for the town, with a concurrent loss of innocence. The final chapters reveal the inner decadence of the town and its final destruction in a whirlwind.

While the novel is fantastic and magical, it also reveals significant information about the history of Colombia, particularly in the nineteenth and twentieth centuries. During the years between 1884 and 1902, Colombia experienced three civil wars. The events of the novel parallel this period of Columbian history surprisingly closely. Indeed, many critics identify one of the novel's major characters, Colonel Aureliano Buendía, as the historical figure Colonel Uribe Uribe. This period in Colombian history is full of chaos and confusion, just as in the novel. Certainly, the characters in the novel seem to have little idea of what they are fighting for or why they are fighting.

The second important historical event treated in the novel is the incursion of American investors and the Ba-

nana Massacre of 1928. In the early years of the twentieth century, United Fruit Company, an American concern, began building huge banana plantations in the vicinity of Aracataca. Likewise, in the novel, Americans arrive in Macondo and begin developing the area. In the novel, the Banana Company engineers magically change the course of the river; in Columbia, the erection of dams and dikes did indeed change the flow of the river.

Further, in the real town of Ciénaga, near Aracataca, labor unrest erupted into violence in 1928. On December 6, a large number of striking banana workers were massacred at the railway station by government troops. It is still uncertain how many people were actually killed, despite the many investigations. It is clear that the government attempted to mask its involvement in the massacre. This event is dramatically rendered in the novel. José Arcadio Segundo is present with the striking workers at the train station when the army opens fire with machine guns. He witnesses two hundred train cars filled with the dead and wounded. Yet, when he attempts to report the massacre, he finds that no one will believe him and that everyone denies any such event took place. Critics suggest that this denial represents the reluctance of the real witnesses of the Ciénaga massacre to speak out about what they had seen.

Riohacha (ree-oh-HAHCH-ah). Coastal town, the birthplace of Macondo's founders, José Arcadio Buendía and Úrsula Iguarán. In the sixteenth century, according to the novel, the pirate Francis Drake attacked the town. It is here that Buendía murders Prudencio Aguilar in response to his taunting about Buendía's supposed impotence. Aguilar's ghost will not leave José and Úrsula alone, and so it is that Macondo's founders set off on their expedition to their new home.

— *Diane Andrews Henningfeld*

THE ORDEAL OF RICHARD FEVEREL: A History of Father and Son

Author: George Meredith (1828-1909)
Type of work: Novel
Type of plot: Tragicomedy

Time of plot: Mid-nineteenth century
First published: 1859

George Meredith uses this novel to rail against the practice of rearing young people in systems that prevent them from developing natural feelings about the world—especially about love. Through his early years, protagonist Richard Feverel is confined closely to the family estate by a father who wants to insulate him from women. Eventually, however, he meets and marries a delightful farm girl, Lucy Desborough, and must struggle to regain his father's approval. Meredith uses setting with great care, establishing verisimilitude for the episodes in the novel by relying on readers' preconceptions about baronial manors, country farming communities, London, and locales traditionally thought of as places for escape.

Raynham Hall. Ancestral seat of the Feverel family. Like many English manorial estates, Raynham Hall is a self-contained city, frequently described as a fortress or citadel sheltering its inhabitants from the outside world. Sir Austin keeps his only son, Richard, a virtual prisoner in Raynham Hall while the boy is growing up, carefully ensuring that Richard will face no temptations, especially from women, during his formative years. Because Raynham Hall provides a practically self-sufficient community, Sir Austin is able to introduce what he believes are the right kinds of people to help shape his son's character and not allow Richard to fall prey to the wrong woman, as happened to Sir Austin himself. The cold, lifeless surroundings of the hall are set in contrast to the grounds outside, and especially to the farms in the surrounding area, where life seems to flourish and relationships develop naturally.

Belthorpe. Home of Farmer Blaize, Lucy Desborough's uncle. Richard and his friend Ripton arrange to burn a haystack on the farm in retaliation for Farmer Blaize's treatment of them when he catches them poaching game. In having to admit guilt for his offense, Richard visits Belthorpe and first meets Lucy. A future chance meeting in the woods brings the young people together again, and the rural setting provides an Arcadian backdrop for their first amatory adventures. Despite his father's instructions, Richard lolls about in the woods and on the waterways in the area, courting Lucy in these idyllic settings.

*****London.** Great Britain's capital serves as the meeting place for people of different backgrounds and social classes. Through a series of coincidences made believable because of their setting in the great city, Richard eventually reunites with Lucy, after she is sent away from Belthorpe at the request of Sir Austin. In London, he marries Lucy and eventually negotiates a reunion with his estranged parent. The city is also a place of intrigue, in which Richard is enticed by a woman hired to keep him away from his wife, whose employer attempts to seduce her.

*****Isle of Wight.** Island off the southern coast of England. Traditionally a spot for vacationers, the island serves as Richard and Lucy's honeymoon getaway. Richard leaves Lucy there when he returns to London to seek a reconciliation with his father. Unbeknownst to him, he leaves Lucy exposed to the machinations of Lord Mountfalcon, a libertine noble who hires a woman to seduce Richard while he himself pursues Lucy. The suggestion that Wight is a spot for carefree play lends credence to the idea that people of seemingly upright social status can behave hypocritically outside the normal boundaries of society.

*****Continent.** European mainland on which Richard wanders aimlessly after abandoning Lucy. On the banks of the Rhine River, he experiences a wild thunderstorm that reveals to him the power of nature and variety of life; the exhilaration he feels later gives him the courage to return home to face Lucy and confess his infidelity.

— *Laurence W. Mazzeno*

THE ORESTEIA

Author: Aeschylus (525/524-456/455 B.C.E.)
Type of work: Drama
Type of plot: Tragedy
Time of plot: After the fall of ancient Troy

First performed: Agamemnōn (*Agamemnon*),
Choēphoroi (*Libation Bearers*), and *Eumenides*,
458 B.C.E. (English translation, 1777)

This trilogy of plays—Aeschylus's examination of revenge, guilt, and the need for human justice—moves from the Greek kingdom of Argos, where Agamemnon is killed by his wife, Clytemnestra, and is later avenged by his son Orestes, to Delphi, home of the famous oracle, and concludes in the Areopagus, supreme law court of Athens, and symbol of democratic Athenian justice, where Orestes is tried and acquitted.

Agamemnon's palace. Royal palace of King Agamemnon at Argos. In ancient productions of this play, at the open-air theater of Dionysus in Athens, the palace was represented by the skene, a two-story wooden building located at the rear of the stage. There, as in most Greek tragedies, place is of much less importance than space. The large central door of the skene provides an entrance into an inner, "private" space concealed from the audience's view. When Agamemnon comes on stage fresh from his victory at Troy, he is greeted publicly by his wife, in full view of both the audience and the chorus, whose members move about in the orchestra, the open space between the skene and the audience. In this open space, Agamemnon is safe; when he enters the palace, however, he will die. In *Libation Bearers*, Orestes confronts his mother outside the palace, but will force her inside—out of the audience's view—to exact his revenge.

*****Temple of Apollo.** Home of the Pythia, Apollo's priestess and oracle, at Delphi; one of the greatest shrines of ancient Greece. The temple contains the *omphalos*, the "navelstone," whis is supposed to mark the center of the earth. *Eumenides* opens here, with the temple represented by the skene. Pursued by the Furies (primal agents of vengeance), Orestes comes to Delphi to implore Apollo's help in cleansing himself of the guilt of his mother's murder. Apollo almost immediately sends him to Athens, directing him to seek sanctuary at the temple of Athena.

*****Athens.** Ancient Greek city-state that is home to the Temple of Athena, atop the Acropolis, and the Areopagus, where *Eumenides* concludes here with a trial presided over by Athena.

— *Michael Stuprich*

ORLANDO: A Biography

Author: Virginia Woolf (1882-1941)
Type of work: Novel
Type of plot: Phantasmagoric

Time of plot: 1588-1928
First published: 1928

This novel takes the form of a biography of an English courtier who not only lives from the time of Queen Elizabeth I into the twentieth century but also changes from a man to a woman. The settings of London and Orlando's castle symbolize the conflicted evolution of British social and cultural history, especially with regard to gender, social conventions, and politics. Together London and the castle are used to critique traditional notions of history and biography as fact and truth, as permanent and reliable.

Orlando's castle. This site inspires Orlando's creative struggle to become a poet. With its 365 rooms and 52 staircases, the castle extends over several acres. Hundreds of servants care for the castle and its grounds, which contain an oak tree that symbolizes the enduring presence of literature and inspires Orlando to write an ongoing poem titled "The Oak Tree." Contrasting with the continual change in London, Orlando's castle remains unchanged from the glorious days when it received Queen Elizabeth in the sixteenth century to its grandeur in the twentieth century.

Although the castle is fictional, it is based on Vita Sackville-West's ancestral home Knole and her later home, Sissinghurst Castle. During the 1920's, Great Britain's laws of entail meant that Vita could not inherit the ancestral house she loved because she was a woman. In transforming Knole into Orlando's house Woolf draws on Vita Sackville-West's own book *Knole and the Sackvilles* (1922) and restores the house to her friend.

*London. As Great Britain's capital and leading city evolves through Orlando's long lifetime, it demonstrates an Einsteinian blend of time and space. Each century in London is represented by specific historical and literary events. Although the city is presented through actual sites, they are fictionalized in order to represent various historical periods. Virginia Woolf prefaces her introduction of Orlando into London society with this disclaimer:

> To give a truthful account of London society at that or indeed at any other time, is beyond the powers of the biographer or the historian. Only those who have little need of the truth, and no respect for it—the poets and the novelists—can be trusted to do it, for this is one of the cases where truth does not exist. Nothing exists. The whole thing is a miasma—a mirage.

Sixteenth century London is seen through Queen Elizabeth's courtier tradition. Grand halls, elaborate furnishings, and elegant costumes suggest the majesty and dignity of Elizabeth's reign. During this century Orlando betrays the queen's love and is ousted from the royal court.

The historically accurate Great Frost, the most severe winter in England's history, characterizes the seventeenth century. This setting is fantasized with the frozen River Thames as site for a winter carnival celebrating King James I's coronation. Huge bonfires, colorful balloons, drinking booths, decorated arbors, elaborate feasting, and musical galas contrast with the meager living conditions of the masses. As an emblem for all of the seventeenth century, the Great Frost suggests the "cold-

ness" of members of the royal family's attitudes toward their constituents, as well as the political tensions of the country—Protestants versus Catholics, Regents versus Parliament, upper versus lower classes, and England versus Scotland, Wales, and Ireland. During this century Orlando grows out of adolescence and discovers his manhood in his social responsibilities and sexual encounters.

In the following century, after a sojourn in Turkey during which Orlando becomes a woman, she returns to England, where the castle staff welcome her home as if there has been no change. Becoming bored with the new expectations for feminine behavior, Orlando escapes into the nightlife of London reverting to masculine dress and befriending prostitutes. In seedy areas of London, Orlando learns the more devious of her feminine characteristics, woos literary figures—such as Alexander Pope and John Dryden—and gains entrance into London salons. Together the salons and red light district create a paradoxical view of London society: "A turbulent welter of cloud covered the city. All was dark; all was doubt; all was confusion. The Eighteenth century was over; the Nineteenth century had begun."

This stormy view of the nineteenth century persists, forcing Orlando inside her castle where she redefines herself. She both writes and takes on womanly domestic duties of redecorating the castle to recreate its past splendor. She hunts and farms. She meets and marries Marmaduke Bonthrop Shelmerdine. Orlando's isolation in her castle is indicative of the Romantics' reflection on individual spirituality as a source for artistic inspiration.

Finally twentieth century London introduces Orlando to a world of modern technology. Various city sites prompt Orlando's reflections on her life, on literary history, on the evolution of English culture, and she discovers from its diversity that life is never concluded but ongoing, continually in flux, never complete.

*Constantinople. Capital of the Ottoman Empire, to which Orlando is sent as ambassador extraordinaire during the eighteenth century. Woolf's use of Constantinople and the Turkish countryside reflects the contemporary interest in exotic locales as places of mystery, romance, and intrigue. Bringing together several story threads, this mysterious city shapes Orlando's character with its emphasis on death, war, and sex. While there, Orlando unaccountably changes from a man to a woman.

After her sex change Orlando flees to Broussa, a rural mountainous area outside Constantinople, where she allies herself with gypsies. The beauty of Nature betrays Orlando's oversensitivity, making the gypsies suspicious. Her escape on the ship *Enamoured Lady* symbolizes her new role as a woman and its codes of behavior.

— *Kathryn N. Benzel*

ORLANDO FURIOSO

Author: Ludovico Ariosto (1474-1533)
Type of work: Poetry
Type of plot: Romance

Time of plot: Eighth century
First published: 1516; second revised edition, 1521; third revised edition, 1532

Settings in this epic poem range far and wide, across Medieval Europe, North Africa, the Middle East, India, and numerous imaginary realms, and the poem is extraordinarily rich in casual geographical references. The story's principal narrative base is the emperor Charlemagne's court in Paris, but it is the many places visited by his busy knights errant—especially the hippogriff-borne Astolpho—that provide the poem with its extraordinary scope and zest.

*Paris. Charlemagne's capital in France. The visit of Angelica, daughter of the emperor of Cathay, signifies the city's importance on the world stage, which is further emphasized when it is besieged and assailed by Islamic invaders—variously described as Moors and Saracens—under the command of Agramant. The attackers are eventually driven back, but they continue to mount an inconvenient blockade on Paris until Astolpho's borrowed Nubian army mounts an assault on Agramant's homeland. (The sequence of these events has no real historical basis.)

*Italy. Although few Italian settings are directly featured in the main story (Mantua is the principal exception), Italy is frequently at the forefront of prophecies uttered in the course of the poem. These include the prophecies vouchsafed in the magician Merlin's tomb, a subterranean chamber reached from the bottom of the chasm near Bordeaux, into which Bradamante descends in canto 3. The prophecies delivered by Andronica in canto 15 and those depicted in paintings viewed in canto 33 also include extensive references to Italian future history. These prophecies proudly celebrate the regeneration of Italy's long-lost glory, flattering Ludovico Ariosto's contemporary Italian readers.

*Spain. Although several specific locations in Spain are featured in the story, most notably Atlas's enchanted palace, there is a more general sense in which that country is one of its main anchorages. Charlemagne's campaigns against Spain's Islamic conquerors form the core of the legend of Orlando (Roland in the original French). Thanks to the hindsight of history, the poem's sixteenth century readers knew that parts of Spain would remain under Moorish dominion for several centuries more. They also knew that the primal text of the Roland cycle, the twelfth century *Song of Roland*, concludes with an ambush in the Pyrenean pass of Roncesvalles in which Roland and many of his companions die; an awareness of this fate adds a certain tacit poignancy to the odysseys of exotic discovery.

Ebuda. Island west of Scotland on which maidens are regularly sacrificed to an orc (a sea-monster) until Orlando arrives in canto 11 to destroy the monster.

*Nubia. Capital of Ethiopia (not to be equated with modern Ethiopia), at the source of Africa's Nile River. Its emperor Senapo is tormented by the depredations of harpies until Astolpho comes to his aid, thus prompting the journey that takes Astolpho to an inconveniently smoky Hell, then to the Earthly Paradise and the Moon.

Earthly Paradise. Beautiful Arcadian plain with gemlike flowers, whose trees are perpetually laden with fruit. At the center of the plain is the residence of the saints: a radiant palace thirty miles around, formed from a single gemstone.

Moon. World whose geographical features are all unlike their earthly equivalent, although the exact differences are unspecified. The palace in which the Fates spin the destinies of humankind is there, as is a valley where everything lost on Earth is stored: reputations consumed by time, insincere prayers, lovers' tears, wasted time, and vain desires. These lost entities take ironically appropriate physical forms: Every flattery is a garland concealing a noose; every authority surrendered to a servant an eagle's talon. The largest heap of all is a mountain of minds, and the largest item in the heap is the lost wits of poor Orlando.

Bizerta. Capital city of Agramant's kingdom, which encompasses all of North Africa's Mediterranean coast except Egypt; located in the Atlas Mountains. Following the assault on the surrounding territory mounted by Astolpho's Nubian army in canto 38, Bizerta's walls are stormed by Orlando's Christian army in canto 40. Its residents are slaughtered, and the city is looted while Agramant is stranded at sea; this prepares the way for the crucial battle on the shore in canto 41, in which three champions of Christendom defeat three champions of Islam.

— *Brian Stableford*

ORLEY FARM

Author: Anthony Trollope (1815-1882)
Type of work: Novel
Type of plot: Domestic realism

Time of plot: Mid-nineteenth century
First published: serial, 1861-1862; book, 1862

Although competition over possession of Orley Farm and its environs drives the plot of this novel, Anthony Trollope is clearly more interested in the psychological states that his characters undergo during the legal struggle to ascertain the estate's rightful owner.

Orley Farm. Country residence not far from London. The title site is actually two plots of land: the Old Farm, three hundred acres that have been let to an area farmer, and the eponymous farmhouse itself, with its adjoining two hundred acres. The house is where Sir Joseph Mason lived with his second wife, Lady Mason; the entire property was supposedly bequeathed to his youngest child, Lucius Mason.

At the time of the novel, Orley Farm consists of three buildings, "commodious, irregular, picturesque, and straggling." This picturesqueness does not imply an unmodified landscape. All the buildings pertaining to farm work, for example, are hidden from view from the house. The immediate surroundings are nonetheless pleasant, including nearby apple trees that produce delicious fruit, even though their size is not up to those produced by modern scientific methods. All in all, the farm seems to be the perfect habitation for one of Trollope's gentlemen, and thus perhaps worth Lady Mason's machinations to secure it for her son; however, it is certainly not worth the splenetic greed that Mr. Joseph Mason displays in trying to retrieve it. Trollope gently pokes fun at Lucius Mason's scientific future plans for farming, including the guano he is at pains to secure for fertilizer. As is the case for many locations in the novel, its features are rarely referred to again after their initial description.

Trollope modeled the farmhouse on Julian Hill, a real farmhouse near Harrow that Trollope's parents built during his youth.

The Cleeve. Ancestral home of Sir Peregrine Orme, which is the ideal gentleman's estate, in Trollope's estimation. The house itself is Elizabethan, last remodeled during the seventeenth century reign of Charles II. This structure, with its imposing lineage, is set amid a landscape that the narrator praises for its "beauty and wildness." The path that the River Cleeve takes through the estate is described in almost Romantic terms, a seemingly distant cousin to the Alph, the "sacred river" of Coleridge's "Kubla Khan" (1816). Its "glorious . . . picturesque beauty" is not entirely untamed: sightseers can view deer drinking from it from one of the wooden bridges that have been built over it. The estate's size is such that the owner himself can be its own land steward, and Sir Peregrine is an ecologically sound steward, being careful not to cut down more trees than he has planted.

Groby Park. Mr. Joseph Mason's estate in Yorkshire. Although the equal of the Cleeve in area and value, Groby Park is not equal to it in fundamental worth, according to Sir Peregrine—a judgment with which the narrator would agree. Possession of the estate does not by itself make Mason a gentleman, and its description—from its "flat and uninteresting" landscape with its new trees to its "pediment and seven Ionic columns" that give it a spurious classical facade—shows that Mason is not to be considered a gentleman merely because of his possessions, a fact that his actions as a character thoroughly bear out. The house's interior is "handsome" but "heavy," a description that is likewise quickly undercut by Mrs. Mason's parsimony in providing food for both guests and family.

Noningsby. Estate of Judge Staveley and his family, a place that is delightful but new, a fault for which the only cure is time. Nonetheless, it seems to harbor the happiest household described in the novel, particularly during the four Christmas scenes that make up the centerpiece of the first volume.

*****London.** Great Britain's capital city is the scene of several briefly described locations. It is the base for its most powerful lawyers. The two words used to describe the chambers of Mr. Furvinal, Lady Mason's chief advocate, are "brown" and "dingy"—evocations, some biographers insist, of the chambers of Trollope's own father. Furvinal's home is now on fashionable Harley Street, but as Trollope makes clear, he enjoyed better domestic relations when he was a struggling lawyer and made his lodgings on the more mundane Keppel Street. In contrast to Furvinal's chambers, the chambers of the win-at-any-cost lawyer, Mr. Aram, are "smart and attractive," an appearance that, like that of Aram himself, is spurious.

— *William Laskowski*

OROONOKO: Or, The Royal Slave, a True History

Author: Aphra Behn (1640-1689)
Type of work: Novel
Type of plot: Didactic

Time of plot: Seventeenth century
First published: c. 1678

Responding to contemporary seventeenth century interest in exotic lands and the New World, Aphra Behn used the story of Oroonoko, a fictional African prince, to explore the cultures of Africa and the West Indies and to comment upon seventeenth century colonial practices. Like other writers, Behn also used her depictions of foreign lands to satirize British culture and comment upon contemporary political events.

*****England.** Setting of the novel's present-time narration. In 1688 England was a nation in crisis. After issuing a series of unpopular laws and producing an heir to his Roman Catholic throne, King James II struggled to retain power. In December, he fled the country and was replaced by the Protestant prince William of Orange. Although many people feared James, Behn remained fiercely loyal to him. Her novel, which chronicles the tragic destruction of a heroic prince, reflects the sorrow she felt during James's political struggles.

*****Surinam.** European colony on the northeastern coast of South America (now independent Suriname) to which the African prince Oroonoko is taken after he is enslaved in Africa. Behn probably visited Surinam during the early 1660's. By the time she wrote *Oroonoko*, the colony had been ceded to the Dutch, a fact that would have underscored for her contemporary readers her themes of futility and loss.

Within the novel, Surinam is not only an exotic land filled with unusual wildlife, but also an edenic paradise.

Behn describes the colony's inhabitants, who live without shame or deception, as "so like our first Parents before the Fall." They represent the "first State of Innocence, before *Man* knew how to sin." In depicting Surinam as a prelapsarian world, Behn follows the satiric tradition of writers such as Michel de Montaigne, who contrasted the primitive virtue of "savages" with the corruption of European society.

By the time Behn wrote *Oroonoko*, Surinam was no longer an entirely primitive land. It had been colonized by the British and participated in the triangular trade of the seventeenth century that brought slaves from West Africa to the New World in order to help produce the raw products sent to European markets. At the same time that Surinam represents an unspoiled Eden, it also represents an abundance of natural resources. In contrast to many modern writers, Behn does not overtly criticize the institutions of colonization and slavery themselves. The English colonists in her novel appear entitled to both the wealth of the land and the labor of their slaves. Only near the end of the novel, when the otherwise peaceful local people threaten to attack their colonizers, does Behn acknowledge the cost of imperialism.

The colonists themselves, however, are not innocents in the novel. Although the slaves and many of the settlers recognize Oroonoko's inherent nobility, the colonial government refuses to restore his freedom and threatens to enslave his unborn child. In this way, Surinam resembles seventeenth century England. Like Behn's fictional Oroonoko, England's King James II faced a nation that sought to deny both his nobility and that of his son. The fact that Behn gave Oroonoko the same nickname that King James had—"Caesar"—suggests further that she used Surinam as a representation of her own country.

Coromantien. West African realm from which Prince Oroonoko is taken into slavery and carried to the New World. Behn took the name from a historical slave-trading station on the coast of what is now Ghana, but her kingdom is imaginary. Because Behn does not condemn slavery, modern readers might expect her to present the inhabitants of West Africa as barbaric, that is to say, a people who might somehow benefit from being enslaved by European Christians. Behn's imaginary Coromantien, however, is anything but uncivilized. Following the practices of popular romances, Behn creates an Africa imbued with heroic notions of honor and nobility.

Although Coromantien's culture contains ideals that were familiar to Behn's contemporary English readers, its social customs are distinctly different. At times Behn appears critical of these customs. Coromantien's laws, for example, allow the king to make Imoinda his concubine in spite of his grandson Oroonoko's love for her. At other times, Behn uses Coromantien to satirize England. For example, while its men practice polygamy, they—unlike Englishmen—never abandon their women. "Such ill Morals," Behn notes, "are only practis'd in *Christian Countries*, where they prefer the bare Name of Religion." Like Surinam, Coromantien provides Behn with an opportunity to criticize her native country while presenting her readers with a fascinating account of an exotic land.

— *Christopher D. Johnson*

ORPHEUS AND EURYDICE

Author: Unknown
Type of work: Short fiction
Type of plot: Mythic

Time of plot: Antiquity
First published: Unknown

This mythical story about the poet-musician Orpheus, who falls in love with the lovely young Eurydice, is set in Thrace, said to be the most musically accomplished area of ancient Greece. After Orpheus's death, his head is buried on the island of Lesbos, whose inhabitants excel in the art of lyric poetry. His body is buried either at Pieria, one of the homes of the Muses, or at Libethra.

*Thrace (thrays). Supposed birthplace of Orpheus, now a region of eastern Greece bordering Turkey, where the love story of Orpheus and Eurydice begins. In ancient times, Thrace's peoples were renowned as being among the most musically accomplished in the Greek world.

Ismarus (is-mahr-as). Village on the southern coast of Thrace and home of the Cicones, a savage Thracian tribe whose women are believed to have attacked Orpheus and dismembered him. At Zone, near this village, mountain oaks grow in an unusual formation after dancing to Orpheus's music—an example of how the story explains unusual geographic features found at Zone.

Hades (hay-deez). Underworld realm of the dead ruled by Queen Persephone and King Hades. Orpheus's journey to Hades dramatizes his immense talent as a poet, as he soothes the tortures of the damned, the terrible, and the dead. His songs even mollify the king and queen of the underworld. In some versions of this story, after Orpheus returns from the underworld, he shares with his followers his newfound knowledge of the dead, and of the salve that poetry and song can bring to the deep wounds memory or "looking back" can cause. Eventually, Orpheus joins Eurydice in the underworld; happy at last, they wander through the fields together.

Acherusia (ak-ah-REW-see-ah). Lake on the border of ancient Pontus, a strip of land along the southern edge of the Black Sea in Asia Minor that was supposed to have been surrounded by hot, steaming mud. Orpheus is said to have traveled to this appropriately ugly and uninviting place in order to enter the underworld.

*Pieria (pee-er-ee-ah). Mythical home of the Muses, located near the village of Vergina in northern Greece. As the home of the goddesses of the arts, including poetry and music, Pieria is an appropriate place to bury the body of Orpheus.

Libethra (li-beh-thra). Ancient city at the foot of Mount Olympus, the home of the gods, where the fragments of Orpheus's body were buried. It is said that nightingales sang more sweetly over his grave than in any other part of Greece.

— *Ginger Jones*

OTHELLO: The Moor of Venice

Author: William Shakespeare (1564-1616)
Type of work: Drama
Type of plot: Tragedy

Time of plot: Early sixteenth century
First performed: 1604; first published, 1622; revised, 1623

Opening in the cosmopolitan seaport city of Venice, with the Moor Othello at the peak of his powers, professionally and personally, the action of the play moves to Cyprus; beyond are the barbarian Turks. Paralleling this move is Othello's deterioration, through the machinations of Iago, from the grand general respected by the Venetian senate to the jealously driven murderer of his wife, Desdemona. The contrast between civility, represented by Venice, and barbarity, represented by the Turks, is one of the major themes of the play.

*Venice. Northeast Italian seaport on the Adriatic that is the setting of the three scenes of the play's first act. This affluent Renaissance city was greatly admired by Elizabethans, and utilized by William Shakespeare in his earlier play *The Merchant of Venice* (c. 1596-1597). Ruled by a duke and a senate, Venice was an autonomous, powerful republic at this time, with a flourishing commercial economy. Venetian ships plied the seas from the Adriatic through the Mediterranean, trading wool, furs, leather, and glass. In the play, Iago cynically describes Venice as a place of moneybags, treachery, and promiscuity, and insinuates that a black man can never be other than an outsider. Playing upon Othello's sense of alienation, he suggests that Desdemona's choice of him was unnatural and thus temporary.

Before Brabantio's house, Iago and Roderigo call out with shouts of alarm and obscene insinuations about his daughter Desdemona, which escalate almost into a brawl, until Othello appears to calm the fray. This outdoor setting, dark and noisy, creates a feeling of unrest and tension.

Duke's council chamber. Awe-inspiring room to which Othello is summoned before the Duke and the special session of Senate. In this Venetian crisis, with the Turkish fleet now bearing down on the island of Cyprus, a possession of Venice, Othello's services are necessary. However, he must defend himself first from the accusations of Brabantio, who claims that he has stolen Desdemona by witchcraft. Although alien to Venetian culture as a Moor, Othello has previously proven his worth to the state and he defends himself from Brabantio's charges persuasively. Into this solemn chamber peopled with the powerful hierarchy of Venice, Desdemona appears to declare her love for Othello, which convinces the Duke to support the marriage and enlist Othello in the war against the Turk.

*Cyprus. Important island trading post in the eastern Mediterranean Sea and a Venetian possession from 1489 to 1571. It provides the setting for the last four acts of the play and, symbolically, represents the edge of the civilized world; beyond is the Ottoman Empire, the enemy infidels. The second act of *Othello* opens at an open place near the quay of a Cyprus seaport. The tempest-tossed, Venetian seafarers reach safety. The location emphasizes the distance from their familiar world. Although the Turks have now drowned, Cyprus is a barren military outpost, a citadel, lacking many of the comforts of Venice. It is a masculine world, isolated and contained; Desdemona is at the mercy of the men around her.

Cyprus citadel. Governor's castle within whose soldiers' quarters, orchard, and halls the remainder of the play unfolds. This citadel is the spot where civility and barbarity merge. There, Iago is free to advance his plans for Othello's destruction, first by making Cassio drunk, leading to his dismissal, and then by using lies and insinuations to increase Othello's jealousy. At a distance, Othello sees the encounter between Cassio and Bianca and his handkerchief pass between them; he is then convinced of the falseness of Desdemona. The isolation of the island from the civilized world contributes to the absolutism of the play.

The setting of Desdemona's murder in her citadel bedchamber is cruelly appropriate. "Strangle her in her bed," says Iago. The room brings together the sexual possessiveness of Othello, Desdemona's innocence, and Iago's passion for destruction. But it also represents a place in which the truth is revealed, where Venice, in the person of Lodovico, brings civility once more, and where Othello can feel remorse.

— *Joyce E. Henry*

THE OTHER ONE

Author: Colette (Sidonie-Gabrielle Colette, 1873-1954)
Type of work: Novel
Type of plot: Psychological

Time of plot: 1920's
First published: La Seconde, 1929 (English translation, 1931)

Setting in this novel is tightly focused. Most of the action of its first half takes place in a villa in Franche-Comté; the story later moves to Paris, primarily to the apartment of the Farou family. Within these geographical limits, Fanny Farou struggles to assert control over her life—in the villa, where disorder at first prevails, and in her apartment—her home, where she takes a stand and defends herself and her marriage.

*Franche-Comté (franshe kohn-TAY). Mountainous area in France southeast of Burgundy and near the border with Switzerland. Franche-Comté is a popular resort area, and it is here that *The Other One* opens.

Fanny Farou and her playwright husband, known simply as Farou, and their son, Jean, are at the Villa Déan for a summer vacation. Also a member of the party is Jane Aubaret, Farou's assistant, sometime mistress, and

Fanny's friend—and rival. Jane is the "seconde"—"number two," or perhaps "second fiddle." Both of these meanings are suggested by the French word.

The heat, the dry terrain, the unkempt vegetation, and the mountainous horizon constitute the principal features—and drawbacks—of the villa setting. Farou comes and goes, frequently commuting to Paris, where he has plays in production. Fanny is initially uncomfortable during the family's first summer at the villa. She finds the landscape dreary, the heat unpleasant; even the beautiful sunsets, she thinks, are for other people on the other sides of the mountains. In her view, Jane too is unnerved by the frequent thunderstorms and begins to weep over lost love affairs. Colette's descriptions here emphasize the shrubbery, flowers, and unpruned trees; the leaves and branches of some of the latter even encroach upon the house.

There is a certain wildness to the place. Sixteen-year-old Jean, who falls in love with Jane, though she is twice his age, often seems to inhabit the shrubs, trees, and shadows, leaping from them unexpectedly. Disorder manifests itself, too, in Farou's infidelity to Fanny—including his ongoing fling with Jane, thus intruding into the tranquillity of Fanny and her household. And finally, Jean's adolescent, young-animal passion is disruptive: he stays out late at night, spies on Jane, makes little effort to conceal his infatuation.

Farou is responsible for Fanny's discomfort in Franche-Comté, as well as in other resorts he chooses for family holidays and in Paris, to some extent. Habitually adulterous, Farou embodies disruption, displacement, and disorientation for Fanny, who would much prefer to remain in Paris. However, even in Franche-Comté, she can find solace in her books, armchair, angora wrap, and chocolates—her ways of making a home. Eventually, after two successive summers at the Villa Déan, Fanny becomes so at home there that she regrets having to leave.

*Paris. France's capital city is home to the Farous, the place where Fanny feels happiest is within her own apartment in the fashionable Champ de Mars-Eiffel Tower area. She is most comfortable, most in control of herself when she is near the apartment's fireplace. Once again however, the Paris sections of the novel are marked by Farou's often noisy invasions of the apartment and its peace and quiet. Ironically, Farou thinks of the apartment as *his* house and of Fanny and Jane as *his* women. (It should be noted that the French word *foyer* means "fireplace," and it approximates the English word "home" in its multiple emotionally resonant senses. Thus the fireplace truly symbolizes the home in French culture.)

During the Paris sections of the novel, the season is winter, in direct contrast to the summer atmosphere of the villa in Franche-Comté. In a stunning scene, Fanny sees Farou passionately kiss Jane in the apartment bathroom. Fanny decides to have it out with her concerning her affair with Farou. This confrontation does not at all flatter Jane physically. Fanny sees her in the apartment salon, as Jane stands in the December sunlight that comes through a window glass—and seems to turn Jane's ash-colored hair green while also exaggerating the flaws in her face.

One of Farou's noisy entrances puts an abrupt end to Fanny's angry argument with Jane. Oddly, Fanny then takes refuge in her home within her home: She draws the curtains, lights lamps, and seems to nearly embrace the fireplace, beside which the novel's moving finale takes place. When Fanny discovers that she and Jane actually have much in common as friends and mutual comforters, she realizes that she needs Jane so that the two of them can stand against Farou's regular depredations. The novel's last image is of Fanny and Jane seated by the fireplace, secure in their solidarity as women—while their men, like all men, enter and exit but seldom stay.

— *Gordon Walters*

OTHER VOICES, OTHER ROOMS

Author: Truman Capote (Truman Streckfus Persons, 1924-1984)
Type of work: Novel

Type of plot: Psychological realism
Time of plot: Mid-twentieth century
First published: 1948

This novel depicts the Deep South as a ghostly and strange place, as the twelve-year-old protagonist, Joel Knox, discovers the adult world. Transported by the vagaries of his family's fortunes from New Orleans to a remote and unfamiliar place, the inquisitive Joel undergoes a journey full of discovery. In the most unlikely places, he witnesses both human kindness and perversity. The rural South, represented by the state of Louisiana, is a bizarre location that severely tests Joel's young mind and heart.

*New Orleans. Louisiana city that is Joel's hometown. It is a place where he feels isolated and alone, but one that nurtures his growing interest in the adult world. He never feels at home in New Orleans. Feeling like an outsider, he often skips school and hangs out with older, African American fruit pickers. His alienation from the gloomy city is not helped by his lack of friends and parents, and he daydreams about stowing away on a banana boat to Central America and becoming an adult with a good job in some foreign city. In his dreams, he wants to be as far away as possible from New Orleans.

Paradise Chapel. Rustic Louisiana village meant to represent rural Louisiana as a whole. During the summer, the town is a dusty place full of truck drivers transporting interstate goods. For Joel, it is a point of transition in his voyage from New Orleans to his new final destination. His genealogical attachment to the land of the American South is symbolized by the big luggage that belonged to his Confederate great grandfather. Joel is carrying a piece of history with him in a rusty and dusty town of the Deep South that pays no attention to a sensitive boy who is alienated from his own geographical roots.

Noon City. Another small Louisiana town. Upon entering Noon City, Joel has a singular experience that is tied to the mysteries and perversions of the location. The town is so rustic that it appears to belong to an era fifty or one hundred years earlier than the time in which the novel is set. The old-fashioned town has a saloon, a confectionery, and a barber shop/dental clinic that is run by a man who is himself badly in need of a shave. With its bizarre cast of characters, Noon City resembles a carnival more than a real town. It is so lacking in culture and refinement that Joel orders a beer in its saloon. In an act of kindness, the proprietor, an obese woman who looks as alien to him as the town itself, instead gives him a soda pop. Joel feels completely out of his element in this place, where similar kindnesses tend to be rare occurrences.

Skully's Landing. Decaying mansion in Noon City where Joel meets his father for the first time. The old mansion seems to contain more human perversity and atmospheric strangeness than all the rest of Noon City. The moment Joel arrives there, he is alienated from the place because there is no sign of his father's presence. Instead, he is greeted by his strange bird-killing stepmother and her debauched brother, who give the environment a morbid atmosphere.

Joel hates Skully's Landing not because it has no running water, proper plumbing, or electricity, but because of the ghosts and strange voices he hears often. He finds no true friends or confidantes, except a good-hearted black woman, whom his stepmother treats as if she were a family slave in the Old South—which seems to lurk just beneath the surface of the place—and a tomboy girl, for whom he develops romantic stirrings. Of all the places to which Joel goes, Skully's Landing is the worst. It tests his inner spirit and his humanity as he desires so badly to discover human goodness. It is not a place than can provide what Joel needs.

Cloud Hotel. Old hotel in Noon City in which Joel makes a shocking discovery. One morning he wakes up and sees that the mule that has carried him and his uncle to the hotel is dead, hanging by its neck from a ceiling beam. Cloud Hotel, like Skully's Landing, tests the limits of Joel's mental endurance. Its perverse sights stand for the aberrations of the Deep South against which Joel can do nothing in this alien place.

— *R. C. Lutz*

OTHER WOMEN

Author: Lisa Alther (1944-   )
Type of work: Novel
Type of plot: Social realism

Time of plot: Early 1980's
First published: 1984

In this novel that focuses on individual crisis and social responsibility, the primary settings comprise homes and medical buildings in New Hampshire. As Caroline Kelly struggles to find a sense of self and acceptance in a world of suffering, she moves almost exclusively from her home to her hospital to her therapist's office, as she attempts to shake off a debilitating depression.

Lake Glass Therapy Center. Place where Caroline has lengthy therapy sessions with Hannah Burke that develop the major themes of the novel. Noting the brown tweed couch, bookshelves, photographs of children, and poorly tended fern in Hannah's office, Caroline initially believes she cannot be helped in such a shallow, comfortable, conventionally suburban atmosphere. However, the sign on Hannah's office door, "Thank you for shutting up while I smoke," is indicative of Hannah's refreshing honesty and self-acceptance—characteristics that the unconventional and rebellious Caroline lacks. During sessions that take place over several months, Caroline eventually recognizes not only her inability to be truthful with herself, but also the presence of suffering everywhere. In the office, Caroline discovers that the apparently comfortable and secure Hannah has suffered the loss of parents to abandonment and death and the loss of two children to accidental carbon monoxide poisoning.

Caroline Kelly's home. Cabin near Lake Glass. Caroline shares the cabin with Diana and her daughter Sharon, occupying the first floor with her sons, Jackie and Jason. Caroline's on-again, off-again relationship with Diana, indicative of her confused sexual identity, and her frustrations as a single mother, are dramatized in the cozy cabin. Beside Caroline's bed stands a loom where Caroline weaves shawls that she sells in a Lake Glass retail shop, her handwoven materials revealing the work she does throughout the novel with the strands of her psyche.

Hannah Burke's home. Yellow Victorian house outside Lake Glass that Hannah shares with her husband, Arthur. The home is comfortable, suburban, and safe, but it, too, was a place of suffering when a carbon monoxide leak killed two of the Burkes' children. The home reveals the novel's vision of suffering, which arises in every place on the planet and affects everyone, including the affluent.

Mass General Hospital. Hospital in which Caroline works as an emergency room nurse and has daily contacts with suffering, particularly of the innocent: people injured in automobile accidents, women and children abused by men, families affected by natural disasters and accidents in their homes.

Lake Glass. Fictional New Hampshire town north of Boston, Massachusetts. Originally created as an outpost for fur traders and loggers, Lake Glass turned industrial in the mid-twentieth century with the development of factories, and was infused with new money in the 1960's and 1970's as a summer resort for the wealthy of Boston. The picturesque lake teems with wildlife but is also a place of destruction, as when Caroline helplessly watches a man commit suicide there. The novel opens with a description of a wintry Lake Glass and ends with details of summer life, revealing the thawing and opening to new life that Caroline has experienced.

— *Mark Walling*

OUR ANCESTORS

Author: Italo Calvino (1923-1985)
Type of work: Novel
Type of plot: Satire
Time of plot: Middle Ages to early nineteenth century

First published: Il nostri antenati, 1960 (English translation, 1980); *Il visconte dimezzato,* 1952 (*The Cloven Viscount,* 1962); *Il barone rampante,* 1957 (*The Baron in the Trees,* 1959); *Il cavaliere inesistente,* 1959 (*The Non-existent Knight,* 1962)

Italo Calvino is frequently more interested in places for their fantastical possibilities than for their historical reality, and that is certainly the case in this trilogy, many of whose key places relate to the division between reality (and real places) and literature (and literary places), a division that Calvino eventually undoes.

*Terralba. Village on the west coast of the Mediterranean island of Sardinia at the time of the Crusades. At the conclusion of *The Cloven Viscount,* the adolescent narrator misses his chance to set sail with his tutor, Dr. Trelawney. Although Trelawney is sailing with the historical Captain James Cook, he is also a character from Robert Louis Stevenson's novel *Treasure Island* (1883). Ultimately, Trelawney's departure represents the loss of childhood adventure stories, and the imaginary spaces of literature more generally, and the narrator is left behind in the real world of "responsibilities" and disappointing "will-o'-the-wisps."

Forest. Woods surrounding the fictional Ombrosa in Northern Italy during the Enlightenment in *The Baron in the Trees.* The woods ultimately extend over much of Europe, permitting Cosimo, who has decided to live in the trees, to range freely over the continent, where he meets characters both literary and historical. His arbitrary decision to live in the trees represents a desire to find a utopia, a true harmony between humanity and nature. At the end of the novel, however, the narrator wonders if this idyllic forest ever existed at all or was merely a tangle of fantasy, like his own story, indeed, like the words on the very page he is writing.

Convent. Nunnery located somewhere in chivalric Europe in *The Non-existent Knight.* Sister Theodora recounts the often parodic story of famous figures from chivalric romances, such as Emperor Charlemagne and the woman warrior Bradamante. The implicit contrast throughout the novel is between the open space of Europe—filled with epic adventure—and the closed, literary space of the convent, where Theodora writes as a penance. At the novel's end, this division is neatly undone when Theodora reveals that she *is* Bradamante, and the division between the two spaces collapses as she dedicates herself to the possibilities the future may hold.

— *Robert A. Rushing*

OUR HOUSE IN THE LAST WORLD

Author: Oscar Hijuelos (1951-   )
Type of work: Novel
Type of plot: Bildungsroman

Time of plot: 1920's-1970's
First published: 1983

From comfortable homes and sleepy, small-town streets of a rural Holguín on Cuba, the newlywed Santinios emigrate to an urban New York where their dreams of America become ensnared in a life of poverty and despair in an impoverished neighborhood. Through the success stories of other new arrivals, who manage to prosper and move out, the Santinios catch glimpses of what life may be like beyond their symbolically dead-end street.

*Manhattan. Borough of New York City in which most of the novel takes place within an upper West Side apartment building. From Cuba, New York City beckons with opportunity, a springboard for "making it" before moving on to settle elsewhere or returning to the island. The self-imposed exile of the adventurous or carefree Cubans of the 1940's was quite different from that of the political refugees several decades later.

After their spending money dwindles, the Santinios—unskilled and speaking no English—discover the harsh reality of surviving in the big city. The kitchen of the luxury hotel in which Alejo works as a cook—a space and job generally reserved for women in Cuba's patriarchal culture—is a microcosm of the downtrodden of the city and epitomizes Alejo's failure to become a man of distinction. Similar to the city, the hotel, a large enterprise, offers opportunities that Alejo passes up.

The Santinios' dilapidated apartment mirrors a dysfunctional family literally falling apart. In the novel, New York can be equated with a place of violence—in the streets, in the home. Ironically, although the Santinios live near "the University," presumably Columbia University, an Ivy League institution synonymous with upward mobility, a higher education is not accessible to them or their children.

*Holguín (ol-GEEN). Picturesque Cuban city of rolling hills in the island's central valley; a fertile region for agriculture and diverse commerce often called Cuba's granary. The novel opens with the family history of Mercedes Sorrea and Alejo Santinio, both of whom come from a lineage of successful Spanish immigrants and respected patriarchs, whose image Alejo is not able to live up to in the United States.

Descriptions of Mercedes' luxurious childhood home and Alejo's leisurely, debonair lifestyle in Cuba contrast starkly with the couple's life in their Manhattan tenement. Mercedes especially resents her husband's failures and comes to remember Holguín as a lost paradise, as her memory selectively recalls what she has left behind and not why she and Alejo left. The Santinios' metaphorical loss of their homeland becomes real and permanent with the triumph of the Cuban Revolution in 1959 that prompts other family members to join the mass exodus of Cubans fleeing the new communist regime of Fidel Castro.

Although the Santinios' New York-born sons spend only one summer in Holguín, Cuba marks their identity formation. Coming into manhood is linked to a search for Cubanness and personal authenticity. For Hector, who contracts an illness during his visit, Holguín represents painful aspects of his life—"Cuba gave the bad disease. Cuba gave the drunk father. Cuba gave the crazy mother"—but he also recognizes that this place is one of original love and happiness that is seemingly out of reach to the Santinios in New York. Cuba is where Mercedes once lived a "life of style and dignity and happiness." Hector wants their apartment to be filled with beams of sunlight, "like in the dream house of Cuba." He also recalls that Cuba was where Aunt Luisa constantly showered him with the hugs and kisses his soul craved.

*Miami. Florida city that has flourished economically and culturally with the entrepreneurial spirit of its large Cuban immigrant population. In Miami, the Cuban way of life thrives outside the Caribbean homeland. The city offers hope—for prosperity, for a better life, and for a return to Cuba. In contrast to his Manhattan neighborhood, Hector observes there are no street gangs, derelicts, or junkies on Miami's Calle Ocho, the small business sector in Little Havana and the heart of a vibrant community of exiles. Members of the Santinio clan who have made it big in the United States live in Miami. Only in Miami does Hector come into contact with strong, successful, and respected Cuban men who, unlike his father, make him feel protected.

Last World. The title of the book alludes to a multivalent place that may or may not be associated with a geographical location. The "Last World" contains the house of memory, the past and one's origins, the life of the spirit and of dreams; however, for the characters in the novel it is ultimately the place where love resides.

— *Gisela Norat*

OUR MUTUAL FRIEND

Author: Charles Dickens (1812-1870)
Type of work: Novel
Type of plot: Domestic realism

Time of plot: Mid-nineteenth century
First published: serial, 1864-1865; book, 1865

Two major geographical symbols in this novel, the river and city dustheaps, show Charles Dickens at the height of his power. The river cuts across all inflated, unreal social distinctions and at times is used overtly as a symbol for the passage of life itself. The novel's other dominant symbol is the dustheaps that accumulated in city streets and often contained enough wealth to create family fortunes. At every level of society, people of all ages are shown in the act of hunting for money.

***River Thames** (tehmz). England's most important river serves as the central thread of the novel, tying together both character and incident. When the novel opens, the river offers both life and death. In a surreal, night scene, Gaffer Hexam is shown making his living from the bodies he finds in the river. During the course of the novel, the river is the setting for seven drownings or near-drownings, including the apparent drowning of young John Harmon, the "mutual friend" of the title.

Upriver, Rogue Riderhood and the schoolmaster, fatally embracing, drown each other in the river. In contrast, Betty Higden finds a peaceful and longed-for death on its shores in Oxfordshire, and it is the scene of Eugene Wrayburn's regeneration after he is left for dead in the upstream shallows. Lizzie Hexam, who has always been ashamed of her father's boat-handling lessons, is able to now use these skills to save Wrayburn from death.

Dustheaps. Mounds of dust that collect in public streets provide a second literal and symbolic portion of the novel's landscape. These are actual representations of the Victorian heaps of soot, cinder, broken glass and crockery, paper and rags, bones, and possibly even human waste, as well as jewels, coins, and other valuables. Dickens's periodical *Household Words* included mention of such heaps, not as fantasy, but as fact. They are evidence of Victorian recycling, for their contents were sifted, sorted, and then sold to brick-makers and road-builders, as well as to makers of soap, fertilizer, and paper.

Marxist critics have suggested that Dickens is making a moralizing connection between capitalist money and dust, trash, refuse, even excrement. In the novel, contents of the mounds were accumulated by a nasty and miserly Old John Harmon who used this wealth to manipulate his family. Also, the dust heaps provide comic scenes of scheming greed as Silas Wegg's wooden leg gets stuck in the refuse when he searches for treasure. However, the "Golden Dustman," Boffin, remains uncorrupted by their wealth. Overall, as with the river, these dust mounds provide unity and coherence in this expansive and complex novel.

Boffin's Bower. Mansion formerly belonging to Old John Harmon that has been inherited by the faithful Boffins. Formerly called Harmony Jail, it is located adjacent to the dustheaps. Although Mr. and Mrs. Boffin, are content with each other, they feel some discomfort in these wealthy surroundings. Their drawing room reflects this displacement, for Mrs. Boffin's somewhat gaudy attempts at fashion are jumbled together with Mr. Boffin's more homely sawdust floor, his comfortable footstool and his nearby well-stocked pantry shelves. Nevertheless, this generous couple graciously shares with others, including the pouting Bella. Later, chastened and enlightened after her secret marriage and content to live in Blackheath in a small dollhouse, Bella proves herself worthy and capable of handling wealth well. Eventually, the Boffins turn over their house to her, her husband John, and their new baby.

Veneering house. The "veneer" of this nouveau riche household consists in the ostentatious display and the tasteless money-grubbing, name-dropping guests. This setting is juxtaposed to the opening, elemental river scene, and thus impresses the reader with its garish opulence. The guests at the Veneerings are dehumanized as body parts: aquiline noses and fingers, nostrils like a rocking horse, a face like one in a tablespoon. Also, they are shown to be unreal and shallow, mere reflections in the great looking glass over the Veneering sideboard: rags, wig, and powder make up Lady Tippins another guest is merely "gingery whiskers and teeth"; others are identified as "Boots" or "Brewer." Their dining room is praised for being as glorious as those of the genies in *The Arabian Nights*, and ironically prove to be just as ephemeral, for the author announces in his closing chapters that the household will soon experience "a resounding smash" when found out by the Insolvent Fates.

— *Marie J. K. Brenner*

OUR TOWN

Author: Thornton Wilder (1897-1975)
Type of work: Drama
Type of plot: Symbolism

Time of plot: 1901-1913
First performed: 1938; first published, 1938

Shunning the conventional use of scenery and props in this play, playwright Thornton Wilder forces audiences to use their own imaginations to "see" his imaginary New England town of Grover's Corners. The absence of a concrete sense of place emphasizes the play's major theme—that people are defined by how well they take note of the smallest aspects of their everyday lives.

Grover's Corners. Fictional New Hampshire town that is the setting for the entire play. The depiction of this small village is primarily dependent upon the descriptions given by the pivotal character of the stage manager. He explains that the town is "just across the Massachusetts line: latitude 42 degrees 40 minutes; longitude 70 degrees 37 minutes." He goes on to describe what a typical morning sky looks like in Grover's Corners, with its "streaks of light" and the morning star still shining brightly within it. The effect of the stage manager's words is both cinematic and hypnotic; it accomplishes what mere scenery could not. Through his words, the audience sees, as if they are behind a moving camera, the heavens that look down upon the town, the town's busy streets and communities, and even more specific spots, such as the stores the townspeople frequent and the schools their children attend.

Finally, when the stage manager approaches the table and chairs that serve as the Gibbs house and points to the spot that is to be Mrs. Webb's garden, vine and flower-covered trellises are rolled out "for those," he says, tongue planted firmly in cheek, "who think they have to have scenery," and the audience then focuses on the individual lives that are to be examined in this play, rather than on superfluous details.

Main Street. Street at the heart of Grover's Corners on which almost every character in the play is, at one time or another, seen bustling along. However, the actions of these people take on far greater meaning against the backdrop of Emily's return visit to earth. Even Howie Newsome's job of delivering the daily milk seems poignant when Emily "listens in delight" to the sound of his voice, along with Constable Warren's and Joe Crowell Jr.'s, sounds she very likely heard every day of her life.

Gibbs and **Webb houses.** Childhood homes of George Gibbs and Emily Webb. The introductory stage directions for act 1 state that the audience is to see nothing but "an empty stage in half-light" upon arriving. Eventually, the stage manager strolls out and places "a table and three chairs downstage left," and another set of table and chairs downstage right. These items, along with a small bench, serve as the Gibbs and Webb houses. These are the sole objects seen as the stage manager begins to describe Grover's Corners in the play's opening lines. When Emily revisits the Webb home in act 3, as Wilder himself once pointed out, even the kitchen table and chairs are gone. "Our claim, our hope, our despair are in the mind—not in things, not in 'scenery,'" Wilder said.

Morgan's drugstore. Grover's Corners's combination pharmacy and soda shop. Again emphasizing the irrelevance of place and props in this play, the stage manager takes two chairs from the Gibbs family's kitchen and places a board across their backs to create the counter of what is presumably the local teen hangout. It is here that George and Emily first realize they want to spend their futures together.

Cemetery. Hilltop graveyard that becomes Emily's final resting place. Given the theme of the play, it is not surprising that its last act emphasizes the specifics of nature. According to the stage manager, the graveyard lies beneath "lots of sky, lots of clouds,—often lots of sun and moon and stars." He also tells the audience that lilacs and mountain laurel cover this hill, and admits to being puzzled when he thinks of people who choose to be buried in a place like Brooklyn when they could spend eternity in this corner of New Hampshire.

As with every setting in the play, the beauty of the cemetery could not have been conveyed in a more effective way than through words alone. Paradoxically, the very absence of concrete place is what makes every aspect of Grover's Corners come so vividly to life. However, as Wilder intended, each audience member's idea of the town will be specific to that individual's own imagination and rendering. "The climax of this play," he said, "needs only five square feet of boarding and the passion to know what life means to us."

— *Paula R. Hilton*

OUT OF THE SILENT PLANET

Author: C. S. Lewis (1898-1963)
Type of work: Novel
Type of plot: Science fiction/fantasy

Time of plot: Early twentieth century
First published: 1938

This first volume of C. S. Lewis's space trilogy takes three human characters to Mars, where they encounter three rational native species. The setting is cleverly employed to make subtle observations, often humorous and ironic, about the follies of human society, particularly the relations between races and species. On Mars, Lewis's hero, Professor Ransom, finds knowledge of the cosmic Christ, though under a different name and represented by different symbols.

*Thulcandra.** Martian name for Earth, meaning "**Silent Planet**," where the narrative begins and ends. Ransom, a Cambridge philologist, is a solitary bachelor starting out on a walking tour, savoring the charms of his native England. Like a classic epic, this tale begins and ends on the native green. Before Ransom has gone far, he is hijacked to Mars by two villains he knows. While on his adventure, Ransom discovers that Thulcandra is presided over by a perverted Oyarsa (demoniac being), who has revolted against Maleldil the Younger (Christ), and therefore has been placed under planetary quarantine. Though Ransom clearly sees why the universe must be protected from the poisonous practices of Earth, when given the opportunity, he does not hesitate to return home.

Decades before the first photos of Earth from space were made, Lewis provided a vivid and accurate description of the planet as seen from Mars. Even as he views that radiant agate ball hanging in the sky, Ransom nostalgically tries to spot England and thinks of the tiny plot where he left his backpack.

*Malacandra (Mars).** Martian name for their own planet. While epic adventures, such as the hnakra (vicious monster) hunt take place, suggesting that not all is paradisiacal on this planet, Ransom discovers that three intelligent species live here in harmony, with a neat division of tasks. These are the intellectual sorns, the artisan pfifltriggi, and the hrossa, skilled in navigation and agriculture. By allowing Ransom to anatomize Malacandrian culture in the manner of an anthropologist, Lewis is able to make, by implication, further comments on the failings of human societies, always competitive and suspicious. For example, Ransom learns that not all hrossa are alike; they exist in different colors, a treasured diversity.

Lewis has sometimes been criticized for his scientific carelessness, especially by readers who prefer "hard science fiction." Though the careful mapping of Mars would take place decades after this book was published, Lewis knew that telescopic observations had demolished Percival Lowell's theory of a carefully engineered network of canals on Mars. However, since canals were part of the popular beliefs about Mars, Lewis chose to retain them in his book.

Lewis felt that fantasy writing should not merely expand experience, as all good literature may do, but should actually enlarge understanding of the range of possible experience. Early critics praised Lewis's Miltonic or Dantesque love of light, which made his descriptions of Malacandrian landscapes exciting. Lewis wrote about how, throughout his life, he had enjoyed conjuring visions of imaginary landscapes while lying in bed at night. With his setting on the still unexplored surface of Mars (in 1938), Lewis was able to describe wonderfully strange scenes, filled with diffused light, aromatic perfumes unknown to Earth, and resounding with panegyric hymns issuing from alien throats deeper and more varied than any known at home.

— *Allene Phy-Olsen*

THE OVERCOAT

Author: Nikolai Gogol (1809-1852)
Type of work: Short fiction
Type of plot: Social realism

Time of plot: Early nineteenth century
First published: "Shinel," 1842 (English translation, 1923)

Nikolai Gogol's story transforms the real Russian location of St. Petersburg into a mysterious realm in which the laws of proportion and logic are suspended. The city becomes a backdrop for events with multiple interpretations.

*St. Petersburg. Russian city founded by Czar Peter the Great to replace Moscow as the capital. The city gradually developed a special reputation. On one hand, it was viewed as a utopian, model city of the future, but on the other, it was seen as a realm of dark, unfriendly forces. By the time Gogol wrote "The Overcoat," the city was rife with stories that highlighted the fantastic and mysterious quality of the place.

After Gogol's hero, Akaky Akakievich, a meek and lowly clerk in the vast government bureaucracy, is assaulted by the bitterly cold wind of this northern city, he must have a new coat made. Gogol's narrative suggests that Akaky's decision may have led him into the clutches of demonic forces, and after his new coat is stolen from him, he strives without success to find a sympathetic figure in the city's impersonal bureaucracy. Akaky dies from illness and sorrow, but after his death, rumors begin circulating that he has returned as a ghost to steal the coats of other people. The entire narrative, however, ends on a note of confusion or uncertainty, and this strange ending accords well with the enigmatic nature of the St. Petersburg setting. Although the tale evokes different aspects of city life—from the simple apartments of the poor clerks to the more elegant homes of the higher officials—Gogol's narrator intentionally refuses to provide specific details and locations, thereby heightening the atmosphere of mystery and uncertainty that permeates the work.

— *Julian W. Connolly*

THE OX-BOW INCIDENT

Author: Walter Van Tilburg Clark (1909-1971)
Type of work: Novel
Type of plot: Regional

Time of plot: 1885
First published: 1940

The subject of this novel, set in Nevada during the late nineteenth century, is the lynching of three men by an angry mob who have falsely accused them of cattle rustling and murder. Walter van Tilburg Clark interjects western characters, settings, and devices into the classical formula. The action begins in town, moves to its tragic climax in an ox-bow valley outside town, then returns to town, where more tragic fallout occurs along with the resolution of the plot.

Bridger's Wells. Nevada town in which most of the novel's characters live or do business. Two cowboys, Croft and Gil, ride into this town after spending the winter in solitude on the range. While in town, rumors quickly spread that a local cattleman has been murdered and his cattle have been stolen.

The town scenes are important for several reasons. First, this is the place of civilization. In contrast to the open range country, the town, with its churches, businesses, and legal authorities, represented by Sheriff Mapes and Judge Tyler, all suggest a civilization where moral and ethical judgment is presumed. Second, in the town scenes, Clark is able to introduce a large number of characters who either live in Bridger's Wells or who are present to do business. These characters all have an economic interest in the town. They are rightly concerned about cattle rustling and murder, and they are eager to make sure evil is punished so that their status will be protected. Third, in front of the saloon, these various characters gather to hear and respond to the announcement of murder and cattle rustling. This is a natural setting where readers can readily see the range of emotional speeches and futile attempts at reason provoked by the announcement.

Finally, after the tragic miscarriage of justice occurs, most of the riders return to Bridger's Wells. Readers see various responses to the deed, including drunken attempts at stoic callousness, guilty introspection, and even suicide. After the foolish hangings occur outside town, the plot returns to where the rush to judgment began, thereby providing a powerful contrast in the characters, from their initial public energy to a secretive, shameful reflection. Readers are brought back to the place of civilization as the characters are brutally reminded that, although justice may not be swift, it must be accurate.

Ox-Bow Valley. Valley outside the town in which the hangings take place at the conclusion of the novel. There, the three falsely accused cattlemen have stopped to spend the night and avoid a snow storm. This place is important because, as the vigilante posse recognizes, it is the only possible place rustlers could have taken the supposedly stolen herd. This valley has only one entrance and is surrounded by steep mountains on the three remaining sides. The posse thinks the rustlers are foolish for stopping here and that a relatively easy capture and enforcement of justice will follow. Ironically, the cattlemen stop here because it is a natural place to wait while the weather clears, and since they are innocent, they have no reason to find a better hiding place or escape route. This valley also reminds readers of a noose and a question mark. Clark seems to use the geographical shape of this valley as an ugly symbol that portends the trap in which the falsely accused find themselves, where the question of justice is arrogantly pretended and where the three die by hanging. After the truth is realized, however, readers more accurately see that those rushing to judgment also trapped themselves in this valley, having committed themselves to a group process that no individual could prevent without serious consequences.

— *Kenneth Hada*

P

THE PAINTED BIRD

Author: Jerzy Nikodem Kosinski (1933-1991)
Type of work: Novel
Type of plot: Social morality

Time of plot: 1939-1945
First published: 1965

This exploration of the horrors of the Jewish Holocaust in Eastern Europe is set among the remote, backward, and harsh villages of an Eastern European country resembling Poland that becomes the inhospitable and terrifying hiding place for an unnamed Jewish boy, whose parents have sent him there for safety at the outbreak of war.

Villages. Much of the horror encountered by the Jewish boy takes place in remote and underdeveloped Eastern European villages. Isolated for centuries, the villages appear almost medieval and lack all modern amenities. Primitive living conditions in these places, the novel suggests, have given rise to a population of genetically similar, hostile, superstitious, and brutal peasants. The peasants' huts, farms, and workplaces are rough and meager, corresponding to the mean and vicious streaks of their owners. For example, on the barren floor planks of a mill, the jealous owner stamps on the eyes he has gouged out of the face of a man he suspects of having committed adultery with his wife. When lightning hits the barn of a carpenter, he blames the black hair of the boy for the strike and tries to kill him.

Germany's occupation of the country lies like a plague on the land, which yields little even in good times. Demanding food and trying to hunt down the last Jewish refugees, the Germans treat the inhabitants harshly and add to the fugitive boy's dread. He must periodically flee from one village to another. One village's peasants eject him by throwing him in a river, on which he lands on the inflated swim bladder of a giant catfish, which carries him downriver.

All the villages the boy encounters come to resemble one another. His ordeal living among callous people ends only when the Soviet Army occupies the land, inflicting yet more violence on its sullen inhabitants.

Cesspit. Pool of human excrement into which the boy is thrown. While staying in a village in which a Roman Catholic priest is protecting him, the Jewish boy accidentally drops a Bible during Sunday services. The enraged villagers then throw him in a large open cesspit, which they have dug close to their church to relieve themselves. After sinking below the surface of the pool of excrement, the boy manages to escape but becomes mute. This is clearly a psychological reaction to the horror of the place. He recovers his speech after the war at a skiing resort deep in the mountains, in a room filled with spring sunlight, among caring people.

Railway tracks. Tracks cutting through the isolated landscape are closely associated with the misery brought to the country by the German occupation. Harbingers of death, the tracks add yet another vicious ingredient to an already infernal landscape. German trains passing over the tracks carry Jews and others to death camps. Peasants living near the tracks loot corpses of prisoners who die trying to escape; they gather the prisoners' photos and mementos, regarding them with boorish fascination. In one savage incident, peasants kill a Jewish woman who survives her jump from a train. Ironically, however, when the unnamed boy is captured by Germans and taken to a railroad outpost, he tries to entertain a would-be executioner by comically trying to walk on a rail while still tied to the soldier's leg. Inexplicably, the man lets him escape.

Soviet army camp. Camp of the Soviet occupying force. Erected on the banks of a river bordering the last village of the boy's ordeal, the encampment offers him safety, education, and two soldiers who serve as his father figures. After driving away the German troops, the Soviets adopt the boy as a mascot, and their encampment becomes the first place where he feels free, loved, and welcome.

Industrial city. Unnamed city resembling the Polish city of Lodz, in which Jerzy Kosinski grew up before the war and later attended the local university. There, his fictional boy is reunited with his parents. He has difficulty readapting to normal life. As the city itself is also not yet back to normal either, he finds release prowling it at night. Meanwhile, outcast people begin appearing; the ruins of the city shelter rapists, and its parks offer places for illicit behavior. Soon the authorities intervene, and the boy is sent to a mountain resort to gain health. There, the novel ends in a serene landscape.

— *R. C. Lutz*

PALE FIRE

Author: Vladimir Nabokov (1899-1977)
Type of work: Novel
Type of plot: Parody

Time of plot: Late 1950's, early 1960's
First published: 1962

Many Vladimir Nabokov novels depict characters who have rich inner lives that are poor fits for the real world. In this novel, however, contrasts between fantasy and reality and between inner desire and outer fact are most clearly rooted in place, principally in the contrast between the mundane Appalachian town of New Wye and the extravagant fictional land of Zembla.

Zembla (zehm-BLAH). Imaginary country located somewhere near Russia that is the homeland of the literary scholar Dr. Charles Kinbote. The name "Zembla" comes from the real Russian island of Nova Zembla, in the Arctic, whose name means "new land."

Nabokov also plays on the similarity of the sound of "Zembla" to such English words as "assemble," "emblem" and "resemble," which relate to one of the novel's most important themes: art as a mirror to reality. However, it is a curious sort of mirror, one that not only reflects but also distorts, refracts, and multiplies. Zembla is a distorted mirror image of the mundane world that Kinbote is forced to inhabit. In the normal world Kinbote is a lonely, obscure, closeted homosexual. In Zembla, he is King Charles the Beloved, whose sexual orientation is regarded as proof of manliness, not as a shameful secret. (The novel *Pale Fire* itself is formed of a similarly distorted reflection—John Shade's poem and Kinbote's commentary on it, a pale and distorted reflection of the original.) In this ideal, "crystal land," art and science

flourish under King Charles's rule, and even taxation becomes "a thing of beauty."

Zembla is not simply Kinbote's escapist fantasy. It has a complex—if invented—history that reads something like a parody or distorted mirror image of Russian history. Like that of the historical Russia, Zembla's aristocracy falls to revolution, and the idyllic Zembla becomes populated by characters such as the assassin Jakob Gradus, who typifies Nabokov's conception of the Soviet mind-set: low, vulgar, and incompetent. Unlike Russia's czar, King Charles escapes to America, where he assumes the identity of Charles Kinbote, or so Kinbote claims. There he meets the poet John Shade, who he hopes will be able to "re-assemble Zembla" in rhyme. Much of Kinbote's commentary recounts the king's flight and Gradus's subsequent attempt to find and kill him.

New Wye (noo wee). Fictional Appalachian town based on Ithaca, New York, where Nabokov lived during the 1950's. Unlike the fantastic and epic Zembla, New Wye is generally depicted realistically and domestically. Shade's poem depicts a world of natural details—such as birds and trees—middle-class trivia, and domestic life. Seen through Shade's eyes, the world of New Wye is a mass of subtle detail—a band of color on a butterfly wing, or the shape taken by a falling rubber band—that is imbedded in the largest of questions: death and the afterlife.

For Kinbote, the Old World king in exile, New Wye is bleak and follows social rules that he finds largely incomprehensible. Much like some of Nabokov's other novels, *Pale Fire* is about the Old World meeting the New World and the inevitable conflicts that arise. While Kinbote may characterize America as middle class, domestic, and, at times, lowbrow, his commentary and Zemblan epic reads much like the absurd paperback mystery novels he claims to despise.

Shade home. Middle-class house in New Wye. Perhaps no other place within the novel so clearly represents Kinbote's isolation and loneliness as the poet Shade's home. Kinbote tries to watch Shade at work on the poem he believes will restore Zembla to him, peering into his neighbor's house with binoculars and at times even peeking in the windows. He daydreams about situations in which he saves Shade's life and imagines being warmly received in the latter's house. However, he is not even invited to Shade's birthday party. In contrast to the "normal" heterosexual family of his neighbors, Kinbote's own home is a rental house, in which he sleeps alone in a "solitary double bed," apart from his brief liaisons.

Wordsmith University. University modeled on Cornell University, where Nabokov taught while living in Ithaca. The fictional university is material for parody—Kinbote mocks the "suburban refinements of the English Department," and its faculty members are largely small-minded and not infrequently vulgar. In this novel, the university is conspicuous for its absence: almost all of the action takes place either in or around the Shade home, or in Kinbote's imaginary Zembla.

— *Robert A. Rushing*

PALE HORSE, PALE RIDER: Three Short Novels

Author: Katherine Anne Porter (1890-1980)
Type of work: Novellas
Type of plot: Psychological realism

Time of plot: Old Mortality, 1885-1912; *Noon Wine*, 1836-1905; *Pale Horse, Pale Rider*, 1918
First published: 1939

The first two novellas of this volume are set in Katherine Anne Porter's native Texas, offering two contrasting pictures of life in this region. The third novella—which gives the book its title—although set in an unnamed city, nonetheless depends on descriptions of place and time for its contemplation of life and death in time of war.

*South Texas. Both *Old Mortality* and *Noon Wine* use Texas as their settings, but the Texases depicted in these stories are very different. *Old Mortality* is the first of Porter's "Miranda" stories, generally agreed to be the most openly autobiographical portions of her work. The story is suffused with the culture of the Deep South, opening with a picture of Miranda's dead Aunt Amy, whose idealized and romanticized memory continues to haunt the family. The family that Porter constructs for Miranda is in many ways the family Porter tries to give herself. While Porter was raised by her grandmother on a south Texas ranch on which money was tight, Miranda lives in something like a plantation, filled with books and music and dancing.

By contrast, *Noon Wine* features a hardscrabble Texas ranch far out in the country, inhabited by the decidedly nonaristocratic Thompson family. In all likelihood, the reality of Porter's childhood is probably closer to this picture than to the one she constructs for Miranda. In contrast to the southern sensibilities implicit in *Old Mortality, Noon Wine* offers the life of plain dirt farmers trying to eke out livings from the soil. The isolation of the ranch provides a sense of the frontier rather than the flavor of the antebellum South.

*Deep South. The idea of the South plays a prominent role throughout *Old Mortality*. For example, New Orleans figures as the center of society for Miranda's family. The city plays a triple role in the story: It is the place where Amy dies after her marriage, the location of the convent school that Miranda and her sister later attend, and the site of Miranda's last glimpse of her Uncle Gabriel. In New Orleans, Miranda sees Gabriel not as the mythologized gallant of family memory, but as a drunk and seedy racer of horses. By offering these contrasts, Porter demonstrates how the mythology of the Deep South may be at odds with its reality.

Western city. Unnamed city in the American West used in another Miranda story, *Pale Horse, Pale Rider*. Details in this story allow readers to identify Denver as the story's setting, although the city is never specifically named. During World War I, Porter lived in Denver, where she worked as a theater editor of the *Rocky Mountain News*—the same job she gives her character Miranda. It is also in the unnamed city that Miranda contracts the dreaded Spanish influenza, just as Porter did in Denver in 1918. *Pale Horse, Pale Rider* opens by connecting Miranda to her Texas roots. In a prophetic dream, she rides her horse Graylie across the plains in a race against the "pale rider," death. Her waking reality in the unnamed city assumes a dreamlike fugue state as she perceives herself and those around her through the fog of the influenza that is overwhelming her body.

Porter's choice of the unnamed western city is an important one for the story. The city is clearly in a place of natural beauty. In addition, the city seems remote from the rest of the country. The vaudevillians Miranda reviews refer to the city as the "boondocks." These edenic images contrast starkly with the reality the rest of the country faces. Porter's use of the isolated Western city lets her demonstrate how deeply World War I infiltrates even the lives of common people living at the edges of their culture.

In many ways, the evil of the war is present metaphorically in the unseen, deadly virus that ravages not only the large coastal cities but the interior of the country as well. Moreover, the pestilence kills indiscriminately, soldiers and civilians alike, in their very homes, thousands of miles from the front lines. The cost of the war is higher than anyone could have expected, and Porter's story, with its dreamy, impressionistic prose brought about by Miranda's illness, explores life and death and life after death.

— *Diane Andrews Henningfeld*

THE PALM-WINE DRINKARD

Author: Amos Tutuola (1920-1997)
Type of work: Novel
Type of plot: Folktale

Time of plot: Indeterminate
First published: 1952

In this episodic West African narrative told in childlike English, the narrator-protagonist visits a series of strange and sometimes terrifying places while searching for his palm-wine tapster, who was killed in a fall from a palm tree. The sparseness of descriptive details adds to the supernatural atmosphere.

African bush. Wild, shrubby landscape through which the drinker of palm-wine (a naturally alcoholic beverage that is tapped directly from trees) travels during most of the novel. Occasionally, he and his wife discover a road, but they are soon driven back into the uncharted bush. The setting is never specifically stated, but it may be inferred. The author is Nigerian, and he incorporates Yoruba myths and legends into his loosely connected narrative. The setting is either West Africa or a magical landscape that physically resembles West Africa.

Death's house. Former residence of the personified Death, an eight-hour journey down Death's road. It is a house and adjoining yam garden where human skeletons are used as fuel woods and human skulls as basins, plates, and tumblers. The palm-wine drinkard ensnares

Death in a net and carries him away. Since that day, he has wandered homeless in the world.

Endless forest of the Complete Gentleman. Forest in which only terrible creatures live. The Complete Gentleman (or Curious Creature) is greatly admired in the market but, when he returns to his forest, he begins to return his body parts to the creatures from whom they were rented. He finally becomes Skull, when that is the only body part he retains. The protagonist follows Skull to his family's house. When Father of Gods who can do anything in this world (as the protagonist now calls himself) saves the daughter of the nearby village's headman from Skull, she becomes his wife.

Wraith Island. High piece of land located in a bush full of islands and swamps. The people of the island are the most beautiful in the world of the curious creatures. They are kind and loving. Other than planting their food, their only work is constantly playing music and dancing. When the protagonist and his wife leave the island, the beautiful people give them valuable gifts.

Unreturnable-Heaven's town. Large town full of perverse creatures who are cruel to human beings. All activities in the town are backward. The residents avoid the flat land near their town and build their houses on a steep hillside. They climb ladders before leaning them against trees. They wash their domestic animals but not their own bodies. They trim the fingernails of these animals but not their own. They sleep on the roofs of their houses. The protagonist is finally able to cut a window in the tall, thick wall surrounding the town, through which he and his wife can escape.

White tree. Giant tree, about one thousand feet tall and about two hundred feet in diameter. Inside the white tree is a big house. Sitting in a chair in a big parlor is an old woman called Faithful-Mother. The house has a beautiful spacious hall with over twenty stages for musicians and dancers, a kitchen employing 340 cooks, and a hospital with many beds. The protagonist and his wife sojourn there for a pleasant year and two weeks before resuming their quest.

Red-town. Town located within the Red-bush, where everything is deep red in color: bush, trees, ground, people, animals, food, water. The town has been under a spell since the Red-king inappropriately caught a red bird in a fish net and a red fish in an animal trap. These creatures, grown to an enormous size, come out from a big hole near the town once each year to receive a human sacrifice. The Red-people choose the protagonist as their victim. However, since he sold his death at the door of the white tree, he is invulnerable. Though terrified, he kills the creatures and lifts their spell.

Deads' Town. Where the qualified dead, both black and white, reside after two years of training. The denizens of Deads' Town, along with their domestic animals, walk backward. In fact, everything they do is opposite to that of living people. There, the protagonist finds his tapster, the only man ever able to satisfy his insatiable thirst. The tapster can not return to the land of the living, but for consolation he gives the palm-wine drinkard a magic egg.

— *Patrick Adcock*

PAMELA: Or, Virtue Rewarded

Author: Samuel Richardson (1689-1761)
Type of work: Novel
Type of plot: Epistolary

Time of plot: Early eighteenth century
First published: 1740-1741

Written in epistolary form, this book is the first English-language narrative to present a dramatic situation and thereby meet the modern definition of a novel. Many Samuel Richardson scholars believe that Pamela *can be read as fiction's first entry in the battle of the sexes and, as such, a parable of Adam and Eve in the Garden of Eden.*

Garden. Walled garden on the Lincolnshire estate of the young squire Mr. B——, where Pamela Andrews has been reduced to a servant because of her family's declining fortunes. The squire wants to seduce the virtuous young Pamela, who uses the garden to meet, or correspond with, Mr. Williams, the local clergyman, who loves her. The plot of the story centers on threats to Pamela's virtue, her successful defense, and the rewards she receives as a result of her steadfastness, just as the biblical story of Adam and Eve centers on the serpent's efforts to seduce Eve from her innocence. Pamela's first temptation, like Eve's, takes place in a garden. The garden of Mr. B——'s Lincolnshire estate becomes a setting that helps chart Pamela's seeming recoiling from, and eventual seduction of, her master. Eventually, Mr. B——'s love for Pamela overcomes his lust and his pride of caste. They are married by Mr. Williams in the restored chapel on his estate. Pamela's virtue is rewarded by marriage and by B——'s reform. She now becomes the mistress of his estates in Bedfordshire and Lincolnshire.

To Pamela, the estate's old-fashioned walled garden at first appears to be a prison, as its high walls serve only to shut her in. Later, however, it also seems to be a refuge, protecting her from external dangers. Similarly, other natural features trace Pamela's progress from captive to captivator. Ultimately, the fifteen-year-old Pamela turns her principal disability—her inferior status—into an impregnable fortress.

The eighteenth century was the great age of the English garden. Tudor gardens, characterized by encircling walls, were redone in the new fashion of sunken fences that opened new floral vistas. Pamela's letters describing Mr. B——'s house and garden lead readers to infer that neither had been much altered. The pleasantly unfashionable nature of the garden suggests fidelity to old values. The garden is also relatively unpretentious. For example, Pamela uses a plain sunflower to mark the hiding places for the letters that her presumably loyal friend Parson Williams will carry to their destinations.

Pond. Pool of water in the Lincolnshire estate's garden. Early during her confinement, Pamela fishes in the garden's pond and catches a carp. After considering the parallel between the fish and herself, she lets the carp go. Later, the pond assumes a more sinister aspect when Pamela contemplates suicide. Finally, as Mr. B—— moves toward proposing marriage to her, he sits beside her as she kneels on the bank of the pond, takes her in his arms, and tells her, "I love you with a purer flame than ever I knew in my life, and which commenced for you in the garden."

— *Richard Hauer Costa*

PARADE'S END

Author: Ford Madox Ford (Ford Madox Hueffer, 1873-1939)
Type of work: Novel
Type of plot: Impressionism

Time of plot: World War I and after
First published: 1950: *Some Do Not . . .* , 1924; *No More Parades*, 1925; *A Man Could Stand Up*, 1926; *The Last Post*, 1928

Locations in the novels of this tetralogy set in World War I shift between the British home front and the trenches of France, tracing the impact of the war on British culture through the experiences of three characters: Christopher Tietjens; Sylvia Tietjens, his estranged wife; and Valentine Wannop, his lover.

*****England.** These novels trace the devastating impact of World War I on England, emphasizing the sharp division between pre- and postwar conditions. Ford Madox Ford represents prewar England as a country on the verge of chaos, with only nationalistic illusions maintaining a semblance of order. The war destroys those illusions, and the postwar changes in British culture are represented by the decline of the Tietjens family from their upper-class position as wealthy, landed gentry.

Groby. Yorkshire country estate of the Tietjens family and the postwar setting for *The Last Post*, the concluding novel in the series. The estate's main house is notable for the gigantic Groby Great Tree that has grown into the structure of the house. After the war, the estate is rented to Americans who have no respect for the history behind it, except from a tourist's perspective. When the Americans try to have Groby Great Tree removed, they do significant damage to the entire structure of the house. These dramatic changes at Groby symbolize the decline in power and authority of the British gentry in the aftermath of the war.

*London. Capital of Great Britain, in which Tietjens recuperates with Sylvia at the end of *Some Do Not . . .* Sylvia moves within London's elite society while Tietjens is stationed in France, and Christopher's older brother Mark works in the War Office near Regent's Park. In addition, Valentine teaches physical education at a London girls' school.

*Western Front. Broad region running from Belgium through France that was the center of the most intense and devastating combat in World War I. Tietjens is stationed there during the war, and Ford provides vivid descriptions of life in the trenches for British soldiers. In *Some Do Not . . .* Tietjens suffers amnesia after being caught in an explosion during 1916. Later, he is assigned to supply duties that keep him behind the lines, but through the influence of his godfather, General Campion, he is reassigned to the front at Flanders. Even at the front, Tietjens's attention is split between his military duties and some "distant locality"—his marriage problems, financial situation, and romance with Valentine back in England. Toward the end of *A Man Could Stand Up*, Tietjens again experiences shell shock after being blown in the air and buried in a shell explosion. Tietjens is hospitalized in Rouen, as was Ford during the war.

In a key scene in *No More Parades*, Sylvia makes an improper visit with Christopher at the front. They later meet at a nearby hotel (from which the sound of shelling can still be heard) and attempt reconciliation. Their reunion, however, is interrupted by Sylvia's lover, Major Perowne, and the ensuing fight is witnessed by General Campion. The positioning of this scene so close to the battle lines collapses and intensifies Tietjens's concerns over his domestic problems at home and his military duty at the front.

Mountby. English country estate, near Rye, owned by Tietjens's godfather, General Campion. The novel opens in 1912, with Tietjens and Macmaster on a train to Rye for a golf outing with Campion. While visiting Campion, Tietjens first meets Valentine Wannop and begins his romantic relationship with her.

Lobscheid. Little-known German resort at which Sylvia conducts her extramarital affair at the beginning of *Some Do Not . . . .* The fact that she vacations at a German resort in the years before the outbreak of war indicates her blindness to the developing crisis in Europe.

— *Andrew J. Kunka*

PARADISE LOST

Author: John Milton (1608-1674)
Type of work: Poetry
Type of plot: Epic

Time of plot: Creation of the world
First published: 1667

While Heaven, Hell, and paradise (Eden) of Judeo-Christian tradition were already established by John Milton's time, his imaginative powers make these settings his own. It is no exaggeration to say that traditional Western images of these three places derive in large part from Milton's epic. Milton's images of Hell rival Dante's, while those of paradise make use of his considerable lyrical powers in offering a sense of the beauty of natural creation before the Fall.

Heaven. Unlike the other places described by Milton in *Paradise Lost*, the scenes in heaven are not memorable for their physical description. When God the Father and his Son Jesus speak in book 3, they do so from the heights of Heaven. All the speaker asserts about the scene of this dialogue is that it is high above both Earth and Hell, and that it is bathed in celestial light. God's throne is mentioned, along with the choirs of angels surrounding it, but traditional images of clouds and stars are absent. The book opens with Milton's famous hymn to light, and the overall effect is the repeated emphasis on the brilliance of the empyrean, the highest heaven which, in the medieval cosmology surviving in Milton's day, was the home of God and the angels.

Hell. The underworld into which the rebel angels fall in book 1 of Milton's epic is the first fully visualized scene. After describing the precipitous fall of Satan and his cohorts amid the chaos of floods and whirlwinds, Milton has the demons remark on how different this place appears in comparison with the Heaven from which they have come. Just as Heaven is characterized mostly by light in book 3, Hell is known by its dimness. Even flames give forth no light, and there is no land, though Milton teases the reader's visual imagination by speaking of lakes of liquid fire and lands of solid fire. Specific locations within Hell include its capital, Pandemonium; the large gates through which Satan flies; and the Paradise of Fools, a borderland where foolish monks believe, in their vanity, that they are in Heaven.

Pandemonium. Word coined by Milton to describe the capital of Hell in this epic that now has a broader meaning. Milton invented the word by analogy with the Pantheon, the temple of all gods in ancient Rome. The Pandemonium is thus an infernal temple honoring all demons. Milton describes it near the end of book 1, and the first half of book 2 takes place there as well. As in Milton's other place descriptions in *Paradise Lost*, the emphasis is on the spaciousness of this capital of Hell, the throngs of demons filling the hall, the wide gates and porches. Yet, since Milton is using this spaciousness as an emblem of greatness, he effects a sudden change in point of view at the end of book 1, making the demons, who seemed gigantic, become minuscule. The change is due to their fall, which has just taken place. In Pandemonium, as elsewhere in Milton's cosmology, place has moral significance.

Garden of Eden. Biblical site in which the bulk of *Paradise Lost* after book 3 takes place. For Adam and Eve, the physical beauty of paradise represents the unfallen world. They are in harmony with all creatures, and they receive all the food they need without effort. To Satan, however, the place represents a painful reminder of all the joys he and the other fallen angels have lost forever. His first reflection on the sight of Eden, near the beginning of book 4, is a curse hurled at the Sun for showing him its beauties. There, it becomes clear that place is a function of one's moral state. For example, Satan, though in paradise, brings his Hell with him because of his unrepentant, fallen nature. Conversely, at the end of the epic, Adam and Eve, though banished from paradise, carry a small reflection of it with them in their love for each other.

— John R. Holmes

PARADISE REGAINED

Author: John Milton (1608-1674)
Type of work: Poetry
Type of plot: Epic

Time of plot: First century
First published: 1671

This brief epic tells the story of how humanity was restored to paradise through the actions of one man, Jesus Christ. Set in the Holy Land, it alludes to many other places in the ancient world, while suggesting that the critical events of only a few hours of time shaped world history. Like John Milton's full-scale epic, Paradise Lost, *this poem foregrounds a single period of temptation. Again, like that epic, it visits unearthly places, such as the "middle region of thick air," where Satan consults with the fallen angels to plan his attack on the Messiah.*

*Judaea. Desert region east of Jerusalem, near the Dead Sea, where Jesus goes to be baptized in the Jordan River. Baptism gives him an overpowering sense of mission to proclaim the kingdom of God the Father, and he spends forty days wandering through the Judaean wilderness, absorbing the new reality. Afterward Satan accosts Jesus and tries to tempt him three times. The first temptation is to feed himself by turning a stone into bread or by accepting delicacies conjured up out of thin air. The second is to prepare himself for his new mission by acquiring the powers of a world ruler. For this temptation, Satan takes Jesus to a mountaintop from which they can see every place in the ancient world.

*Parthia. Mesopotamian territory in what is now northeastern Iran; the center of the Parthian Empire, which overran Israel briefly during the first century B.C.E. Looking east, over Parthia, from the mountaintop, Satan tempts Jesus with all the glory of the Asian king. He includes military victories that would place Jesus among such heroes of later ages as Charlemagne. He also suggests that Jesus can reunite the ten lost tribes of Israel, now scattered over the area. Jesus rejects this offer by saying that his time has not yet come.

*Rome. Largest city in Italy and center of the vast Roman Empire at the time Jesus was alive. Looking west from the mountaintop, Satan points toward Rome and its Capitol building, in which senators and other officials plan the fate of an empire reaching all the way to Britain. Jesus rejects this, too, saying that God's kingdom will be far more permanent.

*Athens. Principal city of ancient Greece and center of intellectual activity in the ancient world. The final temptation that Satan offers to Jesus is the intellectual attainments of ancient philosophy and literature, and he points toward Athens to call attention to the Academy of Plato, the Lyceum of Aristotle, and the Stoa of Zeno and other Stoic philosophers. He suggests that learning of this sort can make Jesus a ruler over himself. Jesus rejects even this offer, countering that his own Jewish culture has plenty of thought and beauty.

*Jerusalem. City situated on a hill in Judaea that is the center of religious life for the Jewish people. After Jesus spurns every sort of power—physical, political, and intellectual—Satan suggests that he has no place in the world. He then leads Jesus to the pinnacle of the Temple of Jerusalem, suggesting that Jesus throw himself off its top and let the angels decide what to do next. Again Jesus resists, knowing that he must let God direct his life.

*Nazareth. City in Galilee, a province north of Judaea that is home to Mary, the mother of Jesus. As Satan begins tempting Jesus, Milton imagines Mary in Nazareth worrying about her son. After Satan makes his last offer, he has Jesus return privately to his mother's house.

— *Thomas Willard*

A PASSAGE TO INDIA

Author: E. M. Forster (1879-1970)
Type of work: Novel
Type of plot: Social realism

Time of plot: c. 1920
First published: 1924

This novel opens in the fictional city of Chandrapore in the early twentieth century during the period of the British Raj in India. Most of the action occurs in Chandrapore or in the vicinity of the neighboring Marabar Hills and Caves. The eclectic environment, personal relationships, and conflicting cultures all affect the setting. Private homes, mosques, and civil and religious functions provide settings for characters from the Hindu, Muslim, and Christian religions to interact.

Chandrapore. Old, remote Hindu city with filthy alleyways and mean streets that is divided into three parts: old Chandrapore on the Ganges River; inland Maidan on higher ground, and the Civil Station on the second hill.

Although it is located on the river, Chandrapore has no riverfront and no bathing steps. Nothing distinguishes Chandrapore except for its proximity to the Marabar Caves. It is home for the Indians.

Maidan. Central section of Chandrapore that contains the hospital in which Dr. Aziz practices medicine and which is the section in which most Europeans live, in houses near the railway station. Maidan has an oval parade field on which polo is played and where soldiers practice.

Civil Station. Section of Chandrapore made up of British civil offices and residences. It is a city of gardens, forests, birds, and streets laid out and named for generals. If not charming, it is functional, with houses for the officials, a grocery store, a cemetery, the Chandrapore Club, Government College, and the official offices. The police station and courthouse are located in the Civil Station. The police station is where Aziz is incarcerated after he is accused of an attack on Adela. The court is the formal courtroom for legal proceedings and is composed of several platforms for various service persons and magistrates who function in the courtroom.

The Civil Station is more formal than some of the other settings of the novel. Mr. Fielding's residence is located near the Government College. Social interaction among Aziz, the British officials, and visitors before and after Aziz's trial occurs here. It is also the only place for Adela to stay after the trial ends. The residence of the superintendent of police is where Mrs. McBryde provides nursing care and sanctuary for Adela after the attack and before the trial. However, because of cultural and religious prejudices, the home is closed to Adela when she recants her accusation of Aziz.

Mosque. Islamic place of prayer that is a peaceful, gracious, but crumbling holy place. It is enclosed with a low wall around the courtyard, with a stream that runs through the garden and a three-sided covered part. Aziz frequents this mosque and one night is disturbed to see an Englishwoman there. After admonishing her for entering the mosque and wearing her shoes inside, he learns of her knowledge and genuine appreciation for the Islamic religion and for India.

Chandrapore Club. Social center for British government officials from which Indians are denied admittance. Instead of bridging the gap between the colonizers and their subjects, this club makes the gap wider.

Marabar Caves. Complex of caverns in the rough Marabar Hills overlooking Chandrapore. The caves are not sacred, contain no sculptures or drawings, and are not tourist attractions. They are all just alike. The entrance is a long human-made tunnel that leads to a circular center room. It is believed that the caves were opened in the seventeenth century by the orders of Shivaji, perhaps for the Hindu military to flee to the hills from Muslim invasions. The ruined water tank near one is probably the remains of the elaborate cistern system that was built to supply water for those who sought refuge in the caves. Kawa Dol is the only cave mentioned by name, but it is not accessible.

The most important scene in *A Passage to India* is Aziz's visit to the caves with the British women. Puzzling and terrifying to both Muslims and Anglo-Indians, the caves form the center of the novel. The caves are elemental. They have been there from the beginning of the earth. They are not Hindu holy places, but Godbole can respect them without fear. Cave worship is the cult of the female principle, the Sacred Womb, Mother Earth. The Marabar Caves, both womb and grave, demand total effacing of ego. The individual loses identity, and whatever is said returns as *Ommm*, the holy word. The caves are terrifying and chaotic to those who rely on the intellect. The outing itself emphasizes the chaos that is India. Once in the caves, the party encounters the Nothingness that terrifies.

Aziz's home. Small hut, simply furnished with minimal furniture, that is the meeting place of Aziz's friends. The only thing of value that Aziz owns is a picture of his deceased wife.

Mau Palace. Beautiful white stucco palace with a courtyard and expensive, exotic furnishings. Inside is a small shrine that serves as the setting of a British ceremony. The streets near the palace provide the setting for the Procession of the Chief God, an evening torchlight procession.

— *Anna Hollingsworth Hovater*
— *Additional material by Michael S. Reynolds*

PATERSON

Author: William Carlos Williams (1883-1963)   *First published:* 1946-1958
Type of work: Poetry

A masterpiece of modern American poetry, this epic explores the physical, natural, and human world around the falls in Paterson, New Jersey, as a poetic landscape. It portrays the Passaic River, industrial city life, tensions of the local people, hidden turmoil between men and women, and the city history, and includes correspondence with the poet. All these elements combine as a living thing into the mind of a central figure, sometimes called "Dr. Paterson" and sometimes the "poet," who struggles to find the language equal to all that is there.

***Paterson.** City in northeastern New Jersey set amid factories, garbage dumps, pollution, and industrial blight, with the much larger cities of New York City and Newark on the horizon. Paterson is perched on the edge of the Passaic River and roaring waterfalls that attracted industry as far back as the time of Alexander Hamilton. The city itself is the poem's main character: a living being, chaotic and shifting through time and differing perceptions, full of energy, beauty, ugliness, cruelty, and crass moneygrubbing.

Sometimes, William Carlos Williams is exhilarated by the masses of workers, immigrants, and ordinary men and women in Paterson; at other times, he is angry at their meanness, immorality, and pettiness, preferring the dogs in the park. Paterson is also the man/poet/doctor who becomes the consciousness and the voice of the city. The poem incorporates bits of conversation on the street, letters, news clippings, historical documents, and geological, economic, and industrial records.

***Passaic River.** New Jersey river that flows about ninety miles to the sea, passing through Paterson and entering the Atlantic Ocean at Newark. In the poem the river, representing life, time, and language, has been polluted and despoiled by human failure, greed, cruelty, and the failure to communicate. In the eighteenth century, however, the river is the place where Alexander Hamilton saw a future for the city and the place where early industrial barons grew rich off cotton and silk mills. As the river pours over its falls, it can cleanse itself; however, humans, who have no such redeeming language, are condemned to an inarticulate and fragmentary consciousness.

***Great Falls.** Seventy-four-foot drop in the Passaic River at Paterson, where the river thunders over a rocky ledge about sixty feet wide into a broad basin. The waterfall has been an attraction since early Native Americans thought the site to be holy, and it continues to draw tourists. In the poem the waterfall represents a potential that has been squandered through commercial exploitation. Williams uses the lip of the falls to represent the risk of inspired speech, the kind of imaginative leap necessary for poetry's rebirth, an action that makes a new language possible.

***Sleeping Giant.** Rock formation that creates the Great Falls and the bend in the river and changes the natural woodland above the waterfall into one of the major manufacturing centers in America. Williams believed that the shape of the rocks resembled the figure of a man lying on his side. In his poem, this imaginary stone figure becomes Paterson itself—the "Genius of the Place"—who becomes the symbol of the masculine, matched by the female symbol, the park, the mountains that overlook the city, and the natural world.

***Park.** Parkland surrounding Great Falls that represents the female principle, often ignored and abused by the male, giving rise to the failure of communication and the divorce of the spirit. In the second volume of this poem, the imaginary Dr. Paterson strolls through the park observing men, women, dogs, and nature. He laments the poverty of imagination in the present-day population, suggesting that culture and poetry will "go on/ repeating itself with recurring/ deadliness," destroying even the trees.

Library. In the third volume, Paterson the poet/city searches the library for historical records looking for an adequate language to recapture the promise of the landscape and the falls. In the library the fragments of history record the destruction necessary to start afresh: the fires, floods, winds, and all the literary, economic, social, perceptual, and emotional breakdowns that have plagued

Paterson and America for more than three centuries. Out of this destruction the "Beautiful thing" arises.

Sea. The fourth book, "The Run to the Sea," begins as an idyll modeled on Theocritus with a dialogue between Corydon and Phyllis and then between Phyllis and Paterson, who is married. The language becomes furtive and mingles with office talk in New York of money and murder and exploitation. The river and the book end in the sea, but a poet triumphantly crawls up out of the surf accompanied by a black female dog.

*Cloisters Museum. New York City art museum housing the famous Unicorn Tapestries, which are one of the subjects in the fifth volume of Williams's poem. There, Williams meditatively focuses on the concepts of the Virgin and the whore, or art and morality. Poetry and art for Williams is sexual in its origin; in his fifth volume, art is seen as combining both male and female, a place for rebirth, and reawakening. The language is whole again for a while.

— *Newton Smith*

THE PATHFINDER: Or, The Inland Sea

Author: James Fenimore Cooper (1789-1851)
Type of work: Novel
Type of plot: Adventure

Time of plot: 1756
First published: 1840

Set in the woods around Lake Ontario during the French and Indian War of the mid-eighteenth century, this novel relies heavily on place for meaning, for it is through place that characters test themselves, learn, and live or die. Like James Fenimore Cooper's other Leatherstocking Tales, this novel began a tradition that focuses on the American frontier and its influence on those who experience it.

*Lake Ontario. Great lake that separates the northwestern part of what is now New York State from Canada—the region in which *The Pathfinder* is set. As a Navy midshipman in the early nineteenth century, Cooper was stationed at Oswego and traveled through the region. When he later wrote the novel, he called his description of the region "as nearly accurate as is required by the laws which govern fiction." He seems to have first proposed setting a novel in the Great Lakes area in 1831; at various times he even referred to the novel's title as "Lake Ontario" and "Inland Sea," thus suggesting the importance place would play.

From the very first page of *The Pathfinder*, the eighteenth century New York wilderness is established as a powerful, awe-inspiring, mythic force, wherein forest training, and neither book learning nor map reading, keeps one alive. Natty Bumppo, here called Pathfinder, appears in these first few pages, establishing his reputation for finding his way "where there is no path" and sharing his vision of the wilderness as God's temple. He is Cooper's archetypal frontiersman, guide, hunter, and trapper, a model of rugged American individualism, de-

mocracy, and transcendental spirituality. As he does in the early pages, Cooper uses place in the remainder of the novel to articulate and test the values and skills that frontier life has given Pathfinder.

*Oswego River. Tributary of Lake Ontario that rises near Syracuse, New York. Cooper's preface and footnotes make it clear that his depiction of his characters' encounter with the Oswego River is based in reality. There, as in the thick of the forests, wilderness training and the frontier's power to shape are spotlighted. Chingachgook, the Iroquois warriors, Pathfinder, and Jasper represent the "cunning of the woods"; Cap is disrespectful yet also afraid of the wilderness; meanwhile, Mabel's experience of the frontier begins to teach her bravery. As in other novels, Cooper is careful to distinguish for his nineteenth century audience the difference between those educated in the wilderness (Pathfinder and Jasper) and those *of* the wilderness (Chingachgook and the Iroquois). Pathfinder's kill-only-when-unavoidable attitude depicts the justice that is learned by "living much alone with God in the wilderness" when one has white gifts.

*Fort Oswego. Frontier outpost near the mouth of the Oswego River on Lake Ontario. Once the characters reach the fort, the fast-paced action of the river scenes slows to a standstill as Cooper uses place to showcase the romance portion of what he once called his "nautico-lake-savage romance." His descriptions here evoke a kind of democratic Eden: perfect climate; boundless game, so much so that every one, not just the wealthy, can feast; Pathfinder as Adam, indifferent to class distinctions and judging only on personal merit. In the midst of Eden, Cooper introduces the historically valid sharpshooting contest, which further spotlights both the great frontier skills of Pathfinder and his generous heart.

— *Anna Dunlap Higgins*

PATIENCE: Or, Bunthorne's Bride

Author: W. S. Gilbert (1836-1911)
Type of work: Drama
Type of plot: Satire

Time of plot: Nineteenth century
First performed: 1881; first published, 1881

A highly topical burlesque of the British aesthetic movement in general and of Oscar Wilde in particular, this play has pronounced Victorian settings. These serve to root the story in a specific milieu, but the setting does not interfere with the universal aspect of the satire.

Castle Bunthorpe. Fictional castle setting that gives W. S. Gilbert the opportunity to dress up his burlesque of English sham. The chorus of twenty-six lovesick maidens with lutes and mandolins hearkens back to the Pre-Raphaelites, and the appearance of Patience the milkmaid in a costume copied from a painting by Sir Luke Filde suggests the kind of decorative taste and sentimentality prevalent in Victorian society. The opera ridicules affectation, nowhere more so than in the fleshly figure of Bunthorne, who has a languid love of lilies and who appears to be an all-purpose amalgam of Oscar Wilde, Sir Edward Coley Burne-Jones, and Dante Gabriel Rossetti.

Glade. Site of the pastoral scene that opens act 2, with the Lady Jane (one of the Rapturous Maidens) playing on a violincello as the chorus is heard singing in the distance. The libretto specified a small pond in the center, a tree stump, and a rock. The tree stump is an essential part of the action; for Bunthorne, it is a surface on which to scribble a poem, a rest stop during the floral procession at the end of act I, and an obstacle in his attempt to evade Lady Jane after their duet. For her, it is a cello stand. Thus, an ordinary piece of stage decor becomes a means to further farcical action and to mock certain attitudes.

— *Keith Garebian*

PATIENCE AND SARAH

Author: Isabel Miller (Alma Routsong, 1924-   )
Type of work: Novel
Type of plot: Love

Time of plot: Early 1880's
First published: 1969, as *A Place for Us*

Set in Connecticut, Massachusetts, and New York, this novel unfolds primarily indoors—within houses, wagons, and boats. These various settings emphasize the restrictions that American women in the early nineteenth century had to endure.

Connecticut farmhouses. Differences between the farmhouses in which Patience and Sarah grow up reveal the differences between the two women. Patience owns half of the family home and has her own kitchen, parlor, and bedroom, willed to her by her father. With her own fireplace and high feather bed, she can entertain Sarah cozily. She also owns two cows, and she and her brother jointly possess a fine barn. In contrast to Patience's affluent surroundings, Sarah's home is small and unpainted, dark inside, without such luxuries as a mirror. She must climb a ladder to sleep in the loft on a corn husk pallet with her sisters. The land which she helps her father farm is rocky and hilly—as Patience describes the state of Connecticut—"stingy country." These farmhouses, though different, are both dominated by men, and they symbolize the restrictive life which the two young women dream of escaping.

Patience and Sarah's home. House in New York's Greene County, near the Hudson River, that Patience and Sarah buy for $640. The house fulfills their dreams, although it is merely an old and small log cabin with sagging roof and collapsing chimney. After taking ownership, the women begin work immediately to make it liveable. On her way there, Patience notices mountains "like lady giants lying together, vast hips and breasts," as well as flowering fruit trees. Patience and Sarah are such fertile giants. The fact that they sleep and make love outside while they are rebuilding their cabin shows that they have escaped their restricted life in Connecticut.

*Genesee. Frontier town in far western New York where Sarah initially dreams of settling because of cheap land. Though willing to travel there with Sarah, Patience fears both its hardships and public opinion. When Patience breaks her promise, Sarah walks across Connecticut but, even though disguised as a boy, soon realizes what problems unescorted women face. When Sarah returns, willing to settle for stolen moments instead of an uninterrupted life together, Patience insists on leaving for Genesee. The women's eventual decision to settle instead in Greene County symbolizes their acceptance of life's reality and their determination and ability to realize their dream as completely as possible.

Parson Dan Peel's van. Vehicle in which Sarah's education about the larger world begins. By traveling across Massachusetts with Dan in his snug, tidy home on wheels, Sarah (Sam) learns to read and write, skills Patience acquired when her father sent her away to school. Sarah spends much of her travel time inside the van learning new concepts from Dan, one of the few times a man liberates rather than restrains her.

Coastal trader. Sailboat that carries Patience and Sarah from Stratford, Connecticut, to New York City. Sarah's one venture outside of the Ladies' Cabin ends when a flirtatious man accosts her. When Patience rescues her, Sarah realizes that she has much to learn from her mate. The two women use the restrictive protection of the small, shabby Ladies' Cabin to improve Sarah's social skills, which helps make the women more equal.

Boardinghouses. Lodgings in New York City and Kaatskill in which Patience and Sarah stay. The house in New York City belongs to the captain of the coastal trader, who has been commissioned by Patience's brother to look after the women. The house in Kaatskill, though safe in many ways, restricts them because the other women overhear Sarah's groans during their lovemaking. These boardinghouses provide transitions between the restrictions of the farmhouses in Connecticut and the freedoms of their new home in Greene County.

Steamboat. Frightening means of transportation up the Hudson River to Greene County. Sarah is especially scared of the steamboat's loud noise and rumored tendency to explode. The rapid boat trip on "the ancient sea" by means of "new wheels" symbolizes to Patience their brand-new life which they must "invent" for themselves "on a razor's edge."

— *Shelley A. Thrasher*

PEACE

Author: Aristophanes (c. 450-c. 385 B.C.E.)
Type of work: Drama
Type of plot: Satire

Time of plot: Fifth century B.C.E.
First performed: Eirēnē, 421 B.C.E. (English translation, 1837)

Two locations are used in this play: a farmer's field near Athens and an open area in heaven where the goddess Peace is buried. As in all ancient Greek plays, outdoor locations are crucial because all city business was conducted in open locations. Private locations for public business were considered dangerous to the well-being of the city, for political plots are conceived in private.

Trygaegus's farm. The play begins in a field in front of Trygaegus's farmhouse outside of Athens where two servants are feeding a huge beetle upon whose back Trygaegus will fly to heaven to plead with the goddess Peace for an end to the Peloponnesian War. In the last part of the play, the group returns to Trygaegus's farm for a celebration of a peaceful and fruitful harvest and a marriage to ensure the propagation of the Athenian population.

Heaven. When Trygaegus reaches heaven, he meets Hermes, messenger of the gods, and discovers that Zeus has "washed his hands" of the Greeks and left control of heaven to the god of War, who has buried the goddess Peace.

Tomb of Peace. Trygaegus goes to the Tomb of Peace and after some difficulty with various helpers from other Greek city-states and other occupations, he calls upon his fellow farmers to aid him in hoisting Peace out of her tomb. They do so and return to Trygaegus's farm with Peace and her two handmaidens, Harvest Fruits and Celebration. At the farm a marriage is celebrated to ensure the ongoing fertility of Peace.

— *August W. Staub*

PEDER VICTORIOUS

Author: O. E. Rölvaag (1876-1931)
Type of work: Novel
Type of plot: Regional

Time of plot: Late nineteenth century
First published: Peder Seier, 1928 (English translation, 1929)

A sequel to Giants in the Earth *(1924), this novel continues the story of Beret and her son, Peder, in Spring Creek, Dakota Territory, where despite the opposition of his mother, Peder is drawn by American schools and culture away from his Norwegian heritage.*

*Dakota Territory. During the 1880's—the period during which the novel opens—Dakota Territory flourished. The grasshopper plagues had ended, and the land again produced bumper crops. Attracted by prosperity, new settlers swarmed in, with the steady westward expansion of the railroads speeding their access. Heading westward from Chicago and St. Paul, railroads linked the Dakotas with markets on both coasts, increasing the wealth of the region. The population of the territory expanded so fast that the territory's growth set off debates in the mid-1880's, dramatically presented in the second section of *Peder Victorious*, over whether to divide the territory into two states. On November 2, 1889, shortly before Peder's sixteenth birthday, North Dakota and South Dakota were admitted to the Union together.

Spring Creek. Town in South Dakota, situated near the state's border with Minnesota. As *Giants in the Earth* ended, a railroad neared Spring Creek on its way to Sioux Falls; O. E. Rölvaag never states whether the railroad builds a station at his fictional settlement; however, Spring Creek clearly shares the prosperity and population growth of the 1880's. Frame houses replace sod huts, farmers build elaborate barns, and newcomers settle all the available land. The entire action of *Peder Victorious* takes place in Spring Creek, especially in its churches and schools.

The town's two major ethnic groups are Norwegians, living mostly on the east side of the creek, and the Irish, dominating the west side. Each group has its own churches, and the two public schools of the village reflect the population of the area they serve.

Churches. Spring Creek has several Christian denominations. Its original Lutheran congregation, St. Luke's Norwegian Evangelical Church, meets in the Tallaksen schoolhouse while its members gradually raise money for their own building. A dissident group of Norwegians, more literal in their reading of the Bible, founds the Bethel Evangelical Lutheran Church, and Beret shifts from one Norwegian church to the other, hoping that membership in one of these churches will slow her son Peder's abandonment of Norwegian language and customs. However, she finds neither church satisfactory because both use English to attract the younger generation.

Where the town's Roman Catholics meet—or whether they even have their own meetinghouse—is never mentioned in the novel. That a parish church has existed there, however, is clear, as the novel mentions a priest who strongly denounces interfaith marriages.

Schools. Two public schools serve as political and cultural centers for the village. Tallaksen School, on the east side of Spring Creek, teaches a standard English language curriculum to its predominantly Norwegian students. The Irish children in Murphy School, on the west side, already speak English, but the schoolteacher who runs the school is determined to Americanize her charges further by teaching them to revere the heroes of American history. She also presides over a community meeting to debate the future of Dakota Territory. Her pupils open the session by reading the Declaration of Independence and Gettysburg Address to the largely immigrant audience. Dissenters from the decision of the first meeting later assemble at the Tallaksen schoolhouse.

Beret regrets the fact that district lines put her home within Murphy School territory. She distrusts the schoolmistress's policy of rigorous Americanization and objects to Peder's being forced to associate with Irish children. Beret has Peder transferred to Tallaksen School, where Norwegian children will surround him, but that school's English-language curriculum also reinforces the process of cultural assimilation. Peder continues to participate in extracurricular activities at Murphy School that are open to the entire settlement and at the novel's conclusion becomes engaged to an Irish American girl.

— *Milton Berman*

PEDRO PÁRAMO

Author: Juan Rulfo (1918-1986)
Type of work: Novel
Type of plot: Psychological symbolism

Time of plot: Late nineteenth and early twentieth centuries
First published: 1955 (English translation, 1959)

Set in rural Mexico, this novel opens with Juan Preciado's journey in search of his father that resembles aspects of the life of the orphaned author Juan Rulfo. Time periods shift among past, present, and future, often employing memories and flashbacks. Characters both living and dead seem to converse and interact. The setting of the novel is memorable, almost like a character in the work, and actually becomes a sort of purgatory full of wandering, lost souls. Juan discovers that his deceased mother's memories of a promised land in her home region are no longer accurate as the place has changed dramatically over the years of her absence.

*Jalisco (hah-LEES-koh). West-central Mexican state in which Rulfo grew up and which he used as a backdrop in most of his work. Rulfo also produced numerous photographs of the area, which vividly portray its people and places, as do his writings. Rulfo's laconic writing style imitates the speech patterns of the region. He depicts the pessimism and despair he felt about much of rural Mexico as it lost residents to better jobs in the cities and across the U.S. border.

Comala. Fictionalized version of a real Mexican town

in the state of Colima, not far from where Rulfo was born in neighboring Jalisco. These places appear both on maps and in Rulfo's novel; however, the real places are greatly transformed in the novel. Comala is described as being so hot that former residents who end up in Hell must come home to fetch their blankets.

Rulfo's fictional Comala is controlled by the iron hand of its *patrón*, Pedro Páramo. When he decides that the townspeople show insufficient respect upon the death of his wife, he turns his back on the town and lets it die. Like many other Mexican villages, it becomes virtually a ghost town after its young people leave to find employment in big cities, leaving behind only the elderly, who stay to care for the graves of their dead.

Pedro Páramo's name itself, which means "rocky barren place" in Spanish, symbolizes the barren place that the town becomes and further links the character to the location.

Media Luna. Ranch that is run by Pedro Páramo, as it had been by his father before him and as it probably would have been run by his son Miguel, if the youth had not died at an early age. The story emphasizes the importance of keeping land in families through the generations. In Spanish, the ranch's name means "half moon."

La Andrómeda. Mine worked by Bartolomé San Juan, father of Susana. Taking its name from a celestial galaxy, it is one of many astronomical references found throughout the novel. Continuing with the theme of depth and death in the work, in some cases local graveyards in the area contain the dead buried on top of one another. They sigh, moan, and apparently converse. By the end of the novel, the reader concludes that all of the characters are actually dead, yet are able to communicate and relive their memories.

— *Margaret V. Ekstrom*

PEER GYNT

Author: Henrik Ibsen (1828-1906)
Type of work: Drama
Type of plot: Satire

Time of plot: Mid-nineteenth century
First published: 1867 (English translation, 1892); first performed, 1876

This play—which was written as poetry, rather than prose, depending on highly stylized language—presents its hero as a world traveler who, like Homer's Odysseus, uses his wiles to attain wealth and renown. In this play, however, Henrik Ibsen seems to disregard realism in order to explore the psychology of the hero. A loutish, self-centered but likable villager, Peer has delusions of grandeur which he feeds through his fantasies. Peer is a man who lives for himself alone, using others to gain pleasure and power. Ibsen uses various locations both in the North Sea region of Europe and in the Mediterranean area to dramatize those fantasies.

North Country. Four of the five acts of the play are set in various locations in the far north, presumably Norway and surrounding regions. Ibsen is intentionally vague about setting, however, in order to suggest the fairy-tale quality of his drama. Farms, towns, and woodlands serve a dual purpose. They are realistic locations in which much of the action takes place, but they are simultaneously places where Peer Gynt's imaginative life is realized. Trolls, elves, and other fantastic creatures populate these regions. Thus, setting comes to symbolize the state of mind of the hero as he strives to become successful, respected, and powerful.

North Africa. The fourth act of *Peer Gynt* is set principally in Morocco and Egypt, where the hero's wanderings take him and give him opportunity to interact with other tycoons and attempt to solve the modern riddle of the Sphinx on the meaning of life. Gynt's astute answer to that riddle lands him in a Cairo madhouse. Through this radical shift in locale, Ibsen further suggests the epic nature of his play, emphasizing the foolish dreams of his hero to become emperor of the world.

— *Laurence W. Mazzeno*

PELLE THE CONQUEROR

Author: Martin Andersen Nexø (Martin Andersen, 1869-1954)

Type of work: Novel

Type of plot: Social realism

Time of plot: Late nineteenth century

First published: Pelle erobreren, 1906-1910 (English translation, 1913-1916)

This classic Danish novel is about the heroic struggle of the working-class poor in the face of horrendous conditions of insensitivity and exploitation. The struggles of the hero as a worker in many different trades mirror author Martin Andersen Nexø's own life of poverty and exploitation, as does the hero's involvement in trade unionism and political action.

***Bornholm.** Danish island to which the young Swedish boy Pelle Karlsson is taken by his father to escape a life of abject poverty in Sweden after his mother dies. Pelle's father, Lasse, expects Bornholm, a place of fishermen, farmers, sailors, and shopkeepers, to be a cornucopia of opportunity. Instead he finds a new life of desperation in a rural farm.

Stone Farm. One of the largest farms on Bornholm, where Lasse is tricked into working for poverty wages and bad food. There Lasse and Pelle spend six years working in fetid cow stables shoveling manure and tending the cattle. Often working in freezing conditions, they start their work at 4:00 A.M. Deceived by scoundrels on the farm, Pelle comes to understand that many people lie and learns to read their eyes instead of listening to their words.

The Koller family, who own the farm, live in a high white house referred to as the Palace and grow wealthy through poor treatment of their workers and by taking advantage of the misfortunes of neighboring farmers. Their debauchery is the talk of the town, but they are not measured by the same standards used for common people. Pelle gets a bare education at the farm's school, taught by the mediocre Mr. Niels, and learns only that the real lessons of life are to be learned outside. After much hardship on Stone Farm, Pelle sets off with a sack on his back to find opportunity in the city.

Jeppe's shop. Shoemaker's shop in which Pelle finds work as an apprentice. The shop is stuffy, dreary, smelly, and cramped, and no ray of sunlight ever enters it. After

Pelle completes five of the six years needed to become a journeyman shoemaker, Jeppe dies, and his apprentices are turned out into the street.

Heath Farm. Run-down farm on seventy rocky acres in the wilderness that Pelle's father buys with his savings and borrowings. Pelle joins him for a short time in near-starvation winter conditions but eventually refuses to be bound to the soil and returns to the city to be a common laborer. Although Lasse improves the farm, he eventually goes bankrupt and loses it.

***Copenhagen.** Capital of Denmark to which Pelle goes, seeking his fortune. He soon finds the city to be merely another battlefield for survival. There, he works as a journeyman shoemaker, employed by exploitative bosses in Meyer's Shoe Warehouse.

Ark. Collection of dilapidated working-class dwellings, located in Copenhagen's Kristianshavn district, where life is like a beehive. In spite of the desperate conditions, the residents generally take care of each other in the Ark. Because Pelle embraces trade unionism and can give moving speeches, he soon becomes president of the Shoemakers' Union and a hero to many of the Ark's inhabitants. Conditions worsen in the Ark as a freezing winter and an economic depression set in. The collection of workers' shanties finally burns down under mysterious conditions, shortly after Pelle leads his union to a victorious conclusion of a strike against employers such as Meyers. Yet Pelle's reward is an arrest on "trumped-up" charges and long-term imprisonment.

— *Irwin Halfond*

PELLÉAS AND MÉLISANDE

Author: Maurice Maeterlinck (1862-1949)
Type of work: Drama
Type of plot: Symbolism

Time of plot: Middle Ages
First published: Pelléas et Mélisande, 1892 (English translation, 1894); first performed, 1893

This play is set in the generalized European past into which all oral traditions eventually fall, to be rediscovered by the modern mind through acquaintance with folktales. The story is replete with fairy-tale motifs, carefully redeployed as symbols of implacable fate.

Allemonde. Kingdom ruled by Arkël, the grandfather of Pelléas and Golaud. The name recalls Allemagne, the French name for Germany (*Allemand* means "German"), but *monde* is French for "world," so it may also be read as a German/French or English/French composite signifying the whole world.

Castle. Arkël's seat, an old and gloomy edifice set on the shore of an ocean; a reek of decay ascends from the cracked walls of its extensive vaults. Like the Brothers Grimm's Rapunzel, Mélisande lets her abundant hair fall from one of the castle's towers as Pelléas climbs up, entangling them both.

Forest. Wild land beyond the park where Golaud hunts. It is there that he discovers the distraught Mélisande beside a spring, and there that he sustains his injuries.

Blindman's well. Spring in the park beyond the castle's gardens, whose water is reputed to have once been able to cure blindness. Mélisande loses her wedding ring there, and it is there that she and Pelléas make their fatal confessions of love on the eve of his intended departure. The association between Mélisande and the two springs is strongly reminiscent of Friedrich de la Motte-Fouqué's novel *Undine* (1811), suggesting that Mélisande is more elemental than human.

Cave. Large, partially unexplored, stalactite-encrusted grotto on the seashore, which Pélleas and Mélisande visit after she lies about the loss of her wedding ring. It is, in effect, an extension of the vaults underlying the castle, symbolic of the dark depths of the human mind where lust and jealousy are born.

— *Brian Stableford*

PENGUIN ISLAND

Author: Anatole France (Jacques-Anatole-François Thibault, 1844-1924)
Type of work: Novel
Type of plot: Satire

Time of plot: Ancient to modern times
First published: L'Île des pingouins, 1908 (English translation, 1914)

This novel uses a fanciful and remote island to take a satirical look at the pious and secular legends of French churchmen, historians, philosophers, and statesmen that concludes with a brief account of the presumed future of human society. Through all this, the island changes in size and shape as its satirical function evolves. This arbitrary variation reflects and subverts the transformations wrought by actual geographers and historians.

Alca. Island in the North Atlantic, close to the Arctic Circle, that is also known as the Island of the Penguins, **Penguin Island**, and **Penguinia**. Its shore was initially circular, surrounding a single, central mountain from whose peak the distant shores of Armorica could be seen. It was then flanked by steep cliffs, except for one place inset with a natural amphitheater formed of black and red rocks; in this amphitheater, while rendered snow-blind by the Arctic ice, the future Saint Maël preached the gospel to a population of penguins, thinking them humans, and then baptized them. (Note that penguins are native to the Southern Hemisphere, not the Arctic.)

Alca subsequently grew considerably in size, changing its shape to that of a mulberry leaf. Its previously desolate landscapes gave way to cultivated fields and woodlands. Much later in its history, the island was redesignated an "insula" following the expansion of its empire by the conqueror Trinco (although the conquered lands were soon lost again, along with the neighboring islands of Ampelphoria and the Dog's Jaws, which had belonged to the Penguins before Trinco's rise to power). These shifts in size and shape are a satirical projection of the alterations that changes in political geography impose on real maps.

The elementary geography of Alca is a conceptual sketch map of various kinds of territory recognized by mythographers and historians. The Coast of Shadows, to the east of the island, remains an ominous place long after the first phase of Penguin expansion—the sort of terra incognita which may be marked (literally, in this case) "here be dragons." The church and monastery built by Maël are in the far more hospitable Bay of Divers to the south, which becomes the site of a trading port. The Penguins' first violent property disputes erupt in the fertile western valleys of Dalles and Dombes, irrigated by the rivers Clange and Surelle, as a result of which disputes the First Assembly of the Estates of Penguinia is convened. From these primal locations, history progresses in Penguinia as a parody of actual social prog-

ress, culminating in a series of cultural cycles that suggests that the future of Penguinia and of the world will never culminate in a just and equitable society.

Abbey of Yvern. Monastery on the northwestern coast of France where Maël becomes abbot, establishing a school, an infirmary, a guest-house, a forge, and several workshops—a little utopia of sorts—before unwisely setting off to proselytize the pagans of the Breton Islands. He returns to the abbey to restore order when the chastity of its inhabitants is threatened by wayward nuns from the offshore island of Gad, after which the Devil diverts his boat to the northern Atlantic, so that he may discover Alca. When the monks of Yvern are dispossessed of their small-scale utopia by pagans in the Middle Ages, King Brian invites them to Alca, where he builds them a new monastery; however, the new one never becomes an entirely adequate substitute for the real thing.

Paradise. Site of the conference called by God to determine the legality of Maël's baptism of the penguins, as a result of which Maël is licensed to perform a miracle transforming the penguins into humans. It is, in essence, a place in which saints engage one another in endless arguments about obscure matters of dogma and propriety.

Gigantopolis. Capital city of **New Atlantis**, the greatest of the world's democracies, briefly visited by Professor Obnubile in the futile hope that the seemingly relentless march of its social and technological progress might bring about an end to war. However, the president of New Atlantis seems to devote all his energies to the promotion of distant wars, with the aim of forcing free trade upon the entire world.

— *Brian Stableford*

THE PEOPLE, YES

Author: Carl Sandburg (1878-1967)
Type of work: Poetry

First published: 1936

The symbolic setting for Carl Sandburg's poems, songs, narratives, and dramatic scenes is the broad landscape of the United States and the earth itself, in which people are constantly constructing, remodeling, tearing down, and reconstructing their places of abode and work, along with their lives.

New York City. America's greatest city typifies the urban metropolis of the industrialized United States. Scenes of wharfs, skyscrapers, tenement dwellings, and even streets form the backdrop for incessant noise and activity. Beginning with workers whose jobs are tailored to the building trades—from architects down to brick-layers and carpenters' helpers—the people of many languages construct their lives as they make their homes and places of work in the busy cityscapes of New York, Chicago, and other urban centers of industry and trade. The skyscraper is the "Tower of Babel," erected by people of all languages who come from all over the world to settle and build their lives in the land of opportunity. From the wealthy industrialist to the poverty-stricken homeless of the city, the voices of the people blend in the raucous song of the big city.

Great Plains. Great central region of the United States, stretching from the slopes of the Rocky Mountains in the west to the Upper Mississippi basin in the east, and from Texas in the south into Canada in the north. As in the great cities, people from "six continents, seven seas, and several archipelagoes," build railroads, bridges, riverboats, and roads that connect their settle-ments. In the Texas Panhandle and the high plains, the cowboys and cattle shiver in the cold winds that sweep from the North Pole to Amarillo, Texas, their only wind-break a barbed wire fence or the North Star. Voices heard on the prairies, in the deserts, and in Pacific Ocean ports define their lives in terms of their jobs—railroad men, meat wholesalers, fishermen, shippers, politicians, trial lawyers, merchants, waitresses, and housewives—and in so doing, describe the breadth and diversity of the land that is their home.

As Sandburg describes the people who construct the nation as they construct their dwellings and workplaces, he defines the character they impart to the "United States of the Earth." It is infused with their contradictory spirits of courage and fear, despair and hope—builders and wreckers blending together in a restless but accommo-dating land with a republican government that guards in-dividual freedom and inspires hope of future success for its people. In a very real sense, the land itself in all its di-versity is the setting for this epic of the rise of the United States and its people's struggle for survival.

— *Marguerite R. Plummer*

PEPITA JIMÉNEZ

Author: Juan Valera (Juan Valera y Alcalá Galiano, 1824-1905)
Type of work: Novel
Type of plot: Psychological realism

Time of plot: c. 1870
First published: Pepita Ximenez, 1874 (English translation, 1886)

This novel is a story of passionate love confused and nearly frustrated by religious faith. The difficulties afflict-ing the relationship are painstakingly mapped out in the geography of the stereotypical Spanish village in which the story is set; their eventual conquest is triumphantly celebrated in the decor of the house in which the affair is consummated.

Village. Typical community of the Andalusian plain in southern Spain to which Luis de Vargas, a young man studying for the priesthood, returns in order to visit his father Don Pedro, the community's reverend vicar. Hav-ing been away from the village since he was a child, the adult Luis observes that everything in it now seems smaller; his father's house pales into relative insignifi-cance by comparison with the seminary in which he is training for the priesthood. The orchards and flowery streams of the surrounding countryside initially seem more beautiful, although Luis soon begins to weary of their monotony and lack of intellectual stimulation.

Beyond the orchards are the vineyards and olive groves that provide the staple crops of the region. A sanctuary consecrated to the Virgin Mary, the patroness of the village, sits on the summit of a neighboring hill, while another small hermitage crowns a smaller hill called Calvary. The ruins of the ancient convent of Saint Francis de Paul are two miles away. The mountains of the Sierra Nevada form a backdrop to the scene.

In spite of all the ostentatious trappings of Roman Catholicism that surround the village, its inhabitants are not entirely disconnected from their ancestors' pagan past. The festival of Saint John's Day, which replaced more ancient celebrations associated with the summer solstice, is still tainted by paganism and primitive naturalism; the whole population moves out-of-doors, moving among little tables laden with confections and booths selling dolls and toys. The village clubhouse is thoroughly secularized; men go there to read newspapers, play cards and chess, and to watch cockfights, while wine-buyers from Xeres strike deals there. It is in the clubhouse that Luis confronts the count of Genazahar, beating him at cards and then wounding him in a duel.

Pepita's house. Home of the young widow Pepita Jiménez; a fine house situated in a small estate that became prosperous due to the exceptional thriftiness of Pepita's uncle and her late husband, the petty capitalist Don Gumersindo. The house is in two parts, each with its own door. The door of the "dwelling-house" opens into the paved and colonnaded courtyard, giving access to the parlors and other family apartments, while the door of the "farmhouse" opens to inner yards, giving access to the stable and coach house, the kitchens, the mill, the wine press, the granaries, the storerooms and wine cellars.

The dwelling-house is very clean, modestly furnished, and filled with houseplants and caged canaries. At the beginning of the story the main room has a small altar bearing a carved image of the infant Jesus, about which a great many wax tapers are always burning. Pepita, who regularly entertains the local doctor and notary, as well as the vicar, hosts a social occasion at the Feast of the Cross, involving a solemn ceremonial dance.

Pepita's personal retreat is a "study" or "library" on the upper floor, adjacent to her bedroom. It has a mahogany bookcase and table as well as a writing desk set on a smaller table; its walls are adorned with religious engravings. It is there that Pepita's crucial confrontations with Don Pedro and Luis take place. After their triumph over convention, the room in which Pepita and Luis first meet is transformed into a "temple" with a portico and white marble columns; it contains two sumptuous pictures, one representing Psyche's discovery of Cupid, the other a scene from the ancient Greek Longus's pastoral romance *Daphnis and Chloë* (which Valera translated into Spanish), but pride of place is given to a copy of the Venus of Medici, with an inscription taken from the Epicurean poet Lucretius.

Pepita's garden is a tract of land at the foot of a waterfall in a sheltered ravine, where Pepita cultivates strawberries, vegetables, tomatoes, potatoes, beans, peppers, walnuts, and figs. She hosts a seductive banquet there.

Don Pedro's villa. House on the bank of the Pozo de la Solana, two leagues away from the village, which is approached by a bridle path. The sight of Pepita on horseback on the way to the villa inspires Luis with a strong desire to learn to ride.

— *Brian Stableford*

PÈRE GORIOT

Author: Honoré de Balzac (1799-1850)
Type of work: Novel
Type of plot: Realism

Time of plot: c. 1819
First published: Le Père Goriot, 1834-1835 (English translation, 1860)

Because Honoré de Balzac believed that place influences the personality of his characters, he chose Paris as the setting for his hero's social and psychological education.

Maison Vauquer (MAY-sohn voh-KAY). Run-down boardinghouse (*pension*) in the Latin Quarter area of Paris. The house's parlor with its ugly decor, the dining room with its sticky furniture, and the kitchen with its nauseating smells, as well as wretched bedrooms, constitute a perfect example of bad taste and squalor. In fact, the entire house, which long ago saw better days, reflects the current low socioeconomic status of both its owner, Madame Vauquer, and its tenants. It is no wonder, therefore, that most of its boarders hope to escape to better lodgings, starting with the poor law student Eugène de Rastignac, who resolutely sets out on his climb up the ladder. Only the archcriminal Monsieur Vautrin prefers to live in such an environment, so he can better hide from the police.

The maison is the novel's main focal point, since all the principal characters live there and have links to the highest reaches of financial and aristocratic society, through family or love connections. Their paths thus crisscross each other in a complex, but plausible, pattern.

Hôtel de Beauséant (oh-TEL deh BOH-say-ant). Elegant mansion in Paris's upper-class Faubourg Saint-Germain des Prés district. As the home of one of the noblest families in France, this fashionable residence is the setting of brilliant balls. This explains why the nouveau riche Delphine de Nucingen, who was born a commoner, would go to any lengths to receive an invitation to at least one exclusive and sumptuous reception, including becoming the mistress of Eugène, a distant cousin of Madame de Beauséant.

Restaud home (ray-STOHD). House in the solidly bourgeois Chaussée d'Antin neighborhood. Although it does not have the cachet of the Beauséants', it is still fancy enough to embolden its staff to snicker at an ill-dressed Eugène, who comes calling on Countess de Restaud, for arriving on foot instead of in a carriage.

Eugène's apartment. Bachelor home of Eugène de Rastignac, the young law student, in another part of the Chaussée d'Antin. Paid for by Delphine's father, the financially strapped Père Goriot, this exquisitely decorated place is to serve as the lovers' nest and also as Goriot's refuge in a quasi-incestuous relationship. Furthermore, in so willingly accepting such a generous gift, Eugène shows that he is in the process of implementing lessons he has learned from Vautrin and his cousin.

***Père-Lachaise** (la-SHAYZ). Famous cemetery in eastern Paris. Completely abandoned by his two daughters and their rich husbands, the destitute Goriot is buried here by an equally penniless Eugène. From the heights where the cemetery is located, the young hero sees in the distance the column in the center of Place Vendôme and the golden dome of the Invalides. These two famous landmarks symbolize for him the topographic limits of a world of wealth and privilege, which he defiantly and grandiosely challenges.

***Théâtre-Italien.** Paris opera house, also called Italiens and Bouffons, located on the rue de Louvois. In their desire to see and be seen, members of high society feel the need to attend the opera; this is true as well for other select theaters. Indeed, it is at the Italiens that Eugène, escorting Madame de Beauséant, first sets eyes on Delphine and is encouraged by his cousin actively to pursue her, rather than the prettier—but unwinnable—Madame de Restaud. Vautrin, in contrast, takes Madame Vauquer to the Gaîté, a theater specializing in lowbrow entertainments.

***Paris.** France's capital city is often compared to the American wilderness, to a jungle, to a battlefield, and to a mudhole. Through cunning, strength, and moral accommodation, however, ambitious men and women may not only survive but actually emerge victorious.

— *Pierre L. Horn*

PERICLES, PRINCE OF TYRE

Author: William Shakespeare (1564-1616)
Type of work: Drama
Type of plot: Historical fantasy

Time of plot: Fifth century C.E.
First performed: c. 1607-1608; first published, 1609

Pericles leaves his blighted homeland, shipwrecks, and becomes a favorite at the foreign court of King Simonides at Pentapolis. He gains a wife and daughter but loses them during the return trip home. When he comes back years later, he regains the wife and daughter, who have become important spiritual icons in Ephesus and Mitelene.

*Tyre. Eastern Mediterranean port city that arose as the center of the Phoenician trading empire in ancient times and afterward remained an important trading port. Located in what is now southern Lebanon. The homeland of Prince Pericles.

*Antioch (AN-tee-ahk). Ancient city in Asia Minor and the capital of William Shakespeare's King Antiochus in this play. Antioch and other cities, such as Tharsus and Tyre, are lands of treachery and blight. To avoid being murdered, Pericles flees Antioch, land of the incestuous Antiochus and his daughter, and hides briefly in Tharsus before taking ship again. Pericles later leaves his daughter in Tharsus, in the care of Cleon and his wife, Dionyza, while he returns to rule in Antioch and Tyre after the deaths of the sinful king and daughter. Years later, Dionyza plots against Pericles's daughter, Marina, who escapes to Miteline.

Pentapolis. Kingdom ruled by Simonides known as a land of opportunity and ethical judgment. Pericles shipwrecks there, wins a contest for the hand of the king's daughter, Thaisa, and marries her. They leave the land after it is revealed that Pericles is the rightful ruler of Tyre and must return home.

*Ephesus (EHF-ah-suhs). Ancient city in Asia Minor that is home to the Temple of Diana. After Thaisa dies in childbirth while traveling to Tyre, her body washes ashore at Ephesus. There, Lord Cerimon restores her to life and places her as a nun at the Temple of Diana. The play's concluding reunion scene takes place at Diana's Temple.

— *Scott D. Vander Ploeg*

THE PERSIANS

Author: Aeschylus (525/524-456/455 B.C.E.)
Type of work: Drama
Type of plot: Tragedy

Time of plot: 480 B.C.E.
First performed: Persai, 472 B.C.E. (English translation, 1777)

The setting of this play, in Persia's Susa at the temple of Xerxes I and the tomb of his father and the former king, Darius the Great, is significant. The only extant Greek tragedy based on a contemporary event, the play glorifies Athens's part in the Greek defeat of forces under Xerxes at Salamis.

*Athens. Powerful city-state of ancient Greece and capital of Attica, a province of east-central Greece. Athenian forces were prominent in defeating the Persians at Salamis and in other battles in a fifteen-year war.

*Persia. Country in western Asia that is now known as Iran. At the time of the play, Persia controlled a vast empire extending from India through Asia Minor to the Aegean Sea, solidified by Cyrus the Great and sustained by his son Darius, who ruled until 529 B.C.E.

*Susa. Capital of the Persian Empire in which the play is set. Darius built the city on an ancient fertile tract on the lower Tigris and Euphrates Rivers, a site now south of Dezfūl in southwestern Iran. The ancient city had a strongly fortified citadel containing the treasury and the palace, consisting of self-contained units with successive rooms opening onto central courts. The city's ruins were discovered in the nineteenth century. Xerxes' father Darius, probably buried in Susa, had sought to reclaim a portion of his empire by invading Greece in 490 B.C.E. but was defeated by Athenian forces. Ten years later, Xerxes invaded Greece only to be defeated and forced to retreat, thus liberating Greek cities in Asia Minor. Queen Atossa, Xerxes' mother, and a chorus of elders mourn her son's defeat on his return.

*Salamis. Island off the coast of Attica in east-central Greece, whose capital was the city-state of Athens. The Bay of Salamis was the scene of the Greek naval victory over the Persian fleet in 490 B.C.E.

— *Christian H. Moe*

PERSUASION

Author: Jane Austen (1775-1817)
Type of work: Novel
Type of plot: Domestic realism

Time of plot: Early nineteenth century
First published: 1818

In her last completed novel Austen tells a story of love lost and redeemed, while contemplating an England caught in the throes of social change. That change is symbolized by contrasts between Kellynch Hall, the ancestral home of Anne Elliot's family, and the neighboring estate Uppercross, as well as the "artificial" social world of Bath and the natural beauty of Lyme.

Kellynch. Elliot family estate in southwestern England's Somersetshire, where the novel opens, with the spendthrift baronet Sir Walter Elliot reading the "Elliot of Kellynch-Hall" entry in a list of baronets. Jane Austen rarely describes buildings in any physical detail and devotes scarcely a single word to Kellynch Hall itself. The house can, however, be imagined to be a fairly impressive structure, probably a manor house dating back to the seventeenth century, as the Elliots are an "ancient and respectable family.")

During Austen's lifetime, the country gentry—prosperous landowners living on estates similar to Kellynch and serving as local landlords and civil magistrates—constituted the backbone of English society. However, Sir Walter, selfish, shallow, hopelessly vain, and near financial ruin, is forced by his circumstances to rent out Kellynch Hall and move to less expensive quarters in Bath. In so doing, he forsakes his social responsibilities as manor lord, leaves his tenants to fend for themselves, and makes of Kellynch Hall and its "deserted grounds" a kind of socially purposeless derelict that his daughter Anne can only think of in pain.

Uppercross. Musgrove family estate, located three miles from Kellynch Hall. It includes both the Great House that is the home of the elder Musgroves and their

daughters, Henrietta and Louisa, and Uppercross Cottage, the home of Anne's sister Mary and her husband, Charles Musgrove. The senior Mr. Musgrove is very much an English squire in the traditional sense—one of which Austen approves. His estate is well managed, prosperous, and generally happy. At the same time, however, Uppercross is in the midst of ongoing renovation. Uppercross Cottage ("elevated" from a farmhouse) now sports a "veranda, French windows, and other features. Even the Great House's old-fashioned parlor has been modernized to such an extent by Henrietta and Louisa that its paintings of Musgrove ancestors seem "to be staring in astonishment." Austen, a social conservative in most ways, nevertheless recognizes that change, when undertaken within reasonable limits, is both a necessary and a healthy process. The Musgroves change, and their estate thrives; Sir Walter does not, and Kellynch is left barren.

*Lyme. Dorset town on the southern coast of England, some twenty miles from Uppercross. Well known as a seaside resort and for its Cobb, a massive stone breakwater enclosing its small harbor, Lyme becomes the temporary home of Captain Harville and his family. When Anne visits Lyme, she is impressed both with the natural beauty of the surrounding countryside and with the "picture of repose and domestic happiness" within the Harville's small house—a telling contrast with the cold, vacant grandeur of Kellynch Hall.

One of the novel's key events occurs on a walking tour in Lyme, when Louisa Musgrove is badly injured in a fall from the Cobb. Significantly, Austen's descriptions of the local landscapes in this section of the novel, with an emphasis on "high grounds" and "dark cliffs," are among her richest and most deeply felt, suggesting an imaginative identification with nature that would seem to connect her with her literary contemporaries, the Romantic poets. Certainly, Anne's appreciative response to Lyme's natural beauty points to her own reawakening after eight years of heartbreak and emotional dormancy—a reawakening outwardly symbolized by her renewed "bloom."

*Bath. Early nineteenth century England's premier resort town, located near Bristol, about fifty miles from Kellynch Hall. Named after its famous hot springs, which are supposed to have curative powers, Bath is fashionably elegant and offers a lively social agenda, including theatrical performances, concerts, dances, and the Pump Room, in which visitors can drink its famous water.

Bath was attractive to most classes of English society, but Anne's impoverished friend Mrs. Smith can only afford to live in Bath in a humble way, "almost excluded from society." Anne herself, however, sincerely dislikes Bath, as did Austen (who is said to have fainted when she found that her family was to move there in 1801). She finds little there but despair: The rain seems unending; the streets are crowded, muddy, and full of mindless clamor; and her snobbish family's evenings are often passed "in the elegant stupidity of private parties." Only the presence of the Crofts (the admiral hopes that "taking the waters" will help his gout) and, later, Wentworth, makes life bearable for her.

— *Michael Stuprich*

PETER IBBETSON

Author: George du Maurier (1834-1896)
Type of work: Novel
Type of plot: Historical

Time of plot: Mid-nineteenth century
First published: 1891

Presented as the autobiography of the title character, this novel combines personal and historical descriptions of nineteenth century Paris and London with the narrator's fantastic dreamworld, which transcends space and time. The two cities and their cultures reflect the duality in the main character and stimulate his romantic view of his childhood and the past.

*Passy (PAH-see). Small community on the western edge of Paris, where Peter Ibbetson spends his childhood. Idealizing his own childhood, George du Maurier created an edenic setting for Peter. Passy is a place of freshness and innocence, filled with beautiful people, music, and flowers such as "roses, nasturtiums and convolvulus, wall-flowers, sweet-pease and carnations," all seeming to be perpetually in bloom. Memories of this childhood home, of idealized family, friends, and school, give Peter a rich inner life which sustains him when his parents die and he moves to England to live with his uncle, Colonel Ibbetson. As an adult, Peter revisits Passy but finds it altered for the worse. The Passy of his youth is the place of his outer life when he is a child and the predominant locale of his inner dream life when he is an adult.

*Paris. Capital of France and the location of many of Peter's boyhood adventures. Through Peter, du Maurier vividly describes the sights, sounds, and scents of old Paris. At times, the novel reads almost like a guide book to Paris, with lists of historical places that Peter and his friends frequent: the Island of St. Louis, the Island of the City, the Pont Neuf, and the winding streets and alleyways that were destroyed when Baron Georges-Eugène

Haussmann undertook the renovation of Paris. Old Paris is further romanticized as Peter's reading of novels colors his vision of the city. Peter, the adult, feels nostalgia for the Paris of his youth when he returns and sees the changes in the city.

***Pentonville.** London suburb in which Peter, the young adult, is an apprentice to an architect. This community represents for Peter the drab, dreary English life of philistinism and respectability. The outward bleakness of the town itself and the people he meets contribute to his growing isolation.

***London.** Capital of Great Britain and the location of Peter's trial and imprisonment. In London, Peter is most isolated, but his prison cell becomes the location of his nightly dreaming so that although he is physically confined, he is mentally liberated.

Magna sed Apta. In Peter's dreamworld, a house based on **Parva sed Apta**, the home of his childhood playmate Mimsey Seraskier, later Mary, Duchess of Towers. If the Seraskiers' house in Passy was "small but fit," this dream house is truly "large but fit." It contains every room that either Peter or Mary has ever seen, allowing them to visit the great museums and theaters of the world. They venture outside and eventually learn to travel through time, seeing the past through their ancestors. This large, expansive house of Peter's inner world sharply contrasts with the physically limited world of the prison cell. Magna sed Apta, located in the dreamworld Passy of Peter's childhood, lets him revisit childhood scenes and watch himself and Mary in their idealized youth. This aspect of the dreamworld expresses the adult's romantic longing for the idealized past and provides a means of recapturing it.

***Mare d'Auteuil** (MAHR do-TUI). Small pond in the Bois de Boulogne, a wooded park, in Passy. Appearing several times during the novel, the pond is associated early on with Peter's childhood happiness, with young lovers, and with dreams. As a young man in England, Peter daydreams about Passy, and has especially fond memories of the Mare d'Auteuil. When he and Mary begin to meet nightly in their dreamworld, the pond is one of the favorite haunts of this young couple. Although in reality the pond, like the rest of Passy, has changed, has become "imperially respectable" with "No more frogs or newts . . . but gold and silver fish in vulgar Napoleonic profusion," the pond of his dreams is ever the pond of his childhood. It is the place he goes when Mary dies, and he believes that he has been left alone on earth and in his dream Mary comes back from the dead to meet him and assure him that they will spend eternity together.

— *Elizabeth A. Hait*

PETER PAN: Or, The Boy Who Wouldn't Grow Up

Author: Sir James M. Barrie (1860-1937)
Type of work: Drama
Type of plot: Fairy tale

Time of plot: Late nineteenth century
First performed: 1904; first published, 1928; first published as novel, *Peter and Wendy*, 1911

This play about a boy who refuses to grow up uses a whimsical version of London's Bloomsbury district as a staging point for the flight of young English children to an even more fantastic Never Land.

***Bloomsbury.** Fashionable district of London. James Barrie lived in Bloomsbury before achieving financial success, which is perhaps his reason for locating the home of the Darling family in a somewhat run-down section of the district. One of the place's fantastic touches is the family's Newfoundland dog, which acts as the children's nurse.

Never Land. Fantastical island home of Peter Pan and other parentless boys that the Darling children glimpse during the moment before they fall asleep. Thus, it is not a dream, but a physical analogue of the state between waking and sleeping, a condition when vivid fantasies can be shaped to fit one's wishes. Barrie describes Never Land as a compact place for adventures, with wild Red Indians in the woods, mermaids in the lagoon, and pirates in the river. Because Never Land also condenses Earth's seasons, the river is frozen in winter (appropriate to its evil inhabitants), while the lagoon and forest remain in summer.

Among the land's inhabitants are fairies, seen as a series of lights projected on the stage; lost boys, who fell from their mothers' perambulators as babies and were taken to Never Land by the fairies; and an assortment of animals, including a musical ostrich and a crocodile with a loudly ticking clock in its stomach.

Since the games of real children in London's Kensington inspired the drama, Barrie writes that Peter first lived with the fairies there before they took him to Never Land. Indeed, Never Land itself combines the comfort and beauty of that park with characters and sites from the adventures the real children imagined they were having while in the Gardens. In Never Land, the lost boys' cavern, with seven hollow trees as entrances, is a place of eternal play, threatened by Captain Hook, who in early drafts of the drama appears as a schoolmaster.

— *James Whitlark*

PHAEDRA

Author: Jean Baptiste Racine (1639-1699)
Type of work: Drama
Type of plot: Tragedy

Time of plot: Antiquity
First performed: Phèdre, 1677; first published, 1677
  (English translation, 1701)

In this comparatively modern version of a Greek tragedy, oppressive family histories enacted in various regions converge on an Athenian kingdom, destroying its order through illicit passions.

***Troezen** (TREE-zun). Greek town in the Peloponnesus, on the Saronic Gulf, opposite Athens, that is the birthplace of Theseus, king of Athens, as well as his son Hippolytus's childhood home. Troezen is a "gentle province" removed from "the blaze of Athens's brawling protocol." However, Hippolytus's return to Troezen to live under the same roof as Phaedra during Theseus's absence makes the province seethe with forbidden desires.

*Athens.** Theseus's seat of government. Before Theseus's reign, Athens's subordination to Crete required an annual tribute of fourteen young people to be devoured by the Cretan Minotaur.

*Crete** (kreet). Fifth largest island in the Mediterranean Sea, located southeast of the Greek mainland. There, in a mazelike labyrinth at Knossos, lives the Minotaur, the creature born from Queen Pasiphaë's coupling with a white bull that the sea god Poseidon gave to her husband, King Minos. Theseus killed the Minotaur

with the help of Princess Ariadne, then married her sister Phaedra. Phaedra's Cretan origins establish not only her foreignness in Athens—in contrast to Princess Aricia's pure Athenian blood—but also her heritage of monstrous passion, embodied at play's end in the bull-dragon from the sea that kills Hippolytus.

*Scythia** (SIHTH-ee-ah). Area in southeastern Europe, around the region northeast of the Black Sea in what is now Moldava, Ukraine, and western Russia. The Greeks considered the Scythians and their Amazon neighbors, a female warrior society, barbarians. Hippolytus, as the son of Antiope, an Amazon whom Theseus carried off to Athens, is both an illegitimate heir and a despised alien.

*Naxos.** Largest and most fertile of Greece's Cyclades Islands, almost at the center of the Aegean Sea. There, Theseus abandons Ariadne before kidnapping Antiope and marrying Phaedra.

— *Margaret Bozenna Goscilo*

PHILOCTETES

Author: Sophocles (c. 496-406 B.C.E.)
Type of work: Drama
Type of plot: Tragedy

Time of plot: Antiquity
First performed: *Philoktētēs*, 409 B.C.E.

Sophocles' penultimate play is about the Greek soldier and master archer Philoctetes, whom Odysseus abandons on an island to nurse a wound from a snake bite. The island setting intensifies Philoctetes' feelings of loneliness and desire for companionship.

*Lemnos.** Barren volcanic island in the north Aegean Sea, across from Troy. There, Odysseus abandons Philoctetes after the Greek warrior is bitten on the foot by a snake while preparing to make a sacrifice at the shrine on the island of Chrysa. Philoctetes' wound never heals, and the smell it emits and Philoctetes' groans are the reasons Odysseus gives for making him an outcast. The play makes Lemnos appear to be far more isolated from the Greek world than the real Lemnos actually was. The island's exaggerated isolation strengthens the play's theme of the difficulty of human survival in nature: Philoctetes lives alone in a cave, a place that reinforces his isolation yet provides him with shelter and some comfort. There, birds and animals constitute his only companions.

When Odysseus returns to Lemnos, he describes the cave in which Philoctetes has been living. Neoptolemus identifies it by the stained bandages he finds drying in the sun, the leaf-stuffed mattress, and a crude wooden cup.

*Euboea.** Long, narrow island along the eastern coast of Greece where Chalcedon ruled and to which Philoctetes begs to be taken. The river Spercheius was opposite the island on the Greek mainland. Trachis is a small coastal town across from Euboea near Oeta, a mountain near the coast in the region of Malis. Philoctetes describes the island and its surrounding terrain to show how deeply he yearns to return to civilization.

*Pactolus.** River in ancient Lydia (in west central Asia Minor, now Turkey) once famous for the gold found in its sands, a source of wealth for the Lydian kings, mentioned by the Chorus as a place of sustenance.

— *Ginger Jones*

PHINEAS FINN: The Irish Member

Author: Anthony Trollope (1815-1882)
Type of work: Novel
Type of plot: Political realism

Time of plot: Mid-nineteenth century
First published: serial, 1867-1869; book, 1869

Access to various places, particularly in London, underscores Phineas Finn's social and political successes and failures in this novel, whose social dynamic is inextricably linked to the political, everywhere Phineas goes. Ultimately, however, access to the political and social heights Phineas seeks requires compromising his principles, which he cannot do. Even though he leaves them, the places in which he has been glow in his memory.

*London.** Great Britain's capital city encompasses the world that the personable young Irishman with political aspirations, Phineas Finn, is trying to reach, as well as the world he is trying to leave. While the characters inhabiting this novel's London are fictional, the novel's places are either real or based on real places. Even though he is a new member of Parliament, Phineas continues to live as he had as a barrister in training, in lodgings in London's Great Marlborough Street and as a member of the Reform Club. As his career advances, he eventually moves to a more fashionable street and joins Brooks' Club, both of which better suit his rising political and social profile.

London's House of Commons and Foreign Office are the world to which Phineas strives. Both government centers are initially forbidding to him, but as his career develops, they become comfortable to him. His experience on a parliamentary committee investigating tinned beans represents how the time of effective politicians can be wasted. However, his time in the Foreign Office shows how budding politicians can be useful when he investigates a shipping question in Canada. Ultimately, he performs his greatest political act in the House, when he votes his conscience by supporting a bill that the rest of his party opposes. His support exiles him from both places, but permits him to leave believing in the importance of his principles.

The private London homes among which Finn circulates offer political and social opportunity. The Portman Square home of Whig cabinet member Lord Brentford, for example, represents the political and titled social establishment, to which Phineas is introduced by Lady Laura Standish, Brentford's daughter. There Phineas meets the other cabinet members and rising Whig politicians. One evening, while departing from the Brentford home with Mr. Kennedy, Finn rescues Mr. Kennedy from an assassination attempt in Park Street, thereby securing his future political success. A small home on Park Lane, the exclusive street overlooking Hyde Park, belongs to the wealthy and well-connected widow Madame Max Goesler. The welcome he receives to her home represents the intimacy which Phineas has achieved within the highest political and social circles.

Loughlinter (LAKH-len-ter). Scottish estate of the wealthy member of Parliament Mr. Kennedy, to which Phineas is invited for a political retreat that the Whig party disguises as a leisure trip to the Scottish Highlands. Loughlinter is first presented as a beautiful and warm home; however, by the end of the novel it is viewed as a chilly and confined place, mirroring the disintegration of Lady Laura's marriage to Mr. Kennedy. The Kennedy house in Grosvenor Square undergoes a similar but accelerated transformation, as Mr. Kennedy withdraws from political life and expects Lady Laura to do so as well.

Loughlinter represents both the social and political spheres into which Phineas is advancing, for he is spending his leisure as the traditional country gentry do and he is socializing with the major party figures. However, it also reveals how social dynamics reflect the political undercurrents. Lady Laura declines Phineas's marriage proposal so that she can marry Mr. Kennedy, through whom she believes she will have greater political influence. Phineas then hides his disappointment so he will not jeopardize his standing with the party leadership.

Loughshane (LAKH-shayn). Phineas's borough in County Clare, Ireland, where he is elected to his first and final terms in the British House of Commons. Loughshane is undistinguished in its own right but provides Phineas with a place from which to stand for political office and a place to return to when that office no longer exists. As a result of the Irish Reform Bill, which Phineas supports against the majority of his party, Loughshane is absorbed into another district. This eliminates his seat in Parliament—and thus another term in office—and prompts him to return home to marry his local sweetheart.

***Loughton** (LAKH-ton). Pocket borough of Lord Brentford, located in Essex in southern England. At the time in which *Phineas Finn* is set, Loughton was still a rural area, although it was becoming more commercialized as a suburb of London. On Lady Laura's recommendation, her father gives the borough to Phineas so he can be elected to a second term in Parliament. Because Finn is the recipient, it represents the favor Finn has won among the political establishment. It also represents the way pocket boroughs are dispensed without regard for a candidate's actual views, so long as he has (and maintains) the favor of the peers who control them.

— *Clare Callaghan*

PHINEAS REDUX

Author: Anthony Trollope (1815-1882)
Type of work: Novel
Type of plot: Political

Time of plot: Mid-nineteenth century
First published: serial, 1873-1874; book, 1874

Like Phineas Finn, *to which this novel is a sequel,* Phineas Redux *is set mostly in London. Whereas the first novel shows how Phineas became accepted into the British social and political world that he idealized, this sequel shows his disillusionment with it. The people and places that welcome Phineas without question ultimately prove themselves to be unreliable, shattering Phineas's faith in the world. What glow his memory has awarded to parliamentary life dissipates as Phineas realizes the superficiality and opportunism inherent in politics.*

*London. Unlike the British capital city of *Phineas Finn*, this London is focused in a political and legal sphere. Phineas seeks to return to the House of Commons, and he joins the Universe Club as part of reestablishing his ties with fellow Whigs. Not all the members are his friends, though, and one evening a political rival is murdered just outside the club. An eyewitness, also a club member, claims to have seen Phineas committing the crime. Phineas is arrested, imprisoned in Newgate, and tried in the Old Bailey. Most of his former friends expect he is guilty, and do little to support him through this experience.

This mirrors the assassination attempt upon Mr. Kennedy in *Phineas Finn* which Phineas foiled. Where that was followed by political acceptance and success in the House, Bonteen's murder is followed by rejection and disillusionment in Newgate and the Old Bailey. The shift of place reflects the shift of fortune; being on trial in the Old Bailey is an inversion of making a speech in the House of Commons. The public galleries in the Old Bailey are filled with morbidly curious crowds that Phineas does not know. The galleries in the House were rarely filled except by an onlooker with a compelling interest.

Ultimately, Finn is proven innocent by evidence that Madame Marie Max Goesler obtains in Prague. His subsequent popularity prompts his party to offer him his old position (*Phineas Finn*) in the Foreign Office, a post he declines because of the party's opportunism and disloyalty.

Harrington Hall. Home in which Lord Chiltern and Violet live now that they are married. Chiltern is Master of the Brake Hounds, gainfully employed in a position that suits his character and principles. Chiltern and Vio-let establish an ideal domesticity at the Hall. They are active in their family pursuits, welcoming and loyal to their friends, and disinterested in pursuits outside their domestic sphere. Chiltern's outrage over dead foxes in a nearby woods, which are under the control of a cabinet member's uncle, is the closest political matter to the Harrington Hall residents. Encountering Madame Max there, outside the usual London political circles, enables Phineas to see her in a nonpoliticized setting and therefore as free from the perverted values of political life.

Loughlinter (LAKH-len-ter). Scottish estate of the wealthy parliamentarian Mr. Kennedy. Initially a beautiful and warm home in *Phineas Finn*, Loughlinter is now changed into a solitary and drab refuge in which Kennedy sequesters himself as he declines into madness and religious obsession. When Phineas goes there on Kennedy's request, he is struck by Loughlinter's air of desolation and neglect. Similarly, **Macpherson's Hotel**, in which Kennedy stays when he visits London to confront Phineas, is also a forlorn and isolated place. Both places reflect Kennedy's increasing mental illness and dourness.

*Dresden. East-central German city in which Lady Laura and her father live in self-imposed exile after she separates from Kennedy. Like Loughlinter, their home in Dresden is chilly and cold, and dramatic changes come over both Lady Laura and her father while living there. Both lose their vivacity, chilled in their souls as much as in their home. Their return to Portman Square in London after Lady Laura is widowed does not restore them.

Tankerville. Borough in which Finn campaigns to recapture a seat in Parliament after his Irish borough loses its seat. Although the borough's vote initially goes against him, he disputes its results on the grounds that his corrupt conservative opponent, Browborough, has bought votes. This development represents the shift from the old style of "pocket boroughs" to a theoretically more independent electorate. Although there are cries for him to resign, Phineas holds this seat while he is being tried for bigamy. He resigns the seat after he is acquitted, but the borough's voters proudly reelect him, demonstrating on a borough level the sentiments of other political friends, who distance themselves from him during troubled times and claim him during good times.

— *Clare Callaghan*

PICKWICK PAPERS

Author: Charles Dickens (1812-1870)
Type of work: Novel
Type of plot: Social realism

Time of plot: 1827-1828
First published: serial, 1836-1837; book, 1837

This novel is a comic whirlwind of picaresque episodes and colorful characters and diverse locations that tie them together. The Pickwickian journeys, primarily by coach, offer vivid portraits of country and city life in pre-Victorian England. Dickens's use of setting and travel provides a sentimental and somewhat idealistic version of a past that belongs not only to England but to Dickens as well. Thus, the novel is both a historical representation and an imaginative creation, a testament to Dickens's powers of verisimilitude. Mr. Pickwick's convoluted travels represent his personal odyssey of spiritual growth, from harmless pomposity and self-absorption to humility and sincere concern for the welfare of others less fortunate than himself.

*London.** Great Britain's capital city is the headquarters of the Pickwick Club. Dickens's acute sense of place enhances his descriptions of the great city, particularly the labyrinthine streets and lanes and inns—such as the **White Hart Inn**, where Sam Weller first appears and identifies the unscrupulous rogue Alfred Jingle. The various characters' lodgings, such as Mr. Pickwick's rooms at Mrs. Bardell's, Mr. Weller, Sr.'s domicile in Dorking, and the rooms of Bob Sawyer, highlight class distinctions.

*Fleet Street Prison.** London institution in which Mr. Pickwick is incarcerated after losing a trumped-up breach of promise suit to Mrs. Bardell. The prison scenes contribute to the thematic concerns of spurious litigation and social abuses and highlight Dickens's own remembered horror and shame over the period in his youth when his father was imprisoned for debt.

As Mr. Pickwick travels about and attempts to uphold the law and bring justice to all those who deserve it, he is manipulated into a legal situation from which his pride will not permit him to extract himself. It is only in the depths of the Fleet, where his kindness and sympathy know no bounds, that Mr. Pickwick is able to put aside his pride and set himself free in order to save Sam Weller and Mrs. Bardell, who have joined him there. The suggestion is clear: The welfare of others is easily considered when one's own will is being fulfilled, but only deep in the prison of the ego, where one is compelled to act out of concern for others at the expense of pride, can altruism and compassion be realized.

*Dingley Dell.** Country location of Mr. Wardle's **Manor Farm**, which nurtures the comic romances that pervade the novel. "Who could live to gaze from day to day on bricks and slates, who had once felt the influence of a scene like this?" asks Mr. Pickwick on his first morning at the farm. The natural world of the country stands in innocent contrast to the fallen world of the cities, particularly London and Birmingham. Though tainted at times and thrown into confusion by the machinations of city types like Jingle or even local politicians and newspapermen, the country and small towns possess a resiliency that restores them from apparent hurts and assaults from the fallen world. When the Pickwick Club is officially disbanded, it is noteworthy that Mr. Pickwick settles in Dulwich, a town near London that possesses the trappings of country living.

Bath. Resort city in western England, noted for its hot springs, to which the Pickwickians repair after Mr. Pickwick is convicted of breach of promise. The sojourn at Bath promotes the romance between Mr. Winkle and Arabella Allen, but the health spa is not beyond the reach of the city law courts, as Mr. Pickwick's retreat is broken by a subpoena calling him back to London for refusing to pay damages to Mrs. Bardell. Bath, like Ipswich and Bury St. Edmonds, functions to remind the reader of the discrepancy between appearances and reality. Jingle is found lurking in Bury St. Edmonds, and he is foiled in Ipswich.

Rochester. Town southeast of London that is the first destination of the Pickwick Club, whose journey begins with Alfred Jingle's insinuating his way into the company, foreshadowing the conflict between idyllic intentions and chaotic circumstances that marks the comic nature of the novel. In this first journey Dickens demonstrates his skills at using travel and destination as devices to advance and complicate the plot, a technique he would employ throughout his literary career.

— *Erskine Carter*

THE PICTURE OF DORIAN GRAY

Author: Oscar Wilde (1854-1900)
Type of work: Novel
Type of plot: Fantasy

Time of plot: Late nineteenth century
First published: serial, 1890; book, 1891

While most of the English settings in this novel have a sketchy existence, a more detailed psychological analysis is applicable to the house where the eternally young Dorian cultivates a fantasy lifestyle, inspired by his reading of a French novel, unnamed in the text but subsequently identified by Oscar Wilde as Joris-Karl Huysmans's À rebours *(1884; Against the Grain, 1922).*

Mayfair. Richest district of London, lying to the east of Hyde Park, bounded on the north by Oxford Street and on the south by Piccadilly. Most of the significant locations featured in the novel are situated there. The exact location of Lord Henry Wotton's house, with its oak-paneled library, furnished with Persian rugs, is left unspecified, but his uncle, Lord Fermor, lives in Berkeley Square, one of the most imposing addresses in London, and is a member of one of the most exclusive gentlemen's clubs, the Albany. Even Alan Campbell, the chemistry expert blackmailed by Dorian into disposing of Basil Hallward's body, lives in Mayfair, although Hertford Street is one of the least prepossessing thoroughfares in the district.

Dorian's own town house, inherited from his grandfather, Lord Kelso, is situated in the other famous Mayfair square, Grosvenor Square. It is here that a study in contrasts is developed between the room in which Dorian hides the portrait, his old schoolroom, located at the very top of the house, and the rooms that he furnishes in an

extraordinarily lavish fashion with all manner of tapestries, textiles, embroideries, and ecclesiastical vestments.

Schoolroom. Symbolizing Dorian's lost innocence, the schoolroom is furnished with a satinwood bookcase, a Flemish tapestry featuring two monarchs playing chess while falconers hover nearby, and a *cassone*, a large Italian trunk with a hinged lid, which features painted panels and gilt moldings. Dorian used to use this *cassone* as a hiding place when he was a child. The remainder of the house undergoes a remarkable transformation as Dorian buries the conventional furnishings handed down by his grandfather in a decorative riot of silks, satins, velvets, and other ultrasoft materials. The obsessively conservative Victorians condemned any tendency to luxury as a sign of moral decadence, prompting radical aesthetes like Oscar Wilde to go to an opposite extreme.

Selby Royal. Site of Dorian's country house. It was standard practice for every nineteenth century family of any real social standing to maintain a town house and a country house, the former being used for "the season," the summer months when all London's key social events took place, while the latter was usually the manor house attached to the family estate. Dorian, like most young aristocrats of his generation, prefers to spend almost all his time in London, but Selby Royal proves a convenient location for the elimination of the vengeful James Vane.

*Euston Road. London street. In the 1880's the streets surrounding Euston Station were a modest residential district, considerably more respectable than the poverty-stricken East End although far inferior to Mayfair. It is not surprising that the working-class Vanes are struggling to pay the rent on their apartment in Euston Road, even though Sibyl is appearing at the Royal Thea-

tre in Holborn. The address signifies that the family is desperately ambitious to move up in the world, which is a significant factor in the frustration that leads Sibyl to suicide.

Basil Hallward's studio. Artist's studio situated in an unnamed suburb of London, conceptually, if not geographically, midway between Grosvenor Square and Selby Royal. Its French windows look out onto a pleasant garden scented in summer by lilac, laburnum, and honeysuckle, but its interior is furnished in a slightly Bohemian style, with sofas and divans. Like the Vanes, Hallward is operating in a social stratum above that in which he was born.

— *Brian Stableford*

PIERRE: Or, The Ambiguities

Author: Herman Melville (1819-1891)
Type of work: Novel
Type of plot: Philosophical

Time of plot: Early nineteenth century
First published: 1852

An abrupt shift of setting in this novel, from an idyllic country location to an abysmal city, epitomizes the stark contrast in its main character's development. The time of Pierre Glendinning's bliss, and ignorance, is embodied in his rural surroundings; his unhappiness, and knowledge, in the urban setting. In this sense, the countryside is his eden, and, after choosing knowledge of his father's secret over ignorance and perpetual happiness, he is exiled to the city, to labor in unhappiness and die in shame. The certainty with which Pierre holds the simple ideas of his pastoral upbringing are challenged by ambiguities that his sister introduces, leading him to a complicated and morally ambiguous life in the city.

Saddle Meadows. Name of both the New York village and the nearby ancestral manor of Pierre Glendinning's family. Herman Melville modeled the estate on his own Arrowhead estate, near Pittsfield, Massachusetts, as well as his Uncle Herman's home at Gansevoort in upstate New York. From the start of the novel, Pierre embodies Saddle Meadows. The grandeur of the countryside is reflected in the physical and spiritual grandeur of this cultivated youth and his heroic lineage. The novel opens with repeated assertions that Pierre is fortunate to have been born and bred in the country; however, he eventually must survive in the city, where his pastoral breeding is of little help.

The residents of the village of Saddle Meadows are a closely knit community; the threat of scandal to the

Glendinning name is made that much more damning because of this. In the early nineteenth century, America's Revolutionary War was still within the cultural memory, and its heroes were still linked with the ancestors who bore their names. Because of their ancestry, the Glendinnings hold a place similar to that of feudal lords in the village: They own most of the property and many of the church pews. Their implicit superiority to the townspeople is based upon the respect—and fear—they collect from these people.

After Pierre chooses to learn Isabel's story, Saddle Meadows becomes a fantasyland for him, to be recalled in solitude in the city as an idealized and untouchable dream that no longer can exist in reality. In the city, Pierre's memories of his home tie the second part to the first and make his situation more miserable in comparison. Emphasizing where he comes from, and how ideal his surroundings were, Melville makes Pierre even more tragic and pathetic as a character.

City. Although the name of the city is unspecified in this book, it is clearly based on New York: It is a large coastal city, of hundreds of thousands of people, edged by a large bay. In the first part of the novel, the city is mentioned only briefly as a remote seat of aristocracy that draws away people like Lucy and Pierre's father for portions of the year. After being expelled from Saddle Meadows, Pierre flees to the city, hoping to enjoy these same aristocratic elements through the supposed generosity of his cousin, Glendinning Stanly.

Far from aristocratic, the city which Pierre, Isabel, and Delly encounter is dark and gloomy. Most of the scenes occur either at night or indoors. The night of their arrival foreshadows their entire experience in the city.

They find the sights, the sounds, and the citizens rude and garish. It is an awakening from their original illusion of Saddle Meadows as a microcosm of the world, an illusion that is shattered on their first night in the city when Pierre enters a hotel. The innkeeper, noting Pierre's address in his book, asks whether Saddle Meadows is anywhere in this country. Once the source of Pierre's identity and pride, the name "Saddle Meadows" is shown to be of no worth in his new life in the city.

The city's dismal atmosphere brings about physical changes in both Pierre and Lucy, who lose their bloom after they begin to live there. These two perfect creations of nature, like spring flowers, lose their beauty and vitality when transplanted to the gloom of the city. Because Pierre's beginnings and formation are entirely in the hands of nature, he is unequipped for his unnatural existence in the city.

— *Shalom E. Black*

THE PILGRIM HAWK: A Love Story

Author: Glenway Wescott (1901-1987)
Type of work: Novel
Type of plot: Psychological realism

Time of plot: May, 1929
First published: 1940

This novel's primary setting is the house and garden of Alexandra Henry, in the village of Chancellet, France, and the adjoining small hunting park of an estate. The house and garden alternately symbolize a safe haven and a prison, as love, contentment, jealousy, hatred, and frustration emanate from the human occupants and their visitors' captive pilgrim hawk.

Chancellet (shahnz-ih-LAY). Village near Paris in France. One of the "least changed" villages after World War I, Chancellet lies along the highway from Paris to Orleans and the tourist country of the Loire River. Busy automobile traffic through the village symbolizes the restless and rootless generation of the postwar 1920's, when foreigners' paths often intersected in France or other popular places during their journeys from place to place.

The Cullens, an Irish couple, seeking to escape the unpleasant consequences of their involvement with Irish revolutionaries, are stopping over in Paris during their automobile trip to Hungary, where they have rented a property. They take advantage of their stopover to visit

their American friend, Alexandra Henry, who has a house in the village, a short distance from Paris. They bring along their Irish chauffeur and a pilgrim hawk named Lucy, an unexpected "guest" that Mrs. Cullen is training to hunt.

Alexandra Henry's house. Chancellet home of the American expatriate Alexandra Henry. Located directly on the village street, the house combines two small dwellings and a large horse stable, rebuilt and furnished in a modern style. Alwyn Tower, Alex's houseguest who narrates the story from a vantage point ten years in the future, points out the architect's mistake in placing the dining room and chief guestroom on the street, where all the noise of the highway traffic and frequent close brushes with heavy trucks interfere with dinner conversation and nightly rest.

The house's living room is a converted stable with the hayloft removed, so that the old chestnut rafters stretching thirty feet to the roof give a Gothic feeling to the otherwise modern room. Painted white, with darkened woodwork, the room features a picture window that takes up a third of the wall. The window frames a broad view of the garden and the hunting park that joins it. The house, garden, and park form a triangular setting for the love-hate triangle among Mr. and Mrs. Cullen and the pilgrim hawk. To the hawk, the huge glass window offers an enticing vista of freedom that she cannot explore. To keep the frustrated bird calm, Mrs. Cullen confines it to her leather wriststrap and blinds it with a hood, a device commonly used for hunting birds. She also denies the bird any freedom in the same manner during a stroll in the park.

Mrs. Cullen talks of nothing but hawks the entire afternoon, comparing them to people in the "great madhouse in Dublin." Hawks, she says, whether in the wild or in captivity, become weak and blind as they grow old and eventually give up and die of discouragement at their loss of hunting ability. Mr. Cullen compares his own declining vigor with that of his rival, the hawk, and grows increasingly resentful of his wife's preoccupation with the hawk. He releases the hawk from its perch in the garden, where Mrs. Cullen leaves it while resting. Mrs. Cullen succeeds in recapturing the bird, but the episode is so stressful that the Cullens depart early, without staying for the dinner that Alexandra's servants are preparing for them.

The house's spacious English-style garden features trees, strolling paths, and a water pond but has no formal flowerbeds. In late May, the surface of the pond reflects a muffled blue sky with foamy white clouds. The garden is the setting for another love-hate relationship—that of Jean and Eva, Alexandra's Moroccan servants, who spend their days quarreling and their evening hours in a corner of the garden where plane trees provide a romantic hideaway. The visiting Irish chauffeur flirts with Eva, evoking a jealous tirade from Jean. The garden is filled with peace or turmoil, as it forms the setting for jealous rages or peaceful romantic interludes.

With the departure of the Cullens, their hawk, and chauffeur, the house and garden settle back into an uncertain harmony. The narrator fears that after observing so much turmoil in others' relationships, Alex will never risk marriage herself. However, he later reveals that upon her return to America, Alex meets and marries his brother. Thus, Glenway Wescott makes his point in this brief novel: Though house, garden, and park take on the aura of tension, frustration, and turmoil emanating from the interaction of the occupants, the setting remains an inanimate reservoir for human passions, not a determining force in the inhabitants' behavior.

— *Marguerite R. Plummer*

PILGRIMAGE

Author: Dorothy Richardson (1873-1957)
Type of work: Novels
Type of plot: Bildungsroman
Time of plot: Late nineteenth and early twentieth centuries

First published: 1938: *Pointed Roofs*, 1915; *Backwater*, 1916; *Honeycomb*, 1917; *The Tunnel*, 1919; *Interim*, 1919; *Deadlock*, 1921; *Revolving Lights*, 1923; *The Trap*, 1925; *Oberland*, 1927; *Dawn's Left Hand*, 1931; *Clear Horizon*, 1935; *Dimple Hill*, 1938; *March Moonlight*, 1967

Readers of this series of novels travel with the protagonist, Miriam Henderson, from her early years in England's fictional idyllic Babington through her pilgrimage into middle age, both in and outside England. Throughout the series' thirteen "chapter-volumes," Babington serves as a symbol in Miriam's search for a lost paradise. Many of her moves represent a means of escape from a situation or persons that have become difficult.

Babington. Idyllic English provincial village in which Miriam lives until she is eighteen years old, when her father's bankruptcy forces her to leave in order to earn money to help support her family. She leaves behind a provincial life of safety, her parents, and her three beloved sisters, to seek her fortune in Germany. Dorothy Richardson based the village on Abingdon in England's Berkshire district, where she herself was born.

Hanover. German city to which Miriam goes to work as a governess after her father's bankruptcy. Germany represents such a challenge in language and culture to Miriam that she returns to England after a single year, sadder but wiser, and depressed by her lack of achievement. *Pointed Roofs*, the title of this chapter volume, refers to the pointed roofs of Hanover.

London. Capital of Great Britain that throughout the novel plays the most significant role in shaping Miriam's cultural and psychological life. Miriam first goes there from Germany to become a teacher in the "backwater" of north London (hence, the title of the second chapter-volume, *Backwater*). There she teaches in a school run by three spinster sisters. The name of their school, **Banbury Park**, is an oblique reference to Richardson's own experience of teaching in north London's Finsbury/Barnsbury Park district. Mirroring Richardson's experience there, Miriam is discouraged by the region's mean streets and the harsh, snarling voices of north London residents. Again, a contrast of cultures looms unpleasantly and frustrates Miriam's intellectual aspirations.

Miriam's later experience as a dental assistant on Wimpole Street takes her deeper into the heart of London life for the first time. For her, London represents the large world, contrasted to her former life in Babington. Richardson fills her descriptions of London with the names of real streets and places. Having a well-lighted room of her own on Tansley Street helps liberate her, and she ever feels the presence of London in her own room, as it is brought in with the light. When she pays a

brief visit to Banbury Park to spend Christmas with the family of one of her former students, she feels an urgent need to return to the freedom of her Tansley Street room.

Miriam's later experiences in London include residence in a gloomy flat in Flaxman's Court, where she is close to the slums of St. Pancras but—significant to her own aspirations as a writer—opposite the rooms of the Irish poet William Butler Yeats. Her final residence is at a boardinghouse in St. John's Wood, far from the center of London, where she finally begins her vocation as a writer in earnest.

Wimpole Street. District in London where Miriam works as a dental assistant in *The Tunnel* and *Interim*. This episode, too, mirrors Richardson's real life experience in London's Harley Street—a district famous for its high-class medical professionals. Wimpole Street's literary fame rests on its association with England's literary star, Elizabeth Barrett Browning.

Brighton. Seaside resort in southeast England's East Sussex County, where Miriam vacations with her sisters. While she is there, she strikes out for freedom from teaching long hours in the little north London school. Her stay by the sea recalls childhood memories; while looking out over the cliff edge beyond Dawlish, she determines to make another change.

Newlands. Town far from London where Miriam takes another governess position with a wealthy family. There she experiences a "Vanity Fair"-like life. The spectacle and pageantry of Newlands life is finally closed, and her real life begins.

Oberland. Fictional Swiss village whose very name (meaning "over land") symbolizes a new height in Miriam's long pilgrimage. Richardson adapted the name from that of the real Adelboden in the Swiss Alps.

Dimple Hill. Quaker farm in the quiet countryside of Sussex, where Miriam rests from her journeys. Richardson based it on Windmill Hill in the East Sussex downs, where she herself had once spent time recuperating.

— *Esther K. Labovitz*

THE PILGRIM'S PROGRESS

Author: John Bunyan (1628-1688)
Type of work: Novel
Type of plot: Allegory

Time of plot: Any time since Christ
First published: part 1, 1678; part 2, 1684

In both parts of this novel, characters set forth on a road that leads toward a city. John Bunyan describes the hills, valleys, and houses his characters pass so well that many have been identified as actual places in his native Bedfordshire district of England. However, like the novel's characters, these places represent realities or temptations in the life of the spirit. Bunyan's travelers are Christians, and their road is the road of life. The novel is meant to warn them of the spiritual dangers they will encounter and to point out the aid that God has provided for them as they move through the years toward their goal: admission into the city of Heaven.

Den. Place where the narrator lies down and begins to dream the story of Christian at the beginning of part 1. Bunyan was undoubtedly remembering the jail on Bedford Bridge where he was confined for preaching illegally, thus putting his religious convictions ahead of his family responsibilities, just as Christian does when he leaves his wife and children behind.

City of Destruction. Christian's home until he becomes convinced that because they have not accepted Christ, all the residents of the city are damned. When he leaves the city in part 1, his wife refuses to follow him. However, after having a change of heart in part 2, she and her four sons take the same road on which Christian has previously traveled.

Slough of Despond (sloo). Bog into which Christian falls, based on the notorious sloughs on the road to Hockley, Bedfordshire. The Slough of Despond symbolizes the paralyzing depression experienced by pilgrims when they realize that they deserve to be damned for their sins. God sends a spiritual guide named Help to point out the steps that lead out of the Slough of Despond.

***Mount Sinai** (SI-ni). Mountain in the Holy Land identified in the Bible as the place where Moses received the Ten Commandments. In *The Pilgrim's Progress*, Mount Sinai lies near a town named Morality, where Mr. Worldly Wiseman tells Christian that he can learn how to reach Heaven simply by following a set of rules. Thus Bunyan voices his objection to the Church of England, which takes a more formal approach to religion than his highly emotional sect. When Mount Sinai flashes fire, Christian knows that he is being warned away from Morality and returns to the right road.

House of the Interpreter. Way station where both Christian and Christiana receive both hospitality and instruction. This is one of a number of places on their road where Bunyan's travelers are strengthened in body and in spirit. It is significant that his description of this house matches that of the rectory of St. John Baptist in Bedford, where Bunyan himself sought counsel on religious matters from William Gifford, a dissenting minister who lived there for a time.

House Beautiful. Place where both Christian and Christiana are armed both mentally and physically for the difficult road ahead. Bunyan's House Beautiful is clearly a composite of two country houses, Elstow Place and Houghton Manor House, the latter a well-known showplace because of the treasures it contained. By contrast, Bunyan's House Beautiful, while described as equally elegant, is filled only with spiritual gifts.

Valley of Humiliation. Deep valley where Christian is attacked by Apollyon, a satanic figure described in the New Testament's Book of Revelation as dominating the bottomless pit, or Hell. By defeating Apollyon, Christian makes it easier for those who follow, including his own family, to pass down the dangerous road of life. Thus Bunyan stresses how important every triumph over evil is, not just to the individual but to the Christian community as a whole.

Valley of the Shadow of Death. Phrase from the Twenty-third Psalm used by Bunyan to denote another valley through which pilgrims must pass. There, the road becomes a narrow path, punctuated with pits and traps, with a ditch on one side of it, a quagmire on the other, and at one spot, the mouth of Hell yawning beside it. Although Christiana's guide protects her from a lion and a giant, darkness brings the Shadow of Death. As in the psalm, the travelers turn to God for help, and he sends light to deliver them from their fears and show them the way.

Vanity Fair. Never-ending fair at the town of Vanity, probably inspired by England's largest fair, held annually at Stourbridge. Vanity Fair offers every kind of pleasure; it is a place where everything and everyone is for sale. When Christian and his companion Faithful reject the life of pleasure, they are attacked by the ruffians who frequent the fair. Christian escapes, but Faithful is killed. Later, Christiana passes through without difficulty, evidently because the inhabitants are ashamed of their earlier actions.

Doubting Castle. Stronghold of the giant Despair, who seizes Christian and his new companion Hopeful and thrusts them into a dungeon. The giant represents profound depression, which arises out of doubt. Only when Christian remembers that he has a key, God's promise, is he able to unlock the door and escape. When Christiana arrives, the men with her kill the giant and purge the castle of evil. It is thought that Doubting Castle was modeled on Cainhoe Castle, near which Bunyan's ancestors once lived.

Delectable Mountains. Another pleasant stop, where shepherds entertain the pilgrims, show them some of those who have fallen by the wayside, and offer them a distant glimpse of the Celestial City. The Delectable Mountains are clearly modeled on the Chiltern Hills of Bedfordshire.

Enchanted Ground. Beautiful area of comfortable seats and arbors, where tired pilgrims are tempted to stop and slumber. However, Christians who sink into a spiritual torpor there will never reach Heaven.

Land of Beulah (BYOO-lah). Pleasant country where pilgrims can pause before they cross the River Jordan to the Celestial City.

Celestial City. Heaven, where Christians who have successfully completed their journey will spend eternity.

— *Rosemary M. Canfield Reisman*

THE PILLARS OF SOCIETY

Author: Henrik Ibsen (1828-1906)
Type of work: Drama
Type of plot: Psychological realism

Time of plot: Nineteenth century
First performed: 1877; first published, 1880 as
Samfundets støtter (English translation, 1880)

This play illustrates Henrik Ibsen's concern about corruption at the core of small-town societies. Its hero, Karsten Bernick, is revered as a pillar of the seaside community in which he lives, but he is actually morally suspect—an indication that the social and moral norms on which the community is built are corrupt. Ibsen subtly plays off the two meanings of "community"—a physical place and the people who live in that area—to suggest that communities built on falsehoods, like edifices built shoddily with inferior materials, are doomed to failure unless real reforms are instituted.

Bernick's house. Home of Karsten Bernick, the leading citizen of the unnamed coastal Norwegian town in which the play is set. The house is the location for all the onstage action of the play. Its opulence suggests the status of its owner, and the irony of Karsten Bernick's situation is highlighted by the physical surroundings. Unfortunately, his good fortune, both at home and in business, is built on a lie.

Shipyard. Although no action is set in the town's shipyard, the yard dominates the drama because of its significance to both plot and theme. Bernick's profitable shipping business has made him one of the town's leading citizens. As the story unfolds, however, readers learn that Bernick has had to commit crimes, vilify his exiled stepbrother, and use others in his family to preserve his good name and keep his unsavory actions from being discovered. While he struggles to keep his business profitable, he treats workers as commodities, replaceable by more efficient machines—showing repeatedly that he puts his own well-being ahead of the interests of the community he claims to love dearly. Ibsen uses a key incident to vivify his indictment of Bernick: In an effort to please a client, Bernick demands that a ship be repaired and set to sea immediately, even though he knows the work done will be inferior and that the ship may sink.

— *Laurence W. Mazzeno*

PINCHER MARTIN

Author: William Golding (1911-1993)
Type of work: Novel
Type of plot: Psychological realism

Time of plot: World War II
First published: 1956

This novel's title character is a British naval officer thrown into the sea when his destroyer is sunk by torpedoes in the North Atlantic. He finds a form of salvation on a tiny, barren, rocky island in the middle of the ocean.

Atlantic island. Desolate rocky island, perhaps near North Africa, where the naval officer Christopher "Pincher" Martin miraculously washes up after his ship has been sunk by a German torpedo, leaving him alone in the ocean, adrift with only a lifebelt.

William Golding served in Great Britain's Royal Navy during World War II, and the early pages of his novel—in which Martin struggles to stay alive in the ocean—have a gritty realism that could well have been informed by experience. However, when Martin discovers a tiny island where no island should be and manages to clamber ashore, the character of the novel itself subtly changes. The foreground of the novel remains realistic, as Golding describes in minute, moment-by-moment detail Martin's continuing struggle to survive on the island. However, behind this struggle, there is a moral dimension, typical of Golding's work, in which the island becomes an expression of what is going on inside Martin's mind.

Golding describes the island in exact detail, from the coarse shingle on which Martin comes ashore to the rocky tower he must climb in order to escape the tides and the barren place where he must figure out how to live. The island offers Martin no comforts whatever; to sleep he must squeeze his body into a narrow crevice between rocks, to drink he must crawl headfirst under another rocky overhang and sip rainwater from a small pool containing disturbing rod growths. For food, he must scramble upon dangerous cliffs in order to reach unappetizing and insubstantial sea anemones.

If Martin's struggle for simple human survival seems like a turn in Purgatory, the impression is heightened as the novel begins revealing the island as a reflection of the inside of Martin's head. Occasionally, the parallels are explicit, as when Martin "looked solemnly at the line of rocks and found himself thinking of them as teeth." More often, however, connections between Martin's mind and the island are metaphorical. Martin's dreams and illusions appear in an irregular sequence of often brief flashbacks—some lasting no more than a sentence or two—in which figures from his past are seen to emerge from and retreat back into the rock.

This struggle to find reference points for hope and a meaning in life is allegorized by Golding in clear references to the Christian faith. First, Martin's own first name, "Christopher," recalls the legend of the man who bore the Christ child across dangerous waters and who was then given his name, meaning "Christ-bearer." Christopher Martin's failure causes readers to question the simplicity of an understanding of life that merely floats along the surface of experience. The rock that Martin imagines himself as having reached is symbolic of the "rock," or St. Peter, upon which Christ founded his church. Again, the rock, as readers learn at the end of the novel, is a figment of Martin's imagination and permits the questioning of the foundations of faith.

Most of Martin's hallucinatory episodes take the form of brief exchanges or glimpses of characters; their settings are imprecise—a theater, a bar—if there is any sense of place at all. The only place that is real is the rocky island. The flashbacks illuminate, in glimpses as sudden and unsettling as a strobe lamp, Martin's own character. As he deteriorates physically, losing weight, flesh, physical definition, at an exaggeratedly rapid rate, so his past is presented to him on the stage of the island in vignettes that make him see who and what he was. Only as he completes his moral journey toward self-knowledge does he complete his physical descent into death.

HMS *Wildebeest*. British naval destroyer on which Martin is an officer before it is sunk by a German torpedo. Flashbacks in the novel reveal scenes from Martin's past as an actor and a naval officer. The scenes on his ship, as befitting Golding's own naval background, are generally the longest and most detailed, providing a sense of the movement of the ship through water and the perpetual lookouts for what other ships in the convoy are doing and also for the telltale signs of approaching enemy submarines.

Scottish island. In an abrupt shift at the novel's end that overturns all the readers' notions of what has gone before, the scene shifts to a small Scottish island, where a naval officer arrives to collect a human body that has been washed ashore. Again the scene is one of dereliction, but this time it is a human dereliction, a ruined building with broken walls and the roof fallen in. There, the officer and a local official connect briefly—the sort of human connection denied to Martin—and readers learn that Martin's dead body could never even have reached the island, let alone gone through that Purgatory. Everything that Martin has experienced after falling into the sea happened only within his imagination in the brief moments before he drowned.

— *Paul Kincaid*

THE PIONEERS: Or, The Sources of the Susquehanna

Author: James Fenimore Cooper (1789-1851)
Type of work: Novel
Type of plot: Historical

Time of plot: 1793
First published: 1823

This historical novel about the settling of the American frontier shortly after the Revolutionary War takes place exclusively in central New York state. James Fenimore Cooper raises questions about property rights, but in the more specific setting of Templeton itself, Cooper explores the need for compromise in a society based on a "composite order."

Templeton. Fictional New York frontier town in and around which all the events of the novel take place. It is modeled on Cooperstown, New York, which was founded in the 1780's by James Fenimore Cooper's father William and is the town in which James was reared. In his introduction to the novel, Cooper locates Templeton in the real county of Otsego which lies in "those low spurs of the Alleghenies, which cover the midland counties of New York." Templeton is on the southern edge of Otsego Lake (as is Cooperstown), one of the sources of the Susquehanna River, and was founded by Marmaduke Temple, the town's judge and patriarch. Clearly in the early stages of development, the town it-self consists of only about fifty buildings, most of them unfinished. Through these buildings, Cooper reveals a society struggling to put into practice democratic principles. On one hand, the buildings exemplify the "composite order," a mixture of seemingly incongruous parts built on principles of utility rather than beauty. In a fledgling community consisting of people from a variety of backgrounds and under threat from nature, the settlers must base their lives, politically, legally, morally, and physically, on what works rather than on tradition and what has worked in the past. The "composite order," then, is at the heart of democratic egalitarianism and individualism and is reflected in such buildings as the

Bold Dragoon and the church. These buildings serve different needs, but both are necessary to town life and both accommodate a variety of social classes, religions, and political stances, coexisting with minimal conflict. However, the superior quality of three or four of the buildings, the dwellings of Templeton's most prestigious citizens, reveals the residues of a class structure not entirely eliminated by the inception of democracy.

Judge Temple's house. Home of Marmaduke Temple; the grandest building in Templeton. Marmaduke's house stands on several acres, on which grow fruit trees, lending a sense of advanced cultivation to the dwelling and to Marmaduke himself. Adding to this sense of superiority is a line of Lombardy poplars which had to have been imported because they are not native to America. If the grounds on which the house is located suggest the elite status of Marmaduke, the architectural structure of the house reflects those democratic principles of the "composite order." Furthermore, the house stands in stark contrast with Natty's humble hut, wherein dwell, at one time or another, a variety of characters, each having his own claim to the land now owned by Marmaduke. It becomes apparent, then, that Marmaduke, the principal occupant of the grandest house in Templeton, the legal authority in town, and the owner of ten thousand acres in and around the town, must learn to provide justice for the "composite order" rather than succumb to motivations of self-interest. Scenes related to this issue of democratic justice as opposed to self-interest occur in the courtroom during Natty's trial.

Mount Vision. Tallest mountain among those surrounding Templeton. This is the site from which Marmaduke first views the valley wherein Templeton will be located. This is also the location of Indian John's death and the place in which a compromise, in the form of marriage, between the former British owners of the land and new American owners, is reached. Thus the land becomes the possession of those who will further the cause of democracy.

— *Michael A. Benzel*

THE PIRATES OF PENZANCE: Or, The Slave of Duty

Author: W. S. Gilbert (1836-1911)
Type of work: Drama
Type of plot: Operetta

Time of plot: Nineteenth century
First performed: 1879; first published, 1880

This play is situated in Penzance, Cornwall, in two settings: a rocky seashore and a ruined chapel by moonlight. These romantic venues provide a fairy-tale backdrop for romantic comedy.

Penzance. Port on the southern coast of southeastern England's Cornwall region. In choosing Penzance, Cornwall, as the setting of his play, W. S. Gilbert situates an improbable plot in a remote town in one of Britain's most remote southern regions. Beautiful and wild, Cornwall was seen in the Victorian era as a place where most anything could happen.

Cornish seashore. This remote outcropping is the site of the pirates' lair. The Pirate King presides over a bumbling group of inefficient buccaneers. Into this scene stumble the many daughters of Major General Stanley, who are promptly seized by the pirates. Fortunately, General Stanley and his policemen are equally inept, and the girls fall in love with the pirates who, in truth, have hearts of gold. The romantic setting of the seacoast encourages the audience to suspend disbelief and accept a ludicrous situation.

Chapel. Ruined Gothic chapel in act 2 that echoes the Victorian love for this style of architecture and provides the backdrop for the inept efforts of the police to capture the equally inept pirates and for romantic interludes between the hero Frederic and his love, Mabel. The pirates finally yield when commanded to do so in the name of Queen Victoria; they in fact are peers of the realm, not pirates, so all is well in the high Victorian setting of a ruined chapel in remote Penzance.

— *Isabel Bonnyman Stanley*

THE PIT: A Story of Chicago

Author: Frank Norris (1870-1902)
Type of work: Novel
Type of plot: Naturalism

Time of plot: 1890's
First published: 1903

This second novel in Frank Norris's projected "Epic of the Wheat" trilogy is set entirely in Chicago. Other places figure in primarily to provide background for the principal characters and to reinforce the novelist's theme. Chicago is presented as a powerful commercial center in which cultural aspirations vie with the economic forces underlying the buying and selling of wheat.

Barrington. "Second-class town" located in Worcester County in central Massachusetts that is the "native town" of Laura Dearborn, the novel's principal female character. Laura's upper-middle-class New England upbringing provides her with a background in literature and a reading knowledge of French, but because of the death of her father, the stilted social climate of the town, and the presence of an aunt living in Chicago, she eventually pulls up stakes and moves west.

*Grand Rapids. Western Michigan town near which the novel's principal male character, Curtis Jadwin, grew up on a farm. Curtis briefly attends high school there but quits to enter the livery stable business and later moves to Chicago. There, he attains great wealth through real estate speculation. Curtis and Laura bring together the economic and cultural strains found in Norris's depiction of Chicago.

*Chicago. Great midwestern commercial center and hub of the nation's commodities trading. The dual character of Chicago, as both a cultural and an economic center, is best seen through individual sites that figure into Norris's novel. At the same time, the city as a whole is wonderfully described in the novel, and there are particularly fine, often poetical, descriptions of the city's changing seasons.

*Chicago Auditorium. Building in which the novel opens, during a grand opera performance. In addition to introducing the novel's main characters, this scene offers a powerful symbolization of the dual character of the city. During the midst of the operatic performance, a background conversation about a big wheat deal is taking place.

*Pit. Huge downstairs room in Chicago's Board of Trade Building in which commodities traders do all their bidding. It represents the focal point of the economic forces presented in the novel. It is here that the nation's wheat is bought and sold on a world stage. It is also the site of Curtis Jadwin's eventual financial downfall, as he attempts to "corner" the wheat market. Numerous descriptions of the enormous scale of the pit's commodities trading appear throughout the novel.

After Curtis Jadwin is ruined in the commodities market, the novel ends with him and his wife leaving Chicago by train. Laura looks back reflectively as they pass the Board of Trade Building, which appears to her "a sombre mass . . . black, monolithic, crouching on its foundations like a monstrous sphinx with blind eyes, silent, grave . . . without sign of life. . . ."

North Avenue house. Chicago house that Curtis buys and has remodeled after his marriage to Laura. It provides another powerful symbol of the novel's central theme. The extravagance of the house—including its art gallery and built-in organ—is fully described. Juxtaposed to the house's opulence is the fact that Curtis is largely oblivious to it, knowing little about the expensive works of art it contains. At one moment, he does not even know the number of rooms the house contains. As Curtis becomes more and more consumed with his wheat deal, the artistic dimension of his house offers a retreat for Laura and a place for her developing relationship with the artist Sheldon Corthell.

*American West. The decision of the Jadwins, at the end of the novel, to "start over again" in the West following Curtis's financial ruin, draws heavily upon the traditional role of the West in American literature as a place of moral regeneration. The novel ends with the Jadwins leaving Chicago. Curtis "studying a railroad folder," is thinking, one assumes, of the future.

— *Scott Wright*